D1596091

CENSORSHIP AND LITERATURE IN FASCIST ITALY

The history of totalitarian states bears witness to the fact that literature and print media can be manipulated and made into vehicles of mass deception. *Censorship and Literature in Fascist Italy* is the first comprehensive account of how the Fascists attempted to control Italy's literary production.

In this study Guido Bonsaver looks at how the country's major publishing houses and individual authors responded to the new cultural directives imposed by the Fascists. Throughout Bonsaver uses rare and previously unexamined archival materials to shed light on important episodes in Italy's literary history, such as the struggles between Mussolini's regime and particular publishers, as well as individual cases involving renowned writers such as Moravia, Da Verona, and Vittorini. Thoroughly researched and persuasively argued, the work charts the development of Fascist censorship laws and practices, including the creation of the Ministry of Popular Culture and the anti-Semitic campaign of the late 1930s.

Examining the pervasiveness of censorship in Fascist Italy, from the entrenchment of Mussolini's role as 'prime censor' to the suppression of works by female writers, this is a fascinating look at the vulnerability of culture under a dictatorship.

(Toronto Italian Studies)

GUIDO BONSAVER is University Lecturer in Italian and Fellow of Pembroke College, Oxford.

GUIDO BONSAVER

Censorship and Literature
in Fascist Italy

UNIVERSITY OF TORONTO PRESS
Toronto   Buffalo   London

978-0-8020-9301-1 (cloth)
978-0-8020-9496-4 (paper)

Printed on acid-free paper

Toronto Italian Studies

Library and Archives Canada Cataloguing in Publication

Bonsaver, Guido
Censorship and literature in facist Italy / Guido Bonsaver.

(Toronto Italian studies)
Includes bibliographical references and index.
ISBN 978-0-8020-9301-1 (bound)
ISBN 978-0-8020-9496-4 (pbk.)

1. Censorship – Italy – History – 20th century.   2. Italian literature –
20th century – History and criticism.   3. Fascism and literature – Italy.
4. Italy – Cultural policy – History – 20th century.   5. Politics and culture
– Italy – History – 20th century.   I. Title.   II. Series.

PQ4088.B655 2007   303.3'76094509041   C2007-900935-2

University of Toronto Press acknowledges the financial assistance to the publishing program of the Canada Council for the Arts and the Ontario Arts Council.

University of Toronto Press acknowledges the financial support for the publishing activities of the Government of Canada through the Book Publishing Industry Development Program (BPIDP).

Ai miei genitori, Gianni e Jerta, cresciuti all'ombra del Littorio

Tendiamo a semplificare anche la storia; ma non sempre lo schema con cui si ordinano i fatti è individuabile in modo univoco ...; la maggior parte dei fenomeni storici e naturali non sono semplici, o non semplici della semplicità che piacerebbe a noi.

Primo Levi, cap. 2 'La zona grigia,' in *I sommersi e i salvati*

We also tend to simplify history; but the pattern within which events are ordered is not always identifiable in a single unequivocal fashion ...; the greater part of historical and natural phenomena is not simple, or not simple with the simplicity that we would like.

Primo Levi, *The Drowned and the Saved*, trans. R. Rosenthal

Contents

Illustrations

Acknowledgments

During a prolonged period of research work, there are countless instances in which progress is made possible by competent friends and experienced specialists. This book is no exception. I owe much to librarians and archivists, and among them I would like to thank Leonardo Lattarulo at Rome's Biblioteca Nazionale Centrale; Mariapina Di Simone, Mirna Mercanti, and Giovanna Tosatti at the Archivio Centrale dello Stato; Alessandro Taddei at 'La Sapienza's' Archivio 900; Paola Villa at Pavia's Fondo Manoscritti; Daniele Sironi at Milan's Fondazione Mondadori; Luisa Gandolfi and Greta Belbusti at Bompiani; and Roberto Cerati for his kind introduction to Einaudi's history and archives in Turin. In Britain, my warm thanks go to the friendly professionalism of library staff at Royal Holloway in Egham, at the Taylorian and Bodleian institutions in Oxford, and in particular to Katherine Melling, liaison librarian for Italian at the Taylorian.

Questions of content have been discussed with history and literature scholars, who have been immensely helpful in clarifying my ideas and pointing me in the right direction. On the historical front, I would like to thank Ruth Ben-Ghiat, Richard Bosworth, Mauro Canali (for his archival tips and conversations), Philip Cannistraro, Christopher Duggan, Giorgio Fabre (for his help during the initial stages of my research), Emilio Gentile, Denis Mack Smith (for kindly allowing me use of his personal library), Paolo Murialdi, Gabriele Turi, and Albertina Vittoria. Closer to home, among literature specialists I would like to thank Pierpaolo Antonello, Giorgio Bàrberi-Squarotti, Paolo Buchignani, Phil Cooke, Jane Dunnett, Robert Gordon, Peter Hainsworth, Debbie Holmes, Laura and Giulio Lepschy, Penny Morris, Martin McLaughlin, Anne Mullen, Daragh O'Connell, Luciano Parisi, and

Lucia Re. Among them, Anne, Daragh, Martin, Peter, Phil, and Robert had the patience to read and comment on parts of the manuscript. To them goes unending gratitude and to me the blame for any remaining flaws. I am similarly grateful to my editor, Ron Schoeffel, for his perfect blend of professionalism and good humour, and to Barbara Tessman, whose attention to detail and abhorrence of redundancies taught many a lesson in copy-editing and good English.

Finally, I would like to thank the British Academy for its generous help in supporting the necessary research trips abroad, and similarly my former department at Royal Holloway, London, and the Faculty of Medieval and Modern Languages, and Pembroke College, in Oxford. Last but certainly not least, I would like to thank those whose hospitality has added warmth and comfort to my archival quests. While in Rome Silvia and Alexander Gavuzzo-Stewart have provided superb company and a quiet space wherein to work. Mauro Maspero ('il grande motorista') has proven once more the priceless value of a lifelong friendship. Similarly, Stefano Genetti added wise advice and friendly banter during a couple of regenerating breaks in Verona and Lake Garda. Back home, *un grazie di cuore* to Rebecca and our two children, Laura and Matthew, who held the fort with good humour.

Abbreviations

ACS	Archivio Centrale dello Stato (Central State Archives)
ASV	Archivio Segreto Vaticano (Vatican Secret Archives)
CAS	Centro Studi Anticomunisti (Centre for Anti-Communist Studies)
Demorazza	Direzione Generale per la Demografia e la Razza (General Directorate for Demography and Race)
DGPS	Direzione Generale di Pubblica Sicurezza (General Directorate of Public Security)
DGSI	Direzione Generale per il Servizio della Stampa Italiana (General Directorate of the Italian Press)
GUF	Gruppi Universitari Fascisti (Fascist University Groups)
MCP	Ministero della Cultura Popolore (Ministry of Popular Culture)
PNF	Partito Nazionale Fascista (National Fascist Party)
RSI	Repubblica Sociale Italiana (Italian Social Republic)

CENSORSHIP AND LITERATURE IN FASCIST ITALY

Introduction

Any study of censorship in a dictatorial state runs the risk of being swayed by a moral urge or, better, a fully understandable ethical desire to give voice and space to the victims of oppression. Such a desire is particularly relevant in the case of Italian Fascism. After the fall of Mussolini's regime, a fundamental underpinning of the newly formed Italian Republic was the *lotta partigiana* – that is, the contribution of the anti-Fascist movement to the restoration of democracy. Stories of resistance and defiance against Fascist totalitarianism were necessary for the reconstruction of a dignified sense of national identity. These stories described real events, and many such acts related to the publishing world will be recounted and documented in this study. However, insistence on episodes of open opposition have tended to produce a rather dualistic vision of the historical picture and to discourage the exploration of the so-called grey zone occupying the vast space between vocal opposition and full collaboration. Italian literary history and, more specifically, the study of censorship are a case in point.

It was twenty years after the end of the Second World War that a young, radical left-wing scholar, Alberto Asor Rosa, convincingly argued against the distorting perspective of dichotomies such as Fascist/anti-Fascist and prewar/postwar culture, pointing instead at the complexity and the degree of permeability of such opposing blocks.[1] What followed was a slow turn towards a more detailed mapping of Italian literature under Fascism. Censorship, however, remained to some degree a taboo subject, and not entirely for ideological reasons. There were first of all practical problems related to the accessibility of archival sources. Fascist ministerial archives were either missing or preserved in the chaotic state in which they were found at the end of the war. A reading of the correspondence of the Allied military team that took copies of the most important ministerial documents found in occupied Italy provides a colourful account of the discouraging state of those archives. Second, the history of publishing (*storia dell'editoria*) is a rather young discipline, and it has often tended to concentrate on earlier centuries. In the case of the Italian publishing industry in the twentieth century, academic studies are relatively recent, mostly less than ten years old. The relationship between book production and state control is also a rather neglected topic. As a result, literary historians dealing with censorship have too often simply relied on personal accounts and memoirs, thus exposing themselves to the risk of offsetting useful facts with potential omissions, distortions, and the lack of detail that are typical of undocumented reconstructions.[2]

The proceedings of a conference on the publishing industry during the interwar years, held in Milan in February 1981, illustrate the lingering reluctance to address such issues. Organized by the Fondazione Arnoldo e Alberto Mondadori, the conference was opened with a welcome speech by Arnoldo's daughter, Mimma Mondadori. Many speakers had first-hand experience of those years, and all of them, including Valentino Bompiani, enriched the discussion with their recollections of Milan as the book capital of Italy and of Arnoldo Mondadori as the greatest of its publishers. However, the contribution by a prolific young biographer, Giordano Bruno Guerri, struck a different tone. His considerations on the relationship between Mondadori and the Fascist regime were received with some frostiness. This is recorded in the concluding remarks by Risorgimento historian and Republican politician Giovanni Spadolini, who was to become Italy's first non–Christian Democrat prime minister only four months after the conference. Spadolini dwelled on every conference paper, but when it came to Guerri's he quickly dismissed it as polemical and simplistic. In fact, subsequent studies of Mondadori, including Enrico Decleva's detailed biography, have shown that, in this particular case, Guerri's account was factual. Arnoldo Mondadori maintained an intricate network of personal relations with Mussolini and other high-ranking officials of the regime, and more often than not he was the initiator of those relations. Yet at the time when the conference was held, Italians were simply not ready for an open discussion of the consensual collaboration between Mussolini's Fascism and Italy's publishing industry.[3]

Before embarking on the present study, I came up against unanswered questions regarding literary censorship while working on a study of Elio Vittorini. Despite the number of monographs already published in Italy on this renowned author and the numerous commentaries on the various instances of censorship involving his fictional and editorial work, I was surprised to find that no literary historian had made full use of the documentary material available at the state archives in Rome and Milan. The censorship of the most famous anti-Fascist novel written and published in Fascist Italy – Vittorini's *Conversazione in Sicilia* – was taken as a mere *fait accompli*. No attempt had been made to investigate problematic issues such as when, by whom, and in what form the novel had been censored. I was also struck by the tendency to write about 'Fascist censors' without providing a more detailed account of who these censors were and how they operated.[4]

As this study will show, Fascist censorship was not a monolithic and tightly coordinated machine of repression. It had many faces and it went through different phases. The many officials involved in the censorship process – prefects, ministers, Mussolini himself – neither shared precisely the same perspective nor imposed their beliefs with complete consistency. Equally important, one ought to avoid approaching censorship as an isolated activity, totally detached from the many other strategies – repressive and supportive – through which Fascism attempted to shape Italian society. Recent studies on modern Italian culture have allowed for a much more sophisticated and inclusive understanding of how censorship fit within the bigger picture of Fascism's cultural policies. The next few paragraphs outline the contribution of the works from which the present study benefited and derived its methodology.

Censorship is an integral part of state–culture relations. It belongs to the complex web of activities through which these two spheres relate to each other, sometimes in oppositional terms but more often in self-adjusting, complicit ones. David Forgacs's seminal study, *Italian Culture in the Industrial Era, 1880–1980,* is fundamental in this context. Its rejection of any Crocean idealization of artistic endeavour, its firm vision of the interaction among social, economic, political, and cultural factors, and its sophisticated embrace of popular forms of culture, made this study a groundbreaking model.[5] Censorship too can only be fully understood if placed within a wider context. It was a weapon in a war for people's minds, a war fought by different armies, on different fronts, and for many different causes, even within the publishing world. Politicians set the boundaries, censors patrolled them, authors defied them, editors worriedly followed or tried to rein in their authors' moves, publishers tried to make peace with politicians while protecting their commercial interests, and so on and so forth, in a hectic merry-go-round to which should be included two other groups: authors censoring themselves in order to comply with their perception of the permissible, and journalists and critics acting as an independent or mercenary army, sometimes on the side of freedom, sometimes on that of power, sometimes taking the initiative and becoming agents of censorship. Within this complex dimension, the scholar who produced the first in-depth analysis of cultural policies during the Fascist years is Philip Cannistraro. His *La fabbrica del consenso: Fascismo e mass-media* is a fundamental contribution to modern Italy's cultural history. It is also the first study to make ample use of archival sources at Rome's Central Archives. Published at around the same time was Maurizio Cesari's *La censura nel periodo fascista*, a work of more limited scope and accuracy, but nonetheless essential for its mapping of the organization of censorship across the entire cultural industry. For a number of years, these three works have been the only academic studies that have tackled general issues related to the censorship of books. To them one could perhaps add the contribution of historian Mario Isnenghi, whose study of Fascist culture, although not directly dealing with censorship, encouraged a redefinition of the actual relationship between the regime and the Italian intelligentsia.[6]

However, the past ten years have seen the publication of a number of influential key works to which this book is greatly indebted. The study by Nicola Tranfaglia and Albertina Vittoria is a milestone in the *storia dell'editoria italiana*, which in its turn was underpinned by focused studies such as Luisa Mangoni's detailed book on Einaudi Editore, Enrico Decleva's biography of Mondadori, and, on a minor scale, other studies on smaller publishing houses such as Corbaccio and Gobetti. Monica Galfré's volume on Fascism's educational policies and the publishing industry has shown the closeness of the relationship between the regime and some of the leading publishers. Gabriele Turi's expertise in the history of modern Italian publishing has generated a number of important works and resulted in the editorship of a journal, *La Fabbrica del Libro*.[7] In the field of censorship, the most important contribution has been Giorgio Fabre's detailed study of the effects of anti-Semitic legislation on the publishing industry. His *L'elenco: Censura fascista, editoria e autori ebrei* is an essential and groundbreaking piece of archival research. The number of citations that the book received during the proceedings of a recent conference on culture and censorship in twentieth-century Italy provides indisputable evidence of Fabre's contribution to our knowledge of book censorship during the Fascist years. Mention should also be made of other detailed archival studies such as Patrizia Ferrara's reference work on the Ministry of Popular Culture and Antonio Fiori's *Il filtro deformante*, which, although concentrating on censorship during the First World War, provides an essential picture of the situation from which Fascist censorship was to develop.[8] Outside Italy, the study of state–culture relations under Fascism has been particularly taken up in the United States, and close to the issues examined in this book are Marla Susan Stone's *The Patron State* and Ruth Ben-Ghiat's *Fascist Modernities*.[9]

A few observations need to be made about the state and accessibility of primary sources. Much ministerial and prefectorial material on censorship was lost during the last months of the war in more or less known circumstances. Practically all the papers related to censorship at the prefecture of Florence have disappeared, possibly removed when the Nazis/Fascists withdrew from the city in August 1944. Many of those held at the prefectures of Milan and Turin are missing too. In addition to the limited material available in the three capitals of the Italian publishing industry, there are serious gaps in the collection of ministerial documents held at Rome's Archivio Centrale dello Stato. Antonio Fiori, himself an archivist at the archives, clarifies the situation in his introduction to the catalogues of the Direzione Generale di Pubblica Sicurezza (the police archives at the Ministry of the Interior). In short, the paperwork related to *Categoria F2 Sequestri di stampa* is entirely missing for the years up to 1926. Even worse, for the years 1926–43, *Categoria F1 Libri nazionali* is also missing.[10] It is possible that the material was moved north in 1943–4, when the ministries of the Repubblica Sociale Italiana were based around Lake Garda. Only the files of the Ministry of Popular Culture remain as an untidy but substantial collection, and this is one of the reasons why it is much easier to reconstruct censorship activity in the second decade of the Fascist regime, during which that ministry was inaugurated. Fortunately, useful material can be found among the collections of other ministries and the Political Police (Polizia Politica). Better still are the archives of Benito Mussolini's office, which are well organized and provide an invaluable source of information.

Myths abound about the existence of many missing files, mysteriously hidden in state or private archives. Any historian working on Italy is well acquainted with the Italian love of conspiracy theories and sinister plots. Journalists refer to it as *dietrologia*, almost a discipline in its own right. These stories might simply be intellectual folklore, but as recently as July 2003 a hoard of documents pertaining to the Ministry of Popular Culture was 'found' collecting dust in the archives of the Prime Minister's Office. However unintentional this example of archival inefficiency might have been, the fact that the material had sat unseen for half a century fuelled speculation about much more being held elsewhere. A frequently whispered piece of hearsay is that the archives of the *Presidenza del consiglio* contain many restricted documents relating to the Fascist period.

Work on theatre censorship has benefited from the excellent state of primary sources. This is due to the work of Leopoldo Zurlo, who from 1931 single-handedly and efficiently held the reins of theatre censorship. As a result of his professional devotion, the archives pertaining to his censorial activity have remained mostly intact. Moreover, the documentation is complemented by Zurlo's long, erudite, and detailed memoirs, published soon after the war. Several studies of specific cases of theatre censorship have also been published, and the recent publication of the complete catalogue of all the scripts examined by Zurlo, enriched by Patrizia Ferrara's long and detailed introduction, means that, at least in this subfield, it is unlikely that new and controversial material will surface in years to come.[11]

The state of historical archives kept by publishing houses is promising although not ideal. Those of Einaudi and Mondadori are well organized and open to researchers. At Bompiani, more discretion is exercised: it is not by chance that a definitive account of the activity of that publishing house is still to be written. However, Valentino Bompiani's editorial correspondence, which has been published, provides great insights. As we will see, there are a number of other publishing houses whose archives have provided material for specific studies.[12]

A few final remarks concern the general organization of this book. As the title suggests, literary publications, and not the publishing industry at large, form the object of study. This is mainly for two reasons. First, given my personal expertise in literary history, it would have been ill-advised to venture into areas such as the censorship of philosophical or scientific publications of which my knowledge is scant. Second, I believe that it is in the field of literature – roughly understood as published writings of a fictional or autobiographical nature – that research is particularly needed. Too often episodes of literary censorship have been passed on from critic to critic without a thorough analysis of existing archival documentation. If this book has a single aim, it is the attempt to provide an overall outline of the literary field in the light of primary sources. A certain amount of trespassing of literary boundaries was sometimes inevitable, particularly so when outlining the history of specific publishing houses. However, the focus of the overall book is on works of literature.

The three parts deal with three distinguishable phases of Fascist censorship. The first part (1922–33) begins with pre-Fascist censorship and moves on to examine how Mussolini adapted the existing system to stifle dissonant voices and proceed to a *fascistizzazione* of Italian culture. Il Duce's personal grip on censorship will become apparent, although he was not a careful planner of censorial policies. In his speech to all chief editors of Italian newspapers on 10 October 1928, Mussolini said that 'La stampa più libera del mondo è la stampa italiana' (The press enjoys more freedom in Italy than in any other country in the world). However, only two paragraphs later he offered a revealing image of this 'freedom.' Journalists were likened to musicians in a huge orchestra in which the diversity of each instrument is counterbalanced by the collective desire to contribute to the same musical piece. Not suprisingly, he refrained from mentioning his role as conductor and composer of the score. Mussolini's idea of a paradoxical coexistence of freedom and all-pervading supervision was a key factor in determining the working practices of Fascist censors.[13]

The second part (1934–9) tracks the establishment of a fully fledged, centralized system of control with the creation of the Ministry of Popular Culture (Ministero della Cultura Popolare). This is the period during which, after an initial crisis, most publishers and authors aligned themselves with a modus operandi that relied on self-censorship and government help as much as on the repression of criticism. These are also the years in which censorship became part of a wider project of 'cultural reclamation' – that is, a utopian and highly illiberal attempt to mould Italian culture, which was to culminate in the barbaric turn towards anti-Semitism.

The third and final part (1940–3) focuses on the new policies and restrictions imposed by Italy's intervention in the war on the side of Nazi Germany. It also examines the regime's attempt to fight its last internal battles, against translations of foreign fiction, and against women writers, defeatism, and, more importantly, the Jews. The development of anti-Semitic policies, which lead to the publication of the List of Unwelcome Authors in the spring of 1942, is a most shameful act of cultural politics for which Fascism and Italy's publishing industry bear collective responsibility.

Each of the three parts is divided into three chapters. In each case, the rationale is that the first chapter outlines the state and organization of the legislation and institutions related to censorship. The second and third chapters concentrate on a number of specific cases related to that period. Publishing houses and, thereafter, individual authors and publications are examined in detail with the aim of providing a clear picture of the number of different strategies, measures, and solutions with which the regime attempted to shape literary culture. The English translation of the many passages quoted from documents and published works in Italian are mine.

Richard Bosworth's reminder to be ready to distinguish between 'legal Italy' and 'real Italy' acquires particular value in a study of this kind.[14] Constant comparison of different archival sources, from ministerial and prefectorial to those of publishers and authors, including their private correspondence, is essential in order not to fall into the trap of taking every piece of legislation and every government memorandum as a mirror of actual practices. Mussolini was the first to make sure that doors would be left ajar, thus allowing useful space for negotiations, self-interested acts of toleration, and plenty of ad hoc solutions. Moreover, in the field of censorship one has to take into account the degree of consensual collaboration through which publishers and authors acquired credit with the regime, which could then be invested in requests for adjustments and exceptions. The system also sometimes operated by 'word of mouth' – that is, instructions were given to publishers and authors via a telephone call or a personal meeting, thus avoiding a potentially embarrassing paper trail. This naturally creates additional difficulties for the researcher; hence the need to use caution before allowing oneself to be swayed by written declarations that sometimes suggest extreme harshness, sometimes extreme liberality. In some individual cases, attention will be paid to another literary censor operating on the Italian peninsula: the Vatican. Although there were no formal links between the Vatican and the Fascist regime in terms of book censorship, it will be interesting to see how challenges to Catholic morality were sometimes taken up by the state thanks to influential personalities such as the Jesuit Father Pietro Tacchi Venturi. Finally, this study will take into account other forms of censorship that fell outside the realm of 'legal Italy.' Bookshop owners could be threatened into withdrawing a certain publication from their shop windows. Theatre perfomances could be stopped through violent protests. Newspaper editors could be strongly 'advised' to ignore a certain author. As we will see, censorship implied much more than just deleting sentences in red ink.

PART ONE

Mussolini Takes the Helm, 1922–1933

1 Towards a New System

Book Censorship in Pre-Fascist Italy

Control over production and distribution of books does not seem to have been a problematic issue for the first governments of unified Italy. Most of the legislative and executive measures were aimed at the press (*stampa periodica*), whereas the publication of books (as part of *stampa non periodica*) was dealt with mainly as a secondary aspect of press-related topics.

The principles of press freedom were established on 26 March 1848 by a royal decree. The *Editto sulla stampa* proclaimed by King Carlo Alberto on the eve of Italy's First War of Independence was later extended from the Kingdom of Sardinia to the entire, unified peninsula. A liberal piece of legislation, it conceived of no pre-publication censorship. Article 7 required printers to deposit one copy of each publication at the local prefecture court (Tribunale di Prefettura) but only at the time of distribution.[1] Control and sanctions were then administered by each prefecture, which was responsible for what was being published within its jurisdiction. A similar approach concerned theatrical censorship, which, since 1864, had been decentralized and handed over to the prefectures.[2] National coordination was tentatively provided by the Ministry of the Interior (Ministero dell' Interno) via its General Directorate of Public Security (Direzione Generale di Pubblica Sicurezza, DGPS) led by the head of police (Capo della Polizia).

The DGPS had been reorganized and strengthened during the years of Francesco Crispi's first period as prime minister (1887–91) as part of an attempt to respond to anarchist and revolutionary unrest, which, in the eyes of foreign observers, was threatening to turn Italy into a hotbed of international terrorism.[3] No specific office was created to coordinate the particular task of book censorship. The Special Office (Ufficio Riservato) – a sub-department of the DGPS – would receive copies of any 'pubblicazioni sovversive' (subversive publication) seized by the prefectures and would alert them whenever a title had to be withdrawn from circulation across the nation.[4] Archival documentation suggests that this task was often aimed at banned publications that had been printed abroad. Indeed, in many cases it was the Foreign Office (Ministero degli Esteri) that alerted police authorities to the existence of subversive publications being smuggled into and circulated in Italy. In the field of theatre, on the other hand, prefectures maintained their leading role, with the Ministry of the Interior acting only as national coordinator and the authority in case of appeal.

A definition of what the *Editto sulla stampa* described as an abuse of press freedom was limited to a generic list of the most sensitive topics: public enticement to commit crime; writings against religion, morality (*buon costume*), the king, parliament, and government; and libellous defamation and public slander against private citizens. In this respect, Italy's framework was not different from that of other European nations that had already introduced similar, liberal legislation. A specific understanding of what could be considered a breach of these boundaries was left to the police and the judiciary. It should also be noted that the seizure of a publication could be instigated only by a court judge, and trial proceedings had to be initiated *per direttissima* – that is, within forty-eight hours of the seizure.

Fear of political unrest was at the root of the circular on the press of September 1898, in which the minister of the interior in Luigi Pelloux's government required prefects to send quarterly reports about subversive periodicals. 'Subversive' in the circular was clarified as meaning 'stampa repubblicana, socialista ed anarchica' (republican, socialist, and anarchic press). Other measures taken by the Pelloux government included steeply increasing the fines for those found guilty of abusing press freedom and giving magistrates the power to suspend the circulation of a periodical for up to three months.[5] With the new century, however, came a relaxation of these measures. After widespread protest from members of Parliament, high-court magistrates, and journalists, a law was eventually passed on 28 June 1906 under Giovanni Giolitti's prime ministership. It stated that magistrates were allowed to seize a periodical only at the end of the trial and following a court order.[6] In June 1912 the ministry decreed that prefects could limit themselves to one annual report on periodicals, and in September 1919 even those reports were made redundant. It is also important to note that all these circulars were related only to periodicals, which underlines the relative lack of interest in the control over books shown by Italy's governments from unification to the Fascists' seizure of power.

A periodical was at the centre of a celebrated case of literary censorship that occurred in 1912, at the height of the colonial war between Italy and Turkey for possession of Libya. On the one side, the poet and self-appointed bard of Italy, Gabriele D'Annunzio, on the other liberal prime minister Giovanni Giolitti. In those months D'Annunzio was a regular contributor to Italy's major newspaper, *Corriere della Sera.* The patriotic excitement unleashed by the military expedition inspired him to compose ten poems, entitled *Canti delle gesta d'oltremare,* which were published between October 1911 and January 1912. The most controversial one was 'La canzone dei Dardanelli,' in which he attacked other European nations for their indifference towards the barbarity of the Turkish state. The poem criticized 'five-meals-a-day Britain' for its passivity while vilifying Germany and Austria as cruel and Italophobic nations. Giolitti decided that such an attack by an internationally renowned poet was against the interests of Italy's foreign policy. On 12 January 1912 he ordered the censoring of the most damning verses of the poem, which then appeared in *Corriere della Sera* with a blank space in place of verses 63 and 81. A similar fate was in store a few weeks later, when the poems were collected in a book entitled *Merope.* D'Annunzio's publisher, Emilio Treves, had personally travelled to France to meet the poet in an attempt to convince him to drop the controversial poem. But he would not relent, and so the first edition was promptly seized by the police (although Treves had wisely printed only 150 copies). A second edition followed with cuts to the poem similar to those that had appeared in the newspaper version. In typical D'Annunzian self-advertising style, a note specified that 'Questa canzone della Patria delusa fu mutilata da mano poliziesca, per ordine del Cavalier Giovanni Giolitti, capo del governo d'Italia, il dì 24 gennaio 1912' (This Canzone of our disappointed Motherland was mutilated by the hand of the police, at the orders of Giovanni Giolitti, head of the Italian government, on 24 January 1912). It was only three years later, in 1915, in the run up to Italy's military intervention against Austria and Germany, that an unexpurgated edition of the book was allowed to be distributed.[7]

During the First World War, as can be expected, the Italian government increased its control over printed matter. This control mainly took the form of two pieces of legislation. In May 1915 a decree law gave prefects the power to ban the publication of news that might harm the nation's war effort and its internal social stability. This law introduced a regime of pre-publication censorship on all periodicals (printers were required to submit the proofs of each issue), which effectively stayed in force until 1920. It also gave prefectures the power to seize publications without prior authorization by the judiciary.[8] In November 1917 a new department was created inside the Ministry of the Interior: the Secretariat for Propaganda Abroad and the Press (Sottosegretariato per la Propaganda all'Estero e la Stampa). The timing of this second measure was not without reason: only a few weeks before Italy had experienced the great military disaster of Caporetto. Both the country's morale and its image abroad had to be supported; fears were also emerging among government officials that communist and revolutionary ideas were fast spreading among the disillusioned masses. Indeed, the new secretariat concerned itself mainly with monitoring and attempting to influence public perception of the war effort, and, once more, this meant almost exclusive attention to journalistic production.[9] With regard to this new, more 'active' role that prefects and the secretariat had to take in order to guarantee the stability of the home front, one can see a forerunner of the mixture of repressive and promotional measures that censorship authorities were to adopt in Fascist Italy, particularly with the creation of the Ministry of Popular Culture.

Two renowned cases of literary censorship during the First World War concern authors at different ends of the political spectrum: the father of futurism and passionate interventionist, Filippo Tommaso Marinetti, and the Milanese socialist councillor and popular novelist, Virgilio Brocchi.

In the autumn of 1916, while convalescing from a wound received in battle, Marinetti had written a humorous book entitled *Come si seducono le donne*. Its preface and various extracts had been published in the Florentine journal *L'Italia futurista*, but when the book edition was prepared in September 1917, its proofs met with government disapproval. Marinetti's narcissistic boastings of his amorous conquests often bordered on the pornographic, and the censors decided to suppress those involving members of the church. Marinetti was quick to exploit the situation for further publicity. The book was published with six blank pages (131–6) marked 'censurato' and was such a success that by the following year it was already in its fourth reprint.[10]

At the other end of the political spectrum, Virgilio Brocchi's novels could hardly be accused of open left-wing propaganda, although his stories sometimes featured working-class heroes with socialist leanings.

Brocchi's literary career had started in 1906 with the novel *Le aquile* published by the Milanese publisher Treves. He subsequently enjoyed great popular success, and his books were frequently reprinted. Between September 1917 and February 1918 Brocchi published in instalments his latest novel, *Casa di pazzi casa di santi*, in the pages of the popular Milanese magazine *Il Mondo*. Set in contemporary times, the novel contained many episodes of war, among which were two examples of fraternization between Austrian and Italian soldiers – one on Easter day and the other concerning an Austrian soldier of Venetian origin who refuses to shoot an Italian soldier approaching his trench. Even more compromisingly, the novel contained extracts from the (real) diary of a fanatical Austrian officer. Before the publication of the penultimate instalment, the novel was accused of defeatism and anti-nationalist propaganda, and its author was brought to trial.[11] In his defence, Brocchi underlined the fact that the novel, published in a periodical, had been regularly vetted by the Milanese censors, who had required no modifications to the text. His lawyers also quoted some extracts taken from the French trial proceedings concerning Flaubert's *Madame Bovary* in 1857. The extracts showed that the French judges had accepted the view that the opinions of a character cannot be interpreted as the author's personal convictions. In the end Brocchi was found not guilty of any crime. The novel was published in book form by Treves in 1919, with the new title *Secondo il cuor mio*. According to Brocchi, the change was made because the original title had been imposed by the chief editor of *Il Mondo*. The book remained in circulation even during the Fascist years, despite the clampdown on those First World War books that were perceived to be defeatist. In 1944 *Secondo il cuor mio* was reprinted for the seventh time.

In the early interwar years, once pre-publication censorship was abolished, book censors in the prefectures returned to the usual patrolling of the moral and political respectability of what was published within their jurisdiction. A case of book seizure for immorality concerned the collection of short stories *Le adolescenti* by Mario Mariani. Published in 1920 by the Milanese house Il Corbaccio, the book was seized but subsequently redistributed after publisher and author won the court case. As can be imagined, the book benefited from the scandal, and after a few weeks the author could celebrate record-breaking sales of 30,000 copies.[12] The first of many controversial and irreverent books by Kurt Erich Suckert, alias Curzio Malaparte, *Viva Caporetto*, was seized in 1921. The first two printings were published by a small press in Prato. Despite Malaparte's later claims that two liberal governments, those of Giolitti and Bonomi, directly intervened to stop the publication, it is more likely, given the then unknown author, that it was simply stopped by the local prefecture. The reason was the implicitly defeatist, anti-militarist, and anti-establishment content of the book, presenting the rout at Caporetto as an act of protest by a proletarian army sick of its commanding officers' privileges and incompetence. A second edition, entitled *La rivolta dei santi maledetti*, came out in April 1923 and was suppressed after episodes of Fascist violence in various bookshops in Rome. This time Malaparte claimed that the order had come directly from Mussolini. No archival evidence supports either of Malaparte's claims but, given the notoriety he had attained by 1923 and the absence of subsequent editions or reprints of the book, it is likely that a blanket ban had been imposed on it.[13] One of Italy's most acute intellectuals at the time, Piero Gobetti – whose tragic fate will be dealt with in the following chapter – spotted an embarrassing case of self-censorship in the second edition of Malaparte's book. In a long article for the Genoese paper *Il Lavoro*, Gobetti took pleasure in exposing the hypocrisy of Malaparte, whose narcissistic thirst for controversy had brought him to a fleeting collaboration with Gobetti's journal *Rivoluzione liberale* back in the months preceding the March on Rome in 1922. By 1924 Malaparte was safely settled in the Fascist camp as a revolutionary Fascist. In his article, Gobetti showed how Malaparte had followed his leader in 'rewriting' his past socialist ideas. The first edition of *Viva Caporetto*, three years earlier, contained a statement in which Malaparte suggested that the lack of patriotism among Italian soldiers was a sign of the internationalism of future societies, and concluded: 'L'Italia e la Russia sono all'avanguardia della civiltà di domani: l'avere saltato uno stadio dell'evoluzione dei popoli, quello patriottico, le rende più elastiche e più permeabili alla mentalità dell'internazionale' (Italy and Russia are at the avant-garde of tomorrow's civilization: having leaped a stage of the evolution of nations, that of patriotism, makes them more flexible and more permeable to the mentality of internationalism). As Gobetti sarcastically pointed out, in the 1923 edition of the book the entire passage was inside quotation marks, followed by this comment: 'Era questo il giudizio che davan di noi molti stranieri, e non tutti socialisti, nel 1919' (This is how many foreigners, and not all of them socialists, saw us in 1919).[14]

Fascism in Power

Once in government, Mussolini concentrated on cementing his grip on the levers of state machinery. His clear aim was a progressive Fascistization of institutions and public opinion in Italy. As a consequence, the Ministry of the Interior was a key centre of his operations. Mussolini himself took the position of minister of the interior and appointed General Emilio De Bono, one of the four commanders of the March on Rome, as head of police. One of De Bono's tasks was to re-establish law and order by reining in the violence of the Fascist squads. His status as a First World War general and a Fascist hero was probably one of the reasons behind Mussolini's choice (De Bono would have actually preferred the Ministry of War). For Mussolini's part, it is not surprising that an experienced journalist and editor such as Mussolini should have decided to be personally involved in issues surrounding printed matter. From the pages of *Il Popolo d'Italia*, an unsigned editorial probably written by Mussolini had already warned his readers as early as 6 December 1922: 'Davanti allo spettacolo d'inco-scienza offerto quotidianamente da certa stampa, chi si meraviglierà se il governo Fascista imporrà la censura o adotterà misure ancora più severe?' (Looking at the daily show of irresponsibility by certain papers, nobody will be surprised if the Fascist government will impose censorship or will adopt even more severe measures).[15]

Cesare Rossi, one of Mussolini's most reliable collaborators at the time, was immediately put in charge of the press office at the Ministry of the Interior. The role of the office was expanded from that of a rather passive monitor of national periodicals to the more disturbing activity of shaping public opinion through a range of legal and illegal means. In a handwrit-ten note to Rossi, dated 28 May 1923, Mussolini indicated that the priority of the press office was going to be the 'razionale sistemazione della stampa filofascista e nazionale' (rational restructuring of the pro-Fascist and national press).[16] This is confirmed by the documentation regarding Rossi's secret accounts, which, together with those of the Ministry of the Interior, show that considerable secret funds were used to finance the publications of pro-Mussolini political factions and to draw some inde-pendent papers under the influence of the government.[17] In order to free Rossi from any potential interference within the Ministry of the Inte-rior, in August 1923 the press office was moved under the direct control of the Prime's Minister's Office. By 1925 it was aptly renamed Press Office of the Head of Government (*Ufficio stampa del Capo del Governo*). Rossi was also at the centre of the creation of a secret group of Fascist militants who were to organize illegal operations such as the physical elimination of opponents of the regime both in Italy and abroad. Amerigo Dumini, the organizer of Giacomo Matteotti's kidnapping and murder in 1924, appeared regularly in Rossi's secret accounts. Indeed, Rossi's involvement in the Matteotti crisis led to the loss of his position. Afraid of becoming a scapegoat for the whole affair, Rossi hid important documents to be used as blackmail material and went underground. He eventually was allowed to flee the country, and, more importantly, Mussolini managed to stave off his own political demise. Indeed, what amounted to the worst crisis experienced by his government was turned into a *casus belli* for the imposition of dictatorial powers. In order to achieve that, one of the first priorities was to muzzle the opposition press. This was accomplished through an escalation of measures that started with the decree law of 8 July 1924. This law had already been signed by the king in July 1923, but Mussolini decided to enact it only when the pressure from the opposition press had become dangerously intense. It gave prefects the power to suppress a periodical after two warnings (*diffide*). And if this were not enough, two days later, a second decree containing the regulations of the law (*norme di attuazione*) granted prefects the power to suppress periodicals without any previous warning.[18] The interior minister, the newly appointed nationalist Luigi Federzoni, added pressure with a welter of telegrams to all prefects, instructing them to apply the new directives and often explicitly referring to certain pieces of news that had to be ignored by the press.[19] The failed attempt to assassinate Mussolini on 4 November 1925 provided one more opportunity to turn the screw on the opposition press. The printshops of socialist, communist, and republican papers were searched by the police and some of them closed.[20]

The final nail in the coffin was provided by the draconian Single Text on Public Security (*Testo Unico di Pubblica Sicurezza*), which came into effect in November 1926. Five articles spelled out the boundaries – or, better, the lack of them – to be observed by police in suppressing publications to immediate effect. Article 112 defined the possible reasons for immediate seizure by the police in just one sentence: it listed writings 'contrari agli ordinamenti politici, sociali od economici costituiti nello Stato o lesivi del prestigio dello Stato o dell'autorità o offensivi del sentimento nazionale, del pudore o della pubblica decenza' (contrary to the political, social, and economic framework that constitutes a state, or damaging to the prestige of the state or its authorities, or offensive to the national sentiment, to moral sense, and public decency). The vagueness of this article was followed by specific instructions related to Mussolini's obsession with demographics and crime news: printers were not allowed to publish writings promoting birth control and abortion; equally punishable was the publication of photographs of murderers and suicides.[21]

Prefects, as local heads of police, played a central role in ensuring the enforcement of these measures. In the early years of government, Mussolini had given up the idea of a massive injection of Fascists among their ranks because of the internal divisions within the Fascist movement. He relied instead on the prefects' commitment to the state and its laws. In 1927 Mussolini clearly spelled out the features of the new role prefects had to perform under the Fascist regime. He did so in a circular sent on 5 January 1927, the importance of which is suggested by the fact that the national press was allowed to quote and discuss it in full on the following day. Prefects, or 'Fascist prefects,' as Mussolini explicitly addressed them, were told that their role extended from that of policing to that of 'tutela *dell'ordine morale*' (guarantor of the *moral order*; emphasis in the original). This implied that 'il prefetto deve prendere tutte le iniziative che tornino di decoro al regime, aumentino la forta e il prestigio, tanto nell'ordine sociale, come in quello intellettuale' (the prefect has to take all the initiatives which benefit the regime's decorum, strength and prestige, and this within the social as well as the intellectual sphere). Essentially Mussolini expected prefects to become the active representatives of the regime and invited them to contribute to the political alignment of all sectors of society. The fact that these directives were accepted without any resistance might be linked to the reality that, not long before, during the First World War, prefects had been similarly instructed to use their powers to defend the social and political status quo.[22]

With regard to the control of printed matter, there is another, less-known circular that set the limits of the prefects' authority. This circular took the form of a confidential letter (*lettera riservata*), which was sent by Mussolini to all Italian prefects on 30 September 1927. In this letter, he spelled out the directives to be implemented during the following year (the Fascist year began on 29 October). The last of the ten directives referred to the press and imposed a stark limitation on the prefects' powers. It ordered them 'non assumere iniziativa alcuna di divieti o di sequestri giornalistici senza la mia personale preventiva autorizzazione che giungerà esclusivamente per mezzo del Capo Ufficio Stampa del Governo' (not to take any initiative with regard to bans or seizures of publications prior to my personal authorization, which will reach you exclusively through the Press Office of the Head of Government).[23] This is a clear sign of Mussolini's intention to give his press office the lead in controling the press. Indeed, as we will see, it is from this office that the centralization of book censorship was to develop.

Press Office versus Ministry of the Interior

After the involvement of Cesare Rossi in the Matteotti affair, Mussolini decided to entrust the direction of the press office to a less controversial figure. As had happened with the Ministry of the Interior, he preferred not to choose a militant Fascist and appointed instead a nationalist, in this case the aristocrat Giovanni Capasso-Torre, who had established credentials as a journalist. During his four years in office, Count Capasso-Torre supervised the expansion of the department. In 1925, the press office was put in charge of the newly nationalized Istituto Luce, whose newsreels were to become one of the strongest vehicles for propaganda. The following year the press office was given authority over the broadcasting of radio news bulletins and, more importantly, it took over the Press Office of the Foreign Office.[24] The Press Office of the Head of Government continued in its role as guardian and 'adviser' of the press and similarly persevered in apportioning secret funds to ensure the political allegiance of certain papers. However, from a strictly procedural viewpoint, this department continued to appear as if it were uninvolved in matters of censorship. The law on public security of 1926 made no mention of the Press Office of the Head of Government, and neither did Royal Decree 773 of 18 June 1931. Article 112 of both decrees stated that censorship was the responsibility of the local police authority – that is, of the prefectures, which were to act against publications that they perceived as a danger to the political, social, and economic structures of the state.[25] Officially, prefects were the only arm of the law with the authority to impose sanctions on printers and publishers. In reality, Mussolini had already begun a progressive centralization of the control over cultural production.

When Capasso-Torre handed in his resignation in 1928 – to begin a diplomatic career – the time was ripe for the reintroduction of grassroot Fascists. The job went first to Lando Ferretti, a *fascista della prima ora* (Fascist of the first hour) with hands-on experience at the Propaganda Office of the National Fascist Party (Partito Nazionale Fascista, PNF), and then, in December 1931, to Gaetano Polverelli, who had worked for Mussolini as editor of *Il Popolo d'Italia* since 1915, was a founding member of the Rome Fascio in 1919, and had become a Fascist MP in 1924. By this time the regime's grip on the national press was a fait accompli, and Ferretti could end his term in office with a long circular to all the directors of papers outlining the rights and duties of the press. Point 1 was absolutely clear: 'Il giornale deve essere organo di propaganda dell'italianità e del Regime' (Newspapers must be an instrument of propaganda supporting 'Italian-ness' and the Regime).[26] However, even during these years of expansion of the press office, it must be underlined that the attention of the regime was closely focused on periodical publications. Indeed, it is under the headship of Polverelli that the press office centralized and intensified the practice of sending the famous 'veline' – that is, brief directives to all chief editors of Italian papers. One of the first *veline* regarding books concerned the memoirs of Prefect Cesare Mori, who had famously fought against the Mafia in the 1920s: *Con la mafia ai ferri corti* (Mondadori, 1932). A press office note of 6 May 1932 requested that newspaper editors ignore its publication; on 21 May 1932 *Lavoro fascista* was warned for having broken ranks. The alleged reason for this unofficial censorship of Mori's book, apart from his difficult relationship with the regime, was that the original front cover presented the picture of a Sicilian armed bandit. This was attacked as offensive to public morality, and Mondadori was forced to replace it with a new one featuring Mori in a black shirt.[27] Occasionally the press office would be contacted by publishers eager to have prior approval of their choices. This is the case with the literary critic Enrico Falqui who, while co-editing an anthology of contemporary Italian writers with a young Elio Vittorini, decided to contact the press office to enquire as to the political advisability of including a particular author. Unfortunately it is not clear which author was the subject of this correspondence (at the time Falqui and Vittorini were discussing the inclusion/exclusion of dozens of them), but a letter by Ferretti, dated 2 December 1929, on Ufficio stampa del Capo del Governo letterhead, stated quite clearly that 'è preferibile che il nome da Lei indicato *non* figuri nell'antologia che Ella sta preparando' (it is advisable *not* to include in your anthology the name you mentioned; emphasis in the original).[28]

We have to wait until 1931 to witness the first circular specifically aimed at books. It was not sent out by the press office but by the Ministry of the Interior, which since November 1926 had returned to be one of the ministries directly run by Mussolini. This would indicate that, until the early 1930s, control over books was mainly in the hands of the prefectures, nationally coordinated by a department of the DGPS, the Division of General and Confidential Affairs (Divisione Affari Generali e Riservati). The first documented example of a complete ban on an author's work comes from the Ministry of the Interior. The object was the anti-Fascist priest and former leader of the Popular Party (Partito Popolare) Don Luigi Sturzo, who since 1924 had been living in Britain in exile. The telegram from the ministry to all prefects ordered the seizure of the recently printed German translation of Sturzo's *L'Italie et le Fascisme*. 'Pregasi inoltre,' the telegram added, 'disporre sequestro di tutte le pubblicazioni avvenire di Don Sturzo come pure delle traduzioni in qualsiasi lingua' (Please make sure all future publications by Don Sturzo are also seized as well as all translations in any foreign language).[29] Similarly, on 30 May

1930 the entire work of the communist author Henry Barbusse was seized after complaints from the editor of a Fascist paper in Massa Carrara. In this case, the seizure included four translations of books printed in Italy; two months later, the prefect of Milan informed the ministry that a total of 6,013 copies had been seized at the warehouse of the Milanese publisher Sonzogno.[30] It must be said that the Ministry of the Interior had also intervened in order to stem a totally different kind of publications – pamphlets, books, and collections of lyrics crassly eulogizing and glorifying the regime. For example, on 1 December 1928 Mussolini sent a stern circular to all prefects stating in no uncertain terms that prefectures were required to prune the nation from the many 'vulgar, grotesque, stupid' publication praising the Fascist revolution with embarrassing superficiality. Showing a high degree of confidence in his prefecture officials, Mussolini did not require them to ask for a higher authorization before proceeding to seize those publications.[31]

There were also cases in which other Fascist authorities intervened and interfered. For instance, on 4 October 1929 Carlo Ravasio, head of the press office of the Milanese branch of the PNF, wrote to the prefect to inform him that their national party leader, Augusto Turati, had found two pro-Fascist publications that were so embarrassingly inaccurate they deserved immediate seizure. The Milanese prefecture was not so easily swayed. It was only 25 November 1929 that the prefect came to a final decision, and, as he informed Ravasio, only one of the two booklets – *Storia dei fatti di Empoli e del Kursaal 'Diana,'* by Francesco Masiani (publisher unknown) – was considered in breach of the law. The booklet was seized and the authors taken to the police station and given a warning. Regarding the second one – *Annunciamo: L'Italia popolo eletto*, by Giulietto Calabrese and Maria Danese (published by Tipografia Venezia) – the prefect found no reason to justify the seizure despite the fact that Turati had defined it 'inconcludente e pazzesco' (inconclusive and mad).[32]

Sometimes it seems that church authorities too were able to obtain satisfaction for their censorial preoccupations. On 26 June 1929 the head of police informed the prefecture of Milan that, following complaints of the Diocese Board (*Giunta Diocesiana*), he had ordered the seizure of the entire oeuvre of novelist Virgilio Scattolini together with individual works by Arthur Rimbaud (his prose poems *I deserti dell'amore*, published by both Sonzogno and Modernissima) and four other unknown authors. The titles of some of Scattolini's works allow a sufficient indication as to their content: *La Cavalcata delle vergini* (1922), *Cesarina impara l'amore* (1928), and *La bocca mi baciò tutta tremante* (1929).[33]

Another case of censorship of a licentious work concerned one of Italy's most popular novelists at the time, Dino Segre, alias Pitigrilli. Since his debut with *Mammiferi di lusso*, published by Sonzogno in 1920, Pitigrilli's risqué novels had dominated the popular end of the literary market. However, in April 1925 a delegation of the Turinese League for Public Morality (*Lega per la pubblica moralità*) – an odd association of conservative moralizers – reported, among others, two of his books to the police. Only one of the two, the collection of short stories *La cintura di castità* (Sonzogno, 1921), was considered liable to public prosecution. The trial began on 12 January 1926, initially involving only the publisher, but Pitigrilli asked to be part of the proceedings and apparently won over the presiding judge with a virtuoso speech in defence of his fictional work. He also had the support of General De Bono, who sent a statement saying that, as head of police in 1921, he had personally authorized the publication of Pitigrilli's book. According to Pitigrilli's biographer, the trial ended with the acquittal of all parties, although it has been suggested that the publisher was actually found guilty. In any case, no other reprints of *La cintura di castità* were allowed. Pitigrilli continued his successful career until, as we will see in chapter 6, his Jewish origin became the source of more serious trouble.[34]

In addition to its other provisions, the circular of February 1931 also instructed all prefects to send to the Ministry of the Interior three copies of each publication that had been seized. A year later, another circular organized what seems to be the first collection of national data with regard to books. Prefects were told to require all publishers to provide the name and title of each publication before its distribution. All data would be conveyed to the Division of General and Confidential Affairs in Rome, which could then piece together a national picture of book production. On 26 May 1932 a new law regulated the number of copies that each publishers had to deposit for public record – that is, in addition to the copy due to the prefecture. Three copies were to be deposited at the nearest Royal Court (*Procura del Re*), which would forward them to the National Libraries of Florence and Rome and the closest public library.[35]

The next stage in the development of the regime's policies on books was greatly influenced by international events. Hitler's seizure of power and Goebbels's immediate creation of the Ministry for Popular Enlightenment and Propaganda (*Reichministerium für Propaganda und Volksaufklärung*) in March 1933 gave Mussolini a clear example of efficient and radical centralization of state control of culture. Two months later Goebbels himself came to Italy to describe his new organization and visit a number of Italian institutions, including Mussolini's press office.[36] The new Nazi ministry had become responsible for all aspects of cultural production and distribution. *Critica fascista*, the periodical of the then minister of corporations, Giuseppe Bottai, devoted several issues to a discussion on the future organization of Italian culture. All the contributors agreed that the Nazis had set the best example of centralization. Mussolini too must have agreed, because in August 1933 he appointed his young son-in-law, Galeazzo Ciano, as chief of the Press Office of the Head of Government. Ciano, soon considered to be Mussolini's future successor, was then a young diplomat whose father, Costanzo Ciano, had been at the head of the Ministry of Communication since its creation in November 1924. Galeazzo's promotion to the press office gave this department an even stronger profile, and the Nazi example accelerated a process that was already *in fieri*. One of Ciano's first initiatives was to make sure that every major prefecture had its Addetto Stampa (press officer). This move strengthened the tie between the Press Office of the Head of Government and prefectures and, as such, overlapped with the central office of the Ministry of the Interior. This created a dualism that, as we will see, was to remain unresolved until the end of the regime.

The growth in power of the press office was accompanied by an equivalent upgrading of its official status. By September 1934 the department had been renamed State Secretariat for Press and Propaganda (*Sottosegretariato di Stato per la Stampa e la Propaganda*), and in June 1935 it finally became the fully fledged Ministry for the Press and Propaganda (*Ministero per la Stampa e Propaganda*).

However, with regard to censorship, it was an apparently unexpected and relatively minor case that, in April 1934, provoked both a radical reorganization of the censorship of books and a tentative clarification of the role played by each authority. The book in question was a novel written by a popular fiction writer, Maria Volpi, alias Mura: *Sambadù, amore negro*. This important case will be dealt with in chapter 4. Before that, however, the next two chapters will examine how, between 1922 and 1934, the system of book censorship actually worked in practice. The combination of the coexistence of old and new centres of authority with the not so rare interference of the regime's charismatic dictator meant that the system was fraught with potential complications. To this, one should add the simple fact that book censorship did not take place only in the arena of printed texts confronted by censors. Publishing houses were an important part of a cultural industry that had to be helped and developed, not simply put under control. Hence, as we will see, policies were often adapted to the circumstances, needs, and 'fortune' of individual books, authors, and publishers.

2 Carrots, Sticks, and Charismatic Ruling

Taming Unfriendly Publishers: The Cases of Gobetti, Monanni, and Corbaccio

This first section of this chapter concentrates on the fate of three publishers that on the eve of Mussolini's seizure of power were clearly identified as anti-Fascist. Each of them was giving voice to different political camps: from Turin, Gobetti represented the most daring and acute voice of liberal anti-Fascism. The Milanese publishers Monanni and Corbaccio were devoted, respectively, to the work of anarchist philosophers and of socialist intellectuals. Their different destinies are emblematic of the range of strategies with which the regime muffled its enemies in the publishing industry.[1]

The case of Piero Gobetti as a publisher is inextricably linked with his activity as a journal editor and an outspoken intellectual. His publishing house was part of Gobetti's project to provide a bulwark against the conversion to Fascism of progressively larger circles of Italian society. On reading Gobetti's sarcastic attacks against both Fascism and the meekness of most opposition politicians, Mussolini must have realized that he was facing an exceptional opponent of unbending determination. Action needed to be taken.

Gobetti's journal, *Rivoluzione liberale,* began its life in February 1922 and quickly established itself as one of the most lucid enemies of Fascism. Its twenty-one-year-old editor showed a unique capacity for leading the debate while rallying a distinguished group of authors (from old *maestri* such as Luigi Einaudi, Prezzolini, and Salvemini, to young intellectuals such as Sapegno, Ansaldo, Caramella, Brosio, and Monti). His contributions as a theatre critic to Gramsci's journal *Ordine nuovo* were also evidence of his sympathy for communism and in particular his belief that only working-class militancy could stop Italy's slide towards Fascist dictatorship.

With Mussolini's seizure of power in October 1922, Gobetti's critique of Fascism became even stronger. In his attempt to reveal the violent and totalitarian core of Fascism, he constantly challenged the regime to show its intransigence. Yet, paradoxically, he often suggested that a period of proper dictatorship was perhaps necessary for the political maturation of Italians. In his articles he warned his supporters to consider themselves as a kind of 'compagnia della morte' (fellowship of the dead) and to prepare themselves for some form of persecution. Finally he resorted to open provocation and polemically asked to be attacked – 'chiediamo le frustate perché qualcuno si svegli, chiediamo il boia perché si possa veder chiaro' (we ask for violence so to wake us up, we ask for the executioner so that we can seee more clearly).[2] Sadly, he did not have to wait for long.

Mussolini did not refrain from personal and direct involvement. As De Felice has shown, it was a telegram by Mussolini to the prefect of Turin that triggered Gobetti's first arrest on 6 February 1923. The text of the telegram deserves to be quoted in its entirety:

> Ordinole perquisire immediatamente redazione amministrazione giornale 'RIVOLUZIONE LIBERALE' sequestrando schedari abbonati corrispondenza libri amministrativi-stop Contemporaneamente procederà arresto nominato Pietro Gobetti e redattori provvedendo a denunciarlo autorità giudiziaria per intelligenza coi comunisti sovversivi – stop Attendo risultato operazione telegraficamente massima energia e durezza – stop[3]

> (Proceed immediately to search administrative offices of journal 'RIVOLUZIONE LIBERALE' seize subscription records and administrative correspondence – stop At same time proceed to arrest Piero Gobetti and editors for conspiring with subversive communists – stop Telegraphic update of operation expected use maximum energy and force – stop)

By the evening Prefect Enrico Palmieri could answer with a telegram confirming the arrest of Gobetti, who had just come back from his honeymoon.[4] The prefect also asked Mussolini for evidence of Gobetti's illegal activities so that he could initiate judicial proceedings. However, the evidence must have failed to arrive from Rome because the following day Gobetti was released and was able to continue his journalistic work.

A month later Gobetti announced the birth of the publishing house bearing his surname. It was destined to last only two and a half years, but the fact that in those twenty-eight months about one hundred volumes were published is a clear testimony to his extraordinary energy and enthusiasm. The publishing house was supposed to complement *Rivoluzione liberale* as a platform for militant anti-Fascism. Gobetti asked for and obtained the collaboration of leading anti-Fascist politicians and intellectuals. Authors such as Salvemini, Nitti, Amendola, Sturzo, Missiroli, and Luigi Einaudi left no doubt as to the sophisticated level of argument that Gobetti was able to employ against the regime. Mussolini continued to keep a watchful eye. A second telegram to the prefect of Turin, on 8 March 1923, suggested Gobetti's arrest and detention for five days. Two weeks later the prefect informed Il Duce that Gobetti had been interrogated at the police station and his offices searched. On 28 March Mussolini reiterated his direct request to keep Gobetti under pressure, once more in fairly explicit terms: 'Non perda d'occhio elementi sedicente rivoluzione liberale renda loro vita difficile dal momento che insistono loro obliquo imbecille atteggiamento' (Do not lose sight of elements of so-called liberal revolution, make their life difficult since they insist with their oblique imbecile behaviour).[5]

On 29 May Gobetti was arrested again, but this time his rising fame meant that the national press publicized the event, and two opposition MPs filed a question in parliament asking the government for justification. The unconvincing reply by Mussolini's deputy minister of the interior, Aldo Finzi, was that the arrest had been warranted by Gobetti's involvement with Gramsci's outlawed *Ordine nuovo*. As if to proclaim his determination to fight on, Gobetti decided to add a Greek inscription to the logo of his firm, its words showing once more his cynical sarcasm: 'Che ho a che fare io con gli schiavi?' (What have I got to do with slaves?).

At around the same time Gobetti was preparing a collection of his *Rivoluzione liberale* articles for the Bolognese publisher Cappelli. The choice of publisher was the result of the collaboration between Gobetti and Marxist historian Rodolfo Mondolfo. The latter, who had been writing for *Rivoluzione liberale*, was editor of a series of social studies for Cappelli and happily agreed to include a book by Gobetti. Their correspondence shows Mondolfo advising his author on giving cohesion to the collection but also suggesting a degree of self-censorship with regard to Gobetti's attacks on both the socialist leader Filippo Turati and Fascism. Gobetti agreed to tone down his criticism of Turati, but the section of the book devoted to Fascism presented an undiluted selection of his harsh attacks against Mussolini. The volume was eventually published in 1924, and, according to the historian Angelo d'Orsi, most copies of its first edition were destroyed by Fascists. Officially it was banned only in 1938, when all the works of anti-Fascists such as Gobetti were included in the first list of proscribed texts.[6]

In the same year, as a publisher, Gobetti took on board the third volume of Francesco Nitti's reflections on the political situation in Europe, which his Florentine publisher, Bemporad, had refused to publish for fear of Fascist reprisals.[7] However, events of a much greater magnitude were raising the temperature of the political debate. First, the April 1924 general elections saw a comfortable Fascist victory thanks to their controversial electoral reforms; two months later, the kidnapping and assassination of Giacomo Matteotti seemed likely to provoke the fall of Mussolini's government. In all his different functions – as journalist, editor, publisher – Gobetti was in the front line of the anti-Fascist battle. In the weeks preceding the general elections he did his best to promote the work of anti-Fascist leaders, including a collection of speeches by the Reverend Don Luigi Sturzo, leader of the Popular Party (Partito Popolare). His indignant articles about the Matteotti affair were also collected in a book this time under his own imprint.

Despite his intense political militancy, Gobetti found the time to devote himself to literature. Since the birth of his publishing house, he had planned to expand its list with a number of literary works. In 1924 he published a variety of poetry books. One of them, a collection of poems by a young Ligurian author – *Ossi di seppia* by Eugenio Montale – was to become one of the most popular works of modern Italian literature. Montale was also a collaborator with the Genoese paper *Il Lavoro*, and his anti-Fascism was to become public in 1925 when he signed Benedetto Croce's a manifesto of anti-Fascist intellectuals. Although *Ossi di seppia* did not encounter any censorship problems, this should not come as a surprise, as Montale's poetry was far from containing explicit, direct political comments.

A week after the Fascist victory in the election, Mussolini was once again putting pressure on the prefect of Turin, sending a two-line telegram on 13 April that read: 'Richiamo energicamente attenzione V. S. su linguaggio provocatorio giornale Rivoluzione Liberale' (Let me forcefully remind you to pay attention to the provocative language used by paper Rivoluzione Liberale). Gobetti's offices were promptly searched by the police and a number of documents seized. A new wave of repression came in June after yet another request from Mussolini's to

the prefect to 'rendere nuovamente difficile vita questo insulso opposi-
tore governo e fascismo' (to make life difficult for this despicable
opposer of the government and Fascism). Two days later the next issue
of *Rivoluzione liberale* was seized while still in proofs, Gobetti's offices
were again, searched and a batch of documents, mainly correspondence, was sent directly to Mussolini for his perusal. In a letter to a
friend, Gobetti complained that the police raid had taken place without
the required mandate from the judiciary. Moreover, he noticed that the
content of one of his letters that had been intercepted back in April had
been used by Cesare Rossi, head of Mussolini's press office, to attack the
publisher from the pages of *Il Popolo d'Italia*.[8]

If Gobetti suffered the attention of the Turin police, a much more
sinister event was taking place in the capital: on Sunday, 10 June 1924,
the outspoken Socialist MP Giacomo Matteotti was kidnapped and mur-
dered by a group of Fascists. What was left of the non-Fascist press
raised its voice once it became clear that the murderers were in close
contact with Mussolini's inner circle of collaborators. That response was
enough to convince Mussolini to tighten the screw on the freedom of
the press. In July 1924 Mussolini decided to apply in full the two decrees
that allowed prefects to close down any publishing activity. Gobetti's
immediate reply from the pages of *Rivoluzione liberale* was that the survival of his own activity, however subdued, was more useful than a
heroic but ultimately sterile martyrdom. It was a sign that Gobetti
intended to move from the provocative opposition of previous years to
subtler forms of resistance.[9] A further sign of this change of strategy was
the creation of a literary journal that was planned to exist in parallel
with *Rivoluzione liberale*. This was *Il Baretti*, which began publication in
November 1924. As one of its editors remembered, a tacit degree of self-
censorship was applied in order to guarantee the paper's survival. This
strategy, though frustrating, was successful, as no issue of *Il Baretti* was
ever seized by the police.[10]

But it was too late to change tactics. Gobetti's criticism of the nationalists
and the liberals who had joined Mussolini's government had already
resulted in a physical attack by a group of Fascist sympathizers on 5 September 1924.[11] After that, more issues of *Rivoluzione liberale* were seized by
the police than were freely distributed. Throughout most of 1925 the journal survived thanks to Gobetti's unbending determination to continue,
but it was only a question of time before the prefecture decided to close it
down. Moreover, it was becoming clear that, even on a strictly financial
ground, the situation had become untenable. If for some time Gobetti had

entertained the idea of expanding his publishing activity abroad, by the end of the year it was quickly becoming the only option left. On 3 October, before the prefecture threatened to close his publishing operation (through a diffida), Gobetti had already mentioned to Prezzolini his plans to open a publishing house in Paris. He hoped that the international profile of his activity might restrain the Fascists from closing down his activity on Italian soil.[12] A few weeks later a second diffida by the prefect was followed by the closure of most of Gobetti's publishing enterprise, books included. The Gobetti publishing house was finished. The last issue of *Rivoluzione liberale* was published on 8 November 1925.

Gobetti was well aware of the fact that Mussolini himself was behind the campaign against him. In a letter to Prezzolini, he concluded: 'Potrei venire a patti ma non lo farò. È probabile che mi decida invece a venire a Parigi' (I could come to a compromise but I won't do it. Instead, it is likely that I will come to Paris).[13] Indeed, it was with the specific intent of exploring the possibility of moving his publishing activities to France that Gobetti set off for Paris on 8 February 1926. However, acute bronchitis was to confine him to his bed as soon as he arrived there and led to his death by the following week.

The literary journal *Il Baretti* continued for more than another two years, closing down in the autumn of 1928. Gobetti's editors at *Il Baretti* also attempted to continue the publication of books under the Edizioni del Baretti imprint. The publication of Gobetti's works was one of their main goals. Four volumes of his collected work came out, together with some volumes on European poetry and politics. But by November 1928 even this publishing activity came to a halt.[14]

There is no doubt that, as a publisher and a journalist, Piero Gobetti had been one of the most outspoken critics of Fascism and perhaps the most prescient in judging the development of Mussolini's movement. The direct role that Il Duce took in the campaign of repression is a testimony to the calibre of Gobetti's activity. It is also an example of the strategies with which, in his early years of power, Mussolini managed to stifle the few remaining voices of open criticism.

The small publishing house Monanni provides another example of early Fascist repression of publishers. Ironically, Monanni's publications were close to Mussolini's early political beliefs. Its founders were two Tuscan anarchists, Giuseppe Monanni and Leda Rafanelli. In 1909 this young couple, who already had experience as editors, journalists, and writers, had moved from Florence to Milan, where they created the Società Editoriale Milanese. The following year it was renamed Libreria

Editrice Sociale, later Casa Editrice Sociale, and ultimately Casa Editrice Monanni. When Mussolini was still the promising socialist chief editor of *Avanti!*, Leda Rafanelli had published an article praising his speech in commemoration of the Paris Commune. As a result the two had started to correspond and had met on a number of occasions (she is often remembered in Mussolini's biographies for her alleged relationship with him). Il Duce's conversion to interventionism, however, violently clashed with her anti-imperialist ideals and their relationship ended in October 1914.[15]

The small publishing house specialized in the publication of foreign works of either fiction or political-philosophical matter. Some space was also devoted to Rafanelli's copious production of pamphlets and fictional works. In the catalogue one could find authors who had greatly influenced Mussolini in his early years as a political activist. Between 1910 and 1915 the Libreria Editrice Sociale published the work of anarchists such as Peter Kropotkin – whose work Mussolini himself had translated in 1904 and 1911 – Errico Malatesta, and Louise Michel.[16] As individualist anarchists, Monanni and Rafanelli also promoted the work of philosophers Max Stirner (*L'Unico*, 1911) and Friedrich Nietzsche (*L'anticristo*, 1913). Mussolini himself had expressed his admiration for these philosophers, referring to them, in a letter written in 1910, as 'queste dolomiti del pensiero' (these Dolomites of thought).[17]

When the Fascists came to power, Monanni and Rafanelli's publishing house continued its activity. In 1923, for example, it published two works of the French anarchist Georges Palante and a volume of collected essays by Max Stirner, and it continued its publication of Russian fiction (Gorky, Tolstoy, Goncharov, among others). In the same year, according to two scholars, the offices of the publishing house were attacked and ransacked by Fascists. This episode is not confirmed by official documentation (it is actually denied, as we will see later on). In any case, the fact that during that year and the following ones books by Casa Editrice Sociale – as it was called between 1919 and 1926 – were still published seems to suggest that, if there were an attack, it was not sufficient to halt the activity of the publishing house.[18] In 1923 Rafanelli published a new edition of her 1910 novel *L'eroe della folla*, which tells of the life of a young revolutionary anarchist. This outspoken pro-anarchist, anti-militarist novel was, perhaps, the reason for the Fascist attack. What we know beyond doubt is that no official measures were taken: the novel was not officially seized nor did Rafanelli's surname ever enter the list of prohibited authors.[19] In 1925 Monanni published a translation of Jack London's most political novel,

The Iron Heel (1908). The book appeared as *Il tallone di ferro*, with its subtitle 'Romanzo di previsione sociale' (a novel of social prediction) pointing to its topical plot: the Dystopia of a democratic state developing dictatorial forces in reaction to the rise of socialism. Despite its potentially anti-Fascist content – although set in the United States, the story could be read as a powerful prophecy of Italy's descent into Fascism – the novel was reprinted in 1928. However, as we will see below, it was to become one of the causes of Monanni's later problems with the police.

When, in 1926, the Casa Editrice Sociale was renamed Casa Editrice Monanni, the change was probably an attempt to weather the dictatorial clamp down on the press following the Matteotti crisis. Schirone suggests that the closure of Casa Editrice Sociale was forced by the police. This notion is based on a police memo dated 27 February 1927, in which Rome's head of police states that 'dopo lo scioglimento dei partiti avversi al Regime Fascista, il Monanni, pur continuando a professare idee anarchiche, ha smesso forzatamente tali pubblicazioni [di libri e opuscoli di propaganda sovversiva]' (after the disbanding of all political parties opposed to the Fascist Regime, Monanni, despite his surviving anarchist beliefs, was forced to stop such publications [of books and pamphlets of subversive propaganda]). A memo from the Milanese police two years later confirms that when the decrees of 1926 were applied, some of Monanni's publishing activities were stopped.[20] Given the fragmentary evidence, we can only guess that Monanni was probably warned by the police to stop any publications with potential subversive content. The creation of a new company – based in the same premises – was arguably part of the adjustment to the new dictatorial times.[21]

There is no doubt that the survival of Monanni's publishing activities came at a price. The promotion of anarchist works was replaced by the publication of books that either were linked to Fascist syndacalism (in 1927 Monanni published a book by the ex-socialist and corporativist syndacalist Angelo Oliviero Olivetti) or were written by foreign intellectuals whose work was still acceptable to the regime. This was certainly the case of Gustave Le Bon, another great star of Mussolini's cultural upbringing. In 1927 Monanni published both his *La psicologia delle folle* and *L'evoluzione dei popoli*. Moreover, the complete works of Friedrich Nietzsche were published between 1927 and 1928, and the publisher sent a complimentary copy of this monumental work to Mussolini, who asked for the books to be delivered to his home address.[22] Monanni's publication of foreign works of fiction also continued, and it was in this area that he would have lingering problems with the Fascist authorities.

On 20 May 1929 a circular was sent to all prefects by the Secretariat of the Ministry of the Interior (which at the time was under Mussolini's personal direction). It warned them about the sales by itinerant booksellers (sui banchi di fiere) of low-priced Russian and American novels. The memo underlined that these books were to be seized if they were perceived to be circulated as a propaganda weapon against the regime. The directive was evidently taken to the letter: only a couple of weeks later, the same government office had to send out a second memo in which prefects were advised not to be too strict in imposing measures that could 'determinare, in caso di persistenza, un rilevante danno alle Case Editrici' (cause, if they were to persist, a major damage to publishing houses). It is very likely that this reversal of policy was determined by the complaints of some influential publishers or booksellers. The following month the prefects of Arezzo and Reggio Emilia answered with reassuring letters stating that the seizure of American and Russian books had been halted. Not so the prefect of Ferrara, whose letter contained an explicit denunciation of Monanni as a subversive publisher:

> L'editore Monanni di Milano mi risulterebbe essere sempre stato editore di libri sovversivi.
>
> Spesse volte la sua libreria sarebbe stata saccheggiata dalle squadre fasciste. Venne anche sottoposta a diverse operazioni di sequestro da parte della questura di Milano. La Sua Ditta, allora, era 'Casa Editrice Sociale.'[23]

(The Monanni publisher from Milan has always been a printer of subversive books.

His bookshop was often ransacked by the Fascist squads. It was also the object of various seizures by the Milan police. His firm, at the time, was called 'Casa Editrice Sociale.')

At this point the ball was in the court of the prefect of Milan, and indeed the Ministry of the Interior forwarded the letter to him. His answer came on 7 August 1929: the prefect admitted that the Casa Editrice Sociale had published subversive works but, he stated, this had stopped in 1926. After that time, the output of Monanni was perfectly legal, and its publications had been accepted by the prime minister as well as by government-sponsored people's libraries (*Librerie Popolari*). Finally the prefect stated that, according to his records, neither the Casa Editrice Sociale nor Monanni had ever been ransacked by Fascist squads.

The storm subsided with no apparent measures being taken. But there is no doubt that, with the anarchist credentials of Monanni and Rafanelli (the police had files on both of them), the Casa Editrice Monanni continued to be subjected to particular scrutiny. This is directly suggested by a letter that Giuseppe Monanni sent to Mussolini in 1931, in which he complained about the fact the some novels by Maxim Gorky had been seized by the police in various bookshops. Gorky's work, Monanni underlined, was published by other houses such as Treves, Voghera, Sonzogno, Bietti, and Mondadori, so it was not clear to Monanni why only his own house's publications should be banned.[24] The prefect of Milan was once more asked to look into the problem. His answer, on 7 July 1931, was that the seizure had taken place in only one bookshop in southern Italy (Bari) and the volumes had been returned after the prefecture of Bari had found that they were not on any black list. It is tempting to think that the titles of two of the three novels seized – *La spia* (1928) and *Confessione* (1930) – might have prompted the attention of some overzealous policeman.

Two years later Monanni sent one more letter to Mussolini, this time complaining that at a Rome bookshop three Monanni novels had been seized by the police. This time it was because of their alleged immoral content. Two of the three books, *Il gesto di Frine: Amori esotici* (1932) and *La voluttà sul mondo* (1932), were by popular novelist Maurice Dekobra, the other by Venceslao Fernandez Florez, *Storia immorale* (1932). Monanni's complaint was passed on to the head of police, who replied that the books had only been withdrawn ('prelevati') so that the police could double-check on their moral content. According to the report the action was the result of a letter of complaint that the police had received with regard to the content of one of the three books, *La voluttà sul mondo*. For good measure, the police must have then decided to have a look at the other two. Again, officially no further action seems to have been taken.[25] In the same year, however, the Casa Editrice Monanni ceased its activity. To what extent are these two events related? There is no evidence that the closure was the result of direct political pressure. We also know that in those same months the relationship between Monanni and Rafanelli had come to an end, and it is possible that the two decided to stop their collaboration as publishers as well (although they remained good friends). Yet, it is important to note that in the same year an officer of the Fascist Militia, in his report about a recent anti-subversive operation in Emilia, suggested that some of the novels published by Monanni (such as Gorky's *La madre* and Jack London's *Il tallone di ferro*) were invariably found in the houses of suspected anti-Fascists. He concluded: 'Non sarebbe il caso di far scomparire da tutte le biblioteche d'Italia la letteratura del genere?' (Wouldn't it be appropriate to get rid of such literature from all the libraries of Italy?). However, the prefecture of Milan had already acted: as shown by a telegram dated 20 February 1931, London's book had been the subject of a search at the two Milan publishing houses producing an edition of the novel: 160 copies were seized at the offices of Modernissima and 790 at the offices of Monanni.[26] Although it remains to be proven that this last seizure triggered the closure of Monanni, it is arguable that if the police or some other authority had ordered Monanni – perhaps off the record – to stop his publication of foreign fiction, there is no doubt that this would have destroyed the financial viability of the publishing house. Moreover, the connection between Monanni's books and left-wing anti-Fascist circles was a real one. This is reinforced by the fact that in 1938 an unsigned internal memo from the General Directorate of Public Security returned to the subject of 'subversive' literature read by anti-Fascists. It was noted that novels by Gorky (this time *La madre* was present together with *La spia*) and Jack London (*Il tallone di ferro*, though the title in the memo was rendered as *Il tallone di Achille*) were constantly found in the house of anti-Fascists. The report added that, once the occupants were queried about the books, 'le dichiarazioni rese dagli arrestati sono state sempre le stesse: "farsi un'anima comunista"' (the statements given by the people arrested were always the same ones: 'to develop a Communist mind'). The memo concluded with the proposal to forbid their circulation. These last lines were highlighted in the margin by a double-stroke in pencil. And with the same pencil appears a 'sì' followed by Mussolini's unmistakable initial (see figure 1).[27]

It seems possible that, although in 1933 Monanni was told to stop his publishing activity, the circulation of his published books had continued, thus prompting the seizure of some of them in 1938. A final, baffling coda to this matter is provided by the last two documents to be found in Monanni's file in Mussolini's office. The first is a letter from the prefect of Milan, dated 7 March 1940. It informs Mussolini that Monanni had been arrested by the Political Police (Polizia Politica) in the previous summer and was now asking for financial compensation. The prefect did not know the reason for Monanni's arrest. Could it be linked to his activity as a publisher? And why should Monanni be asking for compensation seven years after he had stopped publishing books?

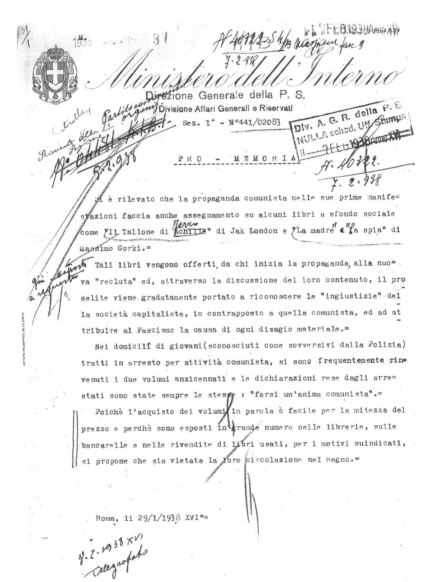

1. Censorship and communist propaganda: police memorandum, 29 January 1938, with Mussolini's authorization in pencil. (*Courtesy of Archivio Centrale dello Stato, Rome*)

The second and final piece of documentation is even more cryptic: it is a request for help that Monanni, through the Milanese prefecture, sent to Mussolini on 28 September 1940. It reads: 'Sono sempre in attesa d'un vostro tangibile segno di ricompensa pel servizio resovi' (I'm still waiting for a tangible sign of reward for the services I provided you with). What services? Lacking any further material evidence, we can only speculate.[28] After the war, Monanni became an editor for the big Milan publisher Rizzoli, and it was thanks to him that Leda Rafanelli's *Una donna e Mussolini* was published in 1946. Could it be that this book had already been written by 1940 and that Monanni's 'service' had been to stop Rafanelli from publishing it? It is a remote but not totally improbable possibility. The publication of the forty love letters might have proved embarrassing for a dictator who at the time of his relationship with Rafanelli was already married with children. At the same time, we should keep in mind that, when this last piece of correspondence reached Mussolini's office, Fascist Italy had just entered the Second World War. There is no proof that Mussolini actually read the message, and even if he did, it is unlikely that, given his commitments, he would have had the time and desire to respond. Monanni's attempt to force Mussolini to do something in his favour might have been a last shot in the dark.

The third anti-fascist publisher that we will consider, Corbaccio, is the only one that was still active at the time of the fall of the regime in July 1943. The Studio Editoriale Corbaccio was established in 1918 mainly to sustain the publication of a new periodical called *La Rivista di Milano* (which was an attempt at an Italian equivalent of the prestigious *Mercure de France*). The actual creation of a fully fledged publishing house was the result of a takeover, in October 1923, by the young self-made publisher Enrico dall'Oglio. Born in 1900, dall'Oglio had worked for publishers such as Società Editrice Libraria and Modernissima, climbing from the lowly position of errand boy to that of director. He was also an enthusiastic socialist and had been a militant syndicalist in the early interwar period.[29] Under his direction the firm was renamed Edizioni Corbaccio, and after a few months it presented itself on the market with an ambitious catalogue of five separate series. One of these, *I classici dell'amore*, which had been inherited by the previous owners, it presented commercial novels of slightly risqué content. The other four showed dall'Oglio's keen interest in covering the extremely sensitive topic of contemporary politics. Their titles were *Cultura contemporanea, Piccola biblioteca di studi politici, Res Publica*, and *Confessioni e battaglie;*

their general editor was another socialist, the literary critic Gerolamo Lazzeri. The intention of dall'Oglio and Lazzeri was for these series to provide a vibrant picture of the political debate within the entire anti-Fascist camp. The first publications were outspoken denunciations of the April 1924 general election, which had given the Fascists an unassailable majority. Giovanni Amendola's *La democrazia dopo il 6 aprile 1924*, Guglielmo Ferrero's *Discorso ai sordi*, and the ex-Fascist Mario Missiroli's *Una battaglia perduta* set the tone for the publisher's output. After the kidnapping and murder of Giacomo Matteotti, the climax was reached with *Reliquie*, a collection of Matteotti's writings introduced by Claudio Treves and with a postscript by Filippo Turati.

It was not difficult to predict that, following Mussolini's intransigent speech of 3 January 1925, Corbaccio was set to become one of the targets of Fascist repression. On 24 January the proofs of the book *Il fascismo senza mito* by another ex-Fascist, Antonio Pescazzoli, were seized by the police.[30] In the same month dall'Oglio's collaborator, Gerolamo Lazzeri, decided to leave the publishing house. We do not know the reasons behind his departure; in the following years Lazzeri continued his activity as a freelance editor for other Milanese publishers, concentrating on works of a non-political nature. Despite that setback, dall'Oglio persevered with the publication of the writings of prominent anti-fascists such as Meuccio Ruini, Mario Borsa, Arturo Salucci, and Luigi Salvatorelli. At the same time, it is noticeable that dall'Oglio must have decided to devote more and more of his list to non-political works. This is exemplified by the destiny of his more militant series, *Confessioni e battaglie*. As Gigli Marchetti recounts in her study of Corbaccio, of the seven titles that were announced in that series in 1925, only two were published, and those two, by the *Corriere della Sera* journalist Luciano Magrini, were far from being polemics against the regime.[31] No other publication followed in that series.

It is not clear whether dall'Oglio's increasing detachment from militant publications was the result of actual pressure, perhaps unofficial, from the Fascists. Given the lack of such indications, even in the memoirs of the people involved, it seems possible that dall'Oglio had simply decided to guarantee the survival of his publishing enterprise by toning down the anti-Fascist content of his list. His improved relations with the regime were indirectly suggested through a short article in the *Giornale della libreria* in June 1927, which announced that Mussolini had thanked dall'Oglio for the donation of the two volumes of a biography of Ugo Foscolo.[32] In the same year Corbaccio published two volumes by Orio

Vergani, a popular Milanese writer and journalist close to the Fascists (he had arrived at *Corriere della Sera* soon after its anti-Fascist editor-in-chief, Luigi Albertini, had been made to resign). The following year the Milanese prefect ordered the seizure of a Corbaccio publication, but it is indicative that the volume in question was a collection of political essays, *Rivolta morale* by Alfredo Misuri, that had been published back in 1924. The volume was a public confession of a former Fascist intellectual who had decided to repudiate his political party, so it is not surprising that by 1928 the prefect had come to the conclusion – probably prompted by some complaint – that the book had to disappear.[33] An investigation must have followed the seizure because on 10 October 1928 the head of the Political Police in Rome wrote to the prefect of Milan with some interesting information about Enrico dall'Oglio. The source of the information was apparently a young writer, Corrado Alvaro, who in those years was close to the Fascists.[34] The document described Dall'Oglio as 'un vecchio massone e irriducibile avversario del regime' (an old mason and a relentless enemy of the regime). It added that 'l'antifascismo del dall'Oglio si dice sia molto noto a Milano ma egli sarebbe riuscito a superare le difficoltà dando commercio a numerosi scrittori fascisti e così riesce a stare in bilico' (dall'Oglio's anti-Fascism is well known in Milan, but he managed to avoid all difficulties and stay in business with the publication of a number of Fascist authors). The reply of Milan's prefect was reassuring: he stated that, according to their investigation, dall'Oglio was not involved in any anti-Fascist activity.

In 1928 there was also an attempt to convince dall'Oglio to leave the directorship of Corbaccio. This came from Orio Vergani, a Corbaccio author who also sat on the governing board of the publishing house. Vergani reported that the trade union representing journalists (which had been 'Fascistized' in 1926) had expressed concern that dall'Oglio was at the head of a publishing house, and it suggested the appointment of a 'una vecchia e fedele camicia nera' (and old and faithful blackshirt). Dall'Oglio promptly presented his resignation to the board, which refused to accept it. Although this attempt to quietly scuttle dall'Oglio did not work, he knew that his activity was going to be constantly scrutinized for any sign of anti-Fascism.[35] His rapprochement with the regime continued. In 1931, when he created a new series of historical essays, the opening book was a volume by the Fascist author Paolo Orano, *Canaglie, venturieri, apostoli del giornalismo*. The following year Orano was invited to join the governing board of the publishing house.

In terms of fictional works, in 1932 dall'Oglio managed to add Guido da Verona to his group of novelists. In the short term it proved a very successful move, as da Verona's sensual novels were particularly popular in Fascist Italy.[36] As we will see, however, in later years da Verona was to encounter the moralism of the Fascist censors, and by 1939 most of his work had been proscribed. Another unlucky move concerned the second edition of Alberto Moravia's debut novel, *Gli indifferenti*. In 1933 dall'Oglio convinced Moravia to allow Corbaccio to reprint the book. However, the novel did not go beyond its first print run, despite the success it had achieved in previous years (three reprints were published by Alpes between 1929 and 1930). Whether this was the product of an unofficial ban on the novel or simply the result of the fact that Moravia had by then become a Bompiani author remains to be proven.[37]

A panoramic look at the entire output of Corbaccio during the 1930s shows that its editor had almost given up any hope to give voice, however indirectly, to criticism against the regime. As we will see in chapter 6, Corbaccio was to be involved in the 'bonifica culturale' (cultural reclamation) of the late 1930s. Perhaps the only sign of a brave choice was the publication in 1937 of a volume by anti-Fascist philosophy professor Giuseppe Rensi. Suspended from lecturing at Genoa University since 1927, Rensi had been arrested in 1930 and had finally been dismissed in August 1934 after a volume of memoirs – *Scolii* (Montes, 1934) – had been seized three months earlier. Despite this, Rensi's study *La filosofia dell'assurdo* was published by Corbaccio in 1937 and was not met with any official reprimand. Perhaps Mussolini thought that there was more to be gained from the occasional exercise of mock liberality, as was extended to the work of Benedetto Croce.[38] However, it is fairly clear that in order to save his treasured enterprise, Enrico dall'Oglio had accepted the unwritten terms of the Fascists. His publishing output became more and more aligned with the times. In 1933, for example, he published the travel writings of Luigi Freddi, the young Fascist leader who, as a correspondent, had followed Italo Balbo's Formation Flight to the Americas and was about to become a powerful figure as head of the Directorate General for Cinematography (Direzione Generale per la Cinematografia) at the Ministry of Popular Culture.[39] Later, Corbaccio books received positive recognition from the regime. In 1936 Emilio Cecchi's *L'osteria del cattivo tempo* received the Mussolini Prize, and in 1938 the Ministry of Popular Culture acquired copies of Corbaccio's fifteen volume *Storia della guerra italiana* for a substantial total of 100,000 lire.[40]

Self-Censorship and Business Deals: Arnoldo Mondadori

When Mussolini was appointed head of his first government in October 1922, he had neither the intention nor the need to impose draconian changes on the publishing industry. Rather, he had friendly publishers to thank and do business with, and old scores to settle with those who had opposed him. Arnoldo Mondadori was certainly a supporter *della prima ora*. His Verona workshops printed Fascist leaflets at the time of the March on Rome. Mondadori had also been the most active among publishers in collaborating with Mussolini. The take-over of the newspaper *Il Secolo* by Mondadori and his major shareholder, Senatore Borletti, in April 1923 was a purely political operation. It responded to Mussolini's desire to 'convert' this old paper into an authoritative pro-Fascist voice capable of competing with Italy's best independent paper, *Corriere della Sera*.[41] However, as Decleva implicitly suggests in his exhaustive biography, Mondadori's support for Fascism was more the result of the publisher's intention to boost his business than a sign of genuine political passion. Indeed, Mondadori's declarations of supposed Fascist militancy before 1922 are contradicted by documentary evidence, and, at the other end of the chronological spectrum, his sudden conversion to anti-Fascism on 26 July 1943 also throws the solidity of his political ideals into question. Mondadori's ambivalence makes for a very interesting case in a study on censorship. Despite his stated dedication to the cause of the regime, Mondadori kept on publishing commercially successful books, even if their content was to some degree at loggerheads with the directives of the regime. In this respect, one could suggest that his collaboration with the Fascists was neither coerced nor consensual: it could probably be most accurately described as self-interested.

One of the early successes of the Mondadori publishing firm had been the signing of one of Italy's most promising young novelists, Virgilio Brocchi, who was also a popular member of Milan's socialist-controlled town council. Mondadori convinced Brocchi to join his firm not just as an author but as editor of one of his literary series, *Le Grazie*, which was to focus on popular middlebrow fiction, mainly by Italian authors. Brocchi's appointment was a blow to his old publisher, Treves, Milan's historic publishing firm. In many respects his move was symbolic of the shift of power from the old guard to the new, more technologically minded generation of publishers such as Mondadori. In the early years of Mussolini's regime, Brocchi continued to work as an editor for

Mondadori, and despite Brocchi's political position there are no records of any interference from state authorities or from his employer. However, in 1926 Brocchi was at the centre of a case of self-censorship that was ultimately resolved within the four walls of the publishing firm. The subject of this episode was the publication of his novel, *Rocca sull'onda*, the story of Pietro Barra, the son of a poor blacksmith who manages to become administrator of a big textile company. On 30 November 1926 Arnoldo Mondadori wrote to Brocchi, cautiously suggesting that future editions should be slightly modified: 'Un solo appunto vorrei muoverti, o, meglio, un suggerimento vorrei darti: quello di eliminare gli accenni politici che pur riferentesi ad epoca passata appaiono oggi o insignificanti o inopportuni, e che, in ogni caso, non sono necessari all'opera. Sono certo che non avrai difficoltà ad accontentarmi in occasione di una tua prossima ristampa' (I would like to note only one point, or, better, I would like to give you my advice: that is, to delete all political references which, despite belonging to a past era, come through as insignificant and inopportune to today's readers, and which, in any case, are not a necessary part of the novel. I am certain that you will be able to do this at the time of our next reprint.)[42] It is not clear whether this reflection by Mondadori was the result of his own reading of the novel or if it followed criticism by some authoritative Fascist. Brocchi's reply was dignified, but at the same time it betrayed his passive acceptance of the political status quo:

Ho meditato a lungo sulla frase segnalatami da te come pericolosa non in sé, ma per la interpretazione che di essa può dare qualche fanatico poco onesto o poco intelligente. Ti confesso che non ho saputo trovare in essa il più lontano pretesto di una possibile accusa, che non possa trarsi da qualunque pagina dei Promessi Sposi o della Divina Commedia. Aggiungo che togliere da una seconda edizione una frase apparsa nella prima può parere ai malevoli la prova di una ... intenzione maliziosa o almeno eterodossa di cui il romanzo intero è la negazione. Tuttavia ho tolto le tre righe; ma unicamente per compiacerti sebbene me ne rincresca, perché quelle tre righe contengono una attestazione di morale professionale che non dovrebbe spiacere a chi ha concepito lo stato corporativo.[43]

(I have thought long and hard about the lines which you indicated as dangerous, not so much because of their actual significance, but because they could be misinterpreted by a fanatic with little honesty and brains. I must confess that I could not find a single line which could give credence to a possible accusation unless one were equally to attack similar passages in *The Betrothed* or *The Divine Comedy*. I must also add that the act of deleting a sentence from a second edition can be interpreted by ill-motivated people as the proof of ... a malicious or bizarre intention, which is totally alien to the novel. Nonetheless, I have deleted the three lines; but only in order to please you, and despite the fact that I regret doing it since those three lines are a statement of professional morality, which should be welcome by those who have created the corporate state.)

Despite the small cut, the work was as popular as most of Brocchi's novels. By 1944 it was in its thirteenth reprint.[44]

Virgilio Brocchi was not Mondatori's only editor with a reputation for being anti-Fascist. In 1926 the publisher's literary series *Le Scie* came under the direction of Giuseppe Antonio Borgese, the Sicilian critic and novelist who was by then a famous journalist and author of the renowned novel *Rubè* (1921). He had recently become a Mondadori author with the publication of a poetry anthology in 1922 and his second novel, *I vivi e i morti*, the following year. Despite his anti-Fascist stance, Borgese had not followed Croce in signing the anti-Fascist manifesto nor had he left the *Corriere della Sera* when its chief editor, Albertini, was forced to resign. Eager to acquire his services, Mondadori probably thought that Borgese's political ideas were sufficiently detached from his literary work. Borgese's strong views with regard to the quality of translations of foreign fiction also struck a chord with Mondadori.[45] Similarly to Brocchi, Borgese did not attempt to use his position as editor to push forward authors whose work was at loggerheads with the regime's cultural directives. He continued his work as editor until he decided to leave the country in response to another form of censorship. In February 1930 his lectures at Milan University were interrupted by a group of young Fascists eager to show their dislike for a professor whom they had identified as anti-Fascist. On that occasion, Borgese complained in person to Mussolini, who immediately sent a telegram to the prefect of Milan asking him to contact the local leaders of the Gruppi Universitari Fascisti (GUF, the Fascist university youth association) and bring the interruptions to an end. The offer of a temporary lectureship in the United States in 1931 became the vehicle for Borgese's departure from Italy to which he was to return only at the end of Second World War.[46] The axe of the censors struck in his absence, in 1940, when his name eventually was included with those of other 'unwelcome authors.' By then he had published his first public attack against Mussolini – the pamphlet *Goliath*, published in the United States in 1937 – which, as it is easy to imagine, did not reach Italy until the end of the war.[47]

In terms of active collaboration, Arnoldo Mondadori's open support for Fascism was reflected in a number of publishing initiatives. The earliest trace to be found in Mussolini's official correspondence dates back to 17 March 1923. On that occasion, Mondadori wrote to inform Mussolini that he had decided to launch a new illustrated periodical, *Annali d'Italia*, that, together with a parallel series of supplements, was to provide the 'most perfect' documentation of the achievements of Fascism. To show his genuine enthusiasm, Mondadori refused to ask for any subvention and even offered to discuss a possible division of profits with the Fascist Party.[48] In later years numerous Fascist leaders were invited to publish their memoirs and other works with Mondadori, beginning with Luigi Federzoni in 1924 and followed by, among others, Italo Balbo, Roberto Farinacci, Margherita Sarfatti, and finally, after years of negotiation, which provided the author with much-needed funds, the national bard and Fascist idol, Gabriele D'Annunzio. Mondadori's determination to become Italy's major publisher depended to some extent on his capacity to establish a privileged status *vis-à-vis* the regime. The fact that Mussolini intervened in person in 1928 to ensure a financial package in favour of Mondadori is a clear indication of the mutual benefits of their relationship.[49] When Mussolini's press office announced that primary schools were going to adopt a uniform textbook for each grade, the race was on for Italian publishers to try to secure as big a slice as possible of this massive state-controlled business deal. Mondadori emerged as the overall winner. In 1928 his firm acquired the rights to print and distribute the *libro unico* in many regions of Italy, and by 1936 it had expanded its monopoly across most of the peninsula.[50]

However, Mondadori 'special relationship' with Il Duce was not always a guarantee of success. On more than one occasion the publisher's ambitious aims were curbed by Mussolini himself, particularly when it concerned his own persona. In 1929, for example, Mondadori asked for permission to publish an Italian edition of Il Duce's autobiography, which had recently been published in the United States and Great Britain, as well as a new edition of Mussolini's anti-clerical novel, *L'amante del cardinale*, originally published in 1909, which had appeared in English and German translation in 1929. The curtness of Mussolini's refusal can be inferred from the size of his handwritten 'NO' on the letter of April 1931 in which Mondadori had tried, once more, to obtain the publishing rights (see figure 2).[51] In both cases, the decision behind this case of 'dictatorial self-censorship' was one of convenience. Mussolini's 'autobiography' was allegedly the work of his brother Arnaldo; hence the embarrassment that an Italian edition would have caused. At the same time his trite anti-clerical novel about the love affair between a cardinal and a noble woman was hardly a diplomatic tool for a prime minister who was doing his best to secure a deal with the Roman Catholic Church.

A third venture involving Mondadori and Mussolini concerned the publication of the latter's conversations with the famous German biographer Emil Ludwig. To everybody's surprise, Mussolini had agreed to a series of encounters with Ludwig, which took place in the spring of 1932. Motivated by the prospect of an international best-seller – the rights to the publication in thirteen other languages had already been sold – Mondadori quickly moved to the production stage. Ludwig's German manuscript was quickly translated. Mussolini personally revised the translation, requiring only a handful of small corrections. By June the book was ready to be distributed. According to people close to Il Duce, the reason why he had agreed to meet Ludwig, a Jewish intellectual with clear democratic principles, was linked to his desire to ignore Adolf Hitler's recent electoral victory (indeed, the latter is almost totally ignored in the conversations, apart from a dismissive judgment regarding his racist policies).[52]

Mussolini had underestimated the negative reaction of some intransigent Fascist militants who, in the pages of *Impero*, attacked Ludwig and Mondadori as profiteers of the good will of their leader. Two days after Mondadori had sent Mussolini his copies of the book, hot off the press and ready to be distributed in a first edition of 20,000 copies, he received a phone call from the head of the press office. Gaetano Polverelli informed Mondadori in no uncertain terms that Mussolini was appalled at the idea of this book being published. Armed with the copy of the proofs containing Mussolini's own handwritten notes, and unable to stop the imminent publication of the *Colloqui* in other countries, Mondadori managed a compromise: the first edition would be allowed to circulate but no further print runs were to follow. On 30 June 1932 Mussolini sent a telegram to the prefect of Milan, ordering him to make sure a second edition would never appear. The reasons were allegedly related to the quality of the translation: 'Avverta anzi diffidi formalmente l'editore Mondadori a non ristampare, esaurita la prima edizione, una sola copia del libro di Ludwig senza che io l'abbia ritradotto in comprensibile lingua

2. Letter from Arnoldo Mondadori to Mussolini's secretary, 29 April 1931, with Mussolini's note in pencil. (*Courtesy of Archivio Centrale dello Stato, Rome*)

italiana poiché quella del testo attuale sarà tedesca, croata, greca, giudaica, ostrogota, ma non è italiana. Siamo intesi e mi informi' (Inform, or
better, formally warn the publisher Mondadori not to reprint, once the
first edition is sold out, a single copy of Ludwig's book without my intervention so that I can translate into comprehensible Italian a text which in
its present form might be German, Croat, Greek, Jewish, Ostrogothic, but
it is certainly not Italian. We are agreed; keep me informed).

It must be said that the editors at Mondadori were equally disappointed by the poor literary quality of the translation and, indeed, they
made small improvements to the text. However, a recorded telephone
conversation between Mussolini and his close collaborator at the time,
Margherita Sarfatti, seems to suggest that the former was more worried
about the frankness with which Ludwig had reproduced his opinions. In
reply to Sarfatti's surprise when she learnt that Mussolini was upset
about a book that he had personally approved in proofs, he said: 'Certe
cose che, in determinati momenti, fanno magari piacere, possono, in
altri momenti, risultare controproducenti' (Some things that, at a certain point in time, might give pleasure, can backfire at other times).[53]

By August 1932 Mondadori had already managed to convince Mussolini to authorize a second edition. This time it was the press office, in the
person of Gaetano Polverelli, that carried out a revision of the text. These
revisions would seem to support the idea that the content of the book was
at least as important as the quality of the translation in provoking Mussolini's second thoughts. Indeed, most of the corrections imposed by the
press office concerned short passages of potentially embarrassing content.
For example, among the cuts were Mussolini's frank statement of his abso-
lute lack of faith in people's loyalty; his description of the Italian-speaking
part of Switzerland as so little that it could be considered as non-existent;
various comments in which Mussolini underlined his independence from
the Roman Catholic Church. By October the book had reached the Italian bookshops once more, and it sold 23,000 copies in the space of a few
months.[54]

Although not a straightforward case of censorship, this episode is
rather symbolic of Mussolini's *modus laborandi* with regard to book censorship. The decision to publish the book was reversed because of the
sudden perception of its potential detriment in the current climate,
then reversed again with nonchalance once a compromise had been
found that would accommodate both the regime and the publisher's
financial commitment.[55] It was a sequence of events that was to repeat
itself throughout Mussolini's dictatorship.

Despite Arnoldo Mondadori's clear sympathies and connections with the regime, it would be wrong to assume that he was intent on turning his industry into a propaganda tool. As we have already seen, editors such as Brocchi and Borgese were guarantors of a diversified range of publications: more central to the operations of the publishing firm was the presence, from 1928, of Luigi Rusca as co-director. His presence had been imposed by the firm's major shareholder, Senatore Borletti, during a period of financial crisis. Yet Rusca was not only famous as a successful advocate of refined culture, he was also openly critical of the regime. Indeed, his move from the Touring Club Italiano had been triggered by his refusal to become a member of the Fascist Party, as was expected of all managers in state-controlled companies. The police had a file on him filled with reports from informers who relayed his constant criticism of the Fascist regime. However, Rusca was not deemed to be actively anti-Fascist and therefore was spared any official sanctions, at least for the time being. Rusca did employ as translators and editors a small group of anti-Fascists, some of whom had collaborated with Gobetti (Arrigo Cajumi, Luigi Emery, Barbara Allason); others, like Vittorio Enzo Alfieri had spent some time under arrest.[56] Rusca's preference for non-Fascists provided a counterbalance to Mondadori's desire to fulfill the expectations of the regime. Moreover, the point where the political opinions of Rusca and the commercial interests of Mondadori met was in the policy not to refrain from producing publications that lay near the very boundaries of the regime's tolerance.

A first case was a translation of Erich-Maria Remarque's famous novel *Im Westen Nichts Neues (Niente di nuovo sul fronte occidentale)*, which was an instant world success on its publication in 1928. Mondadori had acquired the rights for the Italian translation but found the road blocked by Mussolini's dislike for the novel's anti-war and anti-nationalistic message. A few months later, Mondadori's frustration grew even stronger when the other great Milan publisher, Treves, announced in the journal of the publishers' association, *Giornale della libreria*, the imminent publication in Italian of another popular German war novel, this time by Ludwig Renn. Quotes from German papers presented that novel (*Krieg Guerra*), as an even better piece of war fiction than Remarque's. Mondadori was incensed, and on 2 October 1929 he sent a letter to Mussolini asking for permission to circulate his translation of Remarque's novel. Two days later Mondadori reinforced the message by sending a telegram in which he informed Il Duce that at least 25,000 copies of the French translation of the novel had already been sold in Italian bookshops. It was a clever tactic – that is, to suggest that the lack of an Italian translation meant rich sales of the French edition, with the resulting loss of revenue for an Italian company – and Mondadori had used it on other occasions. Developments were to follow, but not entirely as Mondadori intended. Mussolini's secretarial archives show that four days later, the translator of Renn's novel, Paolo Monelli (himself author of a best-selling First World War novel, *Scarpe al sole*), had written to the government to complain about the withdrawal of the authorization to publish *Guerra*.[57] Not content with his competitor's defeat, a week later Mondadori made a third attempt to secure authorization, this time informing Mussolini that he was under pressure to produce an Italian version of Remarque's novel for Switzerland and Latin America. The letter was annotated in the margins by Lando Ferretti, then head of press office, who wrote: 'Risposta negativa al rapporto dell'11 ottobre VII' (Negative response to the report of 11 October 1929). The expression 'risposta negativa' was underlined twice. It is not clear which report Ferretti was referring to, but the case seemed settled once and for all, and indeed the novel was never circulated in Italian under Fascism. Or, rather, was not circulated in Italy. It is interesting to add that two years later Mondadori managed to convince Mussolini to allow the printing of 10,000 copies to be sold in Switzerland and South America. The reason behind this compromise was the fact that Mondadori had discovered that a Swiss publisher was about to produce its own Italian translation of the novel, hence; the need for Mondadori to move in quickly with Il Duce's approval.[58]

When Remarque's following novel, *Der Weg Zurück*, was published in 1931, Mondadori immediately bought the rights for the Italian translation. Once more, the only way to secure the authorization was through the offices of Mussolini. During a meeting on 23 April 1931, Mondadori mentioned the novel to Mussolini and was told to send in a copy in the original. Mondadori promptly did so, but when some weeks later he asked for a response he was told to provide the Italian translation. Because the translation had not yet been commissioned, Mondadori wrote a short presentation on the book in which he praised it while warning Mussolini that it contained indirect criticism of the 'idealità fascista della guerra patriottica' (Fascist ideal of a patriotic war). This time, strangely, the novel ended up in the hands of the regime's theatre censor, Leopoldo Zurlo. In his typical fashion, Zurlo weighed all pros and cons and concluded in a brief report that, indirectly, the book 'può derivarne un sentimento di esagerata prevenzione nei confronti dell'idealità fascista della guerra patriottica' (could engender an exaggerated rejection of the Fascist ideals of patriotic war). There is no trace of Mussolini's personal reaction, but the file contains a copy of a telegram sent on 4 July by the head of police, Arturo Bocchini, to all prefects. It warned them that a French translation of Remarque's novel had just been published. Similarly to what had happened to the novel in its original German (whose circulation had been prohibited on 29 May), no French version was to be allowed to circulate on Italian soil. In the margin of the telegram there is a handwritten note by, presumably, Mussolini's secretary, Alessandro Chiavolini: 'Dopo il mio colloquio con Bruno Mondadori [Arnoldo's brother] come da appunto in Atti. Dal presente telegramma risulta che la questione è stata già risolta per la traduzione francese e perciò a maggior ragione per quella italiana proposta da Mondadori. S.E. però si era già espresso favorevolmente.' (After my conversation with Bruno Mondadori as from my note in the Proceedings. From this telegram it seems that the problem has already been resolved for the French translation hence the same should count for the Italian one proposed by Mondadori. His Excellency, however, had already expressed a favourable opinion.) His Excellency is most likely Mussolini himself (although it could be argued that it might have been Ferretti, then head of the press office, or Arpinati, minister of the interior). In any case, once more the decision was taken at the very top, and a slightly embarrassing change of policy had taken place. Mondadori resigned himself to a blanket ban, but only temporarily so. Copies of Remarque's *La via del ritorno* at the National Libraries of Florence and Rome show that the novel was eventually published by Mondadori in 1932.[59]

During the interwar years, both fiction and non-fiction books about the First World War were very popular. However, they also seem to have been the most unpredictable ones in terms of potential censorship. Another Mondadori publication of this kind was *Die Katrin Wird Soldat (Caterina va alla Guerra)* by Adrienne Thomas, translated from German. The book is the diary of a young nurse serving in the German Army. Mondadori had made sure all the passages of potential pacifist interpretation (when the nurse reflects upon the absurdity of war) would be expurgated. However, he also made the mistake of not asking for an unofficial preview and authorization by the authorities. The novel was published in January 1932 and received a favourable response from critics and readers. Two months later, however, a telegram from the Ministry of the Interior to all prefects ordered the withdrawal of the book and the immediate seizure of all copies. It is not clear how the ministry came to the decision, but once more it seems that it was not the result of a normal process of censorship based in the Milan prefecture, which had jurisdiction over Mondadori. In his defence, Arnoldo Mondadori sent a long letter of appeal to Minister Arpinati with a copy to Mussolini. We do not know what the answer was, but this time too the ban was not lifted.[60]

A different case concerns the memoirs of the maverick businessman Riccardo Gualino, founder of many successful industrial ventures, from Snia-Viscosa to Lux Film, and ex-vice-president of Fiat. In January 1931 Gualino had been sent into *confino* (internal exile) to the isle of Lipari, officially as a punishment for the repercussions to the Italian economy by his recent bankruptcy. Gualino's fame as a businessman and an arts connoisseur, enhanced by the scandal created by his recent financial and political disgrace, seemed to guarantee strong book sales. But before going to press, a cautious Mondadori made sure Il Duce was personally involved in the process. In August 1931 Mondadori sent him a copy of the typescript, softening Mussolini's potential irritation with suggestions about possible cuts. To Mondadori's delight, Mussolini replied with an unconditional *nulla osta*, and confirmed it when, fearing some change of mind, Mondadori asked him a second and, for good measure, a third time. The book was eventually published and, despite a few predictable grumbling sounds among Fascist circles, it was successful enough to go through three reprints and a second, paperback edition. The reasons behind Mussolini's tolerance remain unclear. It can only be speculated that, since the memoirs did not critize the regime in any form, Mussolini might have thought that they indirectly proved its detachment and integrity in dealing with Gualino's financial disaster.[61]

In another area of his activities, when Mondadori created the series *Romanzi della Palma*, which offered popular novels to be sold by news agents, he was to gauge the boundaries of Fascist censorship with regard to immoral content. The taboo nature of any fictional representation of suicide was the first stumbling block. It came up with regard to the translation of the short novel *Musik der Nacht* (*Storia di una notte*) by the Austrian writer Joe Lederer. The suicide with which the book ended was not appreciated by the new head of the press office, Mussolini's powerful son-in-law, Galeazzo Ciano. A ban ensued, to which Mondadori responded by asking for a compromise. Could the book remain in circulation if purged of any reference to suicide? The answer was positive, and the book was modified and republished in 1933. Not surprisingly, a few years later, Mondadori decided not to produce the translation of the crime novel *The Ten Little Niggers* by Agatha Christie because it contained, according to Enrico Piceni (translator from English and head of Mondadori's press office), 'at least two undeletable suicides.'[62]

A Florentine 'Italianissimo': Attilio Vallecchi

A latecomer among Florentine publishers, Attilio Vallecchi had clearly identified his publishing efforts with the promotion of avant-garde Italian literature. His involvement in the publication of the renowned journals *Lacerba* and *La Voce* provided the transition from a printing firm to a publishing house. The official birth of Vallecchi Editore dates back to 1919, but by then Attilio Vallecchi could already boast the publication of works by renowned authors such as Papini, Soffici, Oriani, and Ungaretti in the series *Libreria della Voce*. These writers were shortly followed by other young rising stars such as Bontempelli, Palazzeschi, Cardarelli, Cecchi, and Carrà.[63]

If there was common ground between Vallecchi and Fascism, this was in a shared nationalist spirit. Throughout the years of their correspondence, Vallecchi would constantly remind Mussolini that, as a publisher, he was a most committed supporter of Italian culture. It was a claim that Mondadori, with his efforts to exploit the foreign market, could not match. In *Ricordi e idee di un editore vivente*, a book of memoirs and notes published in 1934, Vallecchi proudly mentioned his contribution to the development of Fascist ideology with the publication of works by Oriani and Corradini. He also repeatedly stated his aversion to foreign publications and the need for the promotion of Italian genius.[64]

Vallecchi's cooperation with the regime started in 1924 with the publication of the official paper of the Florentine branch of the Fascist Party, *Il Bargello*. The paper's founder was Alessandro Pavolini, a young rising leader of Florentine Fascism and future minister of popular culture. He was also a member of the governing body of Vallecchi's publishing house. Another key member of Vallecchi's board was, until 1928, the philosopher, Fascist leader, and powerful figure in the Florentine publishing industry, Giovanni Gentile. In 1931 Gentile directly intervened to convince Mussolini to grant Vallecchi financial help.[65]

Nationalism was not the only issue bringing Vallecchi and Fascism together. The Florentine publisher knew well that the best way to build up the strength of his young firm was to establish it as a service provider for the many printing and publishing needs of the state machine. When Vallecchi wrote to Mussolini in March 1926 – the earliest letter in their correspondence held at the State Archives – the two had already met. Vallecchi sent him some specially bound volumes as proof of his painstaking effort to promote Italian culture. In December of the same year he sent a parcel of similar nature, this time accompanied by a request to have a signed photograph. Mussolini kindly obliged. In May 1928 the then minister for corporations, Giuseppe Bottai, when approaching Mussolini to recommend a publishing venture by Vallecchi, could mention the latter as 'l'editore fascista' (the Fascist publisher). In the same year Vallecchi was chosen to publish the five-volume *Storia della Rivoluzione Fascista* by Giorgio Chiurco. Mussolini himself made some corrections to the proofs and wrote the preface. It was the official publication that marked, the following year, the celebrations of ten years since the foundation of the Fasci. Ten thousand copies were ordered by Mussolini himself (for a massive expenditure of one million lire) to be distributed to all Italian prefectures and other government institutions. Boosted by this publishing success, on 25 August 1928 Vallecchi wrote a seven-page letter to Mussolini in which he proposed a number of collaborative projects. He offered the services of his firm to publish propaganda material ranging from books and pamphlets to periodicals and postcards, as well as Italian grammar books for the foreign market (promising to print one million copies per year). He vowed to sell the *Storia della rivoluzione fascista* to every single Fascist association, 'anche a quelli di dieci iscritti' (even those with only ten members). The final paragraph attempted to distinguish Vallecchi from any other possible competitor: 'Altre imprese editoriali sono sorte e hanno lavorato e prodotto sotto il segno del Littorio: nessuna, data l'impreparazione e data forse la mancanza della necessaria organizzazione, ha potuto compiere quell'opera di decisiva *offensiva* alla quale è mia suprema ambizione dedicarmi se non mi mancherà il Vostro incitante soccorso' (Other publishing firms have emerged and have worked and produced under the Fascist sign: not one of them, due to their lack of preparation and perhaps lack of organization, has been able to accomplish that work of decisive *attack* which is my utmost goal for as long as I have your stimulating help [emphasis in the original]). There is no trace of Mussolini's reply. But it is unlikely that, given his inclination for leaving his options open, he would have committed his government to a single publishing firm. If denied a monopoly, Vallecchi continued nonetheless to receive lucrative contracts. Various ministries regularly reported this to Mussolini and were sometimes asked to justify the fact that Vallecchi had failed to win some competitions (on more than one occasion the reply was that his estimates were substantially more expensive than those of his competitors).[66]

With regard to censorship, there is no evidence that Vallecchi was subjected to the intervention of either the local prefecture or Mussolini's press office.[67] Yet, Vallecchi was rather vocal about the need for a censoring

IL LIBRO ITALIANO

Anno II. - N. 9.   **1° Settembre 1929. VII.**

Conto corrente con la Posta. – PUBBLICAZIONE MENSILE.
ABBONAMENTO: Un anno: Italia e Colonie L. 7 — Estero il doppio — Un numero separato Cent. 80.

Come è stata isti-
tuita la censura ci-
·nematografica, così
si dovrebbe proce-
dere ad un controllo
diretto e severo della
cosiddetta lettera-
tura amena, specie
di quella destinata
a diffondersi tra il
popolo.

Direzione e Amministrazione: Casa Editrice VALLECCHI · Viale dei Mille, 72 - FIRENZE

3. Front cover of Vallecchi's in-house journal, *Il libro italiano*, 1 September 1929.
(*Courtesy of Archivio Centrale dello Stato, Rome*)

authority in the publishing world. This stand was substantiated in Vallecchi's monthly periodical, *Il libro italiano*, which had been created in 1928 to promote publications by Italian authors. The front cover of two 1929 issues presented slogans related to the need to restrain freedom of speech. The first (1 April) read 'Anche in letteratura, se proprio ci tenete, viva la libertà: ma non la libertà di ragliare' (In literature too, if you really want it, let us say long live freedom: but not the freedom to bray). The second (1 September; see figure 3) was more explicit: 'Come è stata istituita la censura cinematografica, così si dovrebbe procedere ad un controllo diretto e severo della cosiddetta letteratura amena, specie di quella destinata a diffondersi tra il popolo' (In the same way as cinematographic censorship was instituted, so we should move on to a direct and strict control of so-called escapist literature, particularly when it is aimed at the people).

The reference to 'letteratura amena' might well be interpreted as an indirect dig at publishers such as Mondadori and Corbaccio who relied on the popularity of some of their risqué fiction. Vallecchi's militancy and commitment were meant to be an example of Fascist activism and moral integrity for the entire publishing industry.[68]

As a result of his close collaboration with Giovanni Papini, Vallecchi was also involved in the promotion of Catholic culture. In a letter dated 6 September 1930 Vallecchi told Papini of his recent meeting with Mussolini during which Vallecchi had presented his future plans of publication and Il Duce had allegedly expressed his approval of both Papini's religious novel *La storia di Cristo* (1921) and Vallecchi's project to publish more books with religious content. In 1930 Vallecchi became the publisher of the newly founded Catholic journal *Frontespizio*. It was a publication that in later years was to bear witness the disillusionment of some young intellectuals and poets of the hermetic school. It contained Carlo Bo's renowned 1938 essay, 'Letteratura come vita.' However, it should be noted that at the time of its foundation, the journal was considered to be perfectly aligned with the newly struck agreement between Fascism and the Catholic Church following the Lateran Pacts of 1929. Yet also from a Catholic background came one of the very few Vallecchi publications that was withdrawn from circulation. In 1923 Vallecchi had published a collection of speeches by the then leader of the Popular Party (Partito Popolare), the priest Don Luigi Sturzo. In 1929 the Vallecchi book was included in a blanket ban on Sturzo's entire oeuvre. The timing was symbolic, as with the Lateran Pacts the Vatican had implicitly rejected Sturzo's call for open opposition to Fascism.[69]

3 The Censor and the Censored

Fascist Censor Supremo: Benito Mussolini

The previous two chapters have described several examples of Mussolini's involvement in episodes of book censorship. For Il Duce, it was clearly not just a matter of setting policies and putting systems in place. He had a passion for detail that contemporary management consultants might define as a serious lack of delegating ability. This is a distinct feature of his *modus laborandi* that those involved in his daily working routine have mentioned time and time again. One of these commentators is Carmine Senise, who was deputy head of the Italian police from 1932 to 1940 and, following the death of Arturo Bocchini, head until July 1943. In his capacity as *Capo della Polizia*, Senise was scheduled to meet with Mussolini every morning for half an hour: 'Un capo del Governo titolare di ben sette dicasteri e che voleva dirigere e seguire personalmente tutti gli affari interessanti le varie Amministrazioni ne aveva abbastanza perché non si occupasse di piccole cose: ebbene queste lo attraevano assai più delle grandi.' (As head of government and cabinet minister of no less than seven ministries, always willing to direct and follow all important matters related to each department, he had more than enough on his plate. He did not need to spend time on small matters. However, those were far more attractive to him than big issues.)[1] Indeed, any researcher working with Mussolini's private papers will be impressed by the sheer quantity of paperwork that Il Duce seemed to find time to cast his eye over, often dealing with fairly minute and secondary issues. This is all the more disturbing when we look at the war years during which, over and above being head of government and minister of seven different departments he was in command of the

Italian Army. As we will see, even in those years his attention to minor detail was as marked as ever.

Philip Cannistraro convincingly argues that it was only after some years in power that Mussolini began interfering in cultural and, more particularly, literary matters.[2] By October 1922 the Fascists had not developed a full-fledged cultural policy. Moreover, with the exception of the school system, the national government had few tools with which to intervene in the cultural life of the country. A brief survey of Mussolini's writings and public speeches in his *Opera omnia* shows that cultural matters did not occupy him for at least a couple of years after his ascent to power. The crisis produced by the Matteotti affair accelerated his direct involvement. Although it might sound incongruous that in times of political crisis the government should place increased importance on cultural matters, during the summer of 1924 Fascism received such a barrage of criticism in the opposition press and in parliament that the need to rally and organize pro-Fascist intellectuals became paramount. Until then Mussolini had gladly accepted the support of famous artists and writers such as D'Annunzio, Marinetti, and Soffici, but he had never effectively responded to their demand to give official Fascist status to futurism or any other cultural movement. Under pressure from opposition forces, the first discussion of Fascist cultural policies took place in August 1924 during a meeting of the directorate of the Fascist National Party (Partito Nazionale Fascista, PNF). The philosopher Giovanni Gentile was to become the forger of the first initiatives, the most important being the conference of Fascist intellectuals that took place in Bologna in March 1925. It was on that occasion that Gentile produced the renowned manifesto of Fascist intellectuals to which Benedetto Croce replied with the equally famous manifesto of anti-Fascism. For the first time, the Fascists were attempting to give themselves a recognizable cultural platform. The cult of the nation, of war, and modernity formed the basic ingredients of the manifesto. More importantly for the subject of our study, Gentile imposed his vision of an 'ethical state' – that is, the idea that the state had the duty to shape the moral and intellectual character of each citizen. By June 1925 Gentile had supervised the creation of the Fascist National Institute of Culture, which, with its vast network of branches, was to become a promoter of Fascist culture throughout Italy. As the leader of the nation and of Fascism, Mussolini was expected to become a guiding force, not just in the political sphere, but also in the ethical and cultural indoctrination of Fascist Italy. Once opposition had been silenced, the time was ripe to lay the foundations of a Fascist national culture.

A guiding hand was provided by Il Duce's collaborator and then lover, Margherita Sarfatti. A highly educated Jewish woman, Sarfatti had been close to Mussolini since his perilous move from socialism to Fascism. An important contributor to *Il Popolo d'Italia*, in March 1919 she led the creation of the monthly literary supplement to Mussolini's paper *L'Ardita*. Sarfatti's refined knowledge of contemporary culture shaped Mussolini's own views, starting from the alliance and collaboration with futurist artists.[3] It is therefore not surprising that one of Mussolini's first public speeches on cultural matters should have been made from an exhibition of the Novecento movement, an artistic school fervently supported by Sarfatti. On that occasion, 14 February 1926, Mussolini affirmed the need for an organic relationship between politics and the arts. The content of his speech was relatively generic, but it suggested a 'Gentilian' turn towards the idea of an ethical state binding all citizens, intellectuals and artists included. The speech provoked a lively debate within Fascist intellectual circles, and, more importantly, it confirmed Il Duce's decision to move to a more interventionist stance in matters of cultural production, censorship included.[4] In the same year, two of the most faithful collaborators of Mussolini, Sarfatti and *Il Popolo d'Italia*'s chief editor, Giorgio Pini, published two biographics of Il Duce, both presenting him as a genius and a Renaissance man. Mondadori published Sarfatti's biography only after Mussolini had read and annotated the manuscript with a series of demands for cuts, which Sarfatti did not entirely accept.[5] Sarfatti's *Dux* was one of the most successful non-fiction books of the interwar period. It sold 25,000 in its first year, by 1928 was in its fifteenth printing, and in 1934 appeared in a new edition containing 250 illustrations and 30 reproductions of handwritten documents. Giorgio Pini's much shorter *Benito Mussolini: La sua vita sino a oggi* was published by the smaller Bologna publisher Cappelli. (Until the mid-1920s Cappelli had been publishing works by anti-Fascist authors such as Labriola, Turati, and Gobetti, but by the second half of the decade had completely converted to publishing pro-Fascist works.)[6] Mussolini was confirmed as a kind of *Über-mensch* whose intuition allowed him to stand out in any field. And, although Mussolini's fleeting past as a fiction writer had been little more than an excuse for political polemic, there is no doubt that he was interested in and opinionated about literary matters. In his conversations on literary subjects, as recorded by Emil Ludwig and Yvon De Begnac, Mussolini showed a fairly sophisticated knowledge of contemporary literature, particularly by Italian authors.[7] His correspondence also shows that he liked to be in contact with famous pro-Fascist authors. Already established figures such as

D'Annunzio, Marinetti, Papini, and Pirandello could count on his sympathetic ear, but he also followed the careers of other, less known figures. One of these was the poet and fiction writer Ada Negri, whose unsuccessful candidature for the Nobel Prize in 1927 was personally sponsored by Mussolini. Negri's autobiographical novel, *Stella mattutina*, originally published by Mondadori in 1921, was reprinted in 1927 with a preface containing Mussolini's 1921 review of the book for *Il Popolo d'Italia* (this same edition was translated in German in 1938 complete with Mussolini's text). In 1931 she received the *Premio Mussolini* for her literary career, and in February 1934, Mussolini ordered the head of police to withdraw a sum of 25,000 lire from the secret funds of the Ministry of the Interior and send it to Negri. Finally, thanks to Mussolini's support, Negri was, in 1940, the first woman to become member of the prestigious Accademia d'Italia.[8]

Given the dictator's obvious influence, it is not surprising that dozens of ambitious journalists and authors were keen to attract his patronage. For instance, Ugo Ojetti and Massimo Bontempelli corresponded with Mussolini in the mid-1920s, both asking for his support. In March 1926 Ojetti accepted the offer to take over the chief editorship of the newly Fascistized *Corriere della Sera*. The following year Mussolini (through the secretary of the PNF, Augusto Turati) asked him to resign; despite the humiliation, Ojetti remained a faithful collaborator. The following year, when he founded the literary journal *Pegaso*, he asked Mussolini's permission to open the first issue with a long article in the form of an 'open letter' to Il Duce entitled 'Gl'Italiani di oggi e di domani.' Mussolini read the article in proofs and gave his approval. As for Bontempelli, the two met in the summer of 1926 during which time Mussolini expressed his support for Bontempelli's and Malaparte's new journal, *900*. Moreover, in 1930 a delighted Bontempelli could thank Mussolini first for his personal comments on his novel *Vita e morte di Adria e dei suoi figli* (Bompiani, 1930) and two months later for having appointed him to the Accademia d'Italia. Ojetti was to join Bontempelli at the Accademia in the same year.[9]

From time to time, Mussolini boasted a degree of liberalism and tolerance towards some adversaries. When the famous theatre actress Emma Gramatica wrote to him asking for help (she was about to bring to the stage a play by the anti-Fascist Neapolitan playwright Roberto Bracco), Mussolini immediately sent a telegram to the prefect of Naples ordering him to make sure that Fascists militants and the press refrained from any criticism.[10] A much more important case concerns the Neapolitan philosopher and historian Benedetto Croce.

Despite his anti-Fascism, Croce was allowed to publish his studies with Laterza throughout the Fascist years. In January 1927 Mussolini sent a telegram to the head of police in Naples: if it were true that his men had Croce's house under surveillance, then the operation had to be halted immediately. The dumbfounded reply from Naples was that the surveillance was meant only as a measure of 'protection.' Some years later Mussolini mentioned his attitude towards Croce as an example of his tolerance. On that occasion, however, he neglected to mention that when, in 1933, he discovered through an anonymous informer that most Italian universities and secondary schools had a subscription to Croce's periodical, *Critica*, he had promptly complained to the minister of national education, Francesco Ercole, describing the situation as 'incredibile.'[11] Another sign of studied tolerance on the part of Mussolini related to the ambitious project of the *Enciclopedia Italiana*, which was developed in the decade beginning in 1925 under the supervision of Giovanni Gentile. Despite the protests of many Fascists and nationalists, hundreds of scholars collaborated on the project regardless of their political credo or nationality. When Mussolini was asked to address the issue, he approved of Gentile's tolerant approach. Through his press office, he ordered the immediate suppression of any public criticism or polemical exchange on the matter.[12]

The few instances we have on record suggest that it was only at the beginning of the 1930s that Mussolini began personally to interfere with the censorship of literary works and, more generally, to assume a dominant role in the cultural policies of the regime. As we have seen in the previous chapter with the case of the memoirs of industrialist Riccardo Gualino published by Mondadori in 1931, Mussolini's judgment was sometimes invoked by the publishers themselves. Another case involving Mondadori concerns the popular poet Trilussa, who wrote in dialect. Since 1927 anonymous and official informers had been supplementing Trilussa's police file with accusations of his anti-Fascist attitude both in his daily conversations and in his poems, some published, some circulated in typescript.[13] There is no doubt that Trilussa's satirical eye had been cast upon the current rulers and the rhetorical vagaries of Fascist Italy. Individual poems from collections such as *La gente* (1927), *Libro 9* (1929), and *Giove e le bestie* (1932), all published by Mondadori, were often discussed for their implicit satire of Fascist Italy. At the same time, Trilussa's bland and tolerant critique was well liked by some Fascist leaders. Giuseppe Bottai was a convivial guest at some of Trilussa's impromptu dinner-table readings, and Mussolini too had revealed his admiration of the poet on more than one occasion.[14] According to two informers' reports, Trilussa had met Mussolini in the late 1920s and, when he asked permission to publish his satirical poems, Il Duce allegedly told him that it was fine to publish them in book form but not individually in the daily papers.[15] However, his poems continued to be discussed and published in the daily press, from *Corriere della Sera* (which on 22 November 1929 published a very positive feature article by Orio Vergani) to *Il Popolo di Roma* and *Il Giornale d'Italia*. The informers' reports occasionally refer to episodes regarding particular poems. This was the case, for example, of the poem 'Però ...,' which was rejected by the Fascist director of *Il Giornale d'Italia*, Virginio Gayda. When Trilussa included it in his next collection, Arnoldo Mondadori asked him to make sure that it was acceptable to the authorities. Through Trilussa's friend Paolo Orano, the poem reached the desk of Mussolini, who sent it back with the comment 'Imprimatur!' followed by his famous stylized 'M'.[16] The poem was eventually included in the collection *La gente* (1927). According to Decleva, Mussolini was also involved in the publication of *Giove e le bestie* (1932). Following Il Duce's go-ahead, an edition of 20,000 copies was circulated and quickly sold despite the criticism of vocal Fascist papers such as Interlandi's *Quadrivio*.[17] Once more, Mussolini was happy to showcase his acts of tolerance, and in his conversations with Emil Ludwig he stated: 'La caricatura è importante e necessaria. Da voi si dice sempre che qui regna la tirannia. Ha letto le satire di Trilussa? Sono pungenti, ma così spiritose che io non le ho proibite' (Caricature is important and necessary. In your country you always say that tyranny reigns here. Have you read Trilussa's satirical poems? They are prickly but so funny that I did not prohibit them).[18]

Mussolini's selective tolerance towards Trilussa did not extend to the entire body of literature in dialect. Indeed, in the summer of 1932 Mussolini launched his famous policy declaring all literature in dialect unworthy of Fascist Italy and therefore deserving of marginalization. Apart from the absurdity of such an order in a country whose dialects were, in many regions, the prime medium of communication and cultural expression, it is interesting to note that the memos from the press office and Mussolini's own comments made on other occasions seem to concentrate on dialect in the press and the theatre. Books seemed to fall outside the area of his concern.[19] On the one hand, it is arguable that this distinction reflected respect for the already existing body of Italian literature in dialect. Such an idea is partially suggested by an anonymous note, dated 10 August 1932 and probably written by Polverelli, then head of Mussolini's press office. In an attempt to provide more articulated rules regarding the censorship of dialect literature, the author distinguished between periodicals and books. For the former, all use of dialect had to be banned, whereas books in dialect were allowed to be published provided they were the work of 'antichi autori' (old authors).[20] Italian intellectuals who publicly supported this viewpoint were personally thanked by Mussolini and Polverelli, as happened, for example, when the Tuscan writer Ardengo Soffici wrote an article in the *Il Gazzetta del Popolo* of 19 January 1933 attacking dialects.[21] A sign that this policy was not only controversial but also a source of embarrassment is implicit in the umpteenth telegram on the subject that Polverelli sent to the prefect of Bergamo on 18 May 1933. He ordered the prefect to warn the editor of *L'Eco di Bergamo* not to publish any more writings on dialects; significantly, however, Polverelli required that the warning should be given 'verbalmente e riservatamente' (verbally and confidentially).[22] Enforcement was an uphill battle, and recent studies have shown that the policy was constantly ignored. Poems in dialect continued to be published in periodicals and books, and one of the most scholarly defenders of vernacular writing Filippo Fichera, was successful in defeating the ban: his periodical, *Convivio letterario*, continued to publish dialect poetry right through the war years, and his propaganda anthology, *Il Duce e il fascismo nei canti dialettali*, despite a ban in 1934, was later republished with a preface by F.T. Marinetti and proved a popular publication.[23]

Another literary field in which Mussolini became considerably involved during the early 1930s is that of theatrical censorship. Fortunately, a considerable number of documents and anecdotes regarding such censorship are available thanks to the survival of the censor's archives and to the detailed memoirs left by Fascism's only theatre censor, Leopoldo Zurlo. However, before we discuss the detail of Mussolini's involvement, some space will be devoted to the organization of theatrical censorship during the first decade of Fascism.

Up until 1931 theatrical censorship was left to the prefects of the towns where the performances were taking place. This was sometimes disruptive for theatre producers: the same play could be allowed to be performed in certain cities and then suddenly prohibited by a less liberal prefect of another town.[24] The centralization of the system in 1931 meant that the theatre industry could rely on a single vetting process, thus guaranteeing untroubled programming of national tours. It was a development that reflected that happening in the field of book censorship through the development of Mussolini's press office. It was also the first time that a formally centralized system of preventive censorship was introduced in Fascist Italy. On 6 January 1931 the Theatrical Censorship Office (Ufficio Censura Teatrale) was created inside the Ministry of the Interior. It was run by a vice-prefect, Leopoldo Zurlo (see figure 4), who reported directly to the head of the police. Zurlo's detailed memoirs, published after the war, present him as a cultured middle-aged man whose censoring activity was strictly formed around the need to defend public decorum and morality, regardless of any Fascist credo. Similarly to his direct superiors – the head and deputy head of the Italian police – Zurlo was a civil servant whose career had started before Mussolini seized power and who had never actively sided with Fascism.[25] His appointment had been proposed by the head of police, Arturo Bocchini, and sanctioned by Mussolini, thus confirming his intention not to 'Fascistisize' the ranks of the Italian police. In any case, Zurlo's literary flair and dry sense of humour made his reports popular not only with his superiors but also with Mussolini himself. Indeed, an important aspect emerging from Zurlo's activity is the fact that whenever he was unsure about a particular case he could count on Mussolini's judgment for a final decision.[26]

As censor, a position he held without interruption until July 1943, Zurlo looked at more than one thousand scripts per year. Of these, about 10 per cent were either rejected or suspended. 'Suspended' works were not allowed to be performed but, for political reasons, were not given an official ban. Although this seems a fairly high percentage, it must be remembered that many works were rejected simply because they were considered offensive to public morality or artistically deficient (particularly if they were naïve works of Fascist propaganda). Other works fell afoul of the regime's dogmatic directives with regard to the representation of suicide or the use of dialect, or because of their satire of Italy's autarkic effort.[27] It is easy to imagine why cases of actual political censorship were few and far between. The preventive nature of theatrical censorship made it nearly impossible for anti-Fascist authors to smuggle their work past the censor. As we will see, it was more typical for Zurlo to have to censor the work of either militant Fascists or their sympathizers.

By the time the Fascists seized power, Sem Benelli was a successful playwright who, on his return from fighting in the First World War and from D'Annunzio's Fiume expedition, had become an independent member of Parliament for the city of Florence. He was a war hero and a fervent patriot who had refused to enter the nationalist or Fascist associations but who had nonetheless supported Mussolini as the only answer

4. Leopoldo Zurlo, in charge of theatrical censorship from 1931 to 1943, photographed in his office at Palazzo Balestra in 1935. (*Courtesy of 'L'Illustrazione italiana'*)

to Italy's social problems. In the general elections of 1924 Benelli had accepted Mussolini's invitation to be part of the 'Listone fascista' (the Fascist list of candidates) and was successfully elected to the Chamber of Deputies.[28] However, during the Matteotti crisis he initially took an anti-Fascist stance and became the head of a short-lived group of nationalist dissenters – the Lega Italica. Mussolini did not take kindly to this and in a letter to Gabriele D'Annunzio described his situation with these resentful words: 'Tre mesi fa mi hanno gettato un cadavere tra i piedi: era pesante: mi ha fatto barcollare e soffrire; adesso – poiché è detto che ogni tragedia deve avere un lato o un elemento di comicità, mi viene tra i piedi quello che si definisce graziosamente *poeta dell'Italia vivente* e vuole anche lui 'salvare' naturalmente la Patria, con una specie di frateria non bene identificata, sottoposta a certe "regole" imprecisate' (Three months ago a corpse was thrown in my way: it was a heavy one: it made me stagger and suffer; now – since it is destiny that every tragedy is followed by comedy, I found in my way the one who graciously defines himself as '*the poet of living Italy*' and he also wants to 'save' the Country, with a sort of ill-defined brotherhood, with ill-defined 'rules').[29] Indeed, Benelli's proclamations in Parliament were rich in literary style but rather convoluted and vague in terms of political action. Only a few weeks later, failing to win the support of D'Annunzio, Benelli decided to disband the *Lega Italica* and announced his resignation from the Chamber of Deputies. After that he returned to his literary work and, apart from signing Croce's anti-Fascist manifesto in May 1925, he refrained from any further involvement in the political debate. Yet, according to Benelli's memoirs, the Fascists did not forget his earlier criticism of the regime and in the following years tried to end his literary career through a campaign of attacks against him involving both the press and the police. The situation seemed to improve three years later when, after a meeting between Benelli and Mussolini, the latter ordered the suspension of any police surveillance on Benelli and invited him to deliver a speech at a First World War remembrance ceremony in the presence of the royal family.[30]

The relationship between Benelli and the Fascists continued to be uneasy in future years. The reason was allegedly the strong element of social critique in his plays. There was little doubt that the performance of his plays provided an opportunity for some Fascists to show Benelli their contempt. Achille Starace, secretary of the PNF between 1931 and 1939, was one of his sworn enemies. This is suggested in various police reports, and Benelli himself made it explicit in a long letter, a *memoir* he sent to Mussolini on 16 July 1933.[31] Benelli complained about the many obstructions that his work was meeting as a result of the opposition of Fascists in positions of power. It should be noted that Benelli's complaints extended only to the programming and production of his plays. His scripts had so far escaped the censors, requiring no drastic intervention on the part of Leopoldo Zurlo.[32] We do not know whether Mussolini responded to Benelli's *cahier des doléances*. A few months later, however, Il Duce was dragged into a controversy surrounding Benelli's latest play. This was *Caterina Sforza*, a historical play containing a powerful critique of the Catholic Church.[33]

The plot of *Caterina Sforza* is based around the life of a popular heroine of Renaissance Italy. An out-of-wedlock but much loved daughter of the Duke of Milan, Caterina Sforza married Pope Sixtus IV's nephew and with him reigned over the cities of Imola and Forlì in the Romagna region. After the pope's death and her husband's murder in 1488, Caterina held the reins of power and bravely fought off all the plots to overthrow her. She eventually capitulated in battle against the infamous Cesare Borgia, son of the even more infamous Pope Alexander VI. It was a time when heads of the church would do their best to raise the fortunes of their family and, in some cases, to enjoy a share of the sensual pleasures offered by their lavish courts. Act 1 begins with a scene at the Vatican, where Pope Sixtus IV, his nephew, and Caterina freely and cynically discuss both their political plans and sensual desires. Almost symmetrically, Act 3 begins with a conversation between Pope Alexander VI and his son, once more revealing the moral and political depravity of the Holy See.

Benelli sent the script of *Caterina Sforza* to Leopoldo Zurlo in December 1933.[34] In his report, Zurlo seemed to be well aware of the potential problems created by the two scenes set in the Vatican. Zurlo felt that the playwright had been particularly unfair and historically inaccurate with regard to Sixtus IV. The depravity and secularism of the Borgia pope, on the other hand, was well known and tacitly accepted by the church itself. However, Easter 1933 marked the beginning of a Holy Year for the Roman Catholic Church, and one could easily predict a wave of protests from the Vatican. Zurlo asked for Mussolini's advice, which arrived in the form of a handwritten note (see figure 5). The note was kept by Zurlo, who published it in his memoirs. It deserves to be quoted in its entirety as it provides a unique example of Mussolini's work as a 'literary censor':

Il dramma di Sem Benelli – Caterina Sforza – è ben congegnato e nel complesso è un forte lavoro. Bisogna togliere tutto intero il 1° quadro perché: a) non è strettamente necessario nell'economia del dramma

b) due papi sulla scena sono troppi

c) mentre la figura di Alessandro Borgia è nota anche al popolo minuto e la Chiesa vi si è ormai rassegnata, quella di Sisto IV è ignota al gran pubblico. E non è bella! Anzi.

Ci sono qua e là espressioni e frasi che potrebbero dar luogo a qualche protesta da parte del clero, ma il censore laico può tirare di lungo.

Comunicare a Sem Benelli.

15 Xbre XII[35]

(Sem Benelli's play – Caterina Sforza – is well put together and on the whole it is a strong piece of work. The entire first scene needs to be cut because:

a) it is not strictly vital to the play

b) two popes in one scene are too much

c) whereas the character of Alexander Borgia is well known to everybody and the church is resigned to it, that of Sixtus IV is unknown to the wider public. And it is not a nice one! In fact, quite the opposite.

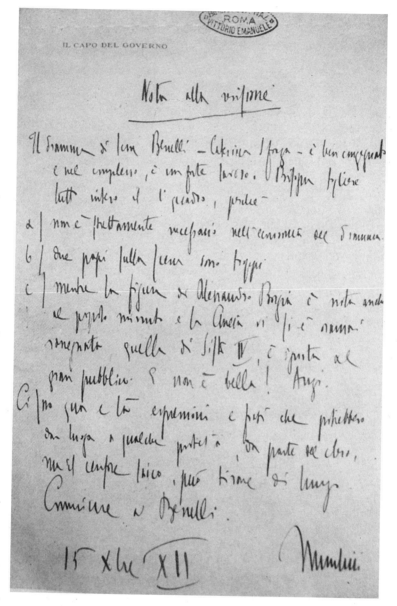

5. Handwritten note from Mussolini to Zurlo, 15 December 1933, concerning the censorship of Benelli's *Caterina Sforza*. (*Courtesy of Biblioteca Nazionale Centrale, Rome*)

Here and there one can find expressions and sentences that the clergy might find offensive. But the lay censor can ignore them.
Inform Sem Benelli.
15 December 1933)

The matter seemed to be settled. However, the note was soon followed by a telephone call from Mussolini's press office: Zurlo was told that *Caterina Sforza* was to be authorized without cuts. Neither Zurlo nor the available documentation throw any light on why Mussolini would have changed his mind. At the time, Zurlo asked for confirmation of the order through the head of the police, and the confirmation arrived. An internal memo in Zurlo's handwriting, dated 14 February 1934, indirectly confirms Mussolini's change of mind.[36] So why did Mussolini decide not to censor the play despite his initial judgment? In the early 1930s Mussolini's relationship with the Vatican was well past the honeymoon period of the Lateran Pacts. The main causes of dissent were the increasing popularity of Catholic youth organizations such as Azione Cattolica and Pope Pius XI's determined intention not to allow the regime to marginalize the church and make it subservient to Fascism's cultural project. The crisis had reached its climax during the summer of 1931, with Pius XI encyclical 'Non abbiamo bisogno' (We Have No Need), and although good relations between state and church were reestablished a few months later, there is little doubt that Mussolini thought of Pius XI as a proud opponent. Benelli's play perhaps gave him an opportunity to embarrass the Vatican, and Mussolini might have decided to allow the controversy to take its course.[37]

The venue chosen for the play's debut was highly symbolic: it was the city of Forlì. Not only did the city have historical connections to Caterina's life (and ancestors, since, as she proudly states in the play, her great-grandfather came from Romagna), but it was also Mussolini's hometown. According to Benelli, the choice had followed an official invitation by the *Podestà* (Fascist mayor) of Forlì, who reassured Benelli that Il Duce had been consulted about the venue. Allegedly Mussolini had approved, following his consent with the remark 'Vi divertirete; specialmente voi di Forlì che siete mangiapreti' (You will love it; particularly you in Forlì who are such priest-eaters).[38] It was not long before the first official notes of protest began to arrive. By February 1934 Benelli's theatre company had already brought *Caterina Sforza* to a number of Italian cities. On 24 February a short article appeared in the Vatican newspaper, *Osservatore romano*: the anonymous author reported the protests of the bishop of Cesena and added that Benelli had replied with a public letter in which he stated that 'l'opera è stata ben considerata e approvata in alto: ed io obbedisco soltanto al governo della mia nazione' (the work has been well received and approved by higher authorities and I only follow the orders of the government of my country). The article ended with a sarcastic remark about the *carabinieri* intervening to arrest a man who protested about the characterization of Pope Sixtus IV. It was a clear signal that resentment was rising among the upper echelons of the Catholic Church.[39] The following day, the prefect of Spezia informed the head of police that the local bishop had complained to him about the production, and the prefect had struggled to convince the bishop to renounce his intention of pinning a declaration of condemnation on the doors of all the churches of his diocese.

Three days later, a memo from the Ministry of the Interior suggested a concession on the part of Mussolini. It stated: 'Su tali lagnanze [di alcuni vescovi e sull' *Osservatore romano*] è stato superiormente riferito e, conformemente alle istruzioni avute, si informa codesta On. Direzione Generale [di Pubblica Sicurezza], per quando del caso, che il lavoro in questione potrà continuare ad essere rappresentato nei vari teatri d'Italia, all'infuori di quelli di Roma ove la rappresentazione di esso non dovrà essere consentita' (Those complaints [by some bishops and in the *Osservatore romano*] have been passed on to superior authority and, according to the instructions received, we inform the Directorate General [of Public Security] that the play in question can continue to be staged all over Italy with the exception of Rome, where any performance will be prohibited).[40] There is little doubt that the 'superior authority' was Mussolini. From the confidential file on Father Pietro Tacchi Venturi in Mussolini's secreterial archives, we know that the Jesuit diplomat had, on the pope's request, met Mussolini on 22 February to discuss 'una questione di alto interesse religioso e sociale della sua Diocesi di Roma' (a question of high religious and social interest regarding his [the pope's] Diocese of Rome). The fact that Benelli was kept out of Rome suggests that a compromise had been reached.[41] A police informer with connections inside the Vatican had reported as early as February that the church authorities were keen to find at least a compromise regarding the Holy City.[42]

A week later, the prefect of Venice informed the ministry that the city's cardinal had asked him to prohibit the play. But the performances continued, and the newspaper of Trieste even announced that *Caterina*

Sforza was going to be staged in Rome. On 5 April the *Osservatore romano* returned to the offensive with a second brief article in which, after characterizing Benelli as 'drammaturgo tosco-ebreo' (Tuscan-Jewish dramatist), attacked the play for its historical inaccuracy.[43] At this point it is beyond doubt that the highest authorities of the church were involved in the *querelle*. Two key figures at the Vatican – Cardinal Pizzardo of the Secretariat of State and the Jesuit father Pietro Tacchi Venturi, both of whom had been involved in negotiations leading up to the Lateran Pacts – reminded Mussolini of his promise not to allow a Roman production of *Caterina Sforza*.[44] The crisis led to a meeting the following day between Zurlo, Benelli, and Guido Buffarini Guidi, then undersecretary at the Ministry of the Interior. Buffarini outlined Mussolini's decision to allow the Roman performance of *Caterina Sforza* on condition that the censor and the author agreed to a series of cuts along the lines of Zurlo's and Mussolini's initial concerns.[45] The two agreed to cut the first scene and to significantly reduce the presence of Alessandro Borgia in the third act. Benelli asked to be allowed to produce a public document explaining that the first scene had been suppressed, but the request was rejected, as shown by Zurlo's note in the margin: 'Risposto no' (I replied no). The play was eventually staged at the Quirino Theatre, and, perhaps not surprisingly, the performance was accompanied by the loud protests of some Catholic viewers. The first disturbance came from a journalist with the *Osservatore romano*. According to a police report, towards the end of the second act, the journalist Andrea Lazzarini stood up and loudly objected to the historical inaccuracies in the play. A policeman invited him first to stop and then to leave the theatre. During the third act a journalist with *Il Tevere* and a young man (later found to be resident in Vatican City) made their objections heard. Both were expelled from the theatre and the police report concluded with 'nessun altro incidente' (no other incident). According to Zurlo, Pope Pius XI was annoyed not so much by the performance of *Caterina Sforza* but by Mussolini's going back on his word.[46] Further insult was provided by the fact that, while these events were occurring, Mondadori published the uncut script of *Caterina Sforza*, which could be bought in any bookshop in Rome. The Vatican could vent its frustration only with another attack in the *Osservatore romano*. The previous two articles had been little more than brief editorials; this time an entire page was devoted to the subject. On 22 April 1934 page 2 of the *Osservatore romano* contained only two articles: the first, signed 'F,' was entitled 'Due drammi.' Most of this long article was devoted to Benelli's *Caterina Sforza*: the second play was mentioned in the final paragaphs as an example of a 'proper' historical play. The article opened by stating that Benelli's play had arrived in Rome despite the disapproval of the Cardinal Vicario. It then proceeded to attack each act of the play, using as a source the Mondadori edition (thus criticizing the parts that had been removed for the Rome performances). The article again had anti-Semitic overtones, with expressions such as 'lo scriba di Prato' (Prato's scribe – a common reference to a Jewish scholar), 'la Caterina semitica.' The two popes appearing in the play were defended and described as much more dignified figures than the characters distorted by Benelli's satire. More importantly, the author of the article directly attacked the Fascist censor for allowing the play to be staged and published. First it asked why the undersecretary at the Ministry of the Interior, despite his speeches about the moralization of Italian culture, had not intervened. Second, Mussolini himself was the subject of a biting remark. The article quoted a speech in which Mussolini exhorted Italians to read the great Italian poets; but since 'il lauro non verdeggia ancora in Campidoglio' (the laurel has not yet grown in Campidoglio), it concluded, contemporaries have to make do with works such as 'Caterina Benelli.' This coded message linking Benelli's play with Mussolini clearly expressed the anger and frustration of the Vatican. The article then concluded with a short analysis of a second play, *El divino impaciente* by the Spanish author José María Pemán. It was a play devoted to the life of the Jesuit saint Francesco Saverio, and the *Osservatore romano* praised it as an example of historical accuracy and moral strength.

The second article that appeared on the same page added weight to the accusations of lack of historical accuracy. It was an article, this time signed 'T,' which was devoted to the newly published sixteenth volume of the history of the popes by Catholic historian Ludwig Pastor. There was no direct reference to Caterina Sforza's times, as that particular volume dealt with the eighteenth-century pope Clemente XIV, but the continuous praise for the historian's brilliant use of historical sources was an apparent counterpoint to Benelli's artistic licence.[47]

Three days later Benelli responded to the attack with a public letter in the Roman paper *Il Giornale d'Italia*. The title was self-explanatory: 'Sem Benelli non è ebreo: Una lettera dell'autore di Caterina Sforza.' In the letter Benelli chose to concentrate on the anti-Semitic tone of the Vatican paper: if his name, Sem, had induced some to think of him as a Jew, they were totally wrong. The name came from his godfather, Sem Nardi, and his family were devoutly Catholic and had been for as far back as family records went.[48] The following day the *Osservatore romano* replied to Benelli's letter with a short, sarcastic article entitled 'Unicuique suum' ('To each his own,' which was also the motto of *Osservatore romano*). The anonymous author announced the end of the performances of *Caterina Sforza* at the Quirino Theatre, once more mocked the play for its historical inaccuracy, and even resorted to a number of innuendos. The first line of attack related to Benelli's public statement that the play had been approved by 'higher authorities.' Benelli lied, stated the *Osservatore romano*, because the play had actually been cut for the Roman performances. It is also interesting to note that, once more, the paper seemed to allude to Mussolini when it mentioned the lives of great Roman emperors. It stated: 'E cosi dobbiamo negare che Adriano fu un grande imperatore a motivo di qualche grave lacuna della vita privata? E' stato detto che nessuno è grand'uomo agli occhi del proprio cameriere' (So should we deny that Hadrian was a great emperor because of some serious fault in his private life? It has been said that nobody is a great man in the eye of his valet). Whether this was a dig at Mussolini's notorious unfaithful love life remains to be proven, but it certainly shows the extent of the Vatican's annoyance. The article also mentioned Benelli's letter defending his Catholic credentials. The *Osservatore romano* was unapologetic. The conclusion was shockingly epigrammatic in its racism: 'Non giudeo. Ma Giuda' (Not a Jew. But a Judas).[49] For the reader of this normally discreet and self-controlled newspaper, the tone taken and the space devoted to Benelli's play must have been a clear sign that the whole affair had caused strong resentment among the church hierarchy.

Finally, it is not clear whether Benelli was specifically rewarded for bearing the brunt of the Vatican's dissatisfaction or was compensated for the loss of revenue that resulted from the controversy. However, it is certainly a sign of Mussolini's approval that some months later, on 7 December 1934, the Press Office of the Head of Government issued Benelli with a payment amounting to the considerable sum of 25,000 lire.[50]

Mussolini was involved in the censorship of another stage production, this time of the opera *La favola del figlio cambiato* by Gian Francesco Malipiero, for which Pirandello had provided the libretto. In November 1933 Zurlo had sent a note to Mussolini warning him that the tale contained a typical Pirandellian twist. The suggestion that the village fool and the king could harmlessly swap identities could be interpreted as lack of respect for the authorities. Given Pirandello's Fascist sympathies, going back to his public support for the regime at the time of the Matteotti crisis, and international renown – the following the year he would receive the Nobel Prize for literature – Zurlo asked for advice from higher up. Mussolini's laconic suggestion was to 'togliere il più forte' (to remove the strongest passages).[51] Zurlo subsequently contacted Pirandello, who promptly agreed to the deletion of a few passages. The following year the opera was staged in Nazi Germany. There, one of the dates was cancelled because the censors of the region of Assia considered the work subversive and contrary to the principles of the German nation. The news reached Italy through various newspapers. On the eve of the Roman premiere of the opera, a cautious Zurlo sent Mussolini a second note of warning. Although he approved Zurlo's tolerant suggestion not to oppose the production, Mussolini informed the head of police that: 'la censura a quell'opera la farò io' (I'll censor this opera myself). Mussolini was present on opening night at Rome's Opera House on 24 March 1934. Various police reports and newspaper articles recorded the loud protests of some of the audience, apparently fuelled by the fact that Mussolini, after having applauded at the end of the first act, registered visible signs of disapproval throughout the rest of the performance. The opera was instantly removed from the calendar, allegedly in response to Mussolini's express instruction. A coda in this event is related in the Paris-based anti-Fascist paper, *Giustizia e libertà*. In its issue of 8 June 1934 a short anonymous article made fun not only of the performance but of Pirandello and Mussolini's angry reaction. It also revealed the existence of a letter to Pirandello from Mussolini's secretary that spelled out Il Duce's decision to stop the performance. This sparked a flurry of correspondence between Rome and Milan police headquarters until the existence of such a letter was denied by Mussolini's office.[52] In the following months both Malipiero and Pirandello reasserted their position as pro-Fascist artists, but it is interesting to note that it is at about this time that Pirandello began to make his allegiance to Fascism much less explicit and public.[53]

Guido da Verona: Censorship and Intimidation

By the time the Fascists seized power, Guido da Verona was a successful novelist specializing in erotic fiction that tested the boundaries of the censors' tolerance. Novels such as *La donna che inventò l'amore* (1915) and *Mimì Bluette fiore del mio giardino* (1916) had, as the author claimed, entertained and consoled thousands of Italian soldiers in the trenches during the First World War. Indeed, since the writer's first commercial success – *L'amore che torna* (1908) – da Verona's novels had regularly sold over 150,000 copies.[54] After the war, he produced other works, such as *Sciogli la treccia, Maddalena* (1920), that established him as a figure in the mould of Gabriele D'Annunzio: sensual, eccentric, a devotee and chronicler of upper-class life and of the excitement of cars and horse racing. However, he lacked the poetic sophistication, the political vision, and the patriotic spirit of D'Annunzio. The timing of his decision to join the Fascist Party is revealing: whereas Pirandello had publicly supported Mussolini during the troubled months of the Matteotti crisis, Guido da Verona decided to act only a year later, in November 1925, when the regime was in total control and Italy's road to dictatorship irreversible. Mussolini did not seem to mind this tardiness; this is at least what one can conclude from the fact that he sent a telegram to the prefect of Milan, asking him to compliment da Verona for having joined the PNF: 'Trovi modo manifestare Guido da Verona mio compiacimento per sua inscrizione ufficiale P.N.F. Congratulazioni per tutto il resto' (Please find a way of manifesting to Guido da Verona my pleasure for his joining the PNF. Congratulations for all else).[55]

Throughout the 1920s da Verona continued his career as a novelist, managing to avoid being caught in the censors' net.[56] However, his luck deserted him when he decided to meddle with one of Italy's sacred cultural icons, the Romantic novelist and poet Alessandro Manzoni. In November 1929 the bookshop of da Verona's publisher, Unitas of Milan, advertised the imminent publication of his latest work, *I promessi sposi*, a parody of Manzoni's nineteenth-century masterpiece. This first advertising campaign earned da Verona a letter of indignant protest and a mock challenge to a duel, both recorded by the Milanese prefecture.[57] The situation degenerated when the book reached the bookshops. Its cover presented the novel as '*I promessi sposi* di Alessandro Manzoni e Guido da Verona' and displayed cameos of both writers (see Figure 6). Da Verona was obviously determined to use Manzoni's fame to trigger interest in and scandal around his own work.

The content of the novel, based on an amusing parody of Manzoni's story, employs two interesting devices. First, there is a clever inversion of the protagonists' personalities. Lucia, for example, in contrast to the virginal creature of Manzoni's pen, becomes a greedy young woman in search of a rich husband. Second, the novel contains recurring links between its nineteenth-century setting and contemporary Italy, thus allowing the author to interject satirical comment and parodic snapshots such as the character of Don Gonzalo, who provides a vehicle for ridiculing Mussolini. Yet the irreverence towards Catholicism and the

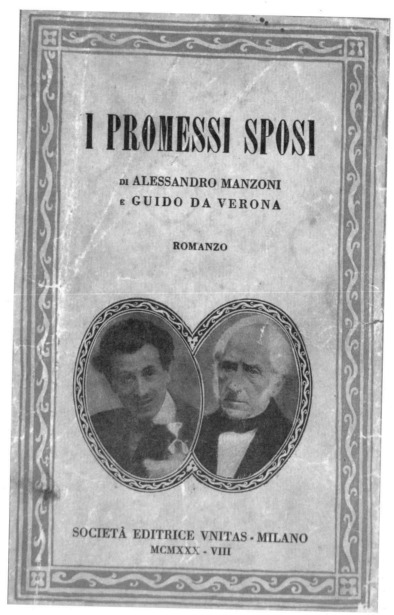

6. Front cover of Guido da Verona's *I promessi sposi* (Unitas, 1930).
(*Courtesy of Biblioteca Braidense, Milan*)

occasional reference to Fascism are bland and were far from insulting; hence the *nulla osta* of the Milanese prefecture.[58] A group of young Fascists, however, disagreed with the police's tolerant stance and decided to take action. On 8 January 1930, they walked into some of the main bookshops in Milan's city centre and ordered the removal of the book from shop windows and shelves. When they walked into the Unitas bookshop in the posh Galleria Vittorio Emanuele near the cathedral, the shop manager called the police. Two of the most excited members of the group were arrested, although they were released the same day. The police report underlined that all the agitators were members of the Fascist University Groups (Gruppi Universitari Fascisti, GUF). The following day, a larger group of about sixty students assembled outside the Unitas bookshop and once more demanded removal of the novel. The police again intervened, arresting three students. This time, in order to pacify the situation, the manager agreed to remove the books from his shelves. According to the police report, the students' protest was directed at the lack of respect shown by da Verona towards one of the fathers of Italian literature. It is interesting to note that on the same day, the Milan prefect had received an official letter of protest from the Diocese of Milan regarding the novel. In the letter, the secretary general of the Giunta Diocesana complained about da Verona's book, which was defined as 'oscena e insulsa parodia di un romanzo tutto nostro e che tutti abbiamo imparato a stimare tra i primi nella produzione mondiale' (an obscene and insulting parody of one of our novels that we have all learned to consider as one of the best in the world). It was of no little importance that with the decree of 21 April 1929, the Holy See had inserted the whole of Guido da Verona's published work in the *Indice dei libri proibiti*.[59]

With the first reviews of the novel, criticism of and insults directed at the author began to be published in the the national press. The most virulent came from Bottai's *Critica fascista*: the review by Cornelio di Marzio judged the novel a total failure, an insult to Italians and Catholicism. It labelled da Verona a Jew, a covert anti-Fascist, and an homosexual. To make matters worst, the review was preceded by a short editorial in which the editorial board gave total support to the article, declaring da Verona an 'antifascista nelle intenzioni, nella sostanza e negli scopi' (an anti-Fascist in matters of intention, substance, and aims).[60] Da Verona replied to the accusation with a letter published on the front page of *Il Corriere Padano* on 22 January 1930. He emphatically denied being Jewish and swore his long-time allegiance to Fascism.

The Milanese prefecture took action the following week. As the documents held in Rome's archives confirm, its move was provoked, once again, by the involvement of Mussolini's office. While students, Fascist press, and church authorities were expressing their outrage, two members of the Manzoni family – the granddaughter and a great-grandson – had presented their complaints directly to Mussolini. If Manzoni's *I promessi sposi* was an cultural icon of unified Italy and of Catholicism, then any attempt to debase it was a direct insult to the nation. A note from Mussolini's office, dated 12 January 1930, stated that 'il Capo del Governo è favorevole a che siano eliminate dalla copertina del libro la dicitura "di Alessandro Manzoni" e l'effigie del Manzoni' (the Head of Government is in favour of eliminating the wording 'by Alessandro Manzoni' and the image of Manzoni from the cover of the book).[61] These were indeed the directives that were passed on to the Milanese prefecture, which in its turn instructed da Verona's publishing house, Unitas. At the same time, the Ministry of the Interior informed all prefects that booksellers around the country were to be instructed to return the book to the publisher so that its covers could be changed.

Despite such directives, the situation in Milan had not entirely settled down. On 20 January, seeking a clarification from the Fascist authorities, da Verona went to PNF headquarters in Milan and asked to speak to the federal secretary. Da Verona was refused an audience, and a few minutes later, while walking back to his hotel, he was attacked by a group of young Fascists. Da Verona reported the brief welter of insults and punches to the local police. No arrests were made – da Verona decided not to make a formal complaint – although his personal protection was guaranteed by a police escort. In the following days da Verona's situation became more vulnerable. On 24 January a telegram from the head of police to all prefects confirmed that all copies of the novel had to be returned to the publishing house. Four days later another telegram informed the Milanese Prefecture that da Verona had been suspended for a month from the PNF, and on 9 February yet another telegram from Bocchini informed all prefects that da Verona's novel had to be stopped from circulation, even in its modified form.[62] What were the reasons behind such a development? It is likely that the scorn of the Milanese Fascists and da Verona's complaints had triggered the temporary suspension from the party. As for the decision to ban any reprint the novel, it is interesting to note that on 29 January a letter was sent to Mussolini by the president of the Italian National Committee for Public Morality (Comitato Nazionale Italiano per la Pubblica Moralità). Based in Turin, the committee was a lobby group directed by Rodolfo Bettazzi, a militant Catholic academic. In rather emphatic tones, Bettazzi had asked for the suppression of the book. More importantly, the Vatican archives show that, on 15 January, Da Verona's case had already been discussed at the highest level by Mussolini and Cardinal Duca Borgoncini, the Vatican's Nunzio Apostolico (ambassador) in Rome. According to Borgoncini, the Pope himself had defined the novel a 'parodia fangosa' (muddy parody). Mussolini briefly replied that the book has been opposed but that it was counterproductive to give the case too high a profile. A week later, the Italian ambassador at the Vatican, Cesare Maria De Vecchi, confirmed that the book has been banned.[63]

Two more details concerning this episode are worth mentioning. First, in a letter to the prefect of Milan, the director of Unitas underlined the fact that he had never received a written confirmation of the order to withdraw the book from circulation. The message had been conveyed over the phone by an officer at the prefecture of Milan. Second, a year later da Verona wrote to ask Mussolini for a meeting so that he could present him with a bound copy of all his novels. Mussolini's handwritten note on the letter agrees to the request, and the two met on 8 May 1931.[64] Nonetheless, as we will see in chapter 6, da Verona's trust in Italy's leader was to suffer a tragic setback in the years to come.

On the Fringes of Fascism: Luigi Bartolini and Vitaliano Brancati

The cases of Luigi Bartolini and Vitaliano Brancati, although in many ways different from one another, are linked by the fact that both authors were at the time eagerly collaborating with Fascist papers. Luigi Bartolini comes from an earlier generation of Italian writers and was already an established author when he encountered problems with the regime. Bartolini was also a successful artist whose etchings were considered to be on a par with those of Giorgio Morandi. His war memoirs, *Ritorno sul Carso*, were published by Mondadori in 1930, followed by two collections of short stories published by Vallecchi in 1930 and 1933. These stories, mainly autobiographical, contained sketches of daily life that often included risqué sensual descriptions. In later years Bartolini's stories were to encounter the regime's disapproval but the first reprimand came from another direction. From his adoptive home in Siena, Bartolini wrote for Maccari's *Il Selvaggio*, which, published in nearby Colle di Val d'Elsa, was the strongest voice of provincial Fascism.

Bartolini also contributed to another Fascist paper, Bottai's *Critica fascista*, which was closer to the heart of the regime. In a series of articles published in 1932, Bartolini presented literary portraits of famous historical figures such as Temistocle, Casanova, Robespierre, and Marat, all reflecting his penchant for anarchic, amoral, law-breaking individu-als. The climax was reached in an article in which Bartolini violently attacked the Sicilian writer Antonio Aniante, who had just published a critical biography of Mussolini with a French publisher. Bartolini's arti-cle was part of a general attack by the *Critica fascista* on any form of anti-Fascism and a call for a more interventionist stance by the regime in the control and development of Italian culture.[65] Bartolini's attack was sav-age. He called Aniante a spy who deserved to be shot in the back and 'un effeminato imbevuto di cocaina' (a cocaine-stuffed effeminate). He also indirectly suggested that the contract with the French publisher had come to Aniante through the chief editor of *L'Italia letteraria*, Curzio Malaparte. This last accusation must have been vigorously rejected by Malaparte – indeed Bartolini himself later admitted that it was false – because in the following issue of *Critica fascista* the editors published a brief anonymous editorial discrediting Bartolini's article. His article on Aniante was to mark the end of Bartolini's collaboration with *Critica fascista*.[66] It was a blow that he took personally.

At the time of the break with *Critica fascista*, Bartolini was in contact with the anti-Fascist art critic Lionello Venturi, who was at the time living in Paris after his refusal to sign the pledge to Fascism imposed on all university lecturers in 1931. Their relationship was mainly due to Barto-lini's activity as an artist, but from their correspondence we learn that Venturi had sent Bartolini some books on contemporary Russia. In a long letter dated 6 February 1933, Bartolini confessed to Venturi his anger at his marginalization, which he attributed to his independence of mind and opposition to the regime. In a rather convoluted line of reasoning, he stated that his attack on Aniante was in reality a indirect attack on the editors of *Critica fascista*, as he knew that the article would bring scorn upon the journal. He then wrote about the need to fight from within the borders of the country instead of doing it from abroad. In the conclusion of the letter, Bartolini somewhat naively suggested that Venturi should replace the original cover of the books he sent so as not to raise suspicion at customs. The letter was detected by the postal censors, and after a second one of similar content – in which he referred to the police officers who had seized some of the publications as 'thieves' – Bartolini was put under police surveillance.

In the following weeks his police file was passed through the hierar-chy of the police forces, ending up on Mussolini's desk. This fact is con-firmed by a memo from the head of police, Bocchini, dated 21 June 1933, in which he states: 'Preso gli ordini da S. E. il Capo del Governo: Riprodurre la pratica il 30 giugno p.v.' (As ordered by H[is] E[xcellency] the Head of Government: Resubmit the file on June 30).[67] We do not have evidence that the file was resubmitted to Mussolini on 30 June, but it is a poignant coincidence that the following day, on 1 July, a police inspector was sent from Rome to Ancona, where he supervised the arrest of Bartolini and a search of his premises. The police officer in charge of the investigation was no other than Guido Bellone, who had a network of informers among which was allegedly listed Ignazio Silone. In the late evening of 1 July 1933, Bellone telegraphed his superior, Bocchini, stating that the house search had produced no further evidence of Bartolini's anti-Fascism. The telegram was followed by a seven-page report in which Bartolini denied all charges of anti-Fascism, justifying his correspondence with Venturi as the frustration following his clash with the editors of *Critica fascista*.[68] Ten days after his arrest Bartolini was sent to *confino* for one year, although he was allowed to retain his occupation as a secondary school teacher. After a short period in Apulia, he spent his time in the South Tyrolean city of Merano, after which he returned to his native Marche region and, in the mid-1930s, again began working for Fascist papers such as Interlandi's *Quadrivio*.[69]

Immediately following the war, Bartolini wrote a pamphlet, *Perché do ombra*, to defend himself from the accusation of having worked for Fascist papers until the end of the regime. In 1945 he also published a second pamphlet, *Scritti sequestrati*, in which he collected some articles written in 1940 but that were not published, allegedly because of their strong social and political criticism. Not surprisingly, Bartolini omitted to mention his article attacking Aniante, published in 1933. The pamphlet also contained the text of a previously published short story, 'La rustica nemica,' which was supposed to strengthen Bartolini's claim that he was *persona non grata* during the Fascist years. Following the original publication of this short story in 1937, the chief editor of *Quadrivio* had been reprimanded by Gherardo Casini, head of the Directorate General for the Italian Press at the Ministry of Popular Culture. The letter from Casini dated 16 December 1937, added that a similar warning had been given for the publication of another short story by Bartolini, 'La giornata del grossista.' Yet both stories had been criticised for their overtly sexual content, and by presenting them as examples of his political persecution Bartolini was considerably distorting the picture.[70]

In conclusion, it is difficult to draw a clear line of demarcation between, on the one hand, the work of Fascists such as Casini, and Interlandi and, on the other, the literary work of Bartolini. His anarchic individualism together with his penchant for polemical essays and risqué fiction certainly brought friction with institutionalized Fascists. However, there is little doubt that his provocative writings for Fascist papers were not so much a threat to the regime as part of an internal debate that allowed space for polemics. The general impression is that Bartolini was considered by many Fascists a valid but volatile writer who needed to be kept under control. To a great extent, the fact that he was allowed to publish his work throughout the last years of the regime is proof not so much of the regime's increased tolerance, but of its capacity to contain and control a certain degree of criticism without resorting to more draconian methods such as arrest, censorship, or exile.[71]

In the early 1930s Vitaliano Brancati was a promising young writer who had recently come to Rome from his native Sicily. Like other Sicilian intellectuals arriving in the capital, he had been helped to settle in by the maverick journalist and editor of *Il Tevere* and *Quadrivio*, the Sicilian Telesio Interlandi. As we have already seen, Interlandi was a militant Fascist whose papers were two of the most radical voices of Fascism, often credited with being very close to Mussolini. In 1931, when still in Sicily, Brancati had started to write for *Il Tevere*. On one occasion he proclaimed his admiration for Mussolini with a poem dedicated to Rome, which contained embarrassing lines such as

> Si sente
> che in piazza Venezia
> un uomo è presente
> come una rupe di cui
> ci si accorge improvvisamente

(One senses that / in Venezia square / a man is present / as a cliff / that suddenly discloses itself to us)

and

> egli dice il suo nome: Mussolini,
> i fiori aprono le corolle;
> il fiume va dal monte al mare[72]

(he says his name: Mussolini, / flowers open their corollas; / the river flows from the mountains to the sea).

This fervent show of admiration had won Brancati a private meeting with Mussolini, which took place in July 1931. The article dedicated by Brancati to this meeting, which praised the highly refined intellect of Italy's Duce, appeared not just in *Il Tevere* but also in Bottai's *Critica fascista*: it was a clear sign that Brancati had been given access to the higher ranks of the regime.[73] His direct contact with Mussolini also gave him access to the pages of the regime's official voice, *Il Popolo d'Italia*. And when Interlandi founded the weekly *Quadrivio*, in August 1933, Brancati came to Rome to take up the position of chief editor.[74]

The preceding year Brancati had produced *Piave*, a play set in the trenches of the First World War, which featured Mussolini as a silent but towering character in the final scene. Mondadori was the obliging publisher, and the play was staged by pro-Fascist avant-garde theatre director Anton Giulio Bragaglia. According to Bragaglia's memoirs, Mussolini had interfered during the rehearsals at Rome's Valle Theatre, asking his press office secretary, Capasso Torre, to phone Bragaglia and enquire about the play.[75] This anecdote is refuted by the fact that Torre had resigned as head of press office in 1928; in 1932 he was no longer part of Mussolini's staff. In addition, there is documented evidence suggesting a different interpretation of events. A recently found letter from Bragaglia to Mussolini shows that not only Bragaglia and Brancati were in contact with Mussolini during the preparation for the theatrical production, but that Brancati submitted to Mussolini three different endings of the final scene. Mussolini eventually chose the version that included an eighteen-foot projection of a photograph of him as a First World War soldier.[76]

On the whole, there is little doubt that at this point in his career Brancati must have thought that the doors of fame and official recognition would stay open and lead him into the inner sanctum of Mussolini's regime. Following his pro-Fascist debut novel *L'amico del vincitore*, published by Ceschina in 1932 (the 'amico' of the protagonist being a fictional alter ego of Mussolini), Brancati's second work of fiction was the short novel *Singolare avventura di viaggio*, published by Mondadori in January 1934. It was the story of a lazy weekend spent in the city of Viterbo by a group of wealthy young people. The protagonists are two Sicilian cousins, Enrico and Anna, who, after some weak attempts to resist temptation, descend into an incestuous relationship. Brancati's descriptions of their passionate cavorting left very little to the imagination. If sex and incest were not delicate enough topics, Brancati decided to add a measure of blasphemy. In the room next to the two lovers we find a man constantly in the act of praying; his presence triggers the imagination of Enrico, who fantasizes about the reasons behind the man's penitential devotion. Towards the end of the narrative Enrico has a dream in which he is in the presence of Jesus Christ. In awe of this silent figure, Enrico confesses his doubts about the roots of Christianity – the ten commandments, the coming of Christ – and expresses his thought regarding the need for a second coming and for new rules. In the end, Enrico wakes up from his stupor brought on by sexual excess and religious musings and decides that action is the only answer. He abandons his cousin in her room – a predictable conclusion given the misogynist undertones of the whole narrative – and decides to return to Rome. By doing this he follows his best friend, who had done the same the preceding day after reminding Enrico of the exemplary role played by Fascist Italy on the European stage (referring to the Austrian political crisis of 1933 in which Engelbert Dollfuss attempted to build an authoritarian state based on Mussolini's Fascism). By the end, young Enrico has reached a new understanding of things, and his return to Rome is symbolic of a return to an active and constructive role in society. From a political viewpoint, *Singolare avventura di viaggio* was hardly a heretical piece of narrative. It certainly pointed towards the sense of dissatisfaction felt by the generation of young men who missed both the First World War and the March on Rome – and indeed the topic is explicitly mentioned in the early pages of the book when one of the characters says: 'La nostra generazione è minacciata dal ridicolo: passa con aria marziale tra guerre e insurrezioni, evitandole con una precisione assai comica' (Our generation is threatened by ridicule: it marches through wars and insurrections avoiding them with comical precision).[77] Moreover, in the final paragraphs the narrative voice seems to detach itself from the character of Enrico, thus presenting but not identifying with his decision to return to active life. However, the sense of decadence and moral weakness in the book is constantly related to Italy's past and to its religious culture (Viterbo, as a medieval city marked by the temporal power of the church, functions as a symbolic backdrop). In contrast, whenever Fascism is mentioned it has connotations of modernity, progress, and political strength.

Once published, the novel received a lukewarm reception, which greatly shocked Brancati. Luigi Chiarini, one of his colleagues at *Quadrivio*, wrote a critical review, presenting the book as a great fiasco and concluding that 'A Brancati (egli appartiene, non fra gli ultimi a questo giornale) potevamo e dovevamo parlar chiaro' ('To Brancati – who is not the last among the staff at this paper – we could and had to speak frankly').[78] A further blow came when the book was seized in all bookshops in Rome by the local police. We have no police records of this event, but the correspondence between Brancati and Arnoldo Mondadori shows that in March 1934 – that is, immediately after Chiarini's negative review – the book was seized by the prefecture of Rome. Strangely, the order to seize the book was not circulated to all other parts of Italy. In a letter dated 15 March 1934, Arnoldo Mondadori confirmed the seizure in Rome and added that he was going to contact Galeazzo Ciano (who was then head of Mussolini's press office) to find out more about the situation.[79] Unfortunately we do not have any more correspondence related to this. In his memoirs, Brancati vaguely remembered this episode, saying that the book was seized 'solo perché vi si notava qualche timido, timidissimo, accenno d'intelligenza' (only because it contained a few humble, very humble signs of intelligence).[80]

Judging from the circumstantial evidence, it seems that something similar to the case of Benelli's *Caterina Sforza* might have taken place. The fact that the sequestration was confined to the city of Rome points to the Holy Year that was celebrated in that period and possibly to the direct intervention of Mussolini in order to appease the likely complaints from the Vatican. The timing of the event is almost contemporaneous with the Roman performances of *Caterina Sforza*; hence it is possible that the two cases received similar treatment. Indeed, we know for certain that the ban had been the consequence of a letter of protest by the same Catholic militant, Carlo Costantini, who had been involved in Benelli's case (see page 292, note 46). As for Brancati, most critics and biographers mention this episode as a turning point in his relationship with the regime. Shocked and disillusioned, he fell out with his colleagues at *Quadrivio*, from which he resigned as chief editor. In the winter of 1934–5 he returned to his native Sicily.[81]

Brancati's correspondence with Mondadori reveals a difficult relationship. After *Singolare avventura di viaggio*, Mondadori was supposed to publish a collection of short stories by Brancati. However, after long procrastination probably related to the recent seizure of the novel, Mondadori wrote to Brancati on 13 February 1935 to inform him of his decision to delay once again the publication. Brancati – who at the time was still writing for *Quadrivio* and *Il Popolo d'Italia* – replied with what amounts to a polite form of blackmail. Mondadori's excuse for delaying the publication was that collections of short stories were not selling particularly well. So Brancati was incensed when some months later Mondadori published a collection of short stories by D.H. Lawrence, *Lo Zingaro e la vergine*. In no uncertain terms, Brancati informed Mondadori of his decision to attack him in the pages of *Quadrivio*, threatening to ask his readers to judge whether it was right that an Italian writer was sidelined in order to accommodate an English one. Considering that those were the months of Great

Britain's strong opposition to Italy's occupation of Ethiopia, it is clear that Brancati was hinting at the political inappropriateness of the situation. Brancati added that he was going to submit this article in ten days' time and would like to know Mondadori's final decision. The publisher's answer, which was sent twelve days later, contained a brilliant mixture of diplomatic flair and negotiating strength. Mondadori reminded Brancati that D.H. Lawrence was hardly an author in harmony with England's official politics. He then boasted the Fascist pedigree of the translator – who, incidentally, was the young Elio Vittorini, defined by Mondadori as 'un giovane e valoroso scrittore nostro, i cui sentimenti e le cui benemerenze fasciste non è il caso di sottolineare' (a young and highly valued writer of ours, whose Fascist sentiments and credentials do not need repeating). Finally, Mondadori added an example of a young Italian author, Ridolfo Mazzucconi, whose work he had recently published. The final blow was a dry reminder of the low sales figures generated by Brancati's previous publications: the play *Piave* had sold 474 copies; the novel *Singolare avventura di viaggio* had sold a mere 339.[82]

Mondadori's letter could not have been more successful. After a short period of silence, Brancati replied with a kind and apologetic letter saying that 'sfogato il dispiacere, m'era tornato il ricordo dell'amico Editore, che so essere anche gentile e affettuoso' (after giving voice to the disappointment, I remembered the friendly Publisher, who I know can also be kind and affectionate).[83] Brancati added that he had received a letter from Ciano, who had assured him that the order to seize *Singolare avventura di viaggio* had not come 'dall'alto' (from above), thus suggesting that he had not lost the approval of Mussolini. Indeed, among the correspondence recently acquired by Rome's Archivio Centrale there is a file on Brancati that proves that in later years, despite living in Sicily, he was still in contact with the Fascist leadership. He sought journalistic work for national papers such as *La Stampa* and *Corriere della Sera* through the recommendation of Ciano and Mussolini. As Minister of National Education, Giuseppe Bottai was asked to recommend his transfer as a teacher to Catania or Rome. And in December 1936 Mussolini personally approved a one-off grant to Brancati to work on a book of essays on Italian romantic poet Giacomo Leopardi, which in 1941 became an anthology of his writings.[84]

Literature from Abroad

Two categories of publications had to be kept under control by the Fascists in an attempt to defend the sacred borders of Italy from outside influence. First, there were books by foreign authors that were deemed unsuitable to be circulated either in the original or in translation. Then there were books by Italian anti-Fascist exiles often published in Italian with the explicit aim of smuggling them into Italy as propaganda material.

Before Fascism there was already an established system regulating publications. It was based on the combined efforts of the General Directorate of Public Security, the prefectures, and the customs police, often helped by the work of the Foreign Office and Italian embassies around the world. Their targets, apart from immoral or pornographic works, were publications labelled as 'subversive' or 'revolutionary,' most often those related to anarchist or revolutionary socialist groups or individuals.[85] The main development during the Fascist period was the predictable introduction of a new category – that is, 'anti-Fascist works.' Apart from this, there is little to distinguish the operation of the police forces involved in regulating publishing before and after October 1922. Similar was also the lack of centralization – at least in the first decade of the regime – which allowed for sometimes erratic and inconsistent mechanisms.[86] In this section I deal briefly on a selection of cases involving various government agencies.

In the run-up to the important general elections of 1924, the police did their best to stop the circulation of anti-Fascist publications from abroad. For instance, as head of police, General De Bono sent a telegram to all prefectures warning them to seize any copies of a pamphlet entitled *Fazioni e patria* written by an Italian anarchist trade unionist and printed in the United States. The author, Carlo Tresca, had been living in the United States since 1904 and was actively involved in the fight against Mussolini's attempt to organize pro-Fascist support among the Italian-American community. Incidentally, Tresca's work in those years was equally censored in the United States. As a consequence of his trade union activities, the U.S. Justice Department kept Tresca under surveillance, and after official complaints from the Italian ambassador, Tresca's periodical, *Il Martello*, was seized in 1923 on the grounds of a two-line advertisement for a book on birth control. Tresca was sentenced to one year in prison and, after surviving a series of attacks and attempted assassinations in the years that followed, was mysteriously killed in July 1943.[87]

Italy's immediate neighbours – particularly France – were more likely bases for anti-Fascist activity. On 19 December 1926 the head of police informed all prefects that the Parisian publisher Hachette was being used as a vehicle for smuggling anti-Fascist publications into Italian territory. Prefectures were instructed to double check all packaging importing Hachette publications.[88] Another French publisher under the scrutiny of the Italian police was the Librairie Valois, run by ex-anarchist, ex-Fascist, and libertarian socialist Georges Valois. This small publishing house had promoted the work of Italian anti-Fascists such as Francesco Nitti and Gaetano Salvemini, and informers of the Italian police were keeping a vigilant eye on its activity. When in October 1930 the writer and translator Paolo Monelli contacted Valois regarding a French translation of his war book, *Le scarpe al sole* (Cappelli, 1921), his movements were reported and an investigation was launched by the Italian Ministry of the Interior. Seven months later it was decided not to proceed against him.[89] In the same months the ministry alerted prefectures to the possible smuggling of overtly anti-Fascist publications such as Emilio Lussu's memoirs, *La catena*, and Pietro Nenni's *Sei anni di guerra civile in Italia*: the former had been published in Paris by Giustizia e Libertà in a miniature edition designed to facilitate its smuggling into the country.[90]

In parallel with the attempt to stop the introduction of anti-Fascist publications, the Fascists were also engaged in the selection of foreign books to be translated and distributed by Italian publishers. It should be clarified that publishers were free to acquire the translation rights and proceed to publish any foreign work without the need for a pre-publication authorization. Indeed, as we will see, the few cases of direct intervention by the government were in reply to queries raised by the publishers themselves. During the first decade of the regime, the most famous case was of Erich Maria Remarque's war novel, *Im Westen nichts Neues* (*All Quiet on the Western Front*). Following its international success, Arnoldo Mondadori rushed to acquire the rights for an Italian edition and had the novel translated and typeset. However, as we have seen in chapter 2, he was allowed only a small print run for the Swiss market and in the process managed to elicit a ban on a previously authorized novel, *Krieg* (*Guerra*), by Ludwig Renn. With regard to Treves's attempt to publish *Guerra*, we can add that, similarly to Mondadori, Treves's chief editor, Carlo Tumminelli, contacted Mussolini's secretary on 8 October 1929 and begged for the removal of the ban on the novel. To his correspondence, Tumminelli attached another long letter in which the Italian translator of the novel tried to convince the authorities of the non-defeatist nature of the book. From the content of the correspondence it is also clear that at Treves they were fully aware of the fact that the source of their recent problems derived from Arnoldo Mondadori's protests. We do not have copy of the official reply of Mussolini's office, but it seems that once more Mussolini allowed for a reversal of policy: Renn's *Guerra* was published and proved a popular success.[91]

Although exceptions were made, Fascist Italy was no place for anti-war sentiment. This is confirmed by another war novel published by Mondadori, *Die Katrin wird Soldat* (*Katrin Becomes a Soldier*) by Adrienne Thomas. This time Mondadori had not asked for unofficial approval, allegedly on the grounds that the editor and translator was a proven Fascist, Enrico Rocca. The book was distributed and was selling well, particularly among the female readership. But on 9 March 1932 the Ministry of the Interior instructed all prefects to seize copies of the novel on sale and in stock. The following week Mondadori complained to both Mussolini and the then undersecretary at the Ministry of the Interior, Leandro Arpinati (Mussolini held the ministerial office), but to no avail. On the internal front, an Italian novel – Carlo Salsa's *Trincee: Confidenze di un fante*, originally published by Sonzogno in 1924 – about the First World War was refused a reprint in February 1932 because of its criticism of the Italian army.[92]

There is no doubt that Mondadori was the most entrepreneurial and daring of all Italian publishers. His desire to exploit publications that were popular abroad often risked overstepping the boundaries of the regime's tolerance. A good example was his decision in 1932 to inaugurate one of his most prestigious series, the *Romanzi della Palma*, with a controversial novel: Ursula Parrott's *Ex-Wife* (1929). The novel had stirred great controversy even in its native United States (the first edition was published anonymously), and Mondadori's choice of the story of an emancipated American woman as the flagship of his series is a clear indication of his desire to take risks for the sake of commercial success. This time he was lucky. Published in 1932, *Ex moglie* reached its fourth reprint by the following year, and Ursula Parrott became a familiar author among the *Romanzi della Palma*.[93] At times Mondadori's boundless ambition produced comical effects, as when he asked Mussolini to write the preface to the Italian edition of a biography of Lenin by the Romanian author Valeriu Marcu. Il Duce refused, but the book was nonetheless published in 1930. Two years later the Ministry of the Interior realized that, while the Italian translation was in the bookshops, the prefectures had been ordered to seize all copies of the French and German editions of the biography. For two years nobody had noticed this bizarre contradiction.[94]

Examples such as these show the extent to which, in the early years of the regime, Fascist censorship was far from being an all-pervading and systematic process. This leads us to the question of whether there was a centralized system for the collection of data and whether all prefectures had access to it. In his study, Giorgio Fabre comes to the conclusion that there must have been one list, although no copies have so far been found in any state archive. His hypothesis is based mainly on a reference in an internal memo at the Ministry of the Interior, dated 27 May 1934, to a 'lista riservatissima' (very confidential list) and the fact that there is a reference to 'pagina 43,' which allows us to assume that it was probably a rather hefty document. However, as even the memo suggests, the list was almost certainly of periodicals and books that had been banned from circulation in Italy – that is, of foreign publications.[95] A reference to the existence of a list was also made in a letter dated 20 July 1930 sent by the administrator of the publishing house Sperling & Kupfer to the prefect of Milan. During a visit of the police, the administrator had heard of the existence of a list of all banned books; he asked if it were possible to consult such list. A handwritten note in the margin of the letter said, 'Dirgli di rivolgersi al Ministero' (Tell him to contact the Ministry). The note was dated 23 July; the following day the administrator was invited to the offices of the prefecture, presumably to let him know – orally – that he had to write to the Ministry of the Interior. Unfortunately we do not know whether the publisher pursued his quest for clarification. In any case, since Sperling & Kupfer specialized in the translation of foreign works, it is likely that the list they were referring to was the list of foreign publications.[96] Even if the Directorate General of Public Security had kept a record of all banned books, the fact that such a list does not survive in any form and, more importantly, no reference to its use is made in the administrative documentation prior to 1934, suggests that if, it was kept, it was almost certainly nor circulated. It seems more likely that prefectures were not given the full picture. Even within the Ministry of the Interior, and probably in Mussolini's press office too, the issue of book censorship was never fully and systematically dealt with until the early 1930s.

If France were the base of most anti-Fascist groups, some attention has to be given to neighbouring German-speaking countries too. In the first years of the regime, Mussolini was busy completing the 'Italianization' of South Tyrol (or Alto Adige as the government renamed it). The province of Bozen (Bolzano in Italian) had been annexed to Italy at the end of the First World War and the Fascists were keen to suppress any reference to the impositions and humiliations suffered by the German-speaking population of the *Alto-Adige*. As a consequence, a selection of unfriendly books on the subject were banned from circulation. These were titles such as *Kleiner Führer durch Sud Tirol* (*A Small Guide to South Tyrol*), published in Austria, and *Tirolo sotto la scure* (also available in English translation as *Tirol under the Axe of Italian Fascism*), published by the Bavarian publisher Beck.[97] From Switzerland, on the other hand, the regime had to defend itself against the arrival of the works by exiles such as Ignazio Silone. On 13 January 1934 the deputy head of the Italian Police, Carmine Senise, sent a telegram to all prefects instructing them to seize all copies of Silone's *Der Fascismus: Seine Entstehung und Seine Entwicklung* (*Fascism: Its Origin and Development*), which had just been published in Zurich.[98]

A final example of foreign publications that met the censors' disapproval relates to Galeazzo Ciano, who, as we have seen, had joined his father-in-law's Press Office of the Government in August 1933 The first documented example of Ciano's activity on the censorship front shows a degree of continuity with Mussolini's own approach. On 3 October 1933 Arnoldo Mondadori contacted him to complain about the ban on two recently translated novels: *Bohème 900* by Roland Dorgelès and *Storia di una notte* by Joe Lederer. They had been blocked because of episodes of suicide and abortion in their plots. Ciano replied to Mondadori saying that the seizure order would be withdrawn provided those passages were deleted. In the case of Lederer's novel this was promptly done, as two weeks later the press office authorized the publication of the newly pruned version of *Storia di una notte*. Given this odd, isolated case of involvement by the press office, it is arguable that the censorship of the two books had once more been provoked by Mondadori's over-zealous approach. In the previous months, Ciano's predecessor at the press office, Gaetano Polverelli, had sent out a number of instructions with regard to themes such as suicide that had to be avoided by the press, but there is no trace that the same rigour was imposed on publishing houses. It is more likely that, keen to make sure he had approval in higher places, Mondadori must have presented the government with a case that, once raised, could not be ignored.[99]

PART TWO

Censorship Fascist Style, 1934–1939

4 From Press Office to Ministry of Popular Culture

The Dictator Dictates: The Mura Case of April 1934

As we have seen in previous chapters, Mussolini's decision making, at least potentially and often practically, played a crucial role in the censoring of literature. The range of channels through which he was alerted to a certain situation or asked for his opinion and, equally, the number of solutions tailored to each case were such that the system was truly unpredictable. So it should not come as a surprise that the single most important act of censorship during the Fascist regime, an act that promoted a dramatic acceleration of the organization and centralization of censorship, was the result of Mussolini's incensed reaction to the cover of a sentimental novel.

The culprit was *Sambadù amore negro*, a novel written by Mura (pseudonym of Maria Volpi), an author and journalist who was particularly popular among female readers.[1] An earlier, shorter version of the novel had been published with a slightly different title, 'Niôminkas amore negro' (Niôminkas being the surname of the protagonist, Sambadù) in the Milan fashion magazine *Lidel* in April 1930 (figure 7). This version was about one-third shorter than the published book and ended with the marriage between Sambadù, a black man, and a young Italian widow.[2] Four years later the novel, with an additional seven brief chapters was published by Rizzoli in Milan as a paperback supplement to its illustrated monthly *Novella*. Its colourful cover illustration showed the photograph of a black man in elegant Western clothes holding an enraptured young white woman in his arms (figure 8). It is not clear how this novel reached Mussolini's office but his reaction was recorded by reliable witnesses. He found the cover to be deeply offensive to a nation that was trying to build an empire in Africa and ordered the head of police, Arturo Bocchini, to act immediately to make sure that such a thing would never happen again. The episode is recounted by Leopoldo Zurlo, who saw Bocchini soon after his meeting with Mussolini. An even more direct witness is Baron Pompeo Aloisi, head of the cabinet of the Foreign Ministry, who made a note in his diary after witnessing Mussolini's angry reaction:

> 2 avril. – A 11 heures chez Mussolini. Il était très contrarié d'une publication, Amour noir, qu'on a fait retirer de la circulation. Il s'agit des amours d'un Italien avec une négresse. Inadmissible de la part d'une nation qui veut créer en Afrique un empire.[3]

> (April 2 – At 11 am with Mussolini. He was very opposed to a publication, Black Love, which he ordered to be seized. It is about the love relationship between an Italian and a black woman. This is unacceptable in nation which wants to create an empire in Africa.)

Apart from Baron Aloisi's misunderstanding – it is a black man not a black woman at the centre of the plot – both witnesses agree that the reason for Mussolini's angry reaction was the illustration's provocative image of interracial romance. It is very likely that Mussolini had not read the novel; had he done so, he would have realized that its content was perfectly in line with the cliché of the superiority of the white race. It should also be remembered that in those months Mussolini had started to draw up plans for the invasion of Ethiopia and therefore it is not surprising that he should be particularly sensitive to issues regarding interracial relationships.

   A comparison of the novel and novella provides some interesting facts. When published in Lidel in 1930 the novella ended with the marriage between the two protagonists and the beginning of their honeymoon. The possibility of giving birth to a mixed-race baby made the young widow apprehensive, but the reassuring presence of her educated and self-assured husband convinced her that theirs was a future worth fighting for. The illustration that appeared next to the title of the novella was highly sensually and likely the inspiration for the cover of the novel. It was only when Mura prepared the expanded version that the racial content was given a more orthodox shape.[4] Indeed, it is in the new last seven chapters of the novel that both protagonists discover their ultimate incompatibility. Sambadù decides that, despite his knowledge of European culture, the

7. First page of Mura's *Niôminkas amore negro*, published in *Lidel*, April 1930. (*Courtesy of Biblioteca Braidense, Milan*)

8. Front cover of Mura's *Sambadù, amore negro* (Rizzoli, 1934). (*Courtesy of Biblioteca Braidense, Milan*)

call of his tribal roots is still too strong, and he literally sheds his Western clothes and goes back to live in the wilderness of 'Dark Africa.' On the other hand, Anita, the Italian widow, is horrified by the idea that 'il sangue del mio bambino sarà inquinato dal sangue di un'altra razza, e porterà in sé i germi selvaggi d'una tribù negra' (the blood of my child will be polluted with the blood from another race, and it will carry the savage germs of a tribe of negroes). The child arrives, although both parents are secretly disgusted by the sight of his half-caste features. By that time Anita is also discovering that below the surface of Sambadù's refined traits lurks a less appealing personality: 'E' pigro, indolente, diffidente, e spesso bugiardo' (He is lazy, indolent, distrustful, and often a liar)[5]. These are no personal traits: they are explictly linked to Sambadù's African origin (along with suspicions of cannibalism). It is therefore not surprising that the novel ends with his decision to leave his wife, son, Western clothes, and education, return to take his rightful place as a chief of his tribe in central Africa. Thus, the moral of the novel was perfectly aligned with widespread white racist attitudes. The sepia illustrations that accompanied the volume publication also tended to diminish the sensual undertones of the tale; the final one in particular adds a clear visual depiction of the moral strength and superiority of the white woman (see figure 9). The expanded version of the text and the accompanying illustrations were clearly designed to present a more orthodox and reassuring ideological picture. Unfortunately for Rizzoli and Mura, the designer in charge of the cover decided to go in the opposite direction. The use of a photograph and the intense sensuality of the couple's embrace unleashed the strong reaction of Italy's Duce. Indirect proof of this is the fact that, as we will see, the designer of the cover illustration was given a police warning whereas the author was not subjected to any formal procedure, although she was to be at the centre of a police investigation.[6]

The immediate political consequence was that on 2 April 1934 Bocchini sent a telegram to all prefects ordering them to seize all copies of Mura's novel. The official reason was that the novel 'offende la dignità di razza' (is offensive to racial dignity). Later that same day Bocchini sent a second telegram, ordering that, from then on, two copies of each new book had to be sent to the Interior Ministry.[7] Even worse, the following day Mussolini himself signed another telegraphic circular to all prefects, setting out the definitive procedures that from that day onward all publishers had to follow.[8] Mussolini's circular ordered that publishers submit three copies of each publication. All three had to be sent to the local prefecture. The prefecture would keep one and

...Mi appare enorme, crollato, come un mucchio di macerie più grande dell'edificio che sostenevano prima. (pag. 97)

9. Illustration in Mura's *Sambadù, amore negro* (Rizzoli, 1934). (*Courtesy of Biblioteca Braidense, Milan*)

forward the other two to Rome, one to the General Directorate of Public Security (DGPS), the other to the Press Office of the Head of Government.[9] It was the first time that the press office had been given an officially recognized role in book censorship. Its pre-eminent role was inscribed in the fourth paragraph of the circular, which stated that 'Se nello stampato si rinvengano elementi contrari agli ordinamenti politici sociali et economici dello Stato aut lesive del prestigio dello Stato et della pubblica autorità aut offensivi del sentimento nazionale le Prefetture ne riferiranno immediatamente all'Ufficio Stampa del Capo del Governo, restandone in attesa di disposizioni' (If the publication contains any elements that are contrary to the political, social, and economic organization of the state, or damaging to the prestige of the State and of public property, or offensive to national sentiment, the prefectures will immediately report this to the Press Office of the Head of Government and await instruction). The DGPS was given a similar role in the case of 'offence to public morality,' but it was clear that any politically charged offence had, from now on, to be vetted and judged by Mussolini's press office.

Another important consequence of this circular is that it implicitly imposed a sort of pre-publication censorship on the publishing world. Although publishers were free to print books without preventive authorization, the circular stated that: 'Tutti gli editori o stampatori di qualsiasi pubblicazione o disegno, anche se di carattere periodico, dovranno prima di metterli in vendita aut comunque effettuarne diffusione, presentare tre copie di ciascuna pubblicazione alla Prefettura' (All publishers and printers of any kind of publication or image, periodicals included, must present three copies of each publication to the prefecture before circulation takes place).

There is no doubt that the circular marked a radical shakeup of the system. Yet, the urgency with which it was put together meant that the new instructions left much to be desired in terms of the practicalities involved. Indeed, the press office and DGPS received several telegrams from prefectures all over the country asking for clarification. What if a prefecture did not have a press office? When did the prefecture have to send the two extra copies to Rome, before it had evaluated its own copy or after? And before distributing the books, did publishers have to wait for final authorization from any of the three authorities involved? These issues were addressed in the following months. What is important to underline is that this type of partially preventive form of censorship was not turned into full-fledged legislation until 1939 and even then, as we will see, it was done in an ambiguous way. Evidently Mussolini was not prepared to admit that any form of pre-publication censorship had been introduced. The hypocrisy lay in the fact that neither the 1934 circular nor the 1939 law stated that publishers were prevented from distributing their books without previous authorization. They were obliged to deposit a number of copies with the authorities (by 1939 the number was to rise to eight), but they were legally free to begin distribution without the regime's *nulla osta*. It is not difficult to imagine how publishers would react to this situation. In order to avoid possible losses from printing expenses, many publishers began to submit their publications when still in proofs (after all, it was already normal practice for some such as Mondadori). The authorities were obliged to deal with an even greater workload after the government decided that books that had been approved at proofs had to be resubmitted to make sure that the published copy did not differ from the proofs.

As to the reasons behind Mussolini's sudden decision to take such a drastic approach, there is more than one hypothesis. For Giorgio Fabre, it was linked to Mussolini's plans to introduce racist policies in Italy, plans that he had been working on from at least the year before.[10] There is also little doubt that the swift efficiency with which the Nazis had imposed their grasp on Germany's state machine as soon as they seized government in 1933 played an important part in making Mussolini more eager to introduce similar policies in Italy. The circular of 3 April marked the beginning of a process that, as we will see, bears similarities with the Nazi one both for its racist nature and for the subsequent centralization of the system. It is very unlikely that Mussolini would have admitted to drawing inspiration from Hitler's policies – certainly not in the early 1930s – but it is arguable that the Mura case gave him the opportunity to accelerate the process of centralization. A third hypothesis is that the decision was not the result of planning or forethought but a knee-jerk reaction to an unexpected event. The way in which the policy was developed seems to support this theory. The factors discussed above certainly played their part, but it is likely that before Mura's book came to Mussolini's attention, the latter did not have a detailed plan of action ready to be implemented. It was not the first case in which Mussolini's policies appeared to emerge from a relatively inconsequential event – even in the field of censorship there are similar instances. According to Zurlo's memoirs, in the early months of 1936 Mussolini happened to switch on his radio to listen to a war bulletin about the Ethiopian campaign. As it happened, the national broadcaster, EIAR, was broadcasting a rather poor variety show that infuriated Mussolini so much that he ordered a blanket ban on all shows of that nature. Zurlo, responsible for authorizing the show, sent an apologetic note to Mussolini in which he explained the need to provide shallow entertainment for the masses. Mussolini apparently appreciated this argument and agreed to withdraw the ban.[11] On the whole, it can be argued that, as much as Mussolini might have already been mulling over the centralization of censorship and the introduction of racial policies, the Mura case acted as an unexpected catalyst that accelerated and gave an irreversible momentum to his policies.

It is also interesting to note that the Political Police (Polizia Politica) at the Ministry of the Interior already had a file on Maria Volpi (aka Mura). It consists of only three documents, all of them anonymous letters by possibly the same informer. What is most intriguing is the fact that the first one predates Mussolini's burst of anger by only a few days. Dated 27 March 1934, it relates to an article written by Mura as part of her regular column for the Milan paper *La Sera*. In the article Mura thanked

Mussolini for allowing three Russian emigrées to be housed in a hospital on Lake Maggiore. The informer also refers to Mura's subsequently receiving an anonymous letter accusing her of singing the praises of Mussolini in the hope of becoming his next lover now that Margherita Sarfatti's place was vacant.[12] There is no sign that the letter was forwarded to higher authorities, but it is nonetheless an intriguing coincidence that the report should have arrived the week before the decision to ban Mura's book. It would not have been the first time that Mussolini was made aware of informers' reports about events of little importance, and it is perhaps especially likely in this case, as his name and that of his former lover were specifically mentioned. The next informer's report, dated 23 April 1934, relates to Mura's dismay about the political storm caused by her novel. The cover illustration of *Sambadù amore negro* is mentioned by the informer as the real source of Mussolini's rage. The informer adds that Mura had asked to see Mussolini but managed to secure a meeting only with Galeazzo Ciano, who dissuaded her from taking the matter any further. The third report is dated 2 October 1934. By this time Mura is described as a possible lover of Alessandro Chiavolini, Mussolini's personal secretary. The suggestion is that compromising letters might have come into Mura's possession through Chiavolini. At the end of the brief report there are two hand-written comments. The first says 'Chi l'ha data? il solito!!!' (Who passed it [presumably the piece of information]? The usual one!!!). The three exclamation marks indicate that the informer was well known, possibly for the unreliability of his/her information or because of his/her anti-Mura attitude. Of equal interest is a second note in the margin, which just says 'Bellone.' This might well indicate that the police officer in charge of either this informer or the overall investigation was Guido Bellone, the officer at the Ministry of the Interior who, as we have seen, was not only involved in other cases involving intellectuals (Silone, Bartolini, and Malaparte) but was also receiving orders directly from the head of police. Was Mussolini made aware of one of these reports during his daily meetings with Bocchini? Did they emerge after Mussolini's interest in Mura's novel? The documentation available makes it impossible to arrive at a definitive answer. However, given the date of the first report, it is arguable that had Mussolini been made privy to it he would have asked for more information, at which point a copy of *Sambadù amore negro* might have landed on his desk. At this stage, however, this is pure speculation.

Whatever the sequence of events, the regime's organization of book censorship had been changed for good. As Fabre rightly suggests, it is interesting to note how the whole event was totally ignored by the the press and went unmentioned even in the official journal of the publishers' association, *Giornale della libreria*.[13] Not only had a new system of implicit pre-publication censorship been introduced, but the high alert created by the welter of telegraphic circulars in the early days of April spurred all prefectures to intensify their control over book production. Indeed, according to ministerial records, no seizures were registered during the first three months of 1934; in contrast, the rest of the year saw a great flurry of activity. Between January and the end of March only three books had been banned, and they were all foreign publications: Ignazio Silone's *Der Fascismus*, published in Zurich; Lauro De Bosis's *The Story of My Death*, published in Great Britain; and Josef Stalin's *U.R.S.S. Bilan 1934*, published in Paris. In the following two months, thirteen circulars were sent to all prefectures, each of them banning books published mainly in Italy.[14] Their titles suggest the possible reason for their seizure. Three were about the French Foreign Legion, which makes one think that perhaps engagement with questions of race relations was behind their ban (they were *Con la legione straniera, 1925–1933* by Giulio Vannini, *Verso la Sfinge buia con la legione straniera francese* by Aldo Camilleri, and *Legione straniera* by Prokovieff, almost certainly a pseudonym for Russian author Victor Fink).[15] Other banned works included a collection of poems in Milanese dialect; a publication entitled *Il Processo a Guido da Verona* by Tom dell'Aquila (almost certainly a pseudonym), a book probably related to da Verona's past censorship problems;[16] two titles, *La vigilia e la carne* by Riccardo Marchi and a new edition of *Perdizione* by Gian Dauli, that were probably targeted for their licentious content; and two works banned for clear political motives – the Italian edition of *Inchiesta sulla gioventù sovietica* by Klaus Mehnert and the memoirs of anti-Fascist professor Giuseppe Rensi, *Scolii: Pagine di diario*. It should be noted that all these texts had been published by relatively small, provincial publishers (Vannini, Casa del Libro, Montes, Corticelli, and Aurora, the only prestigious ones being Ceschina and Laterza/Polo). Established publishers such as Mondadori, Treves, and Sonzogno seem to have been left untouched by this first wave of seizures.

Leopoldo Zurlo, who as we know was in charge of theatrical censorship, interpreted the circular of 3 April to be strictly related to racial policies. On the same day he proceeded to ban the performance of a play featuring a white woman falling in love with an educated black man – *Carne bianca* by the Fascist playwright Luigi Chiarelli – despite the fact that only a few days earlier it had been given the green light. In his memoirs he devotes six pages to other examples of comedies and variety shows that he axed because they featured black people in too positive a light.[17] Another example of the seriousness which which Mussolini's circular was taken comes from the new prefect of Verona, Giovanni Oriolo. Aware of the weight carried by the new directive, Oriolo created a form to be used for all cases of book censorship. The form explicitly mentioned Mussolini's circular as the legal source of the prefecture's actions. It read: 'A norma della circolare telegrafica 3 aprile 1934 XII N. 9532–442 di S. E. il Ministro dell'Interno ...' (Following the telegraphic circular of 3 April 1934 XII No. 9532–442 by H. E. Minister of the Interior ...). From then on, all actions of the prefecture of Verona in matters of book censorship were presented as directly endorsed by Mussolini.[18]

Not everybody was as eager as Zurlo or the Veronese prefect. On 3 June 1934 Ciano sent a long circular to all prefects, complaining about the fact that 'non tutte le prefetture ottemperano sempre con la necessaria scrupolosità alla disposizioni impartite dal Capo del Governo con sua circolare 3 Aprile' (not all prefectures apply the instructions provided by the Head of Government in his circular of 3 April with the same necessary amount of care and attention). Indeed, some prefectures had not even created a press office. For example, the Naples prefecture did so in October 1934, Pisa in December, and Asti in January 1935. Apart from demanding more rigour, Ciano's circular distinguished itself with the first explicit admission that this was a form of pre-publication censorship. The comment concerned novels that were published in instalments: for those, a pre-publication *nulla osta* from the prefecture was a must. The fact that *Sambadù amore negro* had slipped through the net, arguably because it had been first published in a periodical, was therefore addressed with a clear form of pre-publication censorship on this type of publication. On 18 July 1934 Ciano issued another circular, in which he required all prefectures to compile a list of publishers and printshops in their jurisdiction. There is no doubt that the publishing industry had become the centre of attention for Mussolini's press office.[19]

Among the material recently made available at the Archivio di Stato in Rome, there is a file that reveals that even in those weeks of harsh policies Mussolini and Ciano were ready to make exceptions. The object of their personal intervention was radical Fascist writer Marcello Gallian. A follower of Gabriele D'Annunzio in the occupation of Fiume and an early *squadrista*, Gallian was involved in the Roman avant-garde movement of the 1920s. The successful premiere of his controversial play *La casa di Lazzaro* in 1929 had taken place at Anton Bragaglia's Teatro degli

Indipendenti, which was to become the epicentre of experimental theatre during the Fascist years. His rebellious personality and his staunch anti-bourgeois, revolutionary Fascism made him a progressively more isolated figure. As we will see, some of his works were also subjected to censorship, but at the time of this first episode, in the spring of 1934, Gallian was a prolific writer of fiction and journalism for several influential papers (such as *Circoli*, *L'Italia letteraria*, *Corriere della Sera*), and he was working on a short history of Fascism that was part of a propaganda publication officially co-authored by Mussolini himself.[20]

In 1934 Gallian published two books: *Tempo di pace*, with a preface by Giuseppe Ungaretti, an allegorical novel showing black squad Fascism defeating the greed and corruption of the old bourgeoisie, and a collection of autobiographical short stories entitled *Comando di tappa*.[21] The latter encountered the disapproval of the prefecture in Rome. Its press office found the crude realism of some descriptions too harsh and proposed to cut six stories, 'troppo audaci e nel loro verismo anche offensivi del pudore e della morale' (too risqué and, in their realism, also offensive to decency and morality). It was true that Gallian had gone a long way to describe the misery and moral degeneration of the lumpenproletariat in cities like Rome; however, the book contained equally passionate praise of radical Fascism and its potential for engendering social revolution. Its epigraph stated: 'Questo diario strano e arruffato d'uno squadrista è dedicato agli squadristi strani e arruffati' (This strange and scruffy diary by a *squadrista* is dedicated to all strange and scruffy *squadristi*). Mussolini seemed to approve of it because Gallian at the time was receiving funds directly from his press office and Il Duce's signature of approval appears on most of those documents. On 5 April 1934, only two days after he had signed the famous circular, Mussolini had approved press office funds (2,000 lire) to be given to Gallian to pay his expenses for a trip to the rice fields of the Po valley to do research for some articles. Another letter few days later, this time from the chief editor of *Corriere della Sera* to Ciano, tells us that Gallian's collaboration with that prestigious paper had been openly requested by Ciano, presumably following Mussolini's suggestion.[22] So, on 23 June 1934, when the prefect of Rome contacted Ciano to inform him of his intention to censor Gallian's book, it is not surprising to find that Mussolini's press office was not eager to concur. First of all, the press office had already been warned. A note from that office shows that, three days earlier, journalist and writer Nino d'Aroma had telephoned to ask for the press office's intervention in convincing ('sollecitare') the Roman prefecture to give its *nulla osta* to both a publication by d'Aroma and Gallian's *Comando di luppa.* The request might have been successful: a handwritten note at the top of the prefecture's letter repeats d'Aroma's key words: '*nulla osta.*' And, in the end, Gallian's book was neither censored nor seized.

Some months later, on 16 October 1934, Mussolini directly approved the next tranche of money (3,000 lire) to be awarded to Gallian, this time to pay for his children's healthcare and his rent. Another 2,000 lire were to come in February 1935, followed by another 3,000 two months later. In later years Gallian's privileged position was to diminish until his uncompromising and ultimately disillusioned militancy was entirely out of step with the regime's propaganda. Symbolic of this is what happened to his novel *Gente di squadra*, published by Vallecchi in 1941. The book's original title was *Quando siamo disperati*, but to appease the censors, Gallian changed it first to *Come siamo abbandonati* and then to the more neutral *Gente di squadra.*[23] Nonetheless, certainly up until the mid-1930s, and even at the time of his most stringent censoring policies, Mussolini was willing to protect Gallian and other authors whom he deemed useful to the ideals of a Fascist revolution, however evanescent this revolution was to remain.

Galeazzo Ciano at the Press Office

If the Mura case was the sudden catalyst for a radical shakeup of Fascist censorship, the centralization of the system was in many respects a logical consequence of policies set in the preceding months. Hitler's seizure of power in January 1933 not only influenced Mussolini's foreign policy but quickly became a yardstick by which the Fascist regime was forced to measure the development of its own institutions. The patronizing attitude with which Il Duce had followed the rise of the Führer was soon replaced by admiration for and envy of the speed with which Hitler was imposing Nazism both on Germany on the attention of public opinion worldwide. In particular the Nazis implemented their plans for the centralization and Nazification of German culture with enviable efficiency. Hitler had barely been in power for two months when, in April 1933, Joseph Goebbels's new Ministry for Popular Englightenment and Propaganda (*Reichsministerium für Volksaufklärung und Propaganda*) began to mould both Germany's government machine and cultural industries. The creation of the Reich Chamber of Culture in September 1933 and other legislation passed in the following weeks gave Goebbels's ministry total control over newspapers and publishing houses. Private ownership was partly respected, but the ministry was given full powers to guide and to censor, ban, or close down any publishing activity. The Third Reich's publishing industry did not seem to need the kind of semi-preventive censoring measures introduced in Italy with the circular of April 1934. Whether this situation was the result of a lack of Fascist discipline among Italian publishers or of a more pervasive regimentalization of the German press by the Nazis is an open issue. But this kind of difference might help to explain why Mussolini preferred to keep his measures out of the public eye until 1939. Officially, both the Nazi and Fascist regimes were keen to show themselves as presiding over a free publishing industry. In both cases, the coercive methods used in the early years against the opposition press were ignored. The consensual collaboration of publishers and authors was depicted as a product of their enthusiastic observance of the Nazi and Fascist codes. The buzz word for the Nazis was *Gleichschaltung* (regimentation), which referred to the assimilation within the Nazi state of all political and cultural activities. Italian Fascism was already trailing on the cultural front.[24]

Prior to the Mura case, the establishment of Goebbels's ministry in March 1933 had been followed by a less imposing but not dissimilar development on the Italian side. In an internal report presumably written at the time of Goebbels's official visit to Italy in May 1933, Gaetano Polverelli, then head of Mussolini's press office, had made reference to the need to compete with the Nazi propaganda machine. Similarly, from the pages of *Critica fascista*, Giuseppe Bottai had been pressing Mussolini for a reorganization of Italian culture under clear Fascist leadership.[25] Whether or not Goebbels's visit was the actual trigger, it is an undisputable coincidence that a few weeks later Mussolini decided to appoint a new head for his press office. On 1 August 1933 the appointment went to Mussolini's young son-in-law, soon to become his most trusted collaborator. The choice of a public figure such as Galeazzo Ciano was a clear signal that Mussolini had decided not only to enhance the role of this department but also to increase its public visibility. Ciano at the time was a young diplomat (he had spent the previous three years in China), but his ambitious personality coupled with the patronage of his father (Costanzo Ciano, Mussolini's minister of communication from 1924 to 1934) and his recent marriage to Edda Mussolini, quickly propelled him up the Fascist echelons. His accommodating and polite manners – in contrast with the rough edges of Polverelli – also contributed to his popularity among the press and publishing houses.

In his early months in office, the thirty-year-old Ciano seemed to act as little more than an intermediary between Mussolini and the publishing world. He was, understandably, learning the trade. Examples of his secondary role, apart from his totally passive stance during the Musa case, can be found in the correspondence relating to his first year in office. In all cases he was little more than Mussolini's secretary, administering Il Duce's correspondence with cultural institutions and individuals.[26] However, Ciano progressively developed a more authoritative persona and independent decision making. This does not mean that Mussolini was delegating power. If nothing else, Ciano's presence created a new level of authority to which journalists and publishers could appeal and from which they would receive directives and advice. The year 1934 is once more a pivotal one. If the Musa case in April had accelerated the process of centralization and put book censorship in the spotlight, some months later the first stones of the future Ministry of Popular Culture were laid. And Nazi Germany was once more a clear influence.

On 14 June 1934 the first official meeting between Hitler and Mussolini took place in Venice, and in those very weeks Ciano received a detailed report on the organization of Goebbels's Ministry for Popular Enlightenment and Propaganda.[27] Another signal that chance was afoot was the moving of the press office to the larger and more splendid premises in Via Veneto in July. The eventual transformation of the department into the Undersecretariat for the Press and Propaganda (*Sottosegretariato per la Stampa e Propaganda*) was decreed on 6 September 1934. It was the first step towards the creation of a full-fledged ministry.

A look at the expansion of the undersecretariat confirms the influence of the Nazi model. Ciano's department progressively monopolized control over cultural production and propaganda one branch at a time. A similar development had characterized the establishment of Goebbels's ministry. Now it was the turn of Ciano to fend off the protests of various ministries (mainly of Education, Interior, and Corporations) and of the National Fascist Party, which saw its jurisdiction being reduced to benefit the new department. Within its first year of its existence, the Undersecretariat for the Press and Propaganda had grown from its original three divisions (National Press, International Press, Propaganda) to cover a much wider spectrum including cinema, radio, tourism, music, and theatre. Moreover, Italy's seven most important prefectures (Rome, Milan, Turin, Florence, Bologna, Naples, and Palermo) were assigned a press office officer directly appointed by Ciano, who had become a permanent member of the Cabinet Office (Consiglio dei Ministri). Staffing at the undersecretariat had also grown exponentially. In his memoirs, Italian-American journalist Giorgio Nelson Page remembers his friend Ciano trying to entice him to work at the undersecretariat in June 1934, by telling him that 'Fra breve nascerà qui un' organizzazione dre diventerà, la prima in Italia. Tutto passerà attraverso le mie mani' (within a short time this organization will be the first in Italy. Everything will pass through my hands).[28] Indeed, staff was transferred from other ministries (Leopoldo Zurlo was one of them, transferred from the Ministry of the Interior to Ciano's department), and if we compare a report concerning staff at the press office, written in 1933 by Polverelli, with a similar report of July 1936 we can see the magnitude of this expansion. Polverelli's press office had a team of eleven people in its most important section – that for the National Press. This figure allows us to estimate a total of about thirty to thirty-five people in the entire department. By the time the undersecretariat was developed into a ministry, the number of Ciano's employees had risen to 686.[29]

The increasing sphere of interests of the undersecretariat does not mean that book censorship had become less important. The action sparked by the circular of April 1934 coupled with the presence of Rome-appointed press officers had forced the major prefectures to be much more active. The list of all the books banned between April 1934 and August 1935 reaches an impressive total of 260. To this one should add another seventy-four that had been published only after cuts and modifications. It was a staggering figure, particularly if compared to the miserly figure of three books affected in the first three months of 1934. A large number of the banned titles were publications of dubious morality with titles such as *Amanti di un'ora, Amore a cronometro, L'arte di sedurre le donne, Baby, la moglie che cava gli occhi al marito, La bevitrice di perle, La fine della Vispa Teresa*, and so on. Others covered political topics but not necessarily from an anti-Fascist slant – *Amor di patria nella concezione totalitaria dello stato, Bolscevismo e capitalismo, Cenni biografici sulla vita di Benito Mussolini, Giudizi e aneddoti su Mussolini, Inno al Duce, Parole e pensieri del Duce* (published by the Fascist Trade Union Association of the city of Como), *La preghiera del fascista.* As Zurlo mentioned a regard to his activity as theatrical censor, once explicit anti-Fascist works had disappeared from the internal market, censors had to be more careful about embarrassing pro-Fascist publications so badly written that they would produce only scorn and ridicule. Among the list of titles that were distributed after cuts and modifications, it is interesting to note the considerable presence – eleven of seventy-four – of publications relating to religious matters. Produced mainly by Catholic publishers, these publications covered religious topics and included *La mia casa e la famiglia cristiana* by the Jesuit priest Domenico Valle, *I nostri giovani e la purezza* by Monsignore Francesco Olgiati, *Pietre miliari nella storia del cristianesimo* by Ernesto Bonaiuti, and the *Manuale di Azione Cattolica* by Monsignor Luigi Civardi. Unfortunately no records of these particular cases of censorship have been found, so we can only guess that the required modifications related to passages in which there was a lack of consistency between Catholic policies and Fascist ethos. Another missing piece of information concerns the proportion of publications banned by the prefectures and those blocked by Ciano's department. We can conclude only with a general consideration: the 'Elenco delle pubblicazioni di cui è stata vietata la diffusione' (List of the publications whose distribution has been prohibited), which was sent to all prefectures on 8 August 1935, marks the first documented case of efficient centralization and distribution of censorship data by the Fascist government. Moreover, a document that has only recently become available suggests that the initiative for this list did not come directly from Ciano. It was actually the prefect of Mantua who had asked for such a list in March 1935. The obvious usefulness of a complete list must have convinced the undersecretariat to collect data from all prefectures in the following weeks and eventually compile and circulate the resulting document.[30]

The vast increase in the number of banned publications does not mean that publishers and individual authors had stopped successfully pleading and negotiating with the authorities. Archival records are full of such cases, and Ciano's progressively important role simply added another recourse for those seeking to circumvent official policy. As Patrizia Ferrara suggests, Ciano continued Mussolini's policy of ensuring the support of intellectuals through ad hoc financial awards. New recipients were the writers Fabio Tombari, Sibilla Aleramo, and Stanis Ruinas in 1933, and the poets Corrado Govoni and Giuseppe Ungaretti and young novelist Romano Bilenchi in 1934.[31] An already famous writer and controversial Fascist, Curzio Suckert Malaparte, was apparently relying on Ciano for his political survival after he had met the disapproval of Mussolini and the Fascist leader in Ferrara and later governor of Libya, Italo Balbo. The maverick and narcissistic Malaparte was not new to delivering vitriolic attacks in his literary and journalistic work. In the early thirties, both his biography of Lenin and his study of *coup d'état* had been published in France, officially because Malaparte could count on better publishing deals but probably to avoid any problems with the Italian censors. According to

Malaparte both books had been banned in Italy directly by Mussolini, although this is not documented (the first book by Malaparte to appear in any list of prohibited books, *La téchnique du coup d'état*, was listed only in November 1939). A sworn enemy of Malaparte, however, was Italo Balbo. The two had had various polemical exchanges that climaxed, in 1931, with Malaparte's being replaced as chief editor of the Turinese newspaper *La Stampa* (Malaparte alleged that Balbo was behind the conspiracy to dismiss him) and in the publication of a short biography of Balbo, signed by Falqui and Malaparte, which, underneath its grandiloquent glorification, could be read as a malicious parody of the Fascist hero.[32] For years Balbo had repeatedly tried to have Malaparte expelled from the Fascist Party, or even arrested, as is evident from his correspondence with Mussolini. He was finally successful when, on 7 October 1933, Malaparte was arrested on his return to Italy after a long period spent in Paris and London (it was Balbo who had alerted Mussolini of his return three days earlier). Malaparte was sentenced to five years of *confino* on the island of Lipari but after only seven months he was allowed to move the seat of his house arrest to the much more cosmopolitan northern Italian spa town of Forte dei Marmi. This unique treatment was apparently linked to Ciano's benevolence. In his letters to his friend Pierre Bessand Massenet, written between September 1933 and August 1935, Malaparte described Ciano as a brother and mentioned an offer by the latter to write as foreign correspondent for the *Corriere della Sera*. Ultimately, on 11 October 1933 a press office *velina* ordered an end to any public discussion of Malaparte's fall from grace.[33]

Publishers continued to protect their interests, and prominent among them was, as usual, Arnoldo Mondadori. On 20 December 1934 he complained about Marise Ferro's novel *Barbara*, which had been banned (and was to appear in the list of prohibited books in August 1935). Mondadori asked for confirmation that, in a private conversation with Ferro, Ciano had assured her that her novel was going to be allowed in its current edition and only future reprints were going to be banned. We do not have a copy of Ciano's reply, but records in various Italian libraries show that the novel was in fact distributed. Other examples show a friendly relationship between Mondadori and Ciano. On 27 April 1935 the former sent a copy of an anthology of Italian writers to the undersecretariat and expressed his desire to have Ciano help inform the press and Italians in general of this newly published 'opera di propaganda.' Ciano's reply was that he had instructed the press to talk in positive terms of the initiative. A pencil-written note in the margin of the letter says 'C. Sera, dato a Pancrazi'

(C. Sera, given to Pancrazi), Pancrazi being the literary critic of the *Corriere della Sera*).[34] Mondadori was also one of the prime beneficiary of state loans intended to support the publishing industry. Through the government-owned holding IRI, in June 1933 his publishing house received two loans for a total of seven million lire, which allowed Mondadori to reinforce its dominance within the Italian publishing world. It was a fact that book production was entering a period of decline after its peak in 1932–3. As Francesco Chicco suggests in his detailed study, among the reasons were the increase in censorship and the decrease in translation of foreign books.[35] The introduction of a single textbook for each grade in primary schools in 1929 also had a negative impact on book sales, and the regime had shown its willingness to address the matter with ad hoc measures such as reimbursements in the form of book orders. Ceschina, for example, which had been excluded from the selection of publishers allowed to print the *Libro di stato*, received a book order for a total of 200,000 lire after the company complained to Mussolini about its losses. Bemporad, on the other hand, sought to increase its sales of scholastic texts with the help of the Ministry of National Education and the Fascist National Party.[36] As part of its new involvement in the supervision of theatre, Ciano's Undersecretariat for the Press and Propaganda decided to support eight theatre companies with a grant of 400,000 lire each.[37]

With regard to political censorship, the only episode of some importance that took place in the immediate aftermath of the Mura case concerns Carlo Bernari's *Tre operai*. The novel had been published in February 1934 as the first of a new literary series, *I giovani*, created by Cesare Zavattini. The publisher was the same as *Sambadù amore negro*, Rizzoli in Milan, and one has to wonder whether this detail influenced events. The first wave of sales and reviews of *Tre operai* were positive and Zavattini was planning to submit the book for various literary awards. However, on 6 April 1934 he wrote an alarmed letter informing the author that he had just heard that Mussolini's press office had ordered the press not to mention Bernari's novel. This ruined any prospect of new editions and literary awards. From Milan, Zavattini asked Bernari, who at the time was living in Rome, to see if he could get to the source of this unofficial ban. Bernari was able to meet Ciano, who explained to him that it was Mussolini who, after reading the book, had commented: 'Altro che socialista, qui c'è il comunismo!' (This is not socialism, there's communism here!) and had ordered Ciano to take action. The plot of the novel, often considered as a precursor of neo-realist literature, focuses on the frustrations of a group of Neapolitan workers in the years prior to the Fascists' seizure of power. It could not be accused of open anti-Fascism but it certainly presented a bleak view of working-class life, which was at loggerheads with Fascist propaganda. According to Bernari, Ciano's suggestion was to keep a low profile, to keep on publishing, but, prudently, to use a pen name.[38]

Following his father-in-law, Ciano had begun to tailor his censoring role to the individual needs and circumstances of each case. As for the use of funding, an entry from Ciano's diary is revealing of his *modus operandi*. On 8 January 1938, by which time he had joined the Foreign Office, Ciano wrote: 'Gervasi, della "Stampa Hearst," ha chiesto un prestito. Gli ho dato 20.000 lire. Naturalmente a fondo perduto. E' sempre stato un amico. Però io preferisco corrompere coi denari i nemici, che intorbidare col medesimo la spontaneità degli amici' (Gervasi, of 'Hearst Press,' has asked for a loan. I have given him 20,000 lire. Obviously without expecting the money back. He is always been a friend. But I prefer to use money to corrupt my enemies, rather than ruin the spontaneity of my friends with it).[39]

The Ministry for the Press and Propaganda, June 1935–May 1937

It was not long before the burgeoning size and importance of the undersecretariat, coupled with Ciano's ambitious aims, made it inevitable that the department should be elevated to the rank of ministry. This was sanctioned by a decree published on 24 June 1935. The process of centralization carried on as before, with radio and television coming under its jurisdiction four months later when the new Ministry for the Press and Propaganda (Ministero per la Stampa e Propaganda) became roughly equivalent to Goebbels's Ministry for Popular Englightenment and Propaganda. The six directorates of Ciano's ministry mirrored those of Goebbels's (which had seven, but one was simply a finance department), covering propaganda, national and foreign press, radio, film, theatre, and music.[40] More and more institutions came under Ciano's ministry: from Istituto LUCE to all of Italy's Tourist Offices, the SIAE (Italy's copyright office for artistic production), and all national opera theatres.

As for censorship, on 24 October 1935 the Ministry for the Press and Propaganda was given the authority to directly order the ban and seizure of any publication. The department charged with this responsibility was the General Directorate for the Italian Press (Direzione generale per il servizio della stampa italiana, DGSI) under the directorship first of

Francesco Felice and, after July 1936, of the Tuscan Fascist Gherardo Casini – co-editor of Bottai's *Critica fascista* – who was to keep this position until 1942.[41] Until October 1935 this executive power had been a prerogative of the Ministry of the Interior through its head of police. The decision to strengthen the powers of the ministry was strictly related to the international situation. In the same month Mussolini had launched the invasion of Ethiopia, and the new ministry was facing its first real test. Internal and external propaganda required firm coordination as did the supervision of Italy's cultural production. There had to be a unified strategy to support a political and military campaign that had totally isolated Fascist Italy on the international stage – with the predictable exception of Nazi Germany, which had left the League of Nations two years before.

It was a time when propaganda publications abounded, both during and in the wake of the Ethiopian campaign. Mondadori was once more in the front row, acquiring the rights to publish the memoirs of the official protagonists, from Generals Badoglio and Graziani to the secretary of the National Fascist Party, the swaggering Achille Starace. Once he returned from his own service as an airman, Galeazzo Ciano was also asked by Mondadori to write his memoirs but, similarly to his father-in-law some years before, he refused.[42] It was only a minor setback, which did not disrupt Mondadori's fruitful collaboration with the regime. In his study, Scotto di Luzio shows in detail the efficiency with which Arnoldo Mondadori was monitoring the sales of his propaganda publications through official channels such as the branches of the National Fascist Party and the Fascist Institute of Culture. In other cases, Ciano's ministry appeared as a friendly collaborator. On 14 December 1935, alarmed by the request of the Milan prefecture to revise the proofs of Trilussa's *Cento apologhi* and Richard Aldington's *Anche le donne devono lavorare*, Mondadori asked Felice – then head of the DGSI – if the directorate could pre-empt the prefecture's concerns by issuing its own *nulla osta* to publication. The authorization promptly arrived three weeks later. Moreover, on 6 April 1936, when in doubt whether to acquire the translation rights of expatriate German author Leonhard Frank's latest novel *Traumgefährten* (Dream Mates), Mondadori asked the ministry to provide him with their as to the suitability of the book for the Italian market. Mondadori was able to avoid an unwise investment, as the work of Frank – whose pacificist novel *Der Mensch Ist Gut* (The Man Is Good) had been banned in Germany – was deemed by Felice to be 'in contrasto coi sani principi del regime' (at odds with the healthy principles of our regime).

Sometimes favours were sought from the opposite direction, as when Celso Luciano – head of cabinet of Ciano's ministry – informed Mondadori that the government was willing to sponsor the publication of Franz Moedlhammer's anti-Communist work, *Moskaus Hand im Fernen Osten* (Moscow's Hand in the Far East), recently published in Germany with a preface by the Nazi ambassador to Britain and future foreign minister Joachim Von Ribbentrop and the Japanese ambassador to Germany. Mondadori replied on 15 April 1937 that he had already discussed the matter with the new head of the DGSI Gherardo Casini. The commercial prospects of such a publication, however, were rather poor and in the end Mondadori managed not to publish it.[43]

Another anectodal event is related to the *Giornata della fede* (Day of Faith) on 18 December 1935, when Italians were asked to donate their wedding rings and other pieces of gold jewellery in order to support the war effort. To my knowledge, no study has mentioned that the idea to organize such an event might have come from Arnoldo Mondadori himself. On 14 November Mondadori wrote a letter to Mussolini in which he suggested such an initiative. He supported it with some rough calculations according to which if one-third of all Italian families were to donate an average of fifty grams of gold, the state would benefit from a total revenue of about four trillion lire. He also suggested that the donation should be recompensed with state bonds to be cashed in at a time the government deemed appropriate. Mussolini seems to have followed Mondadori's advice to the letter: the initiative, which was successfully launched the following month, was a carbon copy of the publisher's shrewd suggestion.[44]

The Ethiopian campaign accelerated the process of centralization, and the state of war justified a heavy-handed intervention in all cultural matters. Daily meetings between Mussolini and Dino Alfieri, the deputy head of the Ministry of Press and Propaganda, to discuss the regime's propaganda policies became, according to the latter, more than an hour long. A ministerial memo (a famous *velina*) of 5 November 1935 to all newspaper chief editors spelled out the first censorial consequences of Italy's defensive stance in the international community. Alfieri had banned the broadcast of jazz music and other 'musica inglese' by Italian radio, and journalists were warned that he was also studying a plan to ban the staging of plays and operas written by authors belonging to states that were applying the League of Nations sanctions against Italy. Perhaps the most memorable and embarrassing example of state control of the media occurred in October 1936, on the first anniversary of the victorious entry into Addis Ababa: most newspapers were so obliging in following the ministry's instructions that a disconcerting number of them carried exactly the same suggested headline, 'Bandiere al vento' (Flags in the wind).[45] Fascist Italy's high profile on the international stage also had the effect of rocketing young Galeazzo Ciano to an even more important position. On 11 June 1936 Mussolini appointed him foreign secretary. His post at the Ministry for the Press and Propaganda was taken by his deputy, Alfieri, who had temporarily been in charge during Ciano's military service in Ethiopia. Born in 1886, Alfieri was a former lawyer and journalist, a 'fascista della prima ora' elected to the Fascist Chamber of Deputies and senior aid to Ciano from the time of the undersecretariat. His dedication to the job made him an efficient minister – although more than one colleague commented on his legendary absent-mindedness – and it is mainly thanks to him that the ministry remained a fairly tight and efficient organization despite the meteoric rise in its size and importance.[46] Mussolini probably also favoured him because he was not a particularly ebullient or inventive personality. The first important step taken by Alfieri in the field of censorship was a consolidation of all the circulars that had been produced since April 1934 into a single document with clear instructions for all prefects. Alfieri's circular clarified that the press office of each prefecture was supposed to issue a *nulla osta*, and in case of requests for modification or seizure it was supposed to notify the Ministry for the Press and Propaganda and wait for its final decision. The Ministry of the Interior was left out of the loop altogether. In matters of censorship, the prefectures' higher authority was the Ministry for the Press and Propaganda.[47] The prefects' role in terms of censorship was therefore reconfirmed despite the centralization of the system. As we have seen, exceptions would often happen, and large publishing houses continued to look to the authorities in Rome as the best place to negotiate for their interests. The implicit pre-publication character of book censorship was also accentuated by the fact that Alfieri's circular officially allowed publishing houses to submit their publications when still in proofs.[48]

The fiercest competitor to the ministry's progressive centralization of all cultural institutions was the Ministry of National Education, which at the time was run by a Fascist of some intellectual calibre, Giuseppe Bottai. In 1936 his ministry lost control over the Accademia d'Italia and had to fight hard to retain its grip on school texts and state libraries.[49] Incidentally, Bottai, always eager to have the approval of his leader, occasionally had his own work censored directly by Mussolini. During his stint of military service in Ethiopia, in January 1936, Bottai recorded in his diary that Mussolini had read and banned an article that he had written for his journal *Critica fascista*. Ironically, in this article about the need to foster a stronger national ethos, Bottai had written that 'si può limitare la libertà, non la dignità degli uomini' (one can limit people's freedom, not their dignity).[50] As a minister, Bottai also followed the trend by centralizing the power within his own ministry. At the end of 1936 he created a committee responsible for book orders of all school libraries in the country. One of the results was that publishing houses had one more target for their lobbying activities, and it is not surprising to find that the publishing houses benefiting most from this centralization were Vallecchi, Mondadori, and Gentile's Sansoni.[51]

The practice of ad hoc financial help for literary figures and journals was continued by Alfieri in the tradition of his predecessor. In August 1936, for example, Bontempelli gratefully received the sum of 10,000 lire as editor of the ailing *L'Italia letteraria* (which, despite this last-minute injection, folded only a few months later).[52] Mussolini often had the final say, as happened with the decision to give Interlandi's *Quadrivio* a monthly subvention of 2,000 lire, or when the familiar name of Vitaliano Brancati reappeared, asking for a grant so that he could work on a study of Leopardi. As already mentioned, he received 2,300 lire and five years later produced an anthology of Leopardi's writings.[53] All these interventions by Mussolini probably took place during the 'mattinale' – that is, the morning slot allotted to the Minister for the Press and Propaganda for his daily report to the head of government.

More importantly, in March 1936 the Ministry for the Press and Propaganda produced its second list of all publications banned during the previous year.[54] It was less detailed than the previous one (it omitted a list of books that had been partially censored) and much shorter, probably as a result of the diminishing intensity of the alarm created by Mussolini's circular of April 1934. The total number of bans had greatly diminished, from 260 to 93. It should also be noted that the list included books as well as other types of publications such as songs, individual poems printed in *foglietti volanti*, and postcards: once we take those into account, the actual number of book titles decreases to seventy-nine, about one-quarter of those from the previous year. Another sign that prefectures had perhaps higher priorities than targeting books came from a comment in the introduction to the list. Alfieri, then still deputy minister, noted that random checks had clearly shown that several banned publications were still on sale in bookshops. He urged prefects to take more decisive action and to threaten legal prosecution against publishers and bookshop owners (although it is difficult to understand how the latter could have been held responsible, as the list was not public). It is also interesting to note how the criteria reflected the most important issues at the time. If the 1934–5 list contained a high number of licentious and religious publications, the following year everybody's attention seemed to be dominated by the Ethiopian war. Indeed, out of ninety-three titles, twenty-seven were related to the conflict. Most seemed to genuinely support the war effort, either glorifying the deeds of the Italian army or denigrating Ethiopia's Negus or the much hated Albion (Britain being identified as the main mover behind the League of Nation's boycott of Italian imports). The American press also suffered a minor blow: the December 1935 issue of *Readers' Digest* and the January 1936 volume of *Foreign Affairs* were also declared unwelcome on the Italian soil.

The only two notable literary works in the March 1936 list are another novel by Marcello Gallian, *Bassofondo* (whose case will be dealt with in the following chapter), and one by the popular author Dino Segre (alias Pitigrilli). The timing of the ban on the latter is intriguing because the novel, *Vergine a 18 carati*, had originally been published by Sonzogno in 1924, and by the mid-1930s it had already sold about 90,000 copies. What is particularly interesting is the fact that at the time Pitigrilli was working as an informer for the Fascist's political police. He had infiltrated the Turin circles of Giustizia e Libertà, and his reports were instrumental in the police raid of 15 May 1935 that culminated in the arrest of anti-Fascists among whom were Leone Ginzburg and Cesare Pavese of the Einaudi publishing house. It would be tempting to suspect that the ban on this novel was perhaps a form of cover for Pitigrilli's spying activities. However, such a plan would have required a level of coordination between the Political Police and the Ministry for the Press and Propaganda that would have been unprecedented and of which there is no archival trace. It is more likely that it was a coincidence, because it was not common for the Political Police to share the identity of their informers with other departments. Pitigrilli had previously been involved in legal cases in 1926 and 1928, and *Vergine a 18 carati* – whose title is explicit about its risqué content – was probably just another victim of the climate of puritanism created by Mussolini's circular.[55]

Finally, a variation of the general rule was practised by a Fascist who survived many battles and censorial encounters. Flamboyant Curzio Suckert Malaparte did not wait for his publishers to prepare the proofs of his books. Instead he would send his manuscripts directly to the Ministry for the Press and Propaganda, as he did in May 1937 once he had completed a collection of short stories, *Il sangue d'Europa*, subsequently published by Vallecchi.[56]

The Ministry of Popular Culture

By the summer of 1937 the Ministry for the Press and Propaganda was about to go through a final name change that was to remain in place until the fall of Fascism. Back in 1933, the head of the press office, Polverelli, had underlined in a report the negative connotations carried by an expression such as 'Propaganda.' Italians, he wrote, using a neologism, wanted to be informed, not to be 'propagandati' (propagandated).[57] By 1937 even the term 'Press' had become misleading: the functions of the new ministry had developed far beyond the parameters of the press and publishing industry. Once more, it is difficult not to see the influence of Goebbels's Ministry for Popular Englightenment and Propaganda. On 1 June 1937 Alfieri's ministry was renamed Ministero della Cultura Popolare (Ministry of Popular Culture), shortened in internal documents as Micup (and here abbreviated as MCP).[58]

The Book Division (Divisione Libri, often referred to as Divisione III) within the DGSI was the department that oversaw book censorship and provided the necessary coordination between prefectures on the one hand and the minister and Mussolini on the other. Fortunately, for the period March 1937 to May 1938 we have an almost complete set of the monthly reports sent by the head of the Book Division, Gherardo Casini, to Alfieri, by then the DGSI minister. The figures provided by Casini with regard to book censorship are presented in table 1. Considering these figures as a whole, in the twelve months for which we have data, a total of 10,940 publications were submitted.[59] Of these, prefectures flagged 537 (about 5 per cent) for the attention of the MCP. The ministry decided to seize 110 (about 20 per cent) of centrally vetted publications. Although these figures give us a precise picture of the regime's censoring activities, it is much more difficult to draw qualitative conclusions about the level of censorship imposed on the publishing industry. It should be remembered that in previous lists of banned books, the ministry tended to include all types of publications, including songs and postcards. It is therefore impossible to know what percentage of these figures were books, and, even more difficult in our case, to specify how many of these books were literary works. Moreover, official figures mask the number of cases in which an agreement was reached before the

Table 1
Censorship by the Book Division of the DGSI, March 1937–May 1938*

Date	Publications received	Publications earmarked by prefectures for attention of DGSI	Publications seized by the MCP	Banned reprints**	Authorized after modifications**	Banned foreign publications**
1937						
March	777	67	8			
April	980	80	14			
May	762	45	5			
June	668	54	12			
July	346	13	5			
October	725	30	7			
November	858	29	7			
December	860	49	6			
1938						
January	1305	35	5	1	2	5
February	958	60	14	–	2	5
April	1206	40	2	–	2	3
May	1495	35	5	–	–	–

* Data are not available for August and September 1937 and March 1938.
** Data for these categories are not available until December 1937.
Source: ACS, MCP, b. 95, f. 424.

publication was formally submitted as well as all cases of self-censorship in which publishing houses declined to print books because they feared a potential ban. Nonetheless, two interesting facts can be extrapolated. First, the high percentage of publications earmarked by the prefectures but subsequently authorized by the MCP makes one think that the level of control exerted by the prefectures' press offices was relatively low. Or, rather, prefectures probably made a first selection, leaving it to the ministry to use its discretion before deciding what should be banned. Another possible explanation behind the high percentage of publications authorized by the MCP could be that the ministry was much more favourably disposed than the prefectures towards the publishing industry. As we have seen, there are isolated instances suggesting that this might be the case; however, the sheer scale of the differential and the fact that at no stage did prefects seemed to mind the MCP's high proportion of authorizations, allow us to discard the latter hypothesis.[60] Another interesting fact is the extremely low number of publications that were distributed after modifications. We have figures for only three months but their consistency seems to suggest that a very small number of publications (less than 2/1000) were subject to cuts and modifications. Once more, it is difficult to judge whether these figures should be taken as a sign of the MCP's tolerance or inefficiency, or, as is more likely, a sign that by 1938 the publishing industry had successfully adjusted to the expectations of the regime.

The centralization of the system was providing the MCP with a national picture of the situation. This picture came into even clearer focus with the demand in April 1937 that all publishers provide the ministry with monthly lists of every publication coming out of their printshops. Centralization was further enhanced in a delayed reaction to the Mura case: the ministry decided in December 1937 to restrict the circulation of novels published within periodicals. 'Allo scopo di tutelare la sana educazione del popolo' (in order to protect the healthy education of the people), novels in instalments could be authorized only by the ministry, and instalments could not exceed a total of thirty. Another move towards centralization was the decision, in March 1938, that all translations of foreign books had to be vetted by the MCP. Books could be submitted in the original and the ministry would let publishers know its response through the prefectures. Strictly speaking, this process did not correspond to pre-publication censorship – publishers were not obliged to follow this route – yet it is not difficult to see how publishers could respond in no other way than by silent compliance. One should also wonder about the degree of efficiency with which this policy was applied. Three months after the directive had come into force, Casini wrote a note to Alfieri, highlighting the fact that there was no proper office assigned to the examination of foreign publications. Another month passed before a interministerial committee was set up to discuss a similar matter related to how to control the circulation of foreign publications in Italy. The minutes of that meeting show that the participants were preoccupied with making sure that the directives would be applied as discreetly as possible so as not to provoke criticism in the foreign press. As Pietro Peretti (director of the Fascist Federation of Book and Paper Tradesmen) put it, they needed to find a way to 'agire senza apparire' (to act without appearing to do so). By 22 August the committee had come to the conclusion that customs officers should vet all imported books printed by publishing houses that the regime had identified as anti-Fascist; at the same time booksellers were left with the ultimate responsibility to flag any publication that they deemed to be contrary to the values of Italian Fascism. Once more, discretion was paramount: the memo prescribed that booksellers were to receive 'precise istruzioni verbali' (precise verbal instructions), thus leaving no paper trail behind. The following day Mussolini gave the go-ahead for the entire operation. As for the lack of censors, it was eventually decided in late October that the General Directorate for the Foreign Press could employ the readers of the better-staffed General Directorate for the Italian Press. They were to be paid, on a freelance basis, 100 lire per book.[61]

If the centralization of the system proceeded at a constant pace, it was by no means a flawless process. In May and October 1938 Alfieri sent two circulars: the first was a reminder that all requests for bans or seizures had to be signed by him, the second was a circular to all prefects, complaining about inefficient book censorship on the part of some prefectures. Perhaps the changeover from the prefectures' dependence on the Ministry of the Interior to that on the MCP had not been as smooth as one would have expected.[62]

In any case, repression and control were not the first priority of Alfieri's ministry. By the late 1930s the MCP had become a huge promoter and creator of national culture. It is not surprising that, in these years of widespread consensus, the leaders of Fascism should have thought that most of the MCP's efforts needed to be concentrated on enabling and fostering the development of a national culture. Anti-Fascist cultural activity was by then relegated to small groups of activists abroad and, internally, to small pockets of dissidents – such as those grouped around Croce's *La cultura* and the Laterza publishing house – who were often well known but allowed to survive. The ministry's increasing financial help to journalists and writers as well as to publishing houses was not entirely a cynical effort to tie intellectuals and industrialists to the regime. It was also the result of the conviction that the state – which was, after all, at the very centre of Fascism's political philosophy – had almost an obligation to act as a patron and a creator of culture. Moreover, following the international isolation caused by the Ethiopian war, Fascist propaganda put more and more emphasis on the concept of autarky. Such policies of national self-sufficiency spilled from the realm of economics to others, including cultural production. In the field of publishing, Franco Ciarlantini, head of the Fascist trade union of publishers

(Federazione nazionale fascista industriali editori), wrote in 1937 of the need to strive for a cultural autarky that would favour Italy's publishers through its support for national initiatives.[63] The MCP became the prime interpreter of these needs. An official initiative in this respect was the creation, in partnership with Giuseppe Bottai's Ministry of National Education, of a periodical entirely devoted to Italian books. Founded in 1937, *Il libro italiano* devoted ample space to the debate on how to support both Italian culture and the Italian publishing industry.[64]

The costs of implementing such policies provide a measure of the escalating involvement of the ministry: funds apportioned for financing either individuals or private institutions and enterprises rose from a total of 1,541,517 lire in 1933–4 to a staggering 162,831,966 in 1941–2. More particularly, help to journalists and authors rose from about 400,000 lire in 1933-4 to 3,613,000 in 1941–2. These figures, if made public, would have fuelled speculation and criticism – certainly abroad – so it is not surprising to find that the funds were earmarked 'Secret' and were drawn from accounts at the Ministry of the Interior, as was standard practice at the time of Mussolini's press office in the 1920s.[65]

The circle of intellectuals, journalists, and authors drawing some income from their collaboration with, or simply from the patronage of, Alfieri's ministry grew even larger. According to Ferrara, in 1938, Alfieri added fifty new names to his list of intellectuals receiving the ministry's support. Among them were promising young people such as the novelist Carlo Cassola and the Einaudi editor and future Communist politician Mario Alicata.[66] Among the individuals who joined the queue at a different time were, for example, ex-admiral, war hero, and prolific writer Guido Milanesi; the author of successful commercial novels for Bompiani, Arnaldo Frateili; novelist and partner of famous critic Enrico Falqui, Gianna Manzini; and radical Fascist Stanis Ruinas.[67]

It almost goes without saying that the chain of command did not end with Alfieri but would often continue until it reached Mussolini's office. The latter's typical handwritten monogram preceded by a brief comment, for example, can be found on the request for financial help by Alessandro Bonsanti for his literary journal *Letteratura* and in the memo that guaranteed the Tuscan publisher Carabba financial help in the form of book order. A telegram from Mussolini to Giovanni Papini, dated 1 December 1939, contained some positive comments about Papini's recent book, *Italia Mia* (published by Vallecchi), and concluded saying that 10,000 copies had been ordered to be distributed 'tra i giovani' (among the youth).[68]

From the available indexes of the paperwork presented by Alfieri at his daily morning meeting with Mussolini, it is possible to infer that Il Duce was kept informed of all act regarding the promotion and censoring of books. For example, at their meeting of 27 July 1939 Alfieri presented Mussolini with notes regarding grants (*sussidi*) in favour of an invididual and an institution (Palermo's theatre), a report by the Press Office of the Demography and Race Department (*Demorazza*, created in 1938), examples of propaganda leaflets destined for Japan, and Mondadori's request for Stefan Zweig's books not to be banned (more on this in chapter 6). The following day Alfieri presented only two items, another report by *Demorazza* and a request for the translation of a book on Napoleonic Rome by an author identified only as Madeleine.[69] In a more censorial role, Mussolini also directly approved the publication of Croce's *Concezione materialistica della storia*, printed by Laterza in 1938. A year later he manifested his disapproval of the seizure by the MCP of the three Laterza volumes of Herbert Fisher's *Storia d'Europa*. In March 1937, following a theatrical performance during which he had been negatively impressed by a cliched cameo of a Sicilian swindler, he reminded his theatre censor, Zurlo, to be strict about any mocking of Italian regional characteristics.[70] Il Duce acted as arbiter in a case between the prefecture of Milan and the MCP concerning a book published by La Prora, that contained documents related to a recent murder case. The book, entitled *Il delitto di Le Piazze*, had been authorized in 1937 by the prefecture of Milan after some modifications. The MCP, however, had intervened and blocked its distribution. The chief editor of La Prora decided to contact Mussolini himself and ask for his definitive opinion. The letter reached Mussolini's office on 9 October, and, although we have no trace of its reply, the fact that the book did not subsequently appear in any list of prohibited books seems to suggest that Mussolini's answer might have been a benign one.[71] In another case, the prefect of Livorno passed on to Mussolini the request for financial help submitted by a local publisher, Carabba. Handwritten on the publisher's letter, Mussolini's note ordered the government's acquisition of 10,000 books as a token gesture. The order was promptly executed on 16 June 1937.[72]

In a passage from his conversations with his biographer Yvon De Begnac, Mussolini presented himself as a supervisory figure intent on avoiding the overzealousness of his own censors:

Comunque, il vostro caso dimostra che se una censura funziona in Italia, a difesa della cultura della rivoluzione, questa si rivolge primariamente contro i miei camerati fascisti e, spesso, debbo riconoscerlo, ingiustamente. Sono gli inconvenienti derivanti da una burocrazia in formazione, animata più dallo zelo che dalla fede, più desiderosa di potere in proprio che di giustizia per altri. Io debbo spesso intervenire per richiamare all'ordine i pretoriani ministeriali.[73]

(Anyway, your case shows that if there is such a thing as censorship in Italy, to defend the culture of our revolution, this is primarily applied against my Fascist comrades and, often, I have to admit, unjustly. These are the inconveniences resulting from a fledgling bureaucracy, fuelled by zeal more than faith, coveting power more than justice. I often have to intervene to bring my ministerial henchmen to order.)

The case referred to at the beginning of the quotation concerns the publication in 1937 of the second volume of De Begnac's biography of Mussolini. Entitled *La strada verso il popolo*, this volume covered the years 1905–9, including Mussolini's period as a Socialist activist in the Trentino region. The MCP's decision to ban any review of the book had apparently been taken without Mussolini's consent and had been caused by the resentment of various Trentino Fascists and of the widow of the great martyr from the First World War Cesare Battisti, in response to De Begnac's reconstruction of the political climate.[74] Unfortunately no documentation has been found related to this event, but it is rather difficult to believe that Mussolini had not been consulted on the fate of a book devoted to him. It is probable that he might have denied his involvement when speaking to De Begnac simply to avoid reciprocal embarrassment (confirmed by his telephone conversation with Giorgio Pini, as mentioned on page 263). Another interesting aspect of the quoted passage is Mussolini's self-representation as the supreme head of book censorship in Fascist Italy. Archival evidence suggests that this was no exaggeration.

In a dictatorial regime whose leader is always keen to read confidential reports from police informers and spies, it should not come as a surprise to discover that the MCP too was being watched over by informers among its ranks. And, indeed, such a situation is what appears from a number of reports in the files of Mussolini's Political Police. The identity of the informer(s) is not explicit but the fact that all the reports were held by the Political Police in a file called 'Ufficio Stampa Capo del Governo' allows us to infer that the confidential information must have started to flow prior to September 1934 (when the press office became the undersecretariat). Indeed, the earliest report dates back to 27 January 1932, informing the police about the general resentment among journalists at the military rigour of Gaetano Polverelli, then head of the press office and future head of the MCP. Polverelli was again the protagonist of a report dated 2 May 1933. This time we are told that he had called in both Mino Maccari and Leo Longanesi (editors, respectively, of the Fascist *strapaesani* journals *Il Selvaggio* and *L'Italiano*) and had ordered them to curb any literary polemics. The report added that it was thought that other Fascists of dubious reputation, such as Curzio Suckert Malaparte and Antonio Aniante, had moved abroad in order to write more liberally. A cluster of more interesting reports refers directly to the period under scrutiny in this chapter. It begins with a report dated May 1937, which, on the eve of the ministry's change of name, dwells on the negative impression created by the creation of the Ministry of Popular Culture, particularly with respect to its implicit competition with the Ministry of National Education. Two months later the informer could already report on the various nicknames attributed to the MCP. The postwar abbreviation *Minculpop* does not appear; instead we have *Ministero dell'Ignoranza Popolare* (Ministry of Popular Ignorance), *Ministero della Cultura Polare* (Ministry of Polar Culture), and the more cryptic *la Milza* ('milza' being the spleen). On a more interesting political level, there are two reports, dated 1 October 1937 and 24 December 1938, about the alleged influence of the Vatican over the MCP's operations. The first report suggested that Alfieri was very close to the powerful Jesuit diplomat Father Tacchi Venturi (whom we have already met in chapter 3) and would often follow his advice. It added that Leopoldo Zurlo, despite his efficiency, had failed to spot the anti-Fascist spirit of Benelli's play, *L'elefante* (1937). The second report went on to allege that, through Tacchi Venturi's recommendations, the MCP had been infiltrated by the Vatican: among its sympathizers at the DGSI were Annibale Sorge (described as a Jesuit), Gastone Spinetti (a member of Azione Cattolica), Aldo Ricci (Casini's secretary, allegedly a Jesuit), and Gherardo Casini himself, who was accused of protecting the Florentine Catholic journal *Frontespizio*.[75] The honesty, and thus Fascist integrity, of the MCP officials was also questioned. On 14 June 1938 an informer warned the police about the fact that different 'pesi e misure' (double standards) were used in order to censor literary and theatrical works. The accusation of bias was then turned into a suspicion of corruption when the following report, dated 8 November, alleged that two of the three readers at the MCP Book Division, Fernando Gori and Renato Loffredo, were 'corruttibili' (corruptible).[76]

It is obvious that such reports should be taken with more than a grain of salt. Informers were renowned for inflating or sometimes inventing a story in order to justify the money received for their services. The general picture formulated by these reports, however, is not far from what emerges from official documents. We have already witnessed the influential presence of Tacchi Venturi in earlier years, and another insider at the MCP, as we will see in chapter 7, publicly commented on the powerful influence of the Jesuit diplomat even during the last years of the regime.[77] This is far from saying that the MCP had become a branch of the Vatican. Suffice it to say that many publications that the Vatican had for years put on its Index of Prohibited Books were freely available in Italy. Among these were the complete works of Gabriele D'Annunzio, Benedetto Croce, and Giovanni Gentile. Padre Tacchi Venturi was allowed to represent the views of the Vatican on matters of religion and morality, but his role was not formally recognized, and archival evidence suggests that his powers were limited to those of an adviser.[78] The accusation of corruption should be interpreted within the context of the unofficial practices and constant exceptions with which officials at the MCP favoured a number of publishers and authors. I would suggest that it was a system that was less corrupt than conveniently flexible in adjusting to individual cases and circumstances.

A more important question is whether Mussolini was ever made privy to these informers' reports. The documents bear no sign that this might have been the case. However, it is likely that if they reached the head of police, Bocchini might have referred to them during his morning meetings with Mussolini. If we consider the report referring to Benelli's play, it is clear that the informer's suggestion was right: the performance and publication of the play did indeed raise criticism of Zurlo's judgment. We also know that Mussolini was involved in this case, so one could suspect that the informer's report might have been the origin of Zurlo's problems.

5 Shaping Italian Literature

New Publishers in Town: Valentino Bompiani and Giulio Einaudi

Valentino Bompiani began his career in publishing under the wing of Arnoldo Mondadori. Hired in 1922, when the firm was still based in Verona, young Bompiani quickly moved from trusted personal secretary to innovative editor, particularly in the field of foreign fiction. By 1928 his ambition drove him first to become director of the Milanese publisher Unitas and a year later to create his own publishing enterprise. Among his early publications of some importance was *Il volto del bolscevismo* by Fülop Miller, published in 1930 with a preface by Curzio Malaparte. It is, however, in the field of fiction that Bompiani was to concentrate his efforts, carving his own niche within Italy's publishing world. Bompiani was quickly able to secure books by established Italian authors such as Massimo Bontempelli and Giuseppe Borgese and promising young writers such as Cesare Zavattini, Paola Masino, and, some years later, Alberto Moravia and Corrado Alvaro.

A number of censorship cases – most notably the one related to Vittorini's *Americana* in the early 1940s – have helped to establish the view of Valentino Bompiani as a moderate anti-Fascist, discreetly defending the values of freedom and democracy against the regime's authoritarian presence. The archival documentation at both the publishing house and in state archives reveals a more complex situation. Although Valentino Bompiani never reached the levels of militant pro-Fascism of Attilio Vallecchi or the obsequious affectation of Arnoldo Mondadori, there is little doubt that, from the start, he adopted a spirit of collaboration – perhaps the only option to guarantee a financially profitable enterprise – which strongly differed from that of publishers such as Laterza and Einaudi. In this respect, his work experience at Mondadori must have been invaluable. As early as 1931, for example, Bompiani adopted a practice similar to that of his ex-employer: he asked directly for Mussolini's *nulla osta*. This episode relates to the publication of Vincenzo Morello's study of the Lateran Pacts, *Il conflitto dopo la Conciliazione*. A week later Mussolini replied with his imprimatur.[1] During the same period Bompiani requested and was granted a personal meeting with Mussolini which took place on 30 May 1932.[2] Some months later Bompiani sent Mussolini a copy of an article he had published in the newspaper *La Tribuna*, in which he supported the idea of the creation of a publishing consortium to sponsor the sale of Italian books abroad. In Bompiani's words, this initiative was 'in harmony with these times of astounding creation and prodigious expansion of Italianness in the world.[3]

The case of the publication of Hitler's *Mein Kampf* provides a good example of his relations with the regime. In the run up to the German national elections of 1933, Mussolini had secretely acquired the rights for an Italian translation of Hitler's 'bible,' in return for financial help for a total of 250,000 lire. Mondadori was once again Mussolini's first port of call, but after his polite refusal – Mondadori was probably sceptical about the commercial prospects of such a hefty book – the second option was Bompiani who, in July 1933, enthusiastically accepted the offer.[4] In March 1934 Hitler provided a preface, and the book was published in the same month. It achieved some success, as a third reprint was issued by September. In his postwar memoirs Valentino Bompiani attributed the idea of publishing *La mia battaglia* to the Jewish translator Angelo Treves and made no mention of his own correspondence with the regime – a regrettable omission.[5] An interesting detail is that when Gaetano Polverelli, the head of Mussolini's press office, contacted the prefect of Milan to instruct him to get in touch with Bompiani about Hitler's book, he mentioned that Bompiani should be contacted 'verbalmente' (verbally). Once more an effort was made to avoid an embarrassing paper trail. Regardless, Bompiani's interest is documented beyond doubt in his reply to Polverelli of 27 July 1933 in which he fully accepted Il Duce's proposal. The book was eventually divided into two volumes, similar to the original version. However, they did not appear at the same time. The first came out in 1934 in Bompiani's progaganda series *Libri scelti* with the title *La mia battaglia*. It actually corresponded to the second volume of the original, containing Hitler's ideological manifesto. The first volume, which contained an autobiographical account and was considered less interesting to the Italian reader, was shortened to about

10. Publicity poster for the publication of Hitler's *La mia vita* (Bompiani, 1938), which coincided with Hitler's official visit to Italy in May 1938. (*Courtesy of Archivio di Stato, Milan*)

one hundred pages. Four years later Bompiani decided to publish the full first half of *Mein Kampf* in the same pro-Fascist series *Libri scelti*.[6] The timing could not have been more appropriate. The book, entitled *La mia vita*, reached the bookshops on the eve of Hitler's second and most important official visit to Italy, in May 1938. For the occasion Bompiani prepared a publicity poster that, after receiving the *nulla osta* of Gherardo Casini, head of DGSI, on 25 April 1938, was distributed to all the major bookshops in Florence, Milan, and Rome. The caption 'Willkommen!' (Welcome!) was an obvious invitation to display the poster in the shop windows (see figure 10). This new edition proved a commercially astute venture: by 1943 *La mia vita* had reached its nineteenth reprint.[7]

As for censorship, a first case concerning Bompiani relates to Paola Masino's early work. Written in Paris, where Masino and her partner Massimo Bontempelli had been living since the previous year, her first novel, *Monte Ignoso*, was published by Bompiani in 1931. The violent and crude aspects of the plot – a surreal story of domestic madness – had put Bompiani on the alert. He tried to convince Masino to revise the manuscript but to no avail. When it came to her next novel, *Periferia* – a story of children living in the outskirts of a city – he once again tried to convince her of the need to polish some of the rougher edges off the work, particularly its attacks on family life and motherhood. In her study of Masino, Lucia Re describes Bompiani's intervention as 'a first critique (and attempted censorship).'[8] It is arguable that Bompiani's preoccupations were political as much as literary, because the themes touched upon in Masino's novels were the kind of topics that the regime was attempting to eradicate from the national press. Similarly non-committal was the 'fascetta' (the publisher's advertisement) that Bompiani proposed to attach to the book: 'Pubblico per dovere contrattuale questo libro bellissimo e insopportabile' (I publish under contractual obligation this beautiful and exasperating book). To Bompiani's credit, he withdrew his suggestions for modifications to both novels, and the books faced the critics unmodified.[9] *Monte Ignoso* was welcomed by the judges of the well-regarded Viareggio Prize – it won the Gold Medal – but Carlo Emilio Gadda dismissed it in the pages of *Solaria*.[10] Two years later, *Periferia* faced harsh criticism from Fascist papers such as *Il Secolo fascista* and *Provincia di Vercelli* (newspaper of the local Fascist federation), but it found supporters among judges of the Viareggio Prize, and with Fascist papers such as *Bibliografia fascista*, Interlandi's *L'Impero* (an enthusiastic review by Marcello Gallian), and *Quadrivio* (from the pen of film director and co-editor of *Quadrivio* Luigi Chiarini).[11] *Periferia*, like

Monte Ignoso, was never banned by the official censors, but it is interesting to note that Mussolini did not abstain from intervening. The damning review published in *Provincia di Vercelli* must have reached Mussolini's desk because, the following week, he sent a telegram to the prefect of Vercelli instructing him to compliment the reviewer for his harsh criticism of the 'angoli morti della letteratura e relativi romanzi nei quali si ignora la rivoluzione' (the dead corners of literature and the novels produced which ignore the revolution).[12] Clear censorship struck some years later when, in 1938, Masino's short story 'Fame' was published in Cesare Zavattini's literary magazine, *Le grandi firme* (a Mondadori periodical). In keeping with Masino's by then characteristically crude settings, 'Fame' tells the story of a father whose life of misery and starvation ends with the planned murder of his own children. The short story had already appeared in a less renowned journal, *Espero*, in 1933, but it caught the attention of Mussolini when it was reprinted. Enraged and offended by such a despairing portrait of an Italian family, he ordered the closure of the magazine.[13] When Masino prepared a collection of short stories in 1941, 'Fame' was originally to be included. Bompiani once more tried to make her change her mind, and this time he was successful: *Racconto grosso e altri* encountered no opposition from the censoring authorities.[14]

A second case that took place in the mid-1930s concerns a novel by Marcello Gallian. By then Gallian was a relatively popular revolutionary Fascist who, as we saw in chapter 4, benefited from the protection of Mussolini and Galeazzo Ciano. In 1935 Gallian had become a Bompiani author. His sixth novel, *Il soldato postumo,* came out in that year and was positively reviewed by a young Romano Bilenchi in the pages of Mussolini's *Il Popolo d'Italia.* Bilenchi presented his doubts about the crude, *maudit* realism of Gallian but at the same time praised the representation of the sense of disillusionment of revolutionary Fascists who had dreamt of a more radical anti-bourgeois reformation of Italian society.[15]

When it came to the next novel of this prolific author, it seems as if everybody had come to the conclusion that the time had come for Gallian's radicalism to be contained. The novel, *Bassofondo,* tells the story of another disillusioned revolutionary Fascist defeated by the forces of conservatism, this time embodied by the borgeois corruption of Rome – 'la porca città' (the bastard city) as the protagonist describes it. It was printed in December 1935 by the small Milan publishing house Panorama, which was active between 1935 and 1940. On 17 January 1936 the prefecture of Milan proceeded to seize all copies of the book. The prefecture's press office had found the novel to be in need of radical changes: it demanded that some risqué passages and the entire last four chapters be cut. Gallian and Panorama's editors agreed to comply with the orders in exchange for the permission to make use of sections of the already printed and sequestrated edition in order to save some production costs. There is no sign of any intervention from above, and, indeed, Gallian's biographer states that during those very months Gallian seemed to lose the preferential treatment that he had enjoyed for years. However, a letter from Pamorama's director, Rinaldo Galanti to Gallian, written on the same day the police raided the offices of Panorama and seized the novel, suggests that Gallian was about to seek help from Ciano.[16] On 31 January 1936 Gallian's mother had written to Mussolini, asking him to remove the ban imposed by the prefecture of Milan (Gallian at the time was ill in bed). No reply seems to have arrived. An internal memo by an official at the prefecture, dated 2 February 1936, reports that a request had arrived from the Ministry for the Press and propaganda asking the prefecture not to destroy the seized copies of *Bassofondo*. Valentino Bompiani had been informed of the situation by telephone and according to the memo was going to Rome within a fortnight to discuss the matter with Stroppolatini, an official at the ministry. The *nulla osta* from the Ministry for the Press and Propaganda eventually arrived on 17 July 1936 and a modified text of the novel reappeared that autumn under a different title – *In fondo al quartiere* – and without the original last four chapters. In the same year Gallian had published another novel with Panorama, *Tre generazioni*, and its epigraph proclaims the author's relationship with Ciano: 'A Galeazzo Ciano, uomo eroico, questo libro dedico con affetto e con fedeltà' (To Galeazzo Ciano, heroic man, I dedicate this book with affection and faithfulness).[17] Another novel that the prolific Gallian wrote in 1936 and published the following year is *Quasi metà della vita*, printed by Vallecchi and containing another dedication to Ciano. This time the press office of the prefecture of Florence (presumably in the person of Achille Malavasi) considered the proofs in need of some small revisions. On 23 December 1936 Attilio Vallecchi informed Gallian that the prefecture had asked for corrections to five pages of the novel. Unfortunately once more we do not have the original manuscript or proofs, so it is not possible to say with certainty what the changes were to the novel when it was published a few months later.[18]

Despite these setbacks, Gallian continued to receive financial support from the regime. On 19 February 1941 Celso Luciano, then *Capo di*

Gabinetto at the Ministry of Popular Culture (MCP) received a request from Mussolini's office to help Gallian find a permanent position. Luciano's irritable reply of 23 February was that Gallian had been receiving financial help througout the 1930s: a typed list of all the grants awarded showed that between January 1933 and July 1939, Gallian had received a total of 100,856 lire, not including a monthly cheque for 3,000 lire, which he was still receiving.[19]

Another case of a writer whose political commitment and anti-bourgeois stance made him a likely subject of censorship was Corrado Alvaro. At the time of the murder of the Socialist member of Parliament Giacomo Matteotti, Alvaro had publicly stated his opposition to the regime and had signed Croce's manifesto of anti-Fascist intellectuals. In later years, however, he had become closer to intellectuals on the fringes of the regime such as Massimo Bontempelli and Curzio Malaparte (of whose journal, *900*, he became assistant-editor in 1926).[20] Alvaro's most controversial piece of work was the novel *L'uomo è forte*, set in a unspecified totalitarian country that, although clearly modelled on Soviet Russia (which he had visited in 1934 as a correspondent for *La Stampa*), could nonetheless be interpreted as allegory of Fascist Italy. Once the proofs were ready, Bompiani decided to send them directly to the General Directorate for the Italian Press (DGSI) at the MCP for a preventive check. On 13 May 1938 the ministry replied that, after 'contatti con l'Autore,' it had been agreed that the novel would be preceded by a short 'Avvertenza' (Warning) and have nine passages modified.[21] In a postwar introduction to the novel, Alvaro clarified that the *Avvertenza* had been imposed so that he could state explicitly that the story referred to the USSR. He also added that the original title of the novel was *Paura sul mondo*, which was changed to *L'uomo è forte* at the request of the censor. Although this change is not confirmed by the documentation, there is reason to believe that it was part of the negotiations between the MCP and the author. It should also be noted that in a letter of 4 May 1938, Bompiani wrote that he was worried about the fact that Russia was not mentioned in the book. He advised Alvaro to point this out to Casini during their next meeting. On 11 and 13 May 1938 Alvaro was able to write to Bompiani that the meeting with an unnamed official at the MCP (on 11 May Casini was ill in bed) had gone well and only a few changes to the text had been imposed. Alvaro also added that, over the phone, Casini had told him that the first reservations against the novel had been raised by an inexperienced official at the MCP.[22]

By 1938 Fascist propaganda had turned against the Soviet Union. Thus it is not surprising that, particularly because of its clear Soviet connection, *L'uomo è forte* received positive reviews, among which was that of Giuseppe Villaroel, literary critic of *Il Popolo d'Italia*. By March 1939 Bompiani was distributing a third reprint of the novel; the following year he could boast that it was being tranlated into French, Swedish, and Hungarian.[23]

Another interesting case concenrs the novel *Di padre in figlio* by the relatively unknown author Mario Sobrero. Once more, Bompiani sent the proofs of the book directly to the DGSI, whose reply on 30 September 1938 is a good example of the language used by the censors to 'suggest' modifications:

> Nel romanzo che descrive la vita di alcune famiglie italiane durante il periodo compreso tra il 1892 e il 1914 si parla di un deputato antinazionale, Metello Farra, che fa propaganda contro la guerra, che incita i soldati a non partire per l'Africa e manda squadre a tagliare i fili del telegrafo (pag. 163).
>
> Questo Ministero concede il nulla osta alla diffusione, ma nello stesso tempo ritiene opportuno che l'Autore inserisca dove crederà più adatto, anche una sola frase che esprima un giudizio di riprovazione sulla figura morale del deputato Farra.

> The novel, describing the life of some Italian families during the 1892–1914 period, talks about an anti-nationalist MP, Metello Farra, who engages in anti-war propaganda and incites soldiers not to leave for Africa and sends people on missions to cut telegraph wires (page 163).
>
> This Ministry grants its *nulla osta* to the distribution, but at the same time suggests the insertion by the author, where he thinks most appropriate, of even a single sentence in which a negative judgment is expressed with regard to the moral figure of MP Farra.

Sobrero complied with the request, adding some words of condemnation – a simple comment stating that Farra's family was deeply ashamed of his actions. Casini at the MCP gave his final *nulla osta* on 17 October 1938 and the book was duly published a few weeks later.[24]

Let us now move on to Giulio Einaudi Editore. Founded in 1933 around the two journals *La Cultura* and *La Riforma sociale*, Einaudi in its early days was carefully guided by Giulio's father, Luigi Einaudi, the renowned liberal economist and senator who in the postwar years was to become the second president of Italy. The company had a relatively slow start, considering that only nine books were published in 1933 and eleven in 1934. Soon, however, the paternal guidance was supplemented by that of the young duo Leone Ginzburg and Cesare Pavese, whose militant interests in contemporary culture were to expand Einaudi business in the realm of historical and literary studies. As Luisa Mangoni shows in her extensive study, the common aim among the members of this early group, despite their different interests, was to defend a culture that was in many respects an alternative to the Fascist-sponsored one.[25] Ginzburg was to become the prime move behind Einaudi (and his wife Natalia was right, years later, to lament how Giulio Einaudi failed to recognize this in his disappointingly vague postwar memoirs).[26]

The Einaudi family was not unfamiliar with the forces of Fascist law and order. In addition to Luigi Einaudi's passive opposition to the regime, his youngest son, twenty-two-year-old Roberto, had been arrested on 22 March 1929 while in possession of anti-Fascist posters. On that occasion, the police established that Roberto's typewriter had been used to compose articles for the underground journal *L'alto Parlante*. Luigi Einaudi personally wrote to and met with Mussolini to plead for his son and indeed managed to secure his immediate release followed by a simple police warning. As in the case of Benedetto Croce, it is evident that Mussolini intended to show a degree of compassion and tolerance towards some of the most renowned senior members of Italy's liberal culture.[27]

Given the anti-Fascist sentiment reigning in the Einaudi family, it is not surprising that, as soon as the publishing house was set up, a police informer identified it as a centre of opposition to the regime. Giuseppe Bottai was also quick to pigeon-hole Einaudi, together with Laterza, as 'an Italian publisher that ignores the fact that we are in the twelfth year of the Fascist Era.'[28] Indeed, only a few months after the publisher's inception, in March 1934 Leone Ginzburg was arrested as a member of the anti-Fascist liberal group Giustizia e Libertà. He was to spend the following two years in prison, although even in such restricted conditions he continued his work as editor and translator for Einaudi.

Giulio Einaudi was well aware of the dangers to the survival of his company were his books to step too far from Fascist orthodoxy. The first encounter with the censoring authorities was similar to those of other, more orthodox publishers such as Mondadori. It concerned the posthumous publication of a volume of wartime memoirs, *Diario di guerra*, by the ex-socialist leader Leonida Bissolati. As had happened to other memoirs that were partly critical of the conduct of the Italian army during the First World War, the book was earmarked for sequestration. From Einaudi, both father and son wrote in protest, the former to Mussolini, the latter to the prefect of Turin, expressing their disbelief at the categorization of such a book as contrary to the directives of the regime. Luigi Einaudi went so far as to ask for a meeting with Mussolini so that he could explain the choice of Bissolati's work, which he had personally selected. Einaudi's file in Mussolini's office archive Segreteria Particolare shows that Il Duce was involved in the seizure of the book. Among the documents, there is a reader's report, presumably from the press office of the Turin prefecture, highlighting all the passages where the Italian army command is criticized. In the margin, a note says: 'postilla di S. E. il Capo del Governo: "sequestrare / M"' ('note by His Excellency the Head of Government: "seize / M"'). Mussolini must have been on holiday at the time because his order is recorded as coming from the seaside resort of Riccione, near his native Predappio, dated 29 June 1934. A second rider, this time by Mussolini's secretary, Osvaldo Sebastiani, adds: 'telefonare al Prefetto di Torino di sequestrare tutto e di diffidare il figlio Einaudi dal fare l'editore' (telephone the Turin prefect to seize everything and to warn Einaudi to stop his publishing activity).[29] Because only Mussolini could have been the source of such a draconian order, we can guess that Sebastiani added his rider after a telephone conversation with his boss. This might also be the reason why, with the threat of an abrupt end of Giulio Einaudi's publishing activity, his father decided to exercise as much influence as he could over the dictator. And, once more, he was successful. Not only was the publishing house allowed to survive, but Bissolati's memoirs received the *nulla osta*. Eight months after this incident, Giulio Einaudi could inform one of his editors that *Diario di guerra* was about to be published in its untouched original form.[30]

Leone Ginzburg's arrest was not to be Einaudi's only brush with Fascist law and order. Thanks to the help of a police informer with privileged access to Turin's literary circles, particularly among the Jewish community, on 15 May 1935 the police were able to round up most of the militants and more or less all active collaborators with the Turin cell of Giustizia e Libertà. The police informer was the successful commercial novelist Dino Segre, alias Pitigrilli, who in years to come would himself become a victim of Fascist repression. Among the two hundred people arrested on that day figured a number of Einaudi staff: Giulio Einaudi and Luigi Salvatorelli were soon released with no charges, but

Massimo Mila was sentenced to seven years and Cesare Pavese was sent to *confino* for a year. The two Einaudi journals were also suppressed.[31] The publishing house was allowed to continue its existence, although it published only eight books in 1937 and sixteen in 1938. The famous series *Narratori stranieri tradotti* (Translated foreign narrators), edited by Ginzburg and Pavese saws its first volume in 1938. It was the eve of the war before Einaudi was able to establish itself as a full fledged publishing enterprise. One key to its survival was a constant process of self-censorship. Many books never reached the production stage simply because Einaudi's editors predicted a likely intervention by the censors. As Luisa Mangoni suggests, a proper history of Einaudi's struggles in those years should include an account of all the projects that never went past the editors' boardroom.[32]

In its early years Einaudi devoted limited attention to the modern fiction sector. As a consequence, Pavese's activity as a translator of contemporary novels would often find an outlet with other publishers such as Mondadori and Bompiani. There we can find some examples of how, when working as a translator, Pavese was prepared to manipulate his skills in order to avoid censorship. When submitting the manuscript of his translation of Dos Passos's *The Big Money* to Mondadori in June 1937, Pavese made the following comment: 'Ho seguito scrupolosamente i consigli del Ministero cioè inglesizzato i nomi italiani, lasciato cadere gli accenni a Lenin e sovieti, cancellato o sostituito un accenno al fascismo, taciuto o tradotto con dignità *wop* and *dago*' (I have scrupulously followed the ministry's suggestions, that is, I have anglisized all Italian names, cut all mention of Lenin and the Soviets, deleted or replaced any mention of Fascism, omitted or translated with dignity *wop* and *dago*).[33]

Giulio Einaudi also managed to maintain good relations with the regime throughout the second half of the 1930s through the collaboration of personalities such as General Ambrogio Bollati, chief editor of the journal *Rivista coloniale*, whose works on military history had the personal support of Mussolini and fell well within a pan-Fascist interpretation of Italy's history. General Bollati and Mussolini had discussed two of the former's projects: *I rovesci più caratteristici degli eserciti nella guerra mondiale 1914–1918* and *Enciclopedia dei nostri combattimenti coloniali*, both published by Einaudi in 1936. In collaboration with General Giulio Del Bono, Bollati also wrote an openly pro-Fascist two-volume history of the Spanish Civil War (*La guerra di Spagna*), which was published by Einaudi in 1937 and 1939. Both the encylopedia and the volumes on the Spanish

Civil War were dropped from the Einaudi list in 1945 and were left unmentioned in the catalogue that celebrated fifty years of Einaudi's activity.[34]

The Excesses of Left-Wing Fascism: Elio Vittorini and Romano Bilenchi

In the early 1930s Tuscany, and Florence in particular, could boast a vibrant cultural life linked to the Fascist movement. After the violent *squadrismo* of the early years – which climaxed with the assassination, among others, of the Socialist MP Gateano Pilati in October 1925 – Florentine Fascism had been put in the reliable hands of a young, ambitious Fascist, Alessandro Pavolini, who in 1929 became *Federale* – that is, local head of the PNF – of Florence at the young age of twenty-six. Pavolini was sympathetic to revolutionary Fascists – often called left-wing Fascists – and to their demands for an anti-bourgeois renovation of Italian society in line with the radical principles of the first Fascist manifesto of 1919. Pavolini had also founded and directed *Il Bargello*, the official weekly of the Florentine Fascist Federation, a paper that quickly established itself as a lively arena in which young radical Fascists could make their debut as journalists and social commentators.[35] Among them were Elio Vittorini and Romano Bilenchi, both of whom had adopted Florence as their home. Theirs were the voices of young militants who were frustrated and in the long run disillusioned with the lack of progress in Italy's Fascist revolution. And their literary and journalistic production, as we will see, was to test the tolerance of the Florentine prefecture.

Elio Vittorini had various encounters with the Fascist censors: with his novel *Il garofano rosso*, as commissioning editor and translator for Mondadori and Bompiani, and finally with his most famous work, *Conversazione in Sicilia*, in the summer of 1942.

Il garofano rosso was published in instalments in the Florentine literary monthly *Solaria* in 1933–4. At that time Vittorini had published only a collection of short stories and was busy building his reputation as a journalist, critic, and fiction writer. From his native Sicily, he had moved to Florence with his wife and first baby, and he depended on his journalistic work to support his family. His main income came from his collaboration on the third page of Pavolini's *Il Bargello*. By then Vittorini could be described as a radical Fascist, following the lead of Curzio Malaparte, to whom he owed his introduction to the literary world.[36]

Il garofano rosso is a partly autobiographical novel about the first political and sensual experiences of an adolescent living in Syracuse at the time of the Matteotti crisis. The first instalment came out in February 1933 and continued for another five issues until the press office of the prefecture of Florence in August 1934 decided that some of its passages, together with a short story by Enrico Terracini ('Le figlie del generale'), were offensive to public morality. The issue of *Solaria* was ordered to be withdrawn from circulation. The timing of this episode is interesting as it follows by a few months Mussolini's circular of April 1934. Unfortunately, because the archives of the Florentine prefecture have been lost, we can rely only on the correspondence between Vittorini and, among others, the editor of *Solaria*, Alberto Carocci. It is clear from their exchanges that the reason for the censoring was some explicit passages in which the protagonist falls in love with a beautiful prostitute. This is how Carocci announced the censoring of *Solaria* to Vittorini, followed by the latter's reply:

Caro Vittorini,
oramai sei ufficialmente riconosciuto per un pornografo. L'ultimo numero di 'Solaria' è stato sequestrato in questi giorni con decreto prefettizio, a causa del tuo 'Garofano rosso'. Purtroppo è stato un buon profeta. Siccome non voglio sospenderne la pubblicazione, ma d'altra parte bisogna fare in modo di non incorrere in guai più grossi, mandami prestissimo la prossima puntata, più espurgata che puoi: devo sottoporla all'esame dell'Ufficio Stampa della Prefettura.

(Dear Vittorini,
Now you are officially recognized as a pornographer. The latest issue of 'Solaria' has just been confiscated on the order of the prefect because of your 'Garofano rosso.' Unfortunately it has been a good omen. Because I don't intend to suspend its publication, but at the same time we don't want to fall into even more trouble, send me the next chapter as soon as possible, in the cleanest possible form: I must submit it to the press office of the prefecture.)

Caro Alberto,
mi racconti una storia? Io non capisco proprio cosa ci fosse di sequestrabile. Allora perché non sequestrano tutta la buona letteratura italiana dal '300 al '700? Raccontami meglio la cosa e mi rivolgerò a Pavolini per far togliere il sequestro. E *fammi avere una (due) copie della rivista perchè io non ho niente della mia puntata e non posso neanche scrivere il seguito (magari in fogli-macchina).* Però tieni presente che ho moltissimo da fare e che posso mandarti solo una puntata breve se la vuoi proprio presto. (emphasis in the original)[37]

(Dear Alberto,
Are you telling me a story? I don't understand what could have been worth censoring. Why don't they censor all the best Italian literature from the 14th to the 18th century? Let me know about it in more detail and I will contact Pavolini to have the ban removed. And *let me have one (two) copies of the periodical because I haven't got a scrap of my instalment and I can't even write its sequel (even better as typed sheets).* But bear in mind that I have lots to do and that I can send you only a short instalment if you really need it quickly.)

The lack of any political elements in censor's action is confirmed by the wording of the *Decreto Prefettizio* that the editors of *Solaria* were forced to publish in the following issue.[38] It is also interesting that Vittorini should immediately mention Alessandro Pavolini, who at the time had just moved to Rome as an MP and had been appointed by his friend Galeazzo Ciano as head of the Fascist Confederation of Professionals and Artists (Confederazione Fascista Professionisti e Artisti). Indeed, there is little doubt that Vittorini thought of himself as associated with this group of Tuscan Fascist leaders. In a letter of 2 November 1934 to his friend Silvio Guarnieri, he boasted even stronger links with the big and powerful: 'Andrò a Roma da Ciano, quando si tratterà di mettere assieme il volume' (When we get closer to publishing it as a volume, I will go and meet Ciano in Rome).[39] As we will see, the novel was not allowed to appear as a book, but it looks as if Vittorini did receive some personal recognition: the following year Ciano personally awarded him a prize of 2,000 lire for his cultural contribution to *Il Bargello*.[40]

As for *Solaria*, the following issue appeared with the cuts imposed by the Florentine censors, which were, once more, entirely related to risqué passages concerning a prostitute (see figure 11).[41] *Solaria* continued for another two issues, after which it closed down. The financial pressure under which the journal had been straining for years, coupled with the delays created by the interference of the censors, proved too much. Post-war critics have often portrayed this episode as an example of the Fascists' suppression of anti-Fascist culture. Despite its close analysis, Greco's essay is perhaps the most perplexing in its insistence that the explicit passages were censored for political reasons because they challenged the social policies of the regime.[42] Moreover, the hypothesis that the interference might have been an excuse to shut down *Solaria* is unsupported by the facts, including the pre- and postwar memoirs of the people involved. A more plausible interpretation is that the censor believed that the passages were simply offensive to public morality. Vittorini is partly to blame for confusing the issue. In his preface to the postwar edition of *Il garofano rosso*, published in 1948, he stated that the Fascists had censored the fourth instalment (which contains the passages related to the young protagonist's involvement with Fascism). However, as we know, it was the sixth and seventh instalments that were censored (the ones containing the episode with the prostitute). Thus, on the basis of the available documentary evidence it is difficult to support the view of politically motivated censorship. It should also be remembered that Vittorini at the time was a militant Fascist and that *Solaria* had hosted the writings of Fascists leaders such as Giuseppe Bottai and Alessandro Pavolini.[43]

All facts considered, we can suggest that Vittorini's first encounter with censorship was probably a result of the high alert on public morality issues that was created in all prefectures by Mussolini's circular of April 1934. The content of the passages had no political element, excepting that the censor might have found particularly deplorable the notion that the young protagonist, while falling madly in love with a prostitute, was an enthusiastic supporter of the Fascist squads. It should also be noted that by the summer of 1934 Vittorini had already published his thoughts on censorship in the pages of *Il Bargello*. This took the form of an article published in July 1934, 'Censura letteraria.' In the article Vittorini stated his support for the existence of censorship in a Fascist society but pointed to the limitations that resulted from the involvement of conservative-minded civil servants.[44] Vittorini also seemed well informed about the content of Mussolini's circular because, as an example of novels that would always manage to slip through the censors' net, he mentioned 'il romanzetto di Mura.' Judging by the date of Carocci's letter quoted above, it seems as if, by the time he wrote this article, Vittorini did not know what was to going to happen to *Il garofano rosso*. Or perhaps he knew and the article was meant to be a warning signal to the prefecture. Or was the article the reason why the press office decided to bear down on Vittorini's novel? The documentary evidence does not allow for a clear conclusion. However, it can be argued that the censoring of *Il garofano rosso*, if it had any political relevance, had more to do with the boldness of young Fascists like Vittorini, bolstered by the rocketing careers of their Tuscan leaders, rather than with the prefecture plotting to shut down an alleged anti-Fascist journal.[45]

The censor working for the press office of the Prefecture of Florence was Achille Malavasi, former editor of the pro-Fascist Bolognese paper *Il Resto del Carlino* later worked in Florence, teaching German in a secondary

Due volte, alla fine, disse: — Povero piccolo — e mi strinse il mento in una carezza, con un'aria commossa di gratitudine che non riuscivo a capire perché. . . . . . .

. . . .
. . . .
. . . .

A un certo punto il suo sguardo mi riempì di tristezza. Era andata a cercarmi un fazzoletto e nel tornare si fermò d'improvviso con gli occhi traboccanti su di me a guardarni come qualcosa che sarà perduta.

— Mi pare che non vorrei lasciarti più partire — disse, e come io raccolsi la sua mano, piano piano si fece cadere sul letto con parole in bocca da fanciulla.

In quel momento desiderai, e per la prima volta di vero desiderio, ch'ella avesse gli occhi grigi, che fosse in qualche modo anche Giovanna. Pure sentivo che Giovanna era indietro, indietro nella mia vita e che nemmeno a volgermi e ritornare sui miei passi l'avrei più ritrovata vicino al cuore. Solo i suoi occhi scolori erano ancora una grigia bontà rimasta fuori nel mondo, e da andare a raccogliere e condurre dentro alla mia donna bionda.

— Se tu fossi anche Giovanna! — le dissi, impetuosamente.

Ed essa non si rivoltò, non si profuse, come un'altra avrebbe fatto, in affermazioni di se stessa; però non seppe dimenticare, e, divenuta loquace, di continuo tornava sull'argomento.

— Io non capisco — disse tra l'altro — se le volevi bene perché non te la sei presa? . . . .
. . . .
. . . .
. . . .

Pronunciò le ultime parole quasi con un accento d'invocazione. Ma io m'ero fermato a quelle, e m'avevano fatto fremere, che per la prima volta mi davano di Giovanna un'idea di una cosa da prendere. . . . .

75

11. Page of the seventh instalment of Elio Vittorini's *Il garofano rosso*, published with censorial cuts (dotted lines) in *Solaria*, November 1934. (Underlining was added by a careless reader at the National Library.) (*Courtesy of Biblioteca Nazionale Centrale, Florence*)

school and collaborating with the prefecture.[46] A few months after the Vittorini case, Malavasi showed a degree of tolerance when it came to approving the proofs of Cesare Pavese's collection of poems, *Lavorare stanca*, published by Parenti for Edizioni di Solaria. At the time of the second submission of the proofs, in May 1935, Pavese was arrested and sent into *confino*, as shown by his correspondence with his editor at the time of his relocation from Turin to the Calabrian village of Brancaleone. Despite the evident anti-Fascist stigma of Pavese and the fact that some poems ('Il Dio Caprone' in particular) were deemed morally unsuited, Malavasi proceeded to authorize the publication of the book, which came out in the spring of 1936. Even in this case Malavasi's preoccupation seemed to be related to the marginally obscene content of certain passages. As Pavese clearly stated in a letter to Carocci of 11 March 1935, 'Mi attendevo l'onore della censura politica e quelli me la fanno puritana' (I was expecting the honour of a political censorship and instead they come up with a puritanical one).[47]

In the months following the censorship of *Il garofano rosso* Vittorini continued to be a journalist for *Il Bargello* and a supporter of the regime. He particularly admired Galeazzo Ciano, as can be gauged from a brief article that he published in *Il Bargello* at the time of the creation of the Ministry for the Press and Propaganda in 1935. Vittorini hailed the promotion of Ciano's department to a full-fledged ministry with the following introduction: 'I ragazzi in gamba del Fascismo hanno in Galeazzo Ciano il loro rappresentante naturale presso Mussolini.' (The good boys of Fascism have in Galeazzo Ciano their natural representative by Mussolini's side). As the rest of the article made it clear, Vittorini saw in Ciano the leader of the youngest generation of Fascist militants on whose shoulders rested the renovation of Fascism.[48] In five articles published between September 1935 and July 1936, he hailed the invasion of Ethiopia as a perfect occasion for organizing the colonies along corporatist lines and excluding private capital.

The turning point for Vittorini came in the summer of 1936, with the Fascist intervention in the Spanish Civil War. During the initial wavering of the Fascist regime with respect to General Franco's insurrection (in an editorial of 19 July 1936, *Il Popolo d'Italia* dismissed the insurrection as an isolated case), Vittorini immediately sided with the left-wing republican government. He was disgusted by the reactionary, pro-Catholic views of Franco and by the immediate support that the insurrection had been given by the Vatican press. It is at this time that Vittorini had his first encounter with a form of political censorship. An informer (allegedly a waiter at the Caffé Giubbe Rosse) had reported that Vittorini was publicly criticizing Mussolini for his decision to side with Franco. As a result, he was called in by the police on 3 October 1936 and given a formal warning. In response, Vittorini wrote a long letter in which he apologized, listing his Fascist credentials and confirming his firm support for the regime.[49]

We can date the start of Vittorini's disillusionment with Fascism from this time. If the Spanish Civil War had proven to him that Mussolini's regime was becoming reactionary, the warning by the police (who refused to expunge his criminal record despite the letter of apology) had illustrated the diminishing freedom of speech even among Fascists. Another pivotal moment was the assassination of Carlo and Nello Rosselli in the summer of 1937. Vittorini was not a member of Giustizia e Libertà; however, among the papers found in Carlo Rosselli's possession at the time of his death, the police had found a list of addresses to whom propaganda material had been sent, and Vittorini's Florentine address was among them. As a result, an investigation was launched by the prefecture of Florence, but a final report stated that there was no proof of Vittorini's active involvement in any anti-Fascist movement.[50] Without speculating too much, one can say that for Vittorini the news of the assassination of the Rosselli brothers might have come as one more shocking realization of the reactionary, dark side of Fascism.

The novel *Conversazione in Sicilia* was born out of similar tensions. Written in the wake of the Spanish Civil War (not surprisingly, Italo Calvino later described it a 'Guernica novel'), it openly shows Vittorini's disillusionment and, less explicitly, his criticism of the regime. The novel was first published in instalments in the Florentine journal *Letteratura*, which Alessandro Bonsanti had founded in 1937 after the collapse of *Solaria*. It appeared in five instalments between April 1938 and April 1939. At this stage, the publication of the novel did not prompt any negative response among Fascist literary circles, although it was subjected to minor censorship. Bonsanti remembers being contacted by Achille Malavasi about some complaints from Sicily with regard to Vittorini's representation of the island as a poverty-stricken land.[51] The text, however, does not seem to have changed in that respect. The last line of the novel – '"Ed è molto soffrire?" chiesero i siciliani' ('and is suffering too much?' asked the Sicilians) – is missing, but this could have been the author's decision: that ending was to change again between postwar editions. However, a careful look at the text shows one minor sign of the censor's presence, and it is not related to Sicilian poverty. In this case we can infer that the intervention had a political element. Only three lines were cut and substituted with dotted lines: they refer to the end of chapter 43, where the mother of the protagonist receives the news of the death of her son in the Spanish Civil War. A passage that had a woman announcing the news with the expression 'Madre fortunata!' (Lucky mother!) has been cut, presumably because the rhetorical announcement imitated the regime's own rhetoric regarding soldiers who had sacrified their lives for the nation.[52] During the war years, when *Conversazione in Sicilia* was published in one volume, problems were to arise with regard to the novel's second reprint. Because this episode is closely linked to other events taking place at that time, we will postpone its treatment until chapter 6.

In the late 1930s Vittorini had also been working as an editor and as a translator from English. He started as a translator for Mondadori in February 1933 and seemed to be well aware of the self-censoring practices adopted by publishing houses. While working on his very first translation, that of D.H. Lawrence's novel *St Mawr,* he proposed cutting a passage that contained a derogatory reference to Fascist Italy. According to him, it was 'una frase insulsà, giustificabile solo allora, e da parte di uno straniero' (a disgusting sentence, only justifiable at the time and if written by a foreigner). Arnoldo Mondadori gave his approval and added, 'Naturalmente lasciamo a Lei di togliere o modificare quegli altri puntiche, a Suo guidizio, potrebbero riuscire meno accetti al pubblico italiano' (We naturally leave it to you whether to cut or modify other passages which, in your opinion, might be offensive to the Italian public). Interestingly, when the novel was reprinted in 1946, Mondadori personally wrote to Vittorini and asked him to reinstate the self-censored passage.[53]

A similar episode of editorial self-censorship took place some years later, with the translation of Steinbeck's *Tortilla Flat,* published by Bompiani in 1939. Regional pride may have had a part in this as Vittorini omitted to translate some passages containing the scene of the drunken protagonist shouting abuse at a group of Sicilian Americans, calling them 'Sicilian bastards,' 'scum,' and 'dogs.' A year later, while translating Steinbeck's *In Dubious Battle,* it was the turn of Eugenio Montale, who informed Bompiani that he had cut two unfortunate references to Italy, and every reference to communism.[54]

A friend of both Vittorini and Montale, Romano Bilenchi had arrived in Florence from his native Colle di Val d'Elsa in central Tuscany. He had already started to write for Fascist publications, mainly thanks to

Mino Maccari, founder of the journal *Il Selvaggio* and one of the most brilliant and impertinent minds among radical Fascists. In Florence, Bilenchi had become particularly close to Berto Ricci, whose journal *L'Universale*, founded in 1931, was an attempt to create a political platform among young revolutionary Fascists. Bilenchi remembers in 1933 being called in with Ricci by the prefect of Florence, who asked them to justify the radicalism of their ideas. The prefect at the time was Luigi Maggioni, a diplomat who had served in Luigi Facta's liberal government. According to Bilenchi, Maggioni was tolerant and understanding, and the two young men were allowed to continue their activities.

A more tense encounter took place when the two young writers decided to edit the letters of Dino Garrone, a young radical Fascist and close friend of Ricci who had died in Paris on 10 December 1931. Bilenchi finalized the manuscript while Ricci was fighting as a volunteer during the Ethiopian war. Once the book was submitted to the censor of the Florentine prefecture (who had already censored some letters by Garrone that Ricci had intended to publish in *L'Universale*), a number of disrespectful references to living Fascists, including Mussolini, were deemed excessive. Bilenchi was called in by Achille Malavasi, who asked for the removal of a number of passages. Bilenchi stalled the negotiations with the excuse that he wanted to wait for Ricci's return from Palermo, where he had been sent as a secondary school teacher on his return from the war. Ricci was not prepared to budge, as is clear from his correspondence with Bilenchi – suffice it to quote a comment in a letter dated 9 March 1937: 'Mi sembra che si esageri con questo tagliare i coglioni a chi li ha ... Non cedere. Nel libro non c'è da tagliar nulla' (It seems to me that they are going over the top with this cutting the balls off people who really have them ... Do not give in. There is nothing to be cut in that book).[55] From Palermo, Ricci invoked the intervention of another Tuscan Fascist leader, Gherardo Casini, the head of the MCP's DGSI. After some initial promises, however, the manuscript came back from the MCP with even more requests for cuts (among them an irreverent reference to Malaparte). Following an unsuccessful meeting with Malavasi, Ricci decided to aim for the top. Thanks to the help of his friend Giorgio Pini, chief editor of Mussolini's *Il Popolo d'Italia*, Ricci managed to present his case to Mussolini himself. A fortnight later Mussolini returned the manuscript and had a long telephone conversation with Pini. He agreed with most of the censors' requests but in order to show his appreciation for Ricci's work – which he knew from articles for *Il Popolo d'Italia* – he was prepared to allow the editors to leave some of the critical comments directed at his person. Whether intentional or not, it was a cunning move: Ricci and Bilenchi were so touched by his words that they decided to accept the censors' requests.[56] In order to make his approval of the book publicly known, at the time of its publication – in January 1938, by Vallecchi – Mussolini received Ricci, Bilenchi, and Garrone's widow in his office. Yet the regime's support for these figures was not unwavering. In the same year, Bilenchi's project of a literary review was turned down by the MCP and the same fate was reserved for Ricci's *L'Universale*, first closed down during the Ethiopian war – following an order politely given by Ciano during a meeting with Bilenchi – and then after Ricci tried to resuscitate it in 1938.[57]

The debut of Bilenchi's narrative work took place in the pages of Maccari's *Il Selvaggio*, which serialized *Vita di Pisto* between April and September 1931. The following year another work, *Cronaca dell'Italia meschina ovvero Storia dei Socialisti di Colle*, was serialized in *Il Bargello*. But the book that raised a few eyebrows at the prefecture of Florence was a collection of short stories, *Il capofabbrica: Racconti*, published in 1935. Emboldened by his then regular collaboration with Mussolini's *Il Popolo d'Italia*, Bilenchi wrote a short story – 'Il capofabbrica' – that closely reflected his ideals of revolutionary Fascism. The plot, focusing on the contrast and eventual friendship between the young bourgeois Fascist working in his father's factory (an image with clear autobiographical traits) and a militant communist worker, was politically unorthodox to say the least. According to Bilenchi, finding a publisher proved difficult: both Turinese publisher Buratti and Florentine Vallecchi withdrew their interest. Thanks to the help of some friends – among whom were Ungaretti and Bontempelli – Bilenchi eventually managed to secure the publication of the book with the small Roman publisher Edizioni di 'Circoli.'[58] The price was a softening of the pan-communist ending of 'Il capofabbrica.' After its publication, the short story that gave its title to the collection caught the attention of the underground network of militants in the Italian Communist Party. Indeed, on a radio program broadcast in Italian from Moscow by communist militant Ottavio Pastore, the book was quoted as an example of the left-wing aspirations of young Fascists. Bilenchi was called in first at the MCP and then by the deputy head of police in Siena and asked to justify his political ideas.[59] It does not seem that the book was subject to censorship or seizure, but Bilenchi's disillusionment with Fascism eventually saw his progression towards communism and active militancy during the war years. His changed political ideals influenced his own literary output and produced a case of 'retrospective self-censorship.' Bilenchi so resented his early, openly pro-Fascist works than in a letter to Vallecchi, in February 1942, he asked the publisher to withdraw all copies of his *Storia dei socialisti di Colle* from circulation. It was a brave decision, considering the risks involved in asking a publisher with proven Fascist credentials and in contact with Mussolini to withdraw a book that had once been published in a periodical founded by Pavolini, then minister of the MCP.[60]

Close but Not too Close: Massimo Bontempelli and Alberto Moravia

If Vittorini and Bilenchi lent Fascism their youthful enthusiasm and political commitment throughout much of the 1930s, the pair of authors considered in this next section were more lukewarm followers. There is little doubt that both Massimo Bontempelli and Alberto Moravia did not have a particular interest in active politics. Their literary work was by far a more important preoccupation. Yet, they did not refrain from contact with Fascist personalities. Indeed, until the mid-1930s they by and large sought and benefited from these acquaintances. In later years, the nature of these contacts resulted in different groups within the regime adopting a variety of attitudes towards these writers once their work fell foul of Fascist censorship.

After a brief flirtation with the futurist movement, by the early 1920s Massimo Bontempelli was busy forging his own narrative style – realismo magico – and establishing himself nationally as a critic and a leading intellectual. In 1926 he and Malaparte founded the literary magazine *900*, which was meant to widen the horizon of the Italian literary arena. Despite its professed cosmopolitanism, it was fully in tune with the *Novecentismo* art movement openly supported by Mussolini's then lover and influential adviser on cultural matters, Margherita Sarfatti. From the archive of Mussolini's office, we know that Bontempelli wrote to Mussolini on 12 May 1927 to thank him for his promise to openly support *900*. We do not know what form Mussolini's promise took, but in a letter of 12 January 1927 Bontempelli asked Il Duce to defend him from his many enemies. Written in French in its early issues, *900* was accused of lacking the nationalistic approach of a proper Fascist paper. The letter leaves little doubt about Bontempelli's feelings:

> Ho potuto resistere, perché avevo, Duce, <u>la Vostra approvazione.</u>
> <u>Oso chiederVi di rinnovarmela.</u>
> Soltanto la certezza che Voi pensate che io non ho tradito le promesse fattevi quel giorno, e la Vostra fiducia in me e nel mio complicato tentativo

– solo questo può aiutarmi a continuare. Volete darmela?
(Non oso chiedervi un altro colloquio: ogni Vostro minuto è sacro).[61]

(I have managed to resist because I had, Duce, <u>Your approval.</u>
<u>*Dare I ask You to renew it for me?*</u>
Only your belief that I have not broken the promises I made that day,
and your confidence in me and in my complicated attempt, can help me to
continue. Will you grant me this?
(I do not dare to ask for another meeting: Every minute of your time is
sacred)).[61]

We do not know whether Mussolini replied and consented to Bontempelli's request, but the following year, in a letter dated 30 April 1928
Bontempelli asked to be received again by Il Duce so that he could
defend himself from false accusations of anti-Fascism that were prevent-
ing him from being appointed secretary of the Trade Union of Writers.
'Ho documenti precisi e luminosi della mia fede e della mia opera Fasciste' (I have precise and illuminating documents proving my Fascist
faith and Fascist work), he boasted. Mussolini was clearly a reader of
Bontempelli's work: this emerges from a letter dated 5 August 1930, in
which Lando Ferretti, head of Mussolini's press office, communicated
to Bontempelli his boss's appreciation of the book *Vita e morte di Adria e
dei suoi figli.*[62] A few months later Bontempelli wrote to Mussolini to
lobby for his support for the former's nomination to the Accademia
d'Italia. By the end of the month he was appointed Accademico.[63] His
correspondence also shows that in the 1930s Bontempelli was on good
terms with Galeazzo Ciano and Dino Alfieri too.[64]

On the censorship front, Bontempelli's surreal settings kept his
narrative works away from any controversy. The only recorded case of
interference concerned a short story that, perhaps not by chance,
had been censored in May 1934, only a month after Mussolini's
famous circular against Mura's novel *Sambadù amore nego.* Bontempelli intended to publish his short story in *La Gazzetta del Popolo* to
which he was a regular contributor. The reason behind its preventive
censorship on the part of the paper's editors was that it mentioned a
case of suicide. Bontempelli appealed to Ciano, who passed the case
on to Mussolini himself. This time Il Duce decided to stick to his policies: a handwritten note in the margin of the letter abruptly stated
'no.'[65] Collaboration and patronage, however, continued as before.
In August 1936 Bontempelli, as director of the literary journal *L'Italia*

letteraria, received a grant of 10,000 lire from Ciano's Ministry for the Press and Propaganda.[66]

Ultimately, Bontempelli's detachment from political militancy was interpreted as a sign of lack of Fascist commitment. On 4 February 1939 Alfieri, minister of the MCP, ordered the withdrawal from booksellers' shop windows of all copies of Bontempelli's *Pirandello, Leopardi, D'Annunzio: Tre discorsi di Massimo Bontempelli* (Bompiani, 1938). In a letter to his publisher on 29 December 1938, Bontempelli seemed to be aware of a problematic situation. He mentioned the rumour that newspapers had been told not to review his book, then added that this was contradicted by the fact that *Il Popolo d'Italia* and other papers had already written positively. He concluded by asking Bompiani to let him know whether there was any truth to those rumours. On 2 January 1939 Bompiani reassuringly replied that he knew nothing of criticisms about the book and that the many positive reviews were a encouraging sign.[67] The rumour, however, was true. The partial ban was apparently applied on the request of Rome's *Federale* (the local head of the National Fascist Party), Andrea Ippolito, who had found the tone of Bontempelli's speeches to lack respect for the regime. Once more the ad hoc solution should be noted: the book was temporarily withdrawn from shop windows but was never seized. Given that Bontempelli was an Accademico, it would probably have been too embarrassing to impose the full weight of a ban (the working title of the book was actually *Tre discorsi accademici*, which was changed a few weeks before the book went into print, following Bompiani's suggestion). News of the episode was recorded in Giuseppe Bottai's diary, which included a dismissive note regarding the obtuseness of the Roman Fascist official.[68] However, according to a long letter written by Bontempelli, it seems that Ippolito was not the only person behind the attack. Achille Starace, the much maligned secretary general of the National Fascist Party was also involved. In a four-page letter addressed to Starace, Bontempelli defended himself from the accusation that he had omitted to mention D'Annunzio relationship with Fascism and that some of his remarks could be construed as indirect criticism of the regime. But Starace obviously intended to teach Bontempelli a lesson: in the same week the latter was also thrown out of the party and on 15 February 1939 his passport was withdrawn.[69] Certainly the fact that Bontempelli had written, delivered, and published two official commemorations of prestigious figures such as D'Annunzio and Pirandello without a single mention of their links with Fascism amounted, in the eyes of many, to an act of provocation.

In the end Bontempelli managed to rescue the situation and was readmitted to the party. Five months later, in a handwritten note addressed to Mussolini, Bontempelli thanked him for his 'benevola sentenza in mio favore' (benevolent judgement in my favour).[70] The ban on the book was officially revoked on 2 October 1939 by Alfieri, who a week later thanked Bontempelli for his past and future collaborations with a grant of 20,000 lire.[71] A helping hand also came from Galeazzo Ciano, who, as foreign office minister, should not have been involved in this *querelle*. Yet, from Bontempelli's correspondence we know that in October 1939 Ciano had written to the chief editor of *Corriere della Sera*, asking him to employ Bontempelli as a contributor. The initial response was lukewarm (the paper was in those years printed in a reduced four-page format) but five months later Bontempelli received a contract for a monthly contribution.[72] Less successful was a planned collaboration with *Il Popolo d'Italia*. According to Pini's unpublished memoirs, the name of Bontempelli – together with those of Malaparte and Alvaro – had been suggested by Pini in October 1942 in his plan to increase the number of contributors to the paper. Mussolini personally checked the list and struck off those three names.[73] As for the reason behind this decision, we can only speculate that Mussolini probably thought that Bontempelli's lack of Fascist militancy, if defendable at the level of his literary career, precluded his name appearing on Fascism's daily paper.

Bontempelli's open rejection of Fascism during the months of General Badoglio's government in the summer of 1943 earned him the persecution of the Fascists in the last year of the war. Despite this, Bontempelli's collaboration with the regime came back to haunt him. In April 1948 he was elected member of Parliament on the Italian Communist Party ticket. However, the facts of his pro-Fascist past reached the national press, causing a public scandal and forcing him to resign.[74]

Alberto Moravia (né Pincherle) belonged to a younger generation than Bontempelli. Born in 1907, he grew up in a wealthy middle-class family in Rome. His precarious health confined him to hospitals for long periods, which gave him time to nurture his passion for literature. His debut novel, *Gli indifferenti*, was published in 1929 and received critical acclaim. It also opened the doors to journalism and future publications with major publishers. Moravia's father was an architect and painter. More important on the political front, an uncle on his mother's side was Augusto De Marsanich, a powerful Fascist official who represented the government at the League of Nations during the Ethiopan crisis, was undersecretary in the Ministry of Communication from 1935 to 1943, and in the postwar years was to become secretary of the neo-Fascist party Movimento Sociale Italiano. Young Alberto was not attracted to politics, but the publishing house of *Gli indifferenti*, Alpes, had strong connections with the regime. Founded in 1921 and owned by Mussolini's brother, Arnaldo, Alpes was based from 1923 in the old offices of *Il Popolo d'Italia* and had produced various series devoted to Fascism, including collections of Mussolini's speeches.[75] It is probable that the choice of Alpes for the publication of *Gli indifferenti* was linked to Moravia's uncle. Yet, recent studies have shown beyond doubt, Moravia was actively contributing to some Fascist avant-garde journals, and *Gli indifferenti* was well in line with their anti-bourgeois critique. It would be simplistic to assume that Moravia's problems with the regime derived from the alleged anti-Fascist content of the novel, and, criticism to the book tended to come more from conservative and Catholic circles.[76] Moravia's memoirs played a part in postwar interpretations of the novel as a direct attack on Fascist values. In an article written in 1946, Moravia stated that the third reprint was prohibited and only after great efforts was he allowed a fourth.[77] Because records show that the four Alpes reprints did not encounter censorship intervention, it is likely that Moravia's memoirs referred to a failed third edition of the novel by another published. In June 1933 Enrico dall'Oglio had bought the rights to publish *Gli indifferenti*, although he did not go beyond the first printing; the following year the rights were taken over by Valentino Bompiani, who intended to publish a third edition but was not allowed to do it.[78] It should also be noted that, in his conversations with Yvon De Begnac, Mussolini himself made mention of *Gli indifferenti*. He defined it as an example of a novel 'oscenamente borghese e antiborghese al medesimo tempo' (disgustingly bourgeois and anti-bourgeois at the same time), which had powerfully revealed to him the existence of a world of passive anti-Fascism.[79]

The source of Moravia's political troubles came from a different direction. It had to do with another family connection, this time his two cousins Carlo and Nello Rosselli. From Florence – and Paris, after Carlo's adventurous escape from the Fascist *confino* in June 1929 – the Rosselli brothers were active anti-Fascists at the head of the underground liberal group Giustizia e Libertà. Moravia's sister, Adriana, was in contact with them (she was the fiancée of Mario Levi, another Giustizia e Libertà militant), often visiting them in Paris. According to police records, the entire Pincherle family came under the attention of the

Political Police through these connections. Despite the many reports and discreet investigations, Moravia was never accused of being directly involved in any organized anti-Fascist activity. His many requests for passport renewal in order to travel abroad as a journalist were regularly approved, in at least two cases with the final *nulla osta* of Mussolini.[80]

With regard to Moravia's publications, the first encounter with the censorship authorities took place in 1935. It concerned the publication of his second novel, *Le ambizioni sbagliate*. As Fabre accurately reconstructs, in January 1935 one of Mondadori's aids, Mario Pelosini, had sent the manuscript of the novel to the press office of the prefecture of Milan. The press office reader was Mario Pensuti, a journalist who had published a book with Mondadori some years before and was regularly used as a translator from English. His response was, perhaps not surprisingly, positive. As a result, despite some morally debatable passages, Mondadori was allowed to press on with the publication without any requests for cuts. What seemed poised to ruin the smooth progress of the publication was an article that appeared in the journal *Giustizia e libertà*, published in Paris. An anonymous article entitled 'La proibizione del nuovo romanzo di Alberto Moravia' appeared on 4 January 1935. It plainly stated that the book had been seized by the Milan censors and presented the case as the beginning of a campaign by the Fascists against 'la giovane generazione italiana' (the young generation of Italians).[81] The article prompted a frantic exchange of information between the head of police, Arturo Bocchini, and the Milan prefect, Bruno Fornaciari, who resolutely confirmed his *nulla osta* for the publication of the book.[82] Unfortunately, the incriminating issue of *Giustizia e libertà* had reached the desk of Mussolini, and in the end the prefecture was ordered to pass any decision along to the Ministry of the Interior and the Undersecretariat for Press and Propaganda (then run by Galeazzo Ciano). In other words, Rome was going to decide the fate of Moravia's novel.[83] Both the Mondadori publishing house, in the person of Pelosini, and Moravia made attempts at negotiations. Pelosini met Neos Dinale – Ciano's aid at the undersecretariat – in the company of Moravia's uncle Augusto De Marsanich, and Moravia sent a letter to Ciano defending the moral content of his novel. By the time Mondadori submitted *Le ambizioni sbagliate*, other reports had been added to Moravia's file, suggesting that French and American intellectual circles were paying close attention to his fate.[84] According to Fabre, it was probably Mussolini's intention to avoid international indictment that prompted him to allow the publication of the novel in June 1935. The only caveat imposed by Ciano was a *velina* to the press that suggested that the newspapers had to be 'discreet' in their coverage of the publication.[85] It is also at this time that Moravia became the direct subject of police surveillance. Reports on his movements were filed in June 1935, June 1936, and March 1937.[86]

Alberto Moravia's literary career during the Fascist years continued to depend on the relative influence of his various friends and opponents within the regime. To a great extent this was the result of the fact that his fiction lent itself to differing interpretations. His detached representation of middle-class amorality could be interpreted either as an attack against middle-class values (hence in line with the regime) or as a refusal to espouse and foster the nationalistic ideals of Fascism. In March 1935 Moravia also published a collection of short stories, *La bella vita*, with the small publisher Carabba. Once more the Dostoevskian pictures of debased, amoral characters provoked different reactions. The book was not censored, but, almost symbolically, Moravia's file held by the Political Police was supplemented with a copy of two reviews of the book: the first, which came from a Fascist paper, was critical; the second, from *L'Italia che scrive*, was positive.[87]

There were other, indirect ways of making a writer's life difficult. In the weeks surrounding the publication of *La bella vita*, Moravia's journalistic activity seemed under threat. Recently discovered documents show that on 28 March 1935 Moravia wrote to Mussolini to appeal the decision by the chief editor of Rome's *Gazzetta del Popolo*, Ermanno Amicucci, to end Moravia's collaboration with the newspaper. In the letter Moravia paid tribute to the achievements of the regime and of its 'exemplary and extraordinary' leader. Altough he refrained from addressing or saluting Il Duce with any Fascist expression, this humiliating exercise produced the desired effect: a handwritten note by Mussolini, in the margin, states 'può scrivere' (allowed to write). Less successful was a request by Moravia to Ciano, dated 18 August 1935, in which the former asked the Ministry for the Press and Propaganda for some financial help so that he could travel to East Africa. Once more, Moravia stooped to an act of reverence, complimenting Ciano as a role model for Italian youth and saying that his desire to write a book about the Italian invasion of Ethiopia followed his unsuccesful attempt to volunteer in the Italian army. His request was turned down, as stated in a letter by Gherardo Casini.[88] Throughout these years, Casini often displayed tolerance towards Moravia. On 24 November 1936 it was Valentino Bompiani's turn to write to Casini. Bompiani was about to publish a second collection of short stories by Moravia, entitled *L'imbroglio.* In his letter Bompiani asked discreetly to know 'anche in via ufficiosa, se può esservi una qualche obbiezione da parte del Ministero a detta pubblicazione. La mia domanda è in relazione a qualche difficoltà giornalistica di cui mi è giunta eco' (even unofficially, if there are any objections to this publication on the part of the Ministry. My request is related to rumours of journalistic difficulties). Casini's reply was a reassuring *nulla osta,* and the book was published in the following months.[89]

Moravia's roller-coaster relationship with the regime continued in the following years. Various handwritten marginal notes on his letter of request for a meeting with Casini reveal that Moravia's travel as a correspondent for *La Gazzetta del Popolo* had been sponsored partly by the ministry. His claim for $500 towards his expenses for his planned trip to China was considered unlikely to be accepted on the grounds that Moravia had already received $500 and 4000 lire on two previous occasions.[90] More problematic was the 'journalistic difficulty' that Moravia reencountered the following year for a short story published in *La Gazzetta del Popolo* of 14 July 1938. The short story, 'Antico furore,' is a surreal tale of a young man whose life is split between his desire for rational perfection and his sexual drives. More important, in the early paragraphs, the protagonist expresses his repulsion with the vulgarity of politics in his times. There is no explicit indication that the author intended his remarks to refer to contemporary Italy but such was the interpretation of an anonymous reader who sent a copy of the story to the Ministry for the Press and Propaganda. The controversial passages were underlined and a typed note in the margin stated: 'Oh ineffabile apologo! Altro che letteratura Fascista (che roba!) Evviva il giudaismo e gli scrittori ebrei, che come il nostro Moravia, Vi (adopero il voi) prendono in giro' (Oh, what an ineffable apology! Forget about Fascist literature (what a thing!). Long live Jewishness and Jewish authors such as our Moravia who take you (I'm using the Fascist 'you') for a ride). Four days later Casini wrote to the chief editor of *La Gazzetta del Popolo* and ordered the suspension of Moravia's collaboration. Amicucci's reply stated that he had previously questioned the collaboration of Moravia, implying that it was thanks to Casini that Moravia had been allowed to collaborate. When the latter was informed of the ministry decision, he wrote to Mussolini to protest. Moravia went straight to the point: he stated that the racial reasons behind his marginalization were unjustified: although his father was Jewish, his mother was 'di sangue puro' (of pure blood), and his education had been a Catholic one. For good measure, he reminded

Mussolini that his mother was the sister of one of his undersecretaries. Once more, Moravia's self-abasement produced its results: two weeks later Casini wrote to Amicucci to say that Moravia was allowed to resume his collaboration with *La Gazzetta del Popolo*.[91]

In 1938 a police informer's report from Paris described in detail the performance of a theatrical adaptation of Moravia's first novel. *Les indifférents* was performed at the Théâtre de l'Oeuvre in February of that year. In his three-page report, the informer described the lukewarm reaction of the press and stressed underlined that neither the adaptation nor the reviews contained any reference to contemporary Italy, much less to Fascism.[92]

In conclusion, it seems that until the start of the anti-Semitic campaign in 1938, Moravia managed to defend his literary and journalistic work thanks to the self-interested tolerance of various personalities within the regime, Mussolini included. The undignified letters that Moravia was forced to write are testimony to the humiliation that the regime imposed on authors who were not open supporters. As we will see in the following chapter, the anti-Semitic legislation and its impact on the publishing industry were to put Moravia's professional standing even more at risk.

Censorship and Theatre: Sem Benelli's Anti-Bourgeois Plays

Theatre censorship had become one of the Undersecretariat for Press and Propaganda's areas of jurisdiction after its creation, in September 1934. Undersecretariat's. The one-man-office led by the erudite prefect Leopoldo Zurlo stopped reporting directly to the head of the police, instead, Galeazzo Ciano became Zurlo's immediate superior.[93] Ciano's involvement in cultural matters was a considerable change from the total lack of interest shown by his predecessor, Arturo Bocchini. Il Duce's son-in-law was keen to have his say and create a circle of intellectuals and writers devoted to him. He had also been a theatre critic himself, for *Il Nuovo Paese* and *L'Impero*, and had written two plays in the early 1920s. Yet Mussolini continued to have a role as the regime's ultimate censoring authority with regard to theatre. As Zurlo repeatedly suggests in his *Memorie inutili*, it seems that Mussolini had become rather fond of Zurlo's eccentric but always witty and scholarly reports. Similarly to what Bocchini used to do with Zurlo's work, Ciano would often simply act as a go-between. This happened when Anton Bragaglia, director of the Teatro degli Indipendenti, wrote to Ciano only a few weeks after the creation of the undersecretariat. Bragaglia intended to stage Pietro Aretino's satirical play *La cortigiana*. Zurlo, however, was not particularly fond of its scurrilous language and violent satire of the Vatican. His report therefore verged towards the negative, although the final word was left to his superiors. Bragaglia was aware of this – Zurlo would often meet playwrights and theatrical producers in order to discuss modifications – and in an attempt to cut the red tape he wrote directly to Ciano, whom he knew personally. The letter, dated 17 September 1934, asked for Ciano's approval or, preferably, for Ciano to 'intercedere presso il Capo' (to intercede with the Boss).[94] The assumption was that Mussolini was continuing to have a say in theatrical matters. A handwritten, underlined note in the margin indicates the failure of the attempt. It simply says 'Duce' and, below, 'no.' A possible reason is that, after the polemics of Benelli's *Caterina Sforza*, Mussolini might have thought that the idea of staging such an anti-clerical play on the doorstep of the Vatican was simply too confrontational.

Despite his many commitments, Mussolini continued to be the supreme arbiter of what was going to appear on Italian stages. Guspini's *L'orecchieo del regime* provides us with a report of a telephone conversation between Mussolini and Zurlo, from 15 November 1934, which once more confirms the extent to which Mussolini was directly involved. Il Duce had phoned Zurlo to complain about the fact that many intercepted telephone conversations mentioned a play by the famous Italian comedian Antonio De Curtis, alias Totò. Complains had also arrived from the PNF. Zurlo replied that there were only two controversial jokes (puns on the recent introduction of 'Voi' to replace 'Lei') and it would have been too draconian of him to censor the script for such a reason. Mussolini apparently not only laughed at the jokes but added that, with regard to censorship, 'sono stato proprio io a dirvi di essere, in un certo senso, di manica larga …' (it was me who told you to be, in a way, tolerant …). The two agreed to lay the matter to rest by simply ignoring any protest.[95]

Sem Benelli too continued to be the subject of Zurlo's censorial activity. His plays were always popular for their controversial and disrespectful content. In the mid-1930s he produced three works that aimed at a critique of various aspects of contemporary society. The fact that, as the title of this section suggests, they could be put under the umbrella of 'anti-bourgeois plays' might suggest that their content was in line with the regime's social policies and Fascism's long-standing antipathy for the liberal weaknesses of the Italian bourgeoisie. To some extent they were. However, the many derogatory comments on contemporary society could equally be interpreted as a satire of Italian society under Fascism. As we will see, controversy was bound to arise, and this time Mussolini was no longer interested in making use of it for his own goals.

The first play in question is *Il ragno*, which saw its successful debut in March 1935 at Milan's Teatro Odeon. The plot revolves around an impoverished nobleman whose cynical and disillusioned vision of life cuts through the hypocricies of those around him, starting with the successful businessman whose daughter he is expecting to marry. Given the contemporary Italian setting and characters, Zurlo was careful to cut out any possible reference to the Fascist regime.[96] We do not know the extent of his intervention but, judging from the published version, political issues were absent from the play. At most, one could say that the overall display of cynicism and hypocrisy painted a disheartening picture of Italian society. Indeed, this was the interpretation of the police informer who sent a detailed report on 26 March 1935. The informer's conclusion was that Benelli's success had to be judged as 'un vero e solo successo politico' (a true and singular political success) because it had found a way to denigrate contemporary Italy while avoiding political censorship.[97] This report might be the reason why Ciano called in Zurlo and asked him to give *Il ragno* a second look. According to Zurlo's memoirs, on that occasion Ciano had a copy of the play that had been underlined to draw Ciano's attention to certain passages. Zurlo protested that the published version was different from the one that he had allowed to reach the stage. He then agreed to revise the text again and address every passage that had been highlighted in Ciano's copy. We do not know the identity of the second reader of the play. It might have been a disgruntled Fascist from Milan or an official in the Milanese prefecture. In any case, Zurlo was able to convince Ciano that *Il ragno* did not deserve any more cuts.[98] Ricci's theatre company was allowed to tour the peninsula, and *Il ragno* was successfully received in Rome too. All seemed well, but whoever Benelli's enemies were, they were only waiting for a better chance to strike again.

In September 1935, a producer at the Italian state broadcaster, EIAR, asked for authorization to perform Benelli's war play *Eroi, dramma di guerra*. Despite the fact that the play had been successfully staged in 1931, the censors decided that its content was too crude or, rather, 'nobilissimo ma molto verista' (very noble but very naturalistic). In this particular case, it is likely that the act of censorship was less related to Benelli's political ideas than to the fact that the Italian army was only days away from invading Ethiopia. The stark realism of the play and its critique of the officers' behaviour lent themselves to troublesome interpretations.[99] A few months later, driven by his nationalistic pride, Benelli joined the Italian army as a volunteer and served in Africa as a major in an artillery unit. His experiences were later recorded in the book *Io in Affrica* (Mondadori, 1936), but more importantly Mussolini personally received him and asked him for a detailed report of his experience. During that encounter, Mussolini asked Benelli if there was anything that he could do for him. According to Benelli's memoirs, his answer was that all he wanted was to be free to publish and stage his work. Mussolini allegedly refused to give him a clear answer.[100] We have no other documentation regarding that meeting, but it is interesting to note some remarks made by Mussolini during one of his many conversations with Yvon De Begnac. Once more, it is impossible to guess the exact date when the conversation took place but, because Mussolini referred to Benelli's experience in Africa, it certainly took place after 1936. Mussolini refers to the failed appointment to the Accademia d'Italia of Sem Benelli. He explicitly says that on more than one occasion he had refused the suggestion to appoint him because, even after the African campaign, he never believed that Benelli was a genuine supporter of the regime.[101] Mussolini's suspicious attitude was to show itself in the following years.

Benelli's next play, *L'elefante*, premiered at Milan's Odeon Theatre on 17 March 1937. This time Zurlo had suggested a number of cuts and, because Mussolini at the time was on an official visit in North Africa, he authorized the performance without asking for his boss's final approval. Unfortunately, once more Mondadori had made sure that the uncut version of the play was available in all bookshops, and this time the satirical references to the regime were explicit.

In *L'elefante* the central characters expose and discuss several aspects of the hypocrisy of contemporary social etiquette. In particular, the play contained a strong attack on the institution of marriage and various cynical comments about state authority. The first act disingenuously specified that the action was meant to take place 'in un piccolo Stato europeo, possibilmente orientale' (in a small European State, possibly in the east), but there were occasional references to contemporary Italy. For example, when a character in the third act boasts that he is going to employ a lawyer from the party in government, few Italians would have failed to spot the reference to Roberto Farinacci, Fascist leader of Cremona and, as a lawyer, vocal defender of Fascists on trial during the early years of the regime. Or, when commenting on the corruption of a state employee, the mention of the autarkic policies created an immediate link with Fascist economic-policies. These passages were among twenty-nine cuts imposed by Zurlo, but the availability of the uncut version was an invitation to scout for the missing words.

A first report by a police informer, dated 21 March 1937, gave a positive account of the play and of the reaction of the audience. Not so positive was a second informer who, on 2 April, reported that the play was the toast of all the anti-Fascists in Milan, and on 5 April added that the printed book was selling like hotcakes (va a ruba). This second report was swiftly followed by an official investigation. The head of police in Milan sent a report to Bocchini on 6 April 1937 in which he stated that the actors had sometimes failed to omit certain passages that had been censored. The official excuse was that the prompter of the theatre company had mistakenly been using an uncut copy of the script. Four days later the play was suddenly taken off the stage despite the fact that it had been sold out for the previous twenty-four nights. According to a police informer's report dated 10 April, this action followed threats from Rino Parenti, then *Federale* of Milan, to the theatre company director: 'Vietare non lo posso perché non c'è un ordine preciso dalle autorità competenti; ma posso trasformare gli applausi in fischi!' (I can't prohibit it because there's no official order; but I can change applause into whistles!). The *Federale*'s menacing stance had apparently been prompted by a stern rebuke from the secretary of the PNF, Achille Starace. A similar version of the events is given by Benelli in his memoirs.[102]

Benelli went to Rome to protest. He was not allowed to meet Mussolini but in a meeting with Minister of Popular Culture Dino Alfieri, he was given a copy of *L'elefante* with a series of handwritten notes allegedly by Il Duce. Benelli responded with his own comments to every single note and demanded that the play be allowed to be performed. In the end, Alfieri consented to a second revision of the play by the official censor, Zurlo.[103]

On 6 April (the same day that the local head of police in Milan reported about the performances of the play) Zurlo had already written a report in which he had justified his previous action as censor and had reminded his superiors that the printed version of the play had not taken his cuts into account. Replying to Alfieri's demand, on 26 April Zurlo produced a second, long report on *L'elefante* that again concluded that once the play was purged of all references to contemporary Italy, there was no reason to prohibit it. For good measure, he also produced a long table detailing his cuts in a column next to those suggested by 'S.E il Ministro' (His Excellency the Minister, presumably Alfieri, although it might refer to Mussolini as Minister of the Interior). Of the thirty-four cuts suggested by the minister, eighteen were rejected by Zurlo as irrelevant. The official censor was obviously keen to show that his first review of the play had been sufficiently scrupulous.[104]

Once more we have evidence that Mussolini was involved in the decision-making process. A letter sent by Benelli to Alfieri on 26 April 1937 includes the words: 'poi che tu mi dicesti che il Duce non aveva intenzione di ostacolare le recite dell'*Elefante*' (since you told me that Il Duce did not intend to oppose the performance of *L'elefante*). Moreover, a handwritten note in the margin, presumably by Zurlo, provides another clue. It says: 'Autorizzare. Ho chiesto il nulla osta al Duce' (To be authorized. I have asked Il Duce for his nulla osta).[105]

The following month the play was allowed to return to the stage, opening in Genoa. Everything went well until December, when *L'elefante* was performed in Turin. On that occasion, a group of unspecified young men disrupted the play's performance on 2 and 4 December until the play was taken off the calendar on the following day. On 13 December Benelli's friend Alessandro Giuliani – then editor at *Il Popolo d'Italia* – wrote to Alfieri and asked him to forward a letter by Benelli to Mussolini and to discuss with Starace the possibility of allowing Benelli to join the PNF. Starace's answer, handwritten in large letters on the top of the second page of Giuliani's letter, could not be clearer: 'Sono io personalmente responsabile. Benelli è un porco! Non sono mai stato e mai sarò generoso con i traditori, che *sopprimerei fisicamente*' (I am personally responsible. Benelli is a pig! I have never been and I will never be generous with traitors, whom I would *physically suppress*).[106] On 23 December 1937 Benelli wrote directly to Mussolini and once more protested the cancellation of a play that had been directly approved by him. Il Duce once more was forced to have his say. On 1 January 1938 Alfieri informed the Directorate General for Theatre that the head of government had decided that *L'elefante* would be allowed to continue to be performed. The following day Alfieri also sent a personal letter to Starace in which he confirmed Mussolini's decision.[107]

If Benelli had temporarily won his battle against Starace, more problems were about to arise on other fronts. First, Benelli and Alfieri met on 18 January 1938 and on that occasion Benelli consented to suspend *pro bono pacis* (for good peace) the tour of *L'elefante*. Two weeks later a telephone discussion between him and an editor of Swiss state radio was intercepted by Mussolini's Political Police. It revealed that Benelli was going to be interviewed while in Switzerland and that he intended to talk about the censorship of his plays. On 11 February Alfieri wrote that he had been 'told' of the interview and diplomatically suggested to Benelli that 'nel momento attuale, la cosa potrebbe non riuscire gradita' (at this particular time, this would not be appreciated).[108] Benelli did not go to Switzerland. A year later, when the Ministry of Popular Culture circulated a list of recent works that had been prohibited, Benelli's *L'elefante* appeared at the top of the list.[109]

In March 1938, another of Benelli's play, *L'orchidea*, was about to tour Italy's theatres. According to Benelli, the debut took place in the small town of Sanremo, instead of Milan, as the result of an imposition by the MCP. The rationale of the ministry was first to make sure that the play was not going to be another troublesome work before it opened in a major centre.[110] This time the plot focuses on the life of a young woman, Elena Pescova, who, pregnant as a result of an extramarital affair, is able to reconstruct her life thanks to Alberto, a natural scientist who encourages her to fulfill her potential as an artist. There is nothing overtly political about this play, if one excludes the passages where the lack of condemnation for adultery and the promotion of female self-sufficiency risk being interpreted as an attack on Fascist social policies. At the same time, Benelli's play was injected with his usual cynical comments about the many hypocrisies and libertine attitudes of the upper bourgeoisie, and this could well be interpreted as supporting the regime's anti-bourgeois campaign. But the devil is in the details, and once more Benelli peppered the play with impertinent references and double entendres – to the freedom of artists and of individuals, to trade unions and the rights of African citizens – that could be interpreted as indirect jibes at the regime.

Over the course of two months, Zurlo met Benelli on several occasions to review every cut to the play. Zurlo also sent not one but three reports to Mussolini, keeping him informed of all the changes. Reading Zurlo's main report, it is noticeable that the experienced censor was much more cautious than on previous occasions. He constantly referred to the possibility of banning the play altogether and accompanied his comments with snippets of pro-Fascist social critique, which were normally absent from his reports. For instance, when he stated that the debauched demi monde represented in the play was 'cosi lontana dalla nostra realtà e dalla nostra sensibilità morale e politica' (so distant from our reality and from our moral and political sensibilities), the atypical use of the first-person plural and references to politics illustrate a departure from his normal, personal style. The manuscript was littered with cuts, which initially totally 140 (see figure 12). In his second report of 23 February 1938 Zurlo, explained that his comments and cuts had followed a three-pronged approach: they were designed to 1) avoid criticism from the church; 2) reduce the sexual content of the play; 3) delete all lines that had political meaning. In the end, Zurlo's fastidiously accurate table reported that of the eighty-one cuts that were ultimately imposed, fifteen pertained to religion, forty-three to sexuality, and twenty-three to politics.[111]

The maimed play was evenutally allowed to begin its Italian tour and was greeted with lively interest from theatre-goers despite the fact that newspaper editors had been instructed by the MCP not to mention the play until its performances in Milan, and thereafter not to devote more than eight lines to their reviews.[112] Problems arose towards the end of the tour when *L'orchidea* was staged at the Eliseo Theatre in Rome on 18 May 1938. After the first two nights, Benelli remembers being told by the actors that Nicola De Pirro, head of the Directorate General for Theatre, had phoned the theatre to 'inform' its director that the performance of *L'orchidea* was to be stopped after the third night. Benelli at that point tried to contact Ciano, then Alfieri, then Mussolini, but to no avail.[113] The situation took a familiar turn. On the third night, mixed with the usual audience, there were about fifty men whose countenances left little doubt as to their reason for being there.[114] As soon as the curtain rose, insults and mocking shouts were directed at the actors. Some members of the audience tried to intervene, and a chaotic scuffle ensued during which a general in the *carabinieri* and a disabled war veteran were punched in the face. According to Benelli, the *Federale* of Rome, Andrea Ippolito, was loitering in the foyer, supervising the event.[115]

It is difficult to say whether Mussolini was directly involved, but two facts suggest that he was certainly well informed of what was happening. First, a few days after the disrupted performance, Il Duce was sent a detailed report by an MCP official who had witnessed the event. Incidentally, this witness reported that the audience was united in defending the play from the Fascists' provocations (this is actually confirmed by all police informers' reports). Second, we know that among the audience was one of Mussolini's sons, Bruno (who at that time was still living with his parents at Villa Torlonia). It is very likely, however, that the initiative had come from the secretary of the party, Starace, as was suggested in three different informers' reports.[116] The fact that Mussolini does not seem to have done anything to defend Benelli – he refused to answer any of his letters – is a sign that he had decided to withdraw any kind of 'protection.'

12. Page of Sem Benelli's *L'orchidea* (1938) with censorial cuts by Leopoldo Zurlo. (*Courtesy of Archivio Centrale dello Stato, Rome*)

A comparison between Zurlo's cuts and the Mondadori version (which was not in bookshops on the night of the debut) suggests that the publisher had been asked to produce a 'post-censorship' version. A letter was sent to Zurlo on 26 February 1938, in which the head of the press office at the prefecture of Milan asked whether the proofs of the Mondadori version of the play took the censor's cuts into account. Apparently Arnoldo Mondadori himself asked the prefecture to double check in order to avoid any misunderstandings. On 1 March Zurlo asked the prefecture to send him a copy of the proofs. We do not have any more documentation related to this, but the actual published text shows that, apart from some brief passages of no political importance, the Mondadori edition could not have been used by the public as a source of information about what had been cut by the censor.[117]

A clear sign that Benelli's situation had degenerated after *L'orchidea* was the withdrawal of his passport. On 26 June 1938 he wrote a long letter of complaint to the head of police, asking for the return of his passport because, he protested, it was only abroad that he could find any future source of income. Given the previous experience of the attempted radio interview in Switzerland, it is likely that the regime did not intend letting him become an expatriate and spread news of his political persecution. Other solutions had to be found. In this case it is significant that in the copy of a telegram asking Benelli to come to the MCP to see Alfieri on 21 July 1938 there is a handwritten note saying 'l'ha già ricevuto due volte. Deve vederlo ancora et ancora riconvocarlo' (He has already seen him twice. He must see him again and call him again for a meeting).[118] Were these delaying tactics or the result of a prolonged negotiation? Two receipts with Benelli's signature point towards the second hypothesis: he accepted a payment from the MCP of 50,000 lire on 16 October 1938 and of 110,500 on 1 May 1939.[119] In his memoirs, Benelli refers to the second payment, indicating that it was made to free him from the mortgage on his house (the renowned 'castello di Zoagli'). The deal was apparently the result of the mediation of a friend of his, Carlo Delcroix, president of the Association of Wounded War Veterans.[120] On 10 October 1939 Benelli received another cheque from the MCP for 25,000 lire. By then, the ministry had decided that Benelli's latest controversial plays were to be forgotten. On 19 November 1938 Casini's DGSI informed Mondadori that he was allowed to reprint all of Benelli's work, apart from *Il ragno*, *L'elefante*, and *L'orchidea*. The ministry official added that a new title had to be found for Benelli's next play, whose provisional title was *Mangiare da poveri*. (*To Eat Like Poor People*). The play was eventually entitled *La festa*.[121]

Despite the financial compensation with which the regime had silenced the playwright, there is no doubt that Benelli intended to continue his artistic production. On 24 January 1940 his protector Delcroix, with the intercession of Bottai, sent to Alessandro Pavolini – the new minister of popular culture – a letter by Benelli. The letter contained three requests: that he be allowed to bring back to the stage his three anti-bourgeois plays; that the press be allowed to comment on his recently published autobiography, *La mia leggenda*; and that he be allowed to stage his most recent play, *La festa*. The first request was curtly denied. The second was granted (*La mia leggenda* concentrated on the early part of Benelli's life before the Fascists' seizure of power; hence it contained no controversial material).[122] The third was left open as Zurlo had not yet finished his revisions to the play. Zurlo eventually produced an amazing fifteen-page report on *La festa*. The play was purged of every controversial reference, however minute. For example, the protagonist's comment, 'Niente è più civile di un trucco, signorina, tutto è trucco oggi' (Nothing is more civilized than a trick, Miss, in our days everything is a trick), was modified by Zurlo's decision to replace the word 'oggi' with 'nel mondo' (in the world) on the following grounds: '"oggi" dirige tutto il fascio luminoso sul nostro tempo. Critica soltanto morale? – Sarebbe tollerabile. Non la è più se spostiamo il proiettore sul campo politico' ('oggi' draws the spotlight on our own times. Only a moral critique? – Then it would be tolerable. But it is not such if we move the spotlight on to the political arena). With the replacement of 'oggi' with 'del mondo,' Zurlo avoided the possible deduction that all is a trick in Fascist Italy.[123]

In the final years of the regime, Benelli was allowed to work on the film adaptation of his most famous play, *La cena delle beffe* (1909), under the direction of one of Italy's most prestigious filmmakers, Alessandro Blasetti. The Renaissance setting of the film was kept clear of any possible controversial parallels with contemporary Italy. Thanks to this production, Benelli, who by then had sold his house and was living in the gardener's annex, managed to avoid utter poverty. Despite his retirement from any form of political activity, police records show that he was still under surveillance throughout the last years of the regime and, even during the months of the Badoglio government in the summer of 1943. Finally, with the return of Fascism, Benelli fled Italy to live in Switzerland, where, as the last police informer's report suggests, he was welcome as a persecuted anti-Fascist artist.[124]

6 Anti-Semitism and 'Cultural Reclamation'

From Hints to Facts: 1938

Italy's publishing industry was gravely affected by the Fascists' anti-Semitic campaign of 1938. The complex development of these policies has been traced in ample detail by Giorgio Fabre in *L'elenco*, and this chapter is greatly indebted to his archival findings. Until the second half of the 1930s, Italian publishers, similarly to the regime and the Italian public in general, had not adopted a programmatic stance with regard to the Jewish question. The catalogues of major publishers contained works by exiled German-Jewish authors such as Stefan Zweig and Scha-lom Asch as much as anti-Semitic works such as the *Protocolli dei savi anziani di Sion* (Protocols of the Learned Elders of Zion) and Hitler's *Mein Kampf.* Although Mussolini sometimes made more or less casual anti-Semitic comments, he was often sardonic when assessing the Nazis' obsession with Judaism.[1] However, Fascism's involvement in colonial expansion with the invasion of Ethiopia certainly brought to the surface the issue of race relations. As we have seen, the Mura case, which in April 1934 caused a radical realignment of Fascist censorship, was fuelled by an instance of unorthodox race relations. It should therefore not be surprising to find that in the wake of the Ethiopian war Mussolini started to focus on that issue. During a meeting of the Grand Council of Fascism on 19 November 1936 he announced that the time had come to introduce racial policies in Fascist literature and doctrine.[2] It is to this period that we can date the first traces of Mussolini's decision to tackle the Jewish question within the cultural sphere. In December Giorgio Pini, chief editor of *Il Popolo d'Italia*, was discreetly instructed to free his newspaper from its Jewish contributors.[3] At the same time, a number of books (among which was Paolo Orano's influential *Gli ebrei in Italia*, published in March 1937) – and newspaper articles (some by Telesio Interlandi, who was in close contact with Mussolini) seem to suggest that a decision had been taken to change the tenor of the debate on the Jewish question.

Roberto Farinacci, the most vehement anti-Semite among Fascist leaders, joined the campaign from the pages of his newspaper *Il Regime fascista*. A letter by Farinacci to Alfieri throws some light on the involvement of the higher echelons of the regime. In September 1936, Farinacci wrote to Dino Alfieri at the Ministry of Press and Propaganda to complain about an order to stop his anti-Semitic polemics. He asked the minister for Mussolini's final word on the idea of publishing a polemical article by a Jewish author in order to create the impression of a divided Jewish community. Farinacci's final comment makes his position clear: 'Siccome sarà inevitabile che contro questa razza infingarda si dovrà un giorno prendere posizione, è meglio avere anche il pretesto di affermare che contro l'atteggiamento infido degli ebrei italiani sono insorti alcuni stessi correligionari. (Since it is inevitable that one day we will have to do something against this lazy race, it is better to have the pretext to affirm that even some of their co-religionists have rebelled against the devious stance of Italian Jews.) A handwritten note in the margin, presumably by Alfieri and arguably following a discussion with Mussolini, clarifies the regime's position: 'Pubblichi pure come chiusura; va bene per aumentare la confusione ma conferma l'equivoco d'impostazione del problema. Non si tratta di vedere se tra quella giusta vi sono i buoni e i cattivi. La questione è più profonda: i problemi di razza.' (He can publish it to bring the matter to a close; it is okay in order to increase the confusion but it confirms the misunderstanding with which the problem has been tackled. It is not a question of identifying goodies and baddies that have adopted the right approach. The question is deeper: race problems.) Finally, another note in the margin, this time in red pencil and initialled with the by now usual 'M' states: 'Ho già parlato io con Farinacci' (I have already spoken myself to Farinacci). Arguably, the note suggests that Mussolini had discussed the matter with Farinacci before Alfieri could send an official reply.[4] This exchange seems to confirm that in 1936 Mussolini was discreetly stirring the waters of Italian public opinion in order to slowly increase people's awareness of a racial question soon to be addressed. The Italian Jewish community was indirectly warned not to put their religious identity before their allegiance to Fascism and to the Italian nation.

The Ministry of Popular Culture (MCP) seemed to align itself with the new orientation. In September 1937 Gherardo Casini's General Directorate for the Italian Press (DGSI) refused a request by Bompiani to reprint Schalom Asch's *Pietroburgo* and *Varsavia*. A week later it ordered the withdrawal of five books by Jewish author Dino Segre (alias Pitigrilli). And in January 1938 Alfieri was reminded by Mussolini to reduce the presence of works by Jewish composers in the programs of state broadcaster EIAR.[5]

By 1938 the MCP was receiving the help of a semi-official institution that had been created in April 1937: the Centro Studi Anticomunisti (Centre for Anti-Communist Studies, CSA). The CSA was a private institution but its funding came directly from the Ministry of the Interior. Its aim was to provide the regime – mainly the Ministries of the Interior, Exterior, and Popular Culture – with information regarding the activities of the Comintern and other communist associations. Once more the model seemed to come from Nazi Germany, which had set up an Anti-Comintern Office at the time of its Anti-Comintern Pact with Japan in November 1936 (Italy was to join in November 1937). In charge of the Literature Section of the CSA was an impetuous Fascist, Carlo Barduzzi, who as a consular official had already distinguished himself as a fierce persecutor of anti-Fascists abroad. In July 1937 Barduzzi produced a short list of publications in Italian about Soviet Russia. This was followed by a long report, which was passed on to the MCP for information, in which Barduzzi gave details of the many books by Austrian and German exiles, most Jewish, that were circulated by major Italian publishers. Corbaccio and Mondadori appeared as the chief perpetrators and, as we will see, they were to pay for it.[6] In November 1937 Barduzzi managed to receive a copy of a Gestapo list of all anti-Nazi German authors and journalists who had left their country and were working abroad, some of them in Italy. Not surprisingly, the list contained mainly the names of Jewish authors, many of whom he had mentioned in his earlier reports as freely published in Italy. Starting from there and moving on to other nationals, Barduzzi developed a list of authors and publications that in his eyes should have been removed from circulation. However, Barduzzi's virulent anti-Semitism, his vindictive nature, and pedantic correspondence quickly made him unwelcome in government corridors, and by the spring of 1938 he had already been marginalized. Despite this, his lists of unwelcome authors and works were to play a role when the regime decided to implement fully its anti-Jewish campaign.[7]

The first sign that the MCP was about to be involved in a coordinated operation against Jewish Cultural figures appeared on 3 February 1938, when Gherardo Casini gave a speech in Florence entitled 'Bonifica della cultura in Italia' (Cultural Reclamation in Italy). The concept of *bonifica* had been a central buzzword in Fascist propaganda since the glorified projects of land reclamation in central Italy in the late 1920s. The fact that it should be used in a cultural context by a high-ranking official at the MCP was a clear indication that the regime had decided to make its move. At the heart of Casini's speech was the need to defend Italian national culture from 'il pacifismo, l'internazionalismo, il comunismo, la massoneria capeggiati da ebrei o ebreizzanti' (pacifism, internationalism, communism, free-masonry, all lead by Jews or pro-Jews).[8] Casini refrained from announcing the beginning of a racial crusade, but the centrality given to the Jewish question left little doubt about the regime's espousal of the Nazi paranoid dogma on the evil effects of Judaism on the body of the nation. Nor was he the first to have used the expression *bonifica della cultura*. The year before, Cesare De Vecchi, one of the most distinguished leaders of Fascism, who had just finished serving as minister of national education, had published a monumental collection of his speeches and ministerial documents entitled *Bonifica fascista della cultura*. This 700-page book, dutifully published by Mondadori, was meant as an enduring testimony to the Fascistization of the educational system during De Vecchi's tenure. It did not contain any anti-Semitic remarks but there is little doubt that Casini must have thought of his own speech as a further stage in the Fascist *bonifica* of Italian culture that De Vecchi had advertized in such a bold manner.[9]

Fabre's study cannot offer a definitive assessment of Mussolini's role in these developments because we do not have any documented proof of his involvement. However, given the clues mentioned above together with the fact that the head of the MCP, Alfieri, was more a reliable executor of Mussolini's policies than an independent-minded initiator of campaigns, it is most unlikely that such an important development would have taken place without his boss's direct participation.[10] It is also a fact that in early 1938 Mussolini wrote the famous *Informazione Diplomatica n. 14*, which is the first veiled warning that the regime was about to take the initiative on the racial front.[11] A wider and more controversial issue is the rationale behind Mussolini's decision to begin a racial campaign in 1938. Casini's speech was, after all, only part of the slow build-up that was to terminate with the full-fledged anti-Semitic legislation in the latter part of that year.

Historians agree that alignment with Nazi Germany's anti-Semitism was not one of the conditions of the alliance between the two countries that was to be ratified in the Pact of Steel of 22 May 1939. Mussolini seems to have acted of his own volition, although his intention was undoubtedly to show a 'Nazi-like' determination to shape the character and nature of his own people. If the invasion of Ethiopia had brought the issue of race relations to the foreground, by 1938 what seemed to spur Mussolini to action was his annoyance at the clear inferiority of Italian Fascism when compared to the internal and international strength of Hitler's Nazism. On the home front Mussolini decided to accelerate what historian Emilio Gentile calls 'the anthropological project' – that is, an attempt to forge a stronger, warlike Italian race and root out any remnants of a flabby bourgeois lifestyle.[12] These are the months of Starace's much derided directives regarding the imposition of the Fascist salute, the use of 'Voi' to replace the polite form 'Lei,' and the purge of all foreign expressions (the 'bonifica linguistica'). But perhaps the most symbolic act was the introduction of the goose step in the Italian army in February 1938, just in time for Hitler's official visit to Italy in May. Its denomination as 'passo romano' (Roman step) was a rather pathetical attempt to hide its clear Nazi derivation. Within this picture of nationalistic reformation, the Jewish question added a racial element that, given the relatively small dimensions of the Italian Jewish community, promised to be a manageable exercise of 'purification' of the Italian blood. When Mussolini dwelled on these initiatives in his famous speech to National Facist Party representatives in October 1938, he addressed them with one of his crude formulas: 'Alla fine dell'anno XVI ho individuato un nemico, un nemico del nostro regime. Questo nemico ha nome "borghesia"' (At the end of year XVI [of the Fascist era], I have identified an enemy, an enemy of our regime. This enemy is called 'bourgeoisie').[13] The anti-Semitic legislation was part of the climax of a number of measures that desperately tried to redress the failure of the regime to radically change and shape the ethos of Italian society.

On the publishing front, Galeazzo Ciano's diary reveals that in July 1938 Mussolini had a clear idea of the impact that his anti-Semitic campaign was about to have: 'Una prima avvisaglia del giro di vite sarà data dai falò degli scritti ebraici, massoneggianti, francofili. Scrittori e giornalisti ebrei saranno messi al bando di ogni attività ... La rivoluzione deve ormai incidere sul costume degli italiani. I quali, bisogna che imparino ad essere meno "simpatici," per diventare duri, implacabili, odiosi. Cioè: padroni' (A first warning of the turning of the screw will be given by the bonfires of Jewish, pro-Mason, francophile writings. Jewish writers and journalists will be banned from any activity ... Our revolution must now leave a mark on the customs of Italians. And they will have to learn to be less 'sociable' in order to become harder, implacable, hateful. That is: masters).[14] This quotation is important because it shows that Mussolini thought of the publishing and press industry as a first target of his plans for a racial 'toughening up' of the Italian people. In his *taccuini* Yvon De Begnac recorded a similar outburst by Mussolini – undated but presumably from the same period – in which Il Duce made a specific connection between foreign literature circulated by publishers such as Mondadori and Corbaccio and the diffusion of Jewish culture. He considered it an attack on 'the culture of the [Fascist] revolution.'[15]

There is little doubt that Hitler's official visit in May 1938 was a catalyst that pushed various branches of the regime into action. As Voigt has reconstructed in detail, in the weeks before the visit the Italian police made a sweeping round of arrests of all potential opponents of Mussolini's alliance with Nazism. No less than 120 Gestapo and SS officers were posted in Italy for three weeks in order to provide their specialist expertise on German and Austrian exiles.[16] As far as publishers and publications are concerned, Alfieri issued a statement in March 1938 to the effect that all translations of foreign books (with the exception of scientific and 'universally recognized classics') had to be authorized by the MCP.[17] Moreover, it is important to note that at the beginning of April 1938 Mussolini had approved a memo, presumably by Casini, that suggested the need to proceed to a concerted campaign against Jewish and 'decadent' journalists and authors. The campaign was meant to include the creation of a list of unwelcome authors. Mussolini's approval is clearly marked by his initial in the margin of the memo (see figure 13).[18] A few days later, the Ministry of Foreign Affairs sent a circular to all embassies and consulates stating that the MCP had ordered a ban on the circulation in Italy of all foreign books 'il cui contenuto non appaia consono tanto dal punto di vista politico, quanto da quello morale, con i principi del Fascismo' (whose content is incompatible, either politically or morally, with the principles of Fascism). Officials abroad were invited to provide lists of authors and titles.[19] Some days later, it was the turn of Alfieri to order the seizure of twelve books published by Corbaccio, all written by German and Austrian Jews.[20] In May 1938 Mussolini himself ordered the seizure of Mondadori's *Almanacco della Medusa 1934*, a hefty illustrated volume promoting the authors of the famous series *La Medusa*, simply because it contained a write-up on German-Jewish authors.[21] The next month Mondadori was hit with a seizure of ten books by German-Jewish writers. The Fascist Federation of Booksellers got on the bandwagon when, on 6 June, its director, Pietro Peretti, sent a directive to all booksellers ordering the removal from the shop windows of books by Italian and foreign Jewish authors.[22] At the end of July the federation met to discuss ways in which it could collaborate with the regime over the control on imported books. Its suggestion concerning the compilation of a list of foreign publishers with anti-Fascist leanings was later adopted by the MCP: it features in an 'Appunto per il Duce' (Note for Il Duce) on MCP letterhead that Alfieri presented to Mussolini on 22 August 1938. A handwritten note in the margin says 'Ha detto S.E. Alfieri che il Duce ha approvato. 23.VIII' (His Excellency Alfieri says that Il Duce has approved. 23 August).[23]

In these early months of proscriptions, everybody's attention seemed to concentrate on German-Jewish authors. Even the Nazi Embassy in Rome joined in: on 19 July it sent a diplomatic note to Galeazzo Ciano at the Italian Foreign Office containing a list of fourteen books by Austrian and German authors published in Italian by Mondadori whose circulation was unwelcome to the Nazi regime. Among them were Emil Ludwig (although his *Colloqui con Mussolini* was discreetly passed over), Stefan Zweig, and Thomas Mann.[24] Unfortunately it is not clear whether the memo by the Germans followed an explicit invitation by the Italians or whether it was simply their own reaction to the new anti-Semitic initiatives in Italy. Either way, there is clearly a coincidence between this first wave of Italian anti-Semitism and the renewed association with Nazi Germany that was bonded by Hitler's official visit.

This is also the year in which Fascist Italy and Nazi Germany established a program of cultural collaboration concerning the teaching and diffusion of each other's culture. The agreement was signed on 23 November 1938 by Galeazzo Ciano, as Minister of Foreign Affairs, in the presence of Alfieri and Giuseppe Bottai. On the publishing front, both parties agreed to act against the circulation of publications containing a 'tendentious' view of the other country.[25]

It is evident from these first examples of anti-Semitic censorship that Mussolini's inclination towards ad hoc solutions was once more an important factor. When Enrico Dall'Oglio, director of Corbaccio, wrote at length to complain about the losses caused by the seizure of his books – an estimated 200,000 lire – Mussolini approved a compensation package for a total of 100,000 lire, which was transformed into an order for 7,800 books on military subjects.[26]

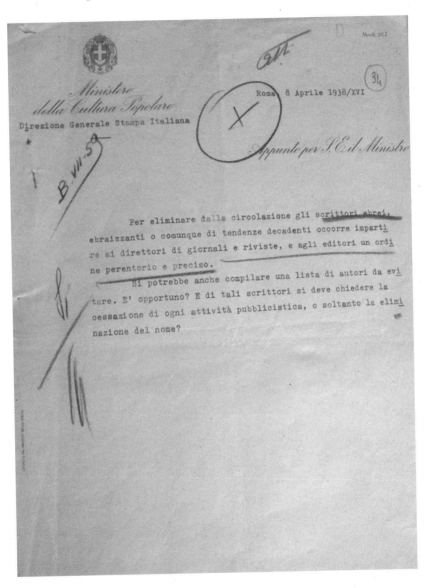

13. Memorandum, presumably by Gherardo Casini, 8 April 1938, concerning the anti-Semitic campaign, with Mussolini's note in pencil. (*Courtesy of the Archivio Centrale dello Stato, Rome*)

The first ministry to put together an official anti-Semitic campaign was Bottai's Ministry for National Education. During the summer of 1938 Bottai distinguished himself as an enthusiastic promoter of the need for a 'racial turn,' both from the pages of his journal, *Critica fascista*, and in his ministerial role. By August he had banned foreign Jews from attending Italian schools and had ordered the elimination of all school texts authored by Jews; by September it was the turn of Italian Jews to be thrown out of schools and all state academies, libraries, and cultural institutions.[27] When the supreme body of the National Fascist Party, the Gran Consiglio del Fascismo, discussed the implementation of anti-Semitic policies on 6 October 1938, Bottai proudly recorded his contribution as a hard-liner.[28] The elimination of school texts written by Jews marked an important stage in the campaign. In August 1938 publishers were asked to take the initiative and prepare a list of Jewish authors involved in writing or editing school texts. It was probably the publishers' compliance with this directive that convinced the regime it could still rely on their collaboration when the campaign was widened to all sectors of book production.[29]

Il libro italiano – the bibliographical journal co-edited by the MCP, in the person of Casini, and Bottai's Ministry of National Education, in the person of Edoardo Scardamaglia, head of the Directorate General of Academies and Libraries – also distinguished itself during the first months of the racial campaign. The issue of September 1938 was entirely devoted to the racial question. It contained a bibliography of studies on racism (continued in the following issue) and a number of articles among which was Riccardo Miceli's 'Razzismo nel libro' (Racism in books). The article contained a bizarre attempt to devalue the Bible because it had been written by several authors, it concluded that 'in questo senso gli ebrei non ebbero "autori" come non ebbero libri' (in this sense the Jews never had 'authors' just as they never had books.[30]

Attempting Book Reclamation

In the summer of 1938 Alfieri began to organize the executive arm of a *bonifica libraria*. The central idea was to form a committee of 'experts' of proven Fascist faith with the objective of drafting a list of authors whose works were somehow contrary to the spirit and values of Fascist Italy. The first meeting of the Commission for Book Reclamation (Commissione per la bonifica libraria) took place on 13 September 1938, chaired by Alfieri and composed by representatives of: interested public bodies such as the MCP (in the person of Casini), the Ministry of National Education, the Reale Accademia d'Italia, and the Institute of Fascist Culture; the National Fascist Party; and the Fascist Confederation of Artists and Writers (Alessandro Pavolini and Filippo Tommaso Marinetti) and publishers (Franco Ciarlantini). According to a note by Casini, the meeting lasted about two hours. There was a general discussion of the time span of the *bonifica* – it was agreed that it should concern post–First World War publications – followed by a discussion of a number of possible cases. Casini's note mentions only those of Karl Marx and Moravia's *Gli indifferenti,* arguably an indication that the committee was inclined to concentrate on Jewish authors and on the political relevance of their work.[31]

In September 1938 Alfieri ordered an accurate census of Jews within the Italian publishing industry. Editors of papers, publishers, and news agencies were ordered to draw up a list of their personnel 'di razza ebraica' (pertaining to the Jewish race). Publishers were given the arguably impossible task of investigating and stating the racial status of all their published authors, including foreign ones. At the same time, prefectures were instructed to proceed with their own census and were to double-check the information released by private firms.[32] The speed with which all bodies were supposed to reply was due to the fact that Alfieri, as much as any minister, knew that during its October meeting the Grand Council of Fascism was going to legislate on the Jewish question; hence the need for the regime's administrative machine to be ready to act.

Alfieri put pressure on the prefectures by asking them to make sure that the books so far seized had actually disappeared from booksellers' shelves. His memo dated 18 September 1938 was accompanied by a list of all books that had been seized since 1 January 1938.[33] It contained 167 titles, of which almost half (71) were published abroad in foreign languages (with the exception of Lussu's *Un anno sull'altipiano* and Giuseppe Garretto *Civiltà nuova* published abroad but in Italian, both in 1938). Among Italian publishers, Mondadori and Corbaccio were the ones who had suffered the heaviest losses. Already singled out by Barduzzi as early as November 1938, and partly on the request of the German Embassy, both publishers had some of their German and Austrian exiled authors axed. Thirty-three titles banned, by Arnold Zweig, Lion Feuchtwanger, Heinrich and Thomas Mann, Arthur Schnitzler, Jacob Wasserman, Emil Ludwig, and Ernst Weiss.[34] Italian authors accounted for only about a quarter of the total of books being banned (figures are approximate because twenty-one titles were published anonymously). A good proportion of these were books of morally debatable content. The author of *Sambadù amore negro*, Mura, was hit again with the seizure of an old novel, *La camerista delle maratone*, first published by Sonzogno in 1920 and reprinted in 1928. There was also a series of five books anonymously published by Hermes in Milan whose titles range from *L'arte di sedurre gli uomini* to *Il vizio solitario* and *Virilità*. The only case with clear relevance to the new racial initiatives was the appearance of seven novels by Guido da Verona, who was widely rumoured to be Jewish. Although the list did not cover da Verona's entire fiction output (at least three other novels had been allowed to circulate) it was not far from a blanket ban. On the whole, da Verona's case and that of German-speaking authors seem to be the only ones directly emerging from the new racial turn during the summer of 1938.

On 17 September 1938 Alfieri wrote to the Jewish owners of two publishing houses, Olschki and Formiggini, and ordered them to replace the names of their firms with Aryan ones. In the case of Angelo Fortunato Formiggini, this brutal imposition led the publisher to commit suicide. At the end of November 1938 he threw himself from a tower in his hometown of Modena. The event went unreported by the Italian press; his gesture of protest was recorded only by anti-Fascist papers abroad. Earlier that autumn Formiggini had completed a manuscript dedicated to his thirty years of activity as a publisher. It was his wish to have it published after his death, but according to his wife the MCP refused to allow the book to be published despite the fact that it contained no reference to Fascism or the recent racial legislation.[35]

The Turin publisher Lattes was later forced to change its name as well: in October 1938 it became Editrice Libraria Italiana, and its owner, Mario Lattes, had to pass the directorship on to a government appointee. In 1939 it was the turn of the prestigious Milan publisher Treves: it changed its name to match the surname of its new Aryan owner, Aldo Garzanti; later, on the Jewish publisher Luciano Morpurgo renamed his firm Dalmatia.[36] Finally, in October 1938 some, perhaps most, Italian publishers were informed verbally by MCP officials that they were expected to proceed to expunge all Jewish authors from their catalogues.[37]

What happened in the following months was a process of collection of information. Publishers were asked to produce lists of Jewish or supposedly Jewish authors. As for the *bonifica* commission, in November 1938 Alfieri decided to divide the field of subjects to be surveyed among its various members. Literary works were assigned to the representatives of the artists' and writers' confederations, Pavolini and Marinetti. As president of the publishers' confederation and a devoted Fascist, Ciarlantini wrote to all Italian publishers, inviting them to proceed – and in effect precede the government – with an exemplary 'self-reclamation' of their catalogues. He also organized a number of meetings. In his memoirs, Luciano Morpurgo remembers the general embarrassment when he was mistakenly invited to and indeed attended one of those meetings.[38] In February 1939 Ciarlantini could already boast that about nine hundred books had been voluntarily withdrawn by the publishing industry. A specific list, however, has never been found nor is it mentioned in any documentation. It is tempting to think that Ciarlantini's claim was partly a bold diplomatic move made by the representative of publishers in order to reassure the government. The uncanny coincidence between the number of books mentioned by Ciarlantini and the number in the MCP's list of officially banned books throws some doubt on the actual dimensions of this act of 'self-reclamation.' Even Fabre, despite his exhaustive analysis of several sources, manages to quote only an undated pamphlet published by the group Azione Cattolica, which contains a list of 231 'spontaneously withdrawn' books published mainly by Salani. Apart from the fact that we do not know when and whether these books were actually withdrawn (the list was presumably drawn up in 1939 or 1940), it should be mentioned that when the Florentine publishing house Salani passed from father to son in 1937, a remarkable change in its output was the move towards the production of religious publications. In other words, the 'withdrawn books' might simply have been a backlog of old titles that were put out of print. We know of only two cases concerning two other publishers, Cedam and La Nuova Italia. In both cases Ciarlantini intervened to complain about the fact that the two publishers had *not* proceeded to 'self-reclaim.' Given the lack of documentation, even a detailed study of the catalogues of individual publishing houses might not produce reliable figures: its presence in or absence from the catalogue of a publishing house does not necessarily mean that a title was available or not. It also remains to be clarified how and with what means Ciarlantini was able to assess the compliance of each publisher with his call for self-reclamation. In any case, given the fact that the self-reclamation of school texts had already produced a list of at least three hundred texts, a total number of nine hundred books for the entire publishing industry is arguably a modest figure, which makes one again wonder about the overall degree of compliance.[39]

With publishers left to proceed only with their own internal expurgations, the *bonifica* commission did not seem to make much progress. When the commission met for the third time, in December 1938, Pavolini and Marinetti were not even present to discuss literature, and once more no clear directives were announced. As Ciarlantini summed up in a reassuring letter to Mondadori: 'In complesso tanto rumore per molto poco. Meglio così' (On the whole much ado for very little. I wouldn't complain).[40] At the end of this first phase, in February 1939 the MCP simply sent to all prefectures lists of books that had been prohibited since 1934. The lists were sent as 'approved' by the *bonifica* commission but in reality Alfieri's ministry had simply put together all the lists of titles that had been seized or denied publication/translation since Mussolini's press office had started to keep censorship records. As specified in the circular sent on 28 February 1939, there were six lists:

1 Italian editions (638 titles),
2 foreign editions (179),
3, 4 anonymous books printed, respectively, in Italy or abroad (both included in the previous two lists),
5 foreign books whose translation had been prohibited (no copy has been found),
6 books whose reprint had been prohibited (64).

Not counting the unknown number of titles in lists, the MCP's master list comprised 881 titles. This is not a high number, and it should be noted that the lists included non-literary works, pamphlets, and so-called *fogli volanti* (unbound pages – that is, one-page publications of a poem, a song, a short tract, or the record of a speech). Twelve titles are explicitly identified as songs and, judging from the titles and the names of the print shops (appearing as publishers), it can be argued that a substantial percentage were publications of local interest and printed in a very limited number of copies. Among the 638 titles in list 1, only about half can be attributed to publishing houses of national or regional importance, the other being print shops whose distribution would be unlikely to go beyond provincial boundaries. Not surprisingly, the publishing houses that were hardest hit were Mondadori, with twenty-nine titles; Corbaccio, with twenty-three, and Casa Editrice Sociale (Monanni's name from 1919 to 1926) with eleven. The Jewish publisher Formiggini and the Florentine Nerbini each had nine titles on the list.

A comparison with the Nazi regime shows that by the late 1930s the united efforts of Himmler's Ministry of the Interior and Goebbels's Ministry for Popular Enlightenment and Propaganda had already reached a much higher figure. At the end of 1938, 4,175 titles together with the complete works of 565 authors had been banned.[41] Fabre's suggestion that, despite this huge quantitative difference, 'il "vantaggio" di più di dieci anni di esperienza dittatoriale si faceva sentire' (one could tell the 'advantage' resulting from more than ten years of dictatorship) is perplexing. The overall figures are so different that it is difficult to see how the Fascist system can be thought of as being ahead of its Nazi counterpart with regard to *bonifica libraria*.[42] It should also be noted that the Italian list of sixty-four books whose reprint had been prohibited specified that publishers and booksellers were allowed to sell existing stock. Among the books in this list were three of Benelli's plays, *L'elefante, Il ragno,* and *L'orchidea*.[43]

At this stage, the MCP's decision to invite publishers to 'declare' their Jewish collaborators and the workings of the *bonifica* commission were distinct and parallel initiatives. But there is little doubt that, in the minds of publishers and authors, the census of Jews in the publishing industry and the campaign to 'reclaim' Italian culture were perceived as offshoots of the same 'racial turn' imposed by Mussolini. There is evidence that officials from the Book Division of the DGSI were keeping an eye on the catalogues of publishers and even on those of antique books dealers. In March 1939, in a memo headed 'bonifica libraria,' the MCP asked the prefecture of Milan to collect nine books from four different antique books dealers. The books went as far back as 1782, with titles that censors must have found morally dubious, such as *Milano equivoca* (1866) and *Raccolta di novelle galanti, ossia avventure delle più avvenenti e spiritose donne del giorno d'oggi* (1783).[44] Yet even that pillar of Fascist cultural policies, Giovanni Gentile, who in those years had become a powerful figure within Florence's publishing industry, was prepared to adopt ad hoc solutions. As Fabre reveals, when in February 1939 Gentile had to face the unpleasant choice of getting rid of an essay by the Jewish scholar Attilio Momigliano from the first volume of the *Annali manzoniani*, he resorted to a cynical solution. He asked his co-editor, Michele Barbi, to contact Momigliano – over the phone, not in writing – and ask him to agree to publish the article anonymously. A few months later the same offer was made to the philologist Ezio Levi regarding a contribution to a Spanish dictionary for Sansoni. In both cases, the Jewish scholars withdrew their contributions. The example of Gentile might be used as an illustration of the degree of flexibility within Mussolini's government; however, it is equally symbolic of the sheer humiliation that Jewish intellectuals were cruelly expected to suffer.[45] For example, on 7 February 1939 Vallardi's *Enciclopedia giuridica italiana* was banned because its twenty-second volume contained entries by Jewish authors Salvatore Ottolenghi and Alfredo Ascoli (the latter being also co-editor of the encyclopedia). The names of both were to appear in the final list of unwelcome authors published in 1942.[46]

The members of the *bonifica* commission seemed to work at different speeds and with different intentions. When between February and March 1939 the commission produced its first two lists of unwelcome books, – totalling 122 titles – it was easy to spot who had done their homework properly. The most devoted member of the group was Giuseppe Bottai. From the pages of his *Critica fascista*, he had raged against the influence of Jewish women writers on Italian children's literature (which, within the commission, was the area assigned to his Ministry of National Education) and, in fact, the names of the writers cited in his article figured prominently in the list of unwelcome books produced in March.[47] The only other branch that seemed to have made some progress was the Reale Accademia d'Italia, which, in charge of historical publications, had contributed about thirty titles of works by non-Fascist historians and anti-Fascist intellectuals such as Piero Gobetti and Don Sturzo.[48] The first list named thirty-one titles, eight of which were in the category of Italian literature. Their authors were Alberto Moravia, Vitaliano Brancati, and Sem Benelli. All three, as we have seen, had had brushes with censorship, but in the case of Moravia's *L'imbroglio* and *Le ambizioni sbagliate* and Brancati's *Singolare avventura di viaggio* the books had not actually been seized across the nation. As for Benelli, the list included his anti-bourgeois trilogy, to which were added two earlier plays, *Amorosa tragedia* (1915) and *L'altare* (1916). Among foreign writers there figured two books by Robert Graves, André Gide's *I sotterranei del Vaticano*, and *Caterina va alla guerra* by Adrienne Thomas (which, as we saw, had been seized back in 1932). The second list consisted of ninety-one titles: seventy-two of children's books, and nineteen published mainly in the early 1920s, related to Italian history and politics. The general impression is that, when approaching literature, the *bonifica* commission mainly reflected the MCP's recent and not so recent activities. The only sign of Marinetti's input was the presence of two works in the first list (a play by Arthur Schnitzler and a critical essay by Ernst Bloch), which he had probably included because they were translated by Telesio Interlandi, a political enemy of his.[49] As for Pavolini, it seems that he was involved in the decision against Moravia's work, a half-hearted attempt that left Moravia's most discussed novel, *Gli indifferenti*, untouched. Such an omission may have resulted from a desire not to raise the interest of the international press or from a recognition that the novel had been originally distributed by a prestigious Fascist publishing house owned by Mussolini's brother.[50] It should also be noted that Moravia once more seemed to have benefited from a privileged status. In a letter to Arnoldo Mondadori, dated 21 June 1939, he wrote: 'A proposito delle *Ambizioni sbagliate* incluse insieme con *L'imbroglio* di Bompiani nella lista della bonifica libraria, io andai a parlare con Casini e lui mi rispose di lasciare esaurire l'edizione attuale' (As for *Ambizioni sbagliate* and Bompiani's *L'imbroglio*, which were included in the list of the *bonifica libraria*, I went to talk to Casini and he answered that we were allowed to let the current printing sell). As we will see in chapter 9, the situation was more complex than Moravia had thought, and his peculiar status was to continue throughout the war years.[51]

In this climate, it is not surprising to find that Guido da Verona and Pitigrilli (Dino Segre), whose risqué novels had for years strained the boundaries of the censors' morality codes, should feel the cold steel of the censor's axe in two other separate incidents. They were the first two writers whose fictional work was almost totally proscribed.[52] In the case of Pitigrilli, a memo by the Ministry of National Education confirmed that by August 1938 five of his seven fictional works had been seized; the decision to extend the ban to all his work was taken by Alfieri in the name of the *bonifica* commission on February 1939.[53] Guido da Verona's work was first hit in 1938. Ten of his novels subsequently appeared on the MCP's list of February 1939, and a total ban followed in the summer of 1939 (after the author's death on 5 April 1939).[54] We do not have any statistical data on the efficiency with which the ban was carried out, but it is revealing that six months later much of da Verona's work was still available in bookshops. Two of his novels – *Il libro del mio sogno errante* (1919) and *Yvelise* (1923) – remained in circulation and were listed in Corbaccio's catalogue as late as November 1941.[55]

These policies made no explicit reference to a parliamentary bill or a government decree. In February 1939 the government introduced a law affecting the number of books that publishers had to submit prior to public distribution. The bill raised the number of copies to be submitted to eight (three for the prefectures, one for the MCP, two for the national libraries of Florence and Rome, one for the provincial library of the place of publication, and one for the Ministry of Justice). In practice, the bill made public the system of implicit pre-publication censorship that had been unofficially introduced with Mussolini's circular of April 1934.[56] The irony is that, after five years, the regime had eventually come clean about its censoring policies while, in those very months, it was adopting a new set of racial policies that were not to be made official until the diffusion of the list of unwelcome authors in 1942. Once more, the Fascist regime was acting outside the normal legal framework, thus making it very difficult for publishers, the international press, and public opinion – and, in this last case, Jewish associations – to question or at least monitor the application of directives.

The application of racist policies accelerated slightly after the interception of a telephone call on 10 August 1939 between an unknown editor and a young official working at the Federation of Publishers. The two sardonically mentioned the fact that, despite the anti-Semitic directives, the works of the famous Jewish author Margherita Sarfatti had not been taken off the shelves. Indeed, this was a rather embarrassing example of the illogical nature of Mussolini's racial stance. As we have seen, Sarfatti had been one of Il Duce's closest advisers (and lovers) and was also the author of a successful biography on him. The transcript of the telephone call unfortunately ended up on Mussolini's desk. His personal secretary's note in the margin provides a clear picture of Il Duce's annoyed reaction. Mussolini asked for a report on the federation's official (who turned out to be a nephew of the federation's director), but more importantly he ordered that Sarfatti's works be removed from circulation. For good measure, he added that the proscription of books by Jewish authors be backdated to the year 1850.[57] The measure taken by Mussolini against his former lover and collaborator was rather undignified and is one more example of the sometimes improvised nature of Mussolini's decision making. Moreover, the designation of 1850 as a time limit is surprising because the *bonifica* committee had settled for the First World War as the earliest period for its project of revision. It is arguable that Mussolini might have decided to propose a broader time span in order to give a more sweeping lesson on anti-Semitism to the Italian nation.

The tragic irony is that the MCP as much as the Ministry of National Education zealously took Mussolini's outburst as official policy. Four days later the DGSI was informed that the *bonifica* committee had to meet 'al più presto' (as soon as possible) to discuss procedures for the identification and elimination of books by Jewish authors published since 1850. Whether or not the committee met to rubber stamp this

order (we lack documentary evidence), it does not seem that the episode caused a wave of activity in any way similar to that following Mussolini's circular of April 1934. The DGSI's reply, presumably by Casini, was
simply that publishers were going to be invited once more to 'self-
reclaim,' thus avoiding the awkward intervention of public officials
from either the MCP or the prefectures. Moreover, there is no proof
that the MCP put any extra pressure on publishers, so one might conclude that on this occasion the regime's officials weathered Mussolini's
sudden directive with aplomb. Indeed, this is an area where it is difficult
to follow Fabre's repetitive use of the expression 'ordine totale,' which
suggests a massive implementation of the directive.[58] In fact Fabre
admits that there is no proof that either the MCP or the prefectures, or
even publishers, through a concerted act of 'self-reclamation,' attempted
a full application of Mussolini's order during the summer of 1939.[59] It
would therefore be inaccurate to consider this period as a turning point
in the development of Fascist anti-Semitic policies. It is arguable that the
'crisis' of August 1939 is more of an example of the fact that Mussolini's
directives were sometimes the result of sudden decisions not always
underpinned by sufficient planning. The analysis of a particular case
adds weight to this hypothesis.

In December 1939 Casini was harassing a Milan publisher, Editrice La
Stampa Commerciale, because its catalogue continued to contain the
work of ten Jewish authors. In the letter sent on 13 December, Casini
asked the publisher to inform the MCP whether fourteen other authors
'belong to the Jewish race.' As usual, the prefecture of Milan acted as a go-
between. The reply of Stampa Commerciale shows how inadequate the
DGSI's measures could be. On 29 December one of its editors (the signature is unreadable) informed the prefecture that only one of the ten
authors (Massimo Grunhut) had published with them. Even more embarrassingly for the DGSI, the editor added that of the fourteen other
authors only one had published with or worked for La Stampa Commerciale (in this case, had published a book for another publisher, Aliprandi,
which had been taken over by La Stampa Commerciale). The editor then
added a list with suggestions as to the possible publishers of the fourteen authors in question. Handwritten notes in pencil suggest that the
letter was used, presumably by the prefecture, in order to further the
'investigation.' Two names were struck off with the note 'non risulta' (it
does not match) and another three with 'non è ebreo' (he is not Jewish).
But this is not the end of it. La Stampa Commerciale's editor wrote a
second letter that reveals that he had been telephoned by the prefecture

of Milan, who had asked him to provide more information about possible publishers of the original ten authors. Obviously well-informed – certainly better informed than the authorities – the editor provided the prefecture with a second list. The publishers associated with the twenty-four authors greatly varied: the majority of them were small provincial publishers but national publishers appeared too – Bompiani (with two authors: Ludwig Paneth and Desiderius Papp), Einaudi (Marco Fanno), Vallardi, Giuffè, and Sperling & Kupfer. Thanks to the help of this editor, on 3 January 1940 the prefect of Milan was able to send a full report to Casini in which he entirely appropriated the editor's suggestions while casually neglecting to add the source of his detailed information.[60]

This embarrassing episode is not entirely surprising. After all, by that time officials were becoming acutely aware of the huge practical problems that directives such as those of August 1939 posed. The idea that publishers should determine the degree of Jewishness of their staff and authors with regard to post–First World War publications was a recipe for inaccuracies and omissions. Expecting them to go back to 1850 was verging on the farcical. Indeed, very little happened for almost a year. It was only with the restrictions following Italy's involvement in the Second World War that, as we will see in the following chapters, the new minister for popular culture and ex-member of the *bonifica* committee, Alessandro Pavolini, was to return to the issue.

This first phase of the anti-Semitic campaign closed with uneven, although still dramatic and deeply undignified, results. Through the MCP, the regime had made a shocking move toward eliminating Jewish publishers, editors, and authors from Italy's publishing industry.[61] Exceptions were made – and, indeed, Fascist legislation allowed for 'positive discrimination' towards Italian Jews who had a proven record as veteran soldiers or militant Fascists – but the general result was devastating. Neither Alfieri nor the *bonifica culturale* commission were distinguished for their commitment and ruthlessness; this debatable honour goes to Giuseppe Bottai, who, through *Critica fascista* and as Minister for National Education, dutifully followed Mussolini's orders. Whether it was the result of personal racism or, as it seems more likely, the desire to show his efficiency and resolution to Il Duce, Bottai ensured that the Fascist axe first and foremost hit the Italian publishing industry in the area of school texts and children's literature. Finally, this first phase showed that publishers and their association were prepared to collaborate on any anti-Semitic operation. It is a shameful record that has rarely been mentioned and, more surprisingly, studied since the end of the war.

PART THREE

A Nation at War, 1940–1943

7 A Turn of the Screw

Alessandro Pavolini at the Ministry of Popular Culture

When the war began to spread throughout Europe, Mussolini must have thought the time had come for a more 'hands-on' minister of popular culture. Alessandro Pavolini was appointed to the post on 31 October 1939, in time to lead the MCP's white-collar army in the war of propaganda. A faithful follower of Mussolini, Pavolini had built his career from his beginnings as a young leader of the Florentine Fascists in the wake of the anti-Socialist pogrom of October 1925.[1] His father was a respected university scholar – Paolo Emilio, professor of Sanskrit – and Alessandro's cultural interests had always been prominent. After a non-descript debut as a novelist at the age of twenty-five (with *Giro d'Italia: Romanzo sportivo*; Campitelli, 1928), Pavolini had coupled his political career with journalism. He was chief editor of the paper of the Florentine Fascist Federation, *Il Bargello*, founded by him in 1929 and printed by Vallecchi. He also worked for the prestigious *Corriere della Sera* as a travel writer, and his articles from Scandinavia had been collected and published with the title *Nuovo Baltico* (Vallecchi, 1935). But the secret to Pavolini's successful career was his friendship with Mussolini's son-in-law, Galeazzo Ciano. When Ciano planned to join the Ethiopian war as a bomber pilot, he looked for an able journalist who could follow him and celebrate his military adventures. Pavolini was by then not only an esteemed journalist and an enthusiastic Fascist but, as was fashionable among young Fascist leaders, he had acquired a flying licence. He became a member of Ciano's bomber squadron, *La disperata*, whose relatively risk-free deeds he fervently recorded for *Corriere della Sera* and later collected in the hefty volume *Disperata* (Vallecchi, 1937). Predictably, Ciano's friendship provided a boost on the political front. Elected to the Fascist parliament in 1934, Pavolini moved with his family to Rome, where he became president of the Fascist Confederation of Professionals and Artists (Confederazione Fascista Professionisti e Artisti). As head of this association, he authored a propaganda publication exalting contemporary Italian literature and fine arts (*Le arti in Italia*; Domus, 1938) and, as we have seen, joined the MCP's Commission for Book Reclamation (Commissione per la *bonifica libraria*). When Pavolini was appointed minister of popular culture, many saw this as a direct result of Ciano's growing influence on his father-in-law. Ciano certainly thought so, as can be seen from his diary entry of 19 October 1939: 'È imminente un grosso cambio di guardia al Governo. Il Duce si accinge a fare Ministri tutti i miei amici: Muti, Pavolini, Riccardi, Ricci. Manda via Alfieri, e ciò mi dispiace perché è un buon camerata. Cercherò di tenerlo io a galla e se non riuscirò a vararlo come Presidente della Camera, vorrei nominarlo Ambasciatore presso la Santa Sede' (A considerable change of guard in government is imminent. Il Duce is preparing to appoint all my friends as ministers: Muti, Pavolini, Riccardi, Ricci. He is dismissing Alfieri, and I am sorry about it because he is a good *camerade*. I will try to keep him going, and if I won't succeed in having him president of the Chamber of Deputies, I would like to appoint him Ambassador at the Vatican). Ciano was true to his word. Alfieri was appointed ambassador, first at the Vatican and later in the even more important position in Berlin.[2]

The Ministry of Popular Culture that Pavolini inherited from Alfieri was a well-oiled propaganda machine and a careful arbitrator of Italy's cultural production. The list of all books seized by the MCP and the prefectures between January and the end of October 1939 totalled 380 Italian titles. Among them were a good number of old anti-Fascist publications that had been out of print for years: for example, Giovanni Amendola's *Una battaglia liberale* (Gobetti, 1924) and *La democrazia dopo il 6 aprile* (Corbaccio, 1924), Piero Gobetti's *La rivoluzione liberale* (Cappelli, 1924), and Arturo Labriola's *Polemica antifascista* (Ceccoli, 1925) – all appearing in the *bonifica* commission list of February 1939 – were unlikely to be found on booksellers' shelves. It is more likely that their ban was aimed at private and public libraries that already held copies of those publications.[3] On another front, among the ninety-five banned publications printed abroad were four works by Ignazio Silone: a Serbian translation of *Il fascismo*, the two novels *Brot und Wein* and *Fontamara* (misspelled *Fontanara* on the list of seized titles), and *La scuola dei dittatori*. The list contained also a sub-list of forty-one titles whose sale was forbidden in street book-stalls. The fact that almost half of them were from the Jewish publisher Formiggini makes one wonder whether his books were by then been sold off to street vendors as remainders. At the same time, the presence of a list specifically relating to street vendors raises the question of whether there was a class-related element behind Fascist censorship. In our discussion of the publisher Monanni in Chapter 2, we have already seen the extent to which there was a suspicion that street vendors were a privileged vehicle for the diffusion of unwelcome literature such as the works of Russian or left-wing American authors. The 1939 list of forty-one titles, however, contains a number of works that were obviously censored because of their immoral content and despite their fame as classics of world literature: among these were Terence's comedies, Rabelais' *Gargantua e Pantagruel*, Bandello's *Novelle*, Belli's sonnets, and even Machiavelli's *La mandragola*. The idea of limiting a ban to street vendors and not to bookshops – presumably frequented by a less casual clientele – is reinforced by the fact that, only a few months later, Corbaccio was allowed to publish the entire edition of Casanova's libertine memoirs; on 13 November 1940 Dall'Oglio received the MCP's *nulla osta* for the publication, although in exchange he was supposed to limit the edition to 3,000 copies and distribute them to bookshops with the recommendation not to put the book on public display and to sell it only to 'persone di serio affidamento' (trustworthy people).[4]

The political and economic restrictions imposed by the war together with the introduction of anti-Semitic legislation presented Pavolini with the chance to toughen the ministry's grip on society. On the whole, however, it seems that Pavolini refrained from taking this opportunity. In terms of legislation on book censorship, he presided over only the obligation of all publishers to request the authorization of the MCP before translating any foreign work. Not surprisingly, the order was sent out soon after Italy entered the war in June 1940; it was hardly a drastic measure, as his predecessor had already issued a similar order in March 1938.[5]

In one instance, Pavolini was stopped in his tracks by the intervention of Mussolini. Laterza, as we have seen, had been allowed to produce non-Fascist publications almost as a showcase for Fascist 'liberalism.' A few weeks after the appointment of Pavolini, Gherardo Casini – who continued to be in charge of the General Directorate for the Italian Press – found Laterza to be in breach of DGSI orders. The publisher had failed to comply fully with the regime's request for the anti-Semitic 'self-reclamation' of Laterza's catalogue. It was the perfect excuse for a clamp down, and Pavolini certainly must have given his go-ahead. Between 14 and 15 December 1939 the prefecture of Bari was ordered to seize twenty-two books by Laterza. Most of them had a Jewish connection, either through their author, as occurred with Attilio Momigliano's *Orlando Furioso* and Sigmund Freud's *Totem e tabù*, or through their translator. Others were the work of anti-Fascists such as Francesco Nitti, Gaetano Solvemini, and Carlo Sforza. Following the usual approach of the MCP, Laterza was also asked to state whether eleven other authors were Jewish.[6] However, by then Giovanni Laterza knew well how to play his cards. He informed Benedetto Croce of the situation and as soon as he received the philosopher's fierce reply he forwarded it to Mussolini. Croce's letter exposed the absurdity of eliminating works that were vital for specialists in the field and concluded with the sarcastic comment that, if things carried on in that vein, one day the government would have had to ban its own racial journal, *La Difesa della Razza*, because it wrote about the Jews! A couple of weeks later Laterza was summoned to Rome by Casini and was informed that the seizure had been withdrawn (with the exception of Nitti's and Salvemini's books).[7] A similar policy reversal took place in the case of Croce's journal, *La Critica*. Using as an excuse the reduction in the quantity of paper available, in June 1940 the MCP informed Laterza of its decision to suppress Croce's journal. Once more Giovanni Laterza responded directly to Il Duce, sending a telegram in which he deplored the MCP's decision; this was followed by Croce's letter.[8] Once more the desired result was achieved: Pavolini sent Laterza a letter informing him that the order had been revoked. Pavolini paraphrased a sarcastic remark by Il Duce: 'Mussolini non vuole propinare al filosofo nessuna coppa di cicuta' (Mussolini is not going to offer a chalice of hemlock to the philosopher).[9] But, sarcasm apart, it was clear that twice within a few weeks Pavolini had suffered his boss's disapproval over an act of censorship. Perhaps it is these early clashes with Mussolini that convinced Pavolini to adopt a more moderate approach.[10]

As for the *bonifica libraria*, the first commission meeting under Pavolini's ministership took place on 8 February 1940. The publishers' representative, Franco Ciarlantini, had died only a few days before, and Arnoldo Mondadori was called in as a replacement. Despite Mussolini's boast that Fascist book reclamation was going to go back as far as 1850, the committee decided to introduce an element of common sense in its proceedings. In a note to Mussolini, Pavolini clarified that the committee intended to concentrate on newly published books, thus avoiding retrospective censorship.

Pavolini reported that commission members had engaged in a fairly intense discussion with regard to such new titles. Mondadori and the representative of the Reale Accademia d'Italia had suggested flexibility in the application of the ban on Jewish authors, whereas the president of the Fascist Confederation of Professionals and Artists was in favour of a blanket ban. In the end, intransigency prevailed. The rationale, added Pavolini, was that such a decision would avoid the confusion created by exceptions such as had been made for Laterza and Moravia.[11] But once more Mussolini must have overruled his minister. As suggested by a circular sent to all publishers on 26 February 1940, the government had decided to leave the door slightly ajar, allowing the MCP an element of discretion. The circular was organized around three points. First, it allowed the publication of scientific works by Jewish author as these publications were not adopted in schools. Secondly, dealing with literary works, it permitted:

> Opere di autori ebrei italiani e stranieri che risultino acquisite alla cultura generale ed in qualche modo 'classiche.' Testi tradizionali di religione e letteratura ebraiche.
>
> Viene consentita su valutazione del Ministero, la loro circolazione, purché non rappresentino un'esaltazione del pensiero ebraico.

> Works by Italian and foreign Jewish authors that are culturally established and are in some way 'classics.' Traditional texts of Jewish religion and literature.
>
> Subject to ministerial evaluation, they are allowed to circulate, provided they do not represent an exaltation of Jewish thought.

Third, it allowed the inclusion of encyclopedic and anthology entries related to Jewish culture, works, or authors, though once again with the proviso that they not glorify Jewish thought.[12.]

However hypocritical, the circular was a rejection of total intolerance in favour of Mussolini's preference for leaving space for exceptions and ad hoc solutions. The only area in which the *bonifica* was supposed to be fully applied was that of children's literature, a field in which Bottai had already operated with some success. Bottai continued to show his particular zeal for the operation. In 1940 his Ministry of National Education published a booklet that grouped all the lists of prohibited books circulated by the MCP.[13] As Fabre rightly says, the 'news' that the government was prepared to contemplate exceptions to its anti-Semitic policies quickly became common knowledge among publishers. In May 1940 La

Nuova Italia advised one of its Jewish authors to work towards finding protection in government circles in order to receive the authorization of the MCP.[14]

For the rest of 1940 and the whole of the following year, the Commission for Book Reclamation assumed a low profile. Pavolini had evidently given up his attempt at a harder line. His biographer, Arrigo Petacco, presents this period as a rather difficult one for him. He still had literary ambitions, which had taken the form of a collection of short stories promptly published by Mondadori in 1940. A bizarre aspect of this publication, *Scomparsa d'Angela*, is the fact that two of the stories contemplate the suicide of the protagonist. The MCP's directives on the removal of suicide from Italian culture obviously did not extend to its minister.[15] But the content of the book was also a sign of his state of mind. Pavolini's wife remembered him writing sentimental poems, which he would immediately destroy because they were not the kind of thing that a Fascist minister was supposed to write in times of war.[16] Pavolini's post as head of the MCP was obviously failing to fulfill his cultural ambitions. Forced to continue the tradition of the *veline*, suggesting topics to be covered or avoided by the papers, he would then complain about the lack of originality of the Italian press.[17] At a time when solidarity and orthodoxy were to be favoured and policed, Pavolini must have found it difficult to sustain his enthusiasm. He developed a relatively hands-off approach to his job, getting involved only when required to do so and being less demanding of Mussolini's time than previous MCP ministers and cabinet colleagues.[18] He also became involved in a much talked about extramarital relationship with one of Italy's femmes fatales, the actress Doris Duranti.

Below Pavolini, Gherardo Casini, head of the DGSI since 1936, continued to deal with all things related to printed material. Publishers and authors often remembered Casini as an efficient deputy, friendly and well disposed towards the industry.[19] Casini too had the pleasure of seeing Mondadori act as publisher of one of his works, a collection of Casini's radio programs for EIAR (*Una volontà, una fede*, 1942). The DGSI was organized in four departments and the third, the Book Division (Divisione Libri), was headed by Amedeo Tosti, a military historian who was to become head of DGSI during the Badoglio government.[20] A memo of January 1940 allows us to form a picture of the Book Division. It was staffed by four people, including Tosti, and the revision of books was partly contracted out to a number of readers, most of whom were journalists. There were ten readers for Italian publications (among whom was the headmaster of one of Rome's most renowned secondary schools, the Liceo Classico 'Tasso') and twenty-two for foreign publications. Here, as reader for French publications, we find the name of Maria Bellonci, future organizer of postwar Italy's most prestigious literary prize, Il Premio Strega.[21]

A valuable source on the Book Division is the memoirs of Bruno Gaeta, who worked at the division after July 1940. Apart from the general impression of the division's benevolence towards unorthodox authors, Gaeta's memoirs record the involvement of the Jesuit Father Pietro Tacchi Venturi, whom we have already encountered as the Pope's emissary in matters of censorship in the early 1930s. Ten years later, he was still a recurrent presence in the offices of the Book Division. Gaeta remembers him having long conversations with Tosti and paints a comic picture of the priest arriving at the MCP with armloads of books that he had bought from street book-stalls. Pointing to the passages revealing their immoral content, Tacchi Venturi would demand an immediate ban, which the censors half-heartedly implemented even if it concerned books that had been out of print for decades. Tacchi Venturi was not the only voice of Catholic morality. The Vatican association Azione Cattolica published its own version of the MCP's list of prohibited books in 1940 through its General Secretariat for Morality (Segretariato generale per la Moralità). Concentrating on allegedly immoral titles, it distributed the list among its members and called on them to help find out which books were still for sale. There is little doubt that many 'segnalazioni' (notices) received by prefectures and the MCP with regard to books still on the shelves of street vendors came from zealous advocates of Azione Cattolica's list.[22]

Some of the MCP's cases must have caused embarrassment for the *bonifica* commission. In the autumn of 1940, for example, the Milanese publisher Sonzogno had reprinted Marinetti's *Come si seducono le donne*, which had already suffered pre-Fascist censorship at the time of its first publication. On this occasion an anonymous reader sent a detailed, ten-page report listing all the passages containing insulting attacks on public morality, the church, and Germany. The report, sent on 14 February 1941, produced the desired effect. The MCP was forced to order the seizure of a book written by one of the members of the very commission that was supposed to purge Italy from any kind of 'non-Fascist' literature.[23] A few months later Marinetti was also forced to suffer the banning of his 'aereopoemi,' which were broadcast by EIAR. It was Pavolini who took the decision on 11 December 1941, after receiving various

complaints about Marinetti's rhetorical and experimental excesses provoking disbelief and sarcastic remarks among the audience.[24]

With regard to the *bonifica*, it seems that the MCP's Book Division did
not take any initiative other than to double check the catalogues of certain publishing houses, making sure that the 'self-reclamation' process
was being carried out. And even this review was not consistently implemented. Fabre's study suggests that only a handful of publishers were
monitored. Cedam and Laterza, as we have already seen, bore the brunt
of the MCP's oversight, after which we know only of the case of Vallardi
and Stampa Commerciale.[25] A different case is that of Garzanti (formerly Treves), which shows the flexibility and debatable efficiency of
the MCP. In November 1939 Casini wrote directly to Aldo Garzanti to
inform him that his *Storia della letteratura italiana*, edited by Ugo Ojetti,
had to be purged of all entries by Jewish authors.[26] At the same time,
more than twenty Jewish authors remained in the Garzanti catalogue,
despite a letter by Casini to the prefect of Milan in February 1940 signal-
ling the problem. Some months later, Aldo Garzanti found himself in
the position of writing a letter of complaint to the Milan prefecture, protesting that two of his books – by non-Jewish authors – had been seized
by the police of seven different Italian towns despite the *nulla osta* previously obtained from the MCP.[27] Some wires were evidently getting
crossed: neither of these works appeared in previous or later lists of
unwelcome books. At the same time, the MCP could target individual
publications. On 4 January 1941 Casini sent to Garzanti (this time
through the prefecture) a detailed response regarding the publication
of Ernesto Kantorowicz's biography *Federico II di Svevia*. The translation
of the book was authorized provided twelve passages were cut (they contained brief references to the mixture of races in Swabian Sicily, to the
church, to marriage, and to the arrogance of Germans). A few months
later, when Garzanti submitted his plan for a new series of foreign books
entitled *Il fiore delle varie letterature in traduzione italiana* (The Best of Foreign Literature in Italian Translation), Casini sent it back with a suggestion that was more political than literary: there were too many French
titles; space should be given to Scandinavian, Eastern-European, and
Oriental ones. It is easy to imagine that he was discreetly asking for
more titles from nations allied with the Axis.[28]

Notable exceptions were even made by the regime in the case of
school texts and children's literature, despite its total ban on anything
published or edited by Jewish authors. Both Principato and Barbera, for
example, continued to print and distribute books by Jewish authors

such as Attilio Momigliano. Whether this was due to interested benevolence or simple inefficiency is an open issue, but certainly there is a
sense that the implementation of the *bonifica* was mainly left to the initiative of the publishing houses.[29]

For its part, at the end of 1941 the MCP sent out a number of circulars deliberating on the range of issues and themes that could and could
not be treated in children's publications. Krieg's wartime study, *La legislazione penale sulla stampa*, devotes an entire section to the five circulars
sent out between October and December 1941. The first one (15 October), imposed pre-publication censorship on any such work, including
illustrated periodicals. The Milanese state archive contains a few examples of this policy in action. A story in the illustrated magazine *Cartoni
animati* was censored because the Italian protagonist, while fighting the
French troops that had invaded Piedmont during the 1705 War of the
Spanish Succession, used inappropriate expressions such as 'accidenti'
(damn) and 'perdio' (for God's sake). Some months later, the *Corriere
dei Piccoli*, Italy's most popular children's magazine, was ordered to
revise a story or, rather, change the introductory part, which revealed
that two little Italian orphans had been driven by sheer poverty to
embark on a ship for the Far East. The editors were told to find a reason
for their departure that was 'più intonata a una vita nazionale nella
quale non ha mai difettato – e meno che mai oggi – l'assistenza affet-
tuosa per i piccoli abbandonati' (more in tune with the life of a nation
that has never failed – today more than ever – to offer its affectionate
assistance to abandoned children).[30]

On a more serious note, thanks to Fabre's archival work, traces can be
found of the dubious means by which some publishers attempted to
protect themselves against the effects of the *bonifica*. For instance,
Giuseppe Morpurgo, the editor of a school edition of *The Aeneid*, saw
Mondadori publish a new edition in 1941 with his name simply replaced
by that of another (anti-Semitic) scholar. When Morpurgo voiced his
complaint, Arnoldo Mondadori simply sought the advice of a lawyer to
make sure Morpurgo could not successfully prosecute the company. To
add insult to injury, the same thing happened with two other Mondadori books edited by Morpurgo. In another instance, the Turinese publisher Utet found a bizarre but equally insulting way of saving twelve
children books written by Jewish authors. A new edition was created
with twelve new 'Aryan' authors who simply paraphrased the content of
the original stories. The rest of the books – title, graphics, illustrations –
was left unchanged.[31]

On the proactive front, Casini's General Directorate for the Italian Press continued to sponsor, promote and finance individual authors, periodicals, and publishing initiatives. The number of papers regularly financed by the MCP rose from fourteen in 1933, at the time of Ciano's arrival, to eighty-four in 1942. Among them were official Fascist journals such as Telesio Interlandi's *Quadrivio*, indirectly pro-Fascist journals such as Marcello Piacentini's *Architettura*, and literary journals at the very margins of Fascist orthodoxy: Alessandro Bonsanti's *Letteratura*, which as we will see was censored when it published Vittorini's *Conversazione in Sicilia*, and Mario Alicata's *La Ruota* were among them.[32] As for individual authors, thanks to Bottai's intercession in March 1940, the poet Alfonso Gatto was assigned a monthly grant of 500 lire. A few months later it was the turn of novelist Gianna Manzini to receive a *sussidio* of 2,000 lire. In addition, from April to September she received a monthly grant of 2,000 lire. Like the earlier grant, the monthly subsidy was arranged with the personal blessing of Mussolini.[33]

In addition to such measures the ministry continued to instruct the press not to give any publicity, even negative notices, to certain books. In the following chapters we will see examples related to famous authors such as Alberto Moravia and Alba De Céspedes. One worth mentioning here concerns popular novelist Giovanni Comisso. In the autumn of 1941 Comisso had edited a collection of historical documents taken from the Inquisitors' Tribunal of the Republic of Venice. Published by Bompiani, the book was entitled *Agenti segreti veneziani nel 700*. It is intriguing that such a book should have been authorized: it portrays a censorial regime relying on spying and anonymous letters, and ends with the fall of the regime and the arrest of the three inquisitors on the orders of Napoleon. Yet, it was only after its publication that the MCP seems to have recognized its potential parallels with contemporary Italy. If that were not enough, one character – a pro-Prussian enthusiast mentioned in an informer's letter of 4 August 1760 – was called 'Moisè Mussolin, ebreo.' On 28 October 1941 Pavolini ordered the immediate seizure of the book. This was followed by a more lenient approach: on 2 November 1941 Casini ordered the prefecture of Milan to inform Bompiani that reissue of the book would be allowed only after Mussolin's name was changed. That directive must have been somewhat too late, though, because three days later an MCP *velina* requested that newspaper editors ignore the publication of the book. Once more, a compromise had to be found. On 5 December 1941 Casini wrote to Bompiani and the prefecture of Milan that Comisso's book could be reprinted only after a number of licentious passages – related to cases of sodomy and to sexual affairs involving members of religious orders – had been cut. Comisso in the meantime had proposed to change the name of Mussolin to Massarin and to delete the reference to his Jewish origin. Despite all the hurdles, by 1945 the book had reached its third reprint, confirming its relative success.[34]

As had long been the case, Il Duce himself often kept his foot in the door. Despite ministerial and military commitments, Mussolini found the time to get involved in publishing matters, some of them of little importance. For example, in February 1940 he read with attention the first issue of *Rivoluzione,* the fortnightly journal of the Florentine branch of Fascist University Groups (Gruppi Universitari Fascisti). Among the articles was a rather cryptic editorial by Vasco Pratolini, who expressed his frustration as a young revolutionary Fascist, using expressions such as 'al fanatismo avevamo rinunziato come a una pederastia reazionaria' (we had given up fanaticism as one gives up reactionary pederasty). As the MCP's head of cabinet, Celso Luciano, reported on 22 February, Mussolini was particularly annoyed by that particular sentence and had sarcastically ordered that Pratolini should be questioned on how he could distinguish between 'reactionary and revolutionary pederasty.'[35] Mussolini's hand was evident again when, a few weeks later, while Italy was preparing to enter the war on Nazi Germany's side, the chief editor of the Turin newspaper *La Gazzetta del Popolo* was informed by the MCP that Mussolini had expressed a wish to see a newspaper from that city publish a cultural article on the Kingdom of Piedmont in the eighteenth century. The reason was that in 1705, during the War of the Spanish Succession, the Savoy army had fought the French with the help of Austrian and German troops. Mussolini even suggested a title, 'press'a poco così: "Quando italiani e tedeschi combatterono assieme per liberare Torino"' (something like: 'When Italians and Germans fought together to free Turin').[36]

Moreover, individual authors could still knock at Mussolini's office door. Some such as Giovanni Papini and Guido Milanesi, did so successfully; others to no avail. In the latter category was the Jewish author-cum-police informer Dino Segre, alias Pitigrilli, whose entire fictional work had been banned. Slightly embarrassing was the case of an old collaborator of Mussolini's, Margherita Sarfatti. She had been allowed to leave the country and settle in South America, where her biography of Mussolini was about to be published in a Portuguese translation for the Brazilian market. In order to downplay the connection between a Jewish author and an official biography of Mussolini, Pavolini sent a confidential telegram to the Italian embassy in Brazil ordering that 'i giornali amici nostri' (the newspapers that are friendly to us) mention Il Duce but ignore the author in their reviews.[37] On a larger scale was Valentino Bompiani's project for a paperback series of propaganda books called *In un'ora*. In October 1940 the project was presented to Mussolini, who agreed to sponsor it with a grant of 10,000 lire. In return Bompiani offered to donate one thousand copies of the first title, the two-volume *Storia della patria* by Piero Operti.[38] In one case, Mussolini seems to have used his authority against one of his own publications. When his book *Parlo con Bruno*, dedicated to his recently deceased son Bruno was published in 1942, he ordered that no reviews should be devoted to it.[39]

As we have seen in previous chapters, Mussolini was particularly interested in theatrical censorship. One of Italy's most famous playwrights, Eduardo De Filippo, seems to have benefited from his protection. Although policy dictated that dialects had to removed from national culture, exceptions could be made for popular figures such as De Filippo. According to his biographer, on more than one occasion Mussolini had expressed both his admiration for De Filippo and his view on the need to keep his work free from censorship.[40] In a way, the playwright could be regarded as a privileged case similar to that of Croce, although in the former no political issues were at stake. Indeed, the only time when the censors intervened was when the setting of one of his plays risked being interpreted as indirectly poking fun at Fascist Italy. In April 1941, for example, De Filippo was asked to modify his play *In licenza*. Since the plot concerned the misadventures of a group of soldiers on leave, the setting was conveniently changed from contemporary times to the nineteenth century, and in times of peace.[41]

Privileged cases such as De Filippo's aside, Mussolini unrealistic attempts to stamp out dialect culture were showing signs of failure on all fronts. In September 1941 the MCP felt it necessary to reissue the 1932 directive on the suppression of dialect in newspapers and periodicals. A letter to Celso Luciano from Cornelio Di Marzio, who in 1939 succeeded Pavolini as president of the Fascist Confederation of Professionals and Artists, shows that in the summer of 1941 the government was contemplating the possibility of banning all literature in dialect. Di Marzio's long letter of complaint made a convincing case about the absurdity of such a policy and the whole project was shelved once and for all.[42] In another attack on theatrical freedom, Pirandello's play *Come tu mi vuoi* was subjected to various cuts when a radio adaptation was made in January 1941.

The references to the brutality of the Austrian and German army during the First World War were deemed unsuitable with Italy now fighting shoulder to shoulder with those troops. Leopoldo Zurlo approved the script only after those passages were removed. He also required that all uses of the polite form 'Lei' should be replaced with the Fascist 'Voi.'[43]

Further insight into the workings of the MCP's Book Division during the war years can be gained from its dealings with a non-Fascist publisher such as Einaudi. Despite the brief arrest of Giulio Einaudi and the *confino* of his two most important collaborators, Leone Ginzburg and Cesare Pavese, the publishing house had survived and had been allowed to carry on limited production of books. Among them was Eugenio Montale's *Le occasioni* (1939) and a new edition of *Ossi di seppia*, which, after prolonged negotiations with the original publisher, Carabba, came out in 1942.[44] Self-censorship was the order of the day. A brilliant example can be found in a dispirited letter by the scholar and translator of German literature Alberto Spaini, who was working on a translation of Schiller's book on the sixteenth-century insurrection in the Low Countries. In a letter of 29 July 1941 Spaini informed Einaudi that the self-censoring of his translation was depriving Schiller's work of all its substance: 'Per non offendere la Chiesa, la Germania, il Regno, l'Impero, l'Esercito e la Marina ho dovuto fare tanti di quei tagli, che di tutto il libro c'è rimasto il titolo – e già quello è notevolmente eretico.' (In order not to offend the church, Germany, the Kingdom, the Empire, the Army and the Navy, I had to make so many cuts that all that is left of the original book is its title – and even that is quite heretical.)[45]

Despite all the difficulties on the political front, Giulio Einaudi decided to expand his publishing activity, particularly of works of fiction. Between 1941 and 1942, new series were created, including *Narratori contemporanei* (whose first volume was Pavese's *Paesi tuoi*), *Libri per l'infanzia e la gioventù*, and a series of classics of world literature *I Giganti*.[46] This activity coincided with the opening of an Einaudi office in Rome, run by another duo of enthusiastic intellectuals, Mario Alicata and Carlo Muscetta, who were among the founders of *La Ruota* and, more importantly, were contributors to *Primato*, Bottai's new cultural periodical.[47] There is no doubt that Alicata and Muscetta fully exploited the degree of tolerance shown by Bottai in attempting to establish *Primato* as a cultural forum open to all young Italian intellectuals. Einaudi benefited from the situation too; both Alicata and Muscetta wrote for *Primato* under pseudonyms, thus allowing them to shower praise on publications that they had sponsored as editors at Einaudi.[48] From Turin,

Pavese too contributed to *Primato* together with another influential collaborator and expert on German literature, Giaime Pintor. In brief,
Einaudi's expansion was led by a group of young intellectuals who were
clearly intent on pushing both the regime and the cultural debate to the
limit. And they sometimes paid the price. Mario Alicata, who was a
member of the Italian Communist Party (Partito Communista Italiano,
PCI) was arrested on 29 December 1942 and was to remain in prison
until the fall of the regime.

As Giulio Einaudi stated in his oft-cited memoir, the need to avoid
direct censorship meant that all editors had to play a game of *dissimu-
lazione* (dissimulation) – that is, assume a level of collaboration that,
while compliant on the surface, allowed the publishing house to push
the boundaries of acceptability further and further. An entry from Bottai's diary suggests the extent to which Einaudi's subtle editorial policies
were hitting the target: 'Paralleli spontanei tra l'uomo Napoleone e
l'uomo Mussolini nelle pagine delle *Memorie* di Madame de Remusat,
maliziosamente ristampate dall'editore Einaudi' (Spontaneous parallels
between Napoleon and Mussolini in the pages of *Memoirs* by Madame de
Remusat, maliciously reprinted by Einaudi). In his memoirs, Bruno
Gaeta dwelled on the publication of this book, suggesting that it was
thanks to his own positive report to Mussolini that the book was allowed
to be published.[49] But examples of self-censorship also abound. For
instance, on 20 April 1942, while giving instructions to Alicata on how to
present the translation of Hans Grimm's *Volk ohne Raum* (1926), Giulio
Einaudi listed a number of cuts that had been made – negative references to Italy and to German politics – in order to make the text acceptable to the censors. On top of that, Einaudi asked Grimm to write a
letter of support, which he passed on to Alicata so that he could hand it
to the staff at the MCP's Book Division. Despite all these efforts, the
book was not authorized.[50]

Despite the odd setback, Einaudi's Rome office was rather successful
in engendering not just the patronage of Bottai but also a general
degree of benevolence on the part of the MCP's Book Division. Mario
Alicata was in charge of keeping in contact with government authorities;
his frequent trips to the MCP's offices often resulted with the desired
nulla osta.[51] At the Book Division, Casini and Tosti were often consulted,
although when the question was of particular importance Einaudi sometimes used his good offices with Bottai to get through to Pavolini more
easily. And favours were returned, as when in January 1942 Einaudi
offered to publish a collection of Bottai's cultural writings. Moreover,

from time to time Casini and Tosti would suggest potential publications to or even collaborate with Einaudi.[52]

Giulio Einaudi's dynamism in the early 1940s is reminiscent of that of Valentino Bompiani in the mid-thirties. Both publishers were keen to expand their range of publications and both were entangled in a game of hide and seek, constantly negotiating, gently pressuring, and, when commercially fruitful, collaborating with the regime.[53] Yet, there are two substantial differences. First, Giulio Einaudi surrounded himself with young intellectuals who had clear non-Fascist tendencies and were determined to push Italian culture in new directions. Second, Bottai's decision to open up the cultural debate with the creation of *Primato* allowed Einaudi and his collaborators unprecedented space for manoeuvring.

It is interesting to note that Il Duce needed some convincing about the loyalty of the publisher. On 5 January 1942 Giulio Einaudi sent him a report on his current and future plans for publication together with some books. Instead of replying, Mussolini asked the prefect of Turin, Francesco Palici di Suni, to provide him with a confidential report on Einaudi. On 6 February 1942 a telegram by the prefect cleared Giulio Einaudi of any suspicion. After listing the problems the publisher experienced in the mid-1930s, the prefect concluded that 'successivamente non ha più offerto motivo a rilievi e ha dimostrato di essersi ravveduto' (he subsequently offered no reason for being reprimanded and he showed that he has acknowledged his faults). Mussolini's mind may have temporarily been put at rest, but his final directive shows that he was still unconvinced. The prefect was instructed to inform Einaudi that the books had arrived but to do so 'senza ringraziare' (without saying thanks).[54]

By the autumn of 1942 Einaudi's 'special relation' with the MCP was losing ground. In a letter of 4 September 1942 Giulio Einaudi complained to Alicata about the increasing difficulties in obtaining *nulla osta* from the Book Division. Perhaps one of the reasons was the departure of Casini in March 1942, replaced by his more hard-line deputy, Fernando Mezzasoma. Alicata also complained about changes in staff that had deprived them of useful contacts – among them, Bruno Gaeta, who had been called up. Alicata's arrest on 29 December 1942 was a major blow even if no other measures were taken against the publishing house. As his correspondence shows, he remained in contact with Giulio Einaudi and somehow continued his role as editor even from the Roman prison of Regina Coeli.[55] But by 1943 everybody was waiting for the end. Einaudi's Roman office was later to result in a split operation. After the fall of the regime, Einaudi's anti-Fascism became public – in August 1943 he had even tried to acquire a newspaper in order to increase his firm's presence in the political debate – and, as in the case of the Mondadori family, the subsequent reinstatement of Mussolini's regime forced Giulio Einaudi to flee to Switzerland. The administration of the publishing house was taken over by a government official, but as soon as Italy's capital was liberated by allied troops the Roman office resumed its activity as an anti-Fascist publisher. Thus, during the last months of the war, there were two squarely opposed Einaudi firms: an anti-Fascist one in central/southern Italy, and a Fascist one in Turin. If the past arrests of Ginzburg, Giulio Einaudi, Pavese, Alicata, and others had borne witness to the publisher's anti-Fascist stance, the end of the war brought even more tragic events. Two of the most important editors were lost: Giaime Pintor died attempting to cross the front line in December 1943, and Leone Ginzburg was arrested and tortured by the Nazis in Rome's Regina Coeli prison in February 1944. There is no doubt that, of all Italian publishing houses, Einaudi was the one that paid the highest price for its opposition to Mussolini's Fascism.

The *Bonifica* Becomes 'Public'

By the time of Pavolini's arrival at the MCP, the ministry was still treading on rather ambiguous ground when it came to the regime's anti-Semitic policies. The process of 'self-reclamation' had forced the Italian publishing industry to revise its catalogues, purging them of a considerable number of publications by Jewish authors. The MCP had led the initiative through its Commission for Book Reclamation, but it is clear that the MCP had preferred to keep a low profile. The purge was never given a legal framework and there is no sign that a detailed list was circulated to all prefectures or publishers. The only printed list was that of all books sequestered up to October 1939, and even that was published by Bottai's Ministry of National Education, which presumably used it for the benefit of its public libraries. At the same time, it is revealing that the expression 'epurato' (purged) began to be used in relation to books. For instance, the two-volume edition by Hoepli of Lancelot Hogben's *La matematica nella storia e nella vita* had been banned following a telegram from Alfieri to all prefects in 27 January 1939. Three months later the MCP sent a strong reminder to the prefecture of Milan, telling it officially to give Hoepli a warning for not complying with the ban.

Hoepli was asked to immediately 'purge' the book from their catalogue. Similarly, on 30 October 1939 a letter from the MCP's DGSI (the signature is unreadable) ordered the withdrawal of Decio Cinti's *Dizionario degli scrittori italiani* (Sonzogno, 1939) because it contained references to anti-Fascist and Jewish authors that needed to be 'purged.'[56]

In the early months of 1940 Casini was still devising ad hoc solutions to individual cases as they were presented by individual publishers. In February, for example, he suggested to Bompiani to cut down in both number and length any reference to works by Jewish authors that were to appear in his *Dizionario delle principali opere letterarie e scientifiche*. Casini allowed the Milanese publisher of scientific books, Società Editrice Libraria, to keep selling Amedeo Dalla Volta's *Il trattato di medicina legale* despite the fact that it had been banned since January 1939. The only conditions were that no publicity and no reprints were allowed.[57] These measures were taken at the time when Pavolini's attempts to adopt a harder line were being thwarted by Mussolini's own intervention. Il Duce seemed to prefer a *modus vivendi* of half-written rules that were subject to change and adjustment according to the situation.[58] His cynical approach is highlighted by a small episode that shows that he was perfectly informed about the situation. In December 1941 Giorgio Del Vecchio, a *Fascista della prima ora*, law scholar, and the first vice-chancellor of Rome University under the Fascist regime, had sent a collection of his poems to Il Duce with an accompanying note highlighting the fact that some of them were of fervent nationalistic content (Mussolini was explicitly mentioned in one of them). The only problem was that he was half-Jewish and his marginalization had already started (for example, his name and entry – together with those of hundreds of Italian Jews – had been removed from the 1940 edition of *Chi è*, the Italian version of *Who's Who*).[59] On this occasion Mussolini was in no mood for exceptions. A handwritten note in the margin of the letter, almost certainly by Mussolini, coldly comments: 'perché hanno fatto pubblicare il libro di un ebreo?' (how come a book by a Jew has been allowed to be published?). The letter was forwarded to Pavolini, who promised to deal with it. On 25 December 1941 newspaper editors were ordered to ignore Del Vecchio's book.[60]

Once more, development of the process was prompted by its Nazi counterpart. A ban on books by Jewish authors had finally been imposed in Hitler's Germany in April 1940, based on a list that had been *in fieri* since 1935. The *Totalverbot*, as it was called, targeted publications in circulation in Germany. Following the invasion of France in the summer of 1940, the Nazis required the collaboration of French publishers to put together a list of banned publications in occupied France. Published in October 1940, the list consisted of 1,060 titles of periodicals and books and was called 'Liste Otto,' apparently from the name of the German ambassador in France, Otto Abetz.[61] It is in the following weeks that Bottai's ministry published the list of books banned by the MCP, which became almost an Italian equivalent of the German one in occupied France. There is no proof of a direct link between the two events, but Fabre's study shows how in the summer of 1940, the German ambassador in Rome, Hans von Mackensen, was putting pressure on Pavolini to increase the level of collaboration on the publishing front.

The following year the MCP's Book Division, in the person of Amedeo Tosti, began to have regular meetings with the consultant for books at the German Embassy in Rome, Gotthardt Maucksch. The first meeting apparently took place in June 1941, after which Maucksch reported to Berlin that he was going to meet Tosti two or three times a week to discuss problems related to both periodical and non-periodical publications.[62] Some individual cases were also discussed: in July 1941 Goebbels's ministry gave its thumbs down to a request by Tosti to allow Italian publishers to print the works of Essad Bey, a biographer of Stalin and Lenin and an expert on the Islam. Another case concerns the publication of Luigi Salvatorelli's *Sommario della Storia d'Italia dai tempi preistorici ai giorni nostri*. The book had been published by Einaudi in 1939 and, when it reached its fourth edition in 1942, a German translation had followed with the title *Geschichte Italiens* (Junker und Dünnhaupt, 1942). Not surprisingly, the MCP considered Salvatorelli's non-Fascist approach unsuitable for Nazi Germany. On 13 January 1942 the MCP's head of cabinet, Luciano, sent a letter to the *Consigliere per la Stampa* (Consultant for the Press) at the German Embassy in Rome: he complained that the MCP had not been consulted about the translation, adding that 'sarebbe stato meglio e più opportuno scegliere un'altra opera' (it would have been better and more suited to choose another work). The embassy's reply arrived only on 22 April 1942 after the consultant, Hans Mollier, had received clarifications from Berlin. His answer was that the authorization to translate Salvatorelli's book had been given back in August 1938, at a time when 'the collaboration between our two nations in the field of publishing was not functioning as it is now.' He laconically ended the letter, 'This way I think we have clarified the issue.'[63]

In at least one case, it was the Fascists who managed to impose their will on their Nazi counterparts. This is related to the publication of an article by German philospher Martin Heidegger in the 1942 volume of the yearly philosophical publication *Geistige Überlieferung* edited by Italian philosopher and Heidegger pupil Ernesto Grassi, then lecturing at the Universities of Freiburg and Berlin. Heidegger's commentary on Plato's doctrine of truth was found to contain an interpretation of humanism that was at loggerheads with the official position of Nazi scholars such as Wilhelm Brachmann, while it supported Grassi's own notion of contemporary humanism. Goebbels's officials entered negotiations aiming at the removal or at least the modification of the article until, on 3 July 1942, they had to accept a *fait accompli*:

> Dr. Lutz of the Ministry of Propaganda has let us know by telephone that Grassi's *Annual* will appear *with* Heidegger's article. At the request of *Il Duce*, the Italian Ambassador Alfieri has spoken personally to Goebbels asking that the *Annual* appear in its entirety. Dr. Lutz knows our opinion and has taken steps to see that the press will not mention Heidegger's article. At the same time, Dr. Lutz has informed us that there is a plan to publish Heidegger's complete works in Italian. We will keep you informed on developments.

Considering that Ernesto Grassi was a friend and in close contact with Bottai, it seems probable that the latter interceded on his behalf. Mussolini must have gleefully seized the opportunity to defend Italian claims to the roots of European humanism.[64]

In the summer of 1941 the Nazis finalized their own list of 'unwelcome authors' and during a meeting in Berlin on 4–6 September 1941 – attended by, among others, by Arnoldo Mondadori as the representative for Italian publishers – it was decided that the Nazis would pass their list on to all Italian publishers, as indeed happened the following month.[65] Although the Fascists returned the favour, they did not do so for a few months. It is not clear what the reasons were for such a delay: theoretically, the list was already at the MCP's disposal. Perhaps it was not in a finished state. After all, there are no extant copies predating 1942. Another possibility is that time was needed to do some final double checking to ensure its reliability. But even this last hypothesis is debatable, given that a considerable number of mistakes were found and corrected after its first publication. Fabre suggests, on the one hand, possible resistance on the Italian's part to the idea of making their racial policies public, and, on the other, the irritation of the MCP at having its German counterpart interfere with Italy's publishing industry. The facts are that only on 23 March 1942 did the MCP sent its 'Elenco di autori non graditi in Italia' (List of authors unwelcome in Italy) to all prefectures and publishing houses (see figure 14). On 11 April the list was passed on to the Ministry of Foreign Affairs but it took another three months before it was finally submitted to the German embassy in Rome on 4 July 1942.[66] While all this was happening, Mussolini's staff was preparing a meeting between Il Duce and Hitler, which took place on 1 May 1942 at Klessheim Castle in Austria. Anti-Semitic directives were certainly in the air, if not openly discussed; indeed, only five days after Mussolini's return to Rome, the Ministry of the Interior introduced forced labour for all Italian Jews between eighteen and fifty-five years of age.[67] As Fabre has reconstructed, in the same period, between 4 and 8 May 1942, there was also an encounter in Rome between representatives of the MCP and of Goebbels's ministry. The German delegation pointed out areas where the Italians were lagging behind their Nazi counterpart and in the following months the MCP made on more than one occasion to act on the 'suggestion' of the German embassy.[68]

A comparison between the Nazy and Fascist lists shows that the German one was shorter. It listed 602 'unwelcome authors' as against the 893 on the Italian one (912 if one disregards mistakes and repetitions). The Nazi list mainly concerned German-speaking authors, ranging from ones already banned in Italy (Schalom Asch, Stefan Zweig, the Mann brothers, Lion Feuchtwanger, Erich Maria Remarque, Arthur Schnitzler) to others such as Bertold Brecht, Alfred Döblin, Franz Kafka, Arthur Koestler, and Robert Musil. The Nazi list also included a handful of anti-Fascist Italians: G.A. Borgese, Ignazio Silone, Curzio Malaparte (obviously as a consequence of his *Technique du Coup d'Etat*, which had disparaged Hitler) and the liberal diplomat and outspoken anti-Fascist Count Carlo Sforza.[69]

The Italian list comprised mainly Jewish authors – about 800 of them – with another hundred 'Aryan' anti-Fascists thrown in. It was not limited to writers but extended to music composers and playwrights (hence its length). It contained a high percentage of foreign authors, although given the number of Italianized names and the difficulty in tracing the nationality of every surname, only approximate figures can be given. Still, the presence of about 300 foreign authors – one-third of the total – shows the much stronger concentration of the Italian censors (or, more accurately, of the publishing houses that helped create the list) on foreign publications. As for names of German-speaking authors, it is interesting to see that most originated from the list that Carlo Barduzzi at the

ELENCO

di autori non graditi in
Italia

A a r o n s o n L.

A b e l s o n

A b r a h a m s Israele

A d l e r Victor

A g h i t o Lorenza

A l e s s i o Luigi

A l g r a n a t i Maria

A l g r a n a t i M a s t r o c i n q u e Regina

A l m a g i à A.

A l m a g i à Guido

A l m a g i à Roberto

A l m a g i à Vittorio

A l m a n Samuele

A l s b e r g Maw

A m o r e t t i Giuseppe

A n c o n a M.

A n d r e m a n n Erich (Pseud. di Hirsch A.Edgar)

A n d r i c h Giuseppe

A n t i c o l i Gabriello

A r i a s Cesare

A r i a s Gino

A r i è Adriano

A r i e t i Cesare

A r t o m Camillo

A r t o m Guido

A s c a re l l i Fernanda

A s c a r e l l i Tullio

14. First page of the *Elenco di autori non graditi in Italia*, circulated in March 1942. (*Courtesy of Archivio Centrale dello Stato, Rome*)

Centro Studi Anticomunisti had obtained from the Gestapo back in 1937. In a couple of instances, it looked as if the Italians had been stricter than the Nazis: both Sigmund Freud and the novelist Hermann Hesse appeared in the Italian *elenco* but not in the German one. Moreover, a bizarre element of the Italian list is that Ignazio Silone appeared only under his real name, Secondino Tranquilli, whereas the German list featured his *nom de plume*. Alberto Moravia too, did not appear as such in the *elenco* but only as Alberto Pincherle. For a list that was supposed to allow censorship officials and librarians to quickly check the status of a certain author, it is certainly odd that these writers' relatively unknown real names should have been preferred to their *noms de plume*. Speculation might arise in revisionist camps that both writers, and for different reasons, were allowed a form of indirect protection by the Fascist authorities.[70] This was not the case for Pitigrilli: his name was mentioned not only under 'S' as 'Segre, Alfredo o Dino (Pitigrilli)' but also under 'P' as 'Pitigrilli (pseud. di Dino Segre).' The case of Pitigrilli also lends itself to a consideration about the dubious efficiency with which the list was compiled. The overlapping of two distinct authors – Alfredo or Dino Segre – is a clear mistake: Alfredo Segre was a local historian of the city of Pisa, a translator from French, and a Mondadori author who had nothing to do with Pitigrilli. Moreover, the mistake was not repeated under the entry for 'Pitigrilli,' in which mention of Alfredo Segre was correctly omitted.[71]

Mussolini's former lover and *consigliera*, Margherita Sarfatti, was also included in the list of unwelcome authors. This time she was not allowed any preferential treatment. An author who was spared any mention was Italo Svevo. Despite being a Jew who had published after the First World War, he was never on the Fascists' lists, either as Svevo or as Ettore Schmitz. Despite this omission, he was 'unwelcome' nonetheless. On 3 February 1942 Arnoldo Mondadori asked Casini for permission to include the work of two Jewish writers, Svevo and Alberto Cantoni, in a new series devoted to nineteenth-century Italian writers, *I venticinque*. On 18 February Casini replied that, after having consulted Pavolini, he could not give his *nulla osta*. As Casini justified his suppression of the two writers, 'Sarebbe inopportuno comprendere proprio due ebrei fra i 25 romanzieri italiani *esemplari*. Del resto, Cantoni non è tra i romanzieri italiani più rappresentativi. Per Svevo, fu usata la liberalità di lasciare in circolazione le opere; segnalarle ora al grosso pubblico con particolare distinzione, sembrerebbe troppo' (italics in the original) (It would be out of place to include two Jews among the 25 most *exemplary* Italian novelists. After all, Cantoni is not very representative of Italian novelists. Svevo benefited from our liberality and his work was allowed to be circulated; to invite mass readership to pay particular attention to it would be too much).[72] Svevo's work was therefore left untouched on the assumption that no publicity was made about it. Some months later, Einaudi attempted to publish Svevo as well, but the plan was scuttled because the publisher Corbaccio refused to sell the rights.[73] Another Triestine Jew who avoided the *elenco* was poet Umberto Saba, *nom de plume* of Umberto Poli. At the time of the anti-Semitic legislation, Saba had asked for, and promptly received, Mussolini's intervention. In April 1939 Saba was *discriminato* – that is, he was spared the effects of the legislation 'per meriti eccezionali' (for exceptional merits).[74] Other young Jewish authors were forced to revert to pseudonyms: Giorgio Bassani's debut collection, *Una città di pianura* (Lucini, 1940), was published under the *nom de plume* Giacomo Marchi, and Natalia Ginzburg's *La strada che va in città* (Einaudi, 1942) was published under the pseudonym Alessandra Tornimparte. The use of a pen name also saved Fortuna Morpurgo, whose clearly Jewish surname would have exposed her to the ban. But her Bolognese publishing house, Cappelli, simply did not name her as a Jewish author, and she managed to continue publishing her popular sentimental novels under the name Willy Dias throughout the last years of the regime.[75]

Given the rather haphazard way with which the *elenco* had been put together, it is not surprising to find that mistakes were made. In the months following its circulation, the MCP received and corrected fourteen queries regarding authors whose names had been inserted by mistake. Perhaps the most embarrassing concerned Mattia Moresco, who was vice-chancellor of Genoa University, a member of the Senate since 1933, and not a Jew.[76] Exceptions were also still made; not surprisingly, Mondadori was one of the beneficiaries. In July 1942 he was allowed to proceed with the fourth reprint of a book by novelist Franz Werfel, a German author whose name not only appeared in the German list but had been part of the Italian one since Barduzzi's notes of 1937.[77] Another exception concerned the author of children literature Olga Ginesi. Two new books plus a reprint were published in 1943 and 1944 despite her name appearing in the *elenco*.[78] Other proscribed authors never disappeared from the publishers' catalogues: this was the case with Federico Cammeo, Paolo D'Ancona, Rosa Errera, and Ezio Levi, whose work was still listed in the catalogue of the Florentine publisher Marzocco in May 1943.[79]

The enormity of the whole operation was also highlighted by the reaction of some directors of public libraries. In February 1942 the ever-efficient Bottai had already turned the screw once more by announcing that Jews were to be barred from entering public libraries.[80] In May he passed the list of unwelcome authors on to all directors of libraries that were under the aegis of the Ministry of National Education. This time he received some replies questioning the practical and cultural implications of applying such a draconian directive. Fabre mentions two such responses, one from the director of the Biblioteca Alessandrina in Rome, Maria Ortiz, and the other from Roberto Paribeni, president of Rome's Institute of Archeology and, more importantly, a member of the Reale Accademia d'Italia. Bottai took their cautious misgivings seriously and, after consultation with the MCP and apparently Mussolini himself, decided to adopt a more flexible approach. He borrowed Maria Ortiz's suggestion and on 23 September 1942 informed all directors of public libraries that they were allowed to leave the unwelcome publications on the shelves. All they had to do was to mark them with a sign – a stamp or a code – that would reveal them as unwelcome. Whenever a visitor asked to consult one of them, library officers were supposed to inform the director, who was authorized to decide whether the user in question would be allowed to peruse the book. Although it was a retreat from the previous position, this measure actually allowed library directors to keep an eye on the identity of those trying to read proscribed publications.[81]

It almost goes without saying that even this final episode of large-scale book censorship was applied with no proper legal framework. Jews were no longer supposed to write and publish books, although no law in the country stated anything to that effect.[82] The Fascist regime found the courage to legislate only in one of its colonies. On 11 August 1942 Mussolini's government approved a law that, among other measures, prohibited all Jews in Libya from publishing their work, even in periodicals.[83] Fortunately, the regime by then was nearing its disastrous end in Africa. The second battle of El Alamein in the autumn of 1942 was to turn this last measure into a final, hollow exercise in state persecution.

Censorship Denied

The process of denial referred to in the title of this section does not relate to the regime's desperate denial of its disastrous war campaigns. Instead it refers to a dual process concerning the press. On the one hand, the regime denied that Jewish authors and editors had been banned (however inefficiently and 'selectively' the ban had been applied). As we have just seen, outside of Libya, no Italian law decreed the proscription of Jewish authors. On the other hand, there was the vain attempt by the regime to convince public opinion that freedom of the press was still alive under Fascism. This was reiterated in a circular by Pavolini to the prefects in February 1941 and was publicly stated in 1942 inside Krieg's *La legislazione penale sulla stampa*, which not only denied the wide application of preventive censorship but also conveniently failed to mention Mussolini's circular of 3 April 1934, which had set the tone for Fascist censorship.[84] At the same time, in its last months the regime produced a law that, despite the excesses created by the anti-Semitic campaign, seemed to clarify the situation and simultenously relax the government's grip on the publishing industry. The law of 18 January 1943, called *Disciplina della produzione libraria e degli stampati per il tempo di guerra* (Discipline of wartime production of books and printed matter), clarified which books were to be subject to preventive censorship: publications related to propaganda, the war effort, international relations, and religious/racial issues of political importance. Scientific and 'entertaining' literature ('letteratura amena') were to be excluded unless – a significant exception – their content related to the war or to politics. An important development was that authors or publishers were supposed to bypass the prefectures and send two copies directly to the MCP's Book Division. A form also needed to be attached in which, among other things, the author's racial status had to specified. The MCP commited to communicating its response within one month. Compared to the previous practice of sending copies of works to prefectures, the Ministry of the Interior, and the MCP, the January 1943 law was an attempt to streamline the censorship process. It also finally gave its due to the MCP's centralization and assigned a secondary role to the press office of all prefectures.[85]

A close look at the books seized in the last weeks during which Pavolini was head of the MCP, January 1943, shows that little had changed on the surface. By then, Gherardo Casini had been replaced by Fernando Mezzasoma as head of DGSI. On 18 January 1943 Mezzasoma ordered the seizure of a book published by Catholic publisher Vita e Pensiero, *Il cristiano e la guerra* by journalist and Catholic priest Mario Busti. There are no comments attached as to the reason for the seizure, but one can guess that it was deemed to be too 'pietistico' (meek), a formula often used to denounce any lack of militaristic stamina. On 25 January another book was seized, this time of crime fiction: *Delitto al sesto piano* by Furio Bonesso di Terzet, published by the Modenese publisher Guanda. On the same day Mezzasoma revoked an order of seizure for Manlio Ciardo's *Illuminismo e rivoluzione francese*, published by Laterza the previous year.[86] It was business as usual on the theatre front too. A report by Leopoldo Zurlo gives some figures related to his activity from August 1931 to January 1943. Over that dozen years he had perused a staggering total of 17,330 scripts (including opera librettos and radio programs). Of those, he claimed that 1,000 scripts had been rejected. Only a detailed comparative study of theatrical censorship in other countries, or in Italy before and after Fascism, can give a sense of how draconian Zurlo's censorship process was. In the absence of such a study, the figures related to the month of January 1943 allow us at least to conclude that by that time Zurlo's ratio of rejection had not changed: out of 158 scripts considered, he had rejected 9. Unchanged also were the reasons behind his acts of censorship: to defend public decorum and religious and political institutions, and to reject embarrassing works eulogizing the regime and its leader.[87]

Another useful indication of the state of affairs in the last months of the regime comes from a second report, this time from Mezzasoma to his new head, Gaetano Polverelli, who had replaced Pavolini only a week before. The report, dated 15 February 1943, concerned the state of affairs with regard to 'letteratura destinata alle nuove generazioni' (literature destined for the new generations) – that is, literature for children and adolescents. Because this is the area on which Bottai had been concentrating since the summer of 1939, one would have expected the *bonifica* to have reached a final stage. Mezzasoma's report in this respect is not entirely clear. He boasts about his team of 'una trentina di revisori' (about thirty readers) having already achieved substantial results: in the area of books (the reports also deals with periodicals) the objective was to tackle five types of publications: 1) old works incompatible with Fascist faith; 2) new works incompatible with current international affairs and with the state of war; 3) awkward works of propaganda with counterproductive content; 4) translations of foreign works of debatable value; 5) immoral works (*malcostume*). Of the works examined to the time of Mezzasoma's report, 34 per cent had been sent back to their publishers with suggestions for revision and 31 per cent had been rejected. Mezzasoma unfortunately does not include the figures of the actual number of books that had been examined. However, it is interesting to note that he mentions that his team of *revisori* still had to examine 'qualche diecina di migliaia di opere' (some tens of thousands of works) and that the work of revision was going to last for another couple of years. This is surprising because, given Bottai's directives of 1939, one would have expected the *bonifica* in this sector to be far more advanced.[88] Another interesting aspect of this report is the total absence of any reference to the Jewish question. Despite his rethoric, even when Mezzasoma listed the types of 'degenerate' literature he wanted to fight against – drenched with 'anglofilia, americanofilia, germanofobia' – he stopped short of mentioning Judaism. It is tempting to see this omission as a sign of Mezzasoma's distancing himself from the anti-Semitic persecution already underway. However, given the fact that, as Minister of Popular Culture in the Repubblica Sociale, he was to have no qualms about anti-Semitism, it might just indicate that by this time Mezzasoma considered the purge of Jewish authors to have been *fait accompli*.[89]

As for the new minister of the MCP, Gaetano Polverelli was hardly an inspiring choice. As a journalist, Polverelli had followed Mussolini since the early days of *Il Popolo d'Italia*, back in 1914. His career had been rather undistinguished, leading to the odd political or diplomatic post without ever achieving a position of prominence. Even as a journalist, after twenty years of militancy Polverelli could boast only the editorship of the Roman edition of *Il Popolo d'Italia*. Since January 1941 – when Pavolini had been temporarily sent to the Greek front – Polverelli had served as undersecretary at the MCP, but even in that position he had never distinguished himself as a policy maker. His sudden appointment on 6 February 1943 was a humiliation for Pavolini – even more so because, in his new position as editor of the Rome paper *Il Messaggero*, Pavolini found himself on the receiving end of the instructions that he himself used to send out to journalists. A similar humiliation had been inflicted on Galeazzo Ciano, Giuseppe Bottai, and most other ministers, who were suddenly deprived of their powerful positions.[90] In his diary, Bottai wrote a long note about Polverelli, remembering him as an uncharismatic and bland presence since the beginning of their Fascist militancy.[91] The shuffle saw Mussolini tighten his grip on the government. He took on the portfolio of Foreign Affairs even though he was already in charge of the ministries of the Interior, War, the Navy, and the Air Forces. It would be natural to think that these many responsibilities were only nominal and that he concentrated only on grand questions of policy. However, there is ample documentation suggesting the opposite. Even for questions of cultural affairs, for which Mussolini had no ministerial responsibility, it is baffling to see how often his opinion was requested and given. Some examples even have a touch of the surreal.

On 12 March 1943 the ousted Giuseppe Bottai, mainly concentrating on his editorial activity for *Critica fascista* and *Primato*, wrote to Mussolini with a query. He had received the manuscript of a pamphlet by journalist Mario Missiroli (who was to become editor of *Il Messaggero* and *Corriere della Sera* in the postwar years) about Italy's role in the Mediterranean. Bottai was wondering whether to print it as a publication of the Ministry of Italian Africa or of the PNF. Apart from the irony that by March 1943 Italian Africa had been reduced to a rapidly disappearing stretch of desert, it is bizarre that Bottai should have thought that the head of government had time and interest to devote to such trivial matters. A handwritten note in the margin, however, shows that the letter was read by Mussolini, who suggested the Fascist Institute for Italian Africa as publisher. The telegraphic note also contained a perhaps sarcastic comment: 'Tu leggi?' (You read?). A week later Polverelli wrote to the Minister for Italian Africa confirming that, following a direct order by Il Duce, the pamphlet had to be published by the Fascist Institute for Italian Africa. Seven weeks later, Italian Africa was no more.

On 23 May 1943 the Catholic paper *L'avvenire d'Italia* denounced a group of writers in Bologna for selling a book of prose and poems by Roberto Mandel. The paper considered *Il cantico dei cieli: Poema cosmico* (Studio Letterario Milanese, 1941) insulting and indecent, and a copy of the article ended up among the papers for Polverelli's daily report to Mussolini. A note in the margin states that Il Duce had asked to see the book and that the prefect of Bologna had been ordered to send a copy as soon as possible. On 29 May the prefect confirmed to Mussolini's secretary that the book had been sent courtesy of a police officer instructed to deliver it by hand. The prefect added that the book had been banned and eleven copies seized. A final handwritten note stated that the book had arrived on 1 June 1943 and had been kept by Mussolini.[92]

A final example concerning Mussolini's involvement pertains to the historian and army officer Ivo Luzzatti, whose book *Andrea Doria* (Garzanti, 1943) had been sent 'in omaggio' to Mussolini on 13 May 1943. A note in response to Garzanti's letter, presumably by Mussolini's secretary, says 'Conservalo' (Keep it) and 'E' stato sequestrato' (It has been seized). We do not know whether this happened on Mussolini's suggestion but certainly the book had been sequestrated on suspicion that the author was of Jewish origin. Indeed, Luzzatti was a Jewish surname: two Luzzattis and seven Luzzattos appeared in the *Elenco di autori non graditi* of 1942. However, on 27 May 1943 Garzanti asked the MCP to lift the ban on the grounds that not only was Luzzatti not a Jew but he was a member of the Fascist Confederation of Professionals and Artists. A note by Mussolini's private secretary, Nicolò de Cesare, shows that even this document had reached Il Duce's desk. It stated, 'restituire ma il DUCE non considera esauriente la risposta' (return it but Il DUCE does not think the answer is satisfactory). Eventually a compromise was found: the ban was revoked, Ivo Luzzatti was not proscribed, and Garzanti was told never to reprint the book.[93]

Mussolini's involvement in such trivial affairs, given the scale of what was happening at the time, has more than a touch of the denial. It would be tempting to think that he willingly sought refuge in details. However, as we have seen, there is ample evidence that he had been keeping a close eye on literary and journalistic affairs throughout the *ventennio*. The degree to which this need to micromanage is partly responsible for Mussolini's failure as a statesman is an issue for historians and biographers to discuss. The speed and scale with which the regime apparatus crumbled after 24 July 1943 bears witness to the ultimate failure of his policies and reforms. Mussolini's Fascism had not taken root. In the field of cultural matters, it is interesting to note that the first two powerful ministers of the MCP, Ciano and Alfieri, both voted in favour of Dino Grandi's resolution, which brought the demise of Mussolini's regime. In contrast, their successors remained faithful. Polverelli voted against the resolution and Pavolini followed Mussolini to become one of the most hated figures in the Republica Sociale Italiana as head of the Fascist Republican Party and founder of the *brigate nere*. So did Mezzasoma, and both paid for this choice with their lives.

In a report to what was one of the last meetings of the PNF Directorate, on 19 June 1943, Polverelli lamented the defeatism widespread among Italian intellectuals. They were detached from Fascism despite the fact that they were 'quasi tutti sovvenzionati' (almost all subsidized).[94] Despite Bottai's calls for a united front and the MCP's financial incentives, the gap between regime and intellectuals had become unbridgeable. The same was true with respect to the Italian publishing industry. Indeed, when the regime fell, most publishers immediately immersed themselves in the new political climate. On 26 July 1943 Mondadori sent a telegram followed by a letter to the new head of government, General Badoglio, complimenting him and offering the services of his publishing house. Einaudi was eventually able to publish works of explicit anti-Fascism, already, on 2 August 1943, it was contacting Ignazio Silone in Switzerland, asking for the rights to publish his works in Italy. Enrico Dall'Oglio was able to revive Corbaccio's old tradition as an anti-Fascist publisher. It proved a brief respite. The restoration of the puppet Fascist government in September 1943 caused all these publishers to flee to Switzerland to escape arrest and detention. Corbaccio was closed down and Einaudi and Mondadori were put under government administration.[95]

For the RSI government, faced with civil war, military defeat, and economic meltdown, the control of the publishing industry was a marginal issue. Tragically, as a result of Giovanni Preziosi's new position as *Ispettore generale per la razza* (general inspector for race) and, more significantly, of ruthless Nazi determination, anti-Semitic persecution entered a new phase. In Italy, too, segregation was to be replaced with concentration camps.

8 Foreign Fiction and Weak Autarky

The War on Translations and the Case of Bompiani's *Americana*

Given the national and autarkic leaning of Fascism, it is easy to imagine that questions related to foreign literature would surface from time to time. As we have already seen in previous chapters, its popularity and profit-making potential was such that publishers made full use of their influence in an attempt to dissuade the regime from taking draconian measures to ban works by foreign authors. The war brought these issues to a head, particularly as Italy found itself at war with some of the most popular exporters of narrative literature – Britain, the Soviet Union, and the United States (France's swift capitulation resulted in a somewhat different status).

If anti-Semitism was the main drive behind the *bonifica della cultura*, the desire to curb the influence of foreign literature was also an important consideration. In a speech of 3 February 1938, Gherardo Casini of the General Directorate for the Italian Press had first reassured the publishing industry that no witch hunt was being planned by the regime. However, only a few weeks earlier the MCP had asked all publishers to provide information with a view to drawing up an inventory of all foreign books being translated in Italy. Even worse, a couple of months later it had decided to impose what equated to pre-publication censorship on all foreign books with the circular of 26 March 1938, which stated in no uncertain terms that 'dal 1° aprile c.a. soltanto questo Ministero potrà autorizzare la diffusione in Italia delle traduzioni straniere' (as of April 1st only this Ministry will be authorized to allow the distribution of foreign translations in Italy).[1] Casini's probable aim was to ensure the collaboration of publishers while securing the MCP's grip over the industry. Regardless of whether its alleged tolerance was genuine or not, the MCP had become the only and final authority with power of veto over any proposal to translate a book into Italian.

If, on the front of Jewish culture, publishers faced a ban that – however selectively applied – it was dangerous to challenge, on the front of foreign publications the field was wide open for negotiation. Both regime officials and publishers knew well the extent to which profits from foreign fiction sales contributed to the economic viability of the publishing industry. Despite the recurrent calls for more emphasis on national authors, there was a general agreement that a strongly autarkic focus suited nobody.

Corbaccio's hefty file at the prefecture of Milan contains numerous examples of the range of excuses used by the MCP to justify its ban on the translation of certain foreign books. Ignaz Jastrow's *Weltgeschichte in einem Band* (1932) was banned on 18 June 1938 because the author 'shows little appreciation of Mussolini and Fascism.' Edmund Gilligan's *Boundary against Night* (1939) was banned because it contained a sarcastic comment regarding the King of Italy. Immorality was often the reason behind the ban on the translation, as in the case of Maurice Dekobra's *Les tigres parfumes* (1931), Mirabeau's *L' oeuvre libertine* (1910 edition), Edward Stucken's *Die Weissen Götter* (1918), and George Bernard Shaw's *The Irrational Knot* (1905), which on 18 November 1939 was considered opposed to the 'Fascist principles on the family.' Unsurprisingly, racial reasons were also the cause for bans, as was the case with Sàndor Hunyady's *Nemes Fém* (1938). Frigyes Karinthy's *Viaggio intorno al mio cranio*, which had been regularly published by Corbaccio since 1937, was subject to a number of 'racial' directives. Its second reprint was banned by the MCP on 16 May 1939 because the author was a Jew; however, only two weeks later, after having received 'clarifications' from the publisher, Casini wrote to the prefecture of Milan and ordered for the ban to be lifted (Dall'Oglio had presumably convinced Casini that Karinthy was not a Jew). The defence of Nazi Germany's reputation was the reason for the ban on Katherine Mansfield's short stories *In a German Pension* (1929), which on 30 November 1939 were deemed to be too 'unappreciative towards the German people.' In other cases, the translation was allowed subsequent to a number of cuts. For example, in June 1938 Eduardo Mallea's *La ciudad junto al rìo inmóvil* (*La città sul fiume immobile*, 1938) had to be purged of all the passages showing the sympathy of both the author and Argentinian intellectuals for communism. In John Steinbeck's *Tortilla Flat* (1935), an insulting reference to

Sicilian Americans made by a drunken character had to be left out, and in June 1939 Margaret Halsey's *With Malice towards Some* (*Piccolo mondo inglese*, 1938) had to be purged of a single simile describing a harsh landscape as 'solidified Fascism'. The translation of a novel by the popular Hungarian writer Miklòs Surany, *A szörnyeteg* (*Il mostro*) had to be modified with the replacement of 'Lei' with the Fascist 'Voi'. Finally, William Von Simpson's novel *Die Barrings* (1937) was approved on 4 January 1941 subject to the translator's toning down its eulogistic references to the Anglo-Saxon race.[2]

Another publisher who was particularly interested in foreign authors was Valentino Bompiani. During the war years he employed Elio Vittorini as full-time editor with the specific task of organizing Bompiani's foreign list. The series *La Corona* was one of its flagships, and on a number of occasions Vittorini had to enter into negotiations with the MCP to defend his choices. He sometimes travelled from Milan to Rome to meet Alessandro Pavolini. The two knew each other from their Florentine years. Pavolini was the founder and first editor-in-chief of *Il Bargello*, Florence's Fascist paper, for which Vittorini had worked up until the Spanish Civil War. The rejection of a number of publication proposals from Bompiani and the ban on the reprint of already published books shows that American fiction was bearing the brunt of the restrictions imposed by the war. A translation of Erskine Caldwell's *Journeyman* (1938) was rejected by the MCP on 20 December 1939 on the ground that it did not comply with 'our racial principles.' On 6 February 1940 Casini also rejected the request for a translation of John Dos Passos's *Adventures of a Young Man* (1939) because of its 'communist and often anti-Italian spirit.' The translation of a collection of short stories by Henry James – entitled *La belva nella giungla* – was refused publication first on 11 January 1941 and again on 14 August 1941. In August 1941, the ministry denied permission to reprint *Il piccolo campo*, Vittorini's 1940 translation of Erskine Caldwell's (*God's Little Acre*, 1933). Similar fates befell John Steinbeck's *La battaglia* (*In Dubious Battle*, 1936) and *Furore* (*The Grapes of Wrath*, 1939). Although both titles were published in 1940, the ministry rejected applications to reprint them in 1942. It is a sign of the popularity of these books that by the time of the ban on *La battaglia*, the novel had already reached its eighth reprint. In an exchange of letters between Bompiani and Pavolini related to the ban on Caldwell's novel and on *Cristo tra i muratori* by Italian-American author Pietro Di Donato (*Christ in Concrete*, 1939, a huge success at the time), Pavolini offered compensation for the publisher's losses with the following words: 'Per il sequestro dei volumi *Piccolo campo* e *Cristo tra i muratori*, precedentemente autorizzati dal ministero, non sarei alieno dal cercare il modo di reintegrare, almeno in parte, il danno che ne è derivato alla vostra Casa' (As for the seizure of the volumes *Piccolo campo* and *Cristo tra i muratori*, formerly authorized by this ministry, I would not be against trying to find a way to reimburse, at least in part, the damage suffered by your firm).

Bompiani's political compliance was rewarded with a recognition of the financial implications of the bans (although we do not know what compensation, if any, was agreed in this instance).[3]

Valentino Bompiani was well aware of the dangerously fine line between commercial success and political disapproval. In a letter to Vittorini, dated 2 July 1942, he wrote: 'Bisogna calmare un poco la tempesta addensatasi sulle nostre teste, accelerando gli italiani' (In order to disperse the tempest gathering above our heads, we need to give priority to the Italians).[4] Indeed, the policy adopted by many publishers in order to convince the MCP of their patriotic intentions was to emphasize their publication of Italian authors. Bompiani also continued in his efforts to be involved in a number of state-funded initiatives. In the spring of 1940 he tried to convince Pavolini to finance a series of paperbacks aimed at providing less-educated readers with good patriotic readings. The titles of the first four books are self-explanatory: *Il re*; *Il genio italiano* (by Giuseppe Bottai); *Storia della Patria* (in two volumes); and *Il volto della patria*. Pavolini initially seemed prepared to cover the cost of a first edition of 50,000 copies to be donated to small public libraries and newlywed couples. In the summer of 1940, however, Pavolini and Mussolini refused to commit themselves, despite the publication of the first volume and Bompiani's offer to cover half the costs. Despite the setback, on 14 September Bompiani reminded Mussolini's secretary that during one of his visits, Il Duce had promised to give him an autographed picture of himself. According to the notes in the margin of the letter, Chiavolini double checked with Mussolini and the photograph was duly sent to Bompiani's headquarters in Milan.[5]

Despite putting a brave face on the situation, there is little doubt that Bompiani was seriously worried about the financial viability of his publishing enterprise. On 17 September 1942 he asked Vittorini for a detailed list of the losses incurred by the many publication bans imposed by the MCP and concluded: 'Se andiamo avanti di questo passo conviene smettere perché le perdite gravano troppo' (If we carry on in this fashion we might just as well close down because our losses are too

heavy). And on 21 September he added, referring to *La Corona*, 'Si dif-
fonde sulla collana una luce di sospetto' (A shadow of suspicion is hang-
ing over the series).[6] The MCP's bans were also hitting non-American
publications. For instance, in the spring of 1942 an anthology of the pre-
Fascist journal *La Voce* (1909–16) had to be scrapped after its editors,
Romano Bilenchi and Mario Luzi, complained about the number of
writings and authors that the censors had cut. The main stumbling
block was that among the founders of *La Voce* were personalities who
were considered *persona non grata* – Giovanni Amendola, Giuseppe Prezzolini, Luigi Ambrosini, and Gaetano Salvemini. Bilenchi seemed partially aware of this, as he explained in a letter to Vittorini: 'Di Salvemini
abbiamo incluso scritti che non offendono alcuno. Anzi! Egli mi pare se
non il padre almeno lo zio delle camicie nere. Anche di Amendola nulla
può offendere. E ti dico che senza loro due un'antologia della "Voce"
sarebbe assurda, anzi una viltà di chi poi avesse la sfacciataggine di met-
ter sulla coperta il suo nome di compilatore' (The pieces by Salvemini
that we have included are totally inoffensive. Even better! We make him
look like, perhaps not the father, but at least the uncle of the black
shirts. The same goes for Amendola. And let me tell you that without
those two it would be absurd to have an anthology of 'La Voce,' and
whoever had the arrogance to put his name on the cover as editor
would be a coward).[7]

What both Vittorini and Bilenchi seemed to ignore was the fact that
Salvemini had been added to the list of unwelcome authors that had
been distributed to prefectures and publishers all over Italy only a few
weeks earlier. As a result, the MCP refused to authorize the anthology
despite Bilenchi's effort to go to Rome and speak directly to Pavolini. It
is not clear whether the meeting took place, but in any case the anthology remained unpublished.[8] A second anthology that suffered from the
cuts of the censors was one devoted to German literature. On 22 September 1942 Vittorini informed Bompiani that the MCP had requested
the removal of two items: a comment by Thomas Mann (on whose work,
as we have seen, there was a blanket ban) and the famous short story
'Die Judenbuche' ('Il faggio degli Ebrei') by Annette von Dröste-
Hulschoff. Vittorini suggested that Mann's comment could easily be
removed but protested that von Dröste-Hulschoff's story was too important to be left out. Moreover, it was not censored in Nazi Germany. Vittorini suggested the MCP should ask the cultural attaché at the German
embassy for clarification. Whether this happened or not, two weeks later
Vittorini wrote to Bompiani that after an exchange of letters with the

MCP's head of the Book Division, Amedeo Tosti, he had decided to comply with the request. 'Il faggio degli Ebrei' was eventually removed from *Germanica*.[9] The MCP's particular sensitivity towards Italy's German ally was also at the root of the ban on a collection of essays by the French Catholic and pro-Jewish writer Leon Bloy, *La fede impaziente*, in September 1942. Vittorini had apparently warned the translator to make sure all negative references to Germany were omitted, but this act of self-censorship was not sufficient to secure the necessary *nulla osta*. Bloy's book was eventually published by Bompiani only in 1946.[10]

There is no doubt that, among Bompiani's anthologies of foreign literature, the most controversial one was Vittorini's *Americana*. As with Vittorini's novel *Il garofano rosso*, discussed in chapter 5, this is another episode that postwar literary historians have often presented as an example of the anti-Fascism implicit in Vittorini's literary activities.[11] Once more, the documentary evidence reveals a more complex situation. Vittorini started to work on the anthology in the early months of 1940. On 5 May 1940 he wrote to Bompiani that he was busy selecting the contents (he claimed to be reading three books a day) and organizing the team of translators. By December 1940 the proofs were ready, and Vittorini believed he had successfully presented them to the MCP's 'medii calibri' (middle management – Vittorini's own expression). However, his optimism must have been misplaced: on 4 December 1940 Casini informed both the prefecture of Milan and Bompiani of the MCP's decision not to allow the publication of *Americana*.[12] The following month, Vittorini tried again and this time managed to arrange a meeting with Pavolini. Given its status part of the Axis, Italy regarded the United States as a political enemy (it would become a military one only after Pearl Harbor in December 1941), so it is not surprising that Pavolini's conclusion was that the timing of an anthology celebrating American literature and brimming with Vittorini's enthusiastic comments and notes was unfortunate. The following is from Pavolini's letter of 7 January 1941, in which he gave his view:

Caro Bompiani,
Rispondo con ritardo alla Vostra lettera anche perché ho nel frattempo veduto Elio Vittorini, col quale m'intrattenni lungamente circa l'antologia americana. Egli me ne consegnò anzi le bozze quasi complete che ho esaminate con molto interesse. Frattanto anche A. Frateili parlò della cosa con il mio Capo di Gabinetto.

L'opera è assai pregevole per il criterio critico della scelta e dell'informazione e per tutta la presentazione. Resto però del mio parere, e cioè che l'uscita – in questo momento – dell'antologia americana non sia opportuna ... Non è il momento di fare delle cortesie all'America, nemmeno letterarie. Inoltre l'antologia non farebbe che rinfocolare la ventata di eccessivo entusiasmo per l'ultima letteratura americana: moda che sono risoluto a non incoraggiare.

Proseguite nella Vostra collezione con gli altri interessanti volumi che avete annunziati e riservate dunque l'uscita dell'antologia americana a un secondo più favorevole tempo. Vittorini può riferirVi come io sia anche per altra via disposto a venirVi incontro.[13]

(Dear Bompiani

My delayed reply to your letter is also due to the fact that in the meantime I have seen Elio Vittorini, with whom I had a long meeting concerning the American anthology. He gave me an almost complete set of proofs, which I read with interest. At the same time A. Frateili spoke about this with my head of cabinet.

The anthology is highly commendable for both its content and presentation. However, I am still of the opinion that the circulation of an American anthology at this time is not advisable ... This is not the right time to do America any favours, not even literary ones. Moreover the anthology would add more impetus to the fashion for contemporary American literature: a fashion that I am determined not to encourage.

Please go ahead with the publication of other interesting volumes of your planned series and keep the American anthology for a later, more favourable time. Vittorini will also tell you of another way through which I would be willing to settle the matter.)

Pavolini's displeasure concerning the popularity of American fiction confirms that American books were often singled out by the MCP's censors. In the particular case of *Americana*, it is interesting to note that no censorial pressure had confronted the three short stories by Ernest Hemingway. Because of his open anti-Fascism and his negative depiction of the Italian army in *A Farewell to Arms* (1929), Hemingway's novels had never been published in Italy. His short stories had appeared from time to time in periodicals such as *L'Italiano* and *L'Ambrosiano*, and the permission to have them appear in *Americana* seems to confirm that the American writer was subject to a peculiar type of ban. His books were proscribed but not his short stories, if published discreetly (no entire volume of his short stories was published in Fascist Italy).[14] Two of the three selected short stories had been translated by Vittorini himself and one of them had been subject to a small but politically motivated act of self-censorship. In 'The Gambler, the Nun, and the Radio' (1933), translated as 'Monaca e messicani, la radio,' Vittorini omitted a sentence that would have certainly raised some eyebrows. Hemingway's disdain for the Mexican peasants' talk of Marxist revolution was revealed in its comparison to Fascist nationalism: 'And now economics is the opium of the people; along with patriotism the opium of the people in Italy and Germany.' Vittorini was by then experienced enough to know what could and could not pass through the censors' net.[15]

As promised in his letter to Bompiani, Pavolini's offered a compromise on *Americana*: he would authorize the circulation of the anthology, provided Vittorini's preface be replaced with a more critical one by the *Accademico d'Italia* Emilio Cecchi.[16] Bompiani and Vittorini accepted, but the slowness with which Cecchi complied with the request meant that the new edition could be ready only by the beginning of 1942. Cecchi's preface was the kind of negative assessment that Pavolini had wished for. Its pro-Fascist character was clear from the comment that Sinclair Lewis's absence from the anthology was justified not only by his diminishing fame but also 'in osservanza alle norme della politica razziale' (in compliance with the norms of racial policy) or from the mention that Henry Miller's *Tropic of Cancer* was so vulgar that it had been rightly banned even by American censors. The concluding comment was that the short stories by Frank Norris and William Faulkner would provide an illuminating picture of America's savage capitalism and racial promiscuity.[17]

By 1942 Italy was officially at war with the United States, and Pavolini's 'tolerance' wavered even further. Despite the fact that the book was ready to be circulated, on 30 March 1942 he raised the issue of the ideological imbalance between Cecchi's critical preface and Vittorini's admiring introductions to each section. He suggested the removal of Vittorini's comments and added that a sentence – taken from Cecchi's preface – should be used in all publicity material: 'Trent'anni fa era stato abdicato all'ineffabile dell'anima slava; ora si abdicava a un ineffabile dell'anima americana. Ed incominciava un nuovo baccanale letterario' (Thirty years ago, people deferred to the ineffable nature of the Slavic soul; now people defer to the ineffable nature of the American soul. And so another literary orgy begins). A letter from Bompiani to Cecchi, dated 28 March, reveals that the publisher had already been thinking about ways to address the problem of Vittorini's introductions. In the end, everybody agreed that the best way was for Cecchi to compile a selection of critical passages that would replace Vittorini's comments. It was also the best solution with regard to minimizing the costs of having to modify the book, which was already typeset.[18] Cecchi received the final instructions over the phone from Pavolini's deputy, Mezzasoma: 'Il successore di Casini, Mezzasoma, mi ha telefonato per conto di Pavolini, in sostanza dicendomi: "se io, Cecchi, *rispondo* dell'aggiustamento del volume, il volume può uscire senz'altro' (Casini's successor's, Mezzasoma, has phoned me on behalf of Pavolini, basically saying: 'If I, Cecchi, take responsibility for the amendments to the book, then the book can be published').[19]

In the last days of December 1942 the anthology was finally ready for distribution, complete with Cecchi's preface and notes replacing those of Vittorini. It did not encounter any particular criticism from the Fascist press, and by the end of January 1943 Bompiani was already producing a second reprint. Among its supporters was the American renegade Ezra Pound, who reviewed it for *Il Meridiano di Roma* on 2 May 1943. Bompiani defined this review 'lusinghiero nonostante le critiche. Ma pericoloso!!'" (complimentary despite its criticism. But dangerous!), arguably thinking that Pound's review might provoke the reaction of those who saw the anthology as an insult to Italy's war effort. The same week Vittorini wrote to Pound and asked him to collaborate on the *Dizionario Letterario Bompiani*.[20] However, by June 1943, in the midst of the allied bombardments of Italy's major cities, there was a renewed reaction against the publication of American authors. On 26 June an anonymous typed note addressed the matter in strong tones: 'Proprio nei giorni dei massacri di Grosseto, di Sardegna e Sicilia, l'editore Bompiani mette sfacciatamente fuori un "mattonissimo" intitolato "AMERICANA"' (Right in the days of the massacres of Grosseto, in Sardinia and Sicily, the publisher Bompiani arrogantly publishes a hefty book entitled 'Americana'). The note continued with an attack not just on the anthology but on Bompiani's and Mondadori's policies in favour of the 'frivolezza e immoralità americana' (American frivolity and immorality). As we know, by then Polverelli had replaced Pavolini as head of the MCP, and at the bottom of the memo there is a typed comment by the new minister that he was going to order the withdrawal of the book from circulation. More importantly, a handwritten comment in the margin says: 'Sì, è ora di finirla!' (Yes, it's time to stop this!), signed with Mussolini's stylized "M" (see figure 15). It is generally accepted that this document was the cause of a final ban on *Americana*. Whether this ban was actually declared and respected is another matter: it is intriguing that *Americana* was still advertised on the dust covers of Bompiani's books as late as 1944.[21] It is also noteworthy that, despite the setback caused by the replacement of all of his introductory pieces, Vittorini should not have thought of them as politically compromising. In a letter to Bompiani, dated 21 January 1943, Vittorini proposed to collect all his American pieces in a publication to be entitled *Breve storia della letteratura americana*. He added: 'Ti sarei molto grato se, in un colloquio amichevole con Tosti o con Mezzasoma, ponessi la questione' (I would be very grateful if you could raise the matter in one of your friendly meetings with Tosti or Mezzasoma). The project never came to fruition, not even in the postwar years. However, the fact that, in 1943, Vittorini should have thought of it as a possible enterprise suggests that, as late as that time, publishers and editors thought negotiations were still possible, even in the highly controversial field of American fiction.[22]

Keeping the Channels Open: Mondadori and Einaudi

Throughout the last years of Fascism, Arnoldo Mondadori managed to maintain the by then customary balance between supporting the regime and stretching its tolerance through the promotion of foreign literature. As already suggested, the most successful strategy to ease any tension was to emphasize his efforts in the promotion of Italian literature abroad. In a long report submitted to Mussolini on 14 May 1940, Mondadori boasted about the commitment of his publishing house. To a long list of publications and book series (some published in collaboration with government institutions, as was the case with *Annali dell'Africa Italiana* and *Il Primo Libro del Fascista*), Mondadori added some figures concerning the publication abroad of works by Italian authors. In 1938 Mondadori had sold the rights for the translation of forty books into eight foreign languages. In 1939 the figure had risen to forty-five into ten different languages, and in the first months of 1940 it had already reached twenty-five titles translated into eleven different languages. Very discreetly, Mondadori's refrained from mentioning the massive trade imbalance between his export of Italian books and the number of translations of foreign novels.[23]

Self-censorship was also a fine-tuned practice aimed at guaranteeing the commercial and political viability of each book produced. Sometimes it extended to the cancellation of a planned translation. But even in cases of this kind, Mondadori would make sure the MCP was informed of his decision. A case relating to the prewar period concerns the translation of Roger Martin du Gard's multi-volume saga *Les Thibault* (1913–40). Martin

26 Giugno.XXI

Proprio nei giorni dei massacri di Grosseto,
di Sardegna e Sicilia,l'editore Bompiani mette sfacciatamente fuori un "mattonissimo" intitolato "AMERICA-
NA" antologia di scarso valore con prefazione di un accademico e traduzione di Vittorini; antologia condotta
sui modelli dell'ebreo Lewis. E lo stesso Bompiani con-
tinua nelle stampe e ristampe di Cronin,Steinbeck,ed
altri, bolscevichi puri e in ogni caso perniciosissimi.

 Mondadori a sua volta,dopo aver per anni ed
anni contribuito ad "educare" alla frivolezza e immoralità americana i nostri giovani con la collana "La Pal
ma", e con i "gialli", oggi prosegue nelle ristampe di
autori inglesi e americani.

Concordo perfettamente. Ho dato disposizioni per un rigoroso catenac-
cio e per il ritiro dalla circolazione dei volumi suindicati.

15. Anonymous letter concerning Bompiani's anthology *Americana*,
with Polverelli's typed note and Mussolini's one in pencil, June 1943.
(*Courtesy of Archivo Centrale dello Stato, Rome*)

du Gard had received the Nobel Prize in 1937, and Mondadori had an option to publish the first volumes of his most famous work. However, in a letter to Casini dated 2 December 1937, Mondadori informed the MCP official that he had decided not to publish Les Thibault because of its 'carattere pacifista e socialisteggiante' (pacifist and pro-socialist tone). A cynical note added: 'Glielo comunico nel caso che lo voglia tradurre qualche casa minore' (I let you know in case some other minor publisher were interested in translating it). The novel remained in Mondadori's hands and was eventually published in Italian in 1951.[24] More daring was the decision to publish the three-volume novel Abele cervello fino (Abel az Országban, 1934) by the Hungarian author Aron Tamási. In October 1939 the MCP had authorized its translation with the proviso that a number of risqué passages be cut, among them an episode of pederasty. When the novel was eventually published in 1941 the MCP officials were surprised to find that none of the specified passages had been deleted. On 5 August 1941 Casini sent a letter to the prefecture of Milan, asking it to inform Mondadori of his disappointment at the clear procedural breach (Mondadori had failed to submit the proofs of the book prior to its publication). Even in this case, Casini refrained from ordering the seizure of the book. Instead, he simply stated that any future reprints of the novel would have to be modified and then vetted and approved by the ministry. However, the resentment raised by this episode seems to have found an outlet a few months later. Mondadori was refused a meeting with Mussolini on the explicit ground that Il Duce was disappointed at what had happened with the publication of Tamási's novel. Alarmed, Mondadori first contacted Pavolini, and then wrote a dossier to Mussolini himself in which he explained that the misunderstanding had been caused by an editorial error.[25]

On other occasions, modifications to publications were clearly related to the anti-Semitic campaign. In October 1940 Mondadori was asked to modify George Meredith's Commedianti tragici (Tragic Comedians, 1880) because it contained too many positive remarks concerning the Jewish protagonist. A few weeks earlier, it had been the turn of the scientific work Storia dell'errore umano (Story of Human Error, 1936), edited by the Jewish-American psychologist Joseph Jastrow. The Milanese state archives contain a copy of a long report written by an obscure but fervent reader at the MCP, Cesare Crispolti. In his seven pages of comments, Crispolti singled out every single direct or indirect reference to Jewish individuals – Einstein and Freud included – or to Jewish culture. He also condemned various parts of the book for their support of scientific, secular observation against traditional religious beliefs. Mondadori was asked to modify the text based on all the reader's observation. The book was eventually published in 1941.[26]

Despite the number of difficulties created by the regime, American fiction remained, as it did with Bompiani, Mondadori's most popular and profitable line of publications. By 1942 Margaret Mitchell's *Via col vento* (*Gone with the Wind*, 1936) had broken the ceiling of 100,000 copies sold. It was followed closely by Louis Bromfield's *La grande pioggia* (*The Rain Came*, 1937), whose publication in 1940 had been subject to the softening of the crude language used in the book's dialogues. Kenneth Roberts's *Passaggio a Nord-Ovest* (*Northwest Passage*, 1937), published in 1939, broke through 50,000 copies by 1942. Even translations of British authors remained popular throughout the war years. Both C.S. Forester's *Le avventure del capitano Hornblower* (*Captain Horatio Hornblower*, 1939) and Somerset Maugham's *Schiavo d'amore* (*Of Human Bondage*, 1915) sold about 40,000 between 1940 and 1943. Even better, John Galsworthy, with the popular *La saga dei Forsythe* (*The Forsythe Saga*, 1906–21) published in Vittorini's two-volume translation in 1939, sold more than 40,000 copies by 1941.[27]

However, as the war went on, the room for negotiation on foreign titles progressively diminished. In 1941 Mondadori was still able to reverse the ban on the translation of Steinbeck's early short stories *I pascoli del cielo* (*The Pastures of Heaven*, 1932). According to a letter from Casini of 30 October 1940, the DGSI had written to the prefecture of Milan and asked it to inform Mondadori that the publisher's request for permission to translate Steinbeck's short stories had been turned down. As a result of a breakdown in communication, the MCP's order never reached Mondadori's editors, and, to the annoyance of the censors, the book was published in February 1941, once more in a translation by Vittorini. Casini protested but Arnoldo Mondadori intervened personally to convince him not to reinstate the earlier ban. On 14 March 1941 Casini informed the prefecture of Milan that, following Mondadori's clarification, the ministry had decided to grant its *nulla osta* for the book.[28]

War restrictions on paper became a recurrent excuse through which the regime justified a drastic reduction in the number of translations. Faulkner's *Il borgo* (*The Hamlet*, 1940), which came out in March 1942, translated by Cesare Pavese, was to become the last American novel published in Mondadori's prestigious Medusa series. Similar restrictions hit the popular end of the paperback market. In October 1941 Mondadori's *Libri gialli* series, which relied heavily on the works of authors who wrote in English, was stifled through a ministerial order to ration itself to one book a month.[29]

Alternatives were needed and, as Decleva has shown, Arnoldo Mondadori found other profitable outlets. The publisher's illustrated magazine, *Tempo*, created in June 1939 on the model of the American weekly *Life*, was granted ministerial funds for its distribution throughout occupied Europe. At its head was Mondadori's young son, Alberto. Still in his twenties but already an expert journalist – he was correspondent for Mussolini's *Il Popolo d'Italia* throughout the war years – he had met both Hitler and Goebbels in November 1940 as part of a delegation of Italian journalists. *Tempo* was meant to rival the Nazi illustrated magazines *Signal* and *Adler* in the race for imposing Axis cultural influences over occupied Europe. By 1942, thanks to substantial funding from the MCP, the magazine was printed in eight languages.[30]

Mondadori's attempt to save his most famous cartoon strip, *Topolino*, was also partially successful. Based on Walt Disney's Mickey Mouse, *Topolino* had survived a first cull of foreign cartoon strips that had been imposed by the MCP in 1938. Later, in March 1941, the MCP ordered the suppression of Topolino's adventures (which constituted only part of each issue of *Topolino*). The cut would have made a mockery of the comic book's masthead. Fearing a huge drop in sales, Mondadori wrote to Pavolini. An exemption was requested on the grounds of Walt Disney's status as a world-class artist. The exemption was granted but lasted only until December of that year, when Italy declared war on the United States. At that point negotiations between the MCP and Mondadori resumed and a second compromise was found. Starting in February 1942, *Topolino* was once again allowed to keep its traditional masthead; in return, the three pages of Topolino's adventures were replaced with human characters – although these continued to evoke Mickey Mouse and his cohort – and the protagonist's name was turned into the bizarre 'Tuffolino.'[31]

In the spring of 1943 Mondadori's relationship with the regime received a serious blow. Luigi Rusca, Mondadori's closest collaborator, as co-director of the press since his arrival in 1928, was arrested for suspected anti-Fascism. Rusca's lack of open support for the regime had been registered by the Fascist police since an anonymous letter had led to a first investigation back in 1935. But it was Rusca's frequent trips to Switzerland, as a consultant for a book distribution company founded in 1939, that had reinforced the police's suspicions. In order to show his allegiance, Rusca became a member of PNF in 1940. This might have delayed his downfall, but in March 1943 Mussolini himself approved the decision to arrest him and send him to *confino*. Given the lack of hard evidence against him, Rusca was condemned for being an 'anti-fascista mormoratore' (a muttering anti-Fascist). In order not to compromise his publishing house, Arnoldo Mondadori apparently refused to take a stand in his defence. Rusca spent the last four months of the regime exiled in a small town in southern Italy.[32] The episode seems not to have had any negative repercussions on Mondadori's operations, although there is no doubt that his position as the publisher closest to the regime must have been seriously dented.

During the interim of the Badoglio government in the summer of 1943, Mondadori openly stated his support for the new regime. His daughter remembered him taking Mussolini's photograph off the wall and sending a telegram of support to Badoglio as soon as the news of Mussolini's fall had reached their household. It was a premature move. When Il Duce was reinstated in September 1943, Arnoldo Mondadori and his two sons fled to Switzerland, and the publishing house was put under government administration.

Despite his reputation as a dormant anti-Fascist publisher, Giulio Einaudi managed to survive most of the war years without any major setback. However, like Mondadori, he lost one of his key collaborators during the last months of the regime. Before his arrest in December 1942, Mario Alicata's diplomatic skills had been extremely useful in leading negotiations over the translation of foreign books. His collaboration with Bottai's journal *Primato* was also used as a vehicle for influencing government policies. In December 1941 Einaudi asked Alicata to use *Primato* to defend the publishing house from imminent government policies aimed at redressing the balance between Italian and foreign authors. Einaudi's hope was that *Primato* might prove a useful platform from which to counter excessive nationalistic policies. It was not a successful campaign: in January 1942 Pavolini decided to impose a blanket limit of one translation of a foreign book for every four publications by Italian authors.[33]

Einaudi's wartime correspondence also reveals a degree of freedom enjoyed by the MCP's officials and readers in matters of translation. Publishers were sometimes directly in contact with the MCP readers, and there is a sense that the two parties occasionally collaborated to secure the publication of a translation. For instance, Alberto Spaini, a translator from German, worked for Einaudi while collaborating with the MCP as a reader. On 6 November 1941, after he had approved the translation of Hans Grimm's pro-Nazi *Volk Ohne Raum* (A People without Space, 1926),

Spaini wrote to Einaudi and warned him to make sure that the translator treaded carefully over such a delicate text: 'Altrimenti si passerebbe un guaio tutti in compagnia, tu, io e lui' (otherwise we would all be in trouble, you, I, and he). A few days later, Alicata's correspondence with a more prestigious reader, Emilio Cecchi, was instrumental in securing approval for Edgar Lee Master's *Spoon River Anthology*.[34] Another example concerns Guido Boezi, an orientalist, who in March 1942 submitted a list of possible translations to Alicata, adding that his position at the MCP would facilitate obtaining the necessary ministerial approval.[35]

MCP officials also lightened their censorial authority with the occasional show of studied tolerance. During a meeting with Casini in February 1942, Alicata was told to give higher priority to Italian books and translations from 'friendly' nations; but, added the head of DGSI, he was not against a number of English, French, and Russian publications, provided they were slipped in with little publicity.[36] Within the MCP's Book Division, Bruno Gaeta was also a 'friendly' presence. In another letter from Alicata to Einaudi, this time dated 14 March 1942, it appears that Gaeta had discreetly supplied some personal suggestions for modifications of a translation of Karl Hönn's biography *Konstantin der Grosse* (Constantine the Great, 1940).[37]

9 Unfinished Business

Moravia, the *Discriminato*

As we have seen in chapter 7, the anti-Semitic legislation and the *bonifica libraria* affected the literary career of Alberto Moravia in a peculiar way. As a journalist, he was allowed to publish without using a pseudonym, but at the same time his name had been removed from the roster of the Albo dei giornalisti (the official register of Italian journalists). Two of his works of fiction – *L'imbroglio* and *Le ambizioni sbagliate* – had been banned, but not his most famous novel, *Gli indifferenti*. According to Italian law, Moravia was 'Aryan' because he had been Christened and educated as a Catholic and only one of his parents was Jewish. His status was recognized by the General Directorate for Demography and Race, Demorazza, on 15 July 1939. Encouraged by his recognition as an Aryan, in the following days Moravia met Casini and asked for the ban on the two books to be removed. The head of the General Directorate for the Italian Press (DGSI) initially seemed prepared to allow the distribution of at least the first edition of these works, but he soon had to go back on his word. On 21 July 1939 he informed Bompiani that *L'imbroglio* – and *Le ambizioni sbagliate*, which was published by Mondadori – appeared in the official list of the Commissione per la bonifica libraria (Commission for Book Reclamation) and was therefore proscribed.[1] The situation was ambiguous: one can only conclude that some of Moravia's books had been banned because of their alleged immoral content and not because the author was half-Jewish. Given the fact that Moravia's name had been included in the proceedings of the *bonifica libraria* commission thanks to Alessandro Pavolini, one could argue that the minister of the Ministero della Cultura Popolare simply had a personal, perhaps racist, dislike for Moravia. This conjecture, however, is contradicted by a number of developments that will be examined in the following paragraphs.[2]

The situation seemed to take a turn for the worse in mid-February 1941, when the MCP sent a *velina* ordering all Italian papers 'di non occuparsi di Moravia e delle sue pubblicazioni' (not to write about Moravia and his publications).[3] Almost at the same time, the MCP had discovered that *Le ambizioni sbagliate* was not only still for sale but also appeared in Mondadori's catalogue. The prefect of Milan was ordered to investigate discreetly. Instead of immediately seizing the books and penalizing the publisher, the prefect was told to 'chiedere e fornire in proposito gli opportuni chiarimenti' (to ask for and supply due clarifications with regard to this). Mondadori's official answer was that it was only a mistake ('un mero errore'). However, the correspondence between Arnoldo Mondadori and Moravia reveals that Mondadori had clearly decided to go ahead with not just the distribution but even a new edition of *Le ambizioni sbagliate*. Whether or not Mondadori thought that the declaration by Demorazza had cleared Moravia from any form of censorship, this is one more example of the liberties that big publishers sometimes dared to take.[4]

During these same months it was the turn of a Bompiani book by Moravia to encounter problems. His most recent work, the novel *La mascherata*, had initially passed through the censoring net of the MCP with only a minor change. According to the memoirs of Bruno Gaeta, there was pressure from the National Fascist Party (PNF) to have the book banned because its plot – the farcical deeds of a tinpot South American dictator – could have been read as a satire of Mussolini. Yet, according to Gaeta, everyone at the MCP, from Tosti to Pavolini, was in favour of its publication; the only modification required was the deletion of a sentence in which the dictator was said to have 'un profilo da medaglia di imperatore romano' (the profile of a Roman emperor on a coin).[5] Gaeta also remembers that in the same period Moravia was summoned at the MCP to discuss some modifications that had been required for a new edition of his collection of short stories *La bella vita*, published by Carabba in 1935. On that occasion Moravia refused to accept any modifications and the project was therefore laid to rest.[6] But even the publication of *La mascherata* was to cause trouble. On 31 August 1941 a police informer wrote a report in which he denounced the novel, suggesting that Moravia – once more wrongly described as an *ebreo discriminato* – had written a parody, which added a political element to his usual 'oscenità e immoralità.' Asked by the Ministry of the Interior to justify its position, on 2 November 1941 the MCP answered that 'già da tempo ha provveduto a vietare la ristampa del romanzo "La Mascherata"' (for some time it has already banned any reprint of the novel 'La Mascherata'). Unfortunately the memo does not reveal the identity of the respondent. To claim to have long banned a second reprint was misleading to say the least when the first edition had just been distributed.[7] It is arguable that the publication of *La mascherata* was the reason for the renewed flurry of interest in the position of Moravia. The *velina* of February 1941 was probably designed to put a lid on any possible discussion of Moravia's unorthodox position. But despite the MCP's initial tolerance towards the new novel, public reaction – and by 'public' one includes Fascist institutions such as the PNF – resulted in a stricter stance and forced the MCP to readdress Moravia's peculiar position.

With regard to Moravia's journalism, the situation was equally ambiguous and unstable. When, on 2 April 1941, the chief editor of *La Gazzetta del Popolo*, Eugenio Bertuetti, asked Casini for his *nulla osta* for the publication of articles by Moravia under a pseudonym, the permission was granted. However, once again the MCP had to go back on its word only a few months later. On 10 September 1941 Bertuetti was informed by the press office of the prefecture of Turin that any publication of Moravia's articles had to stop. A puzzled Bertuetti asked whether the ban applied to those works published under a pseudonyms too, and nine days later Casini replied stating that the ban covered all Moravia's writings. The same answer was given to Alberto Mondadori on 29 September, when he asked to publish a short story by Moravia for *Tempo*.[8] Things seemed to be going from bad to worse, but the direction was reversed once more as a consequence of a family event.

On 30 September 1941, while fighting in north Africa, Moravia's brother, Gastone Pincherle, was killed by a land mine. As a result of he bereavement, the regime reverted to a more tolerant attitude towards the Pincherle family. An unsigned memo dated 15 October 1941 alerted the MCP about the recent event. Ten days later Pavolini sent a note to Mussolini in which he asked for his permission to lift the ban on Moravia's journalistic activity. In order to support his case, Pavolini added that Moravia had recently married 'una donna di razza italiana' (a woman of Italian race). Moravia's recent marriage to Elsa Morante had been sanctified in April 1941 at Il Gesù, the main Jesuit church in Rome. Surprisingly, the priest who officiated at the wedding was no other that Father Pietro Tacchi Venturi, the Jesuit diplomat who, as we have seen, was an influential intermediary between the Vatican and

Mussolini and was involved in many cases of literary censorship. Apparently the presence of Tacchi Venturi was not related to his official role, nor was he close to the Pincherle family. He was the father confessor of Elsa Morante, a devout Catholic. Mussolini's 'Sì' followed by his initial appear on Pavolini's memo to show that he himself approved this latest change of policy with regard to Moravia's status. A week later Casini informed the chief editors of *La Gazzetta del Popolo* and *Oggi* that they could reinstate Moravia among their contributors. A passage in a letter from *Il Popolo d'Italia*'s literary critic, Giuseppe Villaroel, to his chief editor, Giorgio Pini, confirms that something had changed with regard to Moravia. In a letter dated 4 October 1941 Villaroel wrote: 'Prendo nota della "Mascherata" di Moravia. Sapevo che il M. d. C.P. [MCP] aveva posto a Bompiani il veto di ristampa; ma se tu mi dai l'incarico vuol dire che vi sono nuove disposizioni' (I take note of Moravia's 'Mascherata.' I knew that the MCP had vetoed Bompiani's reprint; but if you tell me to deal with this, it means that there are new directives).[9]

On 15 January 1942 Moravia asked for permission to sign his articles with his own pen name. A handwritten note in the margin of his application, presumably by Casini, says 'è ancora troppo presto' (it is still too early). Moravia subsequently submitted a list of periodicals that he would like to work for, and on 27 February 1942 Casini replied that he had given his *nulla osta* to all of them, on the condition that Moravia use a pseudonym.[10] Although Moravia's 'racial' status had been fully clarified, there is a sense that he was still regarded as *persona non grata*. If he could not be silenced for racist reasons, there is no doubt that his political aloofness and his connection with the Rosselli family meant that he was under close scrutiny. It is puzzling, however, that in the spring of 1942 Moravia was still allowed to publish books in his own name. A full-page advertisement by Mondadori, on page 3 of the 1 March 1942 issue of Bottai's *Primato*, includes Moravia's *Le ambizioni sbagliate*. What is more, next to Moravia's book, the ad cited another recent Mondadori publication, the collection of short stories *Scomparsa d'Angela* by the MCP minister Alessandro Pavolini. The juxtaposition could hardly have been more symbolic, and it was quite possibly intentional.[11]

Moravia's ambiguous position continued even after the list of unwelcome authors was made public in May 1942. As we have already seen, the name Alberto Pincherle was present in the list, but that of Alberto Moravia was not. It would have made much more sense to list the surname that appeared on book covers. Instead, censors and police would have to have known the connection between family name and *nom de plume*. One could even suspect that it was a last, hypocritical sign of respect or a subtle way of defending Moravia. After all, not all his books had been banned and, as he had been declared Aryan, there was no reason to proscribe his entire oeuvre. But if that were the case, then what was the point of listing him under his family name? Perhaps it was only a last, indirect threat.

What Happened to Vittorini's *Conversazione in Sicilia?*

Conversazione in Sicilia was first published in instalments in *Letteratura*, a Florentine periodical founded in 1937 by Alessandro Bonsanti, one of the chief editors of the defunct *Solaria*. Bonsanti, a good friend of Elio Vittorini, had already published Vittorini's *Il garofano rosso* in the final issues of *Solaria*, and the first instalment of the unfinished *Giochi di ragazzi* – intended as a sequel to *Il garofano rosso* – appeared in the first issue of *Letteratura*.[12] It is therefore not surprising that Vittorini should have thought of Bonsanti's *Letteratura* when it came to publishing his latest novel. *Letteratura* had been receiving MCP funding since February 1938, and Bonsanti had asked for and obtained a meeting with Mussolini so that he could present his new journal. Regardless as to whether his meeting with Il Duce is proof of tacit cooperation or was an opportunistic move or a cover, there is little doubt that *Letteratura* had received the blessing of the upper echelons of the regime. Bonsanti may have wanted to protect the new journal from the possible opposition of the press office at the prefecture of Florence, which had sealed the fate of *Solaria* only a year before.[13]

Conversazione in Sicilia appeared in five instalments in *Letteratura*, from the sixth issue (April 1938) to the tenth (April 1939). The version published in the journal was, contrary to Vittorini's usual practices, very similar to the final version we read today. The very few modifications to the text before its publication in book form concern a subtle reduction of the realistic elements of the narrative, thus increasing the abstract, universal value of the content. More important, only one cut was imposed by the Florentine censor. Surprisingly, it does not relate to the episode of the train journey, in which Vittorini's critique of the regime becomes almost overt with the repeated mention of the smell coming from the two policemen. Instead, a small cut was required in the closing lines of chapter 44 (45 in the book edition). In the dialogue between the protagonist Silvestro and his mother, which is interrupted by a surreal scene of people shooting at some crows – in which the mother symbolically joins with her shotgun – is followed by the arrival of a woman bringing the news of the death of Silvestro's brother (presumably in the Spanish Civil War). The expression used by the woman when announcing the news –'Madre fortunata!" (lucky mother!) – is reminiscent of the nationalistic rhetoric with which the regime hailed the deaths of soldiers and Fascist militants. This last episode was ordered to be removed, and the *Letteratura* instalment was published with three dotted lines that betrayed the intervention of the censor.[14]

After the novel's appearance in instalments in 1938/9, Vittorini prepared a limited edition of little more than three hundred copies to be published by Parenti, the Florentine publisher of *Solaria* and *Letteratura*. The book appeared in 1941 with a new title, *Nome e lagrime*, which was taken from the short story that was published together with the novel.[15] Such a small print run was perhaps necessary to extricate Vittorini from his contractual obligation towards Parenti. He immediately started to work on another edition for Bompiani, this time without the short story. Bompiani ran a first edition of five thousand copies in October 1941, which was quickly followed by a reprint of another five thousand. Both the Parenti and Bompiani editions ignored the cut imposed by the Florentine censor.

The novel received substantial critical attention, most of which was complimentary. Three Fascist papers – *Primato*, *Documento*, and *Il Popolo d'Italia* – reviewed the Parenti edition. All were positive in judging Vittorini as one of the most promising writers of his generation. They made critical remarks only when noting the too explicit influence of American novelists on his prose style. The reviewers were Mario Alicata, Alberto Moravia (who did not use a pseudonym), and the official literary critic of *Il Popolo d'Italia*, the poet and critic Giuseppe Villaroel.[16] The reception of the Bompiani edition, entitled *Conversazione in Sicilia* (with *Nome e lagrime* appearing as a subtitle within brackets) was entirely positive. Laudatory reviews were published by *Roma fascista*, *Il Fascio*, and *Rivoluzione*.[17] By June 1942 Vittorini, as a Bompiani editor was supervising the preparation of a third reprint, which was announced through an advertisement in the weekly *Sette giorni*. Vittorini asked the writer and *Accademico d'Italia* Massimo Bontempelli if he would write a short promotional comment to be added as a 'fascetta' to the third edition. Bontempelli happily agreed. In the meantime, Bompiani was busy finalizing the contracts for the Spanish, English, and French translations.[18]

The first sign that something was wrong was a brief anonymous article published in *Roma fascista*, the weekly paper of the Roman Fascist University Groups (GUF). Despite a positive review of the book in this journal the previous year, an anomynous author published a short parody of the prose style of *Conversazione in Sicilia*, entitled 'Discussione all'Elba di Vittorini.' It was not a vicious attack, but it suggested that Vittorini's style was implicitly defeatist.[19] A month later, another anonymous article appeared, this time of a much more vitriolic nature. Worse, it appeared on page three of Mussolini's newspaper, *Il Popolo d'Italia*. The title was self-explanatory: 'Una sporca conversazione.' The novel was attacked as immoral – on the feeble ground that the mother of the protagonist at one point admits to having had an affair – and defeatist for its disillusioned and desperate tone. But what must have been more worrying was the virulent tone of its first lines: 'Per ottenere ciò che voleva, cioè una società imbecille materialista atea pervertita, la giudeo-massoneria aveva bisogno di una letteratura mediocre, pornografica, erotica. Questa letteratura venne. Si chiamò Pitigrilli, Mariani, Guido da Verona e via dicendo. Aveva bisogno di libri come questo che, in ritardo, ma gagliardamente, emulano opere di quelli' (In order to reach its goals, that is, an imbecile materialist perverted atheist society, the Jewish-Masons needed a mediocre, pornographic, erotic literature. This literature came. It was called Pitigrilli, Mariani, Guido da Verona, and so on and so forth. It needed books such as this one, which, belatedly but arrogantly, emulates works by those authors).[20]

The attack had clear political connotations. Moreover its anonymity and the high-profile paper in which it appeared raise many questions. Was it the result of a concerted decision? By whom? Why attack a novel that had been in circulation for more than a year? The prefecture of Milan, which was responsible for monitoring both *Il Popolo d'Italia* and Bompiani, immediately registered the attack and alerted Casini at the MCP. The article was also noticed at Bompiani; indeed, the following day Valentino Bompiani's secretary sent a copy to Vittorini, who at the time was on holiday in Tuscany. We also know that on 3 August, Bompiani's secretary sent the author copies of two letters concerning *Conversazione in Sicilia*, one by literary critic Aldo Capasso and one by none other than *Il Popolo d'Italia*'s literary critic, Giuseppe Villaroel. Unfortunately neither letter is at Bompiani or in Vittorini's papers. There is also no mention of this crisis in the correspondence between Bompiani and Vittorini, which might suggest that the two discussed the matter in person, probably over the telephone when Vittorini was away from Milan.[21] In his memoirs, Bompiani quotes Vittorini saying that in April 1942 he had been called to the Milanese office of the PNF, where the *Federale* attacked him for the dubious morality of *Conversazione in Sicilia*. The same episode is related by Vittorini in a postwar recollection, but its timing is moved to autumn 1942. Moreover, Vittorini states that in those months the Fascist press moved from praising the novel on their third pages to attacking it on the front one. This is inaccurate: as we will see, other Fascist papers kept on defending *Conversazione in Sicilia*.[22]

The identity and intentions of the anonymous author have never been mentioned or even discussed in the correspondence or the available documentary material. If the archives of *Il Popolo d'Italia* held answers to these questions, unfortunately we may never resolve the issue.[23] Rome's Archivio Centrale, however, contains letters sent to Giorgio Pini, who was chief editor of the paper from 1936 to 1943 (Mussolini's nephew, Vito Mussolini, was officially editor-in-chief but his presence was purely nominal). Though there are no copies of Pini's letters, the correspondence concerning the summer 1942 sheds some light on Vittorini's case. First of all, during that period – to be more precise between June and November 1942 – *Il Popolo d'Italia* printed a number of anonymous short articles that specifically targeted the home front. Corruption, inefficiency, defeatism, and the privileges of the upper classes were the main targets. There is no direct evidence of who wrote 'Una sporca conversazione.' It is possible, however, to narrow the number of possible authors down to three names. The first and most surprising name is that of one of Italy's most famous architects and designers, Gio Ponti. His letters allow us to identify him as the author of seven of the twenty-three brief articles published in those five months.[24] Ponti's main target was the lack of commitment to the war effort on the part of the upper classes. In a letter written in August 1942, he reminded Pini not to reveal his identity to anybody. He may have been concerned about the consequences for his activity as a designer and architect had he been revealed as the author of these articles. But it seems unlikely that Ponti was the author of the attack on *Conversazione in Sicilia*. In none of his other articles nor in his correspondence does he show any particular interest in literary matters. Secondly the prose style of 'Una sporca conversazione' is very different from that of Ponti's articles, particularly so if one considers the anti-Semitic tone of the former, which was totally alien to Ponti's writings.[25]

The second possible author is a militant Fascist, minor playwright, and journalist from the Friuli region, Giuseppe Castelletti. Despite his turbulent reputation as a militant Fascist – he was suspended from the party in 1932 – he had worked for various newspapers, including *Il*

Gazzettino di Venezia and *Il Popolo di Brescia*. In 1940 Castelletti had started at *Il Popolo d'Italia* on 'il delicato lavoro dei corsivi' (the delicate task of writing editorials), as he himself described it in a letter to Mussolini's secretary of 21 October 1940. During the summer of 1942 Castelletti was certainly the author of three brief articles. That he might be the author of 'Una sporca conversazione' is suggested by similarities in the prose style and by the fact that one of his other articles contains anti-Semitic elements. Moreover, both the available correspondence at the Archivio Centrale dello Stato (ACS) and Pini's memoirs seem to suggest that Castelletti was considered a reliable and brilliant collaborator.[26] It is equally possible, however, that the anonymous author of 'Una sporca conversazione' may be a third, more prestigious personality – Goffredo Coppola, a staunch Fascist academic, professor of Greek and Latin at Bologna University throughout most of the Fascist years. He became vice-chancellor of Bologna University during the Repubblica Sociale Italiana and, being a faithful Mussolinian, he followed Il Duce and died with him at Dongo on 25 April 1945. A good friend of Pini, Coppola sometimes wrote lively polemical pieces for *Il Popolo d'Italia*. In Pini's diary we find a number of entries that, as with Castelletti, show that Mussolini was well informed about the content of his articles. The first entry is dated 1 June 1937. On that occasion Pini reports that Mussolini, after having heard of Coppola's most recent article, enquired about his health, knowing that Coppola had recently been involved in a car accident.[27] More importantly, on 7 May 1938 Pini recorded having asked Mussolini if he could publish an editorial by Coppola. The article was a violent attack on the Vatican for its intransigence towards Nazi Germany and indulgence towards Masonic France and 'la sua classe dirigente laica, gindaice ed estremista' (its secular, Jewish, and extremist establishment). Mussolini's reply, in his usual telegraphic style, was 'Pubblicate.' Similarly, on 14 June 1938 Pini informed him of an article by Coppola attacking French academics; it once more received Mussolini's approval.[28] Pini's telephone conversations with Mussolini became more infrequent during the war and the diary virtually stops at December 1940. Pini's correspondence held at ACS also does not clarify the extent to which Coppola was writing for *Il Popolo d'Italia* during the summer of 1942. A detailed portrait left by Pini in his memoirs related to the 1943–5 period (during which Pini was employed as undersecretary at the Ministry of the Interior) presents Coppola as an affectionate friend who in the years of *Il Popolo d'Italia* would come from Bologna once a month and stay in Milan for a couple of days, writing his pieces and helping Pini with his editorial work. Pini remembers him as passionately idealistic and often intransigent.[29] The fact that the two often met in person would also explain the lack of written evidence in Pini's editorial correspondence. Similarly, 'Una sporca conversazione' might have been written and discussed during one of Coppola's visits in service to *Il Popolo d'Italia*.[30] There are, moreover, other clues.

'Guerra di religione,' a polemical article written by Coppola and published by *Il Popolo d'Italia* on 15 January 1942, is highly relevant. The article was a violent attack on the publisher Einaudi, which it accused of distributing books written by authors whose nations were at war with Italy. Pride of place was given to Einaudi's translation of *War and Peace*. Coppola suggested that the choice of the novel might have been motivated by the intention of creating a parallel between Tolstoy's representation of Napoleon's Russian campaign and the Axis invasion. More important, Coppola also made an underhanded, anti-Semitic reference to the editor of Einaudi's edition, Leone Ginzburg, who was criticized for his 'giudaica scrupolosità di forastiero' (Jewish scrupulousness of a foreigner).[31] In her detailed study of Einaudi, Luisa Mangoni dwells on this article, which caused great anxiety inside the publishing house. As was to happen with the attack on *Conversazione in Sicilia*, there was a distinct fear that, given the high profile of *Il Popolo d'Italia*, this was an official condemnation of Einaudi's work. Using established contacts at Bottai's *Primato*, on 1 February 1942 Giaime Pintor published a cautious but firm reply under the pseudonym 'Testadoro' (normally used by *Primato*'s co-director, Giorgio Cabella). A few days later Coppola returned to the attack, openly accusing *Primato* of supporting the interests of Einaudi. This time it was Cabella himself who, again as Testadoro, strongly replied on 1 March 1942 that *Primato* was not going at accept lessons in Fascism from anybody.[32] The polemical exchange ended there with no apparent damage to Einaudi.

Clear parallels exist between this episode and Vittorini's situation. First, there was an indirect anti-Semitic element in both articles. Second, Bompiani – and Vittorini as editor of *Corona* – were as guilty as Einaudi for insisting on publishing British, American, and Russian authors. In other words, given Coppola's particular interest in the publishing industry, there is a distinct possibility that he might have been the author of 'Una sporca conversazione.' On 2 July 1942 he had written under his own name an article, 'A quattr'occhi,' in which he had attacked Einaudi and, indirectly, the Fascist censors for approving the publication of Johan Huizinga's *La crisi della civiltà* (*In de Schaduwen van*

Morgen, 1936). On that occasion the MCP reacted to the attack. In a letter to Pini dated 3 August 1942, Mezzasoma complained about the polemical excesses of Coppola. The MCP's line of defence was that Huizinga's book had been approved for publication in 1938, a long time before the restrictions against foreign books were enacted.[33] The last piece of information we have regarding Coppola's role comes from Pini's unpublished memoirs. In the first months of 1943, after a short period on the Russian front and a stay in a hospital in central Italy, Coppola begun writing again for *Il Popolo d'Italia*.[34]

At this stage, more documentary evidence is needed to arrive at a clear identification of Coppola as the author of 'Una sporca conversazione.' One cannot exclude the hypothesis that the article might have been the product of a one-off collaboration, possibly by some high-ranking leader of the regime. As we have seen, Mussolini himself would sometimes write anonymous editorials and also encourage young authors to write anonymously for *Il Popolo d'Italia*. Berto Ricci, Ruggero Zangrandi, Romano Bilenchi, and others had done so. In this case, however, there is no trace of evidence that the intervention was Mussolini's. This does not necessarily mean that he was unaware of this particular article either before or after its publication. A letter from the administrator (*Direttore Amministrativo*) of *Il Popolo d'Italia* to Pini, dated 13 September 1942, informed the latter that Mussolini had disapproved of an editorial published on 10 September 1942 (about the Jews and the black market). It added that 'Il Duce mi ha incaricato di dirti che in fatto di corsivi bisogna andare molto cautamente' (Il Duce has asked me to let you know that one has to be careful with publishing editorials).[35]

The extraordinary circumstances of the attack against *Conversazione in Sicilia* are confirmed by the reaction of Giuseppe Villaroel, *Il Popolo d'Italia*'s literary critic. The day after the publication of 'Una sporca conversazione,' Villaroel wrote a resentful letter to Pini, underlining the insult implicit in an attack on a book that he had positively reviewed the previous year in the same paper. Unfortunately we do not know the content of Pini's immediate reply, but the letter must have opened Villaroel's eyes to the political aspect of the question, as Villaroel's following letter adopted a much more servile tone:

Tu sai con quanto scrupolo io lavoro, come l'unica mia preoccupazione sia di servire il giornale e di eseguire fedelmente i tuoi ordini. Ti prego, quindi, di guidarmi e consigliarmi. Non vivendo a contatto con te e con la redazione non mi è possibile avvertire nell'aria il senso dell'orientamento, anche nelle piccole sfumature ... Insomma, sono ai tuoi ordini come sempre; e quando noti o avverti che la mia interpretazione non è precisa richiamami all'ordine e aprimi gli occhi, che altro non desidero.[36]

(You know how scrupulous I am and the extent to which my only worry is to serve the interests of the paper and faithfully follow all your orders. I would be really grateful, therefore, if you could guide and advise me. Since I do not live in close contact with the editors, it is impossible for me to detect the latest orientation, even in its small nuances ... In conclusion, I am at your command, as always; and whenever you should notice that my interpretation is incorrect, call me to order and open my eyes, as this is all I want.)

The only clue as to the possible origin of the attack comes from a comment made by Villaroel in the same letter: 'Non vorrei che Ravasio pensasse che io sia propenso a un genere di letteratura che naturalmente è agli antipodi e del mio concetto dell'arte e della mia arte stessa' (I would not like Ravasio to think that I am inclined towards a kind of literature which is naturally at the opposite pole to my concept of art and to my own art). It is not entirely clear what importance we should give to the mention of Carlo Ravasio, then deputy-secretary of the PNF, head of the press office of the Federazione Nazionale Fascista in Milan, and chief editor of another paper of the Mussolini family's, *Gerarchia*. We know that, as deputy-secretary of the PNF, Ravasio had been publicly given the mandate to police the morality of the party. At his meetings with the press in 1942, Pavolini presented him as his close aid and Ravasio's correspondence with Pini shows that he had an ample mandate to interfere with the organization of the national press.[37] We do not know whether he actively intervened in this matter, but his diary sheds some light on the issue.[38] His entries around the time of the article show that Ravasio was pessimistic about the political situation, and he mentions on more than one occasion his approval of the criticisms of the regime by young Fascists. It seems therefore that he was unlikely to be the person who promoted the attack on Vittorini. Even more interesting is his diary entry for 3 August 1942. At that time Ravasio was under pressure from his superior, Aldo Vidussoni, the young secretary of the PNF, who demanded that he should take action against the criticism of the regime coming from the *riviste giovanili* sponsored by the party. Ravasio asked to express his views directly to Mussolini but was able to secure only a meeting with Pavolini. This is how Ravasio recorded Pavolini's views: 'Pavolini

insiste nel ripetermi che non è lui che sottopone i testi incriminati al
Duce; ma che il Duce stesso li scopre, o li riceve dai suoi funzionari, e si
adira per ciò che legge: e chiede le sanzioni' (Pavolini keeps repeating
that it is not him who submits the incriminated texts to Il Duce; but it is
Il Duce himself who discovers them, or he receives them from his officials, and then gets angry at what he reads: and asks for punishing measures to be taken).[39]

Whether or not Mussolini was involved in or aware of the attack on
Conversazione in Sicilia, there is no doubt that its timing coincided with a
period of high alert among Fascist leaders. We still have no decisive evidence as to the author of the article, but it is probable that it was meant
as part of the disciplinary crackdown on young Fascists which was instigated by Mussolini himself. There is little doubt that its publication in *Il
Popolo d'Italia* must have had the approval of some senior authority, certainly Pini's and possibly even Mussolini's.[40]

What were the consequences of the attack on the distribution of the
book? Nothing seems to have happened at an official level. Neither the
MCP nor the prefecture of Milan took any action. *Conversazione in Sicilia*
does not appear in a list of books whose circulation had been prohibited
between July 1936 and April 1943.[41] The Bompiani archives contain no
trace of any correspondence or documents related to measures taken
against the publisher. Because reconstructions of the events by Valentino
Bompiani and Vittorini are equally inconclusive, it is likely that Pavolini
and Bompiani discussed the incident informally, possibly over the phone.
Bompiani may have then decided simply to halt the distribution of the
third reprint of the novel.

The only documented evidence of some form of censorship is related
to the translations of *Conversazione in Sicilia*. By August 1942 Bompiani
was finalizing the contracts for English, French, and Spanish translations (the contract for a German edition had already been signed in
1941). However, none of these three translations was published before
the end of the war. Strangely, although no French publisher was authorized to translate the book, in March 1943 a contract was granted to the
Belgian publisher Toison d'Or.[42] Given Pavolini's inclination for finding
compromises and his friendly relationship with Bompiani, it is not
beyond the realm of possibility that the Belgian edition was allowed as a
sort of damage control for Bompiani's loss of revenue. Throughout this
period, Valentino Bompiani was in constant contact with Pavolini. In a
letter of 14 December 1941, while proudly presenting his company's
publication figures for the previous year, Bompiani added a curious

remark: 'ho mantenuto la promessa, nonostante i tanti dispiaceri che mi avete dato' (I have kept to my promise, despite the many disappointments I received from you). Pavolini's reply was equally cryptic: 'Nel compiacermi vivamente con voi per una così efficiente e brillante attività editoriale, non posso esimermi dal confessarvi, Caro Bompiani, come siate stato proprio Voi a darci fra tante consolazioni, anche qualche dispiacere ... (In complimenting you for such efficient and brilliant editorial activity, I cannot refrain from confessing to you, Dear Bompiani, that it was you who gave me, among so many consolations, the odd grievance too ...).[43]

Later that year Bompiani described the situation to Vittorini with these words: 'una tempesta addensatasi sulle nostre teste' (a storm gathering above our heads) and 'una nube di sospetto' (a cloud of suspicion).[44] The general impression is that Bompiani was entangled in a chess game, forced to plan his own moves while trying to second guess those of Pavolini and his ministerial aids.

Vittorini continued his activity as commissioning editor. His correspondence with Bompiani and the MCP does not suggest that he was subjected to any kind of repressive measures. Despite the attack in *Il Popolo d'Italia*, support for *Conversazione in Sicilia* continued in the Fascist press. Positive mention was made in *Il Popolo fascista*, in *Roma fascista* (which by this time had printed both positive and critical views on the novel), in Vittorini's old Florentine paper *Il Bargello*, and, most importantly, in Bottai's *Primato*.[45] As already mentioned, in October 1942 Vittorini was officially invited as an Italian representative at the Nazi-organized conference on literature in Weimar. If he had enemies inside the regime, they were counterbalanced by an equal number of friends.[46]

A further element of ambiguity surrounds the third reprint of *Conversazione in Sicilia*, which, despite being ready in the summer of 1942, was probably withheld from distribution. Surprisingly, a small number of copies are held in a few Italian libraries, which leads to some interesting implications. The printer's 'finito di stampare,' which traditionally appears in the last page of each book, shows that some of these copies were printed in 1942 (for example, the one held at the Biblioteca Malatestiana in Cesena). However, a more substantial third reprint must have been prepared the following year: this is suggested not only by the Fascist date on the frontispiece of other copies – Anno XXI – but by the 'finito di stampare' too, which specifies that the volume was printed on 15 June 1943.[47] It seems therefore that Bompiani held back the bulk of the 1942 reprint and waited for better times before going ahead with a 'new third reprint' a year later. It is also possible that the 1943 reprint was put together by simply changing the first and final page of already printed books, thus managing to avoid duplicating the paper and printing costs of the 1942 print run.

In the light of these facts, the entire censorial history of *Conversazione in Sicilia* can arguably be summarized as this: the novel was slightly censored in 1939 for the *Letteratura* edition, withdrawn from the market in 1942 but never officially seized by the Fascist authorities, and finally allowed to circulate in 1943. A disputable although well-informed source seems to support this reconstruction of the events. In his postwar diary, written while serving in the French Foreign Legion, Giuseppe Bottai commented on the publication of a chapter of Vittorini's *Uomini e no* in a French journal. On reading that the introduction presented *Conversazione in Sicilia* as having being banned by the Fascists, Bottai jotted down the following comment: 'Non è vero, e la critica letteraria ne parlò *pro* e *contra*, come volle; e Vittorini (forse tesserato – da appurare) pubblicava senza disturbi novelle su settimanali e quotidiani fascisti' (It is not true, and literary critics were free to speak for or against it; and Vittorini (perhaps he had a PNF card – to be checked) was freely publishing short stories in weekly and daily Fascist papers).[48] Bottai's postwar views certainly cannot be taken as fact, and it is sadly characteristic of his idea of freedom that he should think that the conditions under which Vittorini published his work can in any way be described as 'free.' However, given Bottai's position in 1942 as both an influential Fascist leader and key literary patron, he would probably have been informed if the book had actually being seized by the authorities.

It is only after the collapse of the regime that Vittorini's political activities drastically interfered with his literary career. On the first day of the Badoglio government, 26 July 1943, he was arrested in Milan together with other communist activists. The timing of the event suggests that Vittorini had already been identified as a communist militant although no trace of this can be found in either Milanese or Roman state archives. The police raid was part of Badoglio's preventive action to thwart possible communist uprisings. Vittorini spent four weeks in prison and was released on bail on 21 August. Soon after, he went underground. During the Nazi occupation, he worked as editor of the Milanese edition of *L'Unità* and wrote a new novel, *Uomini e no*. After the war, he emerged as a charismatic communist intellectual, and his past as a young Fascist receded into the background.

Censoring Women's Writing: Gianna Manzini, Alba De Céspedes, and Paola Masino

Women's writing in wartime Fascist Italy seems to have been subjected to a form of unofficial censorship. In two cases we have an indication that both Mussolini's *Il Popolo d'Italia* and Bottai's *Primato* were implementing a tacit embargo of the work of female authors. When Gianna Manzini published her first collection of short stories, *Venti racconti* (Mondadori, 1941), Giuseppe Villaroel, the literary critic of *Il Popolo d'Italia*, wrote to his chief editor on 27 November 1941 and offered to review the book. We do not have Pini's original reply, but Villaroel's subsequent letter of 28 December allows us to reconstruct the tone and content of Pini's argument. Meakly submitting to the chief editor's will, Villaroel wrote: 'Non voglio insistere e trovo che in linea di massima il tuo criterio di escludere le donne è ottimo. Anche Carducci inibiva alle donne la letteratura; ma poi fece eccezione per la Vivanti e fece bene' (I do not want to insist and I find that on the whole your criterion for excluding women is excellent. Carducci too used to deter women from literary activity; but then he made an exception for Vivanti, and he was right to do so).[49]

Although Villaroel's subsequently urged him to read Manzini with attention – 'quest'artista, così diversa dalle donne che scrivono' (this artist, so different from other women writers) – Pini did not change his mind. *Venti racconti* was passed over in silence.

A suggestion that the practice of ostracizing women writers went further than the pages of *Il Popolo d'Italia* comes from another author, Elsa Morante. In the autobiographical preface to the paperbook edition of her novel *L'isola d'Arturo*, she wrote that Bottai's journal *Primato* had a similar unofficial ban on women writers: 'basti ricordare che la rivista officiale del regime, "Primato," escludeva per principio qualsiasi scritto di donna' (it will suffice to remember that the official literary review of the regime, 'Primato,' rejected on principle any kind of writing by a woman). Morante was right. It is a fact that, despite Bottai's alleged open-mindedness, women authors were excluded from Primato. An indirect trace of such a boycott can be found in a letter written by Bottai to Paola Masino on 5 October 1940 to inform her that he had turned down a short story she had offered for publication. The justification for the rejection was that the story belonged to a 'letteratura più sottile e scabrosa' (more subtle and risqué literature) that would have generated moral objections within a journal such as *Primato*.[50]

Such sexist directives may have stemmed directly from Il Duce. Knowing Pini's dependence on Mussolini's advice and the latter's level of
interference with the workings of *Il Popolo d'Italia*, it would not be surprising. There is, however, no supporting evidence. If the ban originated with Mussolini, it either was not in place in 1937 or did not
include a favourite female author of his, Ada Negri. According to Pini's
diary, when he asked Mussolini over the telephone about possible new
contributors to *Il Popolo d'Italia*, Il Duce personally approved the inclusion of Negri.[51]

In her essay on Fascist censorship on female authors, Lucia Re suggests that a sexist attitude in literary matters was already present in earlier years. The famous Mura case of April 1934 (see chapter 4) was, after
all, in response to the work of a female novelist. Moreover, at the time of
the regime's turn to anti-Semitism, Bottai's attack against Jewish authors
of children literature, in 1939, was directed mainly at women writers.[52] A
paradoxical side to this state of affairs, is that, according to archival
records, Gianna Manzini was excluded from public recognition for her
writing, but at the same time was receiving funds from both the MCP
and Mussolini's office to support her activity as a writer.[53] This contradiction suggests at least some lack of consistency in the regime's
approach.

The complexity of the situation is more fully exposed by specific, documented cases such as that of Alba De Céspedes. The daughter of a distinguished Cuban diplomat and politician, De Céspedes had grown up in
Rome, married at the age of fifteen, had a child at seventeen. Since her
separation from her first husband in 1931 she was living in the capital,
supporting herself partly through her journalistic and literary activity.
Her Political Police file shows that her initial problems with the regime
were of an entirely political nature. On 11 February 1935 the police
intercepted two telephone conversations in which De Céspedes spoke in
derogatory tones about Italy's invasion of Ethiopia.[54] The reason why her
telephone should have been tapped is not mentioned but it is likely that
it was the result of information received by the police. The source was
possibly an anonymous letter, as many more were sent in the following
years. The order to arrest her was signed the following day by Bocchini in
person; it may have followed a brief discussion with Mussolini during
their morning meeting. De Céspedes denied any wrong doing – she was
not told of the existence of detailed telephone transcripts – and was
eventually given a police warning and released on 17 February. A few
months later she attempted to renew her passport. Given her recent

problems, her application went all the way to Mussolini (then also Ministry of the Interior), who jotted down a 'No' followed by his initial. She appealed in a long letter dated 26 September 1935 addressed to the Minister of the Interior. She presented herself as a member of PNF and justified her request for the passport by saying she needed to visit her father, then the Cuban ambassador in Madrid. Mussolini relented, and a note in the margin of a police memo confirms that the order had come from him.[55]

Three years later De Céspedes began her career as a novelist. Published by Mondadori and supported by an unusually intense publicity campaign for a young Italian author, *Nessuno torna indietro* was an immediate commercial and critical success. Arnoldo Mondadori had obviously spotted a brilliant new author. Published in December 1938, the novel was reprinted twelve times in 1939 and by the end of 1940 had reached its nineteenth reprint.[56] The only restriction imposed on the novel in its early stages was related to the regime's bizarre linguistic policies. In January 1940 Mondadori was told that future reprints had to be modified to comply with the 1938 directive imposing the use of 'Voi' against the less dignified 'Lei.'[57] In December 1940 Mondadori also published *Fuga*, a collection of fourteen short stories by De Céspedes. That volume was part of the series *Lo Specchio*, which included Alberto Moravia's work and *Scomparsa d'Angela*, a collection of short stories by the minister of the MCP, Alessandro Pavolini. De Céspedes sent a copy of *Fuga* to Mussolini's private secretary, Osvaldo Sebastiani, but the gift might have backfired: her letter in Mussolini's office file is accompanied by a handwritten note saying: 'Il primo racconto (che solo ho letto) confermerebbe in parte l'apprezzamento dell'anonima in atti. Scrittrice capace, ma racconti immorali' (The first story – the only one I read – would partially confirm the comments of the anonymous letter on file. A good writer, but of immoral tales). Presumably an anonymous letter had arrived at that very time and this first negative impression of De Céspedes's work might have been the source of her subsequent problems.[58]

A further complication was added by the fact that, in January 1941, a project for a film version of *Nessuno torna indietro* had been launched under the indirect guidance of Arnoldo Mondadori, whose film production company, Montedoro, was to finance the film.[59] Among the actresses contracted to play a group of female university students was Doris Duranti, who was to play Emanuela, a young mother suffering as a result of being forced to live a separate life from her child (a similar situation to De Céspedes's own life, whose son she had placed in a boarding school in Rome). Mention of Doris Duranti is not gratuitous, as the famous actress was at the time the mistress of MCP's minister, Alessandro Pavolini. The first documented mention that *Nessuno torna indietro* was about to encounter problems comes in a letter from Pavolini to the MCP's head of the General Directorate for Cinematography, Vezio Orazi. In the brief letter dated 25 January 1941, Pavolini wrote the following:

> Ti prego di parlare con Luciano [Capo Gabinetto at the MCP] circa il progettato film tratto dal romanzo della DE CESPEDES.
>
> C'è stato, infatti, del nuovo dopo il mio colloquio con Mondadori e le conseguenti direttive a te date.
>
> Converrà, mi sembra, tener di nuovo in sospeso la cosa; in ogni modo ti informerò dell'accaduto.[60]

> (Can you please talk to Luciano with regard to the planned film adapted from DE CESPEDES's novel.
>
> There are some new developments following my conversation with Mondadori and the directives that were given to you.
>
> It is best, in my view, to put everything on hold; I'll let you know about what happened.)

What these new developments were is open to speculation. However, it is documented that two days later, on 27 January 1941, the MCP's head of DGSI, Casini, sent a letter to Mondadori ordering him to stop any reprints of *Nessuno torna indietro*. The ban included any negotiations regarding contracts for translations of the novel. The opening words of Casini's letter – 'Per superiore disposizione' (Following superior directive) – strongly suggest that the order had come directly from Mussolini. This is also partially confirmed by the postwar memoirs of the MCP's head of cabinet, Celso Luciano, who wrote that Mussolini had personally ordered the ban.[61]

The novel was attacked as an example of immoral literature in the Argentinian illustrated magazine in Italian, *Vita italiana*. The article, by Piero Pellicano, accused *Nessuno torna indietro* of painting a derogatory picture of Italian women. Pellicano grossly distorted the actual content of the book and in more than one place attributed to De Céspedes herself passages that actually relate to her characters' thoughts and intentions. De Céspedes's file at ACS contains a copy of a long article written presumably by her in response to Pellicano's attack. Unfortunately it is not clear whether the article was actually published, although the proof format of the copy would suggest it was. In the article, probably written in early 1941, De Céspedes pointed out all the inconsistencies of Pellicano's attack while highlighting the positive features of characters such as Emanuela, Anna, and Silvia. The final paragraph reminded Pellicano that she was an Aryan mother and held a PNF card. This final note must have been humiliating for her and gives us a sense of the pressure on authors to conform to the regime's ideological directives.[62]

In April and May 1941 two anonymous letters were sent to the Fascist authorities insinuating that De Céspedes's house had become a meeting place for more or less covert anti-Fascists who listened to BBC radio broadcasts in Italian. Reference to a defamatory campaign against her is also made in a letter from Arnoldo Mondadori to Goffredo Costa in June 1941.[63] The situation was obviously deteriorating: on 13 August 1941 the MCP sent a telegraphic directive to all newspaper chief editors ordering them to 'non fare pubblicità Alba De Céspedes' (avoid publicizing Alba De Céspedes).[64] It is likely that the order was designed to stop the polemical exchanges ignited by Pellicano's attack and, more important, to suppress any discussion of a novel that had been banned. De Céspedes's next move was to try to arrange a meeting with Mussolini. She submitted her request on 18 September; Mussolini's usual handwritten note makes it clear that he refused to see her. At the same time, he must have asked for a police report on her: on 13 October 1941 the Political Police sent him a letter summarizing her various encounters with the authorities, although refraining from presenting her as a straightforward anti-Fascist.[65]

De Céspedes turned her attention to the MCP. On 31 October 1941 she wrote to Pavolini and asked for his protection against the defamatory campaign that was victimizing her. The following day she also wrote to the MCP's head of cabinet, Celso Luciano, once more asking for support and notifying him of a second, longer letter to come regarding the film production. That letter, which arrived on 17 November 1941, it provides a revealing look at the working of the film project. De Céspedes stated that she had received an advance payment of 60,000 lire for the rights to the film back in 1939; however, because the recent ban on the novel had included the film rights too, the film company was asking for the money to be returned. She asked to be given the chance to revise the script – she had not been involved in the original adaptation – to make it more acceptable to the censors. She offered to cut the character of Xenia, give Emanuela, Silvia, Anna, and Augusta more positive traits, and write a more uplifting finale. She also proposed to change the title of the film, offering as alternatives titles taken from foreign translations of the book: among the candidates were *L'altra sponda* (from the German edition), *Ragazze* (from the Hungarian), *Gioventù in tumulto* (from the Dutch), and *Pensione Grimaldi* (unspecified). According to her letter, the film production company, Urbe Film, had fixed a court hearing for the end of November, and De Cèspedes feared that she might be forced to pay the money back. A handwritten note in the margin says, 'Visto dal Duce. Si autorizza film con nuovo titolo "Ragazze" o "Pensione Grimaldi"' (Seen by Il Duce. The film is authorized with new title 'Girls' or 'Pensione Grimaldi.'[66] Given the urgency of the situation, three days later, on 20 November, De Céspedes was received by Luciano. He informed her of the regime's decision, probably hiding from her the actual source of the final verdict. Two days later Luciano wrote to Vezio Orazi, and told him the film had been given the go-ahead on the assumption that the title was going to be changed.[67]

The production of the film was resumed in 1942 under the directorship of Alessandro Blasetti (its first director, Amleto Palermo, had died in April 1941). The film – entitled *Istituto Grimaldi* – was probably completed in the summer of 1943, although it seems that it was never released.[68] Whatever the film's fate, there is no doubt that De Céspedes's career as a fiction writer had been destroyed. She was allowed to work only as a journalist, and even in this field her life was made difficult. In November 1942 she asked for her passport to be renewed so she could travel to France, via Germany, to write some articles for an unspecified Mondadori periodical (presumably *Tempo*). An exchange of letters between the passport office at the Ministry of the Interior and Luciano at the MCP shows that her request was again considered by the upper echelons of the regime. On 26 November 1942 Luciano gave instructions not to renew her passport.[69]

A final episode related to De Céspedes sees the reappearance of Pavolini. Throughout most of the *querelle* relating to *Nessuno torna indietro*, Pavolini seems to have avoided taking any direct decision despite his position as head of the MCP. His file in Mussolini's office shows that in 1942 various anonymous letters and police informers' reports had arrived on Il Duce's desk denouncing the scandal provoked by the relationship between Pavolini and Doris Duranti. According to Pavolini biographer, Pavolini and Mussolini had a direct confrontation with regard to this, with the MCP minister refusing to bow to his boss's request to end his relationship.[70] Although full documentary evidence is lacking, it is interesting to note that after Pavolini ceased to be head of the MCP – replaced by Polverelli in March 1943 – he attempted to intercede in favour of De Céspedes. In his new position as chief editor of the Roman newspaper *Il Messaggero*, Pavolini wrote to Polverelli on 21 March 1943 to ask whether De Céspedes could be allowed to resume contributing to *Il Messaggero* as a fiction writer. 'Si accontenterebbe di tre quattro racconti all'anno' (she would content herself with three or four short stories per year), noted Pavolini's. Polverelli replied with an ambiguous 'non sono in grado di darti alcun responso' (I'm not in the position to give you an answer). Such a response from the minister of the MCP must mean either that he had failed to get an opinion from his direct superior – who was running a country on the verge of enemy invasion, after all – or that Mussolini had simply refused to deal with the matter.

The last batch of relevant documentation is an exchange of letters between Polverelli and Mussolini's private secretary Nicolò De Cesare. Mussolini's office had apparently received yet another anonymous letter attacking Alba De Céspedes on the grounds that she had been allowed to go ahead with the film. According to the informer, this was the result of De Céspedes's close friendship with Doris Duranti and of the latter's influence over Pavolini. De Cesare wrote to Polverelli on 7 June 1943 and asked for some explanation. The reply confirmed the rumours surrounding the relationship between the former minister and Duranti and indirectly suggested that this might have been a factor in the authorization to keep the film in production.[71] In the end, the collapse of the regime brought this humiliating affair to an end. With the creation of the RSI in northern Italy, De Céspedes fled in the opposite direction and managed to reach the southern part of the peninsula under Allied control. From there she became a broadcaster for Radio Free Bari using the pseudonym Clorinda, and in the following years she was to assume her rightful position as an outspoken intellectual and a popular writer.

As we have seen in chapter 5, Paola Masino's daring surrealistic fiction had already stirred up some trouble in the 1930s. The short story 'Fame' had led to the closing down of Zavattini's journal *Grandi firme* in 1938. Under pressure from Bompiani, 'Fame' was subsequently excluded from Masino's collection *Racconto grosso e altri*, which received Casini's *nulla osta* in July 1941.[72] A similar story of editorial caution and humiliating self-censorship concerns Masino's next novel, her most famous one. *Nascita e morte della massaia* was first published in instalments in Alberto Mondadori's *Tempo* between October 1941 and January 1942. Arnoldo's son shared fears similar to those of Valentino Bompiani about the acceptability of Masino's surreal but nonetheless savage mockery of social hierarchies, particularly in relation to female characters. An exchange of letters between author and editor prior to the first instalment of the novel suggests that Masino accepted the request for some modifications to the text although she stopped short of rewriting passages relating to motherhood and marriage that were so central to her critique of society.[73] When it came to publishing the novel as a book, Masino opted for her customary publisher, Bompiani, who had recently brought out another collection of her short stories, *Terremoto*, positively reviewed by Vasco Pratolini for *Primato* in April 1942.[74] This time it does not seem that Bompiani exercised any pressure to 'normalize' the novel, although the genesis of the final text is not entirely clear: there are two extant typescripts for *Nascita e morte della massaia*, both with a number of cuts and additions apparently in the author's handwriting.[75] We know for certain that the final typescript was submitted to the MCP in the autumn of 1942. It was approved with only ten small cuts of passages that could be interpreted as indirectly fomenting social unrest. In a memo to Casini, dated 23 November 1942, a MCP official added that the content of the book was obscured by the surrealistic, nightmarish setting typical of Masino.[76] The correspondence between the author and Bompiani shows that the first proofs were ready in October 1942. It was subsequent to this date that Masino was asked to modify the novel according to the censors' indications. This is indicated by a letter of 19 January 1943, in which Masino briefly informed Bompiani that, given the complexity of cutting certain sentences without losing the novel's cohesion and value, she had decided to withdraw the publication altogether. Bompiani reminded her that both she and Bontempelli had agreed with the cuts and urged her to continue. Masino soon reversed her decision and returned the corrected proofs. The final proofs were ready in April and were sent to the printers that June.[77] The collapse of Mussolini's government in July coincided with a number of Allied bombing raids on the city of Milan, one of which destroyed the Bompiani warehouse, where the final proofs of the novel were held.[78] *Nascita e morte della massaia* was eventually published by Bompiani in liberated Italy, in 1945. Masino tried to reinstate some of the passages that had been modified or cut; unfortunately, so much had been withheld or attenuated even in the first version that she was unable to recreate the original draft.

Nascita e morte della massaia was to remain an example of a brilliant work of fiction inextricably marred by the political climate of its time.

There is currently not enough evidence to substantiate the hypothesis that the Fascists attempted a concerted clampdown on women's writing in their last years in power. However, it is arguable that women remained the most easily attacked and marginalized groups of authors, too often at the mercy of the personal preferences of individuals in position of authority. There were confined areas such as Bemporad's *Almanacco della donna italiana*, in which female authors were obviously welcome. Moreover, thanks once more to the regime's lack of detailed monitoring, even Margherita Sarfatti continued to be mentioned in its yearly list of female journalists and authors, despite the fact that her publications had been proscribed since 1938.[79] However, one of the side effects of the austere wartime atmosphere was that of dragging women back to more 'useful' roles. It is easy to imagine that, if fiction writing in general could hardly be defended as a proper contribution to the war effort, even more compromised was the position of authors such as Manzini, De Céspedes, and Masino, whose work indirectly questioned some of the basic values of Fascism's vision of domestic life.

Conclusion

As the nine chapters of this book have illustrated, literary censorship concerns much more than scissor-wielding censors. This was even more the case in Fascist Italy because of the ambiguous patronage and hypo-critical displays of tolerance that characterized the system. Once it had established its grip over the cultural industry, the Fascist regime attempted to promote the creation of a culture it could call its own. But here one must immediately pause and clarify. 'Fascist regime' is a vast container within which dozens of different visions cohabited, allowing clear potential for conflict. Mussolini's idea of Fascist culture – if he had only one – did not coincide with that of other prime movers such as Bottai, Ciano, Farinacci, and Pavolini. Censorship was an important tool but, as we have seen, it was a tool that was taken up and used in many different ways, by different agents, and with different results. An additional complication is that, at an official level, the repressive state of Fascist censorship was totally denied. Krieg's often-mentioned book *La legislazione penale sulla stampa* (1942) is a good example of such denial: it omits any mention of not only Mussolini's circular of April 1934 but also, more seriously, the regime's anti-Semitic legislation.

In a recent essay, Philip Cannistraro adopted De Felice's notion of 'spazi di libertà' to suggest that by allowing for a seductive degree of internal debate, the regime secured the complicity of most of the intellectual class. Moreover, if the Fascists needed the consensus of the publishing industry, many publishers equally needed and looked for the support and patron-age of the government.[1] Within the discussion of these controversial issues, the current study should contribute to our understanding of how the Fascist state influenced the field of literary production. It also shows the relative flexibility with which all parties approached negotiations. Even in the case of the most humilitating and barbarous Fascist policies – the anti-Semitic legislation – the harshness of the directives was weakened by a propensity for exceptions and ad hoc solutions. In his study, Fabre used a most appropriate expression when he wrote that the Ministry of Popular Culture sometimes 'navigava a vista' (navigated without a compass). This is an expression that well illustrates the non-programmatic nature of Fascist cultural policies. A number of factors contributed to this mode of political navigation. Among them we should dismiss the clichéd notion of 'italiani brava gente' – that is, the idea that Fascist totalitarianism was a failure because Italians were too 'good' to implement those policies. The Ministry of Popular Culture had long-serving, efficient officials such as Gherardo Casini and Celso Luciano, who were precise executors of clear political directives. Giuseppe Bottai as Minister of National Education was similarly if not more prepared for draconian measures. Even the erudite and good-humoured Leopoldo Zurlo had little reluctance when it came to forcing Italian theatre to comply with Mussolini's racist turn. But if it is true that every organization eventually reflects the *modus operandi* of its leader, then the first factor to be examined should be the role of the regime's Duce.

In the wartime memoirs of an obscure postal censor from Mantua, the following sentence stands out: 'L'ombra del duce, infatti, dal più al meno, ha sempre accompagnato il lavoro del censore' (Big or small, the Duce's shadow has always followed the work of the censor).[2] This sentence brilliantly encapsulates a central aspect of Fascist censorship. Mussolini's presence was felt by everybody and at all levels, and not just because of the semi-religious myth of an all-seeing and all-pervading dictator. As this book has shown, Mussolini was genuinely and passionately interested in questions of press censorship, whether related to newspapers, books, or an occasional sonnet by Trilussa. It was an interest shaped by two features. First, as De Felice suggested, Mussolini's involvement in cultural matters was not the result of a pure love of knowledge: it was instrumental to his political aims and, as such, it was deeply illiberal.[3] Piero Gobetti was among the first to experience this sinister side of Il Duce's personality; others followed, many of whom preferred to stoop to the more or less explicit acts of deference that he expected from his subjects. The second feature is the unpredictability of Mussolini's interventions. It could be argued that he cultivated this aspect as part of his legendary status. Personally, I would be more inclined to agree that the many sudden corrections to the voyage of the Fascist ship (to return to Fabre's metaphor) derived from the fact that Mussolini too *navigava a vista.* From the many cases of censorship examined here, there emerges the image of a dictator who approached each case without a theoretical yardstick. The approach was illiberal and improvised – attuned to the political needs of the moment.

But there was also a temperamental side to Mussolini's dictates: his bursts of anger or passionate response to a situation could be turned into political directives on the spur of the moment. As the long-standing chief editor of *Il Popolo d'Italia,* Giorgio Pini was on the receiving end of many controversial decisions. He recorded them in his diaries and memoirs. One particular entry, from 8 March 1937, deserves mention here. During one of his daily telephone conversations with Mussolini, Pini enquired about a moratorium on reviews of the second volume of Yvon De Begnac's biography of Mussolini. Il Duce replied that 'Non bisogna fare delle recensioni stupide come quella apparsa oggi sul "Messagero," e con quelle illustrazioni. Ma in quanto al veto, farò dare il contrordine' (one has to avoid stupid reviews like the one accompanied by illustrations and published by the *Messaggero*; but, as for the veto, I am going to have it removed). Next to this, Pini annotated:

È evidente l'influenza dei suoi fugaci malumori personali sulle direttive ministeriali che tanto ci assillano per questioni minute e di nessun conto, ma è pure evidente la trasmissione troppo pedestre e non intelligente degli ordini derivanti da scatti momentanei. Presumo che, al posto del Ministro, saprei essere un interprete più agile e spregiudicato di questi ordini, che io stesso riesco così facilmente a far revocare da questo mio posto. Basterebbe soprassedere un giorno e tornare alla carica per la rettifica dopo ventiquattr'ore, ad evitare molte noie e assurdità.[4]

(It is evident that his short-lived bursts of exasperation have an influence over the welter of ministerial directives that we receive over questions of little or no importance. But it is also evident that they derive from too unimaginative and obtuse a transmission of orders that are given on the spur of the moment. I suspect that if I were in the minister's shoes, I would be a more agile and cunning interpreter of his orders, orders that I am easily able to have changed from my position [at *Il Popolo d'Italia*]. In order to avoid so many problems and absurdities all that is needed is to sit on them for a day, and then ask for rectification twenty-four hours later.)

Pini might have been indulging in a self-congratulatory remark here, but he was equally tapping into an important issue. And he was not alone. Similar considerations about this aspect of Mussolini's personality can be found in the memoirs of the MCP's most zealous minister, Dino Alfieri, and in those of Carmine Senise, deputy and later head of police during the Fascist years.[5] Certainly in matters of censorship, there is a sense that Mussolini's many interventions were rarely the result of careful planning. Moreover, since they were taken up with zeal and bureaucratic fastidiousness, the system often found itself having to cope with unforeseen consequences. Hence the need for everybody to *navigare a vista* in case a sudden storm broke out unexpectedly.

Once we come to the anti-Semitic legislation, matters became vastly more serious. The spectrum of historical debate currently oscillates between the two poles of De Felice's suggestion of 'faciloneria mussoliniana' (Mussolinian sloppyness) and Fabre's determination to trace a lifelong racist motif in Mussolini's persona.[6] The two are not necessarily mutually exclusive. Within the field of censorship, if traces of anti-Semitism can be found in the earlier years of Fascist Italy (and even the Vatican's *Osservatore romano*, as we have seen in the case of Sem Benelli, was not exempt from it), there is little doubt that the sudden racist turn of 1938 created a huge amount of unplanned work for the cultural ministries. The fact that it took four years (and the Nazi spur) before the List of Unwelcome Authors was circulated is in itself an indication of the lack of preparation – and in this case one can perhaps add lack of determination – with which Mussolini's latest policy was applied. Such an observation is far from an attempt to soften the assessment of the policy's barbarity. The complicity of Italy's publishing world in the application of this legislation is shameful evidence of a collective responsibility. It is not surprising that the postwar years should have seen the *bonifica libraria* become one of the industry's best-kept secrets. But even in this case it is difficult not to conclude that throughout the process Mussolini remained at the helm, and the discretion and hypocrisy of implementation somehow reflected his intention not to publicize a policy that, as he probably was the first one to know, had not just a cruel but also an absurd side. Benedetto Croce forcefully reminded him of that in his letter of 9 January 1940, but his remained a solitary voice.

Another factor that influenced Fascist policies on censorship was the regime's attempt to control and at the same time support the publishing industry. This 'carrot and stick' approach had its roots in the autarkic desire to sustain a national publishing industry. Publishers such as Arnoldo Mondadori cunningly exploited this desire, constantly reminding Mussolini of their attempts to create a powerful publishing industry capable of projecting Italian culture to the rest of the world. It was also true that the years after the First World War had brought a financial crisis in the publishing sector and so both injections of cash and lucrative government commissions were greatly welcomed. In return the regime expected self-censorship and consensual collaboration. Within this framework, censorship was only one of a number of tools – often used a last resort – with which the regime and the publishing industry negotiated Italy's book production.

A third important factor relates to Bosworth's distinction between 'legal Italy' and 'real Italy.' Several episodes described in this book have confirmed the impression of a bureaucratic system that was making ample use of off-the-record, 'amicable' ad hoc solutions. This time the cliché of 'italiani confusionari' could be used with some success. However, a more convincing argument is that double standards served the regime well. Particularly from the mid-1930s, Fascist propaganda attempted to present Italians as a cohesive, well-regimented, and powerful community fervently dressed in black shirts. In such an ideal totalitarian Fascist state, censorship should have no reason to exist. This is why propaganda publications vainly continued to repeat, right into the war years, that freedom of expression was a well-protected right of Fascist Italians. There was an element of hypocrisy which created the ground for all sorts of ambiguities. As we have seen, the reluctance to convert general policy into specific legislation was a major factor in allowing state officials, at all levels, a wide degree of discretion. This is confirmed by the memoirs of ministers, censors, publishers, and authors, and by a great deal of archival documentation.

A final complicating factor was the relative autonomy and 'non-Fascistization' of the Italian police. Mussolini's decision in his early years in power not to allow Fascist leaders such as Farinacci, Balbo, and others to turn the prefectures into their own fiefdoms had the result of maintaining most of the police cadres as they were in 1922. As Giovanna Tosatti concluded in her study of the organization of the Italian police in liberal and Fascist Italy: 'In sostanza, proprio il periodo del fascismo al potere sembra essere stato l'unico in cui la polizia abbia goduto di una vera autonomia e di un reale potere decisionale' (On the whole, the years of fascism in power are indeed the only ones during which the police benefited from real autonomy and real decision-making power).[7] This book has shown a certain number of exceptions to this argument. After all, theatre censorship, despite being the responsibility of a non-Fascist prefect such as Zurlo, was heavily influenced by Mussolini. Similarly, prefectures all over Italy were given precise political directives to follow. However, Tosatti's argument is absolutely accurate as regards the actual staffing of the police forces. This fact raises the possibility that central and provincial officers were not as eager as militant Fascists would have been to implement policies that had a clear political agenda. There were no boycotts, not even during the years of anti-Semitic legislation, but the existence of a non-Fascist element among the individuals involved in censorship matters was certainly another complicating factor.

This book has tried to offer a detailed overview of this complex situation. More than one case of literary censorship will have fallen through its net, and more new ones will be caught in the nets as a result of further archival trawls. However, I hope that its general structure will continue to provide a solid base. It is regrettable that more textual analysis of censored texts could not be pursued, but this is a direct consequence of the scarcity of archival evidence.

At a more general level, what no study of censorship will ever manage to do justice to is the price Italian culture paid for twenty years under a repressive regime. It was not just a question of self-censorship and complying with political directives. It was the sheer humiliation of having to conform, to stoop to the expectations of a dictatorial power in all its different manifestations. Against this background, the actions of the few who raised their heads and voices stand out even more starkly.

A final open question concerns the return to a democratic system. How easily were those long-established practices reversed? Authors such as Vitaliano Brancati vocally stated that little changed in the postwar years. Recent work such as Turi's book on the *Enciclopedia Treccani* suggests at least an element of continuity. As Brancati put it in 1952, 'Sono scomparse migliaia di persone ... Ma (e sembra un'allucinazione ottica) i vecchi impiegati sono ancora lì, nel palazzo di Via Veneto, che ora porta il nome di Sottosegretariato per lo spettacolo e le informazioni' (Thousands of people have disappeared ... But (and it feels like an optical illusion) the old officials are still there, in the Via Veneto building which is now called Undersecretariat for Entertainment and Information).[8] Further scholarly study is clearly needed to bring into focus this post-Fascist aspect of censorship. If the legislation and practices in liberal Italy were not entirely alien to the subsequent development of Fascist censorship, it would be naïve to expect a complete sea change after the fall of the regime.

Notes

Abbreviations

A900	Archivio del 900, 'La Sapienza' University, Rome
AB	Archivio Storico Bompiani, Milan
ACGV	Archivio Contemporaneo Alessandro Bonsanti, Gabinetto Vieusseux, Florence
ACS	Archivio Centrale dello Stato, Rome
	CPC: Casellario Politico Centrale
	DAGR: Divisione Affari Generali e Riservati
	DGPS: Direzione Generale Pubblica Sicurezza
	DGTM CT: Direzione Generale Teatro e Musica, Censura Teatrale
	MCP: Ministero Cultura Popolare, Gabinetto, I versatura
	MCP II: Ministero Cultura Popolare, Gabinetto, II versatura
	MPI DGAB: Ministero della Pubblica Istruzione, Direzione Generale delle Accademie e Biblioteche
	MI: Ministero dell' Interno
	MI UC: Ministero dell'Interno, Ufficio Cifra, Telegrammi
	PCM: Presidenza Consiglio dei Ministri
	PP FP: Polizia Politica, Fascicoli Personali
	PP M: Polizia Politica, Materie
	SPD CO: Segreteria Particolare Duce, Carteggio Ordinario
	SPD CR: Segreteria Particolare Duce, Carteggio Riservato
AE	Archivio Einaudi, Turin
AFM	Archivio della Fondazione Arnoldo e Alberto Mondadori, Milan
	FAM: Fondo Arnoldo Mondadori
	FB: Fondo Giuseppe Bottai

APICE	Archivio della Parola, dell'Immagine e della Comunicazione Editoriale, Milan
	AB: Archivio personale Valentino Bompiani
ASDMAE	Archivio Storico Diplomatico del Ministero degli Affari Esteri, La Farnesina, Rome
	MAE: Ministero Affari Esteri, Direzione General Affari Generali
	MCP: Ministero Cultura Popolare
ASMi	Archivio di Stato, Milan
	PG I: Prefettura, Gabinetto, I versatura
	PG II: Prefettura, Gabinetto, II versatura
ASRo	Archivio di Stato, Rome
	PG: Prefettura, Gabinetto
	QR: Questura Roma, Cat. 8
ASTo	Archivio di Stato, Turin
	PG: Prefettura, Gabinetto
ASV	Archivio Segreto Vaticano (Vatican Secret Archives)
	SS: Segreteria di Stato
ASVr	Archivio di Stato, Verona
	PG: Prefettura, Gabinetto
BN	Biblioteca Nazionale Centrale, Rome
	FF: Fondo Falqui
FFT	Fondazione di Studi Storici Filippo Turati, Florence
FP	Fondo Manoscritti, Pavia University
	CG: Carteggio Marcello Gallian
GRL	Getty Research Library, Special Collection, Los Angeles
NAKe	National Archives, Kew, UK (formerly Public Records Office)
Opera Omnia	Benito Mussolini, Opera Omnia, edited by D. and E. Susmel, 35 vols. Florence: La Fenice, 1951–62

Introduction

1 Alberto Asor Rosa, *Scrittori e popolo: Saggio sulla letteratura populista in Italia* (Rome: Savonà e Savelli, 1965).

2 The correspondence of the Allied military team working on the Italian archives can be found in NAKe, Captured Italian Records, GFM 36. The first comprehensive study of the publishing industry in modern and contemporary Italy is Nicola Tranfaglia and Albertina Vittoria, *Storia degli editori italiani* (Bari and Rome: Laterza, 2000).

3 Fondazione Arnoldo e Alberto Mondadori, eds., *Editoria e cultura a Milano tra le due guerre: Atti del convegno* (Milan: Fondazione Arnoldo e Alberto Mondadori, 1983). The papers referred to are Giordano Bruno Guerri, 'La Mondadori e la

politica del ventennio' (87–92), and Giovanni Spadolini, 'Relazione conclusiva del convegno' (212–23). Enrico Decleva, *Mondadori* (Milan: UTET, 1993). By then Giordano Bruno Guerri had already published three controversial biographies of influential Fascists: on Giuseppe Bottai (Feltrinelli, 1976), Galeazzo Ciano (Bompiani, 1979), and Curzio Suckert Malaparte (Bompiani, 1980). Guerri is now a Mondadori author and writes for the conservative paper *Il Giornale.*

4 Guido Bonsaver, *Elio Vittorini: The Writer and the Written* (Leeds: Northern Universities Press, 2000). With regard to Vittorini's encounters with censorship, the sections of this book related to it (chapters 5, 8, and 9) update and supersede those contained in my 2000 monograph.

5 David Forgacs, *Italian Culture in the Industrial Era, 1880–1980* (Manchester: Manchester University Press, 1990); translated in Italian as *L'industrializzazione della cultura italiana* (Bologna: Il Mulino, 1992).

6 Philip Cannistraro, *La fabbrica del consenso: Fascismo e Mass-media* (Bari and Rome: Laterza, 1975). Maurizio Cesari, *La censura nel periodo fascista* (Naples: Liguori, 1978). Mario Isnenghi, *Intellettuali militanti e intellettuali funzionari: Appunti sulla cultura fascista* (Turin: Einaudi, 1979). A strong call for a more thorough use of archival resources in the study of the publishing industry came from Carlo Maria Simonetti in his essay 'L'editoria fiorentina dal 1920 al 1940: Proposte per una ricerca,' *Ricerche storiche* 22.2–3 (1982): 541–68.

7 Luisa Mangoni, *Pensare i libri: La casa editrice Einaudi dagli anni trenta agli anni sessanta* (Turin: Bollati e Boringhieri, 1999); Ada Gigli Marchetti and Luisa Finocchi, *Stampa e piccola editoria tra le due guerre* (Milan: Franco Angeli, 1997); Ada Gigli Marchetti, *Le edizioni Corbaccio: Storia di libri e di libertà* (Milan: Franco Angeli, 2000); Maria Adelaide Frabotta, *Gobetti l'editore giovane* (Bologna: Il Mulino, 1988); Monica Galfré, *Il regime degli editori: Libri, scuola, fascismo* (Bologna: Il Mulino, 2005). See also the following works by Gabriele Turi *Il fascismo e il consenso degli intellettuali* (Bologna: Il Mulino, 1980); *La casa Einaudi: Libri uomini, idee oltre il fascismo* (Bologna: Il Mulino, 1990); and his editorship of *Storia dell'editoria nell'Italia contemporanea* (Florence: Giunti, 1997).

8 Giorgio Fabre, *L'elenco: Censura fascista, editoria e autori ebrei* (Turin: Silvio Zamorani editore, 1998). The above-mentioned conference took place in October 2002 and its proceedings were published as Guido Bonsaver and Robert Gordon, eds., *Culture, Censorship and the State in Twentieth-Century Italy* (Oxford: Legenda, 2005). Patrizia Ferrara, *L'amministrazione centrale pubblica*, vol. 4, *Ministro Cultura Popolare* (Bologna: Il Mulino, 1992); Antonio Fiori, *Il filtro deformante: La censura sulla stampa durante la prima guerra mondiale* (Rome: Istituto storico italiano per l'età moderna e contemporanea, 2001).

9 Marla Susan Stone, *The Patron State: Culture and Politics in Fascist Italy* (Princeton, NJ: Princeton University Press, 1999). Ruth Ben-Ghiat, *Fascist Modernities: Italy, 1922–1945* (Berkeley University of California Press, 2001).

10 Antonio Fiori, 'Introduzione,' in Archivio Centrale dello Stato, *Direzione generale della pubblica sicurezza. La stampa italiana nella serie F.1 (1894–1926): Inventario* (Rome: Ministero per i beni culturali e ambientali, 1995), 7–19. The introductory notes and the *inventario* for the years 1926–43 have not been published but can be consulted in the catalogue room at Rome's ACS.

11 Leopoldo Zurlo, *Memorie inutili: La censura teatrale nel ventennio* (Rome: Edizioni dell'Ateneo, 1952); Patrizia Ferrara, ed., *Censura teatrale e fascismo (1931–1944): La storia, l'archivio, l'inventario* (Rome: Ministero per i beni e le attività culturali, 2004).

12 Sadly, a warehouse fire in January 2003 destroyed the important archives of the Florentine publisher Vallecchi. However, Attilio Vallecchi's copious correspondence is held at the ACGV. I am greatful to Laura Cattaneo, at Vallecchi, for providing useful information about Vallecchi's archives. On Bompiani see Gabriella D'Ina and Giuseppe Zaccaria, eds., *Caro Bompiani: Lettere con l'editore* (Milan: Bompiani, 1988). The proceedings of a recent conference entirely devoted to Valentino Bompiani also promise future detailed work on his publishing house; Lodovica Braida, ed., *Valentino Bompiani: Il percorso di un editore 'artigiano'* (Milan: Edizioni Sylvester Bonnard, 2003). As for Bompiani's Archivio Storico, when I visited the archive between 1998 and 2002, I was allowed to consult only a selection of documents at a time. I am deeply thankful to the new archivist, Greta Belbusti, for opening access to the complete files on each author during my last visit in October 2005. Valentino Bompiani's personal papers have also been made available. They are held at Archivio della Parola, dell'Immagine e della Comunicazione Editoriale (APICE), in Milan.

13 Benito Mussolini, 'Della missione del giornalismo nel regime,' in *Opera Omnia*, ed. D. Susmel and E. Susmel (Florence: La Fenice, 1957), 23: 231–2; see also Giulio Benedetti, ed., *Codice della stampa e degli autori* (Milan: Libreria d'Italia, 1930), 6.

14 Richard Bosworth, *Mussolini* (London: Arnold, 2002), 344.

1. Towards a New System

1 Articles 7, 8, and 42 regulated the obligations of printers towards state authorities. Article 8 stated that a second copy of each publication was required to be deposited in the library of the closest university. These arrangements were confirmed by the *Legge 432* of 7 July 1910. The complete

text of the *Statuto Albertino* can be found in Giorgio Lazzaro, *La libertà di stampa in Italia dall'editto albertino alle norme vigenti* (Milan: Mursia, 1969), 179–91. For a detailed analysis see Valerio Castronovo, *La stampa italiana dall'unità al fascismo* (Bari and Rome: Laterza, 1984), 3–8; Lazzaro, *La libertà di stampa*, 7–32; and Maria Iolanda Palazzolo, 'Le forme della censura nell'Italia liberale,' *La Fabbrica del libro* 9.1 (2005): 2–5.

2 On censorship and theatre in pre-Fascist Italy see Ferrara, *Censura teatrale e fascismo*, 7–12.

3 See Giovanna Tosatti, 'La repressione del dissenso politico tra l'età liberale e il fascismo: L'organizzazione della polizia,' *Studi storici* 38.1 (1997): 217–31.

4 A list of all government directives regarding the press (entitled *disposizioni sulla stampa* and probably compiled in 1940) found among DGPS documents, shows that most of the measures taken in these years targeted periodicals written by extremist political groups. ACS, MI DGPS, Massime S4, b. S4/A (provv.), f. 1, sf. 1. Another sign of Crispi's intention to develop a centralized system of control was the creation in November 1889 of a press office within the Cabinet Office of the Ministry of the Interior. The Ufficio Riservato of the DGPS was developed in 1919 into the Divisione Affari Generali e Riservati.

5 During the political tensions of the years 1896–1900, magistrates tended to make ample use of their authority with the sequestration in that period of 106 periodicals. See Antonio Fiori, 'Per la storia del controllo governativo sulla stampa: Le circolari del Ministero dell'Interno dall'Unità alla prima guerra mondiale,' *Rassegna degli Archivi di Stato* 47.1 (1987): 55–65; and Castronovo, *La stampa italiana dall'Unità al fascismo*, 118–27.

6 Exceptions concerned only cases of offence to public morality. On this law see Lazzaro, *La libertà di stampa*, 95–8; and Umberto Levra, *Il colpo di stato della borghesia: La crisi di fine secolo in Italia, 1896–1900* (Milan: Feltrinelli, 1975), 144.

7 On the censorship of D'Annunzio's poem see John Woodhouse, *Gabriele D'Annunzio: Defiant Archangel* (Oxford: Clarendon Press, 1998), 262–4. Only a year before, in May 1911, D'Annunzio's entire fictional oeuvre had been condemned by the Vatican and inserted in the Holy Office's *Index of Prohibited Books*. This centuries-old institution, however, had no legal powers over the distribution of books other than in its own miniscule territory of Vatican City. Indeed, the appearance in the *Indice dei libri proibiti* was often a guarantee of extra publicity and sales for the 'disgraced' author. Also, given the role that Mussolini was to acquire in Fascist censorship, it should be noted that at the time of D'Annunzio's rhetorical excesses, the future Duce was at the receiving end of government repression. Then a young socialist militant,

he was arrested on 14 October 1911 and put on trial, together with Pietro Nenni and others, for protesting against Italy's colonial adventure. Ironically, an act of suppression of the freedom of opinion was to give the future dictator his first taste of national notoriety. He received a prison sentence of one year, reduced to five and a half months after the appeal. By the autumn of 1912, the twenty-nine-year-old Mussolini had become editor of *Avanti!* and an undisputed leader of Italian socialism. On this episode see Renzo De Felice, *Mussolini il rivoluzionario* (Turin: Einaudi, 1965), 108–11, and Bosworth, *Mussolini*, 85–9.

8 In March 1915, each prefecture had also been ordered to create a Press Censorship Office (*Ufficio Revisori per la Stampa*) with the aim of monitoring and censoring the publication of periodicals. The cabinet of the Ministry of the Interior also regularly sent telegraphic directives to the prefectures regarding items of news that had be ignored by the press. A complete collection of the telegrams for the year 1917 is held at Rome's State Archive. During the month of January 1917, for example, prefectures were sent seventy-four telegrams (ASRo, PG, b. 1233, f. 'Censura sulla stampa'). As for censorship of books, article 7 of the decree of 23 May 1915 suggested that *stampa non periodica* and the press should be treated similarly. However, according to the detailed study of Antonio Fiori, prefectures did not attempt to enforce this provision, although some publishers volunteered to comply. See Fiori, *Il filtro deformante*, 56–77.

9 Fiori, *Il filtro deformante*, 253–90.

10 On Marinetti's *Come si seducono le donne*, see Lucia Re, 'Futurism, Seduction and the Strange Sublimity of War,' *Italian Studies* 59 (2004): 83–111. It is not clear whether the proofs were submitted because its author at the time was an army officer or whether the authorities acted on their own initiative. As we will see in chapter 7, Marinetti's book was also censored during the Second World War.

11 The trial proceedings were published in a long appendix when the novel was published in book form with the new title *Secondo il cuor mio* (Milan: Treves, 1919), 229–66. In the appendix Brocchi says only that the attack came from two newspapers, one in Milan and one in Bari. However, in his postwar memoirs – *Confidenze* (Milan: Mondadori, 1946), 215 – he reveals that the Milan paper was none other than Mussolini's *Il Popolo d'Italia*. The other one indirectly mentioned in the trial proceedings is *Humanitas*. During the proceedings, despite being asked by Brocchi, the presiding judge refused to reveal the identity of the individuals who had denounced the novel to the judiciary. Brocchi eventually discovered that the letter of denunciation had been signed by ten individuals he had never met, one of whom was a professor of

geography at Padua University (*Secondo il cuor mio*, 254). On censorship during the First World War, see also the memoirs of the publisher Angelo Fortunato Formiggini, *La ficozza filosofica del fascismo* (Rome: Formiggini, 1923).

12 On this incident see Ada Gigli Marchetti's *Le edizioni Corbaccio: Storia di libri e di libertà* (Milan: Franco Angeli, 2000), 19.

13 As we will see in chapter 3, Fascist authorities were particularly keen to suppress any publication that was critical of Italy's military effort in the First World War. For a detailed reconstruction of the problematic history of *Viva Caporetto* see the 'Notizie sui testi' by Luigi Martellini in Malaparte, *Opere Scelte* (Milan: Mondadori, 1997), 1489–518.

14 Gobetti's article, entitled 'Profili di contemporanei: L'eroe di corte,' was published in *Il Lavoro*, 17 January 1924 (repr. in *Opere complete*, vol. 1[Turin: Einaudi, 1969], 568).

15 'Verso la censura?' *Il Popolo d'Italia*, 6 December 1922, 1. An indication that the author might be Benito Mussolini and not his brother Arnaldo (then chief editor of the paper) comes from the fact that the brief editorial is introduced by a caption saying: 'Roma, 6 notte' (Rome, night of the 6th). Arnaldo lived in Milan at the time, while Benito residence was in Rome.

16 ACS, SPD CR, Autografi Duce, box. 1. Also quoted in Benito Mussolini, *Corrispondenza inedita*, ed. D. Susmel (Milan: Edizioni del Borghese, 1972), 46–7.

17 See Mauro Canali, *Cesare Rossi: Da rivoluzionario a eminenza grigia del fascismo* (Bologna: Il Mulino, 1984), 207–68; Alessandra Staderini, 'Una fonte per lo studio della utilizzazione dei "fondi segreti": La contabilità di Aldo Finzi (1922–1924),' *Storia contemporanea* 10.4 (1979): 767–810; and Mauro Canali, 'La contabilità di Cesare Rossi, capo dell'Ufficio Stampa del governo Mussolini (novembre 1922–maggio 1924),' *Storia contemporanea* 19.4 (1988): 719–50. It must be noted that such practices had a precedent during the pre-Fascist years of liberal Italy. Ministry of the Interior's secret funds were used by Prime Minister Giovanni Giolitti to finance periodicals that supported him. On this, see Gerardo Padulo, 'Appunti sulla fascistizzazione della stampa,' *Archivio storico italiano* 140 (1982): 92–3.

18 Royal Decree 3288 (8 July 1924); Royal Decree 1081 (10 July 1924). See Nicola Tranfaglia, Paolo Murialdi, and Massimo Legnani, *La stampa italiana nell'età fascista* (Rome and Bari: Laterza, 1980), 4–29; Alberto Aquarone, *L'organizzazione dello stato totalitario* (Turin: Einaudi, 1965), 39–46. An interesting publication written at the time is *La libertà di stampa ed i reati commessi a mezzo della stampa* by anti-Fascist lawyer Giuseppe Nardelli. Published by Treves in 1924, the book contains a detailed analysis of the legislation and its

first uses by prefects together with a denunciation of its unconstitutionality. Finally, according to Philip Cannistraro, these measures represent to some extent Mussolini's first policies aimed at Italian culture (Cannistraro, *La fabbrica del consenso*, 18).

19 Federzoni had been appointed minister of the interior on 17 June 1924 in the wake of the kidnaping and murder of Matteotti. An example of the content of these telegrams is that of 5 March 1925 (n. 4961) in which Federzoni ordered all prefects to ensure that no Italian newspaper would mention a parliamentary motion by the opposition in protest against the limitation of freedom imposed on foreign correspondents. All telegrams can be found in ACS, DGPS DAGR, Massime S4, b. 102 (provv.), f. 'Vigilanza sulla stampa.' On the suppression of cultural periodicals such as *Il Caffè* and *Rivoluzione liberale*, see Cesari, *La censura nel periodo fascista*, 18–19.

20 See Renzo De Felice, *Mussolini il fascista: L'organizzazione dello stato fascista, 1925–1929* (Turin: Einaudi, 1968), 142.

21 Royal Decree 1848 (6 November 1926), Articles 111–15. This decree arrived following the third assassination attempt on Mussolini (31 October 1926), which had also instigated the suppression of socialist and communist press and organizations. See Castronovo, *La stampa italiana dall'Unità al fascismo*, 313–15.

22 The text of the circular can be found in Mussolini, *Opera Omnia* 22: 469. See also De Felice, *Mussolini il fascista*, 301–4. On the instructions to prefects during the First World War see Fiori, *Il filtro deformante*, 471–537, and Philip Morgan, 'The Prefects and Party-State Relations in Fascist Italy,' *Journal of Modern Italian Studies* 3.3 (1998): 241–72.

23 Il Capo del Governo, 'Lettera riservata,' 30 September 1927; a signed copy of the document can be found in ASTo, PG, b. 35, f. 'Prefetto – Fascicolo personale.'

24 Cannistraro, *La fabbrica del consenso*, 74.

25 It is interesting to note that, despite their similarity, article 112 of 1926 placed more emphasis on moral issues whereas that of 1931 concentrated on national sentiment and on 'the prestige of the Nation and of the Authorities.'

26 ACS, MCP, b. 4, f. 10 'Ufficio Stampa'; also quoted in Cannistraro, *La fabbrica del consenso*, 91; the entire report is reproduced in Tullio Gregory, Marta Fattori, and Nicola Siciliani, eds., *Filosofi università regime: La Scuola di Filosofia di Roma negli anni Trenta* (Rome: Istituto di Filosofia della Sapienza, 1985), 207–13. On Mussolini's press office in this period see Paolo Murialdi, 'La stampa quotidiana del regime fascista,' in Tranfaglia, Murialdi, and Lignani, *La stampa italiana nell'età fascista*, 138–45.

27 On Mori's book see Christopher Duggan, *Fascism and the Mafia* (New Haven, CT: Yale University Press, 1989), 250–60 and Arrigo Petacco, *Il prefetto di ferro* (Milan: Mondadori, 1992), 225–7. The term 'velina' comes from the thin carbon paper used to prepare copies of those notes. As we have seen, the practice of 'advising' editors on how to approach or avoid controversial topics was occasionally practised in pre-Fascist years through and by local prefects. On its development and transformation into a government practice see Padulo, 'Appunti sulla fascistizzazione della stampa,' and Bruno Maida, 'La Direzione generale della stampa italiana,' both in Nicola Tranfaglia, ed., *La stampa del regime* (Milan: Bompiani, 2005), 49–56. The *velina* concerning Mori's book can be found in Tranfaglia, *La stampa del regime*, 209.

28 Letter from Ferretti to Falqui, dated 2 December 1929; in A900, Fondo Falqui, f. 'Istituzioni.'

29 Telegram dated 13 February 1929; in ACS, MCP, II, b. 4, f. 'Sturzo Luigi'; copy also in ACS, DGPS DAGR, F4, b. 108, f. F4/AG as mentioned in Fabre, *L'elenco*, 20. To reinforce this ban, in later years the Ministry of the Interior alerted prefects whenever a foreign edition of Don Sturzo's works had appeared abroad. This happened on 19 July 1930, when a work by Sturzo was published in English, *The International Community and the Right of War* (document at ASMi, PG I, b. 424, f. 'Libro di Don Luigi Sturzo').

30 All documents are in ACS, DGPS DAGR, F4, b. 102 (provv.), f. F4 (also mentioned in Fabre, 20). A few months later, on 27 October 1930, the prefect of Milan wrote to the DGPS asking for clarification about copies that were still available in the libraries of public institutions. Unfortunately no documentation survives to clarify whether any measures were taken in this direction.

31 Copy of the circular in ACS, Massime S4, b. S4/A (provv.), f. 7 'Pubblicazioni lesive della dignità e del prestigio del Fascismo.' It is interesting to note that a similar problem was faced by theatrical censors during the first years of the Italian nation. By August 1862 twenty-nine plays dedicated to unification hero Giuseppe Garibaldi had been banned by the censors (see Ferrara, *Censura teatrale e fascismo*, 9).

32 Documents in ASMi, PG I, b. 422, f. 'Varie.' The prefect omitted to mention that, only two months before, Masiani had already been given a warning by the Milan Prefecture for the publication of a long poem about the Lateran Pacts.

33 Document in ASMi, PG I, b. 422, f. 'Sequestro dei romanzi dello scrittore Virgilio Scattolini e altri.'

34 Enzo Magrì, *Un italiano vero: Pitigrilli* (Milan: Baldini & Castoldi, 1999), 101–10. A slightly different version of the event – suggesting the publisher's being found guilty – is given by Bruno Wanrooij in his entry 'Pitigrilli' in Victoria De Grazia and Sergio Luzzatto's *Dizionario del fascismo*, vol. 2 (Turin:

Einaudi, 2003), 384–5. In 1930 Pitigrilli also became an informer for the
Political Police. There is more on this in chapter 4 and 5; the latter is
devoted partly to Einaudi and the arrest of some of its employees as a consequence of Pitigrilli's work as an informant.

35 The circulars dated 14 February 1931 and 10 March 1932 can be found in
ACS, DGPS DAGR, Massime S4, b. S4/A (provv.), f. 7. A copy of the decree
law of May 1932 together with the related correspondence can be found in
ACS, MPI DGAB, b. 73, f. 'Leggi. Deposito obbligatorio stampati.'

36 On Goebbels's visit in May 1933 see Cannistraro, *La fabbrica del consenso*, 103–
4. Documents in ACS, PCM (1931–3), f. 4/12.20 'Viaggio di S.E. Goebbels.'

2. Carrots, Sticks, and Charismatic Ruling

1 Gianfranco Pedullà also singles out Gobetti and Corbaccio as examples of
anti-Fascist publishers in his essay 'Gli anni del fascismo: Imprenditoria privata
e intervento statale,' in Turi, *Storia dell'editoria nell'Italia contemporanea*, 342.

2 The quotations come from articles by Gobetti published in *Rivoluzione liberale* on 25 October and 2 and 23 November 1922. The same message was
reiterated a year later, on 9 October 1923, when Gobetti concluded that 'Se
un fascismo potrebbe avere per l'Italia qualche utilità esso è il fascismo del
manganello' (If Fascism can be of some use to Italy it is the Fascism of the
cudgel). All the above mentioned articles have been reprinted in Piero
Gobetti, *Opere complete*, vol. 1 (Turin: Einaudi, 1960), 415, 420, 434, 527.

3 Telegram no. 2902 by Mussolini to the prefect of Turin, dated 6 February
1923, quoted in Renzo De Felice, 'Piero Gobetti in alcuni documenti di Mussolini,' in *Intellettuali di fronte al fascismo* (Rome: Bonacci, 1985), 252.

4 Palmieri had been prefect of Turin from 1 January 1923 to 1 July 1924. He
was born in Naples in 1876, and his first position as prefect predated Mussolini's first government. He was appointed prefect of Chieti on 21 August
1920. On his career as a prefect, see Mario Missori, *Governi, alte gerarchie dello
stato, alti magistrati e prefetti del Regno d'Italia* (Rome: Ministero per i beni culturali e ambientali, 1989), 454, 605, 737.

5 Quoted in De Felice, 'Piero Gobetti in alcuni documenti di Mussolini,' 254.

6 See Angelo D'Orsi, *La cultura a Torino tra le due guerre* (Turin: Einaudi, 2000),
67. On the genesis of Gobetti's *La rivoluzione liberale*, see Umberto Bobbio,
L'Italia fedele: Il mondo di Gobetti (Florence: Passigli, 1986) 87–117. On the list
of proscribed texts and the 'bonifica culturale' see Chapter 6 below.

7 Francesco Nitti, *La tragedia dell'Europa: Che farà l'America* (Turin: Gobetti,
1924). On the refusal to publish by Bemporad see Frabotta, *Gobetti l'editore
giovane*, 128–31.

8 See Gobetti's letter to Emilio Lussu, dated 12 June 1924, in *Opere complete*, 1: 699. The article in *Il Popolo d'Italia*, signed with the pseudonym *Il pinturicchio*, had been published on 2 April 1924. Mussolini's telegram of 1 June 1924 became a source of political embarrassment when a French paper, *Le Petit Niçois*, publish it the week after the death of Gobetti. The telegram was part of a batch of compromising documents that had been stolen from Mussolini's press office by one of Cesare Rossi's collaborators, Arturo Benedetto Fasciolo. He had taken them with him when he fled Italy following the investigation for the murder of Giacomo Matteotti. For more detail, see Mimmo Franzinelli, *I tentacoli dell'OVRA* (Turin: Bollati Boringhieri, 1999), 38.

9 Piero Gobetti, 'La nostra difesa,' *Rivoluzione liberale* 30 (22 July 1924): 117 (now in *Opere complete*, 1: 761–2).

10 This is how Mario Fubini remembers their activity at *Il Baretti* in his preface to a 1976 reprint of the journal; quoted in D'Orsi, *La cultura a Torino*, 74.

11 Judging from Gobetti's own version of the event, it is not clear whether it was a punitive action organized by the Fascists or a reaction of some nationalists to Gobetti's attack against the war veteran and MP Carlo Delcroix (see Gobetti, *Opere complete*, 1: 769–71).

12 Letter to Giuseppe Prezzolini, dated 3 October 1925; quoted in D'Orsi, *La cultura a Torino*, 101. On Gobetti's French projects see Frabotta, *Gobetti l'editore giovane*, 126–9.

13 Letter to Giuseppe Prezzolini, dated 3 February 1925; quoted in Giuseppe Prezzolini, ed., *Gobetti e 'La Voce'* (Florence: Sansoni, 1971), 150–1.

14 However, some of the books remained in circulation. This is at least implicitly in the fact that on 20 March 1931 the Prefecture of Milan ordered the seizure of all copies of *L'opera di Nitti* written by his son Vincenzo and published by Gobetti in 1924 (documents in ASMi, PG I, b. 423 f. 'Censura libri e opuscoli'). For a detailed list of all books published by Edizioni Gobetti and Edizioni de Il Baretti, see Centro Studi Gobetti, ed., 'La Casa Editrice: Elenco delle edizioni gobettiane,' in Centro Studi Gobetti, ed., *Piero Gobetti e il suo tempo* (Turin: Centro Studi Gobetti, 1976), 112–20.

15 Forty letters by Mussolini have been published, interwoven within Rafanelli's memoirs, in her *Una donna e Mussolini* (Milan: Rizzoli, 1946), 2nd ed., 1975); the full text of the letters is available in *Opera Omnia* 38: 28–70. On Mussolini's relationship with Rafanelli, see also Philip Cannistraro and Brian Sullivan, *L'altra donna del Duce: Margherita Sarfatti* (Milan: Mondadori, 1993), 130–2, and Bosworth, *Mussolini*, 91–5.

16 Mussolini mentioned this in an article published in 1912 (*Opera Omnia*, 4: 195–6). It should also be remembered that, as late as 1920, Mussolini would publish articles with statements of this kind: 'A noi che siamo i morituri

dell'individualismo non resta, per il buio presente e per il tenebroso domani, che la religione, assurda oramai, ma sempre consolatrice dell'Anarchia!' (In the current darkness and for the gloomy future, there is nothing left to us, *morituri* of individualism, other then the religion, absurd but always comforting, of Anarchy!). This article was published in the months following the Fascists' unsuccessful campaign for the 1919 general elections ('Divagazioni: L'ora e gli orologi,' *Il Popolo d'Italia*, 6 April 1920; *Opera Omnia*, 14: 398.

17 Letter to Cesare Berti, 3 November 1910 (*Opera Omnia*, 4: 257); quoted in Rafanelli, *Una donna e Mussolini*, 15.

18 The attack on the workshop is mentioned by Pier Carlo Masini in his long preface to Rafanelli's book *Una donna e Mussolini*, 22, and by Franco Schirone in 'La Casa Editrice Sociale: Appunti sull'attività dell'editore anarchico Giuseppe Monanni,' *Rivista Storica dell'Anarchismo* 2 (1994): 996–1116 (101). Masini benefited from his acquaintance with Leda Rafanelli, so presumably she was his source of information, although no details are given about the date and the actual consequences of the Fascist raid. Schirone in this particular respect seems simply to rely on Masini's word.

19 Leda Rafanelli had been under police surveillance since the years of her pre–First World War militancy. The same happened throughout the Fascist period – until 1940 according to records – although term reports on her activity simply confirmed her detachment from any form of subversive politics (see ACS, CPC, b. 4193, f. 3979). That the content of Rafanelli's fiction contained a risqué element is suggested in one of her letters to a friend in Paris who worked there as a translator. On 20 January 1935 Rafanelli asked her to translate one of her books into French and added: 'Qui non si può pubblicare più nulla di genere erotico. E i miei romanzi arabi, capisci, non sono da signorine!' (Here it is no longer possible to write erotique fiction. And my Arabian novels, you understand, are not for well-mannered girls!). The letter was intercepted by the police and was kept in Rafanelli's file (now in ACS, PP FP, f. Rafanelli Leda'; also quoted by Schirone, 'La Casa Editrice Sociale,' 105).

20 Schirone, 'La Casa Editrice Sociale,' 102. The first memo can be found in ACS, PP FP, f. 'Rafanelli Leda'; the second one, dated 7 August 1929, in ACS, DGPS DAGR, Massime S4, b. 103 (provv.), f. 5. We know that on 12 June 1926 a police raid at both Monanni's publishing house and warehouse led to the seizure of 659 copies of *Vita e pensieri* by the anarchist Errico Malatesta. The book had been printed by the Tipografia Il Martello in New York, but Monanni was apparently distributing it in Italy. The Milan police had been tipped by the Customs Police in Rome, which on 28 April 1926 had noticed the unusually great number of copies of the same book that had been sent

from New York. A second police search, on 19 December 1926, resulted in the seizure of other books, this time published by Monanni's old imprint Casa Editrice Sociale: they were Errico Malatesta's *L'anarchia* (1921) and Peter Kropotkin's *La conquista del pane* (1920) and *Le memorie di un rivoluzionario* (1923). Even this second search had been prompted partially by the interception of illegal material: Monanni had sent illegal anarchist booklets to a private address in France. Documents in ASMi, PG I, b. 423, f. 'Casa editrice Giuseppe Monanni.'

21 Another small, left-wing publisher in Milan that suffered a number of raids and seizures in those very months is Libreria Editrice La Cultura. On 6 June 1926 its offices and warehouse were raided by the police. Three days later the publisher sent a long letter protesting that all the seized publications had been officially granted publication before 1922. It also added an annotated list of all the ten seized publications, asking the prefecture to return them. On 25 June the chief editor at La Cultura sent a second annotated list of another eighteen books that had been seized (the entire series entitled *Problemi della rivoluzione* published by the defunct Società editrice Avanti!, the official publisher of the Socialist Party). A third annotated list was sent on 29 June, listing another forty publications (mainly pamphlets). In the end, on 26 July 1926 the prefect of Milan decreed the seizure of a total of seventy publications from La Cultura. The report of the prefect to the Ministry of the Interior, dated 28 July 1926, suggests that the police raid had resulted from the disturbances caused by a number of unidentified individuals – arguably Fascist militants – who had repeatedly attempted to attack the publishing house. The combination of illegal attacks and police raids worked: Libreria Editrice La Cultura ceased to exist in 1926.

22 Copy of the correspondence can be found in ACS, SPD CO, f. 16.650 'Casa Editrice Monanni.' The books were sent on 24 October 1928.

23 Documents in ACS, DGPS DAGR, Massime S4, b. 103 (provv.), f. 5. This episode is also mentioned by Fabre in *L'elenco*, 21.

24 Letter dated 1 June 1931; copy of all documents in ACS, DGPS DAGR, Massime S4, b. 103 (provv.), f. 5.

25 Letter from Monanni dated 3 May 1933, correspondence in ACS, SPD CO, f. 16.650 'Casa Editrice Monanni.'

26 The report, dated 1 March 1933, can be found in ACS, DGPS DAGR, Sez.1 1933 K 1, b. 31, f. 'Propaganda sovversiva.' It is also quoted by Paolo Spriano in the second volume of his *Storia del Partito comunista italiano* (Turin: Einaudi, 1969), 401, and by Schirone in 'La Casa Editrice Sociale,' 103. The telegram from the prefect, Fornaciari, to DGPS at the Ministry of

the Interior, dated 20 February 1931, can be found in ASMi, PG I, b. 423, f. 'Censura libri e opuscoli.'

27 Memorandum dated 29 January 1938, in ACS, DGPS DAGR, Massime S4, b. 103 (provv.), f. 5. It is also interesting to note that, in his conversations with De Begnac, Mussolini twice mentioned Monanni as an example of an anti-Fascist publisher. See Yvon De Begnac, *Taccuini Mussoliniani*, ed. Francesco Perfetti (Bologna: Il Mulino, 1990), 416, 424. De Begnac's notes, prepared as material for his biography of Mussolini, were collected with no reference to the time when Mussolini expressed a particular view. Therefore, unless a specific time is implicit in a statement, it is known only that De Begnac's conversations with Mussolini took place between 1934 and 1943.

28 It is possible that Monanni might have acted as an informer, although this is undocumented and his name does not appear in the list of Political Police informers. On this see Franzinelli, *I tentacoli dell'OVRA*, and Mauro Canali, *Le spie del regime* (Bologna: Il Mulino, 2004).

29 For this and other biographical details I have relied on the extensive studies of Ada Gigli Marchetti, the already quoted *Le edizioni Corbaccio*, and 'Un editore per la libertà: Enrico dall'Oglio,' in Gigli Marchetti and Finocchi, *Stampa e piccola editoria tra le due guerre*, 9–17.

30 The publication of the book had been announced on the *Gazzettino di Venezia* of 21 January. See Gigli Marchetti, *Le edizioni Corbaccio*, 29.

31 The two books were travelogues about China and Japan. Their incongrous presence in the series *Confessioni e battaglie* was noticed by a reviewer for the *Giornale della libreria*, who underlined the fact that the books contained no confessions and battled against nothing (Gigli Marchetti, *Le edizioni Corbaccio*, 32).

32 Quoted in ibid., 37.

33 Alfredo Misuri, *Rivolta morale: Confessioni, esperienze e documenti di un quinquennio di vita pubblica* (Milan: Corbaccio, 1924). For the document related to the seizure see Corbaccio's police file in ASMi, PG I, b. 423, f. 'Censura libri e opuscoli.'

34 Corrado Alvaro's work will be the subject of a more detailed analysis in chapter 5. The letter by the head of the Political Police can be found in ACS, PP FP, f. 'dall'Oglio Enrico.'

35 On this episode see Gigli Marchetti, *Le edizioni Corbaccio*, 48–9.

36 Dall'Oglio's catalogue already contained a number of licentious novels, which had created censorial problems. On 22 June 1929 the head of police had proceeded to seize all copies of *L'onore perduto alla fiera ed altre novelle* by Domenico Luigi Batacchi because of 'intentionally lascivious sentences and descriptions.' Document in ASMi, PG I, b. 423, f. 'Censura libri e opuscoli.'

37 Moravia's work will be discussed in more detail in chapter 5.

38 Rensi's file with the Political Police shows that in the autumn of 1936 he was attempting to contact Mussolini precisely in order to remind Il Duce of the implications of persecuting an intellectual of international fame (indeed, in October 1934 *Giustizia e Libertà* had devoted an article to Rensi's dismissal, presenting it as a further example of cultural repression in Fascist Italy). Moreover, a report from the head of police in Genoa, dated 3 June 1938, addressed to the head of the Political Police, stated that Rensi had not been actively expressing his anti-Fascism for quite a while ('per qualche tempo'). Indeed, in 1931 Rensi had also resigned himself to swearing allegiance to Fascism, as all university professors had been asked to do. Documents in ACS, PP FP, b. 1110, f. ' Rensi prof. Giuseppe.' See also Gigli Marchetti, *Le edizioni Corbaccio*, 66–7; about Rensi's controversial decision to swear allegiance, see Helmut Goetz, *Il giuramento rifiutato: I docenti universitari e il regime fascista* (Florence: La Nuova Italia, 2000), 29. Another political book that was seized in the 1930s is Ferdynand Antoni Ossendowski's biography of Lenin, published by Corbaccio in 1930 and seized by the Milan prefecture on 2 February 1932 (documens in ASMi, PG I, b. 423, f. 'Censura libri e opuscoli').

39 Luigi Freddi, *Altre terre* (Milan: Corbaccio, 1933). Freddi was a fairly close collaborator of Mussolini's: in 1923 he had been in charge of propaganda for the PNF, had been editor at *Il Popolo d'Italia*, and was one of the official organizers of the *Mostra della Rivoluzione Fascista* in 1932.

40 Gigli Marchetti, *Le edizioni Corbaccio*, 68.

41 See Decleva, *Mondadori*, 73–7. See also Tranfaglia and Vittoria, *Storia degli editori italiani*, 304–5. Senatore Borletti was one of Milan's most prominent financial entrepreneurs. He had financed D'Annunzio's expedition to the city of Fiume in 1919. On Mondadori see also Claudia Patuzzi, *Mondadori* (Naples: Liguori, 1978), although Patuzzi's study has been superseded by Decleva's more detailed and documented biography.

42 Letter from A. Mondadori to V. Brocchi, 30 November 1926, in AFM, FAM, f. Brocchi.

43 Letter from Brocchi to A. Mondadori, 30 November 1926, AFM, FAM, f. Brocchi.

44 Oxford's Taylorian Library holds a copy of the first edition, which has a 'finito di stampare' dated 20 October 1926. In his memoirs, Brocchi makes no mention of this episode despite the many pages devoted to examples of censorship predating his collaboration with Mondadori. For example, apart from the case of *Casa di pazzi casa di santi* mentioned in chapter 1, Brocchi wrote that in 1917, the then director of Treves, Giovanni Beltrami – who similarly to Brocchi was an elected member of Milan's socialist-controlled council – personally

vetted the proofs of Brocchi's novel *La bottega degli scandali* to make sure there were no passages of too strong political content (*Confidenze*, 209). The fact that Mondadori was and remained Brocchi's publisher in the postwar years might have been a factor in the selective content of the latter's memoirs.

45 Decleva, *Mondadori*, 89–91. In the 1920s Borgese had also worked as a translator from German. On the rigorous editorial approach of the series *La Romantica*, set up by Borgese in 1930, see Italo Calvino, 'La Romantica,' in Fondazione Mondadori, ed., *Editoria e cultura a Milano tra le due guerre*, 172–8.

46 On Borgese's political thought, see Fernando Mezzetti, *Borgese e il fascismo* (Palermo: Sellerio, 1978), and Luciano Parisi's *Borgese* (Turin: Tirrenia Stampatori, 2000). Mussolini and Borgese had corresponded in 1922 and 1924; Mussolini's telegram to the prefect of Milan, dated 10 February 1930, can be found in Mussolini, *Corrispondenza inedita*, 112; see also ACS, SPD CR, b. 74, f. 'Borgese prof. Giuseppe Antonio,' and Giovanni Tassani, 'Il "peccato originale" di Giuseppe Antonio Borgese,' *Nuova storia contemporanea* 4 (2000): 105–36.

47 That Borgese's early works were still circulating throughout the 1930s is suggested by a telegram by then minister of popular culture, Dino Alfieri, who, on 15 June 1939, ordered the seizure of any edition of Borgese's *Escursioni in terre nuove*, published by Ceschina in 1931 and still available in the bookshops. A copy of Alfieri's telegram to all prefects can be found in ASMi, PG II, b. 153, f. 044 'Ceschina casa editrice.'

48 ACS, SPD CO, f. 509568/2. In those months, Franco Ciarlantini, then head of the Ufficio Stampa e Propaganda of the PNF and future president of the national association of publishers, had shelved the idea of creating a party-owned publishing house. In a letter to Mondadori, dated 6 December 1924, Ciarlantini informed the publisher that 'the party will deal with individual publishers according to its needs; ... and if we acquire considerable numbers of copies we will agree on favourable terms as it is normal to expect whenever the size of the edition is mutually agreed,' in AFM, FAM, b. 'Ministero Stampa e Propaganda,' f. 66.

49 Mussolini wrote to the president of the Ca.Ri.P.Lo bank in November 1928 to 'suggest' the acceptance of a financial plan in favour of Mondadori. When presenting his plan to Mussolini a few weeks earlier, Mondadori had introduced it as 'arma formidabile che il Regime potrà impiegare per tutti gli sviluppi dei programmi che esso ha già luminosamente tracciati' (a formidable weapon which the Regime can utilize in order to develop its already luminously drawn plans). Documents in ACS, SPD CO, f. 509.568/2.

50 See Tranfaglia, *Storia degli editori italiani*, 235–6; Gianfranco Pedullà, 'Gli anni del Fascismo: imprenditoria privata e intervento statale,' in Turi, *Storia*

dell'editoria nell'Italia contemporanea, 345–7; and Cannistraro, *La fabbrica del consenso*, 425–7. Among Mussolini's correspondence, one can also find an anonymous letter of protest complaining about Mondadori's draconian ways of imposing newly published books on all students. Mondadori had sent a circular to all primary school teachers, prohibiting the use of second-hand books. A handwritten comment next to this particular clause stated, 'con tutta la miseria e la disoccupazione che c'è in giro' (with all the poverty and unemployment surrounding us). Documents related to this event can be found in ACS, SPD CO, f. 509.568/2.

51 Letter from Mondadori to Mussolini's secretary, dated 29 April 1931, in ACS, SPD CO, f. 509.568/2.

52 The political connection between the conversations and Hitler was suggested by Giuseppe Bottai, as reported by the journalist Indro Montanelli in his preface to a recent edition of Ludwig's *Colloqui con Mussolini* (Milan: Mondadori, 2000), ix.

53 Mussolini's Telegram of 30 June 1932 can be found in ASMI, PGI, b. 718. ('Mondadori A. Casa Editrice.') The transcript of the recorded telephone conversation can be found in Ugo Guspini's *L'orecchio del regime: Le intercettazioni telefoniche al tempo del fascismo* (Milan: Mursia, 1973), 102. Guspini vaguely introduces the transcript as being recorded in 1931. This is certainly wrong, because Ludwig's meetings started only in March 1932. It is more likely that the telephone conversation took place in the summer of 1932. For a more detailed reconstruction of the controversial publication of the *Colloqui*, see Arnoldo Mondadori's own preface to the *Colloqui*, published in the 1950 edition, and, more importantly, Decleva, *Arnoldo Mondadori*, 166–72.

54 However, as a note by Polverelli, dated 3 July 1932, suggests, Mussolini refused to allow Mondadori to produce a cheaper 'edizione popolare' of the book. Documents regarding this case can be found at ACS (Mussolini Benito, Autografi-Telegrammi, b. 4) and at AFM, FAM (surprisingly in the file 'Vittorio Mussolini') and at ASMi (PG I, b. 718, f. 'Mondadori A. casa editrice'). See also Mussolini, *Corrispondenza inedita*, 133. For a discussion of the political implications related to this episode, see Renzo De Felice, *Mussolini il duce: Gli anni del consenso* (Turin: Einaudi, 1974), 45–7.

55 The confusing development of the situation is well reflected by the notes of Mussolini's press office (the already mentioned 'veline'), which were sent to all Italian newspapers: on 22 March 1932 editors were warned not to pay attention to Ludwig, who was described as 'incostante amico dell'Italia' (unreliable friend of Italy); on 6 April and on 2 and 27 June 1932, the order came and was twice repeated to ignore Ludwig's *Colloqui con Mussolini*; however, only a day later, on 28 June 1932, the press office allowed editors to

recognize the existence of the book, but with the caveat they could publish only extracts and not ful-fledged reviews. Finally, almost two years later, on 26 May 1934, the *Popolo di Roma* was warned not to accept any more articles by Ludwig. See Tranfaglia, *La stampa del regime*, 209–10, 213.

56 In reality Rusca was suspected of having had contacts with anti-Fascist Italians living in Switzerland. On Rusca see Decleva, *Arnoldo Mondadori*, 133–40.

57 The letter from Paolo Monelli was actually addressed to his friend, the minister for war, Angelo Manaresi, with the request to convince the then minister of the interior, Leandro Arpinati, to lift the ban. A copy of the letter was forwarded to Mussolini by the head of the Treves publishing house, Calogero Tumminelli, with a request for Il Duce's direct intervention. Nothing seems to have happened, but it is interesting to note that this documentation was kept in Mussolini's office as part of Mondadori's file (in ACS, SPD CO, f. 509.568/2). For more on Renn's novel, see chapter 5 below.

58 On 30 May 1931 the prefect of Milan was instructed by the Ministry of the Interior to ensure that all copies of the novel would be sent abroad. All correspondence can be found in ACS, SPD CO, f. 509.568/2 and in AFM, FAM, f. 'Borletti Senatore.' See also Decleva, *Arnoldo Mondadori*, 158–9.

59 All the documentation referring to both Remarque's and Renn's novels can be found in ACS, SPD CO, f. 509.568/2. Bruno Mondadori had been called by his brother Arnoldo to help in the management of the firm. There is no mention of this episode in Decleva's *Arnoldo Mondadori*.

60 Documents in ACS, SPD CO, f. 509.568/2 and ASMi, PG I, b. 423, f. 'Censura libri e opuscoli.' The Mondadori reader's report approving the publication of *Caterina va alla guerra* while highlighting the controversial content of the anti-war comments can be found in Pietro Albonetti, ed., *Non c'è tutto nei romanzi: Leggere romanzi stranieri in una casa editrice negli anni 30* (Milan: Fondazione Arnoldo e Alberto Mondadori, 1994), 126–7.

61 Riccardo Gualino, *Frammenti di vita* (Milan: Mondaori, 1931). On Gualino, see Decleva, *Arnoldo Mondadori*, 143–4.

62 See AFM, FAM, f. 'Ministero Cultura Popolare,' and Decleva, *Arnoldo Mondadori*, 183–5. Piceni's reader's report, dated 1939, can be found in Albonetti, ed., *Non c'è tutto nei romanzi*, 473. The translator of the Lederer novel was Barbara Allason, a Turinese anti-Fascist militant first associated with Gobetti and then with Leone Ginzburg. She was arrested in 1934 as part of the police raid against the Turin cell of *Giustizia e Libertà* in 1934 (see chapter 5). On Allason, see the entry by Jane Slaughter in De Grazia and Luzzatto eds., *Dizionario del fascismo*, 1: 38–9.

63 As already mentioned in the introduction, the historical archives of Vallecchi were lost in a fire in January 2003. Unfortunately no major study of

Vallecchi's history was made before that date. Any reconstruction will therefore have to rely on other sources, including Rome's ACS and the Gabinetto Vieusseux in Florence. An important essay that benefitted from material held at the Vallecchi archives is Giorgio Luti, 'Un editore fiorentino: Vallecchi,' in *Firenze corpo 8: Scrittori, riviste, editori nella Firenze del Novecento* (Florence: Vallecchi, 1983), 161–222; see also Simonetti, 'L'editoria fiorentina dal 1920 al 1940,' 566.

64 Attilio Vallecchi, *Ricordi e idee di un editore vivente* (Florence: Vallecchi, 1934); see in particular 164, 166, 207–8.

65 See Tranfaglia and Vittoria, *Storia degli editori italiani*, 289.

66 The letter and other documents mentioned here can be found in ACS, SPD CO, f. 509.224. The only exception is the letter by Bottai to Mussolini, which is in AFM, FAM, f. 'Bottai Giuseppe.' On Vallecchi's relationship with the regime, see also Simonetti, 'L'editoria fiorentina dal 1920 al 1940,' 541–67.

67 However, as already mentioned, the archives of the Florentine Prefecture were lost at the end of the war, so it is impossible to be absolutely certain about this. Giorgio Luti briefly notes that in 1934, the collection of short stories *Avventure terrene* by Giovanni Comisso was subjected to the intervention of the censors. Unfortunately, Luti's source was the correspondence of the Vallecchi editor Raffaele Franchi, which was lost with the rest of the Vallecchi Archives (Luti, 'Un editore fiorentino,' 209).

68 *Il libro italiano* was eventually closed down by its editors because – as they stated in the editorial published in the final issue of December 1929 – the paper had failed to bring culture to the masses. Among its collaborators had been a group of Florentine radical Fascists, including the key figure of Berto Ricci, whom we will meet again in chapter 5. On *Il libro italiano* see Paolo Buchignani, *Un fascismo impossibile: L'eresia di Berto Ricci nel ventennio fascista* (Bologna: Il Mulino, 1994), 49–66.

69 On Vallecchi and Papini see their correspondence in: Mario Gozzini, ed., *Giovanni Papini – Attilio Vallecchi: Carteggio, 1914–1941* (Florence: Vallecchi, 1984); the september 1930 letter is on 197–8. Sturzo's book published by Vallecchi was *Riforma statale e indirizzi politici: Discorsi*. On Luigi Sturzo see Gabriele De Rosa, *Luigi Sturzo* (Turin: UTET, 1977).

3. The Censor and the Censored

1 Carmine Senise, *Quand'ero capo della polizia* (Rome: Ruffolo, 1946), 43 (but see also xix–xxii, 92–9). For an insider's view of Mussolini's daily tasks, see Quinto Navarra, *Memorie del cameriere di Mussolini* (Rome: Longanesi, 1946), 133–5.

2 Cannistraro, *La fabbrica del consenso*, 12–22, 40.

3 On Margherita Sarfatti see in particular the monograph by Cannistraro and Sullivan, *L'altra donna del Duce*.

4 On this see Cannistraro, *La fabbrica del consenso*, 40–6. Mussolini's speech, entitled 'Il Novecento,' can be found in *Opere Omnia*, 22: 82–4.

5 On this see Decleva, *Mondadori*, 77–9.

6 Giorgio Pini's *Benito Mussolini: La sua vita sino a oggi* (Bologna: Cappelli, 1926) was also very successful: it became a suggested text for all Italian secondary schools, thanks to which it sold about 400,000 copies. On this and on Cappelli as a pro-Fascist publisher see Tranfaglia and Vittoria, *Storia degli editori italiani*, 296–8.

7 I am referring to Ludwig, *Colloqui con Mussolini*, and De Begnac, *Taccuini mussoliniani*. But see also the article by the young Vitaliano Brancati, who discussed contemporary Italian literature during his meeting with Mussolini in the summer of 1931: 'La mia visita a Mussolini,' *Critica fascista* 15 (1931): 292–3. Mussolini's interest in literary matters emerges also in his correspondence with D'Annunzio. In a letter of 1 September 1925, Mussolini had promised D'Annunzio to sponsor the publication of his future works; see Renzo De Felice and Emilio Mariano, eds., *Carteggio D'Annunzio–Mussolini, 1919–1938* (Milan: Mondadori, 1971), 163.

8 On Mussolini and Ada Negri, see the vast correspondence and documentation held in ASMi, PG I, b. 424, f. 'Censura libri'; ASC, SPD CO, f. 509.568/2; ACS, SPD CR, b. 14, f. 209/R 'Negri Ada'; and NAKE, GFM 36/372. Mussolini confirmed his personal choice of Negri for the Accademia in one of his conversations with Yvon De Begnac; see De Begnac, *Taccuini Mussoliniani*, 305. Another poet on whose work Mussolini made positive comments during the same period is Vincenzo Cardarelli. The enthusiastic Fascist poet had sent Mussolini his latest volume, *Il sole a picco*, in July 1930. Through his personal secretary Mussolini answered with some brief critical comments on the book (ACS, MCP II, b. 3).

9 The correspondence during the years 1927–9 between Ugo Ojetti and Mussolini can be found in NAKe, GFM 36/447. The correspondence between Bontempelli and Mussolini for the years 1926–30 can be found in ACS, SPD CO, f. 209.230 and in ACS, MCP, b. 4, f. 10 'Ufficio Stampa.' For Bontempelli's difficult relationship with Fascism in later years, see chapter 6 below.

10 An undated copy of Emma Gramatica's letter and Mussolini's telegram dated 14 June 1929 can be found in ACS, SPD CR, b. 74, f. 'Bracco Roberto.' The ban was not entirely successful, as on 20 June the police had to intervene to stop a small group of young Fascists who had begun to protest during one of the performances. It was, however, to remain an isolated incident,

and on 24 June Gramatica wrote again to Mussolini to thank him for his help. Some years later, it was the turn of Roberto Bracco to receive Mussolini's 'favours,' when Bracco was allowed to join the Fascist Trade Union of Writers and was given some financial help with Il Duce's explicit consent (ACS, SPD CR, b. 74, f. 'Bracco Roberto'). On Bracco and censorship, see also Ferrara, *Censura teatrale e fascismo*, 64–6.

11 The telegram to the Alto Commissario of Naples was sent on 17 January 1927. The handwritten note to minister Ercole was sent on 3 March 1933. Both can be found in NAKe, GFM 36/202 (also partially quoted in De Felice, *Mussolini il duce*, 114). After September 1943 Mussolini wrote about Croce in a short article entitled 'Benedetto Croce, l'intellettualismo anglo-filo e i capi dell'antifascismo divenuti (anche loro!) attendisti.' A copy of the article can be found in NAKe, GFM 36/202. Although the article was probably intended to be published anonymously in *Corrispondenza Repubblicana*, it does not appear among those reproduced in *Opera Omnia*, 32. On Croce and Fascism, see Fabio Fernando Rizi, *Benedetto Croce and Italian Fascism* (Toronto: University of Toronto Press, 2003). For more on Croce and Fascism in the 1930s and 1940s, see chapters 4 and 7 below.

12 Mussolini's order to the prefects was sent in January 1932. On this and more generally on the project of the *Enciclopedia Italiana* see, for example, Cannistraro, *La macchina del consenso*, 51–2, and the recent study by Gabriele Turi, *Il mecenate, il filosofo e il gesuita: L'Enciclopedia Italiana specchio della nazione* (Bologna: Il Mulino, 2002). In his study Turi shows the extent to which the Catholic Church managed to keep firm control of all the entries related to religious matters.

13 Documents in ACS, PP FP, f. 'Trilussa. Salustri Carlo Alberto.' A handwritten comment by a police officer that appears in the margin of a report on Trilussa's satirical poems reads: 'Che cosa vuole che importi alla Polizia la pubblicazione sui giornali di poesie più o meno pepate' (Why on earth should the Police care about the publication of more or less controversial poems?). Some policemen were perhaps reluctant to spend their time following the work of literary authors. Report dated 28 October 1928. According to Guspini (*Le orecchie del regime*, 165–6), Trilussa's private telephone was also under constant surveillance.

14 In 1923 Trilussa personally met Mussolini, who thanked him for the gift of his poems with a signed photograph of himself (which was still in his study when Giuseppe Villaroel went to see him for an interview in 1950). In 1926 Mussolini replied to the gift of a more recent collection with a note of thanks that described Trilussa's poems as 'belle e inobliabili' (beautiful and unforgettable). See Anne-Christine Faitrop, *Trilussa: Doppio volto di un uomo e di un opera* (Rome: Istituto di Studi Romani, 1979), 22–6.

15 The reports are dated 2 July and 27 November 1929, ACS, PP FP, f. 'Trilussa.'
16 On this particular episode see Mario Dell'Arco, *Lunga vita di Trilussa* (Rome: Bardi, 1951), 150–1. A similar episode regarding the poem 'Er sonatore ambulante' (published in *Libro 9* [1929]) is reported by Giuseppe D'Arrigo in *Trilussa: Il tempo, i luoghi, l'opera* (Rome: Scalia, 1968), 86.
17 See Decleva, *Mondadori*, 145; and ACS, PP FP, f. 'Trilussa.'
18 Ludwig, *Colloqui con Mussolini*, 36.
19 On Fascism's linguistic policies see Gabriella Klein, *La politica linguistica del fascismo* (Bologna: Il Mulino, 1986); see also individual studies such as Sergio Raffaelli, 'Mussolini contro il teatro dialettale romagnolo,' *Ariel* 2–3 (1993): 139–46, which confirm Mussolini's personal view that all literature in dialect was destined to disappear in the space of a few years. See also ACS, MCP, b. 3, f. 113 'Dialetti.'
20 Anonymous typescript note dated 10 August 1932 in ACS, MCP, b. 3, f. 113 'Dialetti.' In December 1931 literature in dialect was already one of the topics briefly touched upon by Polverelli in a long circular entitled 'Direttive per la stampa.' The circular was sent to the chief editors of all Italian papers on the eve of his appointment as head of the press office (quoted in Cannistraro, *La fabbrica del consenso*, 422).
21 Letter from Polverelli to Soffici, dated 21 January 1933, in ACS, MCP II, b. 13, f. 'Soffici Ardengo.' Soffici was in correspondence with Mussolini throughout the 1920s and 1930s; a letter by Il Duce containing complimentary critical comments about Soffici's collection of poems *Elegia dell'Ambra* was published on the front page of the Roman newspaper *Il Tevere* on 15 January 1927. Soffici was to become fellow of the Accademia d'Italia in 1939; see ACS, SPD CR, b. 14, f. 'Soffici Ardengo.'
22 Telegram dated 18 May, in ACS, MCP, b. 4, f. 10 'Ufficio Stampa.'
23 Filippo Fichera, ed., *Il Duce e il fascismo nei canti dialettali* (Milan: Convivio Letterario, 1934), republished with a slightly different title and in an enlarged edition as *Il Duce e il fascismo nei canti dialettali d'Italia* (Milan: Convivio Letterario, 1937). On Filippo Fichera, see Aurelio Lepre, *El Duce lo ga dito: I poeti dialettali e il fascismo* (Milan: Leonardo, 1993), 107–13.
24 A first step towards a rationalization of the system was made in December 1929: the *nulla osta* by the prefecture of the town where a play was first staged was valid across the nation. On this see Emanuela Scarpellini, *Organization teatrale e politica del teatro nell'Italia fascista* (Florence: La Nuova Italia, 1989), 77–90. On theatre censorship in Fascist Italy see also: Pasquale Iaccio, 'La censura teatrale durante il fascismo,' *Storia contemporanea* 17.4 (1986): 567–614; Nicola Fano, *Tessere o non tessere: I comici e la censura fascista* (Florence: Liberal Libri, 1999); Clive Griffiths, 'Theatrical Censorship in Italy

during the Fascist Period,' in Bonsaver and Gordon, *Culture, Censorship and the State*, 76–85.

25 Before becoming theatrical censor, Zurlo had worked as secretary in three liberal governments of the pre-Fascist era (under Giolitti, 1912–14, Facta, 1921, and Bonomi, 1922). He was fifty-six years old at the time of his appointment. See Leopoldo Zurlo, *Memorie inutili*. On Zurlo see also Ferrara, *Censura teatrale e fascismo*, 35–90.

26 It should be remembered that by 1931 Mussolini had assumed direct headship of the Ministry of the Interior and was therefore Zurlo's superior within the ministry. Zurlo's memoirs provide many insights into Mussolini's dealings with the upper echelons of the police thanks in part to Zurlo's lifelong close friendship with the police deputy head, Carmine Senise (who was head of police in 1940–3, after Bocchini's death).

27 The figures are presented in a report by Zurlo to be found in ACS, MCP, b. 153, f. 'Censura teatrale.' Also quoted in Iaccio, 'La censura teatrale,' 576–7. According to Patrizia Ferrara, the exact number of scripts received by the Ufficio censura teatrale between 1931 and January 1943 was 17,330. See also Ferrara, *Censura teatrale e fascismo*, 101–7, for a statistical analysis of Zurlo's censorship.

28 On Sem Benelli and his relationship with the regime see Renzia D'Incà, 'Sem Benelli: Un'inquieta passione civile,' *Ariel* 2–3 (1993): 81–95; Giuseppe Pardini, '"La schiavitù delle beffe": Sem Benelli e il regime fascista,' *Nuova Storia Contemporanea* 5 (2002): 131–52. See also Benelli's memoirs, written soon after the war: *Schiavitù* (Milan: Mondadori, 1945), and those of Cesare Rossi, *Mussolini: Com'era* (Rome: Ruffolo, 1947), 215. The official documentation referring to Benelli during the Fascist years can be found in two files in the ACS: PP FP, f. 'Benelli Sem,' and CPC, b. 494, f. 'Benelli Sem.' Various extracts of the documentation are quoted by Pardini, '"La schiavitù delle beffe."'

29 Letter by Mussolini to D'Annunzio, dated 5 September 1924, in De Felice and Mariano, *Carteggio D'Annunzio–Mussolini*, 116–17 (emphasis in original). Police reports confirm that Benelli in those months had become a popular figure among anti-Fascists. Attendance at the performance of this plays was seen as a political gesture and scuttles between Fascists and anti-Fascists took place on more that one occasion, for example at the Valle Theatre, in Rome, for the première of *L'amorosa tragedia* in April 1925. See Scarpellini, *Organizzatione teatrale*, 84–5.

30 It is not entirely clear whether Mussolini and Benelli actually met on that occasion. According to a police report, Benelli met the head of the Divisione Polizia Politica in March 1928. He asked to be left free in his literary work and threatened to leave Italy if this did not happen. The report, dated

27 March 1928 can be found in ACS, PP FP, f. 'Benelli Sem.' The archives' file also contains half a dozen informers' reports describing the anger of many Fascists at the rehabilitation of Benelli, who, in his public speech, had explicitly thanked Mussolini for inviting him to intervene. On 28 August 1928 the prefect of Genoa wrote to Benelli to apologize for the imposition of police surveillance (which, similarly to what had happened to Benedetto Croce, was justified as a 'protective' measure). However, the surveillance was not stopped. As the documents suggest, personal surveillance was replaced by 'vigilanza generica' (generic surveillance), which was supposed to concentrate entirely on Benelli's political activity. See ACS, CPC, b. 494, and Benelli, *Schiavitù*, 112–16.

31 ACS, MCP, b. 4, f. 10 'Ufficio Stampa'; the 'memoriale' also appears as an appendix in Pardini, '"La schiavitù delle beffe,"' 145–9.

32 The only recorded case of Zurlo involvement concerns the comedy *Adamo ed Eva*, which Benelli brought to the stage in 1932. Zurlo alerted the head of police to two sentences with indirect political meaning. Bocchini passed his comments on to Mussolini, who decided to cut the two passages. On this see Zurlo, *Memorie inutili*, 310.

33 It should be added that this was not the first time that Zurlo encountered problems with church authorities. On 17 March 1932 the archbishop of Gaeta had officially complained about a play entitled *Per le mie piume e per il tuo cuore* by Nicola Aletta, which Zurlo had approved. The play presented the story of a nun who rejects her religious order in order to get married. Zurlo defended his decision on the ground that the play was neither vulgar nor against religious sentiment – the nun was a member of a semi-secular order that renewed its vows every year. The Ministry of War was also involved since the author was one of its employees. The head of police personally wrote to the ministry to defend Zurlo's decision in a letter dated 19 April 1932. Documents in ACS, MCP, DGTM, CT, b. 274, f. 4978. On this see also Ferrara, *Censura teatrale e fascismo*, 76–7.

34 The script of *Caterina Sforza* was sent to Zurlo on 7 December 1933. All the documentation relative to the censorship of the play can be found in ACS, MCP, DGTM CT, b. 250.

35 Zurlo wrongly reconstructed the date as 15 September 1934, but the archival documentation confirms that the note was actually written almost a year earlier. See ACS, MCP, DGTM CT, b. 250. Part of Mussolini's comment is also quoted by Benelli in *Schiavitù*, 111.

36 'L'autografo di S. E. il Capo del Governo che fu del pari donato a Zurlo è da questi trattenuto insieme con la disposizione di S. E. il Capo della polizia di autorizzare la recita integrale del lavoro' (The handwritten note by His

Excellency the Head of Government, which was also given to Zurlo, has been kept by the latter together with the directive by his Excellency the Head of police to authorize the integral text of the work); in ACS, MCP, DGTM CT, b. 250.

37 This is also Benelli's interpretation, as reported both in a police informer's report, dated 5 May 1934 (in ACS, PP FP, f. 'Benelli Sem'), and in his own memoirs (Benelli, *Schiavitù*, 109). It is a curious and somehow intriguing coincidence that in those very weeks a letter by the Tuscan pro-Fascist writer Ardengo Soffici to Galeazzo Ciano (at the time head of Mussolini's press office) dwells on the fact that Soffici had been discussing with Mussolini the possibility of writing a historical novel about the Vatican. In his letter, Soffici informed Ciano that he had decided to discontinue his project because of his scarce knowledge of the daily life and customs within the Vatican (letter dated 24 February 1934, in ACS, MCP, Gab. II vers., f. 13). An outline of the novel had actually appeared in a newspaper: Ardengo Soffici, 'Papa Pero I,' *La Gazzetta del Popolo*, 1 February 1934, 3. Pero was the name of the priest in the anticlerical play by Dario Niccodemi, *Prete Pero*, first staged in 1918, and banned in 1924 following a letter of protest by the Catholic youth association *Gioventi Cattolica Milanese* (see Scarpellini, *Organizzatione teatrale*, 85–6). Another example of Mussolini's lukewarm relationship with the Vatican was the request by Father Tacchi Venturi to oppose the publication of D'Annunzio's complete work on the grounds that it had been banned by the Holy Office. Mussolini refused to intervene, and Tacchi Venturi's letter, dated 9 January 1933, is annotated with a handwritten note saying 'Non faccio nulla' (I'm not going to do anything), presumably a quotation from Mussolini's reply to his secretary (in ACS, SPD CR, b. 68, f. 404/R 'Tacchi Venturi padre Pietro'). The Fascist government eventually gave financial support to Arnoldo Mondadori for the publication of D'Annunzio's works. A case in which the Vatican was more successful concerns the Italian translation of *Der mythus des 20. jahrhunderts* (1930, *The Myth of the 20th Century*) by Nazi ideologist Alfred Rosenberg (sentenced to death at the Nuremberg trial in 1946). The Holy Office immediately put the German-language edition of the book on the Index for its anti-Christian ideas, and, in order to avoid direct confrontation with the Vatican, the Fascist government did not allow an Italian translation to be published. Later, in 1939, the German original was banned from circulation throughout Italy. On this last case see Giorgio Fabre, *Il contratto: Mussolini editore di Hitler* (Bari: Dedalo, 2004), 68–9.

38 Benelli, *Schiavitù*, 111. According to Benelli, the bishop of Forlì officially protested against the play with a public letter. Although no documentary

trace could be found of this episode, an official protest, as we will see later, was launched by the bishop of the nearby town of Cesena.

39 Anonymous, 'Caterina Benelli,' *Osservatore romano*, 24 February 1934, 2.

40 Telegraphic memorandum from the Ministry of the Interior to all prefects, dated 28 February 1934, in ACS, MCP, DGTM CT, b. 250.

41 Documents in ACS, SPD CR, b. 68, f. 404/R 'Tacchi Venturi padre Pietro.'

42 Anonymous report dated 6 February 1934, in ACS, PP FP, f. 'Benelli Sem.'

43 Anonymous, 'Pubblicità teatrale,' *Osservatore romano*, 5 April 1934, 2.

44 Two handwritten memos, one from Cardinal Giuseppe Pizzardo to Father Tacchi Venturi, and one from Father Tacchi Venturi to Mussolini, both dated 15 April 1934, are kept in ACS, MCP, DGTM CT, b. 250. As it appears from the confidential file in Mussolini's office, between 1924 and 1934 Father Tacchi Venturi played an important part as a discreet go-between in direct contact with both Pope Pius XI and Il Duce (ACS, SPD CR, b. 68, f. 404/R 'Tacchi Venturi padre Pietro'). In Guspini's *L'orecchio del regime* one can find the interesting transcript of a recorded conversation between Tacchi Venturi and a cardinal, which took place at the time of the Lateran Pacts. It shows the role of discreet diplomat played by Tacchi Venturi thanks to his direct access to Mussolini (93–4). We will return to Tacchi Venturi, a key personality with regard to the relations between the Vatican and the regime, in chapter 4. Turi's study on the *Enciclopedia Treccani*, also shows the extent to which Tacchi Venturi was involved in the supervision of the entries pertaining to religious matters (see *Il mecenate, il filosofo e il gesuita*).

45 This meeting is consistent with the archival documentation and is remembered by both Benelli and Zurlo in their respective memoirs: Benelli, *Schiavitù*, 113; Zurlo, *Memorie inutili*, 311.

46 Zurlo, *Memorie inutili*, 311. In a long report to the Vatican's Secretary of State, dated 17 April 1934, Carlo Costantini, a militant Catholic who led a committee of the Diocese of Rome working on 'controllo della moralità,' stated that he was present at the premiere of *Caterina Sforza*, armed with a copy of the Mondadori edition of the play, and accompanied by the chief editor of the Catholic paper *Avvenire d'Italia* and by some editors from the *Osservatore romano*. ASV, SS, Schedario, r. 324 (1935), F.3, f. 132268.

47 T, 'Il Pastor e il suo XVI volume della Storia dei Papi,' *Osservatore romano*, 22 April 1934, 2. The following day a vague but nonetheless critical article on Benelli appeared in the Roman paper *Quadrivio*, written by the Fascist poet Vincenzo Cardarelli: '25 anni di Sem,' *Quadrivio*, 23 April 1934, 1.

48 Sem Benelli, 'Sem Benelli non e ebreo: Una lettera dell'autore di Caterina Sforza,' *Giornale d'Italia*, 25 April 1934, 3. Four days earlier, the *Giornale d'Italia* had published a short article in which it reported the success of the performances of *Caterina Sforza* at the Quirino Theatre in Rome. According to his

memoirs, in his article Benelli intended openly to attack any form of anti-Semitism but was advised by Galeazzo Ciano – who had read and discussed a draft of the article – to leave the matter out (Benelli, *Schiavitù*, 113–14).

49 Anonymous, 'Unicuique suum,' *Osservatore romano*, 26 April 1934, 2.

50 Benelli does not mention this fact in his memoirs. However, the payment certainly took place, as the receipt signed by Benelli can be found in ACS, MCP, b. 53, f. 597 'Benelli Sem.' Relations and collaboration with the church had other, more constructive times. With regard to *Caterina Sforza*, when in 1941 a second application was made to take the play on tour again, Zurlo allowed Monsignor Montini – then Sostituto at the Vatican's Secretary of State and future Pope Paul VI – to provide his own comments. As a self-congratulating memo by Zurlo, dated 5 August 1941, suggests, Montini's comments and suggestions for cuts were very close to those first proposed by Zurlo seven years earlier. In ACS, MCP, DGTM CT, b. 250; see also Zurlo, *Memorie inutili*, 312.

51 Zurlo, *Memorie inutili*, 130. On this see also Alberto Cesare Alberti, *Il teatro nel fascismo: Pirandello e Bragaglia* (Rome: Bulzoni, 1974), 30–1, 215–17. In his long appendix to the book, Alberti has published all the police and ministerial documents held at ACS that are related to this case.

52 Alberti, *Il teatro nel fascismo*, 31, 56. The article 'Pirandelliana,' published in *Giustizia e libertà*, 8 June 1934, can be found in the appendix to Alberti's book, on 216. *Giustizia e libertà* briefly returned to the subject of the opera fiasco in a short article following Pirandello's Nobel Prize: 'Un dispiacere al duce,' *Giustizia e libertà*, 9 November 1934.

53 In his opening speech at an international conference on theatre held in Rome in October 1934, Pirandello chose to speak about the relationship between politics and theatre. Throughout the speech he made no explicit mention of Fascism and in fact repeatedly affirmed the need for theatrical works to be free of any political influence or even content. As for Malipiero, his later works – including operas such as *Giulio Cesare* (1935) and *Antonio e Cleopatra* (1937) dedicated to famous figures of classical Rome – met the regime's expectations. On Malipiero and Fascism, see Fiamma Nicolodi, *Musica e musicisti nel Ventennio fascista* (Fiesole: Discanto, 1984), 200–3. Malipiero's memoirs of his collaboration with Pirandello were published as 'Favoleggiando con Pirandello,' in *Scenario* (November 1940) and reprinted in Massimo Bontempelli, *G. Francesco Malipiero* (Milan: Bompiani, 1942), 190–3. The Italian scholar and friend of Malipiero, Vittore Branca, was also present at the Roman premiere of *La favola del figlio cambiato*. According to him, Malipiero attracted the malevolence of the *gerarchi* by answering back to their criticism. To one, possibly Starace, who told him, 'Da lei mi sarei aspettato meglio' (From you, I would have expected something better than

this), Malipiero apparently answered 'E io da lei no, nel giudicare la musica e di arte' (From you, I wouldn't have expected any better knowledge of music and art). See Vittore Branca, 'Malipiero musicista da grandi battute,' *Corriere dell Sera*, 4 March 2001. Finally, another example of a libretto that suffered from Mussolini's intervention concerns the composer and Accademico d'Italia Ildebrando Pizzetti. After a meeting with Mussolini, he had submitted the libretto of his latest opera, *Orseolo*. In reply Mussolini suggested the removal of the line 'Giustizia e Libertà son presso a morte' (Justice and Liberty are nearing their death), given their potential reference to the anti-Fascist organization of the Rosselli brothers (see the letter by Mussolini's secretary, Chiavolini, to Pizzetti, dated 27 June 1932, in ACS, SPD CO, f. 538.707). The line was removed when the opera was finally performed in 1935.

54 On da Verona's fiction, see Antonio Piromalli, *Guido da Verona* (Naples: Guida, 1975), and Ezio Raimondi, *Il silenzio della Gorgone* (Bologna: Zanichelli, 1980), 44–53.

55 Telegram dated 23 November 1924, in ACS, SPD CO, f. 209.651.

56 The only case of censorship that I have been able to find concerns the advertising campaign related to da Verona's popular poetic pamphlet *Lettera d'amore alle sartine d'Italia* (1924). On 8 June 1924, as minister of the newly created Ministry of Communication, Galeazzo Ciano informed Mussolini's secretary that, following a number of protests, the ministry had ordered the cessation of the advertising campaign. Da Verona's book was advertised on stamped envelopes thanks a deal with the Post Office. Memo from Ciano to Chiavolini, dated 8 June 1924, in ACS, SPD CO f. 209.651.

57 The letter of protest is dated 23 November 1929, while the report concerning the alleged challenge to a duel is dated 13 December 1929. Both documents can be found in ASMi, PG I, b. 423, f. 'Censura libri e opuscoli.'

58 According to Enrico Tiozzo, da Verona was not attacked because of the irreverent content of *I promessi sposi* but because, with his earlier libertine publications, he was 'un'insopportabile spina nel fianco del fascismo' (an unbearable thorn in the Fascist's side); in Enrico Tiozzo, 'Il rifacimento Daveroniano de *I promessi sposi*,' *Romance Studies* 22 (2004): 69. Whether da Verona can be defined as a thorn in the Fascists' side is rather debatable, particularly since there is no evidence of earlier tensions between the author and the Fascists.

59 Letter from Don Giovanni Pandero to the prefect of Milan, dated 9 January 1930, in ASMi, PG, b. 423, f. 'Censura libri e opuscoli.' In a shortened, annotated version of the *Indice dei libri proibiti*, edited by Orsolina Montevecchi – a lecturer of Milan's Catholic university and a militant of Azione Cattolica – the ban on da Verona's work was justified for containing 'immoralità, scene

voluttuose e sensuali, profanazioni' (immorality, voluptuous and sensual scenes, profanation). See Montevecchi, *La chiesa e i libri: Estratto dall'Indice dei Libri Proibiti* (Milan: Archetipografia, 1944), 29.

60 Cornelio di Marzio, '"I promessi sposi" rifatti da Guido da Verona,' *Critica fascista* 2 (1 January 1930): 15–17. See also the literary review in *Il Popolo di Roma*, by Adriano Tilgher, of 7 January 1930, which condemned the novel as a literary fiasco.

61 The correspondence regarding these two letters is held at ACS, SPD CO 209.651.

62 The telegrams dated 24 January and 9 February are in ACS, SPD CO, f. 209.651; the one dated 28 January is in ASMi, PG I, b. 423, f. 'Censura libri e opuscoli.'

63 Report by the Nunzio to the Segreteria di Stato, 15 January 1930; memorandum of the Secretaria di Stato, 22 January 1930; in ASV, SS A.E.S. Italia, p. 794, f. 389.

64 Letter dated 27 January 1930, in ASMi, PG I, b. 423, f. 'Censura libri e opuscoli.' Letter dated 30 April 1931, in ACS, SPD CO 209.651.

65 Gherardo Casini, co-director of the journal and future chair of the Press Division at the Ministry of Popular Culture, added his weight with an article entitled 'Morte dell'intellettuale.' Bartolini, 'Un cattivo libro,' *Critica fascista* 11.1 (1 January 1933): 13–5. The biography was Antonio Aniante, *Mussolini* (Paris: Grasset, 1932). According to Corrado Alvaro's memoirs, Mussolini himself had read and annotated a copy of this biography that was subsequently kept by Margherita Sarfatti; see Corrado Alvaro, *Quasi una vita* (Milan: Bompiani, 1952), 122–3.

66 The anonymous editorial appeared on page 29 of the issue of 15 January 1933. Bartolini's correspondence with his publisher, Vallecchi, reveals that he was also planning to collect his articles for *Critica fascista* in a volume entitled *12 satire, 20 libelli*. The project came to a halt in the autumn of 1932. See two letters by Bartolini to Vallecchi, dated 18 August and 21 October 1932, in ACGV, Carteggio Vallecchi–Bartolini.

67 The police file containing all the documentation so far quoted can be found in ACS, PP FP, f. 'Bartolini Luigi.'

68 On Bellone, see Dario Biocca and Mauro Canali, *L'informatore: Silone, i comunisti, la polizia* (Milan: Luni, 2000), 23–5, 51–3, and passim, and Franzinelli, *I tentacoli dell'OVRA*, 337. Bellone's involvement in the investigation makes one wonder whether Bartolini was at some stage collaborating with the police forces. No clear evidence has emerged to confirm this. Some elements, however, allow the suggestion that Bartolini might have been contradictory in his actions, if not playing it both ways: first, it is odd that while publicly attacking an

anti-Fascist exile such as Aniante, he should try to foster his contacts with another anti-Fascist living in the same city; second, when Bartolini published his letters to Venturi in a pamphlet produced soon after the war, he neglected to insert a sentence that can be found in the copy in his police file: 'S'è scoperto che tutti giocano la doppia parte. Anch'io sembra che giuochi la doppia parte, ma invece non la gioco' (We've discovered that everybody is playing it both ways. It looks as if I'm playing it both ways too, but I'm not playing that game); see Luigi Bartolini, *Perché do ombra* (Rome: Novagrafia, 1945), 6. During this period Guido Bellone was also involved in the police surveillance of another controversial intellectual, Curzio Malaparte (ACS, PP FP, b. 96/A, f. 'Suckert Kurzio' [*sic*]).

69 *Scritti sequestrati* (Rome: Circe, 1945). In a letter to one of his publishers, Arnoldo Mondadori, dated 12 August 1933, Bartolini mentioned that his *confino* had been shortened thanks to the 'clemenza del Duce' ('Il Duce's forgiveness'). The same information was given in a letter to another publisher, Vallecchi, dated 1 October 1933 (in ACGV, Corrispondenza Vallecchi–Bartolini). Whether this is true or not, it suggests that Bartolini may have been aware that Mussolini was made privy to the investigation leading to his arrest. However, there is no doubt that Bartolini was often prone to exaggeration. In another letter to Mondadori, dated 14 April 1939, Bartolini complained about the neglect of his work and attacked Mondadori by stating that instead of being influenced by intellectuals with debatable morals he should listen to real Fascists like him who were in direct contact with Mussolini. Both letters can be found in FMA, FAM, f. 6 'Bartolini.'

70 Bartolini, *Scritti sequestrati*, 10–11.

71 As we will see in chapter 4, Bartolini, as a literary reviewer for *Quadrivio*, was to be involved in a case of censorship in 1941.

72 Vitaliano Brancati, 'Roma,' *Il Tevere*, 8 May 1931, 3, partially quoted in Francesca Guercio, 'La compromissione di Brancati,' *Ariel* 2–3 (1993): 259.

73 Brancati, 'La mia visita a Mussolini,' 292–3; also in *Il Tevere*, 13 August 1931, 3, and *Il Popolo di Sicilia*, 13 August 1931, 3. Two years earlier, Brancati had also produced a play glorifying Mussolini. Entitled *Everest* – although the first working title was *Mussolini* – the play was dedicated to Margherita Sarfatti and published in *Giornale dell'Isola* in December 1929. It was eventually performed in Rome on 5 June 1930.

74 Antonio Bragaglia, 'Sempre "anni difficili" per il teatro di Brancati,' *Sipario* 103 (1954): 36, quoted in Guercio, 'La compromissione di Brancati,' 275.

75 For *Il Popolo d'Italia* Brancati wrote the article 'Rinnovare gli edifici del teatro,' published on 18 June 1933, 3, and 'Ricordi di un ammarraggio,' 2 March 1934, 3.

76 Letter from A.G. Bragaglia to Mussolini, dated 18 October 1932, in ACS, MCP II, b. 2, f. 'Bragaglia Antonio Giulio.' On 30 January 1934 an adaptation of *Piave* was broadcast on the Italian radio. See, for example, the very positive review published in *La Gazzetta del Popolo*: log. (pseud.), 'La serata alla radio,' *La Gazzetta del Popolo*, 1 January 1934, 4.

77 Vitaliano Brancati, *Singolare avventura di viaggio* (Milan: Mondadori, 1934); reprised in *Opere, 1922–46* (Milan: Bompiani, 1987), 9–85; the quote is in *Opere*, 44.

78 Luigi Chiarini, 'Singolare avventura di Vitaliano Brancati,' *Quadrivio*, 7 March 1934, 1–2.

79 Arnoldo Mondadori to Brancati, 15 March 1934, in AFM, FAM, f. 66 'Ministero Stampa e Propaganda.'

80 Vitaliano Brancati, *Ritorno alla censura* (Bari: Laterza, 1952), 22. This pamphlet is an attack against the continuities between the Fascist and postwar periods in the organization of censorship.

81 In a letter to the Vatican's Segreteria di Stato, dated 10 February 1934, Costantini reported that, following his protest, Brancati's novel has been banned in Rome. He added that he was waiting for the Ministry of the Interior to extend the ban to the rest of Italy. ASV, SS, Schedario r. 324 (1935), F. 3.

82 Arnoldo Mondadori to Brancati, 2 December 1935, in AFM, FAM, f. 'Vitaliano Brancati.'

83 Brancati to Mondadori, 16 February 1936, in ibid.

84 See the letters to Mussolini and Ciano, both dated 1 March 1935, and Ciano's subsequent request dated 8 March 1935, to Alfredo Signoretti, chief editor of *La Stampa*, to keep Brancati among their contributors. Three months later Brancati asked Ciano to put similar pressure on Borelli, chief editor of *Corriere della Sera* (who kindly turned down the offer in a letter to Ciano dated 14 June 1935). Other correspondence to Ciano and Mussolini, relates to Brancati's unsuccessful attempts to be employed on a full-time basis by *Il Popolo di Sicilia*. With regard to the book on Leopardi, see the Ministry for Press and Propaganda memo, dated 7 December 1936, which carries Mussolini's handwritten approval of a grant of 2,300 lire. Other requests for journalistic collaboration were dealt with by Gherardo Casini during 1937; in the same year, Bottai was involved in Brancati's request for his teaching post to be transferred to Catania or Rome. All documents in ACS, MCP II, b. 2, f. 'Brancati Vitaliano.'

85 In the archives of the Italian Foreign Office there are a number of documents relating to the pre–October 1922 period: ASDMAE, 'Ufficio Stampa Estera,' b. 303, f. 'Pubblicazioni italiane e straniere.'

86 Mussolini's press office did not seem to be particularly active on this front. As late as 1932, its chief, Polverelli, sent a memo to the Directorate General of Public Security simply requesting that three copies of all seized foreign publications be sent to his press office. Letter dated 28 June 1932 in ACS, DGPS DAGR, Massime S4, b. S4/A (provv.), f. 1. sf. 1.

87 The documents related to the pamphlet *Fazioni e Patria* can be found in ASMi, PG I, b. 424, f. 'Censura libri.' On Carlo Tresca see for example his entry in Mari Jo Buhle, Paul Buhle, and Dan Georgakas, eds., *Encyclopedia of the American Left* (Champaign: University of Illinois Press, 1992).

88 Documents in ASMi, MCP, PGI I, b. 424, f. 'Censura libri.'

89 The book was eventually published by Valois in 1930 with the title *Les pieds devant*. Documents in ACS, PP FP, f. 'Paolo Monelli.' Some years later the book was turned into a film, *Scarpe al sole*, directed by Marco Elter, which received the Prize of the Ministry of Press and Propaganda at the 1935 Venice Film Festival. A ministerial *velina* of 21 August 1935 invited newspaper editors to give ample space to the premier of the film. See Gian Piero Brunetta, *Storia del cinema italiano*, vol. 1 (Rome: Riuniti, 1993), 42, and Tranfaglia, ed., *La stampa del regime*, 214.

90 Memos dated 18 and 20 March 1930, in ACS, MCP, b. 4, f. 10 'Ufficio Stampa'; also quoted in Cesari, *La censura nel periodo fascista*, 42. Nenni's *Ricordi di un socialista: Sei anni di guerra civile in Italia* was published in Paris in the series *I Quaderni dell'Università Proletaria* by the socialist publisher Cecconi. Emilio Lussu's most famous anti-Fascist publication, *Marcia su Roma e dintorni* (Paris: Casa Editrice 'Critica,' 1933), was also banned. However, it is noteworthy that a copy of the book was kept in Mussolini's private library, now held at ACS, Collezione Mussolini, 59.

91 All the documentation referring to Renn's novel can be found in ACS, SPD CO, f. 509.568/2.

92 On Andrienne Thomas see Decleva, *Mondadori*, 157–8. On Carlo Salsa see Cesari, *La censura nel periodo fascista*, 72.

93 On this novel see Decleva, *Mondadori*, 179.

94 Valeriu Marcu, *Il dramma del dittatore bolscevico* (Milan: Mondadori, 1930). A letter from the prefect of Milan to DGPS, dated 31 May 1930, shows that Mondadori's translation had been queried by the Ministry of the Interior, but the prefect had assured them that since it was 'an objective biography' the publication had been given the prefecture's *nulla osta*. For copy of the prefect's letter and other documents related to this case, see ASMi, PG I, b. 423, f. 'Censura libri e opuscoli.' See also Decleva, *Mondadori*, 146, and Tranfaglia and Vittoria, *Storia degli editori italiani*, 306.

95 Fabre, *L'elenco*, 20. Cesari too states that in his archival research he was unable to find a list of all banned publications during the first decade of the

regime (*La censura nel periodo fascista,* 31). On the other hand, we know that there was a list of all periodicals and books that were banned from circulation in Italy. It was a 413–page list, distributed in the early months of 1931 and then updated in 1932, 1934, and 1936. Because the above-mentioned memo of May 1934 is related to the work of Lenin, it is likely that it referred to the smuggling of Lenin's works from abroad. See ACS, DGPS DAGR, F4, b. 117, quoted in Fabre, *L'elenco,* 20.

96 Documents in ASMi, PG I, b. 424, f. 'Censura libri.'

97 The documents related to these three titles – dated, respectively, 13 August 1928, 6 May 1930, and 9 September 1930 – can be found in ASMi, PG I, b. 424, f. 'Censura libri.' According to Cesari, the American journal *Trentino* was also banned because of its articles on the situation in South Tyrol (Cesari, *La censura nel periodo fascista,* 42). Some years later, on 31 May 1939, the Ministry of Popular Culture ordered the publisher Sonzogno to withdraw all copies of its travel guide *Le cento città italiane* because the photographs related to the city of Bozen still portrayed the city as it was before its 'Italianization' (i.e., showing signboards in German and Germanophile monuments that had since been destroyed); documents in ASMi, PG II, b. 156, f. 044 'Sonzogno casa editrice.'

98 The telegram can be found in ACS, DGPS DAGR, Circolari, f. 11. With regard to Silone's alleged collaboration with the Fascists – as suggested by the studies of Mauro Canali and Dario Biocca – I should note that the censorship material regarding Ignazio Silone seems neither to confirm nor to dismiss Biocca–Canali's hypothesis. For more on this, see in chapter 4.

99 Documents related to this episode can be found in ACS, MCP, b. 4, f. 'Ufficio Stampa.' Polverelli's memos were sent out between April 1932 and February 1933 and included a number of issues, particularly related to crime and morality, which had to be given no space in the Italian press. Ciano himself had reminded newspaper editors of these limitations on 15 September 1933 (see Cesari, *Le censura nel periodo fascista,* 32–3). An example of Mondadori's collaboration with the regime in those months is the 1933 book *La Nuova Italia d'Oltremare: L'opera del Fascismo,* edited by Emilio De Bono and with a preface by Mussolini himself. Lederer's and Dorgelès's case are also mentioned by Christopher Rundle in his article 'Publishing Translation in Mussolini's Italy,' *Textus* 12.2 (1999): 431–2.

4. From Press Office to Ministry of Popular Culture

1 In an article published in *Giornale della libreria* – the official journal of the association of Italian publishers – the publisher Enrico Bemporad praised Mura, Pitigrilli, and Da Verona for the popularity of their novels in Italy and

abroad. Enrico Bemporad, 'La traduzione di libri stranieri in Italia e di libri italiani all'Estero,' *Giornale della libreria* 27–8 (4–11 July 1931): 225.

2 Mura, 'Niôminkas amore negro,' *Lidel* 4.11 (1930): 57–86. In the pages of *L'elenco* devoted to the Mura case, Fabre omits to consider the original version.

3 Zurlo, *Memorie inutili*, 252, Baron Aloisi, *Journal* (Paris: Plon, 1957), 185.

4 With regard to the first version, there is little doubt that Mura was not intending to write a progressive, liberal-minded piece of fiction. It is possible that the magazine version was simply an earlier, shorter draft, conveniently concluding with the marriage of the two protagonists. It is also possible that Mura wrote a first draft, which she then cut or self-censored, perhaps following the advice of *Lidel*'s editors. There are no police records or references to the version published in *Lidel*, so presumably its publication did not encounter any problems with the authorities.

5 Mura, *Sambadù amore negro* (Milan: Rizzoli, 1934), 175, 187.

6 It should be noted that, whereas the cover of *Sambadù amore negro* caused such a stir for its unconventional imagery, book covers showing naked black women were considered perfectly acceptable at the time. This was the case of even serious publications such as Lincoln De Castro's *Etiopia: Terra, uomini e cose*, a study of Ethiopian society published by Treves in 1936. Both its cover and illustrations showed images of beautiful bare-breasted young Ethiopians women.

7 Copies of the telegrams are in ACS, MI UC, In partenza, 2.4.1934.

8 Two telegrams were sent on 3 April 1934, the first one concerned the order to seize all copies of the novel, the second addressed the order to give a police warning to the illustrator of the cover. On 5 April the prefect of Milan directly informed Ciano at the press office that 253 copies of the novel had been seized (documents in ASMi, PG I, b. 423, f. 045 'Sambadù amore negro'). On 8 April the prefect of Mantua sequestrated all copies of the city's paper, *Voce di Mantova*, because it contained a brief review of the novel; ACS, MI, DGPS, Massime, S4 (provv.) f. 1, sf. 5 (the file is marked as *provvisorio* because – in February 2006 – it was still awaiting definitive cataloguing by staff at ACS). See also Fabre, *L'elenco*, 25–6.

9 A copy of the circular can be found in ACS, MI, DGPS, Massime S4 (provv.), f. 1. sf. 5. Cannistraro was the first to mention it, in *La fabbrica del consenso*, 381, followed by Cesari in *La censura nel periodo fascista*, 47–9. Thanks to further archival findings, Fabre has provided the necessary information to contextualize its importance (*L'elenco*, 22–8). All the correspondence related to the circular of 3 April 1934 is held at ACS, MI, DGPS, Massime S4, b. S 4/A (provv.), f. 1, sf. 5. Related correspondence can also be found in ACS, DGPS

DAGR, Circolari, b. 11 (1928–49), and in other regional State Archives (see in particular ASMi, PG I, b. 423, f. 045 'Sambadù amore negro').

10 In *L'elenco*, 28, Fabre suggests that as early as the year before, Mussolini had been making statements showing his interest in introducing racist policies in Italy. Fabre expands on this in his more recent book, linking Mussolini's renewed interest in racism to the publication of the Italian edition of Hitler's *Mein Kampf*, in 1933–5 (Fabre, *Il contratto*, 55–64), and in his *Mussolini razzista* (Milan: Garzanti, 2005), 9–38.

11 Zurlo, *Memorie inutili*, 159.

12 ACS, PP FP, f. 'Mura. Scrittrice.'

13 Fabre, *L'elenco*, 28.

14 Documents in ACS, DGPS DAGR, Circolari, b. 11 (1928–49); and ASMi, PG II, b. 78, f. 045.

15 However, a copy of a circular sent by the Secretariat for Press and Propaganda to all prefectures on 12 April 1935 suggests that the French Foreign Legion had been specifically targeted on its own merit. The circular stated that works on the Foreign Legion had recently been banned because of the 'fallaci illusioni e pericolose suggestioni' (misguided illusions and dangerous influence) created among young readers. The circular ended with an explicit order to the prefectures to inform publishing houses under their jurisdiction to avoid publishing works on the Foreign Legion. Circular in ASVr, PG, b. 11, f. 6 'Affari vari riservati.'

16 Presumably this was a book or a pamphlet related to the problematic publication of *I promessi sposi* in 1930 (see chapter 3 above); unfortunately the ban must have been applied with particular success because I was unable to find any traces of this publication in any of the public or private archives and libraries I visited during five years of field work. The publisher was presented as Laterza e Polo (Polo being the printshops of the Laterza publishing house in Bari); yet neither the author nor the title of the book appear in Laterza's *Catalogo storico* (which was accessible online at http://www.laterza.it/catalogo/cat-sto.asp in July 2006).

17 Zurlo, *Memorie inutili*, 252–8. The text of Chiarelli's *Carne bianca* was actually published by Carabba in 1934, so perhaps only its performance had been banned. See also Iaccio, 'La censura teatrale durante il fascismo,' 604. Ferrara also notes that a play by Maria Bazzi, *L'ebreo errante*, was submitted in May 1934 and prohibited by Zurlo the following September, probably because of its racial content and despite the fact that the play ended with the conversion of the Jewish protagonist to the Christian faith. Ferrara also highlights further examples revealing Zurlo's adherence to government policies related to the anti-Semitic legislation (Ferrara, *Censura teatrale e fascismo*, 82–4).

18 Giovanni Oriolo was prefect of Verona from 20 January 1934 to 1 August
1936 (see Missori, *Governi, alte gerarchie dello stato*, 626). In the files of the
Gabinetto di Prefettura at ASVr there are several examples of this form. One
such example concerns a book on Japanese women, *Il cuore di O-Sono-San* by
Elizabeth Cooper (*The Heart of O-Sono-San*, 1917), which had been translated
by the Verona publisher Estremo Oriente. Unsure whether a passage of the
novel could be regarded as indirectly against Italy's military campaign in
Ethiopia, on 15 June 1935 the prefect asked for the opinion of Ciano's newly
organized Undersecretariat for Press and Propaganda. Two weeks later Neos
Dinale gave the go-ahead of the undersecretariat with the only caveat being
that the incriminated passage had to be cut in future reprints. The prefecture's final report concerning the novel, dated 1 July 1935, was typed on the
form that explicitly mentioned Mussolini's 1934 circular. Documents in
ASVr, PG, b. 11, f. 5/6.

19 The publication of novels in instalments or as supplements to magazines was
to remain a particular preoccupation of the regime: on 28 December 1934
Mussolini's press office (which by then had become the Secretariat for Press
and Propaganda) issued a circular asking prefects to invite publishers to
choose 'narrazioni ispirate a concetti sani e consoni alle direttive segnate dal
Regime' (narratives inspired by healthy ideas and conforming to the directives of the Regime). A circular of 31 July 1935 was along similar lines. All
documents in ACS, DGPS DAGR, Massime S4, b. S4/A (provv.), f. 1 sf, 2. It
must be said that polemics regarding this type of publication preceded the
Mura case. In May 1933 the Milan paper *La Sera* had started a campaign
against the licentiousness of many of the publications sold in instalments by
news agents. Two articles were published, on 18 and 30 May, signed by
Franco De Agazio. These prompted an investigation by the prefecture of
Milan, which had ended on 13 June 1933 with the seizure of a novel published in instalments – *Cuore garibaldino* by Dino Romanelli – and two series
entitled *I banditi celebri* and *Banditi Corsi*. Documents in ASMi, PG I, b. 423,
f. 'Censura libri e opuscoli.' They were all published by Casa Editrice
Moderna, which had been explicitly attacked in *La Sera*.

20 The book that featured his concise history of Fascism and of which he was
co-editor was published as Benito Mussolini, *La dottrina del Fascismo: Storia,
opere e istituti*, ed. M. Gallian, A. Marpicati, and L. Contu (Milan: Hoepli,
1935). Gallian had been receiving financial help from Mussolini – through
Ciano's press office – since at least December 1933 (correspondence in ACS,
MCP II, b. 13, f. 'Gallian Marcello'). In 1933 he had also edited a small propaganda book, funded by the press office of the Fascist Federation of Varese,
entitled *Mussolini nei commenti della stampa nel mondo*. On 5 September 1934

he was asked by Giovanni Gentile to contribute to his Istituto Nazionale Fascista di Cultura with a non-fiction book on a topic of his choice related to contemporary Italy (letter in FP CG, f. 'Gentile Giovanni'). For a biographical study of Marcello Gallian see Paolo Buchignani, *Marcello Gallian: La battaglia antiborghese di un fascista anarchico* (Rome: Bonacci, 1984), in particular 49–108, and his recent *La rivoluzione in camicia nera; Dalle origini al 25 luglio 1943* (Milan: Mondadori, 2006), 178–96, 295–301.

21 Marcello Gallian, *Tempo di pace* (Rome: Circoli, 1934), and *Comando di tappa* (Rome: Cabala, 1934). The latter, thanks to Bontempelli's friendly promotion (the two knew each other well from the late 1920s), had also been runner up for the prestigious *Premio Viareggio*. It is also interesting to note that Gallian's Political Police file contains a copy of an article entitled 'Scrittori fascisti' published in *Giustizia e Libertà* on 23 November 1934. The article ridiculed Gallian's prose style and quoted various passages from *Comando di tappa*, presenting it as an example of the artistic and thematic vulgarity of Fascist literature (ACS, PP FP, f. 'Gallian Marcello').

22 Letter from Aldo Borelli to Galeazzo Ciano, dated 28 April 1934, in ACS, MCP II, b. 13, f. 'Gallian Marcello.'

23 See Buchignani, *Marcello Gallian*, 103–8.

24 For the influence of Nazi Germany on the development of Mussolini's cultural policies, see Cannistraro, *La fabbrica del consenso*, 101–5; Cesari, *La censura nel periodo fascista*, 46–49; Ferrara, *L'amministrazione centrale pubblica*, 30–2; Giovanni Berardelli, 'Il fascismo e l'organizzazione della cultura,' in *Storia d'Italia*, ed. Giovanni Sabbatucci and Vittorio Sidotto vol. 4 (Rome and Bari: Laterza, 1997), 472–6; Alexander De Grand, *Fascist Italy and Nazi Germany* (London: Routledge, 1995), 69–78; and Giovanni Ragone, *Un secolo di libri: Storia dell'editoria in Italia dall'Unità al post-moderno* (Turin: Einaudi, 1999), 160–4. On the Nazi regime and the German publishing industry, see Oron Hale, *The Captive Press in the Third Reich* (Princeton, NJ: Princeton University Press, 1964); David Welch, *The Third Reich: Politics and Propaganda* (London: Routledge, 1993); and Jan-Pieter Barbian, *Literaturpolitik im Dritten Reich: Institutionen, Kompetenzen, Betätigungsfelder* (Frankfurt AM: Buchhändler Vereinigung GmbH, 1993; Munich: Deutscher Taschenbuch Verlag, 1995).

25 Polverelli's note can be found in ACS, b. 4, f. 10 'Ufficio Stampa,' quoted by Cannistraro, *La fabbrica del consenso*, 103. On Goebbels's visit to Italy see David Irving, *Goebbels: Mastermind of the Third Reich* (London: Focal Point, 1996), 167–8. On *Critica fascista* see Giordano Bruno Guerri, *Galeazzo Ciano: Una vita 1903–1944*, (Milan, Bompiani, 1979), 83–4.

26 See, for example, the correspondence with Adriano Grande (chief editor of the Genoase journal *Circoli*) in March 1934 (in ACS, MCP II, b. 6, f. 'Grande

Adriano') or with the authors Ardengo Soffici and Vincenzo Cardarelli, respectively, in June and July 1934 (in ACS, MCP II, b. 13, f. 'Soffici Ardengo' and b. 3, f. 'Cardarelli Vincenzo'), all of whom received funds with the direct approval of Mussolini. At the same time, Mussolini continued to keep personal contacts, as, for example, when he invited the young Ruggero Zangrandi to write for *Il Popolo d'Italia*: between 27 and 29 June 1934, Zangrandi sent Mussolini four articles, which the latter corrected and passed on for publication to *Il Popolo d'Italia*; see ACS, MCP II, b. 15, f. 'Zangrandi Ruggero', and also Ruggero Zangrandi, *Il lungo viaggio attraverso il fascismo* (Milan: Mursia, 1962), 21–32.

27 Proof of Ciano's detailed knowledge of the organization and structure of Goebbels's Reichsministerium can be found in this long report, which was presented to the Council of Ministers in the summer of 1934. The fourteen-page report gave a full picture of the workings of the ministry, complete with a scheme of all the offices and officials at their head. The report is undated, but a reference to the creation of the *Kulturkammer* makes it likely that it was prepared in the first half of 1934. A parallel – this time unintentional – with the Italian institution is that Goebbels's new ministry was in the same building that had been used by previous German governments as the Reich's press office. Finally, the report states that at the time Goebbels's ministry employed a total of about 230 officials. Document in ACS, PCM (1934–6), cat. 1/1.2, f. 2219. See also Cannistraro, *La fabbrica del consenso*, 104–5.

28 Giorgio Nelson Page, *L'americano di Roma* (Milan: Longanesi, 1950), 437, quoted in Guerri, *Galeazzo Ciano*, 91. On Ciano's relationship with young Fascist intellectuals see Zangrandi, *Il lungo viaggio attraerso il fascismo*, 145–54.

29 Polverelli's report is in ACS, MCP, b. 4, f. 10 'Ufficio Stampa.' The data regarding the Ministry of Press and Propaganda come from a draft bill written in the summer/autumn of 1936, in ACS, PCM (1936–7), b. 293. f. 'Schema di regio decreto di approvazione dei ruoli organici del Ministero per la stampa e la propaganda.'

30 It should be added that the list also contained titles of publications that had been published earlier. This is certainly the case of *La rivoluzione liberale* by Piero Gobetti (mispelled Pietre Gabetti in the list) published by Cappelli in 1924 (see chapter 2 above). A later edition of Jewish author Cesare Lombroso's *La donna delinquente, la prostituta e la donna normale* (Milan: Bocca, 1915) was also banned, although under the name of his co-author and son-in-law, Guglielmo Ferrero. The undersecretariat's circular mentioning the request of Mantua's prefect and asking all prefects to supply their censorship data was sent on 30 March 1935, signed by the head of the undersecretariat's National Press Division, Neos Dinale. All documents can be found in

ACS, MI, DAGR DGPS, Massime S 4, b. S4/A (provv.), f. 6 'Elenco delle stampe sequestrate.'

31 Patrizia Ferrara, 'La voce del padrone,' *Storia e Dossier* 10.99 (1995): 57.

32 The biography of Balbo was actually ghost written by the young Elio Vittorini, who was at the time an enthusiastic follower of Malaparte. On this see Lorenzo Greco, 'Vita di Pizzo-di-Ferro: Vittorini e lo pseudo-Malaparte,' in *Censura e scrittura: Vittorini, lo pseudo-Malaparte, Gadda* (Milan: Il Saggiatore, 1983), 13–50, and Bonsaver, *Elio Vittorini*, 23–4.

33 Mussolini's office had a file on Malaparte containing all this correspondence with Balbo (in ACS, SPD CR, b. 61). The correspondence with Massenet can be found in BN, FF, 'Carte Malaparte' b. 25. A report by a police informer concerning Malaparte was passed on to Galeazzo Ciano on 30 January 1935: it stated that, among his French friends, Malaparte openly boasted of being protected by Ciano; ACS, MCP, b. 4, f. 10 'Ufficio Stampa.' A collection of informers' reports concerning Malaparte, written between October 1927 and July 1934, can be found ACS, PP FP, b. 96/A, f. 'Suckert Kurzio' [*sic*]. On the *velina* see Tranfaglia, *La stampa del regime*, 212.

34 Copies of the correspondence can be found in AFM, FAM, b. 66. The seizure of *Barbara*, written by Marise Ferro (wife of famous author Guido Piovene) was recorded by his friend Eugenio Montale in a letter to Irma Brandeis dated 4 October 1934; see Eugenio Montale, *Lettere a Clizia* (Milan: Mondadori, 2006), 96–7. I am grateful to Franca Pellegrini for bringing this to my attention.

35 On Mondadori's loan see Decleva, *Mondadori*, 207. Book production peaked in 1932 with 12,550 units, followed by 12,442 in 1933. The following year saw a fall of about 10 per cent to 11,431, after which figures progressively diminished to 10,293 in 1940. Chicco's study was published in four issues of the journal *Graphicus*: Francesco Chicco, 'Indagine statistica sulla produzione editoriale italiana fra il 1886 ed il 1960,' *Graphicus*, no. 10 (October 1964): 5–9; no. 12 (December 1943): 5–6; no. 1 (January 1965): 5–13; no. 3 (March 1965): 5–17.

36 On Ceschina see the letters dated 8 March 1934 and 19 December 1934 in ACS, SPD CO, f. 204.478. On Bemporad see Adolfo Scotto di Luzio, 'Gli editori sono figlioli di famiglia: Fascismo e circolazione del libro negli anni trenta,' *Studi storici* 3 (1995): 5–6. As far as Florentine publishers are concerned, one should also bear in mind the pervasive presence of the Fascist philosopher Giovanni Gentile, who, in the early 1930s, became involved in the administration and ownership of Sansoni, Bemporad, and Le Monnier (see Tranfaglia and Vittoria, *Storia degli editori italiani*, 263–80).

37 The plan was successfully submitted to Mussolini on 8 May 1935 (documents in ACS, SPD CO, f. 500.007).

38 The correspondence between Zavattini to Bernari can be found in A900, 'Corrispondenza,' f. 27; see also Cesare Zavattini, *Una, cento, mille lettere* (Milan: Bompiani, 1988), 37–8. Bernari's reconstruction of the events can be found in 'Postfazione,' in *Tre operai* (Milan: Mondadori, 1965), 237–59; Filippo Accrocca, ed., *Ritratti su misura di scrittori italiani* (Venice: Sodalizio del libro, 1960), 67; and Eugenio Ragni, 'Intervista a Carlo Bernari,' *Quaderni d'italianistica* 13.2 (1992): 283.

39 Galeazzo Ciano, *Diario, 1937–1943* (Milan: Rizzoli, 1990), 86.

40 For a detailed description of Goebbels's seven departments see Welch, *Third Reich*, 23–6. On the composition of the Italian Ministry for Press and Propaganda see Ferrara, *L'amministrazione centrale pubblica*, 60–3, and ACS, SPD CO, f. 500.007.

41 On the development of the Direzione Generale per la Stampa Italiana, see Bruno Maida, 'La Direzione generale della stampa italiana,' *La stampa del regime, 1932–1943*, ed. Nicola Tranfaglia (Milan: Bompiani, 2005), 29–56.

42 See Decleva, *Mondadori*, 210–16. In 1929, as we saw in chapter 2, Mussolini had also refused Mondadori permission to publish an Italian edition of his autobiography. Mussolini's son, Vittorio, on the other hand, published his own memoirs of the Ethiopian campaign with the Florentine publisher Sansoni (*Vittoria sulla Ambe*, 1937). This is consistent with Mussolini's refusal to allow Mondadori too privileged a relationship with his family and the regime.

43 See Scotto di Luzio, 'Gli editori sono figliuoli di famiglia,' 7–12. For all other cases see AFM, FAM, b. 66.

44 The letter from Mondadori, addressed to Mussolini's secretary and dated 14 November 1935, can be found in ACS, SPD CO, f. 509.568/2. Mondadori's estimate proved to be extremely optimistic. He had calculated a potential total of 189,500 kilograms of gold. In reality the government managed to collect only 36,895 kilograms (figures in De Felice, *Mussolini il duce*, 627).

45 For Alfieri's memo of November 1935 see Tranfaglia, ed., *La stampa del regime*, 178 and Scarpellini, *Organizzazione teatrale*, 186–8. The episode concerning 'Bandiere al vento' is recalled in Cesari, *La censura nel periodo fascista*, 72, and Murialdi, 'La stampa quotidiana del regime fascista,' 184. See also a letter by Alfieri to Galeazzo Ciano, dated 30 November 1935, about the length of the daily meeting between Mussolini and Alfieri (ACS, MCP, b. 8, f. 31 'S.E. Alfieri').

46 On Alfieri see for example Celso Luciano, *Rapporto al Duce* (Rome: Editrice Giornale Mezzogiorno, 1948), 5 and Navarra, *Memorie del cameriere di Mussolini*, 137.

47 Copy of the circular, sent to all prefects on 18 December 1936, can be found in ACS, DGPS DAGR, Massime S 4, b. S4/A (provv.), f. 1 sf, 2. On this see also Fabre's considerations in *L'elenco*, 28–31.

48 It is also interesting to note the language used at a meeting of an inter-ministe-
rial committee set up in June 1936 to clarify the procedures to be followed by
all publishers when submitting a book. The committee decided that publishers had to submit seven copies, two of which went to the National Libraries in
Rome and Florence, two to the relevant provincial library and tribunal, and
three to the prefecture, as stated in April 1934. It is revealing that these last
three copies were defined as 'le tre copie necessarie per il controllo politico'
(the three copies that are necessary for political control). Minutes of the meeting of 12 June 1936, in ACS, DGPS DAGR, Massime S 4, b. S4/A (provv.), f. 1
sf. 2.

49 See Cannistraro, *La fabbrica del consenso*, 136–7. Another standoff concerned
the legislation on the deposit of books which in 1938 was abruptly passed on
from Bottai's ministry to Alfieri's Ministry of Popular Culture (see ACS, MPI
DGAB, b. 73, f. 'Leggi,' and, for a detailed reconstruction, Fabre, *L'elenco*,
60–2).

50 Entry dated 30 January 1936, in Giuseppe Bottai, *Diario, 1935–1944* (Milan:
Rizzoli, 1989), 85–6, 495.

51 See Adolfo Scotto di Luzio, *L'appropriazione imperfetta: Editori, biblioteche e libri
per ragazzi durante il fascismo* (Bologna: Il Mulino, 1996), 56–7.

52 See letter dated 6 August 1936, in GRL, Bontempelli Papers, box 8.

53 On *Quadrivio* see the 'Appunto per il Duce', dated 4 January 1936. As for
Brancati, on 7 December 1936 the request was passed on to Mussolini, who
agreed to award him a grant of 2,300 lire. Both documents contain Mussolini's handwritten approval (in ACS, MCP II, b. 2, f. 'Brancati Vitaliano').
The book was published by Bompiani in 1941 with the title *Società, lingua e
letteratura d'Italia*. The *nulla osta* to its publication, dated 12 July 1941, can be
found in ASMi, GP II, b. 153 'Bompiani Valentino casa editrice.'

54 A copy of the list can be found in ACS, DGPS DAGR, Massime S 4, b. S4/A
(provv.), f. 6 'Elenco delle stampe sequestrate.'

55 As we have seen, in 1926 two of his novels, *La cintura di castità* (1921) and
Oltraggio al pudore (1922), had been denounced as immoral by the Turin
League for Public Morality (Lega per la pubblica moralità). The case
reached court, but the judge found no grounds for proceeding against the
author. Moreover, in 1928 Pitigrilli had been accused of having insulted
Mussolini in private; again the legal case ended in Pitigrilli's favour. According to Pitigrilli's biographer, Enzo Magrì, the ban in 1936 was instigated
directly by Mussolini, who was unaware that Pitigrilli was a police informer.
Magrì adds that another novel by Pitigrilli, *L'esperimento di Pott* (1929), was
banned in the same year. For both events, however, no reference to factual
evidence is provided. Magrì, *Un italiano vero*, 164–76. On Pitigrilli as a police

informer see also Franzinelli, *I tentacoli dell'OVRA*, 283–91. See also Domenica Zucaro, ed., *Lettere all'Ovra di Pitigrilli* (Florence: Parenti, 1961).

56 In a letter to Vallecchi, dated 26 May 1937, Malaparte informed his publisher that he was sending the manuscript himself (ACGV, Fondo Vallecchi).

57 Quoted in Cannistraro, *La fabbrica del consenso*, 130.

58 The other abbreviation, *Minculpop*, often adopted by postwar historians and journalists despite its scurrilous connotation ('cul' meaning 'bum'; 'mincul' suggesting sodomy), was understandably never adopted in official documents or by the press. According to a memo addressed to the government Press Agency, Agenzia Stefani, the order to change the name of the ministry came from Mussolini, who phoned Alfieri on 26 May from his home city, Forlì (ACS, SPD CO, 500.007).

59 All documents can be found in ACS, MCP, b. 95, f. 424.

60 This is indirectly confirmed by some correspondence between the MCP and the prefecture of Milan in March 1939. It shows that the prefecture used to send a simple list of earmarked books, which did not contain a reader's report or a brief outline of the reasons why the prefecture thought those publications should be examined by the ministry. In fact, all copies of readers' reports that are attached to the paperwork come from officials working at the MCP. A similar procedure was adopted by Italian embassies, or at least by the embassy in Paris, which in 1939 sent to Italy copies of newly published books concerning Italy to be examined by the MCP. Documents in ASDAE, MCP, b. 292, f. 'Controllo importazioni.'

61 Circular by Alfieri to all prefects, dated 26 March 1938; note by Casini to Alfieri, dated 14 June 1938; minutes of the meeting of 29 July 1938; note from Alfieri to Mussolini, dated 22 August 1938; memo from Guido Rocco (head of the Directorate General of Foreign Press) to the head of personnel at the MCP, dated 31 October 1838; all documents in ASDMAE, MCP, b. 292, f. 'Controllo importazioni.'

62 The first circular, dated 19 May 1938, was sent to the General Directorate of Italian Press and to the General Directorate of Foreign Press (in ASMAE, MCP, b. 292, f. 'Controllo importazioni'); the second one, dated 25 October 1938, was sent to all prefects and did not specify which prefectures has been lacking in efficiency (in ACS, DGPS DAGR, Massime S 4, b. S4/A [provv.], f. 1 sf. 5).

63 See his articles published in *Giornale della libreria* of 5 June 1937 and 15 January 1938; both are quoted in Gigli Marchetti, *Le edizioni Corbaccio*, 70.

64 On this see Tranfaglia and Vittoria, *Storia degli editori italiani*, 246–8.

65 Figures are taken from Ferrara, 'La voce del padrone,' 60.

66 Ibid., 59.

67 Guido Milanesi was given, with Mussolini's approval, the directorship of
Rome's Museo Napoleonico on 19 February 1937, and, later, on 22 February
1939, 30,000 lire to write a nationalist novel set in Corsica (ACS, MCP, b. 228,
f. 'Milanesi Guido'). Arnaldo Frateili was openly supported by the MCP which,
on the eve of the publication of his travel book *Polonia frontiera d'Europa*,
instructed all newspapers to review the book in a positive light (memo dated
1 March 1938, in ACS, MCP II, b. 11, f. 'Popolo d'Italia'). The following year
Frateili won the Viareggio Prize for his novel *Clara fra i lupi*. Gianna Manzini
began to receive MCP's financial help in July 1937 (3,000 lire), and the grants
continued on an irregular basis, sometimes prompted by Enrico Falqui's
request, until March 1943 (ACS, SPD CO, f. 534.645, ACS, MCP, b. 258 and b.
271, ff. 'Sussidi'); Stanis Ruinas received 20,000 lire for the publication of his
travel book *Viaggio nelle città di Mussolini* (1939), again published by Bompiani
(ACS, MCP II, b. 11, f. 'Ruinas Stanis').
68 Alessandro Bonsanti received 5,000 lire in February 1938, was allowed to
meet Mussolini on 7 December of the same year, and subsequently received
another two grants in February (5,000 lire) and October (3,000 lire) 1939;
documents in ACS, MCP, b. 271, f. 'Sussidi.' On Carabba see the entire file
in ACS, SPD CO, f. 515–615; the book order was drawn in June 1937. The
original signed version of Mussolini's telegram of 1 December 1939 can be
found in ACS, SPD, Autografi del Duce, box 16, f. 17.
69 The two indexes can be found in ACS, MCP, b. 36, f. 'Rapporti al Duce.'
Using the scarce information in the report, I have been unable to find a
French publication on Napoleonic Rome by a Madeleine either among the
index of the Italian National Library or in the French National Library or
the French national Sudoc catalogue.
70 On Croce's book see Fabre, *L'elenco*, 164–5. Zurlo's memoirs, referring to the
play *Impresa trasporti* by Umberto Morucchio, performed in Rome in March
1937, are in his *Memorie inutili*, 29–30. As for theatre censorship, a delegation
of playwrights from an official Fascist trade union group representing
'Autori Drammatici' asked to meet Alfieri in May 1938. The reason was to
express their frustration with regard to the unclear parameters used by the
MCP to censor their work. The meeting took place on 31 May 1938, with
Massimo Bontempelli among the thirty-two delegates. Unfortunately no
archival documentation is available with regard to the minutes of the meeting or to the minister's reply. See ACS, MCP, b. 138, f. 'Autori, riunione.' On
this see also Ferrara, *Censura teatrale e fascismo*, 49–50.
71 Documents in ACS, SPD CO, f. 513.379, also mentioned in Fabre, *L'elenco*,
31.
72 Documents in ACS, SPD CO, f. 515.615.

73 De Begnac, *Taccuini mussoliniani*, 419.
74 On De Begnac's volume see Francesco Perfetti's 'Introduzione,' ibid., 19–21.
75 In his diary, Bottai suggests that Tacchi Venturi's influence extended to the appointment of officials within the PNF. See his entry for 23 September 1938 (*Diario, 1935–44*, 135).
76 All reports in ACS, PP M, f. 'Ufficio Stampa Capo del Governo.'
77 With regard to Alfieri's friendly relationship with Father Tacchi Venturi, it is interesting to note that, in his published memoirs related to his years as ambassador (1939–43), Alfieri dwells on two telelegrams of congratulations that he received. One of them was from Padre Tacchi Venturi, who hailed Alfieri's appointment as ambassador at the Vatican with the following words: 'Veni, vidi, vici.' In Dino Alfieri, *Due dittatori di fronte* (Milan: Rizzoli, 1948), 12.
78 On the internal front of Vatican censorship, it seems that Father Tacchi Venturi had tried to avoid the 'messa all'Indice' of Gentile's work. See Guido Zapponi, 'La condanna all'Indice delle opere di G. Gentile e di B. Croce nei ricordi di Rodolfo de Mattei,' *Storia contemporanea* 17.4 (1986): 715–19.

5. Shaping Italian Literature

1 Letter from Bompiani dated 15 December 1931; reply from Mussolini dated 23 December 1931; copy of documents in ACS, SPD CO, f. 509.109/1 and ASMi, PG II, b. 153, f. 'Bompiani Valentino casa editrice.' Morello's study was published in 1932.
2 At the end of a later meeting Bompiani was promised a signed photograph of Il Duce, and after a couple of reminders he eventually received it on 19 November 1938. In his letter of acknowledgment, Bompiani thanked Mussolini, saying the 'l'ambitissimo dono' (this most desired gift) had filled him with profound gratitude (documents in ACS, SPD CO, f. 509.109/1). A sign of Mussolini's benevolence towards Bompiani can also be found in one of his anonymous editorials published on the front page of *Il Popolo d'Italia*. The editorial, entitled 'Un libro,' appeard on 3 February 1937. It was a positive review of Joseph Bernhard's history of the Vatican (*Il Vaticano potenza mondiale*), and, more importantly, it contained a number of complimentary remarks about Bompiani's acumen as a publisher. For a copy of the article see *Opera Omnia*, 28: 114–15. Not all publishers were personally received. Some months later Aldo Garzanti, who had recently taken over the Milan publisher Treves (sold as a consequence of the anti-Semitic legislation), was less fortunate. Because he was not a member of the National Fascist Party he was refused a meeting with Mussolini in January 1939 (see documents in ACS, SPD CO, f. 509.257). For more on Garzanti see chapter 7 below.

3 Letter from Bompiani, dated 14 July 1933, in ACS, SPD CO, f. 509.109/1. Around the same time, Bompiani had contacted the head of Mussolini's press office, Gaetano Polverelli, to enquire whether the publication of a study of the Jews in Nazi Germany by journalist Andrea da Silva was advisable. On 12 June 1933 Gaetano Polverelli instructed the prefect of Milan to inform Valentino Bompiani 'verbally' and 'confidentially' that such publication was not considered advisable. Bompiani followed the advice. Documents in ASMi, PG II, b. 153, f. 'Bompiani Valentino casa editrice'; see also Fabre, *L'elenco*, 41. According to Fabre, Andrea da Silva was a Brazilian journalist who was subsequently extradited from Germany in August 1935.
4 For a detailed analysis of this episode see Fabre, *Il contratto*.
5 On Bompiani's partial reconstruction of the events see ibid., 137–9.
6 On 'Libri scelti' see Irene Piazzoni, 'Una collana militante nell'Italia Fascista: "Libri scelti" di Bompiani,' *La Fabbrica del Libro* 9.1 (2005): 19–26.
7 Memo from Casini to the prefecture of Milan, in ASMi, PG II, b. 153, f. 044 'Bompiani Valentino casa editrice.' The file contains a copy of the poster.
8 Lucia Re, 'Women and Censorship in Fascist Italy: from Mura to Paola Masino,' in Bonsaver and Gordon, *Culture, Censorship and the State*, 71.
9 Copy of the correspondence between Masino and Bompiani can be found in both A900, Fondo Masino, and AB, f. 'Masino Paola'; see in particular the letters from Bompiani dated 7 and 10 March and 25 and 28 April 1933. Some of the sentences that Bompiani highlighted as needing modification were: 'Mi piacerebbe tanto avere un marito morto e tutto il giorno ricevere insulti che spezzano il cuore' (I would love to have a dead husband and every day receive heart-breaking insults); 'alla nostra età si deve somigliare a bambini morti' (at our age we have to look like dead children); 'Io sono contento che ci sia l'inferno perché mamma mia ci va di sicuro' (I'm pleased there is hell because my mum is certainly going to end up there); 'la mia mamma sarebbe felice di trovare una scusa così bella per farmi ammazzare' (my mum would love to find such a brilliant excuse for killing me (all taken from the letter dated 3 March 1933).
10 Carlo Emilio Gadda, 'Monte ignoso,' *Solaria* 7–8 (July-August 1931).
11 Marcello Gallian, 'Paolo Masino: "Periferia," *L'Impero*, 10 June 1933; G.N. Serventi, 'Paola Masino: Periferia,' *Il Secolo Fascista*, 15 August 1933; Leandro Gellona, 'Da un romanzo sballato e premiato ai vari angoli morti letterari,' *Provincia di Vercelli*, 29 August 1933; P.M. Bardi, *Bibliografia Fascista*, 9 (September 1933): 704–5 Luigi Chiarini, 'Periferia,' *Quadrivio*, 17 September 1933. All reviews are collected in A900, Fondo Masino.
12 The content of the telegram was quoted by the newspaper *Il Popolo biellese* on 7 September 1933 (copy in A900, Fondo Masino).

13 See Re, 'Women and Censorship in Fascist Italy,' 71; Beatrice Manetti, 'Biografia,' in *Paolo Masino*, ed. Francesca Bernardini Napoletano and Marinella Mascia Galateria (Milan: Fondazione Arnoldo e Alberto Mondadori, 2001), 38–63; and Decleva, *Mondadori*, 239. Masino's books, however, were unaffected, as is indirectly proven by the fact that in March 1939 Bompiani could advertise *Monte Ignoso* and *Periferia* as both having reached their second reprint. The publicity appears on the dust jacket of Corrado Alvaro's third reprint of *L'uomo è forte* (Bompiani, 1939).

14 See Bompiani's letter, undated but written in June 1941, in A900, Fondo Masino. See also Manetti, 'Biografia,' 74–6.

15 Romano Bilenchi, 'Il soldato postumo,' *Il Popolo d'Italia*, 20 August 1935, 3. Bilenchi and Gallian knew each other well. A letter from Bilenchi, dated 1 May 1934, reveals that the two had met in Florence on the occasion of the performance of Blasetti's experiment of mass theatre, *18 BL*.

16 Galeazzo Ciano, moreover, was already in contact with Gallian at the time, as suggested by a brief letter dated 18 December 1935, in which Ciano thanked Gallian for keeping him informed of an unmentioned case, presumably the publication of the novel (FP, CG, f. 'Ciano Galeazzo'). Rinaldo Galanti's letter dated 17 January 1936 is in FP, CG, f. 'Galanti Rinaldo.'

17 The internal note can be found in ASMi, PG II, b. 153, f. 044 'Bompiani Valentino casa editrice,' See also Buchignani, *Marcello Gallian*, 49–74 and 96–7. There is no explicit indication that the change of title was imposed by the censors. However, a letter to Gallian by Panorama's editor, Gianni Mazzocchi, dated 15 September 1936, states that, at the last minute, the entire book had been reprinted (instead of making use of the seized copies, which had been returned) in order to obliterate every trace of the old title and to avoid possible 'noie' (problems) (letter in FP CG, f. 'Mazzocchi Gianni'). Copies of both the 1935 and 1936 version of *Bassofondo / In fondo al quartiere* can be consulted at BN, FF. A new and short-lived publishing arm of Milan's Editoriale Domus, Panorama concentrated on the work of contemporary Italian writers such as Gianna Manzini, Massimo Bontempelli, Enrico Falqui, Emilio Cecchi, and Indro Montanelli. The correspondence of Gallian with its directors, Rinaldo Galante and Gianni Mazzocchi, suggests that initially Gallian was also given the role of editor. He also published a collection of short stories for Panorama, *Racconti Fascisti*, in 1937. The correspondence at FP between Gallian and Galante suggests that Panorama tried and managed to obtain orders of the book from Alfieri's Ministry of Press and Propaganda but failed with respect of Bottai's Ministry of National Education. A copy of *Racconti-fascisti* can be found in Gallian's private library now at FP. It contains handwritten notes by Gallian that indicate that in the postwar years he might have planned a new edition with a

more neutral title, *Racconti*, with its preface cleansed of all the references to Gallian's radical Fascism. As for Valentino Bompiani, I have been unable to find any documentantion explaining the reason behind his involvement in *Bassofondo*, a book that was being published by Panorama. Considering that in the same year Bompiani was publishing Gallian's *Il soldato postumo* and in March 1936 Valentino Bompiani was in contact with Gallian regarding the publication of *Tre generazioni*, which he eventually declined, there is the possibility that the publisher might have been asked for help, given his contacts at the Ministry of Press and Propaganda. Indeed, in a short letter to Gallian, dated 7 March 1936, Bompiani mentioned that while in Rome he had heard of Gallian's illness and asked if he could do anything to help (copy of the letter at both AB, f. 'Gallian Marcello,' and FP, CG, f. 'Bompiani Valentino'). Bompiani's publication of *Il soldato postumo*, on the other hand, took place with no intervention of the censorship authorities. Gallian's correspondence with Attilio Vallecchi also shows that in November 1937 Casini wrote directly to Vallecchi to support the publication of Gallian's *Combatteva un uomo*, which was eventually published in 1939 (FP, CG, 17 and 19 November 1937).

18 Letter by Vallecchi to Gallian in FP, CG, f. 'Vallecchi Attilio.'

19 Mussolini, however, never agreed to accept Gallian's request for permanent employment within a ministry or as a journalist for *Il Popolo d'Italia* (documents in ACS, SPD CO, f. 510.601 'Gallian Marcello'). Gallian's file with the Political Police also reveals that he was arrested in Rome on 31 July 1934 by the *Carabinieri*, accused of drunken behaviour and insults to public officials; immediately released, he was declared innocent at the end of court proceedings on 15 February 1935 (documents in ACS, PP FP, f. 'Gallian Marcello'). Gallian's correspondence with the chief editor of *Corriere della Sera*, Aldo Borelli, shows that throughout the mid-1930s he was asked by Borelli to tone down and self-censor his articles for the Milan paper. (See, for example, the letters dated 20 June 1934, 2 October 1934, and 25 April 1935; in FP, CG. I am greatful to Paola Villa for bringing this to my attention.) Finally, it should be noted that Gallian received some financial help during the postwar years too. As his correspondence shows, the Federazione Nazionale della Stampa Italiana granted Gallian a sum from its Fondo Assistenza of 10,000 lire on 14 November 1958, 15,000 lire on 20 December 1958, and 10,000 on November 1959 (documents in FP, CG, f. 'Azzarita Leonardo').

20 In 1935 Alvaro had also written a propaganda book about the land reclamation projects, *Terra nuova*, published by Giovanni Gentile's Istituto Nazionale Fascista di Cultura.

21 Letter from the MCP to the prefect of Milan, dated 13 May 1938, in ASMi, PG, b. 153, f. 044 'Bompiani Valentino casa editrice.' In a letter from Alvaro to

Bompiani, dated 6 May 1938, it appears that Alvaro was going to meet Casini to discuss the cover and publicity poster illustration for the novel. In the letter it also appears that Alvaro was still making changes to the novel following Bompiani's suggestions. Letter in D'Ina and Zaccaria, *Caro Bompiani*, 294–5. No letter specifying the content of Bompiani's suggestions could be found. On the relationship between Alvaro and Valentino Bompiani before and after the Second World War see Giuseppe Zaccaria, 'Bompiani e Alvaro: un "rapporto esemplare,"' in Braida, *Valentino Bompiani*, 122–43.

22 Alvaro, 'Avvertenza' to the 1974 edition of *L'uomo è forte*, published by Bompiani. In this prefatory note Alvaro also stated that the changes imposed by · the Fascist censors were not reinstated at a later stage because they were 'without importance.' The collection of Alvaro's articles on Russia had been published under the title *I maestri del diluvio: Viaggio nella Russia sovietica* (Milan: Mondadori, 1935) and reprinted in 1943. Bompiani's letter of 4 May and Alvaro's replies of 11 and 13 May 1938 can be found in AB, f. 'Alvaro Corrado.' For an analysis of the parallels between the *L'uomo è forte* and *I maestri del diluvio*, see Rocco Paternostro, *Corrado Alvaro: 'L'uomo è forte,' ovvero la poetica della colpa-espiazione* (Rome: Bulzoni, 1980), 47–62.

23 Bompiani's 16 December 1940 letter to Alessandro Pavolini concerning the translations of *L'uomo è forte* can be found in ACS, SPD CO, f. 511.102. On Corrado Alvaro and the reception of *L'uomo è forte*, see Ben-Ghiat, *Fascist Modernities*, 143–7 and 187–8. Mention should be made of Bottai's very critical comment in his postwar diary, in which he attacked Alvaro for his ambiguous position during and after the Fascist period; see the entry for 25 May 1946, in Giuseppe Bottai, *Diario, 1944–1948* (Milan: Rizzoli, 1982), 367–8. See also the polemical study by Communist MP and journalist Enzo Misefari, who interprets *L'uomo è forte* as a hypocritical homage to the anti-Bolshevism of the Fascist regime. Enzo Misefari, *Alvaro politico: Analisi di un comportamento* (Soveria: Rubbettino, 1981), 110–15.

24 Documents in ASMi, PG II, b. 153, f. 044 'Bompiani Valentino casa editrice.'

25 Mangoni, *Pensare i libri*, 3–17. A good example in this respect is Ginzburg's decision in 1934 to publish Antonio Labriola's essays *Bolscevismo e capitalismo* in competition with a similar edition sponsored by Giuseppe Bottai (see Mangoni, *Pensare i libri*, 9). Ginzburg was also behind the editing of the series *Biblioteca di cultura storica*, which attempted to offer an original inter- · pretation of Italian history with non-Fascist studies such as Luigi Salvatorelli's *Il pensiero politico italiano dal 1700 al 1870*, published in 1935 (see Turi, *Casa Einaudi*, 75–8).

26 Natalia Ginzburg, 'Memoria contro memoria,' *Paragone* 462 (August 1988): 3–9. Ginzburg was referring to Giulio Einaudi's memoirs: *Frammenti di memoria*

(Milan: Rizzoli, 1988), which had been recently published. See in particular her comment: 'Leggendo il suo libro, non si capisce come questa casa editrice sia venuta al mondo' (From his book it is difficult to understand how this publishing house could have come to exist).

27 With regard to the arrest of Roberto Einaudi, see the letter to Mussolini by the prefect of Turin, dated 29 March 1929, in ACS, SPD CR, b. 74, f. H/R 'Einaudi Luigi.' At the National Archives at Kew there are four letters by Luigi Einaudi and a copy of Mussolini's telegram, dated 5 April 1929, ordering the prefect of Turin to release Roberto Einaudi immediately (NAKe, GMF 36/299).

28 Unsigned letter, dated 9 March 1934, in ACS, SPD CR, b. 74, f. H/R 'Einaudi Luigi'; also published in Giuseppe Carlo Marino, *L'autarchia della cultura: Intellettuali e fascismo negli anni trenta* (Rome: Editori Riuniti, 1983), 220, and quoted in De Felice, *Mussolini il duce*, 115. Bottai's quote is taken from the article, 'Appelli all'uomo,' *Critica Fascista* 12 (1934): 4, quoted also in Turi, *Casa Einaudi*, 24.

29 Document in ACS, SPD CO, f. 528.771.

30 Documents in ACS, SPD CR, b. 70, f. 438/R, and SPD CO, f. 528.771; AE, b. Ruini and NAKe. GMF 36/299. See also Mangoni, *Pensare i libri*, 19; Turi, *Casa Einaudi*, 85. Another minor but nonetheless indicative sign of Einaudi's fragile position relates to a book by Henry Wallace that Giulio Einaudi had sent as a gift to Mussolini in March 1935. In this situation, publishers would normally receive a note of thanks from Mussolini's secreterial office. However, in this particular case the book was forwarded to Neos Dinale, then general director of the Undersecretary for Press and Propaganda, who returned it two days later with a note suggesting that no note of thanks should be sent to the publisher (letter dated 19 March 1935, in ACS, SPD CO, f. 528.771).

31 See Turi, *Casa Einaudi*, 69–71. The police raid of May 1935 hit another small Turin publisher, Frassinelli. The arrest and subsequent *confino* of its editorial director, Franco Antonicelli, caused the folding of the groundbreaking series, *Biblioteca europea*. On this see Albertina Vittoria, '"Mettersi al corrente con i tempi": Letteratura straniera ed editoria minore,' in Gigli Marchetti and Finocchi, *Stampa e piccola editoria tra le due guerre*, 215–17).

32 Mangoni, *Pensare i libri*, 25–7.

33 Cesare Pavese, *Lettere, 1924–1944* (Turin: Einaudi, 1965), 527, quoted in Mangoni, *Pensare i libri*, 21.

34 In a letter to Giulio Einaudi, dated 2 February 1937, General Bollati informed him that an anonymous review of his encyclopedia in *Il Popolo d'Italia* had been written by Mussolini himself. On this see Mangoni, *Pensare i*

libri, 19–21. The catalogue that celebrated fifty years of Einaudi's activity is *Cinquant'anni di un editore: Le edizioni Einaudi negli anni, 1933–1983* (Turin: Einaudi, 1983). On this see Turi, *Casa Einaudi*, 86.

35 Alessandro Pavolini was also the director of the first meeting of the inter-university competition *Littoriali della cultura*, which took place in Florence in 1934. Bilenchi, together with Bontempelli and Cecchi, sat on the committee of judges for *Narrativa* (reference to this can be found in a letter by Bilenchi to Enrico Falqui, undated, in A900, Carte Falqui). On Florence during the Fascist years see: Andrea Binazzi and Ivo Guasti, eds., *La Toscana nel regime Fascista* (Florence: Olschky, 1971); Marco Palla, *Firenze nel regime Fascista, 1929–1934* (Florence: Olschki, 1978); Luti, *Firenze corpo 8*; and Paolo Buchignani, 'Il caso "Montale Vieusseux" e Marcello Gallian,' *Nuova Storia Contemporanea* 2 (2002): 133–50.

36 On *Il Bargello* see Anna Panicali, 'Sulla collaborazione al *Bargello*,' *Il Ponte* 7–8 (1973): 955–70, and Peter Hainsworth, 'Florentine Cultural Journalism under Fascism: *Il Bargello*,' *Modern Language Review* 953 (2000): 696–711. The discussion of Vittorini in this section owes much to an article of mine, 'Fascist Censorship on Literature and the Case of Elio Vittorini,' *Modern Italy* 8.1 (2003): 165–86.

37 Carocci's letter, dated 14 August 1934, can be found in Guido Manacorda, ed., *Lettere a Solaria* (Rome: Editori Riuniti, 1979), 524. The letter by Vittorini, dated 16 August 1934, can be found in Carlo Minoia, ed., *Elio Vittorini: I libri, le città, il mondo. Lettere, 1933–1943* (Turin: Einaudi, 1985), 39.

38 The decree spoke of 'espressioni licenziose riportate in varie pagine, e per il loro contenuto in genere sono contrari alla morale e al buon costume' (licentious expressions to be found in various pages, whose content is generally offensive to public morality); in *Solaria* 4 (1934), quoted in Anna Panicali, *Elio Vittorini* (Milan: Mursia, 1994), 113.

39 Minoia, *Elio Vittorini*, 53.

40 The prize is mentioned by Vittorini in a letter to the prefecture of Florence, dated 6 October 1936, in ACS, PP FP, f. 'Elio Vittorini.'

41 The cuts are visible in the form of nine sections of dotted lines for a total of forty lines (see figure 11). A more detailed analysis can be found in Raffaella Rodondi, *Il presente vince sempre* (Palermo: Sellerio, 1985) 13–86; Greco, *Scrittura e censura*, 99–132; and Panicali, *Elio Vittorini*, 109–29.

42 Greco, *Censura e scrittura*, 101–2.

43 In his memoirs Silvio Guarnieri, a contributor to *Solaria* and a close friend of Vittorini and Bonsanti, attributed the closure of *Solaria* to the internal divisions among its editors, particularly between the literary interests of Bonsanti and the political mindset of Carocci. See Silvio Guarnieri, *L'ultimo*

testimone (Milan: Mondadori, 1989), 266–8. After the closure of *Solaria*, Carocci was to found a new journal, *La Riforma letteraria*, together with Giacomo Noventa. As Guarnieri remembers, the first issue contained an article by Giuseppe Bottai, which is a clear indication that the journal had the support of the then minister of national education. It should be noted that an anonymous memo dated 1 April 1933 and produced within the Press Office suggests that in those months the office had increased its activity related to 'vigilanza dei periodici che ignorano il Regime' (control of periodicals that ignore the Regime). Within this context, it is possible that *Solaria* might have been identified as such a periodical. However, a link between this memo and *Solaria*'s problems the following year remains to be substantiated. A copy of the memo can be found in ACS, MCP, b. 13, f. 180; it is reproduced in Gregory, Fattori, and Siciliani, eds., *Filosofi università regime*, 215.

44 'Censura letteraria' appeared in *Il Bargello* on 23 July 1934, 3; it is reprinted in Raffaella Rodondi, ed., *Elio Vittorini: Letteratura, arte e società. Articoli e interventi, 1926–1937* (Turin: Einaudi, 1997), 793–5.

45 A more explicit case of political pressure being exerted on the editors of a Florentine periodical concerns Luigi Russo's *La Nuova Italia*. In the summer of 1931 Russo was identified as a 'Crociano' and attacked in the pages of *Il Bargello*. In order to save the journal and the publishing house from possible reprisals, Russo agreed to step down as chief editor. He was replaced by an editorial committee that included the orthodox Fascist intellectual Francesco Ercole (who was to become minister for national education in 1932). On this see Alessandro Piccioni, ed., *Una casa editrice tra società, cultura e scuola: La Nuova Italia, 1926–1986* (Florence: La Nuova Italia, 1986), 38–45.

46 Alessandro Bonsanti, 'Questo libro è timbrato "fragile,"' *Il Giorno*, 17 November 1971, 3.

47 The correspondence between Alberto Carocci and Pavese allows a reconstruction of this episode, although it contains no mention of the specific textual modifications. It begins with a letter of 7 March 1935 in which Carocci announces to Pavese that the prefecture of Florence has demanded a number of changes to the first proofs. In an attempt to bypass the prefecture, Carocci asked for the help of Adriano Grande, then undersecretary at the Ministry of Press and Propaganda. In his reply of 8 April 1935 Grande wrote that it was not possible to avoid the judgment of the prefecture of Florence. The correspondence continues until May 1936, when the book was published. On this see Manacorda, *Lettere a Solaria*, 568–609; Pavese's own letters are also published in Cesare Pavese, *Lettere, 1924–44*. According to the biographical entry in *Chi è?* of 1940, Achille Malavasi was born in Bologna in 1887, had a degree in philosophy from the University of Heidelberg, was

chief editor of *Il Resto del Carlino* from 1930 to 1933, and wrote short pamphlets on Emmanuel Kant (1924), Saint Francis of Assisi (1926), and San Francis and Savonarola as examples of 'religiosità italiana' (1927). He was also correspondent for *Il Popolo di Roma*, the Roman newspaper founded in 1925 from the ashes of the unsuccessful Roman edition of Mussolini's *Il Popolo d'Italia*. See *Chi è? Dizionario degli italiani d'oggi* (Rome: Cenacolo, 1940), 557–8. According to Paolo Murialdi, the appointment of Malavasi to the editorship of *Il Resto del Carlino* had been the result of a compromise between Mussolini and Arpinati, the Fascist leader in Bologna. The latter insisted on reinstating the old editor, Mario Missiroli, but Mussolini was strongly against this and would accept only the appointment of a less prominent journalist – but one still linked to Missiroli – which turned out to be Achille Malavasi. See Murialdi, 'La stampa quotidiana del regime Fascista,' 135–6.

48   Elio Vittorini, 'Propaganda e Stampa, dicastero dell'intelligenza Fascista,' *Il Bargello* 26 (30 June 1935): 1; reprinted Rodondi, *Elio Vittorini*, 874–5.

49   The correspondence can be found in ACS, PP FP, f. 'Elio Vittorini.' The episode is also recounted by Romano Bilenchi in his memoir 'Vittorini a Firenze,' in *Amici* (Turin: Einaudi, 1976); reprinted in Bilenchi, *Opere* (Milan: Bompiani, 1997), 799–800. The allegation that a waiter at the Giubbe Rosse café was a police informer comes from Silvio Guarnieri, *L'ultimo testimone*, 242, 273. This is also suggested in a detailed report by an Allied officer of the Psychological Warfare Branch, dated 9 October 1944, entitled 'Conditions in Tuscany' and containing a section: 'Information regarding the Florentine Caffè "Le Giubbe Rosse," Piazza Vittorio Emanuele,' reprinted in Roger Absalom, ed., *Gli alleati e la ricostruzione in Toscana (1944–1945): Documenti anglo-americani*, 3 vols. (Florence: Olschki, 1988), 1: 284.

50   ACS, PP FP, f. 'Elio Vittorini.' The letter by the Divisione Polizia Politica is dated 3 November 1938; presumably the Fascist police had acquired the papers some months after Rosselli's death.

51   Bonsanti, 'Questo libro è timbrato fragile,' 3.

52   The cut was noted by Raffella Rodondi in her notes to the Mondadori edition of Vittorini's narrative works (*Vittorini: Le opere narrative*, vol. 1 [Milan: Mondadori, 1974] 1203). That the cut was imposed by the censor is indirectly confirmed by a memo by Casini, then director of the DGSI at the MCP. Casini's memo was directed at Dino Alfieri and addressed Bonsanti's request for a grant in support of his journal *Letteratura* (as already mentioned in chapter 3). Casini's memo was positive in tone (it reminded the minister that Bonsanti was also a member of Ministerial Committee for the Regulation of Literary Prizes) but in its last paragraph it mentioned the fact that

the latest issue of *Letteratura* had been subjected to the intervention of the prefecture with regard to Vittorini's novel. Interestingly, despite this negative mention, Bonsanti continued to receive government grants to support his journal: 5,000 lire in February 1939 and 3,000 lire in January 1940. Bonsanti also met Mussolini on 7 December 1938. Documents in ACS, MCP, b. 271, f. 'Sussidi.'

53 Letters dated 14 March 1933, 27 March 1933, and 9 April 1946, in AFM, FAM, f. 'Vittorini.' A more detailed analysis of Vittorini's translating activity can be found in Gian Carlo Ferretti, *L'editore Vittorini* (Turin: Einaudi, 1992), 4–68, and in my article 'Vittorini's American Translations: Parallels, Borrowings and Betrayals,' *Italian Studies* 53 (1998): 67–93.

54 Letter dated 31 March 1940, in D'Ina and Zaccaria, eds., *Caro Bompiani*, 36.

55 Letter quoted in Buchignani, *Un fascismo impossibile*, 149. The book was eventually published as: Dino Garrone, *Lettele* (Florence: Vallecchi, 1938). On Dino Garrone see Anna Panicali, 'Appunti sul realismo degli anni Trenta: Dino Garrone,' *Angelus Novus* 23 (1972): 55–79.

56 It was not a total surrender. The irreverent reference to Malaparte, in a letter to Berto Ricci of 3 July 1929 (Garrone, Lettere, 171) was left untouched. Moreover, at the end of the book, the two editors added a brief *Avvertenza* in which they mentioned that, for reasons beyond their control, some letters had not been included in the book. However, all passages referring to Mussolini were highly positive, beginning with the mention that in December 1928 Garrone was planning to found a periodical, which was going to be entitled *M* in honour of Mussolini (ibid., 79). As for Mussolini's appreciation of Ricci's work, according to Pini's diary on 7 January 1939, Mussolini not only told Pini over the phone to compliment Ricci on his article but also enquired whether it was possible to employ Ricci at *Il Popolo d'Italia* on a permanent basis. Giorgio Pini, *Filo diretto con Palazzo Venezia* (Bologna: Cappelli, 1950), 187. Mussolini's conversation with Pini is also recounted by the latter in his unpublished memoirs in ACS, Carte Pini, b. 22. Ricci later volunteered to fight in the war and was killed on the African front in February 1941. After his death he was treated as a national hero; his wife received decorations and funds directly from Mussolini's office, and in March 1943 Vallecchi published a collection of Ricci's articles for *L'Universale.*

57 See Bilenchi's memoirs in 'I silenzi di Rosai,' in *Amici*, and *Opere*, 762–6. See also Buchignani, *Un fascismo impossibile*, 147–51 and 259–64 and the correspondence between Ricci and Pini in ACS, Carte Pini, b. 15.

58 Bilenchi's correspondence with Marcello Gallian also shows that, through the help of the latter, Bilenchi had tried to place *Il capofabbrica* with Interlandi's *Quadrivio.* Letter dated 4 May 1934, in FP CG, f. 'Bilenchi Romano.'

In this letter as well as in the subsequent one dated 14 May 1934, Bilenchi insisted that if *Il capofabbrica* were to be accepted he would expect to be allowed to modify the text slightly 'perché ci sono cose che non vanno' (because there are things that do not work).

59 The episode is remembered by Bilenchi in 'Nota dell'autore,' in *Il capofabbrica* (Milan: Rizzoli, 1991), 121–2, quoted in Bilenchi, *Opere*, 973–4. See also Paolo Buchignani, 'Da "Strapaese" a "L'Universale": Il fascismo rivoluzionario di Romano Bilenchi,' *Nuova storia contemporanea* 4 (2000): 76–7.

60 Letter from Bilenchi to Attilio Vallecchi, dated 10 February 1942, in ACGV, Corrispondenza Vallecchi. According to Bilenchi's memoirs, even the novel *Conservatorio di Santa Teresa* was published with some delays, in 1940, because the Florentine censor did not approve of the relationship between the young protagonist and his mother and aunt. Bilenchi does not specify whether the novel was subjected to any cuts. See the interview 'Bilenchi: Scrivendo sfuggivo al Fascismo,' *Corriere della Sera*, 23 October 1985, quoted in Bilenchi, *Opere*, 1011.

61 Letter from Bontempelli to Mussolini, dated 12 January 1927, in ACS, SPD CO, f. 209.230.

62 Letter from Ferretti to Bontempelli, dated 5 August 1930, in ACS, MCP, b. 4, 'Ufficio Stampa.' On 25 August 1930 Bontempelli forwarded a copy of the letter to Bompiani with suggestions on how to make use of it for future publicity material. Letter in AB, f. 'Bontempelli Massimo.'

63 Letter from Bontempelli to Mussolini, dated 15 October 1930, in ACS, SPD CO, f. 209.230. Bontempelli was nominated as an Accademico d'Italia on 29 October 1930.

64 In ACS, MCP, b. 4, f. 'Ufficio Stampa,' there are various instances of general correspondence addressed to Galeazzo Ciano. As for Alfieri, in one case he asked for and obtained Bontempelli's intervention regarding a literary polemic in March 1935. On this see Ruth Ben-Ghiat, *La cultura Fascista* (Bologna: Il Mulino, 2000), 33 (this particular note has been omitted in the English version of this study, *Fascist Modernities*).

65 Letter from Bontempelli to Alfieri, dated 14 May 1934, in ACS, SPD CO, f. 209.230.

66 Letter from Ciano's secretary to Bontempelli, dated 6 August 1936, in GRL, Bontempelli Papers, b. 8.

67 Both letters in AB, f. 'Bontempelli Massimo.'

68 Entry dated 1 February 1939, in Bottai, *Diario, 1935–44*, 140–1; documents in ACS, SPD CO, f. 209.230; ASMi, PG, b. 78. A few months later, when Bottai founded the journal *Primato*, he invited Bontempelli to collaborate in order to show publicly the editors' support for the chastized author. In his postwar

memoirs the Jewish jurist and historian Eucardio Momigliano offered
another version of the events: according to him, Bontempelli was disciplined
because of an exchange he had with Bottai during the reception following a
speech Bontempelli gave on D'Annunzio. Bontempelli apparently told Bottai he should be ashamed for signing the decree that expelled non-Fascist
academics from Italian universities. Starace took action when he heard of
Bontempelli's impertinence. Judging from Bottai's diary entry, and given the
fact that no mention of this episode is made in any memoirs or correspondence, including Bontempelli's, it is difficult to fully accept this version of
events. Bontempelli's partner, Paola Masino, recorded that after the speech
on D'Annunzio in November 1938, she and Bontempelli had had a long conversation with Bottai. On that occasion Bottai had offered Bontempelli
Attilio Momigliano's chair of Italian at Florence University (which
Momigliano had been forced to vacate following the anti-Semitic legislation). According to Masino, Bontempelli replied that he was going to consider the offer for the following year, although he subsequently declined it.
See Eucardio Momigliano, *Storia tragica e grottesca del razzismo Fascista* (Milan:
Mondadori, 1946), 133–4, and Paola Masino, *Io, Massimo e gli altri* (Milan:
Rusconi, 1995), 78–9.

69 Correspondence in ACS, SPD CO, f. 209.230.

70 Letter to Mussolini, dated 27 July 1939, in ibid. The news of his readmission
to the PNF reached Bontempelli through a letter from Luigi Federzoni
(then head of the Accademia d'Italia), who on 22 July 1939 congratulated
him for his readmission to the party; in another letter, loosely dated July
1939, Federzoni warned Bontempelli to adopt a more reserved and disciplined attitude in the future (both letters in GRL, Bontempelli Papers, b. 4;
my thanks to Ruth Ben-Ghiat for drawing these letters to my attention).

71 Letters from Alfieri to Bontempelli, dated 2 and 8 October 1939, in GRL,
Bontempelli Papers, b. 7. In his letter of 2 October, Alfieri informed Bontempelli that he had also withdrawn the order to seize his book of essays
Avventura novecentista published by Vallecchi in 1938. As for his expulsion
from the party, Bontempelli's readmission was sanctioned by a letter of the
party's deputy secretary, Vincenzo Zangara, dated 17 August 1939 (GRL,
Bontempelli Papers, b. 4).

72 Letters dated 9 October 1939 and 30 March 1940 (the second one from *Corriere della Sera's* chief editor to Bontempelli); both in GRL, Bontempelli
Papers, b. 12. The contract envisaged the payment of 1,300 lire for each article and 1,600 lire (raised to 2,000 two months later) for each short story.
Bontempelli's *Pirandello, Leopardi, D'Annunzio* must have also been 're-
accepted,' as on 15 October 1940 the chief editor of the Nazi periodical

Italien asked Bompiani to translate and publish a number of extracts from the book. This is mentioned in a letter by Valentino Bompiani to Bontempelli, dated 15 October 1940, in AB, f. 'Bontempelli Massimo.'

73 ACS, Carte Pini, b. 50, vol. 5 'Crinale,' 186. Among the approved collaborators were Cesare Zavattini and Alessandro Pavolini's brother, the literary critic Corrado Pavolini.

74 Bontempelli's position had been legally challenged with reference to the Electoral Bill of 5 February 1948, which specified that authors of school textbooks containing Fascist propaganda were not allowed to run for the Italian Senate for five years. Bontempelli had been the editor of an anthology of Italian literature for junior secondary school children, *Oggi* (Milan: Editrice Dante Alighieri, 1939), whose selections were aligned with Fascist propaganda. The most popular authors in the anthology were Gabriele D'Annunzio, Benito Mussolini, Corrado Alvaro, and Massimo Bontempelli: each had four pieces.

75 On Alpes see Tranfaglia and Vittoria, *Storia degli editori italiani*, 252–3. Before Moravia's novel, Alpes had published a number of literary works such as Federigo Tozzi's collection of essays *Realtà di ieri e oggi* (1928). In his conversation with Alain Elkann, Moravia mentioned the fact that Alpes' publication of his novel had been sponsored by his father with a subvention of 5,000 lire. See Alberto Moravia and Alain Elkann, *Vita di Moravia* (Milan: Bompiani, 1982), 39.

76 A positive review was published in *Il lavoro fascista* on 14 August 1929. It should be noted that Moravia's uncle was the director of this official Fascist journal and Gherardo Casini was its chief editor. *Il lavoro fascista* was the journal of the Fascist Trade Union of Professionals and Artists. In *Il Popolo d'Italia* of 25 September 1929 Margherita Sarfatti also published a positive review of *Gli indifferenti*. She noted the lack of moral strength on the part of the protagonists, but compared Moravia to masters of literature such as Balzac, Shakespeare, Manzoni, and Verga. See also Ben-Ghiat, *Fascist Modernities*, 55–7.

77 Alberto Moravia, 'Ricordi di censura,' *La Rassegna d'Italia*, December 1946, 95–106. In the article Moravia also mentions that Mussolini's brother, Arnaldo, had attacked his novel. This is somewhat surprising given the fact that, as we have just seen, Arnaldo was the owner of Moravia's first publishing house. Perhaps the attack, in whatever form, took place after Moravia had left Alpes for Corbaccio and then Bompiani.

78 For dall'Oglio see Gigli Marchetti, *Le edizioni Corbaccio*, 60; for Bompiani see Ben-Ghiat, *Fascist Modernities*, 57. A letter from Moravia to Arnoldo Mondadori, dated 22 July 1933, suggests that Mondadori was also involved in the attempt to print a new edition of *Gli indifferenti* (in AFM, FAM, f. Moravia). Accord-

ing to Ben-Ghiat, *Gli indifferenti* was actually published by Bompiani (*Fascist Modernities*, 57), but despite several searches I was unable to find either documentary or bibliographical evidence of this edition. There are three possible reasons behind this: (1) Bompiani was stopped from producing his edition because the copyright was held by dall'Oglio; (2) both publishers were unofficially told not to reprint the novel; or, (3) the least likely option, interest in the novel had diminished to the point that a third edition was no longer commercially viable. On Moravia and Bompiani see also Turchetta, 'Alberto Moravia diventa un autore Bompiani,' 86–121. Turchetta's interesting article, however, does not benefit from the archival material available at Milan's and Rome's Archivio di Stato.

79 De Begnac, *Taccuini Mussoliniani*, 483–4. Once more we have to mention the degree of unreliablity of this memoirs, which was collected thematically with no chronological reference to the time Mussolini made any particular statement.

80 Moravia's first entry in the police files is related to a trip to Paris in December 1929. His sister Adriana Pincherle, too, although under surveillance, was not directly accused of being a member of Giustizia e Libertà. Mussolini countersigned memos related to Moravia's request for the renewal of his passport in November 1937 and in December 1938. On this see Giorgio Fabre, 'Sul "Caso Moravia,"' *Quaderni di storia* 42 (1995): 181–96. The file of the Political Police on Moravia can be found in ACS, PP FP, f. 'Pincherle Alberto.' When I consulted the papers in April 2003, five documents had been 'scremati' (excluded from public access by the archive officer responsible because of their libellous content): these documents are dated 3 January 1930, 25 March 1934, and 1 January, 12 March, and 2 May 1935.

81 A copy of the article is kept in Moravia's file: ACS, PP FP, f. 'Pincherle Alberto.' On Mario Pensuti see Albonetti, *Non c'è tutto nei romanzi*, 49–50.

82 At the fall of the Fascist regime in July 1943, Bruno Fornaciari was to become minister of the interior in General Badoglio's first government. See Missori, *Governi, alte cariche dello stato*, 174.

83 Mussolini's involvement is suggested by a memo from the Political Police to Galeazzo Ciano, dated 12 January 1935. It mentioned 'orders from His Excellency the Head of Government' (see Fabre, *L'elenco*, 35).

84 Mention of discussions of Moravia's case among French intellectuals came from a police informer's report from Paris, dated 9 February 1935. Moravia's file also contained copy of a letter by Curzio Malaparte, dated 7 March 1935, discussing various options concerning the French translation of Moravia's books. Moreover, the article in Giustizia e Libertà had been cited by the Parisian newspaper *Le Figaro* on 10 February 1935 (and from there had bounced into the pages of *L'Italia che scrive* the following April).

85 Fabre, *L'elenco*, 37; see also his 'L'indifferente Moravia', *Panorama*, 28 November 1993, 142–50, and George Talbot, 'Alberto Moravia and Italian Fascism: Censorship, Racism and *Le ambizioni sbagliate*,' *Modern Italy* 11.2 (2006): 127–45. Ciano's *velina* of 2 March 1935 can be found in Francesco Flora, *Stampa dell'era Fascista: Le note di servizio* (Rome: Mondadori, 1945), 83; it is also reprinted in Brancati, *Ritorno alla censura*, 16. *Le ambizioni sbagliate* was published in French translation in 1937 and in English in 1938. For the correspondence between Mondadori and Moravia see AFM, FAM, f. 'Moravia.'

86 ACS, PP FP, f. 'Pincherle Alberto.'

87 The anonymous critical review, entitled 'Cronaca nera,' was published in *Ottobre* on 4 April 1935, 4. A positive review appeared anonymously in *L'Italia che scrive* (the journal of the publisher Formiggini), entitled 'Alberto Moravia. La bella vita,' 13 (April 1935): 89. A police informer's report, dated 20 January 1934, described Moravia's past collaboration with Fascist groups as instrumental to his ambitions and concluded 'che il Moravia non sia Fascista non è un mistero per nessuno' (that Moravia is not a Fascist is not a mystery to anybody); in ACS, MCP II, b. 8.

88 The letter by Casini to Moravia is dated 24 August 1935. All quoted documents are in ACS, MCP II, b. 8, f. 'Moravia Alberto.'

89 Letter by Bompiani to Casini, dated 24 November 1936; letter by Casini to Bompiani, dated 30 November 1936; both in ACS, MCP II, b. 8, f. 'Moravia Alberto.'

90 Moravia's request for a meeting is dated 2 February 1937. Moravia was to travel to China in the summer of that year. His feature articles 'Aspetti settecenteschi della vita di Pechino,' 'Nel quartiere delle Legazioni,' and 'Nelle vie di Pechino falegellate del vento distruttore' were published in *La Gazzetta del Popolo*, 1, 14, and 31 July 1937. Memo in ACS, MCP II, b. 8, f. 'Moravia Alberto.'

91 Letter from Moravia to Mussolini, dated 28 July 1938; and correspondence between Casini and Amicucci, in August 1938, both in ACS, MCP II, b. 8. In his memoirs, Moravia mentioned two other short stories that met with some trouble: 'Le donne fanno dormire' and 'Domenica con lo scirocco.' The first was lampooned in a journal edited by Mussolini's sons; the latter was returned to Moravia with a handwritten note by Mussolini himself saying 'visione non Fascistica né ottimista della vita' (neither a Fascist nor an optimistic vision of life). Unfortunately no mention is made of the exact date when these events took place. See Moravia, 'Ricordi di censura,' 99, 101.

92 ACS, PP FP, f. Pincherle Alberto.

93 It should be noted that, according to the legislation, Zurlo should have worked in conjuction with an appointed committee (similarly to what was happening in film censorship). However, because all interested parties agreed to give Zurlo almost total autonomy, no committee was ever formed. See Ferrara, *Censura teatrale e fascismo*, 42–3, 90.

94 Letter by Bragaglia to Galeazzo Ciano, dated 17 September 1934, in ACS, MCP II, b. 2, f. 'Bragaglia Antonio.' Reference to the censorship of Aretino's play can be found in Zurlo's *Memorie inutili*, 62–3. It should also be mentioned that despite Ciano's involvement in the censorship of *La cortigiana*, it was only a few months later, in April 1935, that Zurlo was officially moved from the Ministry of the Interior to Ciano's Undersecretariat for Press and Propaganda. See also Ferrara, *Censura teatrale e fascismo*, 61.

95 Guspini, *L'orecchio del regime*, 122–3. The play by Totò referred to in the correspondence could be either *La mummia vivente* or *I tre moschettieri*, both performed in 1934. Another case in which Mussolini decided to rule against Zurlo's view concerns a play with Napoleon as protagonist, *Sant'Elena* by Robert Casalis-Sheriff, submitted in November 1937. Despite Zurlo's positive view of the artistic integrity of the play, Mussolini disliked the representation of Napoleon's everyday life as a prisoner (see Ferrara, *Censura teatrale e fascismo*, 42).

96 The manuscript with Zurlo's cuts is not at ACS. I could find only a letter by Benelli to Zurlo, dated 4 February 1935, in which Benelli informs the latter of some small changes regarding the lines of one character (ACS, MCP, DGTM CT, b. 660). Those changes are not recorded in the published version distributed by Mondadori when the play was staged. Once more, this suggests that the published version of the play would often fail to include the censor's cuts. This is confirmed by Zurlo, as we will see below.

97 ACS, PP FP, f. 'Benelli Sem.'

98 Zurlo, *Memorie inutili*, 312–13. According to Benelli, the success of *Il ragno* was such that the regime found it impossible to stop it once it was on stage. Benelli also mentions hearing from a friend at *Il Popolo d'Italia* that Mussolini himself had phoned the paper to find out more about the success of the play in Milan. (*Schiavitù*, 120–1).

99 ACS, MCP, DGTM CT, b. 520.

100 Benelli, *Schiavitù*, 129–32.

101 De Begnac, *Taccuini Mussoliniani*, 360.

102 All the informers' reports can be found in ACS, PP FP, 'Benelli Sem.' Starace's rebuke is included in a report dated 5 May 1937. See also Benelli, *Schiavitù*, 140. Although the performances had been stopped, the printed version continued to be available. On 30 April a police informer complained that the play was still available in Milan's bookshops.

103 Benelli, *Schiavitù*, 143–4.

104 ACS, MCP, DGTM CT, b. 654.

105 The letter and Zurlo's report can be found in ACS, MCP, DGTM CT, b. 654.

106 Letter by Giuliani to Alfieri, dated 13 December 1937, in ACS, MCP, b. 53, f. 'Benelli Sem'; emphasis in the original text.

107 ACS, MCP, b. 53, f. 'Benelli Sem.'

108 Ibid.

109 Circular dated 1 August 1938 sent by the Ministry of National Education informing all directors of libraries and other institutions of the MCP's recent prohibitions. ACS, MPI DGAB, b. 226, f. 'Libri di vietata diffusione.' On Benelli's *L'elefante* see also the (factually disappointing) article by D'Incà, 'Sem Benelli,' 93.

110 Benelli, *Schiavitù*, 153.

111 Zurlo, *Memorie inutili*, 318–20. The reports can be found in ACS, MCP, b. 53, and the manuscript with Zurlo's cuts in ACS, MCP, DGTM CT, b. 426. A thematic analysis of the cuts imposed on *L'orchidea* and the earlier *L'elefante* can be found in Leena Erika Vainio's article 'Operato della censura teatrale italiana negli anni Trenta: Il tormentato caso di Sem Benelli,' *Romansk Forum*, 16.2 (2002): 985–96.

112 Benelli, *Schiavitù*, 153–4. This is confirmed by a letter of protest that Benelli wrote to Mussolini on 2 May 1938 to which he attached a copy of the brief reviews published by *Giornale di Genova*, *Secolo XIX*, *Il Lavoro*, and *Corriere Mercantile* (in ACS, MCP, b. 53). A collection of reviews in the play's file at MCP shows that after its debut in Sanremo the play had been widely reviewed, with long positive articles in national papers such as *Corriere della Sera*, *La Gazzetta del Popolo*, and *La Stampa* (when the play arrived in Turin on 16 April 1938). Not surprisingly a strong moralistic attack was made by the Catholic paper *L'Avvenire d'Italia* in a review by Cesare Jacomelli, dated 24 March 1938. The generally positive critical response to the play might be the reason why the ministry decided to send a *velina* on the eve of the Roman premiere, on 18 May 1938, requesting that all papers ignore the event. See Tranfaglia, *La stampa del regime*, 215.

113 Benelli, *Schiavitù*, 158–9. A copy of Benelli's short letter to Mussolini, dated 20 May 1938, can be found in ACS, MCP, b. 53. In it Benelli asked Mussolini to intervene and stop the MCP's plans to cancel the run.

114 According to Benelli (as reported by a police informer), the Rome Federation of the PNF had raised his suspicions when it booked fifty seats for the evening performance (report dated August 1938, in ACS, PP FP, 'Benelli Sem').

115 Benelli, *Schiavitù*, 162. General mention of the problems of *L'orchidea* is made in Fano's *Tessere o non tessere: I comici e la censura Fascista*, 38–9. It

should be mentioned that the practice of 'censoring' the performance of a play through open protest and disturbance was not such a rare event in Fascist Italy. The police files of the Milan prefecture are replete with reports of such occurances, not always caused by Fascist militants. One unusual case deserves mention, although the report may be unreliable: two members of Don Sturzo's Partito Popolare were arrested on 1 February 1924 for disturbing the performance of the comic opera *Fifì e l'immoralità*, allegedly armed with batons. Report by *Carabinieri* Colonel Ferlosio, dated 1 February 1924, in ASMi, PG I, b. 432, f. 'Revisione teatrale 1924.'

116 There are several informers' reports regarding *L'orchidea*, dated 20, 22, 24 (four different ones on that day), 26, 27, 28 May, and 4 June 1938, in ACS, PP FP, 'Benelli Sem.' Benelli was also accused of being an outsider vis-à-vis Fascist culture in a short anonymous article published in Bottai's paper *Critica fascista* on 1 June 1938.

117 ACS, MCP, DGTM CT, b. 426. On pages 17 and 25 of the Mondadori text published in 1938 it is possible to find brief passages that had actually been cut by Zurlo (pp. 4 and 10 in the original manuscript). Presumably they might be cuts that had been imposed at a later stage, although by the beginning of March Zurlo's role as censor of *L'orchidea* had come to an end. Finally, Mondadori's 1946 reprint of the play did not reintegrate the cuts made in 1938, hence the work never regained the political edge originally conceived by Benelli (see, for example, a long passage about Europeans and Africans on page 89 of the original manuscript).

118 ACS, MCP, b. 53. According to a police informer's report dated August 1938, Benelli claimed that Alfieri had ordered him 'a nome del Capo' (on behalf of the Boss) to stop his activity as a playwright (ACS, PP FP, 'Benelli Sem').

119 ACS, MCP, b. 53.

120 Benelli, *Schiavitù*, 170–1. Indeed a letter from Delcroix to Alfieri, dated 25 June 1938, can be found in the MCP records, ACS, MCP, b. 53.

121 ASMi, PG, b. 155, f. 'Mondadori Arnoldo casa editrice.' By October 1939 another two of Benelli's earlier plays had been added to the list: *L'altare* (1915) and *L'amorosa tragedia* (1925): all five works appear in the list of books sequestrated by the MCP between January and October 1939. See ACS, MI DGPS, Massime S 4, b. S4/A (prov.), f. 'Elenco delle stampe sequestrate.'

122 The *nulla osta* for the publication of *La mia leggenda* was granted by Casini on 22 July 1939. Mondadori was asked to delete three short sentences from the book, all three vaguely suggesting the author's disillusionment with contemporary Italy. The most explicit one, on page 206, read: 'A petto alla

quale la nostra vita è vita che va sempre più verso il servaggio e l'ingiustizia'
(In front of which, our life is moving more and more towards serfdom and
injustice). As a copy of the book's first edition shows, the three passages
were effectively removed from the text. Casini's letter can be found in
ASMi, PG II, b. 155, f. 'Mondadori casa editrice.'
123 ACS, MCP, b. 53. Benelli's plays were not the only ones being subjected to
the MCP's censorship. Luigi Pirandello was asked to delete a generic reference to a minister and an undersecretary from his radio play *Cecè* on 7 July
1939 (ACS, MCP, DGTM CT, b. 483). Another radio play, by Michele Galdieri entitled *Divertiti stasera*, was heavily censored for containing reference
to suicide and the meta-theatrical presence of two censors (Zurlo's report is
dated 17 November 1939; in ACS, MCP, DGTM CT, b. 654). On Galdieri see
Pasquale Iaccio, *La scena negata: Il teatro vietato durante la guerra fascista,*
1940–1943 (Rome: Bulzoni, 1994), 31–3.
124 On police surveillance in 1942–3 see ASRo, QR, b. 77, f. 'Benelli Sem.' The
last report, sent from Lugano on 3 February 1945, is in ACS, PP FP, 'Benelli
Sem.'

6. Anti-Semitism and 'Cultural Reclamation'

1 On Mussolini and the Jewish question see Renzo De Felice, *Storia degli ebrei*
sotto il fascismo (Turin: Einaudi, 1961); Meir Michaelis, *Mussolini and the Jews*
(Oxford: Clarendon Press, 1978); Michele Sarfatti, *Mussolini contro gli ebrei:*
Cronaca dell'elaborazione delle leggi del 1938 (Turin: Zamorani, 1994);
Bosworth, *Mussolini*, 334–46; and Fabre, *Mussolini razzista*. Annotations
regarding anti-Semitic comments by Mussolini can be found in the diaries
of Galeazzo Ciano and Giuseppe Bottai. For example, on 30 August 1938
Ciano recorded Mussolini's idea to resettle the Italian Jews in Ethiopia,
where, among other things, they could occupy themselves with shark-
fishing industry and possibly get eaten in the process (Ciano, *Diario, 1937–*
1943, 170). On another front, as early as July 1933, in a letter to Mussolini,
Luigi Einaudi had praised Il Duce's disdain for Hitler's anti-Semitism (ACS,
SPD CR, f. H/R; quoted in De Felice, *Mussolini il duce*, 124–5).
2 A detailed summary of Mussolini's speech is reported in Bottai's diary, (*Dia-*
rio, 1935–1944) 114–15).
3 This is recorded in Pini's diary on 23 December 1936 and on 20 January 1937,
in Pini, *Filo diretto con Palazzo Venezia*, 58, 72–3. See also Fabre, *L'elenco*, 51.
4 Letter dated 26 September 1936, in ACS, MCP II, f. 12 'Regime fascista.'
The letter is not discussed by Fabre in *L'elenco*, as it is part of a cache of
material found at ACS after the publication of his study.

5 Fabre, *L'elenco*, 49–51
6 The report is dated 28 July 1937 (in ACS, MCP, b. 12, f. 144 'Centro studi anticomunisti'). The list on Soviet Russia can be found in ACS, DGPS DAGR, b. 3, f. 'CSA Affari speciali.'.
7 From the start, the Centro Studi Anticomunisti was destabilized by the conflict between Barduzzi and another of its members, the Russian scholar Tomaso Napolitano. Barduzzi repeatedly tried to discredit Napolitano, although the latter was generally considered a reliable and scholarly collaborator. On the CSA and Carlo Barduzzi see Klaus Voigt, *Il rifugio precario: Gli esuli in Italia dal 1933 al 1945* (Florence: Nuova Italia, 1993), 93–8; Fabre, *L'elenco*, 52–7, 169–72.
8 Quoted in Fabre, *L'elenco*, 67. The expression *ebreizzanti* had been coined by Paolo Orano in his *Gli ebrei in Italia*. According to Ciano's diary, on 6 February 1937 Mussolini said that he intended to keep the anti-Semitic writing under control although 'senza soffocare la cosa' (without silencing it); a week later Ciano recorded the visit of Margherita Sarfatti, who manifested her worries about an escalation of rhetoric regarding the Jewish question (Ciano, *Diario, 1937–1943*, 95, 98).
9 Cesare De Vecchi di Val Cismon, *Bonifica fascista della cultura* (Milan: Mondadori, 1937). An important letter by Franco Ciarlantini, then president of the Fascist association of publishers, to Arnoldo Mondadori confirms that it was in the early months of 1938 that publishers heard the first warnings that something was about to happen. In a letter dated 27 August 1938 Ciarlantini stated that six months earlier he had warned publishers of 'quello che bolliva in pentola' (what was being prepared); in AFM, FAM, b. 28, f. 'Ciarlantini Franco,' twice quoted in Fabre, *L'elenco*, 69, 116.
10 At the end of January 1938 Mussolini was also involved in the seizure of three books by Stefan Zweig. In *L'elenco* (67) Fabre originally attributed the order to Casini but in a more recent study has corrected himself, stating that a note by Bocchini suggests that the order actually came from Mussolini himself (see Giorgio Fabre, 'A proposito dell'antisemitismo fascista dell'inizio del 1938,' in *Studi sulla tradizione classica per Mariella Cagnetta*, ed. Luciano Canfora (Bari: Laterza, 1999), 231, 237.
11 On Mussolini's diplomatic note of 16 February 1938 see De Felice, *Storia degli ebrei*, 271–5. Its importance was implicit in a MCP *velina* of the same day requesting that newspaper editors publish it in the front page. See Tranfaglia, *La stampa del regime*, 149.
12 Emilio Gentile, 'The Fascist Anthropological Revolution,' in Bonsaver and Gordon, *Culture, Censorship and the State*, 22–33.
13 Speech delivered at the National Council of the PNF on 25 October 1938, in *Opera Omnia*, 29: 186.

14 Entry dated 10 July 1938, in Ciano, *Diario, 1937–43*, 156. Four days later the
Giornale d'Italia published the *Manifesto degli scienziati razzisti* (Manifesto of
racial scientists).

15 De Begnac, *Taccuini Mussoliniani*, 388.

16 Voigt, *L'esilio precario*, 118–38. According to Goebbels's diary, shortly before
and after the visit to Italy in May 1938, new anti-Semitic measures had been
discussed at length between him and Hitler. Total elimination of Jewish cultural influence in Nazi Germany was one of Goebbels's highest priorities at
the time. See Irving, *Goebbels*, 251–3.

17 Telegram dated 26 March 1938 from Alfieri to all prefects's, ACS, MCP, b.
56, f. 1075.

18 The memo, dated 6 April 1938 in a first version, then slightly rewritten on 7
and 8 April until it reached the fourth and final version reproduced in figure
13, is an 'Appunto per S.E. il Ministro' ('Note for His Excellency the Minister'). It is typed on DGSI; paper hence it is likely that its director, Gherardo
Casini, was the author. Mussolini's approval appears in the margin. Documents in ACS, MCP, b. 12, f. 141 'Scrittori ebrei.' For a detailed discussion see
Piccioni, *Una casa editrice*, 69–70, and, in more detail, Fabre, *L'elenco*, 75–9.

19 Circular signed by Giuseppe Bastianini, undersecretary at the ministry, sent
on 13 April 1938, in ASDMAE, MCP, b. 292, f. 'Controllo importazioni libri
stranieri.'

20 This is confirmed by a memo dated 27 May 1938 sent by Bottai's education
ministry to all directors of national libraries; ACS, MPI DGAB, b. 226, f.
'Divieto diffusione scrittori ebrei.' On Corbaccio, see documents in ASMi,
PG II, b. 153, f. 044 'Corbaccio casa editrice.'

21 Mussolini's personal order of 21 May 1938 to seize Mondadori's *Almanacco
della Medusa* is confirmed by his personal secretary, Celso Luciano, in a
handwritten memo; both documents in ACS, SPD CR, b. 146, f. 402. Among
the Jewish authors hit by Alfieri's order of 13 April 1938 were Lion Feuchtwanger, Arthur Schnitzler, and Stefan Zweig. The 1934 *Almanacco della
Medusa* contained a five-page introduction by Arnoldo Mondadori himself.
Reference to its seizure is made in Albonetti, ed., *Non c'è tutto nei romanzi*, 83.
As for Stefan Zweig, even the news of his suicide in 1942 was censored by the
MCP, whose *velina* of 24 February 1942 required newspaper editors to ignore
the event. See Tranfaglia, ed., *La stampa del regime*, 155.

22 On this see Fabre, *L'elenco*, 85, 88.

23 Documents in ASDMAE, b. 292, f. 'Controllo importazioni.'

24 The seizure was ordered by Alfieri on 25 August 1938. However, his telegram
was followed by a second one, on 27 August, in which he suspended the
operation, adding that Mondadori had been allowed to withdraw the books

without the intervention of the authorities. Documents in ACS, MI UC, telegram nos. 44053 and 44408; see also Fabre, *L'elenco*, 92, 98.

25   See Jens Petersen, 'L'accordo culturale fra l'Italia e la Germania del 23 novembre 1938,' in Bracher Karl Dietrich and Valiani Leo, eds., *Fascismo e nazionalsocialismo* (Bologna: Il Mulino, 1986), 330–48; Voigt, *Il rifugio precario*, 86–106.

26   On this see Fabre, *L'elenco*, 56, 82–3, 91, and Gigli Marchetti, *Le edizioni Corbaccio*, 67, 72–4 (Gigli Marchetti fails to mention the link between Dall'Oglio's complaint and Mussolini's decision to partly compensate Corbaccio for its losses).

27   It is a sad reflection on the sudden development of Italy's racial campaign to note that when Ignazio Silone wrote an article on Italian universities under Fascism in 1935, he had come to the conclusion that Italy's situation differed from that of Nazi Germany only in the fact that there was no place for anti-Semitism in the Italian system. Ignazio Silone, 'Die Italienische Universität,' *Die Neue Weltbühne* 37 (14 September 1935): 1150–2, quoted in Voigt, *Il rifugio precario*, 418. As for Bottai's latent anti-Semitism, traces of it can be found even in his postwar diaries; see, for example, the entry for 26 May 1946 in Bottai, *Diario, 1944–1948*, 370. On Bottai's anti-Semitic policies within the school system, see Teresa Maria Mazzatosta, *Il regime fascista tra educazione e propaganda, 1935–1943* (Bologna: Cappelli, 1978), 59–62, and Piccioni, *Una casa editrice*, 71–4. Giordano Bruno Guerri's disappointing biography of Bottai is an example of an unconvincing attempt to accept the reality of his anti-Semitic measures while trying to keep the image alive of Bottai as a moderate and morally upright leader. According to Guerri, Bottai's efficient implementation of the anti-Semitic legislation was part of a move to defend himself from the accusation of being pro-Jewish. See Giordano Bruno Guerri, *Giuseppe Bottai: Un fascista critico* (Milan: Feltrinelli, 1976), 166–73. See also De Felice, *Storia degli ebrei italiani*, 278–9.

28   Bottai, *Diario, 1935–1944*, 136–7, entry dated 6 October 1938 (see also Ciano's own entry, in which he recorded his surprise at the intransigence of Bottai, in Ciano, *Diario, 1937–1943*, 193). It should be noted that earlier diary entries suggest that Bottai was not among the inner circle of decision makers when the policies were first discussed during the summer. On 16 July 1938 he mentions 'hearing' about the launch of Fascism's racial manifesto during a phonecall with Adelchi Serena, then deputy secretary of the PNF (*Diaro, 1935–1944*, 125). On 27 August 1938, after mentioning that, through Alfieri, Mussolini had converged his approval of Bottai's articles in *Critica fascista*, Bottai notes that he was informed by his cabinet of Mussolini's decision to widen the school ban to Italian Jews (ibid., 131). If Bottai were initially left

out of the decision-making process, his slew of initiatives in the summer of 1938 is explainable partly as an attempt to regain a position of prominence in Mussolini's eyes. It should also be noted that Bottai convinced Mussolini to give publishers partial compensation for their losses with an *una tantum* grant of 1.5 million lire, which was divided among thirty publishing houses. Sadly, publishers thankfully cashed in the compensation but 'forgot' to provide any of these funds to their proscribed Jewish authors and editors (Fabre, *L'elenco*, 246–57). As we will also see in chapter 7, Bottai's approach was less draconian when it came to dealing with prohibited books kept in public libraries. On Bottai's initiatives see ACS, MPI DGAB, b. 226, f. 'Divieto diffusione scrittori ebrei'; also Centro Furio Jesi, eds., *La menzogna della razza: Documenti e immagini del razzismo e dell'antisemitismo fascista* (Bologna: Grafis, 1994), 319–24.

29 This first initiative led to the compilation of a list that on 30 September 1938 included 114 authors and corresponded to about 300–400 texts. In a letter to Bottai on 3 October 1938, Mondadori boasted of having adopted the anti-Semitic directives 'severamente e chirurgicamente' ('with strictness and surgical precision'). See Galfré, *Il regime degli editori*, 153, 155.

30 Riccardo Miceli, 'Razzismo nel libro,' *Il libro italiano*, September 1938, 382.

31 Casini's note dated 6 October 1938 can be found in ACS, MCP, b. 56, f. 1075; quoted in Cannistraro, *La fabbrica del consenso*, 118; reproduced in Gregory, Fattori and Siciliani, eds., *Filosofi, università, regime*, 221, and quoted in Fabre, *L'elenco*, 133.

32 Fabre, *L'elenco*, 135–8. Publishers and police forces were often at a loss as to how to identify the Jewish origin of staff and authors. Published lists of Jewish names were often used as a first source. Among them was a 1938 edition of the *Protocolli dei Savi anziani di Sion*, edited by Giovanni Preziosi, which contained a long appendix entitled 'Gli Ebrei in Italia.' It contained a list of 9,800 Jewish families. On this see Centro Furio Jesi, ed., *La menzogna della razza*, 261–5. Bizarrely, the department that was a central engine of the regime's racial policies, the Direzione Generale per la Demografia e la Razza (General Directorate for Demography and Race, shortened as Demorazza) was not involved nor did it help. According to Fabre, a possible reason is the combination of Alfieri's intention to keep cultural matters under his control and Demorazza's unwillingness to share its data (Fabre, *L'elenco*, 237–8).

33 ASMi, PG II b. 33, f. 045 'Sequestro libri.'

34 Interestingly, a French translation of James Cain's *The Postman Always Rings Twice* appears as published by Corbaccio. Given the fact that Corbaccio did not have a series of books published in a foreign language, the presence of Cain's novel makes one suspect that the MCP's list mentioned not just books

published and sequestrated but also titles of books that publishers had asked for permission to translate and that had received a negative reply from the ministry.

35 The book was published in 1951 with the title *Trent'anni dopo*. In a polemical preface, Formiggini's wife accused the postwar Associazione Italiana Editori of postponing the publication of the book year after year. She eventually asked for the manuscript to be returned and published it wth the reborn firm Formiggini. On Angelo Fortunato Formiggini see also Alberto Cavaglion and Gian Paolo Romagnani, eds., *Le interdizioni del Duce: Le leggi razziali in Italia* (Turin: Claudiana, 2002), 364–76. It is also significant that, in the annotated version of the *Indice dei libri proibiti*, published in 1944, the only publisher that was explicitly listed was Formiggini because of its by then defunct series *Classici del ridere* (Montevecchi, *La chiesa e i libri*, 16).

36 Tranfaglia and Vittoria, *Storia degli editori italiani*, 324–5, 329–30, 353–7. In the case of Olschki, however, the publishing house was temporarily allowed to retain its name after a protest directly to Mussolini. The change to Bibliopolis finally took place in September 1940. It should also be borne in mind that, in order not to upset the financial viability of those companies, the Fascist government allowed most Jewish shareholders and Jewish managing directors to remain in control of their firms, despite the change in the companies' names. (Fabre, *L'elenco*, 375–8). Another Florentine publisher that was forced to change its name was Bemporad. Despite the fact that since 1935 it was no longer controlled by Enrico Bemporad, the publishing house was renamed Marzocco in October 1938 (see Tranfaglia and Albertina, *Storia degli editori italiani*, 269–72).

37 Fabre, *L'elenco*, 157–8. Fabre's assumption is based on a quotation from a letter by the owner of the Padua publishing house Cedam to Franco Ciarlantini, dated 1 March 1939 (in ASPd, Pref. Gab., b. 507). Indeed, later on in his study, Fabre admits that 'quanti furono contattati in questa fase non si sa' (we do not know the number of publishers who were contacted in this phase), *L'elenco*, 202.

38 Luciano Morpurgo, *Caccia all'uomo* (Rome: Dalmatia, 1946), 39–41. According to his memoirs the event took place in March 1939. Morpurgo also mentioned that a recently published book of his, *Quando ero fanciullo* (Rome: Morpurgo, 1938) had been taken out of the shop windows in July 1938 (14–18). On Franco Ciarlantini's credentials as a Fascist see his collection of speeches and articles, many of which published in *Il Popolo d'Italia: Vicende di libri e di autori* (Milan: Ceschina, 1931). Ciarlantini had also been one of the speakers at Gentile's *Primo congresso della cultura fascista* in March 1925.

39 On Ciarlantini's claim and on his pressure on Cedam and La Nuova Italia see Fabre, *L'elenco*, 176, 195–8, 227–31. On Salani see Tranfaglia and Vittoria,

Storia degli editori italiani, 282. On the case related to La Nuova Italia, see also Piccioni, *Una casa editrice,* 61–79.

40 Letter dated 19 December 1938, in AFM, FAM, b. 28, f. 'Ciarlantini Franco,' quoted in Fabre, *L'elenco,* 208.

41 Barbian, *Literaturpolitik im Dritten Reich,* 528. Hitler's determination to 'convert' German art and literature to Nazi ideology was made explicit as early as 1919 in his party manifesto. In the months following his seizure of power in January 1933, these political aims were put into practice in a variety of forms. Famous writers such as Heinrich Mann were made to resign from state academies, books were burnt in various towns in May 1933, and Nazi groups drew up lists of unwanted publications, which by April 1935 were fused into 'Liste 1 des schädlichen und unerwünschten Schrifttums' (List 1 of harmful and unwanted writings); List 2 was to be devoted to Jewish authors). For a detailed overview of Nazi censorship on books see Barbian, *Literaturpolitik im Dritten Reich,* 517–66; Leonidas Hill, 'Nazi Attack on "Un-German" Literature,' in *The Holocaust and the Book,* ed. Jonathan Rose (Amherst: University of Massachusetts Press, 2001), 9–46; Klaus Siebenhaar, 'Buch und Schwert: Anmerkungen zur Indizierungspraxis und "Schrifttums-politik" im Nationalsocialismus,' in *'Das War ein Vorspiel nur ... '. Bücherver-brennung Deutschland 1933: Voraussetzungen und Folgen,* ed. Hermann Haarmann, Walter Huder, and Klaus Siebenhaar (Berlin: Medusa, 1983), 81–96; Hans Sarkowicz and Alf Mentzer, *Literatur in Nazi-Deutschland* (Hamburg: Europa Verlag, 2000); and the entry on Nazi Germany in Derek Jones, ed., *Censorship: A World Encyclopedia,* vol. 2 (London: Fitzroy Dearborn, 2001), 926–37.

42 Fabre, *L'elenco,* 321. Yet, only a few pages later, Fabre admits that 'Il ministero della Propaganda di Goebbels, nella sua aspirazione totalitaria, era molto avanti rispetto all'omologo italiano' (Goebbels's Ministry of Propaganda, in its totalitarian aspirations, was much ahead of its Italian equivalent), *L'elenco,* 339. Similarly contradictory is the discussion on page 345, where Fabre first states that 'In Germania le autorità naziste furono durissime con gli autori ebrei e incominciarono le eliminazioni dei loro libri molto per tempo' (The Nazi authorities in Germany were extremely harsh against Jewish authors, and they began to eliminate their books at a very early stage), after which he repeats the statement that Fascism's longer hold on the state was clearly apparent. By 1938 the Nazi regime had vastly surpassed the Fascist one in terms of anti-Semitic censorship, so it is difficult to see when and how Fascism's alleged superior experience showed in this regard. Fabre is right in pointing out that the degree of centralization of censorship achieved by Mussolini in the late 1930s was superior to that of Goebbels, who did not

manage entirely to suppress the interference of other institutions such as Himmler's Ministry of the Interior and the Gestapo (see also Barbian, *Literaturpolitik im Dritten Reich*, 522–3). Decentralization, however, was far from meaning lack of determination. As early as 1934 the Bavarian police alone had banned 6,843 books by 2,293 different authors (see Leonidas Hill, 'Nazi Attack on "Un-German" Literature,' 12–13). For a study of the popular consensus and media coverage surrounding the anti-Semitic policies of the Nazi regime see Robert Gellately, *Backing Hitler: Consent and Coercion in Nazi Germany* (Oxford: Oxford University Press, 2001).

43 Copies in ACS, MI, DGPS DAGR, Massime S4, b. S4/A (provv.), f. 1. sf. 7. See also Fabre, *L'elenco*, 214–16, 318.

44 Four memos were sent between 11 and 13 March 1939, giving the prefectures the precise address of the Milan book dealers that had advertised the books. The memos concluded reassuringly that the books would be returned as soon as the MCP had examined them. ASMi, PG II, b. 394, f. 'Disposizioni stampa.'

45 In the mid-1930s Gentile became a member of the managing board of Florence's most prestigious publishers, Sansoni, Bemporad, and Le Monnier. His rise to power was also facilitated by a crisis in the Florentine publishing industry. Book production in Tuscany had plummeted from 1,995 titles in 1930 to 1,366 in 1933 (figures taken from Pedullà, 'Gli anni del fascismo,' 346.). On Gentile and the publishing industry see Tranfaglia and Vittoria, *Storia degli editori italiani*, 263–80; on Gentile and anti-Semitism see Rosella Faraone, *Giovanni Gentile e la 'questione ebraica'* (Cosenza: Rubbettino, 2003). On Momigliano and Levi see Fabre, *L'elenco*, 385, and Galfré, *Il regime degli editori*, 15–18. Jews were also banned from printing non-commercial scientific publications. For instance, on 3 February 1939 the DGSI informed the small Milanese publisher Unione Tipografica that it could not grant permission to publish three medical publications, even though they were not for sale, because their three authors (L. Lattes, C. Foà, and M. Donati) were Jewish. Letter in ASMi, b. 156, f. 044 'Unione Tipografica casa editrice.'

46 Alfredo Ascoli and Eugenio Florian, eds., *Enciclopedia giuridica italiana*, vol. 22 (Milan: Vallardi, 1939). The link between the Jewishness of the authors and the seizure of the volume is not apparent in the documentation. However, a copy of the volume held in the prefecture's file with the two names underlined in red pencil strongly indicates the actual reason behind an otherwise inexplicable seizure. Documents in ASMi, PG II, b. 156, f. 044 'Vallardi Francesco casa editrice.'

47 The article in question, symbolically signed '*Critica Fascista*' and aptly entitled 'Bonifica libraria,' contained a brutal attack against the negative influence of

female Jewish writers. The following quotation illustrates this point: 'Ci accorgiamo che i nostri fanciulli cantano sulla lira di Lina Schwarz, ebrea, e le nostre giovinette sospirano con Cordelia, ebrea, o sognano con Emma Boghen-Conigliani, ebrea, o s'immalinconiscono con Haydée, ebrea, o si erudiscono con Orvieto ed Errera, ebree ... Ogni personaggio uscito da penna ebraica talmudeggia, il che è quanto dire erra interpretando, e interpreta errando stati d'animo, impulsi, desideri, e passioni. (We realize that our children sing to the sound of Lina Schwarz, a Jew, and our girls think of love with Cordelia, a Jew, or dream with Emma Boghen-Conigliani, a Jew, or are saddened by Haydée, a Jew, or learn from Orvieto and Errera, both Jews ... Every character created by a Jewish pen is "talmud-preaching," which means that it is wrong, and it wrongly interprets feelings, impulses, desires, and passions), in *Critica fascista* 18.5 (1 January 1939), 66–7. Starting from the fact that this group of Jewish writers is made up entirely of women, and linking it with Mura's case in April 1934, Lucia Re argues that the regime's censorship policies treated women as a constituency that needed similar repression to that exacted on Jewish authors. See Lucia Re, 'Women and Censorship in Fascist Italy,' 64–75. A list of children's books that had been banned was published in *Giornale della libreria* in January 1939; on this see Gabriele Turi, *Un secolo di libri* (Turin: Einaudi, 1999), 164.

48 Copies of the two lists sent on 22 February and 11 March 1939 are at ACS, DGPS DAGR, b. 117, f. 'Elenco stampe estere sequestrate e vietate'; both are reproduced in the appendix in Fabre, *L'elenco*, 450–2. The Reale Accademia d'Italia might also have been involved in the censoring of an entire series of books about famous court proceedings, *I processi celebri*. On 7 January 1939 the Milan prefecture ordered Corbaccio to withdraw the four books already published and cancel any further publications. The prefecture's letter specified that the series had been 'condannata dalla Commissione per la bonifica del libro' (condemned by the Committee for Book Reclamation). Documents in ASMi, PG II, b. 153, also mentioned in Gigli Marchetti, *L'editore Corbaccio*, 75–6. A second case that might have originated from the historians of the Reale Accademia d'Italia concerns the modifications imposed on the three-volume *History of Europe* (1935) by English historian Herbert Fisher. Although the Italian translation of the volumes, *Storia d'Europa*, published by Laterza, had been on the market since 1936, on 4 February 1939 the books were seized on the order of the MCP and modifications to all three volumes were required. According to a note by his personal secretary, Sebastiani, when Mussolini found out about this seizure he remarked: 'Find out about the reasons for this ban; if they had asked me I would have refused to allow it.' Mussolini's comments can be found in the margin of a letter that Giovanni Laterza had written to him on

20 July 1939. In the letter Laterza cunningly mentioned that apparently a 'studioso' (scholar) had noticed the presence of Fisher's *Storia d'Europa* on Mussolini's desk (in ACS, SPD CO, f. 531.336, copy in NAKe, Captured Italian Records, GMF 36/202).

49 As Fabre shows in detail, in the autumn of 1938 Interlandi's papers had initiated a pro-Nazi debate on the pernicious Jewish influence on modern art, which Marinetti, as father of the futurist movement, had hotly contested. The seizure of these two works (and it is significant that the name of the translator was explicitly mentioned) was, in other words, little more than an act of political revenge on the part of Marinetti. On top of that, it was later discovered that Bloch was not Jewish and indeed his name was removed from the list published in 1942 (see Fabre, *L'elenco*, 184–98). Copy of Interlandi's article that initiated the controversy, 'Arte e razza,' published in *Quadrivio*, 6 November 1938, can be found in Cavaglion and Romagnani, eds., *Le interdizioni del Duce*, 147–50. See also De Felice, *Storia degli ebrei italiani*, 304–7.

50 Although not documented, Pavolini's involvement is suggested in a letter by Ciarlantini mentioned in Fabre, *L'elenco*, 222.

51 Moravia's letter can be found in AFM FAM, f. Moravia. Another author mentioned in the second list, Barbara Allason, author of *Il tesoro dei Nibelunghi* (Milan: Sonzogno, 1921), appealed the decision on 8 May 1940, followed six days later by a supporting letter from Sonzogno. The appeal was successful, and the ban was revoked the following month, on 8 June 1940, with a letter by Casini to the prefecture of Milan, followed on 11 June by a telegram sent by the head of police, Bocchini (documents in ASMi, PG II, b. 156, f. 044 'Sonzogno casa editrice'). Barbara Allason was a militant anti-Fascist who had been arrested together with other Turinese militants from Giustizia e Libertà in 1934.

52 A slightly different case is that of popular anti-Fascist historian Guglielmo Ferrero. Most of his many books on classical Rome appeared in the 1939 list of banned titles. Among them – thirty in total – were two historical novels, *Le due verità* (1926) and *La rivolta del figlio* (1927), published by Mondadori. The two novels were supposed to be part of a tetralogy entitled *La terza Roma*, which was never completed as such. A third novel, *Gli ultimi barbari: Sudore e sangue*, published by Mondadori in 1930, does not appear in the list. However, the fact that a fourth novel, entitled *Gli ultimi barbari: Liberazione*, was published in Italian by the Swiss anti-Fascist publisher Nuove Edizioni di Capolago in 1936 suggests that by then the entire tetralogy had been banned in Italy. As soon as the war was over, Mondadori reprinted Ferrero's fictional work with slightly changed titles.

53 Circular from Bottai's cabinet at the Ministry of National Education to all general directors, dated 1 August 1938, in ACS, MPI DGAB, b. 226, f. 'Divieto

diffusione scrittori ebrei.' On the final decision of February 1939 see Fabre, *L'elenco*, 221.

54 In the few critical writings on da Verona, it is taken for granted that he took his life in desperation (see, for example, Piromalli, *Guido Da Verona*, 180). Sadly, even his death was censored: on 5 April 1935 the MCP sent a *velina* requesting that newspaper editors limit the news of da Verona's death to a brief announcement 'senza alcun commento' ('with no comment whatsoever'). See Tranfaglia, ed., *La stampa del regime*, 217. On the ban of da Verona's work see also Fabre, *L'elenco*, 221–2.

55 A visit by a prefecture official to Corbaccio's warehouse on 4 November 1941 resulted in the seizure of seventy-five copies of the two novels. ASMi, GP II, b. 153, f. 044 'Bompiani Valentino casa editrice.' See also Gigli Marchetti, *L'editore Corbaccio*, 80–1, and Fabre, *L'elenco*, 221–2, 263, 279.

56 Copy of Bill no. 374 of 2 February 1939 can be found in ACS, DGPS DAGR, Massime S4, b. S4/A (provv.), f. 1, sf. 3.

57 In a memo by Casini to Pavolini, dated 12 August 1939, the former had warned that large numbers of Sarfatti's books were in circulation, particularly her biography of Mussolini and her recent work published by Mondadori, *America, ricerca della felicità*. Two days later, the MCP's head of cabinet, Luciano, decided to require the publishers of Sarfatti's works to withdraw all copies that had already been distributed. The memo specified that prefectures would be involved only if this measure were deemed to be insufficient. Discretion was obviously the order of the day. The documentation regarding this episode can be found in ACS, MCP, b. 56, f. 1075. See also Fabre, *L'elenco*, 258–62. The transcript of the telephone conversation and Celso Luciano's memo related to Mussolini's orders have been reproduced in Gregory, Fattori, and Siciliani, eds., *Filosofi università regime*, 227–8.

58 Fabre, *L'elenco*, 260, 265, 273, 286, and passim.

59 See ibid., 278–9.

60 Documents in ASMi, PG II, b. 156, f. 044 'Stampa Commerciale casa editrice.' The prefect's next move was to send letters to those publishers in the province of Milan. There are similar but less embarrassing cases. One concerns Margherita Sarfatti herself. As Fabre shows, one of her books, *Segni, colori e luci* (1926), published by Zanichelli, remained unaffected throughout the last years of the regime (*L'elenco*, 309).

61 At times the attention of the MCP's censors would extend to individual contributors to edited volumes. This was the case with Ugo Ojetti's *Storia illustrata della letteratura italiana*. On 25 November 1939 Ojetti's Milan publisher, Garzanti, was ordered to remove from that volume all articles by Jewish writers (ASMi, PG, b. 154).

7. A Turn of the Screw

1 For a non-academic but factually reliable biography of Pavolini see Arrigo Petacco, *Il superfascista: Vita e morte di Alessandro Pavolini* (Milan: Mondadori, 1998). See also Frank Snowden's entry on Pavolini in De Grazia and Luzzatto, eds, *Dizionario del fascismo*, 2: 351–4. Pavolini also maintained good relations with Florence's publishing world. In the 1930s his father had sat on the administrative board of Sansoni, and Alessandro was on that of Vallecchi (on this see Simonetti, 'L'editoria fiorentina dal 1920 al 1940,' 554–5, and Tranfaglia and Vittoria, *Storia degli editori italiani*, 289).

2 Ciano, *Diario, 1937–1943*, 360. In his memoirs Alfieri suggests that possibly the main reason for his removal from the MCP was his divergence of opinion with the then head of the PNF, Achille Starace. He then adds that, thanks to Ciano's support, Mussolini offered him the prestigious position of ambassador to Moscow, which Alfieri declined in exchange for the equally strategic one of ambassador to the Vatican. See Alfieri, *Due dittatori di fronte*, 3.

3 However, small numbers of proscribed books remained for sale, often surreptitiously, in bookshops managed by anti-Fascists. In a brief memoir, Italian politician and former prime minister Giovanni Spadolini remembers finding Gobetti's publications among the shelves of a communist bookstore in the heart of Florence long after the books had been banned. See Giovanni Spadolini, 'Prefazione,' in Alberto Marcolin, *Firenze in camicia nera* (Florence: Edizione Medicea, 1993), 7–10. Again in Florence, critic and literature scholar Silvio Guarnieri remembers finding a copy of Silone's *Fontamara* for sale in the mid-1930s despite the total ban on this openly anti-Fascist novel. See Guarnieri, *L'ultimo testimone*, 282–3.

4 The list is in ACS, MI DGPS, Massime S4, f. S4 (provv.), f. 5. For Corbaccio see Gigli Marchetti, *Le edizioni Corbaccio*, 79. The MCP's letter is in ASMi, PG II, b. 153, f. 'Corbaccio casa editrice.'

5 Circular sent to all prefectures on 26 July 1940, quoted in Fabre, *L'elenco*, 294. According to Ugo Krieg's *Le legislazione penale sulla stampa* (Milan: Giuffrè, 1942), 19, 253–4, the circular that finalized the situation was sent out on 14 February 1941. Reference to the earlier directive of March 1938 can be found in chapter 4 above.

6 See Fabre, *L'elenco*, 286–8.

7 ACS, PCM, Gab. 1940–43, b. 2988, f. 3.2.6.79; the letter, dated 9 January 1940, can be found in the appendix of Fabre's *L'elenco*, 464.

8 Copy of the telegram in NAKe, GMF, 36/202. Croce's letter can be found in ACS, PCM, Gab. 1940–43, b. 2988, f. 3.2.6.79. On the relationship between

Croce and Mussolini in the late 1930s and early 1940s see also Rizi, *Benedetto Croce and Italian Fascism*, 196–212.

9 Pavolini's letter was sent on 24 June 1940, in ACS, MCP, b. 117, f. 7981; Mussolini's remark was also recorded in his personal waiter's memoirs: Navarra, *Memorie del cameriere di Mussolini*, 193. Bruno Gaeta, who worked at the MCP's Book Division in the war years, stated that he was involved in a delicate case concerning the reprinting of some of unspecified works by Croce. Once more, the *nulla osta* was conceded only when Gaeta's report reached Mussolini's desk. See Gaeta, 'Minculpop, censura libri,' 922–3. One more instance of an about face related to Laterza took place on 25 January 1943, when the MCP sent a telegram to all prefects waiving the seizure order against the recently published *Illuminismo e rivoluzione francese* by Manlio Ciardo (curiously mispelled in the telegram as Guido Cirdo), in ACS, SPD CO, f. 500.007. Finally, in the case of Luigi Russo's *La critica letteraria contemporanea*, published by Laterza in 1942, the MCP issued a velina asking newspaper editors not to review the book (memo dated 29 August 1942, quoted in Petacco, *Il superfascista*, 91).

10 A few months later Pavolini and Mussolini agreed on the suppression of a Florentine journal. Gherardo Casini had sent Pavolini a report in which he had suggested the closure of the Florentine periodical *Argomenti* (called *Riforma letteraria* when founded in 1936 by Alberto Carocci and Giacomo Noventa). The main argument was that the periodical showed the influence of Crocian thought. On 12 December 1940 Pavolini sent Mussolini a note in which he announced his intention to close the periodical down. Mussolini's approval is suggested by a 'tick' in pencil on the note. The following day Casini proceeded to act, sending a letter to Celso Luciano, who presumably passed the order on to the prefecture of Florence. All documents in ACS, MCP, b. 16, f. 226, and reproduced in Gregori, Fattori, and Siciliani, eds., *Filosofi università regime*, 216–19.

11 My suggestion that this comment was probably penned in by Pavolini comes from the fact that in Casini's report to Pavolini of 9 February, there is no mention of Laterza and Moravia. However, when, three days later, Pavolini wrote his memo for Mussolini, he paraphrased Casini's report and added the reference to the two individual cases. Both documents in ACS, MCP, b. 56, f. 1075.

12 The third point concluded with an Orwellian example of Newspeak, advising authors of encyclopedic works to mention pre-Fascist institutions only via 'brevi citazioni in forma di positivo esame ai fini di una efficace critica di tale passato politico nazionale' (brief quotes allowing a positive evaluation aimed at an effective critique of such national political past). Circular sent by the

Fascist Federation of Publishers, dated 26 February 1940, quoted in Alessandro Piccioni, ed., *Una casa editrice tra Società, Cultura e Scuola: La Nuova Italia, 1926–1986* (Florence: La Nuova Italia, 1986), 222. A book that did fit the regime's expectations was a biography of Jewish philosopher Benedict Spinoza. On 18 October 1940 the MCP informed the prefecture of Milan that the request to publish E.G. Kolbenheymer's *Amor Dei* had been rejected because the ministry allowed publications related to Jews only if they were classics of world literature or texts that did not praise Jewish thought. Kolbenheymer's biography did not fall within either category. Similarly, on 9 April 1940 Casini had ordered the removal of any mention of the 'Jewish Heine' from Ludwig Klages's *L'anima e lo spirito* (Bompiani, 1940) because the German writer had been mentioned as a great master of world literature. Documents in ASMi, PG II, b. 153, f. 044 'Bompiani Valentino casa editrice.'

13 Ministero dell'Educazione Nazionale, *Elenchi di opere la cui pubblicazione, diffusione o ristampa nel Regno è stata vietata dal Ministero della Cultura Popolare* (Rome: Istituto Poligrafico dello Stato, 1940). It is reasonable to assume that the publication was supposed to be sent out to all public libraries dependent on Bottai's ministry. This was of particular importance because public libraries were supposed to hold copies of banned books in reserve collections for the use of 'studiosi' (scholars). Strangely, hardly any libraries in Italy have kept the booklet among their holdings. I am grateful to the librarian at the Biblioteca di Storia Contemporanea 'Alfredo Oriani,' Ravenna, for providing me with a photocopy of their rare holding. It was Bottai who, as early as June 1937, had ruled that public libraries were allowed to store banned books (on this see Fabre, *L'elenco*, 346–7).

14 ACS, MCP, b. 56, f. 1075, also quoted in Fabre, *L'elenco*, 288–9. On La Nuova Italia see Fabre, *L'elenco*, 391.

15 The presence of a suicide as part of the plot was the reason for the refusal to allow an Italian translation of the novel *Il figlio del giocatore* (*A játékos fia*, 1940) by Hungarian author Aradi Zsolt. A macabre suggestion was also given to Garzanti in order to camouflage the suicide of one of the characters in the novel *Il calmo Don* (*Tichji Don*, 1928–40) by Mikhail Sholokhov: Casini suggested that the suicide of a character Acsinia could have easily been disguised as natural because the character was already 'corroded by syphilis.' Letters by Casini to the prefecture of Milan, dated respectively 4 December 1940 and 2 April 1941, in ASMi, PG II, b. 154, f. 44 'Garzanti casa editrice.'

16 See Petacco, *Il superfascista*, 101–4. In his diary, Bottai recorded having read Pavolini's book in February 1940. He did not add any critical comments to his note (Bottai, *Diario, 1935–1944*, 177).

17 For a summary of Pavolini's statements during his regular meetings with newspaper editors, see Cesari, *La censura nel periodo fascista*, 80–9.

18 An example of Pavolini' intervention 'on request' concerns the publication of a number of letters by Italy's late Queen Margherita (wife of King Umberto I and mother of King Vittorio Emanuele III) addressed to General Osio, who had been tutor to the future king. Prompted by the royal family, who was not in favour of such publication, in August 1942 Pavolini investigated the matter and eventually ordered a total ban on the content of the letters (documents in ACS, MCP, b. 141, f. 11 'Osio').

19 In the postwar years Alessandro Bonsanti wrote in defence of Casini when the latter was depicted in an article of the weekly *L'Espresso* as a particularly zealous censor. We will return to this episode in chapter 9, when discussing the censorship of Vittorini's *Conversazione in Sicilia*.

20 Reference to Tosti as head of DGSI can be found in a letter by Valentino Bompiani to Bontempelli, 7 August 1943 (in AB, f. 'Bontempelli Massimo'). In the postwar years Tosti was to write a biography of General Badoglio, published by Mondadori in 1956.

21 The list is attached to a memo by Casini to Celso Luciano, head of cabinet at the MCP, dated 13 January 1940, in ACS, MCP, b. 56, f. 1075. Bellonci's name appears in a later list, in November 1940, in which the total number of readers has decreased from forty-three to forty. Details of their payment is also specified: readers of Italian books were regularly paid 1,000 lire a month; readers of foreign publications received 500 lire per book.

22 Gaeta, 'Minculpop, censura libri,' 927–8. On Azione Cattolica's list see Fabre, *L'elenco*, 280–3. It should also be noted that during the war prefects were asked by the Undersecretary at the Ministry of the Interior, Guido Buffarini Guidi, to keep a particular eye on Catholic publications for traces of 'sentimentalismo pacifista aut pietistico verso i nostri nemici' (pacifist and pityful sentimentalism towards our enemies). Telegram dated 19 December 1940, in ACS, DGPS, Massime S4 (provv.), b. 103, f. 8 'Pubblicazioni cattoliche.'

23 The report can be found in ACS, MCP II, b. 8, f. 'Marinetti Filippo Tommaso.'

24 Documents in ACS, MCP, b. 53, f. 583 'Marinetti Tommaso Filippo.'

25 Fabre, *L'elenco*, 304–10. Moreover, as we have seen in chapter 6, the case of Stampa Commerciale is more indicative of the regime's inefficiency than of a cogent plan of action.

26 Letter by Casini, dated 25 November 1939, in ASMi, PG II, b. 154, f. 44 'Garzanti casa editrice.'

27 See letters dated 24, 25, and 31 July 1940, ASMi, PG II, b. 154, f. 044 'Garzanti casa editrice.' Italo Sulliotti's *Entra la corte* had been seized by the police in Ancona, Abano Terme, Benevento, Prato, and Grosseto;

Marise Ferro's *Trent'anni* had been seized in Udine; and Luciano Berra's *Polonia* in Milan.

28 The publication of Kantorovicz's *Federico II di Svevia* was particularly difficult. After the first submission of the proofs, on 10 July 1939 the MCP asked for a new round of modifications. Garzanti's plan for a new series was sent in December 1941. Documents in ASMi, PG II, b. 154, f. 44 'Garzanti casa editrice.'

29 Fabre, *L'elenco*, 306.

30 Krieg, *La legislazione penne sulla stampa*, 254–5. The case of *Cartoni animati* took place in September 1941, which would suggest that, even before the circulars of the following months, some magazine editors were already submitting their work in advance (documents in ASMi, b. 154, f. 9519). Il *Corriere dei Piccoli* was asked to modify the story 'Lo strano viaggio del Sig. Re' on 12 August 1942 (documents in ASMi, b. 284, f. 045).

31 Fabre, *L'elenco*, 305, 307. It is sad to note that, to my knowledge, once the war was over and democratic civil rights re-established, no attempts were made to compensate the authors for their financial losses.

32 Journal figures are quoted in Ferrara, 'La voce del padrone,' 60. On the MCP's funding of *Quadrivio* and *Architettura* see ACS, MCP II, b. 6, f. 'Garzanti' and b. 11, f. 'Quadrivio.' About *La Ruota*, a letter by its chief editor, Mario Meschini, dated 12 March 1940 shows that the journal was assured financial backing from the MCP before it had even published its first issue (in ACS, MCP II, b. 12, f. 'La Ruota'). According to Albertina Vittoria, Meschini was at the time a MCP official (Vittoria, 'Fascist Censorship and Non-Fascist Literary Circles,' in Bonsaver and Gordon, *Culture, Censorship and the State*, 60.

33 The documentation regarding Alfonso Gatto can be found in ACS, MCP II, b. 6, f. 'Gazzetta del Popolo,' while that on Gianna Manzini, beginning in January 1941, is in ACS, MCP, b. 258, f. 'Sussidi.' Mussolini initialled his approval on both requests for funding in favour of Manzini.

34 The first *nulla osta* for the publication of Comisso's book was given by Casini on 25 July 1941; documents in ASMi, PG II, b. 153, f. 044 'Bompiani Valentino casa editrice.' The MCP's *velina* is quoted in Flora, *Ritratto di un ventennio*, 164. The book was also translated into French and published by Grasset in 1944 in an edition that reflected both the imposed cuts and the replacement of 'Mussolin, ebreo' with 'Massarin' (p. 72 in the French edition). Comisso wrote about this episode in a postwar edition of *Agenti segreti di Venezia* (Milan: Longanesi, 1984; repr. Milan: Neri Pozza, 1994), 9–19. Comisso had already encountered problems with the censors for an earlier collection of short stories, *Avventure*, published by Vallecchi in 1935. The content of

some stories had been considered either obscene or irreverent with regard to Italian nationalism (in one story the protagonist finds the skeleton of an Italian soldier from the First World War and in the end unceremoniously scatters around his bones. According to Comisso's memoirs, four short stories were eventually left out of the collection. See Giovanni Comisso, *Le mie stagioni* (Milan: Garzanti, 1951), 149.

35 Attached to Luciano's memo dated 22 February 1940 there is a copy of *Rivoluzione*'s first issue with passages from various articles underlined in pencil. Pratolini's front-page editorial was entitled 'Attendere gli ordini.' Documents in ACS, MCP, b. 44, f. 154 'Appunti al Duce (1937/43).' In November 1943 the name of Vasco Pratolini was included by Mussolini in the list of thirty-three authors – the so-called 'canguri giganti' ('giant kangaroos') – who had publicly hailed the fall of the Fascist regime despite the fact that they had previously received financial help from the MCP. Sem Benelli and Massimo Bontempelli were also listed. See the anonymous article that was credited to Mussolini by the editors of his *Opera Omnia*, 'Canguri gigantic,' *Corrispondenza Repubblicana*, 11 November 1943, in *Opera Omnia*, 32, 264–6.

36 Letter dated 5 April 1940, in ACS, MCP II, b. 6, f. 'Gazzetta del Popolo.' The idea of exploiting the War of the Spanish Succession as an example of Italian-German military collaboration must have been picked up in various quarters. As we have just seen in the case of the children's magazine *Cartoni animati*, a year after Mussolini's 'suggestion,' the magazine ran a story about Italians in Piedmont fighting against the French invaders during that particular war.

37 In February 1941 Mussolini ordered a payment of 100,000 lire to Vallecchi to sponsor a new edition of Giovanni Papini's *Italia mia* (documents in ACS, SPD CO, f. 509.224 'Vallecchi Attilio'; see also Simonetti, 'L'editoria fiorentina dal 1920 al 1940,' 560–1). Following a letter asking Il Duce for financial help (dated 15 April 1942), Guido Milanesi was handed a cheque for 50,000 lire (documents in ACS, SPD CO, f. 510.632). As for Pitigrilli, his March 1942 request for a meeting with Mussolini was turned down, and no reply was given to a letter of recommendation by Augusto Turati, ex-secretary of PNF (28 June 1942), and a letter by Pitigrilli himself (18 March 1943) in which he attached a photograph of the ruins of his home in Turin, which was destroyed in a bombing raid (documents in ACS, SPD CO, f. 532.422). Pavolini's telegram concerning Margherita Sarfatti, dated 19 November 1940, can be found in ACS, MCP, b. 124, f. 9362.

38 The correspondence took place between 8 October and 6 November 1940; documents in ACS, MCP, b. 258, f. 'Sussidi.'

39 Benito Mussolini, *Parlo con Bruno* (Milan: Hoepli, 1942). Mussolini's order is mentioned in one of his letters to Ada Negri, dated 16 January 1942, in ACS, SPD CR, b. 14, f. 209/R.

40 Maurizio Giammusso, *Eliseo: Un teatro e i suoi protagonisti* (Rome: Gremese, 1989), 123; see also his *Vita di Eduardo* (Milan: Mondadori, 1994). A sign of the regime's attempt to monitor theatrical performances in dialect comes from a circular sent by then head of DGSI, Neos Dinale, on 21 February 1935, demanding that all prefects carry out an inventory of all the theatre companies performing plays in dialect within their jurisdiction. Circular in ASVr, PG, b. 11, f. 5/6.

41 On this see Cara Casaburi, 'Eduardo De Filippo e la censura fascista,' *Ariel* 2–3 (1993): 290–1. Zurlo briefly refers to this episode in his *Memorie inutili*, 261. This is an example of how Pavolini, in contrast to Alfieri, did not pass every report by Zurlo on to Mussolini. As Casaburi shows, Pavolini dealt with this case without consulting Il Duce.

42 Di Marzio's letter, dated 29 August 1941, can be found in ACS, MCP, b. 89, f. 7, sf. 2 'Ritiro dalla circolazione dei libri di letteratura dialettale.' Long passages of the letter are quoted in Cesari, *La censura nel periodo fascista*, 111; the episode is also mentioned in Cannistraro, *La fabbrica del consenso*, 141. See also Klein, *La politica linguistica del fascismo*, 148.

43 ACS, MCP, DGTM CT, b. 320/5897. Another play by Pirandello, *Cecè*, had been censored in 1939. Zurlo asked for a brief reference to a minister and an undersecretary to be removed. See ACS, MCP, DGTM CT, b. 483.

44 During the war years these two collections enjoyed, respectively, five and seven reprints by Einaudi. See Giulio Einaudi's *nota* in the publication of the correspondence between him and Montale in Carla Sacchi, ed., *Il carteggio Einaudi–Montale per 'Le occasioni'* (Turin: Einaudi, 1988), vii-ix.

45 Spaini had offered to translate Friedrich Schiller's *Geschichte des Abfalls der Niederlande* in February 1939 but the project was given the go-ahead only in 1941. Spaini's letter can be found in AE, b. Spaini; it is also quoted in Mangoni, *Pensare i libri*, 22. Alberto Spaini occasionally worked as reader of German books for the MCP (Mangoni, *Pensare i libri*, 21).

46 In 1941 Einaudi's project of expansion went as far as planning a takeover of Garzanti (ex-Treves). Both Bottai and Casini were involved in the preliminary negotiations, although the takeover was eventually cancelled since Garzanti in the meantime had managed to secure the funds necessary to the survival of the publishing house. On this see Mangoni, *Pensare i libri*, 86.

47 On *La Ruota* see Vittoria, 'Fascist Censorship and Non-Fascist Literary Circles.' On Alicata see Gianfranco Tortorelli, 'Contributi sulla formazione culturale e politica di Mario Alicata,' *Italia contemporanea* 25.1 (1978): 93–8.

48 Turi, *Casa Einaudi*, 113. It is interesting to note that a rare case of a negative review of an Einaudi book on the part of Bottai's *Primato* concerns Natalia Ginzburg's *La strada che va in città* (1942), which, following the ban on Jewish authors, had been published under the pseudonym of Alessandra Tornimparte (see Turi, *Casa Einaudi*, 115–16). On *Primato* see Luisa Mangoni, *L'interventismo della cultura: Intellettuali e riviste del fascismo* (Bari: Laterza, 1974). But see also De Felice's critical notes questioning the motives of Bottai's interest in young non-fascist intellectuals (Renzo De Felice, *Mussolini l'alleato*, vol. 2, *Crisi e agonia del regime* [Turin: Einaudi, 1990], 851–65). The day after the fall of Mussolini's regime, on 26 July 1943, Muscetta wrote a letter to Einaudi suggesting a takeover of *Primato* (which did not take place); see Turi, *Casa Einaudi*, 147–8. For various examples of Bottai's role as Einaudi's favourite interlocutor among Fascist leaders see the correspondence between him and Giulio Einaudi, which begins on 27 October 1938 with a request by Einaudi for a meeting (AE, b. 'Bottai Giuseppe').

49 Einaudi, *Frammenti* di *menoria*, 72. Entry dated 6 September 1942, in Bottai, *Diario, 1935–1944*, 321. Gaeta, 'Minculpop, censura libri,' 329–30.

50 Documents in AE, b. 'Alicata' and b. 'Einaudi.' The most detailed account of this period in Einaudi's history is certainly Mangoni, *Pensare i libri*, 70–165. But see also Turi, *Casa Einaudi*, 109–47.

51 An unsuccessful case was that of a collection of short stories by the German author Kilian Kerst (pseudonym of Wilhelm Fath), *Tumult des Herzens* (1941). Despite two positive opinions by German readers, it was turned down because of the suicide of one of the characters (AE, b. 'Mario Alicata,' see letters dated 26 November and 7 December 1941).

52 In the early months of 1942 Casini suggested a number of publications, among which was a novel by a friend (an editor of *Giornale d'Italia*), an anticommunist book by Gilberto Severo, *L'oscura filosofia del comunismo* (for which the MCP was prepared to award a grant of 5,000 lire), and his own translation of Metternich's memoirs. Einaudi replied giving his consent only to Casini's translation of Metternich, which was eventually published in 1943 (AE, b. 'Alicata,' letter dated 21 February 1942, also 1 June 1942; AE, b. 'Benedetti,' letter dated 24 April 1942, also mentioned in Mangoni, *Pensare i libri*, 115, and Turi, *Casa Einaudi*, 110, 152).

53 In the spring of 1942, for example, Alicata negotiated a project with Einaudi to publish an entire series of books sponsored by the Ministry of Italian Africa. The project was eventually abandoned (presumably because by the end of that year very little was left of Italian Africa). On this see Alicata's letters in AE, b. 'Mario Alicata,' 15 and 18 April 1942; also Mangoni, *Pensare i libri*, 114.

54 It is interesting to note that the week before Mussolini asked the prefect of Turin to investigate Einaudi, a Fascist university professor at Bologna University, Goffredo Coppola, had published in *Il Popolo d'Italia* a vicious attack against publishers who were still distributing books written by foreigners whose countries were at war with Italy. Among them, Einaudi's edition of Tolstoy's *Guerra e pace* had been singled out. It remains to be seen whether Coppola's article had prompted Mussolini to order an investigation, or whether the article might have actually been 'caused' by Mussolini's disapproval when reading Einaudi's plans for publication. All documentation in ACS, SPD CO, f. 528.771. Coppola's article, 'Guerre di religione,' was published on 15 January 1942 (on this see Mangoni, *Pensare i libri*, 121). For more on Coppola's activity for *Il Popolo d'Italia*, see chapter 9 below.

55 Mario Alicata, *Lettere e taccuini di Regina Coeli* (Turin: Einaudi, 1977). See in particular the long historical introduction by Albertina Vittoria, xvii–lviii.

56 Letter by Casini, dated 18 March 1940, in ASMi, PG II, b. 154, f. 044 'Hoepli Urlico casa editrice'; and letter dated 30 October 1939, in ibid., b. 156, f. 044 f. 'Sonzogno casa editrice.'

57 Documents in ASMi, PG, b. 78 and b. 153, f. 044, quoted in Fabre, *L'elenco*, 290, 292. Around the same date, however, on 9 February 1940, the Commissione per la Bonifica Libraria had met and, despite the opposition of Arnoldo Mondadori as representative of the publishing industry, decided on a course of intransigence towards contemporary Jewish writers (rejecting Mondadori's suggestion that the ministry should judge each individual case on its merit).

58 This is consistent with Mussolini's general approach to the Jewish question. The decree of 13 July 1939, for example, instituted 'race tribunals' that had the authority to give a patent of 'arianizzato' (Aryanized) to Jews who would have not qualified for it under earlier legislation. This opened the door to a number of exceptions and instances of favouritism and corruption. In August 1940 Demorazza planned the 'arianizzazione' of all 'mixed Jews' (i.e., those with Catholic ancestors) and the expulsion of all Jews. Mussolini approved, although the war took priority and the project was never accomplished. On this see De Felice, *Storia degli ebrei sotto il fascismo*, 335–71, and Michaelis, *Mussolini and the Jews*, 276–90.

59 *Chi è: Dizionario degli italiani d'oggi* (Rome: Cenacolo, 1940). Del Vecchio's entry was reinstated in the postwar edition of 1948 (Rome: Scarano). I am grateful to Professor Denis Mack Smith for allowing me free use of his unique collection of *Chi è* of the 1930s and 1940s.

60 Del Vecchio's letter is in ACS, SPD CO, f. 207.715. On this see also Giorgio Del Vecchio, *Una nuova persecuzione contro un perseguitato: Documenti* (Rome: Tipografia artigiana, 1945), 26, and Fabre, *L'elenco*, 313.

61 On Nazi anti-Semitic policies and the publishing industry see Barbian, *Literaturpolitik im Dritten Reich*, 505–66. On the Liste Otto see Natalie Zemon Davis, ed., *Liste Otto: The Official List of French Books Banned under the German Occupation* [facsimile of the 1940 publication] (Cambridge, MA: Harvard College Library, 1992). The collaboration of the publishing industry was highlighted by two facts: the list was organized around individual publishing houses and its title page presented it as 'Works Withdrawn from Sale by the Publishers or Forbidden by the German Authorities' (Ouvrages retirés de la vente par les éditeurs ou interdit par les autorités allemandes). A similar operation had also been accomplished after the Nazi occupation of Czechoslovakia in 1939. See Fabre, *L'elenco*, 330–1. An Italian copy of the Liste Otto can be found in ACS, MCP, b. 56, f. 1075.

62 Fabre, *L'elenco*, 332–9. The meeting might well have been prompted by Pavolini's first official visit to Berlin on 19–21 June 1941, during which he met his Nazi opposite number, Goebbels. The visit had been organized by the MCP's previous minister, Dino Alfieri, who was subsequently Italian ambassador to Berlin (reference to it can be found in Alfieri's memoirs, *Due dittatori di fronte*, 235–6). It is not surprising that at this time the ministries of culture and the embassies of the two nations should have decided to keep in closer contact. The cultural collaboration, however, did not extend to military matters. Pavolini was kept totally in the dark about the Nazi's invasion of Russia, which began on the last day of his visit. Goebbels and Pavolini met again in September 1941, this time on the occasion of the Venice Film Festival. On Pavolini's visit see also Petacco, *Il superfascista*, 116–17.

63 Both letters can be found in ACS, MCP II, b. 13, f. 'Luigi Salvatorelli.'

64 For a detailed reconstruction of this episode see Victor Farias, *Heidegger and Nazism* (Philadelphia: Temple University Press, 1989), 260–8. The quoted memorandum of 3 July 1942 is held at Archiv del Instituts für Zeitgeschichte, Munich, and is quoted and translated by Farias (263). Only one volume of Heidegger's work was published in Italian during the war years: *Che cos'è la metafisica?* (Milan: Bocca, 1942).

65 Fabre, *L'elenco*, 335–6.

66 The documents are in ASDMAE, MAE, b. 171, f. 36/26. See also Fabre, *L'elenco*, 336.

67 See De Felice, *Storia degli ebrei italiani sotto il fascismo*, 364–7, 583–4, Michaelis, *Mussolini and the Jews*, 293.

68 For example, on 5 October 1942 the German embassy successfully requested the seizure of a work by a writer who appeared in the Nazi list of 'unwelcome authors': Carl Zuckmayer's *Maddalena*, published by Bompiani. On this and other cases see Fabre, *L'elenco*, 338–9.

69 A copy of the German list that was passed on by Casini to the MCP's General Directorate for the Foreign Press on 29 December 1941 can be found in ASDMAE, MCP, b. 294, f. 4/II. The file also contains two lists for a total of thirty-five Jewish and 'half-Jewish' authors from Hungary. The first one had been prepared by the Italian Legation in Budapest, the second one by the Hungarian Legation in Rome. The overlap of five names – struck off the first list – suggests that the two lists had been prepared independently by the embassies of the respective countries.

70 Moravia's situation, already discussed in chapter 5 will also be touched upon in chapter 9. As for Silone, the notorious *querelle* relative to his alleged collaboration with the Fascist police is still raging. The book that initiated the debate is Biocca and Canali, *L'informatore: Silone, i comunisti e la polizia.* For a recent discussion of the debate see the chapters by Elizabeth Leake ('Ignazio Silone and the Politics of "Archive Malice"') and Stanislao Pugliese (The Double Bind of Ignazio Silone: Between Archive and Hagiography) in Bonsaver and Gordon, *Culture, Censorship and the State,* 134–41 and 142–9, respectively. As for censorship, the first instance regarding Silone is a telegram of 13 January 1934 from the deputy head of police, Carmine Senise, informing all prefects that Silone's essay *Der Fascismus: Seine Entstehung and seine Entwicklung,* recently published in Switzerland, was to be banned from entry into and circulation in Italy. A second instance concerns the German translation of *Pane e vino* (*Brot und Wein*), which on 3 February 1936 was banned from circulation in Italy. No other documentation has been found concerning Silone's fiction, in particular *Fontamara.* Senise's telegram can be found in ACS, DGPS DAGR, b. 11, f. 'Circolari.' Among the Silone papers at the Fondazione Turati, there is an exchange of letters between Silone and his Swiss publisher, Verlag Oprecht, that shows that in April 1942 the Swiss censorship office asked for some sentences of *Il seme sotto la neve* to be altered (in FFT, b. 'Corrispondenza Silone,' f. 'Editori svizzeri: Oprecht'). A copy of the circular of the Ministry of the Interior related to *Pane e vino* can be found at the Centro Studi Siloniani in Pescina. I am greatful to the Silone scholar Deborah Holmes for pointing this out to me.

71 Alfredo Segre published two novels with Mondadori: *Agenzia Abram Lewis* (1934) and *Cantiere Francesco Silvia* (1938). After leaving Italy, he helped Jewish emigrants in France during the Second World War and eventually moved to the United States, where he worked for the U.S. Army. His personal papers are held at the Immigration History Research Center at the University of Minnesota.

72 AFM, FAM, b. 65 'Ministero Cultura Popolare.'

73 Letter from Giulio Einaudi to Mario Alicata, dated 12 November 1942, in AE, b. 'Alicata Mario.' Reference to Corbaccio's refusal is made by Mangoni

in *Pensare i libri*, 141. In his hometown, the memory of Italo Svevo had at least once been the target of Fascist anti-Semitism. A statue in his honour was smashed by a group of Fascists on 21 September 1939 (see Michaelis, *Mussolini and the Jews*, 282). Trieste was obviously a hotbed of Fascist anti-Semitism: various episodes of attacks on Jewish institutions took place in 1941, July 1942, and May 1943 (see De Felice, *Storia degli ebrei italiani sotto il fascismo*, 389–91).

74 On this see Elisabetta Rasy, 'Caro Mussolini, sono il poeta Saba ...,' *Panorama*, 31 July 1997, 103; Stelio Mattioni, *Storia di Umberto Saba* (Milan: Camunia, 1989), 123–7; and, in more detail, Fabre, *L'elenco*, 366–7.

75 Fabre, *L'elenco*, 397.

76 Fabre has found three other names that simply should not have been on the list but had been mistakenly assumed to be Jewish. They were the professor of statistics Pier Paolo Luzzatto Fegiz, the novelist Annie Vivanti, and the German law scholar Ernst Heinz, whose name did not appear in the Nazi list (*L'elenco*, 372–3). In the case of Annie Vivanti, the fact that by June 1943 the MCP minister, Fernando Mezzasoma, was still ordering the seizure of three of her works (*Circe*, *Naja Tripudians*, and *Salvate le nostre*) is one more sign that the list was perhaps not as efficiently administered as one would imagine (see the telegram dated 15 June 1943, in ACS, SPD CO, f. 509.568/2). Vivanti had also been the subject of a fortnightly *Rapporto riservato* (Confidential Report) by Pavolini to the press: on 2 February 1942, Pavolini explained that Vivanti was an ex-Jew, converted first to Protestantism and then to Catholicism; any publicity, concluded the brief note, was inopportune. The report can be found in Claudio Matteini, *Ordini alla stampa* (Rome: Polibraria Italiana, 1945), 277.

77 See Fabre, *L'elenco*, 343.

78 Fabre refers to two books published by Carroccio (Fabre, *L'elenco*, 395). In 1944 a reprint of Ginesi's *La fuga dei giocattoli* was also published by Vallardi. Another author of children's literature, Maria Ettlinger Fano – whose work appeared in one of the earliest lists, of March 1939 – was allowed to appear as a translator from Russian and English throughout the last years of the regime. See, for example, her translation and abridged version of *Marussia: Leggenda ucraina*, which was reprinted by the Turinese publisher Paravia in 1944, and the translation from English of Giuliana Orazia Ewing [Julia Horatia Ewing], *Jan of the Windmill* (*Gianni del Mulino a Vento*), reprinted by Paravia in 1945.

79 Fabre, *L'elenco*, 309. Unfortunately this is the only 1943 catalogue that Fabre has uncovered. At Bologna's Istituto Gramsci there is a substantial collection of Italian publishers' catalogues (Fondo Cataloghi Editoriali) but not a sin-

gle one for this particular year. I am grateful to Greta Belbusti at Bompiani for attempting to locate such material in the publisher's archives. Apparently Bompiani did not publish an annual catalogue during the war years but only lists of books that were sent to bookshops and libraries. None of these lists for the years 1940–5 has been kept. Further research in this area is clearly needed.

80 See Michele Caterinella, 'Un esempio locale: La Biblioteca Universitaria di Bologna,' in Centro Furio Jesi, *La menzogna della razza*, 326–31. Caterinella's article also shows how, throughout the early 1940s, Bottai's ministry had kept libraries informed of all the books that the MCP had decided to withdraw from circulation.

81 See Caterinella, 'Un esempio locale,' 328–30; Fabre, *L'elenco*, 355–9.

82 It is comforting to see that sometimes even anti-Semitic works would fall under the axe of the censors. On 19 April 1941 Casini rejected the distribution of a short book by Angiolo Maros Dell'Oro entitled *Razzismo* and published by Sonzogno, on two grounds: first, it gave too much space to German racial thought – seventeen pages, in contrast to seven devoted to Italian racism; second, because the references to Nazi theories about the German origin of the Italian Renaissance were likely to cause resentment among the Italian readership. Letter by Casini to the prefecture of Milan, in ASMi, PG II, b. 156, f. 044 'Sonzogno casa editrice.'

83 Fabre, *L'elenco*, 298. As governor of Libya, Italo Balbo had repeatedly defended the Jewish community. His death in 28 June 1940, when his plane was mistakenly shot down by the Italian anti-aircraft defences, had left the field open to the anti-Semites. On Balbo's involvement in the Jewish question see De Felice, *Storia degli ebrei italiani sotto il fascismo*, 196–203, 368–70.

84 Pavolini's statement can be found in Circular 5510 'Disciplina delle pubblicazioni non periodiche,' which was sent to all prefectures on 14 February 1941, in ACS, MI, DGPS, Massime S4, b. S4/A (provv.), f. 1 sf. 1. See also Krieg, *La legislazione penale sulla stampa*, 18. The book was positively reviewed in *Il Popolo d'Italia*, 21 March 1942. The absence of pre-publication censorship in Fascist Italy was also mentioned in a letter from Casini to the prefect of Verona on 11 December 1939 (ASVr, PG, b. 41, f. 526 'Disposizione per la stampa').

85 On 19 February 1943, on the eve of the publication of the bill in the *Gazzetta Ufficiale* (after which the bill would take effect), the MCP's DGSI sent out a circular with instructions on how to apply the law. It is only in this document that the exclusion of *letteratura amena* from preventive censorship is mentioned. The original text of the bill mentions only what was going to be subjected to preventive censorship. Both documents were published in the

Giornale della libreria, 10 March 1943, 1–3. A copy of both documents can be found in ACS, DGPS DAGR, Massime S4, b. 103 (provv.), f. 7 'Controllo della stampa in tempo di guerra.'

86 All documents can be found in ACS, SPD CO, f. 500.007. The telegram revoking the seizure of Laterza's book was seriously mispelled: the author's name, Manlio Ciardo, was spelled 'Guido Cirdo.'

87 The report, undated but arguably written between February and July 1943, can be found in ACS, MCP, b. 143, f. 426 'Teatro.' On theatre censorship during the war see Iaccio, *La scena negata*, which contains the text of six censored scripts. All six pieces were written by pro-Fascist authors and were censored by Zurlo because of their inappropriate treatment of war and politics.

88 The MCP's attempt to tackle children's literature in the spring of 1943 is confirmed by a circular sent to all publishers on 25 March 1942. Polverelli's circular had a form attached, entitled 'Revisione della cultura giovanile' (Revision of youth literature), in which publishers were supposed to provide details of all their children's books whose first printing dated from before 1922. The operation was supposed to tackle books that had been authorized in pre-Fascist years. It is interesting that in the accompanying circular Mezzasoma should have written of the MCP's intention to 'proceed to a gradual, but integral, reclamation of book production,' thus suggesting that by March 1942 the overall operation was still in its early stages. See Piccioni, *Una casa editrice*, 64–6.

89 On this see also Cesari, *La censura nel periodo fascista*, 95–8.

90 Polverelli's appointment was typical of the entire shuffle, which saw prominent personalities being replaced by a team of secondary figures of long-standing service to the regime and the PNF. On this last, sterile government shuffle see De Felice, *Mussolini l'alleat*, 2: 1047–62.

91 Bottai, *Diario, 1935–44*, 367–8.

92 ACS, SPD CO, f. 500.007 'Ministero della Cultura Popolare.' Roberto Mandel was a prolific writer of fiction, poems, and historical works. He had also published pro-Fascist works among which *Il duce: Gli atti e le opere, i discorsi e le direttive, l'azione di governo* (Sonzogno, 1928) and *Celebrazioni fasciste: Prose oratorie* (ISI, 1940). Although seized by the police in Bologna, *Il cantico dei cicli* was never officially banned. It does not appear in a list of books banned between July 1936 and April 1943 that was kept among the papers at DGPS in ACS, DGPS DAGR, Massime S4, b. S4/A (provv.), f. 1.

93 ACS, SPD CO, f. 500.007 and f. 509.257/I; also mentioned in Fabre, *L'elenco*, 303. During the last week before the fall of the regime, we have a final example of Zurlo's asking the views of Mussolini. It concerned a radio play entitled *L'uomo nuovo*, which attempted a biographical tale of Il Duce. In his

handwritten note on Zurlo's memo dated 21 June 1943, Mussolini simply and almost symbolically wrote: 'Niente. M' (Nothing. M). On this last episode see Ferrara, *Censura teatrale e fascismo*, 80.

94 Quoted in De Felice, *Mussolini l'alleato*, 2: 863.

95 The contract for the Italian publication of Silone's work eventually went to Mondadori, who offered the writer an advance of 100,000 lire. Mondadori's telegram and letters ended up in Mussolini's hands after Badoglio's hurried flight from Rome on 8 September 1943. Both were found among the stash of documents that Mussolini was attempting to take with him to Switzerland in April 1945. On Mondadori see Decleva, *Mondadori*, 272–5, 368. On Einaudi see Mangoni, *Pensare i libri*, 166–82. On Corbaccio see Gigli Marchetti, *Le edizioni Corbaccio*, 88–91, 105–9.

8. Foreign Fiction and Weak Autarky

1 Documents in ACS, MCP, b. 56, f. 1075, and ACS, DGPS DAGR, Massime S4, b. 103 (provv.), f. 5, quoted in Voigt, *Il rifugio precario*, 95, and in Fabre, *L'elenco*, 32. For some general considerations on the debate over the translation of foreign works in the late 1930s, see Fabre, *L'elenco*, 62–4. Once more, in Krieg's official publication the picture is presented in rather biased terms. According to it, pre-publication control over foreign literature was introduced only when Italy was at war, with the circular no. 3041/B of 15 October 1941 (Krieg, *La legislazione penale sulla stampa*, 19).

2 Documents in ASMi, PG II, b. 153, f. 044 'Corbaccio casa editrice'; for a more detailed analysis see Gigli Marchetti, *Le edizioni Corbaccio*, 76–9 (which, however, fails to mentions Casini's letter regarding Karinthy's book). The modification of replacing Lei with *Voi* in Surany's novel on 4 December 1938 was also imposed in June and October 1940 on the proofs of two collections of short stories, one by Maria Chiappelli (*L'oca minore*) and the other by Ugo Dettore (*Nel nostro cuore*) both to be published by Bompiani (ASMi, PG II, b. 153, f. 044 ' Bompiani Valentino casa editrice'). An exception was made for Anna Franchi's novel *La mia vita* (Garzanti, 1941), as the historical setting in nineteenth-century Italy justified the use of *Lei*. The need for publishers to make sure that the 'abolizione totalitaria' (totalitarian abolition) of *Lei* was adopted by all authors was stated in a letter to all Italian publishers sent by Dino Alfieri on 13 September 1938 (ASMi, PG II, b. 154, f. 44 'Garzanti casa editrice'). In the midst of the crisis, Dall'Oglio sent a long letter of protest to DGSI, listing the economic damage caused by the many bans. The letter also mentioned the fact that while Corbaccio had been heavily hit, other publishers were left free to distribute books by the

same authors. No answer to the letter could be found. However, the letter might be connected to the fact that on 24 August 1938, the MCP's head of cabinet, Celso Luciano, informed Corbaccio that the ministry had decided to provide some financial help through the acquisition of a number of copies of Corbaccio's *Storia della guerra italiana* for a total of 100,000 lire. Corbaccio's letter had estimated a loss of about 120,000 to 150,000 lire. Both documents can be found in ASMi, PG II, b. 153, f. 044 'Corbaccio casa editrice.'

3 Documents in ASMi, PG II, b. 153, f. 044 'Bompiani Valentino casa editrice,' and D'Ina and Zaccaria, eds., *Caro Bompiani*, 37–8. The letter from Pavolini to Bompiani, dated 2 October 1941, is quoted in Valentino Bompiani's memoirs, *Il mestiere dell'editore*, 12. With regard to Di Donato's novel, despite its seizure in October 1941, it is puzzling to see that a new edition of *Cristo tra i muratori* was authorized under the RSI in 1944. It is interesting to note that some intellectuals regarded the publication of works by contemporary American novelists such as Caldwell and Steinbeck as effective anti-American propaganda. The famous architect Gio Ponti, who, as we will see in the next chapter, was at the time in contact with Mussolini and writing anonymously for *Il Popolo d'Italia*, wrote a letter to Mussolini on 14 February 1940 in which he recommended that Il Duce read Steinbeck's *Furore*. 'Descrive l'estendersi del latifondo in America, ... E' il contrario di quel che il Fascismo ha fatto e fa nel Pontino, in Sicilia, in Libia. E' un libro che tutti gli italiani dovrebbero leggere e tutti i giornali segnalare' (It describes the growth of large-scale farming in America, ... It is the opposite of what Fascism has been doing in the Pontino, Sicily, and Libya. It is a book that all Italians should read and all papers should recommend). Letter in ACS, SPD CO, f. 511.102. The potential anti-American content of Steinbeck's novels had also been spotted by the MCP: we know that the translator of *La battaglia*, no other than Eugenio Montale, had been asked to add a short preface drawing attention to the social conflict represented in the novel. Montale complied with the request but on 15 July 1940 insisted that the preface should be signed as 'Nota dell'Editore' without mention of his name. Montale's letter is quoted in D'Ina and Zaccaria, eds., *Caro Bompiani*, 570. Casini's request for a preface underlining the representation of social struggles and the economic conflicts of American democracy was dated 1 July 1939. A similar request had been made earlier, on 20 June 1939, for the translation of Millen Brand's *Eroi* (*The Heroes*, 1939). This time Casini asked the editor to underline the fact that the novel is about American unemployed ex-soldiers. Both letters are in ASMi, PG II, b. 153, f. 044 'Bompiani Valentino casa editrice.' On Vittorini's activity as an editor see also Ferretti, *L'editore Vittorini*.

4 D'Ina and Zaccaria, eds., *Caro Bompiani*, 122.

5 Documents in ACS, SPD CO, f. 509/1, and ACS, MCP, b. 116, f. 'Bompiani Valentino.'
6 D'Ina and Zaccaria, eds., *Caro Bompiani*, 125–6.
7 Letter dated 22 May 1942, in ibid., 87.
8 According to his correspondence, Bilenchi had to cancel the meeting because Pavolini was not receiving visits as a result of a recent bereavement. In his postwar memoirs Bilenchi reconstructs this event and suggests that he did meet Pavolini, although with no success. See Bilenchi's letter to Vittorini, dated 30 September 1942 in D'Ina and Zaccaria, *Caro Bompiani*, 88; see also 'Vittorini a Firenze,' in Bilenchi, *Amici*, 136–8.
9 Letters dated 22 September and 6 October 1942, in D'Ina and Zaccaria, eds., *Caro Bompiani*, 129, 131. During the month of October, Vittorini had taken part in an international conference of writers in Weimar, understandably attended by representatives of only Nazi-allied nations. On that occasion, as reported in a letter to Bompiani dated 31 October 1942, Vittorini had contacted a number of French and German authors with a view of securing their translation rights for Bompiani (*Caro Bompiani*, 134).
10 See Bompiani's letters to Vittorini of 17 and 21 September 1942 and Vittorini's reply of 25 September (Ibid, 125–30). I have been unable to trace the original French title of this publication.
11 The first detailed analysis of the publication of *Americana* is Giuliano Manacorda's 'Storia minore ma non troppo: Come fu pubblicata *Americana*,' *Rapporti*, December 1973, 21–6, reprinted as 'Come fu pubblicata "Americana,"' in *Elio Vittorini: Atti del Convegno Nazionale di Studi*, ed. Mario Sipala (Catania: Greco, 1978), 63–8. Of some help for the contextualization of *Americana* is Marina Guglielmi's 'La letteratura americana tradotta in Italia nel decennio 1930–1940: Vittorini e l'antologia *Americana*,' *Forum Italicum* 29 (1995): 301–12. See also Christopher Rundle, 'The Censorship of Translation in Fascist Italy,' *Translator* 6.1 (2000): 76–81.
12 Letters from Vittorini to Bompiani, dated 5 May and 6 December 1940, in D'Ina and Zaccaria, eds., *Caro Bompiani*, 38, 39. Casini's letter of 4 December 1940 can be found in ASMi, PG II, b. 153, f. 'Bompiani Valentino casa editrice.'
13 The letter can be found in D'Ina and Zaccaria, eds., *Caro Bompiani*, 39–40 (also quoted by Manacorda in 'Come fu pubblicata *Americana*,' 65–6). Arnaldo Frateili was a relatively popular, pro-Fascist, fiction writer publishing with Bompiani (and a personal friend of the publisher). He was not involved in the *Americana* project but was asked to add his plea and personally deliver a letter from Bompiani to Pavolini during a visit at the MCP.
14 It is interesting in this respect to note that in 1938 Elio Vittorini had approved the translation of Hemingway's *To Have or Have Not* (1937) for

Mondadori. His reader's report was annotated by Enrico Piceni with a comment highlighting the possibility that the author was *persona non grata*, after which Mondadori's co-director, Luigi Rusca, concluded the exchange with a laconic 'decidere negativamente' (come to a negative decision). It is arguable that Rusca or Mondadori himself might have double checked with the Fascist authorities and received a negative reply. Copy of the report can be found in Albonetti, ed., *Non c'è tutto nei romanzi*, 429–30.

15　With regard to *A Farewell to Arms*, there is also an interesting episode of an attempted censorship of its film adaptation. On this see Stephen Gundle, 'Hollywood, Italy and the First World War: Italian Reactions to Film Versions of Ernest Hemingway's *A Farewell to Arms*', in Bonsaver and Gordon, *Culture, Censorship and the State*, 98–108. In the postwar years, Hemingway was to become one of Mondadori's best-selling authors. A situation similar to that of Hemingway concerned Italian-American author John Fante, whose contribution appeared in *Americana* despite the fact that his novel *Wait Until Spring, Bandini* (1938) had been banned in 1938 (as mentioned in a memo by a MCP official, Armando De Pedys, to the prefecture of Milan, dated 12 March 1940, in ASMi, PG II, b. 153, f. 'Bompiani Valentino casa editrice.'

16　Emilio Cecchi, by then a member of the *Reale Accademia d'Italia* and one of Italy's most famous literary figures, had already expressed his critical views of American culture in his collection of articles *America amara* (Sansoni, 1940). Closer to the publication of *Americana*, Cecchi had also confessed his disapproval of the popularity of American fiction in an article for *Corriere della Sera* dated 30 March 1941. Despite this, Cecchi was sometimes contacted for his advice, particularly by Mondadori, on matters related to American fiction. Archival evidence shows that he gave his advice to the MCP too. His correspondence at ACGV shows that on 15 December 1941 and 20 November 1942, Amedeo Tosti contacted Cecchi and asked him for his views 'circa il valore dell'opera stessa e l'opportunità di autorizzarne una traduzione in italiano' (with regard to its literary value and the desirability of an Italian translation). The books reviewed by Cecchi were Henry James's *The Portrait of a Lady* and Lee Masters's *Spoon River Anthology*. A handwritten note in margin of the letter of 20 November 1942 states that Cecchi sent his report the following week, on 27 November. Correspondence in ACGV, Fondo manoscritto Emilio Cecchi.

17　Cecchi's preface was reprinted as an appendix to a postwar edition of *Americana*, which reinstated Vittorini's original texts (Milan: Bompiani, 1984).

18　Letters dated 28 and 30 March 1942, in D'Ina and Zaccaria, eds., *Caro Bompiani*, 42–3. In his second book of memoirs, *Il mestiere dell'editore* (Milan: Longanesi, 1988), Valentino Bompiani quotes Pavolini's letter and surprisingly comments: 'Questa imposizione non fu da noi accettata' (We did not accept this imposition) (121). The facts prove beyond doubt that Bompiani's memory failed him on this particular instance.

19 Letter from Cecchi to Bompiani, dated 29 April 1942, in D'Ina and Zaccaria, eds., *Caro Bompiani*, 45.

20 See the letter from Bompiani to Vittorini, dated 25 May 1943, Vittorini's reply of 29 May, and Bompiani's letter to Vittorini, dated 7 June 1943; all in ibid., 47, 148. On 11 January 1943 a copy of *Americana* had also been sent to Mussolini's office (ACS, SPD CO, f. 509.109).

21 The MCP's memo dated 26 June 1943 can be found in ACS, MCP, Gab. b. 116, f. 'Bompiani Valentino (Editore).' *Americana* was advertised in the publicity insert occupying the entire back cover of Alberto Savinio's *Narrate uomini la vostra storia*. The first edition of Savinio's book was published in June 1942 but it is its third reprint, dated February 1944, that contains this publicity blurb. A copy of this book is held in a private collection donated to Reading University Library; I am grateful to Professor Christopher Duggan for facilitating its consultation.

22 Letter from Vittorini to Bompiani, dated 21 January 1943. Bompiani's letter of 13 February 1943 makes no mention of the project. See D'Ina and Zaccaria, eds., *Caro Bompiani*, 138–40. Bompiani's historical catalogue is of no help in this instance, as it does not provide details of the various reprints of each publication. For its entry on *Americana* see Giuseppe Zaccaria, ed., *Catalogo generale Bompiani, 1929–1999* (Milan: Bompiani, 1999), 549.

23 Letter from Mondadori to Mussolini, dated 14 May 1940, in ACS, SPD CO, f. 509.568/2. On Mondadori and the financial importance of translation of foreign fiction see Pietro Albonetti, 'Trafile di romanzi,' in Albonetti, *Non c'è tutto nei romanzi*, 96–102.

24 Letter from Mondadori to Casini, dated 2 December 1937, in AFM, FAM, b. 65 'Ministero Cultura Popolare.'

25 Letter from Casini to Mondadori, dated 5 August 1941, in ASMi, PG II, b. 155, f. 'Mondadori Casa Editrice.' Letter from Mondadori to Celso Luciano, dated 17 October 1941, and to Mussolini, dated 23 October 1941, in ACS, SPD CO, f. 509.568/2. The episode is briefly mentioned in Decleva, *Mondadori*, 254. An exchange of letters between Celso Luciano and Mussolini's personal secretary, Osvaldo Sebastiani, shows that in May 1941 Mondadori had published a propaganda pamphlet entitled *Vincere o mendicare*. Mussolini had asked for the MCP's opinion (presumably following a request by Mondadori for financial support), which on 10 May came via Luciano saying that Pavolini had no intention of sponsoring its publication (documents in ACS, SPD CO, f. 509.568/2).

26 Documents in ASMi, PG, b. 155, f. 'Mondadori Casa Editrice.'
27 For more detail on Mondadori's translations during the war years see Decleva, *Mondadori*, 223–31, 251–4.
28 Documents in ASMi, MCP, PG II, b. 155, f. 'Mondadori casa editrice.'
29 ASMi, MCP, PG II, b. 156, f. 'Sonzogno Casa Editrice'; Decleva, *Mondadori*, 253.
30 Another non-Mondadori paper that benefitted from ministerial funds for a similar initiative was Interlandi's *Quadrivio*. Very close to Mussolini's ear, Interlandi had secured funding for his paper since January 1936. In June 1941 Mussolini personally approved a grant of 32,000 lire to be awarded to Interlandi towards the creation of an edition of *Quadrivio* in modern Greek. However, it was a much smaller operation than Mondadori's *Tempo*, which, in the same month, received a grant for its Greek edition of 120,000 lire. According to a handwritten record of all the grants awarded to periodicals during the period 1933–43, *Tempo* received by far the highest total, with 47,191,280 lire. On *Tempo* see AFM, FAM, b. 'Tempo' and ACS, MCP II, b. 9, f. 'Mondadori: Edizioni Straniere di "Tempo."' The above-mentioned handwritten document – possibly a list compiled at the MCP soon after the fall of the regime in July 1943 – is held at NAKe, GFM 36/82. See also Decleva, *Mondadori*, 256–9. On *Quadrivio* see ACS, MCP II, b. 2, f. 'Quadrivio.'
31 On *Topolino* see Forgacs, *Italian Culture in the Industrial Era*, 62–3, and Decleva, *Mondadori*, 261–2.
32 On Luigi Rusca's political views see Decleva, *Mondadori*, 268–71. The police file on him can be consulted at ACS, PP FP, f. 'Rusca Luigi.'
33 Letter from Einaudi to Alicata, dated 27 December 1941, in AE, b. 'Einaudi Giulio,' partially quoted in Mangoni, *Pensare i libri*, 116. Pavolini's directive – which also included initiatives for the promotion of Italian books abroad – was given ample space in the journal of the publisher's association, *Giornale della libreria* 19 (20 May 1942): 1–2. It should also be noted that even this drastic directive contained the proviso that exceptions to this limitation could be made for publishers specilizing in translations and those that had distinguished themselves in the export of Italian books abroad.
34 AE, b. 'Spaini Alberto' and b. 'Alicata Mario.' Both cases are mentioned in Mangoni, *Pensare i libri*, 115. The translation of Grimm's book was ready by April 1942. In a letter from Einaudi to Alicata, dated 20 April 1942, it appears that the translator had self-censored a page containing injurious remarks about Italy and various passages on obscure aspects of German home politics. The book, however, was never published. Although there is no documentary proof that the decision not to proceed was imposed by the MCP, this is arguably the most likely cause.

35 Letter from Alicata to Einaudi, dated 2 March 1942, in AE, b. 'Alicata Mario.'
36 A report of the meeting can be found in a letter by Alicata to Einaudi, dated 25 February 1942, in ibid.
37 For reasons unexplained by the available documentation, even this translation was never published. Letter from Alicata to Einaudi, dated 14 March 1942, in ibid.

9. Unfinished Business

1 Moravia was recognized as an 'Aryan' not as an 'ebreo discriminato,' which was the category for Italian Jews whose past services to the state – soldiers decorated during the First World War, for example – exempted them from anti-Semitic legislation. Moravia wrongly used the expression 'discriminato' when referring to his own situation in an interview with Giacomo Debenedetti in *16 ottobre 1943: Otto ebrei* (Milan: Il Saggiatore, 1973), quoted in Fabre, 'Sul il caso Moravia,' 193. Gherardo Casini's letter of 21 July 1939 can be found in ASMi, PG II, b. 153, f. 044 'Bompiani Valentino casa editrice.'
2 In the meantime, Moravia's mother was making use of her legal right to change the family surname from the Jewish Pincherle to the Aryan Piccinini. She formally applied in July 1939 although the procedure, as we will see, was only completed two years later. On this see Fabre, 'Sul "caso Moravia,"' 190–3.
3 The *velina*, dated 13 February 1941, has been reprinted in Flora, *Ritratto di un ventennio*, 164. Also partially quoted in Fabre, *L'elenco*, 398.
4 The novel was apparently withdrawn from sale. On this see ASMi, MCP, PG II, b. 155, f. 044 'Mondadori Arnoldo'; Fabre, *L'elenco*, 398–400; Decleva, *Mondadori*, 263.
5 The modification could have been unofficially imposed, as the *nulla osta* for its publication, dated 4 April 1941 and signed by Casini, gave full approval without requiring any modifications. Letter in ASMi, PG II, f. 044 'Bompiani Valentino casa editrice.'
6 Gaeta, 'Minculpop, censura libri,' 927–8.
7 The informer's report and the memo from the Ministry of the Interior summarizing the MCP's answer to their query can be found in ACS, PP FP, f. 'Pincherle Alberto.' At the same time, it is interesting to note that Corbaccio had asked to publish a new edition of *Gli indifferenti*, to which Tosti at the MCP replied negatively on 5 July 1941 (letter in ASMi, PG II, b. 153, f. 044 'Bompiani Valentino casa editrice').
8 Documents are in the recently discovered files in ACS, MCP II, b. 8, f. 'Moravia Alberto.'

9 ACS, Carte Pini, b. 30. On 11 December 1941 the application to change the family surname had also been to successful. It does not seem, however, that Alberto Moravia made use of this opportunity.

10 Pavolini's memo in response to Mussolini and Casini's letters can be found in ACS, MCP II, b. 8, f. 'Moravia Alberto.' About the marriage to Elsa Morante see Moravia's own recollection in Siciliano, *Alberto Moravia*, 47–8. In a note for Pavolini informing the minister that the editor of *Documento* had asked for permission to publish articles by Moravia, it was suggested that Elsa Morante was the 'figlioccia' (Goddaughter) of Padre Tacchi Venturi (mispelled 'Tocchi Venturi'); document in ACS, MCP II, b. 8, f. 'Moravia Alberto.' Even this memo contains Mussolini's 'Sì' in the margin.

11 A similar advertizement was published on page 3 of *Primato* of 1 April, 1 June, and 1 and 15 August 1942.

12 *Giochi di ragazzi* was left unfinished by Vittorini, partly because of the enthusiasm with which he had embraced the new project of *Conversazione in Sicilia*.

13 The observations in this section are indebted to my 2003 article on Vittorini; however, as a result of new archival and bibliographical findings, they supersede the results of my previous work. On the financing of *Letteratura* see chapter 5, in particular note 51. It should also be added that on 31 August 1940 Bonsanti wrote to Pavolini on *Letteratura* letterhead, asking to be employed by the MCP. On 3 September Pavolini replied that he was unable to fulfill Bonsanti's wishes. On 18 November 1940 Pavolini wrote to Bonsanti again, saying that, in compensation for his failure to employ him at the MCP, he was going to award him a grant of 5000 lire 'affinché possiate più tranquillamente attendere alla Vostra attività letteraria' (in order that you may go about your literary activities without problems). Letters in ACS, MCP, b. 271, f. 'Sussidi.'

14 The fact that this was a coerced cut is suggested by two details. First, later on in the novel the mother makes reference to being called 'Fortunata,' a detail that becomes obscure once the earlier passage has been cut. Second, in a memo by Casini dated 2 December 1938 and related to the financing of *Letteratura*, there is a brief reference to *Conversazione in Sicilia* having been censored during its publication in *Letteratura* (ACS, MCP, b. 271, f. 'Sussidi'; for more on this, see the following pages). For a detailed analysis of the variations between the *Letteratura* publication and the Bompiani version of 1941 see Antonio Girardi, '*Conversazione in Sicilia*: Dalla prima alla seconda redazione,' *Studi novecenteschi* 7 (1974): 111–21, and his *Nome e lagrime: Linguaggio e ideologia di Elio Vittorini* (Naples: Liguori, 1975), 98–105. On 17 July 1939 Bonsanti wrote to the critic Enrico Falqui and asked him to contact Marcello Gallian in order to obtain a statement in support of Bonsanti's 'fede e attiv-

ità e contegno fascista' (Fascist faith, activity and behaviour) (letter in A900, Carte Falqui). This happened at the time of Vittorini's publication of *Conversazione in Sicilia* in *Letteratura*; hence there is a chance that the need for support was related to the censorship problems encountered by Vittorini's novel.

15 Some critics, such as Raffaella Rodondi in her notes to the complete works ('Note ai testi,' *Vittorini: Opere narrative*, vol. 1 [Milan: Mondadori, 1974], 1200), have suggested that the different title might have been part of a ploy to 'smuggle' *Conversazione in Sicilia* past the censors' eyes. A brief passage in a letter by Vittorini of 9 November 1939, to a young scholar who wanted to write an essay on him, confirms that the book edition was encountering some problems: '*Conversazione in Sicilia* non uscirà tanto presto in volume. Vi sono delle difficoltà di censura da superare, e poi voglio correggere molte cose' (*Conversazione in Sicilia* won't be out soon as a volume. There are censorship problems to be overcome, and I also want to change various things) (in *I libri, la città il mondo: Lettere, 1933–1943* [Turin: Einaudi, 1985], 98). To this day there is no documentary evidence or statements by Vittorini or Bompiani suggesting that the change of title had been thought of as a ploy or was an imposed choice. We know, in fact, that at that very time *Conversazione in Sicilia* had been offered with that title to Arnoldo Mondadori. He declined to publish it on 27 March 1940, following two negative assessments by his readers, one of whom was Enrico Piceni (AFM, FAM, f. 'Vittorini Elio'). Moreover, the idea of a different title in order to avoid censorship is not convincing because the short story has a tone and style similar to the novel – that is, it conveys a similar sense of disillusionment and lack of hope. The fact that, with the Bompiani edition, Vittorini immediately returned to the original title *Conversazione in Sicilia* suggests that, by then at least, the title did not present problems of a political nature. Another case of censorship that should be added to the picture regards the short story 'Nome e lagrime' itself. It was first published in *Corrente di vita giovanile* in October 1939. The journal was at the time in its second year of life, and a few months later it was closed down apparently following an order from the MCP. On *Corrente di vita giovanile* see Alberto Folin and Mario Quaranta, eds., *Le riviste giovanili del periodo fascista* (Treviso: Canova, 1977), 349–82. Finally, in his memoirs concerning his friendship with Vittorini, Romano Bilenchi remembers that he and Bonsanti had been asked by Vittorini to write to Casini at the MCP to support the publication of *Nome e lagrime*. See Bilenchi, 'Vittorini a Firenze,' 807.

16 Alberto Moravia, 'Vittorini "Gran Lombardo,"' *Documento* 4 (April 1941); Don Ferrante (pseudonym of Mario Alicata), 'Corriere delle lettere,' *Primato*

7 (August 1941); Giuseppe Villaroel, 'Poeti e prosatori nuovi,' *Il Popolo d'Italia*, 29 June 1941.

17 Luciano Salce, 'Aspetti di Vittorini,' *Roma fascista*, 20 October 1941; Mario De Michelis, 'Conversazione in Sicilia di Elio Vittorini,' *Il Fascio*, 22 November 1941; Fredi Chiappelli, 'Conversazione in Sicilia,' *Rivoluzione* 8–9 (April 1942).

18 The preparation of the third reprint is discussed in a letter by Vittorini to Bompiani, dated 8 July 1942. See D'Ina and Zaccaria, eds., *Caro Bompiani*, 124. The correspondence between Vittorini and Bontempelli, dated 9 and 13 July 1942, can be found in the Bontempelli Papers at GRL.

19 Il revisore (pseudonym), 'Discussione all'Elba di Vittorini,' *Roma Fascista*, 4 June 1942, 3. In previous weeks, parodies by the same author had appeared teasing the prose style of other writers linked to Florentine literary circles such as Carlo Bo and Vasco Pratolini.

20 Anonymous, 'Una sporca conversazione,' *Il Popolo d'Italia*, 30 July 1942, 3. The only censorship problem that Vittorini and Bompiani seem to have had in the weeks before the end of July is related to the publication of *Nozze di sangue* by García Lorca. This is suggested in a handwritten note in a letter to Bompiani, dated 12 July 1942, in which Vittorini sarcastically commented on the fact that a devout Catholic such as Lorca could be found to be 'a poet of the communists' (AB, f. 'Vittorini Elio'). According to Bompiani's historical catalogue, García Lorca's work was nonetheless published in 1942. See Zaccaria, ed., *Catalogo generale Bompiani*, 348.

21 Memorandum by the prefecture official Franco Fuscà to the prefect, dated 31 July 1942, at ASMi, PG II, b. 381, f. 'Bompiani Valentino casa editrice.' Transcript of the letter by Bompiani's secretary to Vittorini, dated 31 July 1942, in AB, f. 'Vittorini Elio.' On 10 August Bompiani's secretary recorded the arrival of a telegram by German scholar Luciano Foà concerning *Conversazione in Sicilia*. This document too, unfortunately, has been lost. Subsequent correspondence allows us to infer that it was about the German translation of the novel and it did not necessarily contain reference to the recent attack in *Il Popolo d'Italia*. By 12 August 1942 the French and English translations were also in proofs. The contract for the Spanish translation of the novel is dated 25 September 1942. Vittorini's correspondence with Bompiani, held in AB in a hefty file, has not a single entry between 25 July 1942 and 7 September 1943. This gap is made even more frustrating by the fact that a number of letters written in that period have been published in D'Ina and Zaccaria's *Caro Bompiani* and were at the time held at Bompiani's archive. According to the current archivist, this incongruity is possibly the result of inadequate procedures at the archives in the years up to the late

1980s; hence the restrictions imposed at a later stage, when it was found that some material had gone missing or was incorrectly refiled.

22 See Bompiani, *Via privata*, 148; Vittorini, *I libri, le città, il mondo*, 425.

23 A veil of mystery surrounds what happened to these archives. We know that they existed and were carefully organized at the head office in Milan. At the end of July 1943 the offices were attacked by a group of protesters celebrating the fall of the regime. During the period of the Republica Sociale Italiana, Mussolini decided not to revive *Il Popolo d'Italia*. The building was sold to a Milanese businessman, Gian Riccardo Cella, but it is not clear what happened to the archives. Mention of this can be found in Pier Giuseppe Murgia's *Il vento del nord: Storia e cronaca del fascismo dopo la resistenza (1945–50)* (Milan: SugarCo,1975), 36. For the attack on the offices see Giorgio Pini's memoirs, *Itinerario tragico (1943–1945)* (Milan: Omnia, 1950), 18–20 and, for more detail, his unpublished memoirs (Carte Pini, b. 50. vol. 6 'Bufera,' 19–24). According to Pini the 'piccolo gruppo di energumeni' (small group of maniacs) did not manage to break in and simply threw stones against the windows. The storming of the Milan offices of *Il Popolo d'Italia* was also recorded by Joseph Goebbels in his diary entry of 28 July 1943. See Louis Lochner, ed., *The Goebbels Diaries* (London: Hamish Hamilton, 1948), 331. I have consulted Professor Emilio Gentile and Dott. Paolo Murialdi and both agree that historians of Fascism or of Italian journalism have so far not discovered what happened to the archives. Once *Il Popolo d'Italia* ceased to exist, Pini attempted to find work within a publishing house. Mondadori and Bompiani did not reply to his request (despite the fact that he had published with both houses); a post as supervisor was eventually offered to him by Rizzoli (Carte Pini, b. 50, vol. 6 'Bufera,' 26–7).

24 Although never mentioned in biographical studies on Ponti, the correspondence with Pini reveals beyond a doubt that during that summer he was a contributor to *Il Popolo d'Italia*. See ACS, Carte Pini, b. 30. Six of the seven articles were published with the pen name 'Dirus'; the seventh, similarly to 'Una sporca conversazione,' was signed only with three asterisks. The file on Ponti at the Segreteria Particolare del Duce (ACS, SPD CO, f. 511.102) shows that Ponti had been sending articles and letters to Mussolini since 1936. Mussolini's replies are limited to formal thanks delivered by his secretary. Ponti also asked for a private audience in 1938, 1941, and 1943, but it is not clear whether he actually met Mussolini. According to a letter dated 2 February 1942, Mussolini had expressed his approval of Ponti's ideas in the book entitled *La casa per tutti* (which Garzanti had showed in proofs to Mussolini). In February 1942 Ponti sent Mussolini an article on the Italian ceramics industry, which – after a check with the prefecture of Milan as to

Ponti's political and moral status – was passed on to *Il Popolo d'Italia* for publication (which took place on 26 March 1942). The beginning of the correspondence between Pini and Ponti, who immediately offered to write anonymous editorials for the paper, also dates from the same period. The sparse documentation held at the Fondo Ponti in Milan only confirms that the correspondence between Pini and Ponti started in the spring of 1942. I would like to thank Massimo Martignoli, curator of the Fondo, for examining Ponti's correspondence.

25 Gio Ponti's support of Fascism was mainly related to his strong patriotic feelings. In 1934 he had received the Mussolini Prize from the Accademia d'Italia for his contribution to Italian architecture. He drew up the plans for the Faculty of Mathematics at La Sapienza and lectured on interior architecture at Milan's Politecnico. Although a sincere Fascist, he was never involved in any political initiatives. His collaboration with *Il Popolo d'Italia* seems to have been a consequence of his critical view of the upper classes' lack of contribution to the war effort. As an architect, he was battling in those years for a campaign to provide affordable accommodation for workers and farmers. He continued to back such causes as well as lecturing at Milan's Politecnico after the end of the war.

26 Castelletti's file at SPD begins with a letter dated 11 June 1926, which accompanied a play by Castelletti, *La madre vera*, sent to Mussolini as a gift. A week later the prefect of Udine sent Mussolini a report in which he described Castelletti as a good Fascist but 'molto discusso' (very controversial) and as having a 'carattere irritante' (irritating personality). On 2 March 1937 Castelletti sent an article of his to Mussolini, after which we find a most important letter dated 7 February 1940 in which he thanks Il Duce for his 'elogio per i miei corsivi sul *Popolo d'Italia* trasmessomi dal camerata Giorgio Pini' (praise of my editorials for *Popolo d'Italia* passed on to me by comrade Giorgio Pini). This means that by 1940 Castelletti was already in the position of anonymous author, and that Mussolini was keeping an eye on his writings. Documents in ACS, SPD CO, f. 512.428. Mention of Castelletti's work as an anonymous writer of editorials with Mussolini's approval can also be found in Giorgio Pini's diary, under the entries 18 February 1939 and 5 February 1940 (*Filo diretto con Palazzo Venezia*, 189, 202). Unfortunately Pini's diary contains very little information about the summer of 1942, by which time Mussolini had stopped ringing Pini every evening to be informed about the coming issue of *Il Popolo d'Italia*. In his postwar memoirs Pini remembered Castelletti as a faithful and brilliant collaborator (*Itinerario tragico*, 36, 77, 268).

27 Pini, *Filo diretto con Palazzo Venezia*, 102–3.

28 Ibid., 151, 153.

29 Pini, *Itinerario tragico*, 300–3.

30 The available correspondence suggests that Coppola would sometimes pay working visits to the Roman branch of *Il Popolo d'Italia*. A letter probably written in July 1942, accompanying an article for Pini, was sent on the letterhead of the Redazione romana. In the letter Coppola made some polemical remarks about hermetic poets such as Quasimodo and Gatto and the fact that they all had been appointed school or university professors thanks to their patron (Bottai as minister of national education) and despite their evident anti-Fascism. In another letter dated 7 July 1942 Coppola told Pini that he was planning to write a number of articles. To complicate matters even more, in a letter to Pini dated only July 1942, Coppola made the following comment: 'Ho letto il corsivo di Castelletti. Bene! Ma continuate sodo e sempre più forte' (I've read Castelletti's editorial. Well done! Keep things going and get tougher and tougher). Letters in ACS, Carte Pini, b. 30.

31 Goffredo Coppola, 'Guerra di religione,' *Il Popolo d'Italia*, 15 January 1942, 3. As a consequence of the anti-Semitic legislation, Ginzburg had lost his Italian nationality; hence Coppola's cruel definition, 'forastiero,' was technically precise. In Coppola's article there is also a second derogatory reference to Judaism when he refers to Soviet Russia's commissars as 'commissari del popolo giudei' (Jewish people's Commisars).

32 Goffredo Coppola, 'Il califfo Omar,' *Il Popolo d'Italia*, 20 February 1942, 3. This article contains a series of anti-Semitic remarks and a critical reference to Moravia's *Gli indifferenti*. For a detailed analysis see Mangoni, *Pensare i libri*, 121–3. Coppola had also published another article, this time against the translation of French, English, and Russian books: 'Le "colonne" infamy,' *Il Popolo d'Italia*, 1 February 1942, 3. A detailed view of this controversy can be found in a letter from Villaroel to his chief editor, Pini, dated 1 June 1942. The main topic of the letter was whether writers suspected of anti-Fascism should be treated as equals. By quoting the example of the polemics between Coppola and Einaudi/*Primato*, Villaroel suggested that there were groups of anti-Fascist writers who were protected by Fascist leaders such as Bottai. It is also interesting to note that in the following letter, of 13 June, Villaroel mentions an exchange between Pini and Bompiani with regard to the translation of foreign books. Unfortunately we do not have copy of the letter but from Villaroel's comment it transpires that Pini had been strongly opposed to foreign books. Both letters can be found in ACS, Carte Pini, b. 29.

33 ACS, Carte Pini, b. 30. This was also not the first time that Coppola had provoked a critical reply from the MCP. Another article for *Il Popolo d'Italia*,

published on 19 June 1942 with the title 'Otto lire,' had made some inflam-
matory remarks about a Swiss cultural journal that according to Coppola
should have been banned. This time it was Pavolini himself who wrote to
Coppola on 27 June to warn him that his statements were both inaccurate
and inappropriate. Interestingly, Pini wrote back on 1 July 1942 and, despite
admitting the inaccuracy of the article in question, strongly defended Coppola's work. After listing all the academic and journalistic achievements of
Coppola, Pini concluded the letter with a remark that could have been interpreted as a veiled threat: 'Credo di poter aggiungere che di lui puoi chiedere anche al Duce, il quale varie volte mi ha lodato i suoi articoli mano a
mano che apparivano sul giornale' (I think I can also add that you can ask Il
Duce about him, since on numerous occasions he has praised Coppola's articles as soon as they appeared in the paper; (ACS, MCP, b. 141, f. 'Coppola
Goffredo').

34 Carte Pini, b. 50, vol. 6 'Bufera,' 10.
35 ACS, Carte Pini, b. 30. The habit of publishing anonymous articles and editorials was obviously not limited to *Il Popolo d'Italia*. In Bottai's correspondence at AFM there is an interesting letter, sent to Mario Missiroli, a
journalist at *Il Messaggero*, on 12 March 1943. In the letter Bottai asked the
famous journalist if he would be prepared to write brief notes, 'precise e
pungenti' (accurate and stinging), which would be published in *Critica fascista* either anonymously or in Missiroli's own name (AFM, FB, f. 52). On
another front, the diary of Giuseppe Bottai succintly informs us that he had
read *Conversazione in Sicilia* in February 1942 (Bottai, *Diario, 1935–1944*,
299). But, as we have seen, Bottai was certainly not on the side of those
opposed to foreign literature, so there is no reason to speculate that he
might have been behind the attack on Vittorini, particularly because he had
no influence over what was published in *Il Popolo d'Italia*.
36 Letter dated 2 August 1942, in ACS, Carte Pini, b. 30. Among Villaroel's credentials as a Fascist intellectual one should also mention his publication of a
propaganda book entitled *Realtà e mito di Mussolini* (Turin: Chiantore, 1938).
It would obviously be of extreme interest to consult Villaroel's private
papers, among which one might find Pini's letter. My attempts, however,
have been successful only in tracing Villaroel's current literary executor,
who in August 2003 declined to allow me access to her uncle's private
papers.
37 Ravasio's 'mission' to guard the morality of the party was made public by
Mussolini in his speech to the Direttorio Nazionale on 3 January 1942. In his
report of 17 April 1942 Pavolini announced that, with Ravasio, he had reorganized the administration of some newspapers. He then concluded the

meeting with a invitation to promote a 'giornalismo di punta e polemico, ma sul cammino e nella traccia di una Rivoluzione che vuole continuare ma che in nessun modo rinnega se stessa e non permette a nessuno che la si rinneghi' (cutting-edge, polemical journalism, but within the path of a revolution that is still alive, does not contradict itself, and shall not allow anybody to step away from it). In Pavolini's meetings with the press on 14 February, 23 April, and 3 May 1942, there are other brief references to his collaboration with Ravasio (see ACS, MCP, b. 50, f. 'Pavolini. Rapporti stampa'). Pini and Ravasio were in correspondence with regard to the appointment of journalists for *Il Popolo d'Italia* and other newspapers (ACS, Carte Pini, b. 29). Ravasio's role is also considered in De Felice's detailed survery of the crisis among young Fascists in the last years of the regime (*Mussolini l'alleato*, 2: 865–921, see in particular 898, 901; also noteworthy is the episode of the arrest of a group of young anti-Fascists in Rome on 1 April 1942 (887).

38 It appears as an appendix of Giordano Bruno Guerri, *Rapporti al Duce* (Milan: Bompiani, 1978), 387–406.

39 Ibid., 397.

40 Unfortunately no mention of this episode is made in Pini's eight volumes of unpublished memoirs (held at ACS, Carte Pini, b. 49 and 50).

41 'Elenco tratto dalla pratica generale 11 Divieti di diffusione' (p. 7), in ACS, Ministero Pubblica Istruzione, Direzione Generale Accademie e Biblioteche, b. 226, f. 1110.

42 I would like to thank Luisa Gandolfi at Bompiani for supplying me with details of the translation contracts for *Conversazione in Sicilia*. That the Belgian edition was actually circulated is confirmed by an article by Albert Beguin, who mentions buying the translation of the novel while in Belgium in 1943/4. Albert Beguin, 'Deux romans de Vittorini,' *Témoignage chrétien*, 14 July 1950, quoted in Giovanna Finocchiaro Chimirri, *Due 'solariani' altrove: Gianna Manzini – Elio Vittorini* (Messina: CUECM, 1986), 153–5. A French edition was published in 1948 by Gallimard.

43 ACS, MCP, b. 116, f. 'Bompiani Editore.'

44 Letters from Bompiani to Vittorini, dated 2 July and 21 September 1942, in D'Ina and Zaccaria, eds., *Caro Bompiani*, 122, 126.

45 Do-re-mi [pseudonym], 'Conversazione in Sicilia,' *Il Popolo fascista*, 7 September 1942; F. Ulivi, 'Asterisco letterario su Vittorini,' *Il Bargello*, 46 (October 1942); L. Chiavarelli, 'Caratteri per una nuova letteratura,' *Roma fascista*, 8 October 1942. A strongly positive comment in favour of Vittorini, in contrast to the 'decadence' of pro-Nazi author Jünger, was made by Einaudi's Germanist Giaime Pintor in his review of Jünger's *Scogliere di marmo* (*Auf dem Marmorklippen*, 1939) published in *Primato* on 15 September 1942 (now in

Pintor, *Il sangue d'Europa*, 132). Vittorini also continued his collaboration with high-profile journals such as Mondadori's *Tempo*, for which on 4 March 1943 he published the short story 'Una bestia abbraccia il muro.' It was a story closely related to Saroyan's 'La belva Bianca,' which Vittorini had translated and inserted in *Americana*, and like *Conversazione in Sicilia* and 'Nome e lagrime' it could easily have been accused of being defeatist and implicitly anti-Fascist.

46 The file at ACS relating to the organization of this conference shows that a host of institutions were involved in the selection of Italian writers to be sent to Weimar, including the Fascist trade union of writers, the Ministries of the Interior, of Foreign Affairs, and of National Education, the MCP, and the Nazi-led European Union of Writers. Vittorini was invited by the last. His letter of acceptance was written on Bompiani's letterhead and sent to Celso Luciano at the MCP on 16 September 1942. Eugenio Montale too had been invited but he declined, alleging health reasons. Documents in ACS, MCP, b. 68, f. 446 'Weimar.'

47 Copies of the 1943 edition are held at the public library of Trezzo sull'Adda (Milan) and at the library of the Department of Italian, Linguistics, and Drama at Trieste University. I am grateful to the librarians of both institutions for their help.

48 Bottai, *Diario, 1944–1948*, 279 (entry for 29 January 1946).

49 Letters in ACS, Carte Pini, b. 30.

50 Elsa Morante, 'Cenni sulla vita e sulle opere,' *L'isola d'Arturo*, 2nd ed. 'Oscar Mondatori' (Milan: Mondadori, 1969), 6; reprinted as an appendix to Marco Bardini, *Morante Elsa, italiana: di professione poeta* (Pisa: Nistri-Lischi, 1999), 682–4. Bottai's letter, written on *Primato* letterhead, is held at A900, Fondo Masino. From the letter it appears that Masino had personally given the manuscript to Bottai when the two had met in Siena. Unfortunately the title of the short stories is left unmentioned.

51 Entry dated 24 February 1938, in Pini, *Filo diretto con Palazzo Venezia*, 84. Moreover, as we will see later on in this chapter, Alba De Céspedes's *Nessuno torna indietro* was positively reviewed in *Il Popolo d'Italia*, 18 March 1939.

52 Re, 'Women and Censorship in Fascist Italy,' 54–63. Bottai's article is 'Bonifica libraria,' which appeared in the 1 January 1939 issue of *Critica fascista*.

53 A request for financial support written by Enrico Falqui – Manzini's husband – on 13 January 1941 went all the way to Mussolini, who approved a grant of 2,000 lire. On 15 January Pavolini personally wrote to Gianna Manzini to inform her of the grant. Manzini replied with a letter of thanks on 23 January 1941. Documents in ACS, MCP, b. 258, f. 'Sussidi.' Subsequently Manzini sent copies of *Venti racconti* and *Rive remote* (1940) to Mussolini, and the

accompanying letter, dated 27 April 1942, suggests that Ada Negri had interceded on her behalf. On 28 June 1942 Manzini sent Il Duce a copy of *Boscovivo* (1932). A memo on MCP letterhead, dated 2 December 1942, states that by then Manzini had been receiving a monthly cheque of 2,000 lire and was requesting its renewal for another four months. A handwritten note in the margin says: 'Il Duce ha annotato: "Sì."' Documents in ACS, SPD CO, f. 534.645.

54 Among other documents, De Céspedes's police file contains the transcript of the two incriminating telephone calls. In one of them, when asked about the reasons why Italy was intervening in Ethiopia, De Céspedes answered 'Perché siamo i più stupidi!' (Because we are more stupid than anybody else!). Documents in ACS, PP FP, f. 395 'De Cèspedes Alba.'

55 Typed memo on clear paper stamped with the words 'Presi gli ordini da S.E. il Capo del Governo' (Orders taken from H.E. the Head of Government), dated 26 September 1935, in ACS, PP FP, f. 395 'De Cèspedes Alba.'

56 In the photographic book on Alba De Céspedes published by Fondazione Mondadori in 2001, one of the editors states that *Nessuno torna indietro* was banned after its fourteenth reprint. However, this is contradicted by the fact that copies of subsequent editions are available in a number of public libraries. The editor unfortunately does not mention the source of this piece of information, which might have been referring to the nineteenth reprint. See anonymous, 'Roma: La città dell'impegno,' in *Alba De Céspedes*, ed. Marina Zancan (Milan: Fondazione Arnoldo e Alberto Mondadori, 2001), 29.

57 On the publication of and modifications to the novel see Decleva, *Mondadori*, 231, 252. According to a letter written by De Céspedes in the postwar years, the novel did not win the Viareggio Prize because of the opposition expressed in a mysterious message from unknown political quarters in Rome, which arrived only three hours after the prize panel had been assigned to *Nessuno torna indietro*. Unfortunately no documentary or autobiographical material of that period corroborates this version of the events, although Alberto Cadioli fully adopts it in his recent essay 'In nome della passione comune: Il lavoro con Mondadori,' in *Alba De Céspedes*, ed. Marina Zancan (Milan: Il Saggiatore/ Fondazione Arnoldo e Alberto Mondadori, 2005), 353. The letter was addressed to journalist Ottavia Vitagliano and dated 22 April 1953. Apart from the two collections of essays edited by Zancan, there are other, strictly thematic studies of De Céspedes's work; see, for example, Carole C. Gallucci and Ellen Nerenberg, eds., *Writing beyond Fascism: Cultural Resistance in the Life and Works of Alba de Céspedes* (Cranbury, NJ: Associated University Press, 2000), and Carole C. Gallucci, 'Alba De Céspedes's *There's No Turning Back*: Challenging

the New Woman's Future,' in *Mothers of Invention: Women, Italian Fascism and Culture*, ed. Robin Pickering-Iazzi (Minneapolis: University of Minnesota Press, 1995), 200–19.

58 De Céspedes's letter, dated December 1940, and the handwritten note, presumably by Mussolini's secretary, Sebastiani, are held at ACS, SPD CO, f. 200.812. The file also contains the short anonymous letter that accuses De Céspedes of trying to use her friendships among politicians in order to meet Mussolini, and this despite both her arrest at the time of the Ethiopian war and the immoral content of her fictional work. There is no archival documentation related to the fate of *Fuga*, but no censorial intervention seems to have taken place because, as late as 1943, the book was still available and had reached its eighth reprint.

59 On Montedoro see Decleva, *Mondadori*, 254, and the file at AFM, FAM, 'Montedoro.'

60 Letter in ACS, MCP, b. 134, f. 'De Céspedes.'

61 Copy of the letter in ASMi, PG II, b. 155, f. 'Mondadori Arnoldo casa editrice.' Luciano's brief memoirs were published as *Rapporto al Duce* (Rome: Editrice Giornale Mezzogiorno, 1948). Reference to the ban on De Céspedes' novel is at on p. 11. In his reconstruction Luciano gives no dates and simply says that the novel was banned by Mussolini after its third reprint. This is certainly not the case, but it is possible that Luciano misremembered the number of reprints. Unfortunately Luciano's memoirs are generally vague, with little attempt at factual accuracy.

62 Piero Pellicano, 'Potenze occulte,' *Vita italiana*, January 1941, 83–5. Copies of both Pellicano's article and De Céspedes's reply are held at ACS, MCP, b. 134, f. 'De Céspedes.' It is possible that the article was intended for publication in *Vita italiana*. According to the detailed bibliography of De Céspedes's work by Laura Di Nicola, however, De Céspedes's only article in 1941 was on a different matter. Di Nicola's bibliography is in Zancan, *Alba De Céspedes* [2005], 421–82.

63 Letter from Arnoldo Mondadori, dated 23 June 1941, held at AFM, FAM, f. 'De Céspedes Alba.' I am grateful to Penny Morris for pointing this letter out to me. Copy of the anonymous letters and attached police reports can be found in ACS, PP FP, f. 'De Céspedes Alba.'

64 The text of the MCP's *velina* has been reproduced in Flora, *Ritratti di un ventennio*, 164.

65 Documents in ACS, SPD CO, f. 200.812.

66 Letter dated 1 November 1941, in ACS, b. 134, f. 'De Céspedes Alba.' On the film production of *Nessuno torna indietro* see Jacqueline Reich, 'Fear of Filming: Alba de Céspedes and the 1943 Film Adaptation of *Nessuno torna indietro*,' in

Gallucci and Nerenberg, *Writing beyond Fascism*, 132–52. The essay unfortunately does not benefit from archival documentation at ASMi and ACS.

67 All documents related to the meeting between De Céspedes and Luciano on 20 November 1941 are in ACS, MCP, b. 134, f. 'De Céspedes Alba.' In some postwar interviews De Céspedes remembered being called to the MCP to defend her novel. See, for example, Sandra Petrignani, *Le signore della scrittura: Interviste* (Milan: Tartaruga, 1984), 40, and Ulderico Munzi, 'Addio Alba de Céspedes, narratrice dello scandalo femminile,' *Corriere della Sera*, 19 November 1997.

68 According to Reich, *Istituto Grimaldi* was finished by the autumn of 1943 although it is not clear whether it was actually released. In his biography of Mondadori, Decleva states that the production of the film was stopped in June 1943 as a consequence of the folding of Mondadori's film production company, Montedoro. Reich, 'Fear of Filming,' 132–3; Decleva, *Mondadori*, 254.

69 Documents in ACS, MCP, b. 134, f. 'De Céspedes Alba.'

70 Petacco, *Il superfascista*, 107–13. Unfortunately Petacco does not quote his source regarding the alleged face-to-face meeting between Pavolini and Mussolini.

71 Documents, including Poverelli's reply of 21 June, in ACS, MCP, b. 134, f. 'De Céspedes Alba.'

72 Letter from Casini to Bompiani, and copied to the prefecture of Milan, dated 12 July 1941, in ASMi, PG II, b. 153, f. 'Bompiani Valentino casa editrice.' Paola Masino had been informed of Bompiani's decision to leave 'Fame' out on 4 June, and in a letter of 6 June she informed Bompiani that she had made some modifications to the text to make it more acceptable (through a more explicit treatment of the reasons that had led the father to murder his own children). Masino also attached a typed copy of the short story with some handwritten amendments. Bompiani, however, must have been relentless, as in another letter, of 26 June 1941, Masino acknowledged and accepted the sacrifice of 'Fame' (AB, f. 'Masino Paola').

73 Letters dated 24 January, 9 April, and 16 and 29 October 1941, held at A900, Fondo Masino. On this see also Re, 'Women and Censorship in Fascist Italy,' in Bonsaver and Gordon, *Culture, Censorship and the State*, 72–3. See also Masino's diary entry, dated 27 January 1941, in Masino, *Io, Massimo e gli altri*, 95.

74 Vasco Pratolini, '"Terremoto" di Paola Masino,' *Primato* 3.7 (1 April 1942): 140. Incidentally, the publication of this review in Bottai's *Primato* suggests that the ban on women writers was not as draconian as Elsa Morante might have thought.

75 One copy, which had remained in Masino's possession, is now at A900, and the second one is among Bompiani's personal papers at APICE, Archivio Bompiani, b. 14, f. 'Masino: Nascita e morte della massaia.' In her article, Re agrees that it is likely that most of the cuts and changes 'were made preventively on the manuscript itself' (Re, 'Women and Censorship in Fascist Italy,' 75). In the copy held at A900 it is clear that as some stage all references to the Italian setting were removed. For instance 'la cugina di Biella' (the cousin from Biella) was replaced with 'la cugina di provincia' (the cousin from the countryside) (18), and the military position of 'maresciallo' was replaced with a more exotic 'commodoro' (65).

76 Memo to Casini, copy held at A900, Fondo Masino. Also quoted in Re, 'Women and Censorship in Fascist Italy,' 73.

77 All documents, including Bompiani's letter of 2 February 1943 and Masino's reply of 4 February, in AB, f. 'Masino Paola.'

78 On 6 July 1943 the printers were still working on the book cover. According to a letter from Bompiani to Masino, dated 21 March 1944, the proofs *Nessuno torna indietro* were destroyed during a bombing raid in August 1943. Copy of the letter in AB, f. 'Masino Paola,' and A900, Fondo Masino.

79 On the *Almanacco della donna italiana* see the study by Elisabetta Mondello in her *La nuova italiana: La donna nella stampa e nella cultura del ventennio* (Rome: Editori Riuniti, 1987), 159–96 (for Margherita Sarfatti see page 191). Both De Céspedes and Manzini contributed to the *Almanacco della donna italiana*.

Conclusion

1 Philip V. Cannistraro, 'Mussolini and the Italian Intellectuals,' in Bonsaver and Gordon, *Culture, Censorship and the State*, 34–41.

2 Giuseppe Pollorini, *La censura e il censore* (Milan: Pan, 1971), 9. Despite its promising title, the book unfortunately provides little factual material for the historian.

3 De Felice, *Mussolini il duce: Gli anni del consenso, 1929–1936*, 107.

4 Pini, *Filo diretto con Palazzo Venezia*, 89–90. De Begnac's book is *Vita di Benito Mussolini*, vol. 2, *La strada verso il popolo*. (Milan: Mondadori, 1937).

5 Alfieri, *Due dittatori di fronte*, 11. Senise, *Quand'ero capo della polizia*, 92–9, 123.

6 De Felice, *Storia degli ebrei italiani sotto il fascismo*, in particular 335, and Fabre, *Mussolini razzista*.

7 Tosatti, 'La repressione del dissenso politico tra l'età liberale e il fascismo,' 255.

8 Brancati, *Ritorno alla censura*, 23; Turi, *Il mecenate, il filosofo e il gesuita*.

Bibliography

Cited Books Subjected to Censorship, Seizure, or Withdrawal

Alvaro, Corrado. *L'uomo è forte*. Milan: Bompiani, 1938
Amendola, Giovanni. *Una battaglia liberale*. Turin: Gobetti, 1924
– *La democrazia dopo il 6 aprile*. Milan: Corbaccio, 1924
– *Almanacco della Medusa*. Milan: Mondadori, 1934
– *L'arte di sedurre le donne*. Milan: Hermes, 1922
Anonymous. *L'arte di sedurre gli uomini*. Milan: Hermes, 1922
– *Virilità*. Milan: Hermes, 1929
– *Il vizio solitario: cause, effetti, rimedi*. Milan: Hermes, 1923
Asch, Schalom. *Pietroburgo*. Milan: Bompiani, 1935
– *Varsavia*. Milan: Bompiani, 1936
Bandello, Matteo. *Novelle* (various editions)
Bassani, Giorgio. [Giacomo Marchi, pseud.]. *Una città di pianura*. Milan: Lucini, 1940
Batacchi, Domenico Luigi. *L'onore perduto alla fiera ed altre novelle* Milan: Corbaccio, 1922
Benelli, Sem. *L'altare* Milan: Treves, 1916
– *L'amorosa tragedia*. Milan: Treves, 1925
– *Eroi*. Milan: Mondadori, 1931
– *Caterina Sforza*. Milan: Mondadori, 1934
– *Il ragno*. Milan: Mondadori, 1935
– *L'elefante*. Milan: Mondadori, 1938
– *L'orchidea*. Milan: Mondadori, 1938
– *La mia leggenda*. Milan: Mondadori, 1939
– *La festa*. Milan: Mondadori, 1940
Bernari, Carlo. *Tre operai*. Milan: Rizzoli, 1934

Berra, Luciano. *Polonia e i polacchi*. Milan: Garzanti, 1939

Bilenchi, Romano. *Il capofabbrica: Racconti*. Rome: Circoli, 1935

– *Conservatorio di Santa Teresa*. Florence: Vallecchi, 1940

Bissolati, Leonida. *Diario di guerra*. Turin: Einaudi, 1934

Bonesso di Terzet, Furio. *Delitto al sesto piano*. Modena: Guanda, 1942

Bontempelli, Massimo. *Pirandello, Leopardi, D'Annunzio: Tre discorsi di Massimo Bontempelli*. Milan: Bompiani, 1938

– *Avventura novecentista*. Florence: Vallecchi, 1938

Brancati, Vitaliano. *Everest: Mito in un atto*. Catania: Studio Editoriale Moderno, 1931

– *Singolare avventura di viaggio*. Milan: Mondadori, 1934

Brand, Millen. *Eroi*. Milan: Bompiani, 1939

Brocchi, Virgilio. *La bottega degli scandali*. Milan: Treves, 1917

– *Secondo il cuor mio*. Milan: Treves, 1919

– *Rocca sull'onda*. Milan: Mondadori, 1926

Bromfield, Louis. *La grande pioggia*. Milan: Mondadori, 1940

Buonaiuti, Ernesto. *Pietre miliari nella storia del cristianesimo*. Modena: Guanda, 1935

Busti, Mario. *Il cristiano e la guerra*. Milan: Vita e pensiero, 1943

Calabrese, Giulietto, and Maria Danese. *Annunciamo: L'Italia popolo eletto*. Milan: Tipografia Venezia, 1929

Caldwell, Erskine. *Journeyman*. New York: Viking Press, 1938

– *Il piccolo campo*. Milan: Bompiani, 1940

Camilleri, Aldo. *Verso la Sfinge buia: Pagine di vita con la legione straniera francese*. Rome: Casa del Libro, 1934

Chiarelli, Luigi. *Carne bianca*. Lanciano: Carabba, 1934

Ciardo, Manlio. *Illuminismo e rivoluzione francese*. Bari: Laterza, 1942

Cinti, Decio. *Dizionario degli scrittori italiani*. Milan: Sonzogno, 1939

Comisso, Giovanni. *Avventure*. Florence: Vallecchi, 1935

– *Agenti segreti veneziani nel '700*. Milan: Bompiani, 1941

Cooper, Elizabeth. *Il cuore di O-Sono-San*. Villafranca: L'estremo Oriente, 1935

Dalla Volta, Amedeo. *Il trattato di medicina legale*. 2 vols. Milane: Società Editrice Libraria, 1933–8

Da Verona, Guido. *Lettera d'amore alle sartine d'Italia*. Milan: Bottega di Poesia, 1924

– *Il libro del mio sogno errante*. Florence: Bemporad, 1919

– *Yvelise*. Milan: Bottega di Poesia, 1923

– *I promessi sposi*. Milan: Unitas, 1930

D'Annunzio, Gabriele. *Merope*. Milan: Treves, 1912

De Begnac, Yvon, *Vita di Benito Mussolini*. Vol. 2. *La strada verso il popolo* Milan: Mondadori, 1937

De Céspedes, Alba. *Nessuno torna indietro.* Milan: Mondadori, 1938

Dekobra, Maurice. *Les tigres parfumes.* Paris: Les Éditions de France, 1931

Dell'Oro, Angiolo Maros. *Razzismo.* Milan: Sonzogno, 1941

Del Vecchio, Giorgio. *Haec est Italia* ed altri sonetti. Modena: Soc. Tip. Modenese, 1941

De Bosis, Lauro. *The Story of My Death.* London: Faber & Faber, 1933

Dell'Aquila, Tom. *Il processo a Guido Da Verona.* Bari: Laterza e Polo, 1934?

Dekobra, Maurice. *Il gesto di Frine: Amori esotici.* Milan: Monanni, 1932

– *La voluttà sul mondo.* Milan: Monanni, 1932

Di Donato, Pietro. *Cristo tra i muratori.* Milan: Bompiani, 1940

Dorgelès, Roland. *Bohème 900.* Milan: Mondadori, 1933

Dos Passos, John. *Un mucchio di quattrini.* Milan: Mondadori, 1938

– *Adventures of a Young Man.* New York: Harcourt, Brace & Co., 1939

Fante, John. *Wait until Spring, Bandini.* New York: Stackpole, 1938

Fernandez Florez, Venceslao. *Storia immorale: Romanzo spagnuolo.* Milan: Monanni, 1932

Ferrero, Guglielmo, and Cesare Lombroso. *La donna delinquente, la prostituta e la donna normale.* Turin: Bocca, 1915; Milan: Rava, 1934?

Ferro, Marise. *Barbara.* Milan: Mondadori, 1934

– *Trent'anni.* Milan: Garzanti, 1940

Filippo, Fichera, ed., *Il Duce e il fascismo nei canti dialettali.* Milan: Convivio Letterario, 1934; republished in an enlarged edition as *Il Duce e il fascismo nei canti dialettali d'Italia.* Milan: Convivio Letterario, 1937.

Fischer, Herbert. *Storia d'Europa.* 3 vols. Bari: Laterza, 1936

Freud, Sigmund. *Totem e tabù.* Bari: Laterza, 1930

Gallian, Marcello. *Comando di tappa.* Rome: Cabala, 1934

– *Bassofondo.* Milan: Panorama, 1935. Reissued under the title *In fondo al quartiere* (Milan: Panorama, 1936)

– *Quasi metà della vita.* Florence: Vallecchi, 1937

– *Combatteva un uomo.* Florence: Vallecchi, 1939

– *Gente di squadra.* Florence: Vallecchi, 1941

Garrone Dino, *Lettere.* Florence: Vallecchi, 1938

Garretto, Giuseppe. *Civiltà nuova.* Paris: Libres internationals, 1938

Ghidoni, Gino. *Il delitto Le Piazze.* Milan: La Prora, 1937

Gide, André. *I sotterranei del Vaticano.* Milan: Mondadori, 1933

Gilligan, Edmund. *Boundary against Night.* London: Jonathan Cape, 1939

Ginzburg, Natalia [Alessandra Tornimparte, pseud.]. *La strada che va in città.* Turin: Einaudi, 1942

Gobetti, Piero. *La rivoluzione liberale.* Bologna: Cappelli, 1924

Gorky, Maxim. *Spia: Romanzo della rivoluzione.* Milan: Monanni, 1928

– *Confessione: Romanzo russo*. Milan: Monanni, 1930

– *La madre: Romanzo russo*. Milan: Monanni, 1930

Gualino, Riccardo. *Frammenti di vita*. Milan: Mondadori, 1931

Halsey, Margaret. *Piccolo mondo inglese*. Milan: Corbaccio, 1940

Hemingway, Ernest, *A Farewell to Arms*. New York: Scribner, 1929

– *To Have and Have Not*. New York: Scribner, 1937

Hogben, Lancelot. *La matematica nella storia e nella vita*. 2 vols. Milan: Hoepli, 1938–40

Hunyady, Sàndor. *Nemes Fém*. Budapest: Athenaeum, 1938

James, Henry. *La belva della giungla*. Milan: Bompiani, 1941

Jastrow, Ignaz. *Die Weltgeschichte in Einer Band*. Berlin: Ullstat, 1932

– *Storia dell'errore umano*. Milan: Mondadori, 1941

Jodice, Vincenzo. *L'amor di patria nella concezione totalitaria dello stato*. Turin: Paravia, 1935

Kantorowicz, Alexander. *Federico II di Svevia*. Milan: Garzanti, 1941

Karinthy, Frigyes. *Viaggio intorno al mio cranio*. Milan: Corbaccio, 1937

Klages, Ludwig. *L'anima e lo spirito*. Milan: Bompiani, 1940

Kropotkin, Peter. *La conquista del pane*. Milan: Casa Editrice Sociale, 1920

– *Le memorie di un rivoluzionario*. Milan: Casa Editrice Sociale, 1923

Labriola, Artura. *Polemica antifascista*. Naples: Ceccoli, 1925

La Motta, Giovanni. *La preghiera del fascista*. Termini: Donato, 1934?

Lawrence, D.H. *Il purosangue*. Milan: Mondadori, 1933

Lederer, Joe. *Storia di una notte*. Milan: Mondadori, 1933

London, Jack. *Il tallone di ferro: Romanzo di previsione sociale*. Milan: Casa Editrice Sociale, 1925; Milan: Modernissima, 1928

Lorca, Federico Garcia. *Nozze di sangue*. Milan: Bompiani, 1942

Ludwig, Emil. *Colloqui con Mussolini*. Milan: Mondadori, 1932

Lussu, Emilio. *La catena*. Paris: Respublica, 1930

– *Marcia su Roma e dintorni*. Paris: Casa Editrice 'Critica,' 1933

– *Un anno sull'altipiano*. Paris: Edizioni italiane di cultura, 1938

Luzzatti, Ivo. *Andrea Doria*. Milan: Garzanti, 1943

Machiavelli, Niccolò. *La mandragola*

Malaparte, Curzio [nom de plume Kurt Erock Suckert], *Viva Caporetto*. Prato: Martini, 1921

– *La téchnique du coup d'état*. Paris: Grasset, 1931

Malatesta, Errico. *L'anarchia*. Milan: Casa Editrice Sociale, 1921

– *Vita e pensier*. New York: Il Martello, 1925

Mallea, Eduardo. *La città sul fiume immobile*. Milan: Corbaccio, 1939

Mandel, Roberto. *Il cantico dei cieli: Poema cosmico*. Milan: Studio Letterario Milanese, 1941

Mansfield, Katherine. *In a German Pension*. London: Constable, 1929

Marcu, Valeriu. *Il dramma del dittatore bolscevico*. Milan: Mondadori, 1930

Marga. *Aneddoti e giudizi su Mussolini*. Florence: Bemporad, 1925

Marinetti, Filippo Tommaso. *Come si seducono le donne*. Florence: Vallecchi, 1917

Masiani, Francesco. *Storia dei fatti di Empoli e del Kursaal 'Diana'*. Milan: n.p., 1929

Masino, Paola. *Racconto grosso e altri*. Milan: Bompiani, 1941

– *Nascita e morte della massaia*. Milan: Bompiani, 1945

Meredith, George. *Commedianti tragici*. Milan: Mondadori, 1941

Mirabeau, Honoré Gabriel de Riquetti. *L' oeuvre libertine*. Paris: Bibliotheque des Curieux, 1910

Misuri, Alfredo. *Rivolta morale: Confessioni, esperienze e documenti di un quinquennio di vita pubblica*. Milan: Corbaccio, 1924

Momigliano, Attilio. *Saggi sull' 'Orlando furioso'*. Bari: Laterza, 1932

Mondina, Carlo, ed. *Parole e pensieri del Duce*. Como: Cavalleri, 1934

Moravia, Alberto. *Le avventure sbagliate*. Milan: Mondadori, 1935

– *L'imbroglio: Cinque romanzi brevi*. Milan: Mondadori, 1937

– *La mascherata*. Milan: Bompiani, 1941

Mori, Cesare. *Con la mafia ai ferri corti*. Milan: Mondadori, 1932

Morpurgo, Luciano. *Quando ero fanciullo*. Rome: Morpurgo, 1938

Mura [Maria Volpi, pseud.]. *La camerista delle maratone*. Milan: Sonzogno, 1920

– *Sambadù amore negro*. Milan: Rizzoli, 1934

Nenni, Pietro. *Sei anni di guerra civile in Italia*. Paris: Cecconi, 1929

Nitti, Francesco. *La tragedia dell'Europa: Che farà l'America*. Turin: Gobetti, 1924

Nitti, Vincenzo. *L'opera di Nitti*. Turin: Gobetti, 1924

Ojetti, Ugo et al. *Storia illustrata della letteratura italiana*. Milan: Garzanti, 1942

Olgiati, Francesco. *I nostri giovani e la purezza*. Milan: Vita e pensiero, 1920

Ossendowski, Ferdynand Antoni. *Lenin*. Milan: Corbaccio, 1930

Pavese, Cesare. *Lavorare stanca*. Florence: Parenti, 1936

Pirandello, Luigi. *Come tu mi vuoi*. Milan: Mondadori, 1930

– *La favola del figlio cambiato*. Milan: Ricordi, 1933

Pitigrilli [Dino Segre]. *La cintura di castità*. Milan: Sonzogno, 1921

– *Vergine a 18 carati*. Milan: Sonzogno, 1924

Rabelais, François. *Il buon gigante Gargantua e suo figlio Pantagruel*. Turin: Società Editrice Internazionale, 1935

Remarque, Erich Maria. *Niente di nuovo sul fronte occidentale*. Milan: Mondadori, 1931

– *La via del ritorno*. Milan: Mondadori, 1932

Renn, Ludwig. *Guerra*. Milan: Treves, 1930

Rensi, Giuseppe. *Scolii: Pagine di diario*. Turin: Montes, 1934

Reut-Nicolussi, Eduard. *Tyrol Unterm Beil*. Munich: Beck, 1928; English translation *Tyrol under the Axe of Fascism*. London: Allen & Unwin, 1930

Ricci, Berto, and Romano Bilenchi, eds. *Lettere: Dino Garrone*. Florence: Vallecchi, 1938

Rimbaud, Arthur. *I deserti dell'amore, Le illuminazioni, Una stagione all'inferno.* Milan: Sonzogno, 1919; Milan: Modernissima, 1923

Romanelli, Dino. *Cuore garibaldino*. Milan: Edizioni C.E.M., 1932

Rosenberg, Alfred. *Der mythus des 20. jahrhunderts.* Munich: Hoheneichenverlag, 1930

Russo, Luigi. *La critica letteraria contemporanea.* Bari: Laterza, 1942

Salsa, Carlo. *Trincee: Confidenze di un fante.* Milan: Sonzogno, 1924

Salvadori, Ferdinando. *Inno al Duce.* Prato: Niccoli, 1934?

Sarfatti, Margherita. *Segni, colori e luci.* Bologna: Zanichelli, 1926

– *Dux.* Milan: Mondadori, 1926

– *America, ricerca della felicità.* Milan: Mondadori, 1937

Scattolini, Virgilio. *La Cavalcata delle vergini.* Milan: Facchi, 1922

– *Cesarina impara l'amore.* Milan: Facchi, 1928

– *La bocca mi baciò tutta tremante.* Milan: Facchi, 1929

Shaw, George Bernard. *The Irrational Knot.* London: Constable, 1905

Sholokhov, Milchail. *Il calmo Don.* Milan: Garzanti, 1928–40; translation banned in 1940

Silone, Ignazio. *Fontamara.* Zurich: Oprecht, 1933

– *Der Fascismus: Seine Entstehung und Seine Entwicklung.* Zürich: Europa-Verl, 1934

– *Brot und Wein.* Zurich: Oprecht, 1936

– *Die Schule der Diktatoren.* Zurich: Europa, 1938

Stalin, Joseph. *U.R.S.S. bilan 1934.* Paris: Denoël et Steele, 1934

Steinbeck, John. *Pian della Tortilla.* Milan: Bompiani, 1939

– *Furore.* Milan: Bompiani, 1940

– *La battaglia.* Milan: Bompiani, 1940

Stucken, Edward. *Die Weissen Götter.* Berlin: Zsolnay, 1934

Sturzo, Luigi. *Riforma statale e indirizzi politici: Discori.* Florence: Vallecchi, 1923

– *La libertà in Italia.* Turin: Gobetti, 1925

– *Pensiero antifascista.* Turin: Gobetti, 1925

– *L'Italie et le Fascisme.* Paris: Alcan, 1927

– *The International Community and the Right of War.* London: Allen & Unwin, 1929, New York: Rihard Smith, 1930

Sulliotti, Italo. *Entra la corte.* Milan: Editori Associati, 1940

Tamási, Aaron. *Abele cervello fino.* Milan: Mondadori, 1941

Thomas, Adrienne. *Caterina va alla guerra.* Milan: Mondadori, 1932

Traverso, Leone, ed. *Germanica.* Milan: Bompiani, 1942

Tresca, Carlo. *Fazioni e patria.* New York: Il Martello, 1924

Trilussa. *La gente*. Milan: Mondadori, 1928
– *Giove e le bestie*. Milan: Mondadori, 1932
– *Cento apologhi*. Milan: Mondadori, 1936
Uchard, Marius. *La bevitrice di perle*. (Milan: Casa per edizioni popolari, 1934
Valle, Domenico, S.J. *La mia casa e la famiglia cristiana*. Turin: Marietti, 1935
Vittorini, Elio. *Il garofano rosso*. Milan: Mondadori, 1938
– *Conversazione in Sicilia*. Milan: Bompiani, 1941
– ed. *Americana*. Milan: Bompiani, 1942
Vivanti, Annie. *Circe*. Milan: Quintieri, 1912
– *Naja Tripudians*. Florence: Bemporad, 1921
– *Salvate le nostre anime*. Milan: Mondadori, 1932
Von Simpson, William. *I Barring*. Milan: Corbaccio, 1941
Zsolt, Aradi. *Il figlio del giocatore*. Milan: Garzanti, 1940
Zuckmayer, Carl. *Maddalena*. Milan: Bompiani, 1938

Secondary Literature

Absalom, Roger, ed. *Gli alleati e la ricostruzione in Toscana (1944–1945): Documenti anglo-americani*. 3 vols. Florence: Olschki, 1988
Accrocca, Filippo, ed. *Ritratti su misura di scrittori italiani*. Venice: Sodalizio del libro, 1960
Alberti, Cesare Alberto. *Il teatro nel fascismo: Pirandello e Bragaglia*. Rome: Bulzoni, 1974.
Albonetti, Pietro. 'Trafile di romanzi,' in Albonetti, ed., *Non c'è tutto nei romanzi*, 7–117
– ed. *Non c'è tutto nei romanzi: Leggere romanzi stranieri in una casa editrice negli anni '30*. Milan: Fondazione Arnoldo e Alberto Mondadori, 1994
Alfieri, Dino. *Due dittatori di fronte*. Milan: Rizzoli, 1948
Alicata, Mario. *Lettere e taccuini di Regina Coeli*. Edited by Albertina Vittoria. Turin: Einaudi, 1977
Aloisi, Baron. *Journal*. Paris: Plon, 1957
Alvaro, Corrado. *Quasi una vita*. Milan: Bompiani, 1952
Aniante, Antonio. *Mussolini*. Paris: Grasset, 1932
Aquarone, Alberto. *L'organizzazione dello stato totalitario*. Turin: Einaudi, 1965
Asor Rosa, Alberto. *Scrittori e popolo: Saggio sulla letteratura populista in Italia*. Rome: Savonà e Savelli, 1965
Barbian, Jan-Pieter. *Literaturpolitik im Dritten Reich: Institutionen, Kompetenzen, Betätigungsfelder*. Munich: Deutscher Taschenbuch Verlag, 1995
Bardini Marco, *Morante Elsa, italiana: di professione poeta*. Pisa: Nistri-Lischi, 1999

Bartolini, Luigi. *Scritti sequestrati*. Rome: Circe, 1945
– *Perché do ombra*. Rome: Novagrafia, 1945
Bemporad, Enrico. 'La traduzione di libri stranieri in Italia e di libri italiani all'Estero,' *Giornale della libreria* 27–8 (4–11 July 1931): 224–6
Benedetti, Giulio. ed. *Codice della stampa e degli autori*. Milan: Libreria d'Italia, 1930
Benelli, Sem. *Schiavitù*. Milan: Mondadori, 1945
Ben-Ghiat, Ruth. *Fascist Modernities: Italy, 1922–1945*. Berkeley: University of California Press, 2001
Berardelli, Giovanni. 'Il fascismo e l'organizzazione della cultura,' In Vittorio Sidotto and Giovanni Sabbatucci, ed. *Storia d'Italia*, vol. 4 Rome and Bari: Laterza, 1997
Bernardini Napoletano, Francesca and Marinella, Mascia Galateria, eds., *Paolo Masino*. Milan: Fondazione Arnoldo e Alberto Mondadori, 2001
Bernari, Carlo. 'Postfazione,' In *Tre operai*, 237–59. Milan: Mondadori, 1965
Bilenchi, Romano. *Amici*. Turin: Einaudi, 1976
– 'Nota de l'autore.' In Bilenchi Romano, *Il capopabbrica*, 121–2, Milan: Rizzoli, 1991.
Binazzi, Andrea, and Ivo Guasti, eds. *La Toscana nel regime fascista*. Florence: Olschky, 1971
Biocca, Dario, and Mauro Canali. *L'informatore: Silone, i comunisti, la polizia*. Milan: Luni, 2000
Bobbio, Umberto. *L'Italia fedele: Il mondo di Gobetti*. Florence: Passigli, 1986
– *Il mestiere dell'editore*. Milan: Longanesi, 1988
Bompiani, Valentino. *Via privata*. Milan: Mondadori, 1973
Bonsanti, Sanro. 'Questo libro è timbrato "fragile,"' *Il Giorno*, 17 November 1971, 3
– 'Vittorini's American Translations: Parallels, Borrowings and Betrayals.' *Italian Studies* 53 (1998): 67–93
Bonsaver, Guido. *Elio Vittorini: The Writer and the Written*. Leeds: Northern Universities Press, 2000
– 'Fascist Censorship on Literarure and the Case of Elio Vittorini,' *Modern Italy* 8.2 (2003): 165–86
Bonsaver, Guido, and Robert, Gordon, eds. *Culture, Censorship and the State in Twentieth Century Italy*. Oxford: Legenda, 2005
Bosworth, Richard. *Mussolini* London: Arnold, 2002
Bottai, Giuseppe. 'Appelli all'uomo,' *Critica fascista* 12 (1934): 4
– *Diario, 1935–1944*. Milan: Rizzoli, 1989
– *Diario, 1944–1948*. Milan: Rizzoli, 1982
Braida, Lodovica, ed. *Valentino Bompiani: Il percorso di un editore 'artigiano'* Milan: Edizioni Sylvester Bonnard, 2003

Branca Vittore. 'Malipiero musicista da grandi battute' *Carriere della Sesa*, 4 March 2001, 3

Brancati, Vitaliano. 'La mia visita a Mussolini,' *Critica fascista* 15 (1931): 292–3
– *Ritorno alla censura*. Bari: Laterza, 1952
– *Romanzi e saggi*. Milan: Mondadori, 2003

Brocchi, Virgilio. *Confidenze*. Milan: Mondadori, 1946

Brunetta Gian 'Piero. *Storia del cinema italiano*. Volume 1. Rome: Riuniti, 1993.

Buchignani, Paolo. 'Il caso "Montale Vieusseux" e Marcello Gallian,' *Nuova Storia Contemporanea* 2 (2002): 133–50
– 'Da "Strapaese" a "L'Universale": Il fascismo rivoluzionario di Romano Bilenchi,' *Nuova Storia Contemporanea* 4 (2000): 49–78
– *Un fascismo impossibile: L'eresia di Berto Ricci nel ventennio fascista*. Bologna: Il Mulino, 1994
– *Marcello Gallian: La battaglia antiborghese di un fascista anarchico*. Rome: Bonacci, 1984
– *La rivoluzione in camicia nera: Dalle origini al 25 luglio 194.3* (Milan: Mondadori, 2006

Cadioli, Alberto. 'In nome della passione comune: il lavoro con Mondadori,' In Marina Zancan (ed.), *Alba De Céspedes* (2005 ed.), 350–73

Calvino, Italo. 'La Romantica,' In Fondazione Mondadori, ed., *Editoria e Cultura a Milano tra le due guerre*, 172–8

Canali, Mauro. *Cesare Rossi: Da rivoluzionario a eminenza grigia del fascismo*. Bologna: Il Mulino, 1984
– 'La contabilità di Cesare Rossi, capo dell'Ufficio Stampa del governo Mussolini (novembre 1922–maggio 1924).' *Storia contemporanea* 19.4 (1988): 719–50
– *Le spie del regime*. Bologna: Il Mulino, 2004

Cannistraro, Philip V., *La fabbrica del consenso: Fascismo e Mass-media*. Bari and Rome: Laterza, 1975
– 'Mussolini and the Italian Intellectuals,' in Bonsaver and Gordon, eds., *Culture, Censorship and the State*, 34–41

Cannistraro, Philip V., and Brian Sullivan. *Il Duce's Other Woman: Margherita Sarfatti*. New York: Morrow, 1993

Casaburi, Cara. 'Eduardo De Filippo e la censura fascista,' *Ariel* 2–3 (1993): 289–94

Casini, Gherardo. *Una volontà, una fede*. Milan: Mondadori, 1940

Castronovo, Valerio. *La stampa italiana dall'Unità al fascismo*. Bari and Rome: Laterza, 1970

Caterinella, Michele, 'Un esempio locale: La Biblioteca Universitaria di Bologna,' In Centro Furio Jesi, ed., *La menzogna della razza*, 326–31

Cavaglion, Alberto, and Gian Paolo, Romagnani, eds. *Le interdizioni del Duce: Le leggi razziali in Italia*. Turin: Claudiana, 2002

Centro Furio Jesi (ed.), *La menzogna della razza: Documenti e immagini del razzismo e dell'antisemitismo fascista.* Bologna: Grafis, 1994

Centro Studi Gobetti, ed. *Piero Gobetti e il suo tempo.* Turin: Centro Studi Gobetti, 1976

Cesari, Maurizio. *La censura nel periodo fascista.* Naples: Liguori, 1978

Chicco, Francesco. 'Indagine statistica sulla produzione editoriale italiana fra il 1886 ed il 1960.' *Graphicus,* no. 10 (October 1964): 5–9; no. 12 (December 1964): 5–12; no. 1 (January 1965): 5–13; no. 3 (March 1965): 5–17

Ciano, Galeazzo. *Diario, 1937–1943.* Milan: Rizzoli, 1990

Ciarlantini, Franco. *Vicende di libri e di autori.* Milan: Ceschina, 1931

Ciurco, Giorgio. *Storia della rivoluzione fascista.* 5 vols. Florence: Vallecchi, 1929

Civardi, Luigi. *Manuale di Azione Cattolica.* Volume 1. *La teorica.* Pavia: Artigianelli, 1932

Comisso, Giovanni. *Le mie stagioni.* Milan: Garzanti, 1951

D'Arrigo, Giuseppe. *Trilussa: Il tempo, i luoghi, l'opera.* Rome: Scalia, 1968

Davis, Natalie Zemon, ed. *Liste Otto: The Official List of French Books Banned under the German Occupation.* Cambridge MA: Harvard College Library, 1992

De Begnac, Yvon. *Taccuini Mussoliniani.* edited by Francesco Perfetti. Bologna: Il Mulino, 1990

De Begnac, Yvon. *Vita di Benito Mussolini. Vol. 2. La Strada verso il populò.* Milan: Mondadori, 1937.

Debenedetti, Giacomo. *16 ottobre 1943: Otto ebrei.* Milan: Il Saggiatore, 1973

Decleva, Enrico. *Mondadori.* Milan: UTET, 1993

De Felice, Renzo. *Mussolini l'alleato.* Volume 2. *Crisi e agonia del regime, 1940–1943.* Turin: Einaudi, 1990

– *Mussolini il duce: Gli anni del consenso, 1929–1936.* Turin: Einaudi, 1974

– *Mussolini il fascista: L'organizzazione dello stato fascista, 1925–1929.* Turin: Einaudi, 1968

– *Mussolini il rivoluzionario, 1883–1920.* Turin: Einaudi, 1965

– 'Piero Gobetti in alcuni documenti di Mussolini,' In Renzo De Felice, *Intellettuali di fronte al fascismo.* Rome: Bonacci, 1985, 250–8

– *Storia degli ebrei sotto il fascismo.* Turin: Einaudi, 1961

De Felice, Renzo, and Emilio, Mariano eds. *Carteggio D'Annunzio–Mussolini, 1919–1938.* Milan: Mondadori, 1971

De Grand, Alexander, *Fascist Italy and Nazi Germany.* London: Routledge, 1995

De Grazia, Victoria, and Sergio Luzzatto, eds. *Dizionario del fascismo.* 2 vols. Turin: Einaudi, 2003

Dell'Arco, Mario. *Lunga vita di Trilussa.* Rome: Bardi, 1951

De Rosa, Gabriele. *Luigi Sturzo.* Turin: UTET, 1977

Del Vecchio, Giorgio. *Una nuova persecuzione contro un perseguitato: Documenti.* Rome: Tipografia artigiana, 1945

De Vecchi di Val Cismon, Cesare. *Bonifica fascista della cultura.* Milan: Mondadori, 1937

Di Marzio. '"I promessi sposi" rifatti da Guido da Verona,' *Critica fascista* 2 (1 January 1930): 15–17

D'Ina, Gabriella, and Giuseppe Zaccaria, eds. *Caro Bompiani: Lettere con l'editore.* Milan: Bompiani, 1988

D'Incà, Renzia. 'Sem Benelli: Un'inquieta passione civile.' *Ariel*, 2–3 (1993): 81–95

D'Orsi, Angelo. *La cultura a Torino tra le due guerre.* Turin: Einaudi, 2000

Duggan, Christopher. *Fascism and the Mafia.* New Haven: Yale University Press, 1989

Einaudi, Giulio. *Frammenti de memoria.* Milan: Rizzoli, 1988

Fabre, Giorgio. 'A proposito dell'antisemitismo fascista dell'inizio del 1938,' in *Studi sulla tradizione classica per Mariella Cagnetta*, ed. Luciano Canfora, Bari: Laterza, 1999

– *Il contratto: Mussolini editore di Hitler.* Bari: Dedalo, 2004

– *L'elenco: Censura fascista, editoria e autori ebrei.* Turin: Silvio Zamorani editore, 1998

– 'L'indifferente Moravia.' *Panorama*, 28 November 1993, 142–50

– *Mussolini razzista.* Milan: Garzanti, 2005

– 'Sul "Caso Moravia."' *Quaderni di storia* 42 (1995): 181–96

Faitrop, Anne-Christine. *Trilussa: Doppio volto di un uomo e di un opera.* Rome: Istituto di Studi Romani, 1979

Fano, Nicola. *Tessere o non tessere: I comici e la censura fascista.* Florence: Liberal Libri, 1999

Farìas, Victor. *Heidegger and Nazism.* Philadelphia: Temple University Press, 1989

Ferrara, Patrizia, *L'amministrazione centrale pubblica.* Vol. 4. *Ministro Cultura Popolare.* Bologna: Il Mulino, 1992

– 'La voce del padrone,' *Storia e Dossier* 10.99 (1995): 50–60

– (ed.), *Censura teatrale e fascismo (1931–1944): La storia, l'archivio, l'inventario.* Rome: Ministero per i beni e le attività culturali, 2004

Ferretti, Gian Carlo, *L'editore Vittorini.* Turin: Einaudi, 1992

Fichera, Filippo, ed. *Il Duce e fascismo nei canti dialettali.* Milan: Convivio Letterario, 1934

Fiori, Antonio. *Il filtro deformante: La censura sulla stampa durante la prima guerra mondiale.* Rome: Istituto storico italiano per l'età moderna e contemporanea, 2001

– 'Per la storia del controllo governativo sulla stampa: Le circolari del Ministero dell'Interno dall'Unità alla prima guerra mondiale,' *Rassegna degli Archivi di Stato* 47.1 (1987): 9–102

Flora, Francesco. *Stampa dell'era fascista: Le note di servizio.* Rome: Mondadori, 1945

Folin, Alberto, and Mario, Quaranta eds. *Le riviste giovanili del periodo fascista.*
Treviso: Canova, 1977

Fondazione Arnoldo e Alberto Mondadori. *Editoria e cultura a Milano tra le due guerre: Atti del convegno.* Milan: Fondazione Arnoldo e Alberto Mondadori, 1983

Forgacs, David. *Italian Culture in the Industrial Era, 1880–1980.* Manchester: Manchester University Press, 1990. Translated in Italian as *L'industrializzazione della cultura italiana.* Bologna: Il Mulino, 1992

Formiggini, Angelo Fortunato. *La ficozza filosofica del fascismo.* Rome: Formiggini, 1923

– *Trent'anni dopo: Storia della mia casa editrice.* Modena: Levi, 1977

Frabotta, Maria Adelaide. *Gobetti l'editore giovane.* Bologna: Il Mulino, 1988

Franzinelli, Mimmo. *I tentacoli dell'OVRA.* Turin: Bollati Boringhieri, 1999

Galfré, Monica. *Il regime degli editori: Libri, scuola, fascismo.* Bologna: Il Mulino, 2005

Gallucci, Carole C., 'Alba De Céspedes's *There's No Turning Back*: Challenging the New Woman's Future,' in Robin Pickering-Iazzi, ed., *Mothers of Invention: Women, Italian Fascism and Culture,* 200–19

Gallucci, Carole C., and Ellen Nerenberg, eds. *Writing beyond Fascism: Cultural Resistance in the Life and Works of Alba de Céspedes.* Cranbury, NJ: Associated University Press, 2000

Garin, Eugenio. *Editori italiani tra '800 e '900.* Rome and Bari Laterza, 1991

Gellately, Robert. *Backing Hitler: Consent and Coercion in Nazi Germany.* Oxford: Oxford University Press, 2001

Gentile, Emilio. 'The Fascist Anthropological Revolution.' In Bonsaver and Gordon, eds. *Culture, Censorship and the State,* 22–33

Giammusso, Maurizio, *Eliseo: Un teatro e i suoi protagonisti.* (Rome: Gremese, 1989

– *Vita di Eduardo.* Milan: Mondadori, 1994

Gigli Marchetti Ada. 'Un editore per la libertà: Enrico dall'Oglio,' In Gigli Marchetti and Finocchi, eds., *Stampa e piccola editoria tra le due guerre,* 9–17

– *Le edizioni Corbaccio: Storia di libri e di libertà.* Milan: Franco Angeli, 2000

Gigli Marchetti, Ada, and Luisa Finocchi, eds., *Stampa e piccola editoria tra le due guerre.* Milan: Franco Angeli, 1997

Ginzburg, Natalia. 'Memoria contro memoria,' *Paragone* 462 (August 1988): 3–9

Gobetti, Piero. *Opere complete.* 2 vols. Turin: Einaudi, 1969

Goetz, Helmut. *Il giuramento rifiutato: I docenti universitari e il regime fascista.* Florence: La Nuova Italia, 2000

Gozzini Mario, ed. *Giovani Papini: Attilio Vallecchi. Carteggio, 1914–1941.* Florence: Vallecchi, 1984

Greco, Lorenzo. *Censura e scrittura: Vittorini, lo pseudo-Malaparte, Gadda.* Milan: Il Saggiatore, 1983

Gregory, Tullio, Marta, Fattori, and Nicola Siciliani, eds. *Filosofi università regime: La Scuola di Filosofia di Roma negli anni Trenta.* Rome: Istituto di Filosofia della Sapienza, 1985

Griffiths, Clive. 'Theatrical Censorship in Italy during the Fascist Period,' in Bonsaver and Gordon (eds.), *Culture, Censorship and the State,* 76–85

Guarnieri, Silvio. *L'ultimo testimone.* Milan: Mondadori, 1989

Guercio, Francesca. 'La compromissione del regime.' *Ariel* 2–3 (1993): 259–79

Guerri, Giordano Bruno. *Galeatto Ciano: Una vita 1903–1944.* Milan: Bompiani, 1979

– *Giuseppe Bottai: Un fascista critico.* Milan: Feltrinelli, 1976

– *Rapporti al Duce.* Milan: Bompiani, 1978

– 'La Mondadori e la politica del ventennio,' In Fondazione Mondadori, *Editoria e cultura a Milano tra le due guerre,* 87–92

Guglielmi, Marina. 'La letteratura americana tradotta in Italia nel decennio 1930–1940: Vittorini e l'antologia *Americana,*' *Forum Italicum* 29 (1995): 301–12

Gundle, Stephen. 'Hollywood, Italy and the First World War: Italian Reactions to Film Versions of Ernest Hemingway's *A Farewell to Arms,*' In Bonsaver and Gordon (eds.), *Culture, Censorship and the State,* 98–108

Guspini, Ugo. *L'orecchio del regime: Le intercettazioni telefoniche al tempo del fascismo.* Milan: Mursia, 1973

Haarmann, Hermann, Walter, Huder and Klaus Siebenhaar, eds. *'Das War ein Vorspiel nur …'. Bücherverbrennung Deutschland 1933: Voraussetzungen und Folgen.* Berlin: Medusa, 1983

Hainsworth, Peter. 'Florentine Cultural Journalism under Fascism: *Il Bargello.*' *Modern Language Review* 953 (2000): 696–711

Hale, Oron. *The Captive Press in the Third Reich.* Princeton, NJ: Princeton University Press, 1964

Hill, Leonidas. 'Nazi Attack on "Un-German" Literature.' In Rose, ed., *The Holocaust and the Book,* 9–46

Iaccio, Pasquale. 'La censura teatrale durante il fascismo,' *Storia contemporanea* 17.4 (1986): 567–614

– *La scena negata: Il teatro vietato durante la guerra fascista (1940–1943).* Rome: Bulzoni, 1994

Irving, David. *Goebbels: Mastermind of the Third Reich.* London: Focal Point, 1996

Isnenghi, Mario. *Intellettuali militanti e intellettuali funzionari: Appunti sulla cultura fascista.* Turin: Einaudi, 1979

Jones, Derek, ed. *Censorship: A World Encyclopedia.* 4 vols. London: Fitzroy Dearborn, 2001

Klein, Gabriella. *La politica linguistica del fascismo.* Bologna: Il Mulino, 1986

Krieg, Ugo. *La legislazione penale sulla stampa.* Milan: Giuffrè, 1942

Lazzaro, Giorgio. *La libertà di stampa in Italia dall'editto albertino alle norme vigenti.* Milan: Mursia, 1969

Lepre, Aurelio. *El Duce lo ga dito: I poeti dialettali e il fascismo.* Milan: Leonardo, 1993

Levra, Umberto. *Il colpo di stato della borghesia: La crisi di fine secolo in Italia, 1896–1900.* Milan: Feltrinelli, 1975

Lochner, Louis, ed. *The Goebbels Diaries.* London: Hamish Hamilton, 1948

Luciano, Celso. *Rapporto al Duce.* Rome: Editrice Giornale Mezzogiorno, 1948

Ludwig, Emil. *Colloqui con Musoslini.* Milan: Mondadori, 1932; new ed. Milan: Mondadori, 2000

Luti, Giorgio. *Firenze corpo 8. Scrittori, riviste, editori nella Firenze del Novecento.* Florence: Vallecchi, 1983

Magrì, Enzo. *Un italiano vero: Pitigrilli.* Milan: Baldini & Castoldi, 1999

Maida, Bruno. 'La Direzione generale della stampa italiana,' In Tranfaglia, ed., *La stampa del regime, 1932–1943,* 29–56

Malipiero, Gian Francesco. 'Favoleggiando con Pirandello,' *Scenario* (November 1940); repr. *G. Francesco Malipiero,* ed. Massimo Bontempelli, 190–3. Milan: Bompiani, 1942

Manacorda, Giuliano. 'Storia minore ma non troppo: Come fu pubblicata *Americana.' Rapporti,* December 1973, 21–6; repr. as '*Come* fu pubblicata "Americana,"' in *Elio Vittorini: Atti del Convegno Nazionale di Studi,* ed. Mario Sipala, 63–8. Catania: Greco, 1978

– ed. *Lettere a Solaria.* Rome: Editori Riuniti, 1979

Mangoni, Laura. *L'interventismo della cultura: Intellettuali e riviste del fascismo.* Bari: Laterza, 1974

– *Pensare i libri: La casa editrice Einaudi dagli anni trenta agli anni sessanta.* Turin: Bollati e Boringhieri, 1999

Marcolin, Alberto. *Firenze in camicia nera.* Florence: Edizione Medicea, 1993

Mariani, Mario. *Le adolescenti.* Milan: Corbaccio, 1920

Marino, Giuseppe Carlo. *L'autarchia della cultura: Intellettuali e fascismo negli anni trenta.* Rome: Editori Riuniti, 1983

Masino, Paola. *Io, Massimo e gli altri.* Milan: Rusconi, 1995

Matteini, Claudio. *Ordini alla stampa.* Rome: Polibraria Italiana, 1945

Mezzetti, Fernando. *Borgese e il fascismo.* Palermo: Sellerio, 1978

Michaelis, Meir. *Mussolini and the Jews.* Oxford: Clarendon Press, 1978

Miceli, Riccardo. 'Razzismo nel libro,' *Il libro italiano,* September 1938, 379–82

Ministero dell'Educazione Nazionale. *Elenchi di opere la cui pubblicazione, diffusione o ristampa nel Regno è stata vietata dal Ministero della Cultura Popolare.* Rome: Istituto Poligrafico dello Stato, 1940.

Minoia, Carlo, ed. *Elio Vittorini: I libri, le città, il mondo. Lettere, 1933–1943.* Turin: Einaudi, 1985

Misefari, Enzo. *Alvaro politico: Analisi di un comportamento.* Soveria: Rubbettino, 1981

Missori, Mario. *Governi, alte gerarchie dello stato, alti magistrati e prefetti del Regno d'Italia.* Rome: Ministero per i beni culturali e ambientali, 1989

Momigliano, Eucardio. *Storia tragica e grottesca del razzismo fascista.* Milan: Mondadori, 1946

Mondello, Elisabetta. *La nuova italiana: La donna nella stampa e nella cultura del ventennio.* Rome: Editori Riuniti, 1987

Montale, Eugenio. *Lettere a Clizia.* Milan: Mondadori, 2006

Montevecchi, Orsolina. *La chiesa e i libri: Estratto dall'Indice dei Libri Proibiti.* Milan: Archetipografia, 1944

Moravia, Alberto. 'Ricordi di censura.' *La Rassegna d'Italia,* December 1946, 95–106

Moravia, Alberto, and Elkann Alain. *Vita di Moravia.* Milan: Bompiani, 1982

Morgan, Philip. 'The Prefects and Party-State Relations in Fascist Italy.' *Journal of Modern Italian Studies* 3.3 (1998): 241–72

Morpurgo, Luciano. *Caccia all'uomo.* Rome: Dalmatia, 1946

Murgia, Pier Giuseppe. *Il vento del nord: Storia e cronaca del fascismo dopo la resistenza (1945–50).* Milan: Sugar Co, 1975

Murialdi, Paolo. 'La stampa quotidiana del regime fascista,' in Tranfaglia, Murialdi, and Lignani, *La stampa italiana nell'età fascista,* 34–257

Mussolini, Benito. *Corrispondenza inedita,* edited by D. Susmel. Milan: Edizioni del Borghese, 1972

– 'Divagazioni: L'ora e gli orologi.' *Il Popolo d'Italia,* 6 April 1920; repr. *Opera Omnia.* Volume 14. Ed. Edoardo and Dwilio Susmel, 398. Florence: Lafenice, 1955

– 'Verso la censura?' *Il Popolo d'Italia,* 6 December 1922, 1

Nardelli, Giuseppe. *La libertà di stampa ed i reati commessi a mezzo della stampa.* Milan: Treves, 1924

Navarra, Quinto. *Memorie del cameriere di Mussolini.* Rome: Longanesi, 1946

Nicolodi, Fiamma. *Musica e musicisti nel Ventennio fascista.* Fiesole: Discanto, 1984

Orano, Paolo. *Gli ebrei in Italia.* Rome: Pinciana, 1937

Padulo, Gerardo. 'Appunti sulla fascistizzazione della stampa.' *Archivio storico italiano* 140 (1982): 83–115

Page, Giorgio Nelson. *L'americano di Roma.* Milan: Longanesi, 1950

Palazzolo, Maria Iolanda. 'Le forme della censura nell'Italia liberale,' *La Fabbrica del libro* 9.1 (2005): 2–5

Palla, Marco. *Firenze nel regime fascista, 1929–1934.* Florence: Olschki, 1978

Panicali, Anna. 'Appunti sul realismo degli anni Trenta: Dino Garrone,' *Angelus Novus* 23 (1972): 55–79

– 'Sulla collaborazione al *Bargello.*' *Il Ponte* 7–8 (1973): 955–70

– *Elio Vittorini.* Milan: Mursia, 1994

Papini, Giovanni. *Italia mia*. Florence: Vallecchi, 1939

Pardini, Giuseppe. '"La schiavitù delle beffe": Sem Benelli e il regime fascista,' *Nuova Storia Contemporanea* 5 (2002): 131–52

Parisi, Luciano. *Borgese*. Turin: Tirrenia Stampatori, 2000

Paternostro, Rocco. *Corrado Alvaro: "L'uomo è forte," ovvero la poetica della colpa-espiazione*. Rome: Bulzoni, 1980

Patuzzi, Claudia. *Mondadori*. Naples: Liguori, 1978

Pavese, Cesare. *Lettere, 1924–44*, edited by Lorenzo Mondo. Turin: Einaudi, 1966

Pavolini, Alessandro. *Le arti in Italia*. Milan: Domus, 1938

– *Giro d'Italia: Romanzo sportive*. Foligno: Campitelli, 1928

– *Nuovo Baltico*. Florence: Vallecchi, 1935

– *Scomparsa d'Angela*. Milan: Mondadori, 1940

Pedullà, Gianfranco. 'Gli anni del Fascismo: Imprenditoria privata e intervento statale,' In Turi, ed., *Storia dell'editoria nell'Italia contemporanea*, 345–67

Pescazzoli, Antonio. *Il fascismo senza mito*. Milan: Corbaccio, 1925

Petacco, Arrigo. *Il prefetto di ferro: L'uomo di Mussolini che mise in ginocchio la mafia*. Milan: Mondadori, 1992

– *Il superfascista: Vita e morte di Alessandro Pavolini*. Milan: Mondadori, 1998

Petrignani, Sandra. *Le signore della scrittura: Interviste*. Milan: Tartaruga, 1984

Piazzoni, Irene. 'Una collana militante nell'Italia fascista: "Libri scelti" di Bompiani'. *La Fabbrica del Libro* 9.1 (2005): 19–26

Piccioni, Alessandro. ed. *Una casa editrice tra società, cultura e scuola: La Nuova Italia, 1926–1986*. Florence: La Nuova Italia, 1986

Pickering-Iazzi, Robin. ed. *Mothers of Invention: Women, Italian Fascism and Culture*. Minneapolis: University of Minnesota Press, 1995

Pini, Giorgio. *Benito Mussolini: La sua vita sino a oggi*. Bologna: Cappelli, 1926

– *Filo diretto con Palazzo Venezia*. Bologna: Cappelli, 1950

– *Itinerario tragico (1943–1945)*. Milan: Omnia, 1950

Piromalli, Antonio. *Guido da Verona*. Naples: Guida, 1975

Pollorini, Giuseppe. *La censura e il censore*. Milan: Pan, 1971

Prezzolini, Giuseppe, ed. *Gobetti e 'La Voce.'* Florence: Sansoni, 1971

Rafanelli, Leda. *Una donna e Mussolini*. Milan: Rizzoli, 1946

Raffaelli, Sergio. 'Mussolini contro il teatro dialettale romagnolo,' *Ariel* 2–3 (1993): 139–46

Ragone, Giovanni. *Un secolo di libri: Storia dell'editoria in Italia dall'Unità al postmoderno*. Turin: Einaudi, 1999

Ragni, Eugenio. 'Intervista a Carlo Bernari,' *Quaderni d'italianistica* 13.2 (1992): 280–4

Raimondi, Ezio. *Il silenzio della Gorgone*. Bologna: Zanichelli, 1980

Re, Lucia. 'Futurism, Seduction and the Strange Sublimity of War,' *Italian Studies* 59 (2004): 83–111

– 'Women and Censorship in Fascist Italy: From Mura to Paola Masino,' In Bonsaver and Gordon, eds., *Culture, Censorship and the State*, 64–75

Reich, Jacqueline. 'Fear of Filming: Alba de Céspedes and the 1943 Film Adaptation of *Nessuno torna indietro*,' In Gallucci and Nerenberg, eds., *Writing beyond Fascism*, 132–52

Rizi, Fabio Fernando. *Benedetto Croce and Italian Fascism*. Toronto: University of Toronto Press, 2003

Rodondi, Raffaella. *Il presente vince sempre*. Palermo: Sellerio, 1985

– ed. *Elio Vittorini, Letteratura, arte e società: Articoli e interventi, 1926–1937*. Turin: Einaudi, 1997

Rose, Jonathan, ed. *The Holocaust and the Book*. Amherst: University of Massachusetts Press, 2001

Rossi, Cesare. *Mussolini: Com'era*. Rome: Ruffolo, 1947

Ruinas, Stanis. *Viaggio nelle città di Mussolini*. Milan: Bompiani, 1939

Rundle, Christopher. 'The Censorship of Translation in Fascist Italy,' *Translator* 6.1 (2000): 67–86

– 'Publishing Translation in Mussolini's Italy,' *Textus* 12.2 (1999): 427–42

Sacchi, Carla, ed. *Il carteggio Einaudi-Montale per 'Le occasioni.'* Turin: Einaudi, 1988

Sarfatti, Michele. *Mussolini contro gli ebrei: Cronaca dell'elaborazione delle leggi del 1938*. Turin: Zamorani, 1994

Sarkowicz, Hans, and Alf Mentzer. *Literatur in Nazi-Deutschland: Ein Biographisches Lexicon*. Hamburg: Europa Verlag, 2000.

Scarpellini, Emanuela. *Organizzazione teatrale e politica del teatro nell' Italia fascista*. Florence: La Nuova Italia, 1989

Schirone, Franco. 'La Casa Editrice Sociale: Appunti sull'attività dell'editore anarchico Giuseppe Monanni,' *Rivista Storica dell'Anarchismo* 2 (1994): 96–116

Scotto di Luzio, Adolfo. '"Gli editori sono figliuoli di famiglia": Fascismo e circolazione del libro negli anni trenta.' *Studi storici* 36.3 (1995): 761–810

– *L'appropriazione imperfetta: Editori, biblioteche e libri per ragazzi durante if fascismo*. Bologna: Il Mulino, 1996

Senise, Carmine. *Quand'ero capo della polizia*. Rome: Ruffolo, 1946

Silone, Ignazio. 'Die Italienische Universität,' *Die Neue Weltbühne* 37 (14 September 1935): 1150–52

Siebenhaar, Klaus. 'Buch und Schwert: Anmerkungen zur Indizierungspraxis und "Schriftumspolitik" im Nationalsocialismus.' In Haarmann, Huder, and Siebenhaar, eds., *'Das War ein Vorspiel nur...'*, 81–96

Simonetti, Carlo Maria. 'L'editoria fiorentina dal 1920 al 1940: Proposte per una ricerca.' *Ricerche storiche* 22.2–3 (1982): 541–68

Spadolini, Giovanni. 'Relazione conclusiva del convegno,' in Fondazione Mondadori, *Editoria e cultura a Milano tra le due guerre*, 212–23

Spriano, Paolo. *Storia del Partito comunista italiano*. Turin: Einaudi, 1969

Stone, Marla Susan. *The Patron State: Culture and Politics in Fascist Italy*. Princeton, NJ: Princeton University Press, 1999

Staderini, Alessandra. 'Una fonte per lo studio della ulitizzazione dei "fondi segreti": La contabilità di Aldo Finzi (1922–1924).' *Storia contemporanea* 10.4 (1979): 767–810

Talbot, George. 'Alberto Moravia and Italian Fascism: Censorship, Racism and *Le ambizioni sbagliate*,' *Modern Italy* 11.2 (2006): 127–45

Tassani, Giovanni. 'Il "peccato originale" di Giuseppe Antonio Burgese.' *Nuova Storia Contemporanea* 4 (2000): 105–36

Thompson, Doug. *State Control in Fascist Italy: Culture and Conformity, 1925–1943*. Manchester: Manchester University Press, 1991

Tiozzo, Enrico. 'Il rifacimento Daveroniano de *I promessi sposi*,' *Romance Studies* 22 (2004): 63–74

Tortorelli, Gianfranco. 'Contributi sulla formazione culturale e politica di Mario Alicata.' *Italia contemporanea* 25.1 (1978): 93–8

Tosatti, Giovanna. 'La repressione del dissenso politico tra l'età liberale e il fascismo: L'organizzazione della polizia.' *Studi storici* 38.1 (1997): 217–55

Tranfaglia, Nicola, ed. *La stampa del regime, 1932–1943: Le veline del Minculpop per orientare l'informazione*. Milan: Bompiani, 2005

Tranfaglia, Nicola, Paolo Murialdi, and Massimo Legnani. *La stampa italiana nell'età fascista*. Rome and Bari: Laterza, 1980

Tranfaglia, Nicola, and Albertina Vittoria. *Storia degli editori italiani*. Bari and Rome: Laterza, 2000

Turchetta, Gianni. 'Alberto Moravia diventa un autore Bompiani (1934–37). In Braida ed., *Valentino Bompiani*, 86–121

Turi, Gabriele. *La casa Einaudi: Libri uomini, idee oltre il fascismo*. Bologna: Il Mulino, 1990

– *Il fascismo e il consenso degli intellettuali*. Bologna: Il Mulino, 1980

– *Il mecenate, il filosofo e il gesuita: L'Enciclopedia Italiana specchio della nazione*. Bologna: Il Mulino, 2002

– *Un secolo di libri: Storia dell'editoria in Italia dall'Unità al post-moderno*. Turin: Einaudi, 1999

– ed. *Storia dell'editoria nell'Italia contemporanea*. Florence: Giunti, 1997

Vainio, Leena Erika. 'Operato della censura teatrale italiana negli anni Trenta: Il tormentato caso di Sem Benelli.' *Romansk Forum* 16.2 (2002): 985–96

Vallecchi, Attilio. *Ricordi e idee di un editore vivente*. Florence: Vallecchi, 1934

Villaroel, Giuseppe. *Realtà e mito di Mussolini*. Turin: Chiantore, 1938

Vittoria, Albertina. 'Fascist Censorship and Non-Fascist Literary Circles.' In Bonsaver and Gordon, eds. *Culture, Censorship and the State*, 54–63

– '"Mettersi al corrente con i tempi." Letteratura straniera ed editoria minore.' In Gigli Marchetti and Finocchi, eds. *Stampa e piccola editoria tra le due guerre*, 197–218

Vittorini, Elio. 'Censura letteraria.' *Il Bargello*, 23 July 1934, 3; repr. in Rodondi, ed., *Elio Vittorini*, 793–5

– 'Propaganda e Stampa, dicastero dell'intelligenza fascista.' *Il Bargello*, 30 June 1935, 1; repr. Rodondi, ed., *Elio Vittorini*, 874–5

Voigt, Klaus. *Il rifugio precario: Gli esuli in Italia dal 1933 al 1945*. Florence: Nuova Italia, 1993

Welch, David. *The Third Reich: Politics and Propaganda*. London: Routledge, 1993

Woodhouse, John. *Gabriele D'Annunzio: Defiant Archangel*. Oxford: Clarendon Press, 1998

Zaccaria, Giuseppe. 'Bompiani e Alvaro: Un "rapporto esemplare,"' In Braida, ed., *Valentino Bompiani*, 122–43

Zancan, Marina, ed. *Alba De Céspedes*. Milan: Fondazione Arnoldo e Alberto Mondadori, 2001

– ed. *Alba De Céspedes*. Milan: Il Saggiatore/Fondazione Arnoldo e Alberto Mondadori, 2005

Zangrandi, Ruggero. *Il lungo viaggio attraverso il fascismo*. Milan: Mursia, 1962

Zapponi, Guido. 'La condanna all'Indice delle opere di G. Gentile e di B. Croce nei ricordi di Rodolfo de Mattei,' *Storia contemporanea* 17.4 (1986): 715–19

Zavattini, Cesare. *Una, cento, mille lettere*. Milan: Bompiani, 1988

Zuccaro, Domenica, ed. *Lettere ali Ovra oli Pitigrilli*. Florence: Parenti, 1961

Zurlo, Leopoldo. *Memorie inutili: La censura teatrale nel ventennio*. Rome: Edizioni dell'Ateneo, 1952.

Index

402 Index

Tozzi, Federigo, 322
Tranfaglia, Nicola, 6, 268
Tresca, Carlo, 88
Treves, Angelo, 130
Treves, Claudio, 40
Treves, Emilio, 15
Treves (publishing house), 17, 43,
    50–1, 89, 104, 179, 300, 310
Trilussa (Carlo Alberto Salustri),
    62–3, 115, 262
Tumminelli, Calogero, 89, 284
Turati, Augusto, 24, 61, 344
Turati, Filippo, 29, 60
Turi, Gabriele, 6, 266, 269, 287, 336

Ungaretti, Giuseppe, 54, 106, 111,
    149
Unione Tipografica, Casa Editrice
    (publishing house), 335
Unitas, Casa Editrice (publishing
    house), 76–81, 129
UTET Casa Editrice (publishing
    house), 199

Vainio, Leena Erika, 326
Vallardi, Casa Editrice (publishing
    house), 183, 198
Valle, Domenico, S.J., 111
Vallecchi, Attilio, 54–7, 129, 134, 150,
    295, 296, 313
Vallecchi Editore (publishing house),
    54–7, 107, 118, 120, 134, 149, 191,
    270, 285, 321, 339, 343, 344
Valois Librerie (publishing house), 89
Vannini, Giulio, 104
Venturi, Lionello, 81–2
Vergani, Orio, 41, 63

Vidussoni, Aldo, 248
Villaroel, Giuseppe, 136, 240, 242,
    243–4, 247–8, 252, 365
Vita e Pensiero (publishing house),
    215
Vittoria, Albertina, 6, 268, 315, 343,
    347
Vittorini, Elio, 4–5, 23, 87, 129,
    140–7, 223–30, 233, 241–51
Vivanti, Annie, 350
Voigt, Klaus, 174, 329, 353

Wallace, Henry, 315
Wanrooij, Bruno, 275
Wasserman, Jacob, 178
Weiss, Ernst, 178
Welch, David, 303
Werfel, Franz, 213
Woodhouse, John, 271

Zaccaria, Giuseppe, 314
Zancan, Marina, 369
Zangara, Vincenzo, 321
Zangrandi, Ruggero, 247, 304
Zanichelli Editore, 338
Zapponi, Guido, 310
Zavattini, Cesare, 113, 129, 133, 258,
    322
Zsolt, Aradi, 341
Zucaro, Domenico, 308
Zuckmayer, Carl, 348
Zurlo, Leopoldo, 8, 51, 64–75, 96,
    102, 104, 110, 125, 127, 128,
    158–69, 203, 216, 262, 265, 301,
    325, 345, 352
Zweig, Arnold, 178
Zweig, Stefan, 125, 169, 175, 210, 330